PRACTICAL

UNIX

Steve Moritsugu
DTR Business Systems

with

James Edwards

Sanjiv Guha

David Horvath

Gordon Marler

Jesper Pedersen

David Pitts

Dan Wilson

Contents
at a Glance

201 W. 103rd Street
Indianapolis, Indiana 46290

Practical UNIX

International Standard Book Number: 0-7897-2250-X

Library of Congress Catalog Card Number: 99-66230

Printed in the United States of America

First Printing: December 1999

02   01   4   3

Trademarks

Warning and Disclaimer

Associate Publisher
Dean Miller

Acquisitions Editor
Gretchen Ganser

Development Editor
Maureen A. McDaniel

Managing Editor
Lisa Wilson

Copy Editors
Krista Hansing
Rhonda Tinch-Mize

Indexer
Cheryl Landes

Proofreaders
Juli Cook
Bob LaRoche

Technical Editor
Eric Richardson

Team Coordinator
Cindy Teeters

Cover Designer
Rader Design

Production
Stacey Richwine-DeRome
Ayanna Lacey
Heather Hiatt Miller
Mark Walche

Contents at a Glance

About the Authors

Steve "Mor" Moritsugu got his B.S. at Caltech, and for over 20 years has specialized in computer operating systems. He is a senior software engineer and is the support supervisor at DTR Business Systems. He has been a featured speaker at computer conferences world-wide and has written articles for various computer magazines. In addition, he also teaches UNIX Operating System, System Administration, Shell Script Programming, and Perl CGI classes at Santa Ana College in Southern California. He has used a number of UNIX books in his classroom and has a unique perspective on what is needed to make an effective book on UNIX.

Acknowledgments

I would like to thank my co-workers and management at DTR for making time and resources available for me to work on this book, DTR's customers for a steady stream of questions and technical challenges, my students at Santa Ana college for their feedback and fresh insights, my friends and family for love and understanding, and of course, to all the UNIX experts who help me when I get stuck.

—**Steve "Mor" Moritsugu**

introduction

Welcome to UNIX!

UNIX systems are valued because of their great reliability. Often they run for months or years without any system problems or crashes. UNIX systems usually offer the best performance, the most throughput, and the easiest support for large numbers of concurrent users when compared to any other computer configuration. UNIX offers unparalleled scalability, allowing a computer system to serve as a single-user workstation or as a server supporting hundreds or thousands of concurrent users accessing a common database.

Tip for Beginners

Look for a "Tip for Beginners" at the start of every chapter in this book. This introduction lists the types of readers that will benefit from this book. It also summarizes each chapter to give an overview of how they fit together.

UNIX also offers a wealth of utilities, networking and programming tools, and custom applications for almost every business and industry. UNIX rewards the time and effort that you put into it by giving you shortcuts to make you more productive and by allowing experienced users to get in under the hood to find and fix things that go wrong. You can customize the system according to your own preferences and even create new commands (called scripts) to automate repetitive tasks. As new CPU chips are developed, the great portability of UNIX will enable you to retain your software investment as you migrate to newer, faster machines.

UNIX commands have odd names such as ls, mv, awk, grep, and sed; with them, UNIX experts can do almost magical things to accomplish in a few lines what might otherwise take hours of work or special programming. In fact, Microsoft provides a Windows NT Services for UNIX Add-On Pack, which, among other things, allows more than 25 UNIX commands and the Korn shell to run under Windows NT.

On the other hand, some people don't like UNIX commands because they find these commands cryptic, terse, and unfriendly. UNIX assumes that you know what you are doing and usually does not give any warning if you enter a command that makes no sense or can damage your files. UNIX error messages often give no clue as to what you are doing wrong, and beginners may not even realize that their commands have failed. Beginners can find themselves in a hung state where they must ask for help to get going again. Each UNIX command can be like a separate kingdom with its own language, customs, procedures, and lore. These kingdoms reward the explorer with new capabilities, but at first it is no fun being a stranger in so many strange lands.

Who Is This Book For?

If you are new to UNIX, you should read through the "Tip for Beginners" sidebar at the start of each chapter to guide your exploration. Chapter 2, "Getting Started— A Guided Tour of UNIX," gives a general overview of UNIX and how all the pieces work together. This book will help you with the underlying concepts to the UNIX rules and commands so that they will make more sense and so that you will remember them better. It will help you avoid the pitfalls and traps most beginners fall into. You do not have to be a programmer or a Windows user—if you are familiar with MS-DOS, you will find some things in UNIX that are similar, but even a background in MS-DOS is not required.

If you have used UNIX for several years and want to learn how to be more productive, this book will help you. The material is grounded in the years I have spent supporting UNIX and teaching an ongoing sequence of three full-semester classes on UNIX at Santa Ana College in Southern California. In particular, Chapters 11, 18, and 19, illustrate difficult subjects that I have organized into a series of concepts that build layer by layer to overall mastery.

If you are a Linux user, you are part of an exciting movement in open computing. One of the strengths of Linux is that the commands are compatible with commercial UNIX systems. However, a large part of most Linux books cover installation and setting up users, disks, printers, modems, networks, PPP, TCP/IP, Web servers, DNS, and so on. There is often little room left to go as deep into UNIX commands and concepts as you will in this book. If you use UNIX on a particular type of computer, you may wonder if this book will be useful for that computer. The answer is yes. Traditional UNIX documentation is usually divided into user manuals, programming manuals, and system administration manuals. This book concentrates on user documentation and script programming documentation, which are uniform for all types of UNIX, Linux, and BSD systems (with small variations). Some topics in this book cover installation and system level administration, but the specific steps can vary widely depending on the type and revision level of the UNIX system. For detailed installation and setup, consult the system documentation for your computer.

What's in This Book?

Part I of this book covers UNIX Fundamentals. Part II shows how to work with files. Part III covers installing UNIX and general concepts of system administration. Part IV shows how UNIX can process and manipulate text output and pattern matching. Part V discusses networking between UNIX and Windows PC systems. Part VI shows three powerful scripting languages available on UNIX systems. A synopsis of each chapter follows.

Part I: UNIX Fundamentals

Chapter 1, "Introduction to UNIX and the Shell," discusses what UNIX is, its history, and why it comes in so many different flavors. It brings the history up-to-date with the recent release of the 64-bit SVR5. This chapter also introduces some basic but essential UNIX concepts that you will need throughout the rest of the book.

Chapter 2, "Getting Started—A Guided Tour of UNIX," illustrates all the important UNIX concepts that users are expected to know and shows how they work together. This is a great chapter for beginners, with analogies to explain difficult concepts.

Chapter 3, "UNIX Directories and Pathnames," shows how to access UNIX directories and files. This chapter covers absolute versus relative pathnames, which is of critical importance in forming UNIX file commands.

Chapter 4, "Rules for Entering UNIX Commands," explains command syntax so that you'll know which spaces are required and which are illegal. This chapter describes the man command, which enables you to look up command usage and options. It also shows common errors made on the command line and how to interpret common UNIX responses. Furthermore, this chapter describes what to do if your station is hung up and tells you how to save the output or errors from any command in a file. It also shows you when and what types of quotes are required in various situations.

Chapter 5, "The UNIX Graphical User Interface (GUI)," describes the X Window system, which enables you to use a mouse and graphical icons under UNIX. This chapter covers the common desktop environment that is found on Sun Solaris, SCO UnixWare 7, IBM AIX, HP-UX, and other UNIX systems. It also describes how to use a mouse and graphics to edit a text file, copy and manipulate files, and send and receive email with attachments.

Chapter 6, "Miscellaneous UNIX Utilities," describes date and calendar commands, how to count things, and how to perform calculations. One application suite for UNIX, StarOffice, is presented with detailed coverage of how to download and install the whole package under Solaris 7.

Part II: Working with UNIX Files

Chapter 7, "Listing and Finding Directories and Files," describes UNIX files in general and covers listing files using ls and finding files using find. These commands have extensive options that are covered in detail.

Chapter 8, "Displaying and Printing Files and Pipelines," covers displaying files (in full and in part) with line numbers and with or without embedded control characters. It also covers printing files, checking the queue, canceling a print job, moving print jobs, and formatting output using pr.

Chapter 9, "Copying, Moving, Renaming, Removing, or Linking Files," covers how to do these actions with simple examples and strategies and tells when different directories are involved. It also covers creating multiple names for the same file using hard and soft (symbolic) links.

Chapter 10, "Comparing, Sorting, Modifying, Combining, and Splitting Files," covers how to compare files, even if they are not on the same system. This chapter discusses the powerful UNIX sort command with the capability to designate primary and secondary sort fields. Other important topics include how to display just the beginning or the end of a file; how to encrypt, compress, and encode a file to a printable text form; how to combine files with sort, cat, paste, and join; and splitting files.

Chapter 11, "Generating and Using File Lists," covers how to use filename generation wildcards to generate a list of desired files for those UNIX commands that can operate on multiple files. It also describes how backquotes and xargs can be used to process lists of files, particularly when there are too many matching files for wildcards to handle.

Part III: System Administration

Chapter 12, "Installing UNIX at Home," gives practical, detailed, step-by-step instructions on how to obtain and install two different major commercial versions of UNIX on a home PC (UnixWare 7 from SCO, and Solaris 7 from Sun Microsystems).

Chapter 13, "Users, Groups, and Logins," covers UNIX commands that deal with individual users and all users on the system, in groups, and in the login session. It shows how to create a user on three different types of UNIX systems (IBM AIX, Solaris 7, and SCO UNIX).

Chapter 14, "File Permissions and System Security," discusses login and password security and tells how users and groups can be set up under UNIX to share some files and directories while others are restricted. It covers file and directory permissions and the chmod command in both numeric and symbolic mode. It also covers how umask affects permissions assigned to new files and directories and discusses the security implications of the SUID and SGID bits.

Chapter 15, "System Startup, Shutdown, and Managing Jobs," covers how to start up and shut down a UNIX system. It discusses how both users and the system administrator can automate jobs at system startup, on login, and at predefined times or periodic intervals. It also covers job priorities and how these can be set and changed, and it discusses job control and how to suspend, resume, and kill background jobs.

Chapter 16, "System and File Backups," covers UNIX device names, in particular those for tape and disk. It covers how to use tar for backing up a directory or selected files, how to list the contents of a backup, and what strategies and precautions to use for restoring files. This chapter then covers the same material for cpio. Next, it discusses the process of saving files on a DOS disk and also how to back up and restore the UNIX operating system itself.

Chapter 17, "Managing System Resources," discusses disk filesystems and quotas. It shows how to use sar, vmstat, and iostat for system performance monitoring.

Part IV: UNIX Text Processing

Chapter 18, "Searching for Lines in a File or Pipeline," describes how to use grep to display lines that contain a pattern. It covers regular expressions, an extremely important but difficult topic that is broken down into a series of layered lessons. It covers extended regular expressions in egrep and discusses how to use perl and awk from the command line to provide additional capabilities to search for patterns.

Chapter 19, "Replacing or Removing Text from a File or Pipeline," describes how to use sed to modify lines using the power of regular expressions. It covers using perl and awk from the command line to provide additional capabilities for replacing and removing text. It also covers cut, tr, and uniq to modify or remove lines or characters.

Chapter 20, "Using vi to Edit a Text File," shows the first 10 vi commands to learn that enable you to do all basic editing. This chapter then covers the next eight commands to learn and lists various vi commands for inserting text and moving the cursor, introducing the concept of separated words versus contained words and non-words. It also lists vi commands for deleting and changing text.

Chapter 21, "Letting the vi Editor Work for You," shows the power of vi in zipping through any repetitive editing chores. Rather than learning separate built-in vi commands, you can invoke sed and awk for search and replace operations, sort for sorting, and grep -v for selectively deleting lines, encrypting sections, inserting a banner, printing a section, and counting lines in a section. This chapter also shows how to cut and paste and how to set desired vi options.

Chapter 22, "Command-Line Editing in the Korn Shell," shows how to recall previous commands and then modify and execute them. The simplicity of this chapter belies its usefulness because it enables the UNIX expert to build elegant command-line structures in layered stages, as illustrated in a detailed example.

Chapter 23, "Introducing the Emacs Editor," describes another UNIX editor that has great power and flexibility. Many users prefer this alternative to vi.

Part V: Networking

Chapter 24, "Accessing Other UNIX Systems by Modem," describes how to use dial-up modems with the cu command to log in to a remote UNIX, use uucp to transfer files, and use PPP to access a remote network.

Chapter 25, "Accessing Other UNIX Systems on the Network or Internet," covers the basics of TCP/IP, how to use telnet and rlogin to log in to another system in the network, how to use ftp and rcp to transfer files, and how to execute commands using rsh (called rcmd on some UNIX systems). This chapter discusses NFS to access remote directories, and it covers the mail command to send and receive email.

Chapter 26, "Accessing UNIX from Windows," shows how to set up TCP/IP on Windows, how to use Windows FTP to transfer files both to and from UNIX, and how to use Windows Telnet to log in to UNIX. This chapter also covers how to use a modem on Windows and how to use Netscape to read your UNIX mail and send replies.

Chapter 27, "UNIX and the Internet," shows how to surf the Internet from UNIX, how to download software using your Web browser, and how to download and use Lynx, a character-based Web browser useful on UNIX terminals for Internet browsing. This chapter also illustrates how to use make to compile the software, how to access UNIX vendors and get help on the Internet (for example, Year 2000 patches needed for UNIX), how to access security bulletins, and how to read the Network News on UNIX.

Part VI: Script Programming

Chapter 28, "Writing Bourne Shell Scripts," covers writing programs in the Bourne shell scripting language. It describes shell variables, prompts, input from the user, command-line arguments, if tests, checking command results, calculations, special variables, usage errors, looping through command-line arguments, debugging, looping to process a group of files, and the case statement.

Chapter 29, "Writing Perl Programs," covers programming in the perl programming language, which is commonly used both on UNIX and Windows to look up and display information on Web sites. This chapter covers built-in variables, if statements, loops, functions, arrays, file access, hashed arrays, strings, and debugging. It does not cover CGI Web programming, but all the elements in this chapter are useful in CGI Web programming.

Part VII: Appendixes

Appendix A, "UNIX Commands," is a reference of UNIX commands, syntax, and useful options.

Appendix B, "Glossary," lists some terms used in this book and their meanings.

Contacting the Lead Author

Several authors wrote chapters for this book to meet the publishing deadlines, and I much appreciate their help. As the lead author, I would enjoy hearing from readers with comments or questions about this book; simply email me at mori@dtrbus.com.

The company I work for, DTR Business Systems, has provided my services as lead author for this book. DTR supports a network of UNIX Value-Added Resellers (VARs) across the country. I regret that I cannot provide free UNIX support by email, but I can likely refer you if you need commercial UNIX products of services.

part

1

UNIX FUNDAMENTALS

chapter

1

Steve "Mor" Moritsugu

Introduction to UNIX and the Shell

Basic hardware and software terms •

What is UNIX •

Different types of UNIX •

UNIX versus Windows •

The UNIX shell •

Standard input, output, and error •

Pipes and filters •

The UNIX way •

Tip for Beginners

Each chapter in this book begins with a tip for beginners, to give you an idea of which topics in the chapter you can benefit from immediately and which topics you should postpone until you have familiarity with other sections. Each topic begins with the basics and then progresses to more advanced usage. Beginners should read all of this chapter. Skim sections that are dry, but concentrate on terms and concepts that are introduced.

UNIX Is an Operating System

To explain what UNIX is, this chapter first covers some very basic terms dealing with computer hardware and software and explains applications versus operating systems. If you already know all this, feel free to skip these next two sections on computer hardware and software generalities.

Computer Hardware in General

Computer *hardware* refers to physical elements that make up the computer—things you can touch. Most computers have a keyboard where you type, for example, and a monitor or screen where you view the computer's output. The box where the computer is housed (its chassis) contains more hardware elements, such as one or more hard-disk drives that enable you to store data. You may have heard of disk drives with capacities as large as 500MB or 2GB. *Mega* means 1 million, and *giga* means 1 billion. A *byte* is a unit of computer storage equivalent to one character in a document. Therefore, a 500MB disk drive could hold 500 documents, each containing 1 million characters. A 2GB disk can hold four times as much data as a 500MB disk.

Another hardware component is memory, also called RAM (Random Access Memory). Memory is the computer's workspace, which holds the code, data, and other information for programs that are currently running. Having more memory allows the computer to work faster. Often, the amount of memory is a power of 2, such as 32MB (megabytes) or 256MB. Some very powerful (and expensive) computers have gigabytes of memory.

The *central processing unit (CPU)* is an essential hardware element. This is the brain of the computer that allows it to follow a set of program instructions to do computations and process information stored in memory or on the disk drives. You have probably heard of Intel processors such as the Pentium chip, but there are also other types of CPUs that are not like Intel processors at all. For example, the PowerPC is used instead of an Intel processor in many computers. It is based on a totally different type of computer architecture called RISC (reduced instruction set computers). Sun Microsystems' computers use still another type of processor called SPARC. Some computers have multiple CPUs to improve performance.

A computer can also contain other system components, such as one or more tape drives, floppy-disk drives, or CD-ROM drives. These components may also be called peripheral devices and auxiliary devices, but these terms are often reserved for attached devices such as terminals, printers, and modems.

Computer Software in General

A set of instructions for the computer is a called a *program*. Programs reside on the hard disk, run from RAM, control the CPUs, and use the peripheral devices. To distinguish this programming from the hardware pieces of the computer, it is referred to as *software*. Computer software can be grouped into these categories:

- Applications
- Languages
- Operating system
- Utilities

Applications are programs designed to provide a particular set of capabilities to a user. A word processing application program, for example, enables the user to key in and modify documents and then to print them out. Application programs are available for almost every aspect of business, such as accounting, payroll, inventory, point of sale, and scheduling appointments. Application programs also can be found for scientific or financial calculations, personal and home use, and games. The person who uses the application program is called the *end user*.

Computer languages are software programs that enable people called programmers to create computer programs. Computer languages such as BASIC, FORTRAN, and COBOL have been around for a number of years and are still used today. New computer languages are developed to give programmers better tools for writing programs. Visual BASIC provides graphics tools, for example, to write programs to run under Windows. Java provides graphics tools for applications that run on the World Wide Web. The C programming language is an older, multipurpose, highly efficient language that is still very much in demand today along with C++, a revised version of C that supports newer object-oriented programming methods that make it easier to write complex programs.

An operating system is the central controlling program for the entire computer, controlling the jobs that are run. It also organizes the hard disk into files, where a file is a collection of disk blocks that store information that the user wants to keep together. The operating system allows each file to be given a name, called a filename, to make it easy for a human to tell the computer which disk blocks to access.

Files can be grouped into directories that in turn can be grouped into larger, more inclusive directories.

An operating system enables a user to run application programs and to perform system functions such as creating directories and copying files. An operating system schedules and runs all the jobs on the computer. It also enables users to log on and use the system. What's more, it controls all the system resources such as memory, files on disk, tape drives, CD-ROM drives, modems, printers, terminals, and the network connection. UNIX, MS-DOS, Windows 95, Windows NT, and Apple Macintosh are all examples of different operating systems that are commonly in use today. UNIX is an operating system, not an application—don't expect to find it as a program on a Windows system.

Many users are more aware of available applications than available operating systems and what they do. When you first power on the system, the operating system must be started before you can run any application programs. This process of starting the operating system is called "bringing up" or "booting up" the system. During this bootup process, the operating system initializes all the devices, which means that it sends them any needed instructions so that they will be ready for use. After the system is up, the operating system has full control over most or all the system hardware—especially the disk drives. When application programs want to access or create files on the disk drive, they don't do this directly. Instead, they ask the operating system to do this for them. Several application programs can access different files at the same time. The operating system keeps track of which programs are using which files. If several programs all request a disk access at the same time, the operating system decides which request to service first. The operating system also determines whether a user has permission to access a file, and it can block access if not.

Utilities are smaller, independent programs that are usually narrow in scope, providing a single capability or a single area of functionality, such as a backup utility. Utilities may be strongly coupled with the operating system or an application, which means that they are an essential, indispensable part. Utilities may also be loosely coupled, as in the cases where the utility is optional, costs extra, is shareware or freeware, must be downloaded from the Internet, or is sold by a different company than the one that provides the operating system or application.

The History of UNIX

UNIX is an operating system that was developed at AT&T's Bell Laboratories in the early 1970s by Ken Thompson, Dennis Ritchie, and others. In those days, interaction with a computer was much different than it is today. A computer user was usually also a programmer who would write a program and then punch each line onto a computer card. The user would also put the data to process onto these punch cards.

The user would assemble these cards into a deck and pray that he didn't accidentally drop them, because trying to put a large deck back together again in the right order could take hours. The deck would be submitted to the computer operators, who would feed each deck into the computer. The computer would run the program, process the data, and print out the results. The operators would then put the deck and printouts into public bins. Users would have to check these bins periodically to see whether their job was done. If the computer was very busy, the job might not be done until the next day. If your program had any errors, you would have to analyze your listing and printout, repunch the incorrect cards, resubmit the whole job, and wait for the new results. The middle of the night was often a good time to submit jobs because the results would come back quickly and you could change and resubmit the job several times with a minimum of waiting. This style of computer usage is called batch operation because the computer runs only one job at a time; it does not run the next job until the current job has totally completed.

In the late 1960s, a new way of using computers, called *time-sharing*, was being developed. Under time-sharing, the computer can run several jobs simultaneously by switching from job to job and giving each job a small, limited piece of time to run until it is time to switch to the next job. Time-sharing enabled multiple users to interact directly with the computer. The computer could immediately show them any errors in their programs, and the users could correct the errors and rerun the job without the large delays that occurred in batch processing. Bell Laboratories, along with GE and MIT, was working on a time-sharing system called Multics. In 1969, however, that project was canceled because Multics was too complex and difficult. Thompson, Ritchie, and other Bell Laboratory people continued to work on their own time-sharing system. They called it UNIX because it was a simpler, more efficient operating system than Multics.

Many other computer operating systems, as well as faster and more powerful computers, were being developed at this time. And in those days, each new computer had its own unique operating system. Whenever a computer manufacturer developed a new computer, it would have to provide an operating system to run on that computer. The manufacturer would also provide new utilities and applications to run on that new operating system. These were called *proprietary systems* because the computer manufacturer owned the only operating system that would run on this computer. Users were locked into that vendor to supply the basic and necessary software for that machine.

A key part of the UNIX story is the fact that, at this time, AT&T could not branch out into the computer business because of legal restrictions. Therefore, AT&T did not develop and sell its own computer systems; it purchased computers from other companies. Because the company was using UNIX on more computers, designers wanted to find a way to easily move it to run on different computers that they might purchase.

Most operating systems, including early UNIX, were written in assembly language. Assembly language is called a low-level computer language because each instruction is a basic operation of the computer hardware. Low-level languages work with the registers and memory accesses that form the basic operation of the computer. Hence, an assembly language programmer can code very tight, efficient loops, which is essential for operating system code used repeatedly. High-level languages such as BASIC, FORTRAN, and COBOL are far removed from the machine level. They provide programming tools and concepts that make it much easier to write programs, but the code produced is not as efficient as assembly language coding.

> **Whatever Happened to C?**
>
> C and its object-oriented spin-off, C++, are widely used programming languages on all operating systems today. C was so good that the designers never went to D.

Thompson and the others realized that it was important to be able to port UNIX to run on new computers as they became available. They also realized that if they continued to write UNIX in assembly language, it would take far too much effort to port the whole system to new computers. Thompson developed a language called B, and Ritchie improved it and called it C. By 1973, they had rewritten almost all of UNIX in this new high-level C programming language that was still very efficient for writing operating system code. The programmers could now provide the same operating system on several different types of computers. They continued to add new functionality to UNIX, wrote papers on UNIX internals, and made the system available to universities, who were intrigued by the design concepts and the fact that it would run on many computers. New features and variants of UNIX were offered by universities and other computer companies that started to use UNIX and extend it for their own needs.

I first encountered UNIX in the mid-1980s, when I was part of an operating system group that wrote and supported a proprietary operating system for the Point 4 minicomputer. In those days, the whole proprietary operating system and all the user data could fit in a 20MB disk drive, and it could run with only 128KB of memory. UNIX was not a threat to the proprietary systems of those days because UNIX required much more disk space, memory, and CPU power; therefore, it was not as cost-effective. All the computer manufacturers offered their own highly optimized proprietary operating systems that could run with a minimum size disk and with minimum memory. These proprietary time-sharing systems still locked computer users into the computer products from one company. This resulted in higher prices because the one company had to do all the program development; therefore, there was little competition.

By 1990, the computer landscape had changed considerably. UNIX had won the battle against the proprietary systems. The hardware costs of memory and disk space had gone down so much that the extra memory and disk space required by UNIX was no longer a major consideration. The big selling point of UNIX was that it was an open system, meaning that users would no longer be locked into a proprietary system. Because UNIX was written in a higher-level language, it could easily be ported to other types of computers, and all the application software that ran on the old computer could be easily ported to the new computer. Prices on open UNIX systems were much more competitive than on proprietary systems. At the same time, UNIX had an extremely rich set of utilities and capabilities as a result of the combined efforts of Bell Laboratories, universities such as Berkeley, and companies such as Sun Microsystems. As UNIX gained momentum, companies writing new software applications chose to write for the UNIX platform so that their software could run on a variety of hardware, which again hastened the demise of the proprietary systems. Although some computer vendors still offer or support a proprietary operating system, they also usually offer an alternative UNIX product line.

How UNIX Built the Internet

The Internet began as a Defense Department project (DARPA) to connect government, military, and university computers. As the number of host systems in the network grew, an efficient method was needed to send information in packets from one system, through other systems and routers in the network, to a desired destination. As the network grew larger, dynamic routing was required to bypass down computers or bad connections. The packet routing protocol that was developed, called TCP/IP, was first implemented in UNIX at the University of California at Berkeley. UNIX and TCP/IP became the backbone of the Internet, tying thousands and then millions of computers together. UNIX and other servers on the Internet make vast amounts of data, research, news, current events, business, and human interest information available via the World Wide Web. In this way, millions of people use UNIX systems and are not even aware of it.

The Diversity of UNIX

As computer vendors ported UNIX to their own machines, they often gave it a unique name. The following section provides a partial list, in no special order, of some computer companies that sell UNIX systems.

Types of UNIX Systems

Table 1.1 shows companies that have ported UNIX and the various names they have given their versions of UNIX.

Table 1.1 Companies That Have Created Versions of UNIX and UNIX-like Systems	
Computer Company	UNIX OS
AT&T	UNIX SVR3
AT&T	UNIX SVR4
Sun Microsystems/SunSoft	SunOS (which is a component of Solaris)
Sun Microsystems/SunSoft	Interactive UNIX
Hewlett-Packard (HP)	HP-UX
Data General (DG)	DG-UX
Novell	UnixWare (early version)
Santa Cruz Operation (SCO)	UnixWare
Santa Cruz Operation (SCO)	OpenServer
Santa Cruz Operation (SCO)	XENIX
Microsoft	XENIX (early version)
IBM	AIX
SiliconGraphics (SGI)	IRIX
Digital Equipment Corp. (DEC)	ULTRIX
Digital Equipment Corp. (DEC)	Digital UNIX
NCR	NCR UNIX
Siemens Nixdorf (SNI)	Reliant UNIX
Caldera	Caldera OpenLinux
Red Hat, Inc.	Red Hat Linux
Noncommercial Sources	UNIX OS
UC Berkeley	BSD (Berkeley Software Distribution)
FreeBSD Project	FreeBSD
Free Software Foundation	GNU/Linux
Linus Torvalds	Linux kernel
Debian	Debian GNU/Linux

This list is by no means complete. Other companies such as Bull and Motorola, for example, sell computer systems using the AIX operating system. Unisys sells computers running UnixWare. Other well-respected companies sell UNIX and Linux systems. In addition, some of the products listed in Table 1.1 may be old products that have been superseded by newer ones; some of the listed companies may no longer sell the particular UNIX product listed.

Non-AT&T UNIX

If you watch a UNIX system as it is first powered on, you may see a long series of copyright notices acknowledging the various companies and organizations that have contributed software to UNIX over the years. One of the copyright notices you might see is from the Regents of the University of California for the considerable work done at Berkeley on UNIX. The UNIX produced at this university is called BSD, for Berkeley Software Distribution. Many of the BSD utilities have become standard in all UNIX packages. FreeBSD is an extension of BSD in which the copyrighted AT&T UNIX code has been removed or rewritten so that it can be distributed without the usual UNIX royalties and source code restrictions. For more complete information, see www.freebsd.org on the World Wide Web.

> **GNU Is A Recursive Acronym**
>
> Most computer acronyms are formed by taking the first letter of each word in the name. The G in GNU does not refer to a separate word, but self-referentially points to the acronym itself. You find this off-beat approach to naming in many UNIX terms.

Linus Torvalds wrote his own UNIX-like kernel that is the main executable part of the operating system. He called this kernel Linux, and although it emulates the main features of UNIX, it does not use any restricted source code. Torvalds' kernel is distributed with utilities from the Free Software Foundation's GNU project, which stands for "GNUs not UNIX." The goal of this project was to create a free UNIX system. The Free Software Foundation had created many significant free software utilities such as the GNU C Compiler and the GNU emacs text editor. Combining the Linux kernel with the GNU utilities at last created a complete UNIX-like system that was free of AT&T UNIX copyrights and royalties. This version of UNIX can be used for commercial purposes. It is governed by a special license called the GPL, which prevents the operating system source code from being restricted or copyrighted. For complete information, see www.gnu.org and www.linux.org.

Commercial UNIX systems usually run on expensive computers that support a large number of users. These systems are usually maintained by a computer operations staff. The average user never even sees the UNIX machine—just terminals that are attached to it. All system administration functions are done by the computer staff. The average user cannot even view most of the system configuration files. On the other hand, these free non-AT&T UNIX systems have enabled UNIX to be loaded on a home computer, so users can install and administer their own personal UNIX systems. In fact, users usually have no choice because private homes rarely have their own data processing departments. These free UNIX systems can be connected to the Internet as a Web server, email handler, or DNS server.

Dedicated volunteers add new modules to the free UNIX so that it stays current with new hardware as it becomes available. Although some companies provide commercial support for Linux, there is still a hesitancy to use free UNIX in large commercial enterprises. Still, this free, fully functional UNIX is certainly playing an important role in the evolution of UNIX.

How UNIX Differs from MS-DOS/Windows

UNIX, MS-DOS, Windows 95, and Windows NT are different operating systems. UNIX was designed to be a multiuser, time-share operating system that could efficiently handle a large number of user stations running different programs simultaneously. Personal computers, or PCs, developed along a totally different path. PCs have one keyboard, one screen, and one mouse; therefore, they accommodate only a single user. The same Pentium processor that supports a single user under MS-DOS or Windows might support 100 concurrent users under UNIX.

The look and feel of Windows software is quite different from traditional UNIX character-based software. If a Windows user starts a job, the processor normally has a lot a spare computing power available; therefore, Windows users are used to busy screens and colorful indicators that graphically show a job progressing. In contrast, traditional UNIX software outputs few messages until the job is done. Keep in mind that UNIX may be running 100 other jobs at the same time it is running your job. Any wasted effort or output would slow down someone else's job.

Today, the differences between UNIX and Windows are not so clear cut. Many UNIX systems are single-user workstations, in which the user utilizes a mouse to click on icons and manipulate windows. Some Windows systems directly run jobs for other users logged on from serial ports or from another Windows PC. Some Windows NT and UNIX servers have no direct users at all; they provide services to a network, such as print sharing, file sharing, email, or Internet access. Many UNIX systems can run Windows programs (for example, through WABI). Likewise, many Windows systems can run UNIX utilities such as vi, awk, and shell (through MKS tools).

One large difference between UNIX and Windows is where users get applications for their system. A wide range of general purpose utilities are available for Windows systems at the local PC store. Word processing, spreadsheet, checkbook balancing, and similar programs are generally useful no matter what business you are in. On the other hand, you will rarely find any UNIX applications at the PC store. One of great strengths of UNIX is that it is an excellent platform to write custom software for a particular industry. UNIX supports many programming languages, databases, and program development tools. It is an open system, so it runs on many different hardware systems. UNIX software developers often study one industry, such as dental offices, lumber stores, auto parts, or flower shops. They then create a set of applications to computerize all the business functions needed by that particular business, using the jargon and special regulations, forms, and accounting needed. These are called vertical applications: They're a complete set of applications for one target business, whereas PC stores often sell horizontal applications in which one application is general enough for a wide range of businesses. The software developer uses UNIX to create a turn-key system—that is, the end user turns the key to power on the system and then uses just the supplied custom programming to run his business.

Today, Windows systems are being networked together to provide the multiuser capability that UNIX provides. Software developers are creating Windows graphics multiuser programs that have a jazzier look and feel than traditional UNIX character-based applications. UNIX can support graphic applications by using special X Windows stations; however, these stations cannot run Windows software from the PC store. Led by Sun Microsystems and its support of the Java language, there is an effort to capitalize on the success of the World Wide Web to provide multiuser graphics and Web-based applications. Running the application through a Web browser is a way to provide the jazzier graphic look and feel that traditional UNIX character-based applications lack. These applications can run on local networks and also over the Internet. They can run on low-cost network computers that are minimal computer stations specially designed to run these browser applications. The host server can be Windows or UNIX, which should be appealing for software development companies. Will browser-based applications become a new application standard? Only time will tell.

UNIX Standards and Revisions

Table 1.1 listed many companies that have modified UNIX and that distribute the operating system under some name other than UNIX, such as HP-UX or SunOS. In this book, you will sometimes see two or three different ways to do one task because some types of UNIX computers can do it only the first way, some only the second way, and some only the third. At one company, you may regularly use several different types of UNIX servers, where the commands have such differences. If you connect to a wide area network such as the Internet, you will encounter even more UNIX hosts in which UNIX is slightly different than what you are used to. At first, you may find this variety disconcerting.

Lack of Administration Standards

Standards for UNIX commands do not extend to how the system is installed and configured. Each version of UNIX can be quite different in the utilities and procedures used to set up the disk, add users or printers, and so on. This book describes user commands common to all versions of UNIX. For UNIX administration, consult a manual specifically for your version of UNIX.

In answer to that, it's important to understand that UNIX works like a car radio. All car radios can play music, adjust the volume, and change the station. Radios differ considerably, however, in the placement and use of knobs, buttons, or sliders. The volume control is not always on the left. Yet, if you rent a car, you can usually still get the radio to work. People are accustomed to fiddling with the controls until they get it to do what they want. In the same way, there is no need to panic when you work on a UNIX system in which the commands are slightly different than the UNIX you are used to. After you know the major varieties, if a command does not work one way, you just try the other standard methods.

Efforts to standardize UNIX abound, attempting to make the commands uniform across different hardware and vendor platforms. POSIX is a standard from an organization called IEEE, to which many types of UNIX adhere. The international X/Open organization provides UNIX standards called XPG3, XPG4, and Spec 1170. Many companies—such as IBM, HP, Sun, and SCO—have adopted the common desktop environment (CDE) to provide a common look and feel for graphic UNIX. System V Interface Definition (SVID) is another standard to help keep UNIX more uniform.

It helps to see how UNIX evolved to anticipate what command variations to expect on an unknown UNIX system. In the beginning, UNIX was developed at AT&T Bell Laboratories, who gave these names to successive revisions of AT&T UNIX:

- Sixth edition
- Seventh edition
- System III
- System V (That is, Roman numeral five; they skipped System IV.)
- System V, Release 2 (abbreviated as SVR2)

- System V, Release 3 (SVR3)

- System V, Release 4 (SVR4)

SVID describes a standard for UNIX based on AT&T's System V UNIX.

While this AT&T development was occurring, an early version of UNIX was being modified at the University of California at Berkeley. This version of UNIX is called BSD, which stands for Berkeley Software Distribution. BSD added many important capabilities to UNIX, but some of these overlapped new features added by AT&T.

Today, all UNIX systems can be classified by the extent to which they are based on System V UNIX versus BSD UNIX. The presence of the directory /etc/rc2.d denotes System V-based UNIX, whereas the absence of this directory usually indicates a BSD-based UNIX. Here are some specific examples of how some specific commands differ between System V and BSD:

System V	BSD
shutdown -g3 -i0 -y	shutdown -h +3
lp -dlaser2 -n2 acme	lpr -Plaser2 -#2 acme

If your system does not support the System V lp command for printing, it probably uses the BSD lpr command. Some systems support both printer commands. SunOS rev 4, for example, was a BSD UNIX variant. The next major release, SunOS rev 5, switched over from BSD to SVR4, which combined features from (System V) SVR3, XENIX, BSD, and Sun. SunOS rev 5 still supports the rev 4 BSD versions of utilities as optional alternatives. Users on SunOS rev 5 can customize their UNIX session to use System V, BSD, or XPG4 versions of utilities by default. (This is done by changing the PATH variable.)

UNIX After AT&T

Initially, AT&T developed and licensed UNIX, controlled the restricted source code, and collected royalties from other companies that sold UNIX. Around 1991, AT&T created a company called UNIX System Laboratories to do this. Around 1993, Novell purchased UNIX from AT&T. Novell integrated some of its NetWare technology and changed the name of UNIX to UnixWare, which is based on AT&T UNIX SVR4. Novell transferred the UNIX trademark to the X/Open Company Ltd., which publishes standards and certifies whether a version of UNIX or UnixWare meets the UNIX standard. Novell retained the right to license UNIX System V source code. Around 1995, the Santa Cruz Operation (SCO) purchased

UNIX from Novell. SCO then had two major lines of UNIX it supported: its own OpenServer UNIX and UnixWare. In 1998, SCO, in conjunction with a number of major UNIX vendors, released UnixWare 7, which contains the next major release of UNIX: SVR5, a 64-bit UNIX operating system. This is not the only 64-bit UNIX operating system, so there is still healthy competition in the UNIX marketplace. As of August 1999, SCO UnixWare 7 has been tested on the new Intel 64 bit processor. This UNIX will be one of the first operating systems to take advantage of the 64-bit processors when they are ready for general release.

Important UNIX Concepts You Must Know First

The following sections cover the basic features of the UNIX operating system you need to understand.

The UNIX Kernel

In Figure 1.1, you can see the UNIX operating system represented as three concentric circles. The innermost circle is called the kernel, which refers to the nucleus or core of the operating system. The kernel is the most hidden part of the operating system. It contains code called drivers; these allow the system to control all the system hardware, the disk drives, the peripherals, and so on.

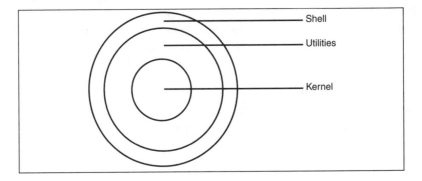

FIGURE 1.1
UNIX kernel, utilities, and shell.

The next circle represents the system utilities and commands. When you run a command such as vi, it uses routines within the kernel to display output on your screen, get input from the keyboard, and save files on the disk.

The UNIX Shell

The outermost circle represents the UNIX *shell*. The shell is a program that accepts commands from a user and starts the requested commands. The shell is all that the user sees of the UNIX operating system, just as when you view an egg or a nut, all you see is the outermost shell layer and none of the complexity inside.

The shell does more than just pass on the commands you type in; it enables the user to run commands in the background. This means that the user's station is not tied up while the command runs. The shell enables the user to use wildcards to indicate which files should be processed. The shell actually supports a complete programming language that allows conditional execution of commands based on the results of other commands and loops to repeat sequences of commands.

A number of shell programs are actually available on UNIX, and different users can be using their preferred, different shells at the same time on one system. A shell is also known by the command used to start that shell. The Bourne, C, and Korn shells are usually available on most commercial UNIX systems today. The Bash and tcsh shell are usually found only on Linux systems; however, there is much cross-pollination, so this is not an absolute rule. Table 1.2 lists these shells with the command used to invoke the shell and a description of the shell.

Table 1.2   Available UNIX shells

Shell Name	Command	Description
Bourne shell	sh	Is available on all UNIX systems
C shell	csh	Uses C programming-like syntax
Korn shell	ksh	Is a superset of the Bourne shell
Bash shell	bash	Contains both C and Korn shell features
tcsh shell	tcsh	Works like the C shell

Because each shell is a system utility, you can start using a particular shell just by entering the command shown in Table 1.2.

The Bourne shell is the oldest shell. It is an adequate programming environment, but it is weak in user conveniences; it offers no way to repeat or re-edit previous commands and no way to control background jobs. Some older systems did not have the C shell or the Korn shell, so many programmers today still write programs (called scripts) primarily for the Bourne shell, even though they use other shells when they are typing in commands.

Although the C shell represented an improvement in user convenience over the Bourne shell, some of its syntax is not compatible with the Bourne shell. Because Bourne shells scripts are common, C shell users must learn the syntax for both shells and must avoid confusing them.

The Korn shell offers similar user conveniences as the C shell. It has a powerful command-line editing capability that is not available in the C shell, using either vi or emacs editing commands that enable you to retrieve previous commands, edit, and execute them. The Korn shell is a superset of the Bourne shell, so no syntax conflicts exist between them. The Korn shell offers more powerful programming constructs than the Bourne shell, but these should be avoided if you need to run your programs on older UNIX systems that did not offer the Korn shell.

The Shell Prompt

To use a UNIX system, the system administrator (called "root") must create an account for you to use. The start of a UNIX session will look something like this:

```
acme login: fred
Password:
TERM = (vt100)
$ _
```

Root Warning

The root logon is the all-powerful system administrator. If you are a beginner, do not use the root logon. If you make mistakes as root, you can crash or corrupt your UNIX (or Linux) system. UNIX will usually try to carry out your commands because it will assume that you know what you are doing. It will usually not warn you if your command makes no sense or will wipe out important files. There is usually no way to undo a mistake, so use a non-root account while you are first learning UNIX, even if you are the only system user.

At the logon prompt, you must identify yourself and enter your password (which will not display as you type it, for security). The dollar sign ($) is the shell prompt that shows that UNIX is ready for you to enter commands. The underline character (_) following the dollar sign represents the cursor waiting for commands to be input. Here are the standard shell prompts:

```
    Bourne shell or Korn shell:    $
                      C shell:     %
root login regardless of shell:    #
```

The shell prompt can be customized to contain your system name, your current directory, or other characters. Here are some shell prompts you might encounter:

```
acme$ _
/usr/fred> _
[acme] _
```

You must be at the shell prompt before you can enter UNIX commands. You can also use UNIX through a graphical user interface (GUI), as described in Chapter 5, "The UNIX Graphical User Interface (GUI)."

Shell Variables

Each shell is a programming language that supports variables, even when typing separate commands at the command line. Words, phrases, and other information can be saved in a named variable and can be used later. Some variables have special meaning to the shell and control how the system operates. These are also called environment variables. The TERM variable, for example, should be set to the type of terminal you are using; otherwise, your screen output may contain garbage. Many shell variables have names in all uppercase to avoid confusion with UNIX commands (which are usually in lowercase).

The following list details some common environment variables:

- HOME (your home directory)
- LOGNAME (your username)
- SHELL (your current shell command name)
- TERM (your current terminal type)

Standard Output, Standard Error, Standard Input

Programs under UNIX usually do not display messages directly to your screen. Instead, they call a special output routine called Standard Output (or stdout, for short). stdout is normally set up to go to your screen, but it can easily be redirected to go to a device such as a printer or a disk file. This is one of the elements of UNIX that is truly elegant: Programs and utilities do their output to stdout so that they have no idea where the output is really going. The shell can easily redirect stdout to a device or file as desired.

```
$ cal
$ cal > /dev/lp0
$ cal > /usr/fred/year
```

The preceding three examples use the UNIX cal command, which outputs a calendar of the current month to stdout. In the first example, stdout has not been redirected; therefore, the output goes to your screen. In the second example, the greater than sign (>) redirects stdout to a printer device (/dev/lp0) so that the output appears on that printer. In the third example, stdout has been redirected to a disk file so that the output is saved on disk.

A special routine also can be used to display error messages. This is called Standard Error (or stderr, for short). stderr usually goes to your screen so that you can see any error messages. But again, the shell can easily redirect stderr to a device or file, totally independently of stdout. Therefore, stdout can be saved in a separate file from stderr.

A special routine for input also is available. This is called Standard Input (or stdin, for short). If a program gets its input from stdin, the shell can provide this input by redirecting it from a device or a disk file. If a utility always asks three questions before it starts to run, for example, you could put the answers to those three questions into a disk file and then redirect that disk file to provide the input so that you don't have to type the input yourself.

SEE ALSO
➤ *For more information on standard I/O, see page 45*

Piping and Filters

stdout from one command can be redirected as stdin to another command, creating a direct pipeline from one command to another. This operation is called *piping*, and the vertical bar (|) is used as the pipe sign character.

```
$ ls | pg
```

In the preceding example, ls is the UNIX command to list the current files. If you run ls by itself and there are more than 25 files, some names will go off the screen before you can read them. pg is a UNIX command to display output one screen at a time. It waits for user input before displaying the next screen. You can pipe the output from ls directly to pg so that you can see the filenames one screen at a time.

Some UNIX commands display so much information that the lines you are looking for get lost. grep is a UNIX command that displays only lines that contain a desired pattern, as the following example shows:

```
$ ls | grep acme
```

In the preceding example, ls will output all the files. These will not go directly to your screen but will be piped instead to grep. At that point, grep will display only those filenames that contain *acme* somewhere in their name. You can think of grep like a coffee filter: Both the hot water and the coffee grounds go into the filter. The filter removes the things you don't want (the grounds) and passes through what you do want (the liquid coffee). In the same way, the grep filter removes the lines you don't want and passes through only the lines that contain the desired pattern. The term *filter* works for any UNIX utility that can be used in a pipeline to modify the output as desired. While a filter normally screens out what you don't want, UNIX filters can also add text or simply rearrange the output.

Users and Groups

UNIX is a multiuser system. Normally, each user must log on with a unique logon name so that the system knows who just logged on. This system keeps track of the files and mail for this user.

A group is a collection of users. Users can belong to more than one group, and each group has a group name. Each file has an owner: the user who owns the file. Each file also belongs to a group that is usually the primary group of the user who created the file. Chapter 14, "File Permissions and System Security," discusses users, groups, and permissions in more detail.

UNIX Access

Commercial UNIX tends to run on more expensive computers in data processing departments. Companies and institutions may have terminals where you can log on to a UNIX server. However, you must be given a UNIX account before you can use the UNIX system.

Linux/GNU, and FreeBSD are non-AT&T UNIX that are sold in magazines, at computer swap meets, at PC stores, in technical book stores, via mail order, and via the Internet. You can get a free SCO UNIX license over the Internet from www.sco.com. You can also order the installation media for a modest price. This offer is just for educational, noncommercial purposes. Sun also offers a low-cost, noncommercial version of its operating system, called Solaris x86, for Intel computers.

Windows and UNIX on the Same Computer

Intel-based systems have the capability to partition the hard disk so that DOS, Windows, or UNIX can reside in their own sections of the disk (called partitions). The fdisk utility can be used to set the active partition whose operating system will come up when you boot the system. Windows is not available while UNIX is running, and vice versa.

These UNIX systems can be loaded on a home computer. However, this process requires an available partition and is not for the beginner. (Linux can load into a DOS file system or run directly from CD-ROM also.) If you have Windows on the same computer, do not load UNIX unless you are confident that you can restore

Windows and all the files in case something goes wrong. You will learn a lot about UNIX and computers in general if you load your own UNIX system.

How to Do Things the UNIX Way

In the following chapters of this book, we will learn many different UNIX commands. In teaching these commands to beginners, I find that it helps if you understand three general principles that apply to all UNIX commands. The following sections cover these three principles.

No News Is Good News

Because the output of one command is often piped as input to another UNIX command, commands do not output unnecessary messages. If a command is successful, it just goes back to the shell prompt without any other output. Don't expect a completion message or a status message. On the other hand, if any output is generated, this is cause for alarm. Study this output carefully because it could be an indication that something went wrong.

Commands Are Building Blocks

Many UNIX commands seem to be primitive or unfinished. Think of them as raw building blocks. You can create your own commands by putting a series of commands in a pipeline. Most commands do not have a print option because you can pipe the output to the printer. Most commands also do not have a sort option because you can pipe the output to sort.

Use Minimum Keystrokes

UNIX enables the skilled user to accomplish marvels using a minimum of keystrokes. You can see this tendency to minimize keystrokes in the names of the common commands:

ls (list files)

rm (remove files)

cp (copy files)

mv (move files)

cd (change directory)

pg (page the output)

Chapter 22, "Command-Line Editing in the Korn Shell," shows how a small wild-card pattern can save typing long lists of filenames. Chapter 11, "Generating and Using File Lists," explains how the shell can facilitate keying in commands. Throughout this book, you will see cases in which UNIX provides features and tools that enable you to automate situations that would normally require tedious repetitive keyboard entry.

chapter

2

Getting Started—A Guided Tour of UNIX

Steve "Mor" Moritsugu

Access and connect to UNIX

Commands and command options

Absolute vs. full pathnames

Pagers, filters, regular expressions

Understanding Standard I/O

Tip for Beginners

This chapter is an overview of UNIX especially for you! It shows how the different UNIX concepts covered in various parts of this book interrelate. Don't worry about the details—those are all covered elsewhere. Concentrate on the concepts.

Traveling in the Land of UNIX

UNIX Adventure Vocabulary

Several UNIX terms are consistent with an adventure/quest theme. Background processes are called daemons. You may have to kill your child processes, lest they become zombies. You might not be able to access a file because it has a bad magic number.

Working with UNIX is like playing an adventure game where you travel through unknown terrain, engage in battles, and pick up magic talismans and incantations. Seasoned travelers can use their bag of tricks to prosper, while newcomers are hard-pressed to just stay alive. People adept at UNIX are like wizards that can pull magic command lines out of the air and accomplish in a few keystrokes what otherwise might require hours of programming.

Unlike Windows, UNIX is not intended for beginners: There are few paternalistic protections to hamper the experienced user. Imagine Windows to be like Disneyland, where everything is safe but limited. Imagine UNIX to be like a tropical rain forest, teeming with life and unimagined possibilities, but also with real dangers for the inexperienced.

When you travel in a foreign country, there are local customs that you must follow to avoid severe consequences. The purpose of this chapter is to give you an overview of UNIX (how everything fits together), and provide a guided tour through the Land of UNIX. So sit back, relax, and let the tour begin. ("I don't think we're in Kansas anymore, Toto.")

Getting Access to UNIX

If you are a beginner, do not rush out to the PC store and buy Linux and expect to be up and running in a couple hours. This is also true if you order low-cost noncommercially licensed versions of commercial brands of UNIX, such as Sun Solaris 7, SCO OpenServer 5, or SCO UnixWare 7, to install at home. Installing UNIX or

Linux on a home computer is a very complex process. Commercial UNIX systems are usually installed only by system administrators with years of experience.

Usually UNIX is the only operating system software on the computer. If you want to run both Windows and UNIX or Linux from the same machine, you have added an extra layer of difficulty to the project. There is a good chance that you will have to reload all your Windows software as well as UNIX or Linux more than once before you are successful.

People usually do not get started with UNIX or Linux by installing it. They might first get a UNIX shell account for login because of a project at work or at school or through an Internet provider. Some people encounter UNIX through friends, computer groups, and user meetings.

To access UNIX, you must be given two things:

- A valid system user name (john or jdoe, for example)
- A password for that account (v5j799t, for example)

If you have no access to a UNIX account, go ahead and install UNIX or Linux at home, but don't be surprised when you find that this is very difficult to do. The initial comments in Chapter 12, "Installing UNIX at Home," will help you whether you are installing UNIX or Linux.

SEE ALSO

➤ *For more information on installing UNIX for your home PC, see page 317*

Connecting to UNIX

You must first get a connection to the UNIX system. If you are at work, your terminal may be directly connected and you can get a login prompt just by pressing Enter.

If you access UNIX via the Internet, you must first connect to the Internet and then to the UNIX system. Some people must first access a router or server and then access the UNIX system. Others must use their modem to dial a phone number before they can connect. There are a myriad of equally valid possibilities and methods. If someone else already knows how to connect to your UNIX system, ask that person to show you how to do it.

The Login Prompt

When you connect to the UNIX system, you should see a login prompt something like this:

```
SCO OpenServer(TM) Release 5 (dtr.dtrbus.COM) (ttyp1)
```

```
login:
```

At this point, the system is waiting for you to identify yourself by typing in the username you have been assigned by the system administrator. Login prompts can differ widely from this. They may refer to the type of UNIX or the name of the company. They may contain a logo or design.

A login prompt on a graphical console might look like this:

```
Welcome to acme.COM
    UnixWare 7
```

```
Please enter your user name
```

After you enter your username, it will ask for this:

```
Password:
```

Enter the password you were given with that username.

If the username or password is not correct, you will be prompted to enter that information again. Make sure that you are using the correct uppercase and lowercase letters.

Once the username and password are verified, you will often then see a message of the day, like this:

```
Printer 14 will be down for maintenance at 2 pm Thurs 9/17.
```

You might also see a humorous or well-known quotation, or have your fortune predicted, just to brighten your day.

The Shell Prompt

After you have logged in, you should see a prompt from a program called a shell, like this:

```
$
```

The shell will accept your commands and cause them to be executed. Several different shells exist (as described in Chapter 1, "Introduction to UNIX and the Shell"), and they have different features. As you become more familiar with UNIX, you will be able to choose your favorite shell.

The shell prompt can be customized. It can contain the system name, the current directory, or any other preferences.

SEE ALSO

➤ *For more information on the UNIX shell, see page 25*

Simple Commands

In the following example, the date command was typed at the shell prompt. The shell caused this command to run and display the current system date and time to the screen. Then the shell prompt reappeared so that another command could be entered.

```
dtr> date
Sun Sep 19 16:00:42 PDT 1999
dtr>
```

Another simple UNIX command lists the files that exist:

```
dtr> ls
mp0095
mp0096
mp0097
mp0098
mp0099
mp0100
mp0106
mp0107
mp0107.old
mp0108
mp0109
mp4.0.1a
mp4.1.2
mp4.1.3
mp4.1.3a
mp4.1.4
dtr>
```

In this example, ls shows you the names of the files in the current directory. Files are just collections of text or data that you can access by name. Directories are just collections of files and other directories.

SEE ALSO

➤ *For more information on UNIX directories, see page 60*

Command Options

Most UNIX commands enable you to specify options that modify how the command works.

For example, -C is an option to ls. It modifies ls to list the files in columns, as you can see in the following example:

```
dtr> ls -C
mp0095      mp0098      mp0106      mp0108      mp4.1.2      mp4.1.4
mp0096      mp0099      mp0107      mp0109      mp4.1.3
mp0097      mp0100      mp0107.old  mp4.0.1a    mp4.1.3a
dtr>
```

The next example shows that the -l option will produce a long listing that includes the file owner, group, size, and date last modified, as well as the name:

```
dtr> ls -l
total 48
-rw-rw----  1 gota    dbhelp      1488 Sep 18  2000 mp0095
-rw-rw----  1 mori    dbhelp      1467 May 27  1993 mp0096
-rw-rw----  1 mori    dbhelp      1110 May 27  1993 mp0097
-rw-rw----  1 mori    dbhelp      1407 May 26  1993 mp0098
-rw-rw----  1 mori    dbhelp       776 Jul  6  1994 mp0099
-rw-rw----  1 mori    dbhelp      1381 Jun 10  1994 mp0100
-rw-rw----  1 mori    dbhelp       737 Jan  4  1994 mp0106
-rw-rw----  1 mori    dbhelp      1593 Jun 17  1997 mp0107
-rw-rw----  1 405     dbhelp      1548 Jun 17  1997 mp0107.old
-rw-rw----  1 405     dbhelp       955 Sep 24  1997 mp0108
-rw-rw----  1 mori    dbhelp       952 Mar 17  1998 mp0109
-rw-rw----  1 mori    dbhelp      1045 Jun  3  1998 mp4.0.1a
-rw-rw----  1 mori    dbhelp       948 Jul 17  1996 mp4.1.2
-rw-rw----  1 lazar   dbhelp       948 Jul 29  1996 mp4.1.3
-rw-rw----  1 stull   dbhelp       951 Mar 24  1998 mp4.1.3a
-rw-rw----  1 mori    dbhelp       948 Apr 13  1998 mp4.1.4
dtr>
```

Almost all the UNIX commands have a rich set of options that enables them to be customized to do just the job you want. An option letter for one command can mean something totally different when used with another command.

Many UNIX commands exist, and each can have many options. How do UNIX people keep track of them all?

Man Pages for Online Help

You can get online help for any command by using the `man` command. This is an example of the man page for the `ls` command.

```
dtr> man ls

ls
  *****
```

```
ls, l, lc, lf, lr, lx -- list contents of directories

Syntax
======

ls [ -1ACFLRabcdfgilmnopqrstux ] [ -Ws ¦ -Wv ] [ directory ¦ file ... ]
```

The man page starts by showing the syntax and allowed options. More than 25 option letters can be used with `ls`, either singly or in combinations. Later in the man page, you see a list of each option and what it does, as in the following:

```
Options are:
```

- `-1`   Forces an output format with one entry per line, for lc, lf, lr, and lx.

- `-a`   Lists all entries; ``.'' and ``..'' are not suppressed.

- `-A`   Lists all entries. Entries whose name begin with a dot (.) are listed. This option does not list current directory ``.'' and directory above ``..''.

- `-b`   Forces printing of non-graphic characters in the \ddd notation, in octal.

- `-c`   Uses the last time that the file was changed for sorting. The change time refers to modification of the file's data, modification of the information stored in the inode, or creation of the file.

          This option is used with -t option.

- `-C`   Lists in columns with entries sorted down the columns. If the argument(s) are filename(s), output is across the page, rather than down the page in columns.

```
...
-l        Lists in long format, giving mode, number of links, owner, group,
          size in bytes, the time that each file was last modified. The -l
          option is assumed.

          Unless one of the -c or -u option is specified, the modification
          time refers only to changes made to the file's data, or the
          creation of the file. It does not record the time that changes were
          made to the information stored in the inode.

          If the file is a symbolic link, the filename is printed followed by
          ``->'' and the pathname of the referenced file.

          If the file is a special file, the size field will contain the major
          and minor device numbers, rather than a size. A total count of
          blocks in the directory, including indirect blocks, is printed at
          the top of long format listings.

          A description of the mode listing is given in ``File modes''.
```

Notice how many option letters are possible for this one command. Since the man pages are on-line, it is easy to look up the options for any command. Some man pages are 40 or 50 screens long, giving copious information on each command including available options, examples of usage, limitations, and related files.

SEE ALSO

➤ *For more information on the* man *command, see page 88*

File Commands

In Chapters 7 through 11, you learn about many UNIX commands that work with files and directories. You can copy, move, delete, find, and print files, among other commands. Let's take one file command as an example:

```
dtr> rm report1 report2 report3
dtr>
```

UNIX Has No Undelete Command

You must be careful when you remove files. If you mistakenly remove the wrong file, there is no way to bring it back. All you can do is restore the file from the last backup that you made.

In this example, the `rm` command removes or deletes the three filenames given. Most file commands will accept a list of files. Put a space, not a comma, between each filename.

No News Is Good News

In the previous `rm` example, notice that `rm` simply shows the shell prompt when it is done. No summary or Good Completion message appears.

In this example, `report2` generated some output. It could not be removed because `report2` did not exist in the first place.

```
dtr> rm report1 report2 report3
rm: report2 non-existent
dtr>
```

In UNIX, no news is good news. Because `report1` and `report3` generated no news, we know they were successfully deleted.

Conversely, any time you run a command and get some output before the next shell prompt, it is likely that something went wrong. Study any output carefully: It is probably an error message that you must resolve before you can go on.

SEE ALSO
➤ *For more information on errors, see pages 94, 98, 102*

Filename Wildcards

UNIX provides a rich set of wildcards that can be used to generate a list of files whose names match a pattern. For example, this command will delete all files whose name starts with acme, as well as some report files:

```
dtr> rm acme* report[1-3]
dtr>
```

In the previous example, `report[1-3]` is a wildcard pattern that will match and delete any of these files if they exist:

- `report1`
- `report2`
- `report3`

The previous example would not delete report7 or report.acme because they do not match the pattern given.

SEE ALSO
➤ *For more information on filename wildcards, see page 292*

Absolute or Full Pathnames

> **The Root Directory**
> The root directory is the base directory that contains all other directories and files.

Up to now, the text has referred only to files in your current directory. You can refer to files in other directories by specifying an *absolute pathname* that tells you how to go from the system's root directory, through each subdirectory, to the desired file. An absolute pathname is also called a *full pathname*. For example, see the following:

```
dtr> rm abc /tmp/abc /usr/fred/reports/abc
dtr>
```

The previous command removes these three files:

- abc in the current directory
- abc in the tmp subdirectory of the root directory
- abc in the reports subdirectory of the fred subdirectory of the usr subdirectory of the root directory

SEE ALSO

➤ *For more information on directories and absolute pathnames, see page 66*

Relative Pathnames

If files are in a subdirectory of your current directory, you can refer to them easily by using a relative pathname. A relative pathname tells you how to go from where you are now to the desired file. These are usually shorter pathnames than absolute pathnames that start all the way at the root directory. The following is an example:

```
dtr> rm abc reports/abc reports/acme/abc
dtr>
```

The previous command removes these three files:

- abc in the current directory
- abc in the reports subdirectory of the current directory
- abc in the acme subdirectory of the reports subdirectory of the current directory

SEE ALSO

➤ *For more information on relative pathnames, see page 70*

File Permissions

Each UNIX file and directory has a set of permissions that controls who is permitted access. In the `ls -l` output seen earlier in this chapter, the permissions can be seen as a set of letters at the start of each line:

```
dtr> ls -l
total 48
-rwxr-x--x    1 gota      dbhelp      1488 Sep 18  2001 mp0095
-rw-r--r--    1 mori      dbhelp      1467 May 27  1999 mp0096
```

There are nine permissions, always in this order:

r	means the user who owns the file can read it (else -)
w	means the user who owns the file can write it (else -)
x	means the user who owns the file can execute it (else -)
r	means the users in the file group can read it (else -)
w	means the users in the file group can write it (else -)
x	means the users in the file group can execute it (else -)
r	means other users can read it (else -)
w	means other users can write it (else -)
x	means other users can execute it (else -)

SEE ALSO

➤ *For more information on users and groups, see page 358*

➤ *For more information on understanding file and directory permissions, see page 377*

Filesystems

UNIX systems do not have a standard name for physical or logical disk drives. Sometimes they are called *slices*, *volumes*, *divisions*, or *partitions*. No matter what the disk area is called, an empty filesystem must be created there before it can be used. The term *filesystem* is standard on all types of UNIX systems. A filesystem is an area on one or more disk drives where files and directories can be created. Before a filesystem can be used, it must be mounted. Most UNIX systems have several mounted filesystems available. If a filesystem becomes full, no more files can be created there, even if other filesystems have available disk space.

The `df` command shows the mounted filesystems and how many free disk blocks each one has:

```
$ df -v
Mount Dir  Filesystem          blocks      used      free   %used
/          /dev/root          1433600   1112914    320686    78%
/stand     /dev/boot            30720     17606     13114    58%
/u         /dev/u             2494444   2197484    296960    89%
/u2        /dev/d1150         8462336   2818482   5643854    34%
```

Don't Get 100% Full

It is important to run the `df` command periodically to make sure that no filesystem is heading towards being 100% full. Once at 100% full, programs could abort, transactions could be left half updated, or the entire system could hang or crash. Users should trim their disk usage periodically, like a spring cleaning, to prevent running out of disk space problems.

Filesystems are accessed through special directories called mount points or mount directories. UNIX does not use the DOS/Windows scheme of drive letters. Anytime you access a mount point directory or any of its subdirectories, you are accessing a separate disk drive or disk area.

Before you create any really large files, you should check the `df` command and see what filesystems, and hence what directories, have enough disk space to hold these new files.

SEE ALSO

➤ *For more information on filesystems, see page 472*

Hard and Soft Links

UNIX allows the same file to be accessed by two different pathnames. This could be useful if you have a directory of customer files and a different directory of vendor files. If a company is both a customer and a vendor, you can put the same file in both directories by using either a hard or soft link. Both types of links mean that there is only one file, but it can be accessed from two different names or two different directories. A link is not a copy.

Here is a soft or symbolic link in the customers directory that allows the acme file to be in both the customers directory and the vendors directory. The real file is in the /vendors directory but it can be accessed using this soft or symbolic link in the /customers directory.

```
lrwxrwxrwx   1 mori      group        13 Oct 31 20:31 acme -> /vendors/acme
```

The next example shows the jupiter file which is a hard link to another file in another directory. The only way we know there is a second name for this file is because the hard link count in field two is 2:

```
-rw-rw----   2 mori     group      25501 Oct 31 20:30 jupiter
```

SEE ALSO

➤ *For more information on hard and soft links, see page 233*

Redirecting Standard I/O

Most UNIX commands invoke a special routine called standard output (or stdout) to display information. They invoke a different routine called standard error (or stderr) to display any error messages. There is a similar routine to get input called standard input (or stdin).

In the following example, mp0094 could not be listed, so an error message went to standard error (stderr):

```
dtr> ls mp0094 mp0095
ls: mp0094 not found: No such file or directory (error 2)
mp0095
dtr>
```

Here, mp0095 was found and listed to standard output (stdout). Using the standard error routine for error messages allows the shell to redirect the errors from the screen to a file, as in the following example:

```
dtr> ls mp0094 mp0095 2> myerrors
mp0095
dtr>
```

In this example, 2> is a special directive to the shell to redirect any errors away from the screen and save them instead in the given filename (myerrors, in this case). Notice that the 2> prevents the error message from appearing on the screen in the previous example.

In the following example, a filename wildcard is used to list all files whose name starts with my. There is now a file called myerrors, created in the previous example:

```
dtr> ls my*
myerrors
dtr> cat myerrors
ls: mp0094 not found: No such file or directory (error 2)
dtr>
```

In this sequence, the cat command is used to display the contents of myerrors. You can see that it contains the error message from the previous example.

Standard error allows errors to be saved in a file so that you can look at them later. Then you don't have to worry about error messages going off the screen before you notice them: You have a hard copy if you want to review each error later in detail.

Similarly, you can use the sign>> sign to redirect (save) standard output (stdout) in a file:

```
dtr> ls mp0094 mp0095 > myoutput 2> myerrors
dtr>
```

Notice now that no output appears on the screen in the previous example. The data output is saved in a file called myoutput. Errors are saved in a different file. You can choose any names for these, and you can use absolute or relative pathnames to save these files in different directories.

Redirection Danger

When you redirect output or errors to a file, you must carefully check the filename you use. If you give the name of an existing file, it will be overwritten with the new output. The old contents will be lost, and there is no way to get it back. You will not get a warning before or after the old data is lost.

This is one of the dangers mentioned at the start of this chapter. UNIX does not warn you that you are about to lose data; it assumes that you know what you are doing.

Piping

In the same way that standard output can be saved in a file, it can also be fed as the input to a second command. This is called process piping because a data pipeline is created from the output of one command to the input (stdin) of a second command.

This is an extremely elegant mechanism that allows UNIX commands to be easily combined together right on the command line. It is also a very efficient mechanism because output from the first program is paced to feed directly into the second program without the overhead of temporary disk file writes.

This is a simple example you saw earlier, where piping would be useful. The ls command lists the files in the current directory. If there are more files than will fit on the screen, the first files go off the screen and all you see are the last screenful:

```
mp0095
mp0096
mp0097
mp0098
mp0099
```

```
mp0100
mp0106
mp0107
mp0107.old
mp0108
mp0109
mp4.0.1a
dtr>
```

You can use the vertical bar symbol (¦) to pipe the output of ls to a program that will pause after each screen page of output. You can then press the spacebar or the Enter key when you are ready to go to the next page:

```
dtr> ls ¦ pg
mp0051
mp0053
mp0054
mp0057
...
mp0095
mp0096
mp0097
mp0098
mp0099
mp0100
:
```

The colon at the bottom of the screen indicates that the pager is waiting for input before displaying the second page. The three dots (...) in the example just mean that some of the lines have been pulled out to take up less space on the page, but this still represents one complete screenful of filenames.

Understanding Standard I/O

The following is a frequently asked question about standard I/O:

I'm still confused about standard input, standard output, and standard error. What should I picture in my mind for these?

Good question. The following comments about standard output (stdout) also apply to standard input and standard error. First stdout is not a piece of hardware; it is not a keyboard, a screen, or a card in your computer. It is actually implemented as a virtual file in UNIX. A UNIX command or program will open stdout as a file and write to it as if it were a file. The shell determines the real destination for those characters.

Here is a follow-up question:

How is standard I/O related to redirection and piping?

When a UNIX command or program sends characters to stdout, the shell can then redirect those characters to go to a file. This command says to send stdout generated by myprog to a file called myfile instead of going to the screen:

```
myprog > myfile
```

If myprog outputs directly to the screen instead of to stdout, then the redirection and piping is ignored. The output will go to the screen and myfile will be empty.

The following command says to pipe stdout from prog1 as stdin to prog2:

```
prog1 ¦ prog2
```

This makes sense only if prog1 sends its output to stdout and prog2 reads its input from stdin.

Standard I/O: An Analogy

Take a look at this analogy to further explain standard I/O.

Imagine that Acme Co. has a phone system. Each phone at Acme Co. has buttons for different extensions, such as the warehouse, shipping department, mail room, and accounting department. To transfer a call to shipping, the user just presses the shipping button.

Now imagine that a new extension is added to the building, called the document room. Someone must go to each phone and add an additional button to be able to access the document room. As Acme Co. grows, you can see that the phone technician will be kept busy adding buttons to everyone's phone.

So far, this analogy represents programs before standard I/O. Each program needed special software to be capable of outputting to a printer or a file. If a new printer is added to the system, all the programs would have to be modified to be capable of sending output to that printer. Programmers would be kept busy modifying programs as new output devices were added to the system.

Now imagine that three new buttons are added to each Acme phone:

- channel 0
- channel 1
- channel 2

To transfer a call, you just push the channel 1 button and tell the operator where you want the call to go. The operator will redirect the call to the desired destination. To transfer a call, you now have two choices: Press the Shipping room button or the channel 1 button. However, if you push the shipping room button, the call goes only to the shipping room and the operator cannot pick it up and redirect it. The advantage of the channel 1 button is that the operator can send the call anywhere, even if you don't have a button on your phone for that destination.

Channel 1 in this analogy represents stdout. The phone operator represents the shell. If a program sends its output to stdout, the shell can redirect it. If the program sends its output to a specific device or file, there is no stdout generated, so the shell cannot redirect it.

Now imagine that at Acme Co., channel 2 is for complaints. To transfer a complaint call, you push the channel 2 button and tell the operator where you want the call to go. Acme Co. allows its people to decide if a call is a complaint call or not. Sometimes the complaint line is used just because the call is out of the ordinary.

Channel 2 in this analogy represents stderr. Like stdout, stderr can also be redirected to different destinations. Each program decides what text should go to stdout versus stderr. Sometimes the decision between stdout and stderr is not clear: Some programs output headings and statistics to stderr so that they will not interfere with piping data to another command.

Imagine that at Acme Co., you can set up a conference call by pressing channel 1 and telling the operator that you want a conference call with another Acme person. That person will see his channel 0 button flash. If he picks up channel 0, he will join your call. If he is busy, he can choose to ignore channel 0.

Channel 0 in this analogy represents stdin. A conference call represents piping. Output from one phone (stdout) can be connected as the input to a second phone (stdin) by the operator (the shell) when you use the pipe symbol (|). If a command or program does not read from stdin, then the pipeline will not work.

Pagers: One Screen at a Time

You are expected to know how to use the system pager utility. This is trickier than it sounds because you will encounter three different utilities on different types of UNIX and Linux systems:

- pg
- more
- less

Some utilities, such as the man pages, will automatically invoke the default pager utility, and you cope with whatever pager you end up in. These pagers have many capabilities, such as jumping ahead a certain number of pages, going back a certain number of pages, going back to the start, skipping ahead to the end, and finding the next occurrence of a string. However these pagers do not use the same commands to do these functions.

SEE ALSO

➤ *For more information on pagers, see page 211*

UNIX Filters

Piping enables you to use several UNIX commands to filter your output so that you can discard the uninteresting part and focus on what you are interested in. The grep command is the quintessential UNIX filter. Like a coffee filter, grep processes the data flow and removes the coffee grounds (the lines you are not interested in) and passes through only the liquid (the lines you want to see):

```
dtr> ls -l
total 48
-rw-rw----  1 gota      dbhelp       1488 Sep 18  2000 mp0095
-rw-rw----  1 mori      dbhelp       1467 May 27  1993 mp0096
-rw-rw----  1 mori      dbhelp       1110 May 27  1993 mp0097
-rw-rw----  1 mori      dbhelp       1407 May 26  1993 mp0098
-rw-rw----  1 mori      dbhelp        776 Jul  6  1999 mp0099
-rw-rw----  1 mori      dbhelp       1381 Jun 10  1994 mp0100
-rw-rw----  1 mori      dbhelp        737 Jan  4  1994 mp0106
-rw-rw----  1 mori      dbhelp       1593 Jun 17  1997 mp0107
-rw-rw----  1 405       dbhelp       1548 Jun 17  1997 mp0107.old
-rw-rw----  1 405       dbhelp        955 Sep 24  1997 mp0108
-rw-rw----  1 mori      dbhelp        952 Mar 17  1998 mp0109
-rw-rw----  1 mori      dbhelp       1045 Jun  3  1998 mp4.0.1a
-rw-rw----  1 mori      dbhelp        948 Jul 17  1996 mp4.1.2
-rw-rw----  1 lazar     dbhelp        948 Jul 29  1996 mp4.1.3
-rw-rw----  1 stull     dbhelp        951 Mar 24  1998 mp4.1.3a
-rw-rw----  1 mori      dbhelp        948 Apr 13  1998 mp4.1.4
dtr>
```

The previous code is the long listing example from earlier in this chapter. Imagine that you are just interested in files that were modified back in 1998:

```
dtr> ls -l ¦ grep 1998
-rw-rw----  1 mori      dbhelp        952 Mar 17  1998 mp0109
-rw-rw----  1 mori      dbhelp       1045 Jun  3  1998 mp4.0.1a
-rw-rw----  1 stull     dbhelp        951 Mar 24  1998 mp4.1.3a
```

```
-rw-rw----    1 mori      dbhelp        948 Apr 13   1998 mp4.1.4
dtr>
```

The grep command displays only lines that contain the given pattern.

SEE ALSO

➤ *For more information on* grep, *see page 493*

Regular Expressions

When examining the contents of files or piped data, you can use another set of wild-cards called regular expressions. These wildcards look similar to the filename wild-cards referenced earlier in this chapter, and many UNIX users don't realize that there are two distinct sets of wildcards.

Assume that you are interested only in files modified back in 1996 and 1997. 199[67] is a Regular Expression pattern that will match either of those years. It will filter out (reject) lines that do not reference those years:

```
dtr> ls -l ¦ grep '199[67]'
-rw-rw----    1 gota      dbhelp       1488 Sep 18   1997 mp0095
-rw-rw----    1 mori      dbhelp       1593 Jun 17   1997 mp0107
-rw-rw----    1 405       dbhelp       1548 Jun 17   1997 mp0107.old
-rw-rw----    1 405       dbhelp        955 Sep 24   1997 mp0108
-rw-rw----    1 mori      dbhelp        948 Jul 17   1996 mp4.1.2
-rw-rw----    1 lazar     dbhelp        948 Jul 29   1996 mp4.1.3
dtr>
```

SEE ALSO

➤ *For more information on regular expressions, see page 502*

Quoting Rules

In the previous example, notice the single quotes around the Regular Expression pattern. This is necessary for the wildcards to work consistently in all situations. Many UNIX users are not aware of when they need single quotes ('), double quotes ("), or backquotes (`) for commands to work properly.

A set of quoting rules can help you know when quotes are needed and what type of quotes to use.

SEE ALSO

➤ *For more information on quoting and these quoting rules, see page 119*

Commands as Building Blocks

UNIX commands don't have built-in code to show one screen at a time because it is assumed that you will pipe the output to a pager if you want it paged. Similarly, UNIX commands don't have built-in code to sort the output because you can pipe the output to the system sort command.

This section demonstrates how rich the system sort command is in features. The following example sorts the files by the year they were last modified. If files were modified in the same year, they will be sorted in order of size from smallest to largest for that year:

```
dtr> ls -l ¦ sort +7 -8 +4n
total 50
-rw-rw----   1 mori     dbhelp      1110 May 27  1993 mp0097
-rw-rw----   1 mori     dbhelp      1407 May 26  1993 mp0098
-rw-rw----   1 mori     dbhelp      1467 May 27  1993 mp0096
-rw-rw----   1 mori     dbhelp       737 Jan  4  1994 mp0106

-rw-rw----   1 mori     dbhelp      1381 Jun 10  1994 mp0100
-rw-rw----   1 lazar    dbhelp       948 Jul 29  1996 mp4.1.3
-rw-rw----   1 mori     dbhelp       948 Jul 17  1996 mp4.1.2
-rw-rw----   1 405      dbhelp       955 Sep 24  1997 mp0108

-rw-rw----   1 405      dbhelp      1548 Jun 17  1997 mp0107.old
-rw-rw----   1 mori     dbhelp      1593 Jun 17  1997 mp0107
-rw-rw----   1 mori     dbhelp       948 Apr 13  1998 mp4.1.4
-rw-rw----   1 stull    dbhelp       951 Mar 24  1998 mp4.1.3a
-rw-rw----   1 mori     dbhelp       952 Mar 17  1998 mp0109
-rw-rw----   1 mori     dbhelp      1045 Jun  3  1998 mp4.0.1a
-rw-rw----   1 mori     dbhelp       776 Jul  6  1999 mp0099
-rw-rw----   1 gota     dbhelp      1488 Sep 18  2000 mp0095
-rw-rw----   1 mori     group         58 Sep 19 17:25 myerrors
dtr>
```

With piping, there is no need to overlap functions within the commands. Each separate building block has its own rich set of features. The UNIX sort command is a good example of that. One pipeline made of these rich building blocks enables you to create composite commands on the fly that would otherwise require hours of programming.

SEE ALSO

➤ *For more information on the* sort *command, see page 255*

The vi Text Editor

You need to know how to use vi to edit a text file. Many applications and system files are configured via simple text file tables that you are expected to edit. vi does not have to be your editor of choice, but it is the only editor that is standard on all UNIX and Linux systems.

vi is difficult for some people because it offers no pull-down menus or command lists to select from. In the spirit of UNIX, you simply have to know the basic commands from memory.

When forced to use vi against their will, many UNIX people pull out a reference card of more than 70 different commands and try to edit the text file. Chapter 20, "Using vi to Edit a Text File," shows you first how to edit anything with just 10 vi commands; then it introduces you the next eight commands to learn. This chapter even shows you how to make a help reference of those 18 commands. Keep this around for those times when vi is your only option.

On the other hand, vi is an extremely rich editor that allows all the other UNIX building block commands to be applied when editing part or all of your text file. Chapter 21, "Letting the vi Editor Work for You," shows how to use vi to easily handle repetitive editing tasks that would drive you crazy with a mouse.

SEE ALSO

➤ *For more information on the vi text editor, see pages 563, 587*

vi Command-Line Editing

As another bonus to being proficient in vi, you can avoid retyping commands on the command line by using vi commands to retrieve past commands, edit them, and execute them. You can even correct mistakes you discover at the start of the current command, without having to backspace and retype the whole command.

Chapter 22, "Command-Line Editing in the Korn Shell," gives you an example of using vi command-line editing to build up a complex pipeline, piece by piece. You can test each stage of the pipeline before adding the next piece on the end. Command-line editing is essential to this process so that you can retrieve the previous command and just add the new piece to the end of it.

SEE ALSO

➤ *For more information on vi command-line editing, see page 613*

Scripts

The last and most powerful weapon in the UNIX wizard's bag of tricks is a powerful scripting language that allows new commands to be created. Use vi or any text editor to create a file of commands called a script. This script can accept filenames on the command line or prompt the user for input. It can test the input to make sure it is valid. It also can execute other UNIX commands and take appropriate action if there are problems.

Any time you find yourself wasting time by repeating the same commands or key strokes, there is probably a way under UNIX to automate the process. No other operating system has such powerful features to avoid repetition. This is the reason UNIX gurus moan so much when forced to work on other operating systems.

Scripts can be written in a variety of languages. Three scripting languages are covered in this book: Bourne shell, awk, and Perl. You can also compile C and C++ programs if your UNIX system has a C or C++ compiler. This is often an extra-cost option or you could download the GNU C Compiler. C programming is not covered in this book.

SEE ALSO

➤ *For more information on Bourne shell programming, see page 753*

➤ *For more information on* awk *programming, see page 801*

➤ *For more information on perl programming, see Chapter 29.*

chapter

3

UNIX Directories and Pathnames

By Steve "Mor" Moritsugu

> **Tip**
>
> This is an important chapter for you to read and understand. All UNIX commands and documentation assume that you can move to a given directory using the command line, as covered in this chapter. Also read about and practice using relative and absolute pathnames in this chapter because you will encounter both types all the time you use UNIX. You can postpone the final sections on increasing productivity until you have a desire to learn some of these shortcuts.

Introducing the UNIX Directory Tree Structure

UNIX stores information such as user data on one or more disk drives. Each disk drive typically has a capacity measured in megabytes (MB), where each megabyte is equivalent to roughly 1 million characters. For example, a 500MB disk drive could hold 50,000 documents, where each document has 10,000 characters of text. Some disk drive systems have capacities measured in gigabytes (GB) or terabytes (TB). Here is a summary of the units used to measure disk capacity.

- 1 KB = 1,024 characters (or bytes) (roughly 1,000)
- 1 MB = 1,024 KB = 1,048,576 characters (roughly 1 million)
- 1 GB = 1,024 MB = 1,073,741,824 characters (roughly 1 billion)
- 1 TB = 1,024 GB = 1,099,511,627,776 characters (roughly 1 trillion)

> **How Fast Things Change**
>
> When I started in computers, my system had 10MB of disk space. Today the specifications for a new release of UNIX, called UnixWare 7, call for 76,800TB of disk space. This is inconceivably larger than my old 10MB drive. Amazing!

Because there is so much data to keep track of, all this information is grouped into collections of related information, called files. If you write a letter to send to a relative, the text of that letter would all be stored as one file. Files can serve different functions on the system. Some files are documents, some are programs, and some are data files or other types. Each file under UNIX has a number called an inode number that UNIX uses to access the file. To make it easier for humans to work with files, each file can also be accessed by a name.

Filenames under old versions of UNIX could contain only 14 characters. Most current UNIX systems allow much longer filenames, sometimes those with several hundred characters. Filenames can start with or contain any letters, digits, punctuation, or spaces, but in practice, you should avoid putting spaces and most punctuation into filenames because that makes them difficult to use in command lines.

UNIX systems can have hundreds of thousands of files—or more—to keep track of. To simplify this, files are grouped into collections of related files called directories. Think of a directory as a folder or container into which you can put related files. For example, if you wrote 20 letters to your Aunt Alice, you could put all 20 of those files into a directory of Aunt Alice letters. I might call the directory *AuntAlice* because I don't want any spaces in my file or directory names.

Similarly, directories can be collected together and put into larger directories. For example, I might create a directory called correspondence that contains a directory for each person, which is contained by another directory. AuntAlice would be a sub-directory of the correspondence directory. The correspondence directory is said to be the parent directory of the AuntAlice directory.

A Hierarchical Directory Structure

Both UNIX and DOS have a hierarchical directory structure that allows files to be organized by categories and subcategories. For example, suppose that I had one file for each city in the world that contained data about that city. I could create one directory called cities and put all the files into that one directory. This is analogous to having one big heap of files, which would make it cumbersome to find what you want.

Alternatively, I could take advantage of the hierarchical directory structure and create a small number of high-level subdirectories within the overall cities directory:

- NorthAmerica
- SouthAmerica
- Europe
- Asia

I could then create subdirectories in each of the high-level directories:

- NorthAmerica/Canada
- NorthAmerica/UnitedStates
- NorthAmerica/Mexico
- SouthAmerica/Brazil

In the preceding example, the UnitedStates directory is a subdirectory of the NorthAmerica directory. The Brazil directory is a subdirectory of the SouthAmerica directory. I could then create subdirectories of those directories:

- NorthAmerica/UnitedStates/Alabama

- NorthAmerica/UnitedStates/Alaska

- NorthAmerica/UnitedStates/Arizona

Notice how a hierarchical organization has levels. At each level, I have a small, manageable number of choices. By making simple decisions at each level, I get to where I want to go.

The files for each city would then be placed in the appropriate subdirectory:

- NorthAmerica/UnitedStates/Georgia/Athens

- Europe/Greece/Athens

The preceding example shows how two city files can have the same name (Athens), but there is no ambiguity due to the hierarchical structure.

The Root Directory Contains All the Other Directories

Figure 3.1 shows a pictorial representation of the way that files and directories are organized under UNIX. One directory or folder contains all the other directories and files. This is called the *root directory* because an entire tree structure of other directories and files grows from it.

The root directory is always denoted by a single slash (/). Whenever you see the slash (/) symbol, picture that slash (/) as a tree root growing diagonally into the ground, anchoring the UNIX tree structure.

How to Find a Path to a Name (Full Pathnames)

Figure 3.1 shows three files coming out of the root directory (/): report7, usr, and tmp.

These three files reside in the root directory. In a real UNIX system, many more files would reside in the root directory, so Figure 3.1 shows just a portion of an example UNIX directory tree.

The usr and tmp directories contain other directories and files, as shown in Figure 3.1. Under UNIX, a directory exists on the disk as a file that keeps track of the contents of that directory. A *directory*, then, is a special type of file.

There are other types of files as well. For example, character and block device node files allow UNIX to access hardware devices in the system. The majority of all files on a UNIX system are called regular files, which are files that contain text, data, or programs. The next most common type of file is the directory. All the other file types, such as device node files, are rarely encountered.

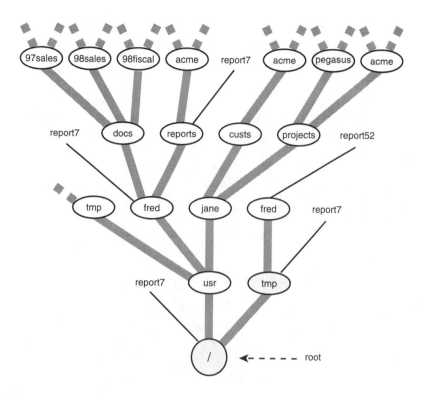

FIGURE 3.1
UNIX directory tree structure.

In Figure 3.2, the tmp directory is shown to contain a regular file called report7. Notice that the root directory (/) also contains a regular file called report7. In fact, this tree example shows four report7 files in different directories. UNIX allows different files with different contents to have the same filename as long as they are in different directories.

Within any one directory, all filenames must be unique. This is true whether or not the file is a directory. For this reason, I could not have both a regular file called usr and a directory called usr in the root directory.

Figure 3.3 highlights one of the report7 files in this tree. The complete name for a file includes all the directory folders that you must go through to get to the desired file. You can see that, when highlighted as a chain, this sequence of directories makes a path through the tree structure, leading to your desired file; hence, this complete name is called a *full pathname*. With a full pathname, there is no danger that someone will mistakenly think that you are referring to one of the other report7 files in the tree. A full pathname is also called an *absolute pathname*.

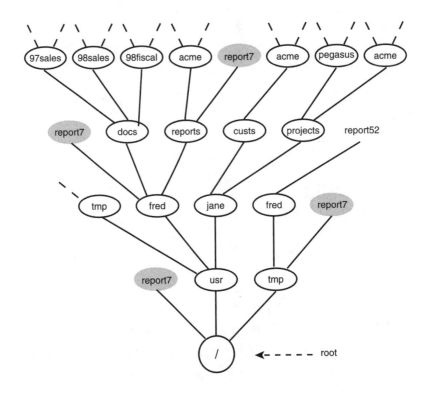

FIGURE 3.2
The same filename in different directories.

Using Directories in UNIX

You will encounter some standard directory names on most UNIX systems. You already know that all UNIX systems will have a root directory (/). The following sections look at some other common directories.

Standard UNIX Directory Names

The /tmp and /usr/tmp directories are used by the system to store temporary files. Users may also store temporary files there. but beware: The system may purge (or delete) older files from tmp directories periodically, without any warning.

The /dev directory in root contains the special device node files that access hardware on the system, such as tape drives and floppy disks. These device node files can exist anywhere, but by convention they are put into /dev or its subdirectories to remind users that they are dealing with a device instead of a regular file.

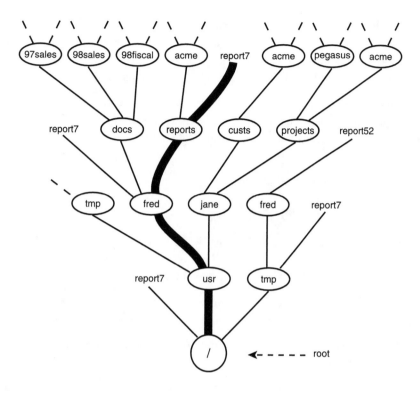

FIGURE 3.3
The full pathname /usr/fred/reports/report7.

How Long Will Files be Left in /tmp?

This can vary from system to system. Often the system will delete files from /tmp or its subdirectories that have not been accessed in 7 or 14 days. Sometimes if the system administrator faces a sudden lack of disk space, he will delete all files in /tmp regardless of age.

The /bin directory in root holds system utility programs such as the ls command. The abbreviation *bin* is short for binary executable files. The term *bin* today may also be used to name other directories of executable files, whether they are binary or text files, as in /usr/fred/bin.

The /usr directory in root holds user files and system utilities needed to support user programs. For example, /bin holds system utilities required for essential system operation, whereas /usr/bin holds system utilities needed by users and user programs. The /usr/lib directory holds libraries of useful system tables and subroutines, and /usr/spool holds spool files that are temporary copies of files queued up for printing until they are finished printing. /usr/spool also holds many temporary files held by other system processes, such as uucp. /usr/bin, /usr/lib, and /usr/spool are important parts of the operating system, and it is often wise to dedicate /usr to system purposes and to place actual user data and programs into other directories.

The lost+found directory exists in root and in other directories where the system stores file data if the filename has been lost due to system crashes. If you are missing important data after a system crash, you might find it here.

SEE ALSO
➤ *For more information on* lost+found, *see page 480*

Directories in newer UNIX systems

Newer UNIX systems are based on the SVR4 kernel, like Solaris 7, and the newer SVR5 kernel, like SCO UnixWare 7. This section lists several directories you may find on these newer UNIX systems that you may not find on older systems.

The /home directory is specifically for users' home directories, where they can store their individual files. (See the following section on home directories.)

The /sbin and /usr/sbin directories contain executable files specifically for system administration and system operation.

The /stand directory is a special directory on some SVR4 systems (but not Solaris) to specifically house the UNIX kernel and boot files.

The /var directory contains files with system variable information—that is, temporary files and logs whose contents vary with time. /var replaces the older /usr/spool directory.

Changing to Another Directory

Being able to freely move around in the UNIX directory tree is a very important skill for UNIX users. In this section, we will cover UNIX commands that are useful when changing to a different directory. We will see how directories have a basename and a dirname and we will cover the important distinction between absolute and relative pathnames.

Changing to a Directory and Viewing its Contents

UNIX would be very difficult to use if you had to specify a full pathname every time you referenced a file. As always, UNIX offers a shortcut to reduce typing. You can specify a directory to be the current directory, which enables you to reference filenames in that directory without giving the full pathname. The current directory acts as a default directory because it will be used whenever you don't specify which directory to use.

Other names for the current directory are *working directory*, *present directory*, *present working directory*, and *default directory*.

Picture in your mind that you have started walking the path from the root directory through the UNIX tree structure and have decided to stop somewhere to see what you can see from that point of view. Imagine that you are sitting on a branch of the tree structure. You can sit only in directories, not in regular files. The directory in which you are sitting is called your current directory.

You can change your current directory by using the UNIX cd command, followed by the directory name you want to change to.

Look back at Figure 3.1. In that figure, if you execute this code:

```
cd /usr/fred
```

then your current directory will be /usr/fred. By changing to /usr/fred, it will be easy for you to access any files in that directory. You can list all the files in your current directory by entering the ls command at the shell prompt (shown here by a dollar sign [$]). The following example shows the output you would see if your files were the same as Figure 3.1:

```
$ cd /usr/fred
$ ls
docs
report7
reports
$
```

DOS Users: Slash versus Backslash

DOS uses a similar directory tree structure that also grows from a root directory. However, DOS uses the backslash (\) symbol for the root directory and to separate directory names, whereas UNIX uses the slash (/) symbol, which is also called the forward slash (/).

If report7 is a regular file in your current directory, you can simply access it as report7. You don't have to specify which report7 file in which directory because the system assumes your current directory whenever you don't specify a full pathname.

For DOS Users on the cd Command

The UNIX **cd** command is similar to the one in DOS. The following are the differences:

1. UNIX requires a space between **cd** and the directory name.

2. UNIX does not allow `chdir`.

3. Use **pwd** under UNIX to see your current directory name.

4. Under UNIX, **cd** without a directory takes you to your home directory.

Using *Basenames* and *Dirnames*

A pathname has a directory portion (which is called the *dirname*) and a final base name (which is called the *basename*). This basename does not include any slashes (/), and hence does not include any preceding directory names. The basename may indicate a regular file or a directory. The dirname indicates how to get to the desired basename.

UNIX provides two routines that will display the basename and dirname of a given pathname:

basename *pathname*

dirname *pathname*

If the pathname is given as just a basename (that is, with no slashes), then the dirname command will output only a period (.), which you will see later is a symbol that represents the current directories. See Table 3.1 for dirname and basename examples.

Table 3.1 *dirname* and *basename* examples

Pathname	Dirname	Basename
/usr/fred/report7	/usr/fred	report7
custs/acme/docs	custs/acme	docs
report7	.	report7

Table 3.2 shows other properties of basename and dirname with page references where these properties are described.

Table 3.2 Other properties of the *basename* and *dirname* commands:

Property	See page
Allows only one relative or absolute pathname	70
Allows output to be piped or redirected	116

Displaying Your Current Directory Name

The pwd command displays the name of your current directory:

```
$ pwd
/usr/fred/reports
$
```

The preceding example shows that /usr/fred/reports is the current directory. To remember pwd, think *print working directory*.

Changing to Your Home Directory

/home is (usually) not your home directory

There is no way to predict the name of your UNIX home directory because each UNIX system may follow different conventions for this. Your system may have a directory called /home that contains the home directories of many users. Some people think that /home is their home directory just because it has the word home but this is wrong.

On most UNIX systems, all users of the system are given a special directory called a home directory to hold the files that they create and to hold the special system files to customize system and utility operations for their preferences. When you first log in to the UNIX system, your current directory is usually set automatically to your home directory (but not necessarily).

To change to your home directory, enter cd.

When you use the cd command without specifying a directory, it takes you to your home directory—that is, your home directory becomes your current directory.

The name of your home directory can vary from system to system, but it will normally contain your login name. For example, if you log in as user jane, your home directory on one UNIX system might be /usr/jane. On another UNIX system—especially SVR4 (for example, Solaris—it might be /home/jane or even something else. To display the name of your home directory, enter the following:

```
$ cd
$ pwd
/home/fred
$
```

The cd command takes you to your home directory, even if you don't know its name. The pwd command then tells you where you ended up, which is the name of your home directory. In the previous example, /home/fred is this user's home directory.

Changing to an Absolute Directory

As you have seen before, you can set your current directory by using the cd command with an absolute (that is, full) pathname.

If you don't know the exact spelling of the full pathname, use the procedure described later in the section "Changing to a Directory in Little Steps." If you know the exact spelling, you can change to that directory in one cd command. Make sure that you start your directory with a leading slash (/).

For example, to change to directory /usr/fred/reports, enter the following:

```
cd /usr/fred/reports
```

To change the root directory, enter the following:

```
cd /
```

Changing to a Subdirectory of the Current Directory (Relative)

If you want to change to a subdirectory of the current directory, you can use another shortcut. You can specify a relative pathname that shows how to get from where you are to where you want to be. For example, in Figure 3.1, assume that the following is true:

- /usr/fred is the current directory.
- /usr/fred/docs/98sales is the directory to which you want to change.

You could get there by using a full pathname:

```
cd /usr/fred/docs/98sales
```

However, because /usr/fred is the current directory, it would be easier to use a relative pathname as follows:

```
cd docs/98sales
```

Notice that relative pathnames do not begin with a slash (/)because they do not indicate the path all the way back to root. For that reason, relative pathnames are also called partial pathnames. They are called relative because they are based on the current directory. For example, Table 3.3 shows how the relative pathname changes as the current directory changes.

Table 3.3 How the Relative Pathname to Get to */usr/fred/docs/98sales* Changes Based on Your Current Directory

Your Current Directory	cd Command Needed
/usr/fred/docs	cd 98sales
/usr/fred	cd docs/98sales
/usr	cd fred/docs/98sales
/	cd usr/fred/docs/98sales

Changing to a Directory in Little Steps

Sometimes you have a vague idea of your desired destination directory but don't know exactly how to get there, or maybe you don't know the exact spelling of each intermediate directory. Sometimes you know these things, but your cd command fails with the error: No such file or directory. Here is an example of this error, using the cities example given earlier in this chapter:

```
$ cd /cities/NorthAmerica/UnitdStates/Georgia
sh: /cities/NorthAmerica/UnitdStates/Georgia: No such file
or directory
$
```

Notice in the preceding example that UnitedStates is misspelled. I have seen beginners repeat a long command over and over, making the same error or a different one each time. The next time you are in this situation, try little steps like this:

```
$ cd /cities
$ cd NorthAmerica
$ cd UnitdStates
sh: UnitdStates: No such file or directory
$ ls
Canada
Mexico
UnitedStates
$
```

In the preceding example, /cities was reached successfully, as was NorthAmerica (but notice that you must enter NorthAmerica without a leading slash). Then an error occurred in response to the command to go to UnitdStates. The ls command shows that the directory name is misspelled. Changing directories one step at a time allowed the problem to be found and corrected so the desired destination can be reached.

SEE ALSO

➤ *For more information on listing files, see page 180*

➤ *For more information on viewing output a page at a time, see page 211*

Accessing the Current Directory

Every directory contains two special subdirectories. One has a name that is a single period (.), and this is called the "dot" directory. The other's name is two periods (..), called the "dot-dot" directory. Both of these directories are special, and you should never try to delete them. A directory is considered to be empty if it contains only dot (.) and dot-dot (..). The dot (.) directory is actually a pointer to the current directory. Many UNIX commands use the dot (.) directory to determine what the current directory is.

What is the difference between these two filenames?

```
./report7
```

```
report7
```

The answer is nothing. They both reference the `report7` file in the current directory.

Going Back One Directory to the Parent

The dot-dot (..) directory is a pointer to the parent directory of the current directory. Thus, it is correct to say that every directory contains itself as a subdirectory (.), and it contains its own parent directory as a subdirectory of itself (..).

You can use the dot-dot (..) subdirectory of your current directory to change to the parent directory. If your current directory is `/usr/fred/docs/98sales/NorthAm`, then after

```
cd ..
```

your current directory will be `/usr/fred/docs/98sales`.

Root Is the Only Directory That Is Its Own Parent

If your current directory is root, `cd ..` is legal and leaves you still in the root directory. `cd ../../../..` would have the same result.

You can also go to the parent directory of the parent directory. If your current directory is /usr/fred/docs/98sales/NorthAm, then after

```
cd ../..
```

your current directory will be /usr/fred/docs.

Changing to a Subdirectory of the Parent

In Figure 3.1, imagine that your current directory is /usr/fred/docs/98sales. How would you change to /usr/fred/docs/97sales? You cannot just cd to 97sales because that is not a subdirectory of your current directory. You could change to that directory by either of these two commands:

```
cd ../97sales
```

```
cd /usr/fred/docs/97sales
```

In Figure 3.1, if /usr/fred/docs/98sales is again your current directory, how can you use dot-dot (..) to change to /usr/fred/reports/acme? The answer is the following:

```
cd ../../reports/acme
```

If you are not sure how many dot-dots (..) to go back, use the technique of changing by little steps, for example:

```
cd ..
ls -CF
cd ..
ls -CF
cd reports
ls -CF
cd acme
```

Each ls command lists the contents of the current directory so that you can see the available directories to go to next. Remember, do not start any of the directory names with a slash in any of the little steps because that would take you all the way back to root.

Returning to the Previous Directory

The cd command under the Korn shell has an extra option not available in the Bourne shell. The following returns you to the previous directory that you were last in:

```
cd -
```

This command can also be used to easily toggle back and forth between two directories, as in this example:

```
cd /data
# now do some work in /data
cd /usr/fred
# now do some work in /usr/fred
cd -
# now you are back in /data
cd -
# now you are back in /usr/fred
cd -
# now you are back in /data
# etc.
```

Using Absolute versus Relative Pathnames

Absolute Pathnames Start with Slash (/)

Learn to pay attention to the very first character of a pathname. If it begins with a slash (/), then it is an absolute or full pathname and includes all directories back to root (/). If the pathname begins with a letter or a dot (that is, a period), it is relative, not absolute.

Frequently in this book, instructions will specify to enter either an absolute or a relative pathname to a desired file. An absolute pathname includes all the parent directories back to the root directory. This is easy to understand but requires a lot of keyboard entry.

If your current directory is the directory that contains the desired file, you can access that file simply by its basename, which is much shorter to enter than an absolute pathname. A *basename* is an example of a relative pathname because the path to follow to get to the indicated file starts from your current directory. Do not put a slash (/) in front of the basename because that would indicate an absolute pathname, telling the system to look for that basename in the root directory, not your current directory.

Here is an example using the cities directory that was described earlier in this chapter. If you are currently in the /cities/NorthAmerica/UnitedStates/Georgia directory, you can print the Athens file using this lp command:

```
lp Athens
```

Athens is a basename that accesses that file in the current directory. You could also print that same file using an absolute pathname:

```
lp /cities/NorthAmerica/UnitedStates/Georgia/Athens
```

Notice how much easier it is (and how much less typing is involved) to use a pathname relative to the current directory instead of an absolute pathname. Assume now that you want to print the same file, but the following is your current directory:

```
/cities/NorthAmerica/UnitedStates
```

In this case, you can use a relative partial pathname, like this:

```
lp Georgia/Athens
```

Notice that there is no leading slash (/) before Georgia in the preceding command. The lack of the slash says to go to the Georgia subdirectory of the current directory, and display any Athens file found there. This is a partial pathname because it is more than a simple basename, but it is less than a full or absolute pathname. This is another example of a partial relative pathname:

```
lp NorthAmerica/Georgia/Athens
```

The advantage of such relative pathnames is that you don't have to specify every directory back to root.

To access a file in the parent directory of your current directory, enter this relative pathname:

```
../filename
```

Dot-dot (..) indicates the parent directory, as you saw earlier in this chapter.

Using multiple dot-dot (..) entries, it is possible to use a relative pathname to access any other file or directory in the whole system, for example:

```
../../../usr/jane/accounts/progs/acme
```

In practice, multiple dot-dot entries are difficult to comprehend and are not found very often.

Relative pathnames are used in UNIX much more often than absolute pathnames because they reduce the amount of typing needed to enter a command. People use cd to change to a directory just so they can use basenames or simple relative pathnames to access the desired files.

Commands that Allow Relative and Absolute Pathname Arguments

Many UNIX commands—but not all of them—enable you to specify one or more filenames on the command line for the command to process. If you have more than one file, separate their filenames with one or more spaces or tabs, but not commas or other punctuation, as shown in the following examples.

correct: lp report3 acme1 acme2

wrong: lp report3, acme1, acme2

In the previous example, the `lp` command is used to print three files to the default system printer. This example uses simple file basenames, covered earlier in this chapter, to refer to files in the current directory.

The following example shows that you can use different types of pathnames within one command. In this example, there is a basename (`acme1`) relative to the current directory, a relative pathname (`reports/acme1`), and two absolute pathnames (`/tmp/acme1` and `/usr/fred/documents/acme1`). The decision of whether to use a relative or absolute pathname is purely based on which one is easier for you to use.

```
lp acme1 reports/acme1 /tmp/acme1 /usr/fred/documents/acme1
```

The following example uses the asterisk (*) wildcard, covered in Chapter 11, "Generating and Using File Lists." It illustrates that relative and absolute pathnames containing wildcards can also be freely mixed:

```
lp acme* /tmp/acme*
```

Commands That Allow Only One Relative or Absolute Pathname

Most UNIX commands that process filenames accept a list of files to act on. A few UNIX commands allow only a single filename. Look for this property in the list of properties that is given whenever a new command is introduced in this book. The single filename argument may be a relative or an absolute pathname, as described in the previous section. Wildcards mentioned in that section cannot be used to generate a list of files, since only a single file is allowed. (The only exception is that wildcards can be used to access a single file, as described in the section "Reducing Typing of Long Filenames," in Chapter 11.)

Creating New Directories

Use the `mkdir` (make directory) command to create new directories, such as the following:

```
mkdir acme reports/acme
```

This example creates an `acme` directory within the current directory; it also creates one in the `reports` subdirectory of the current directory.

You can use the `mkdir -p` option to create a new directory and automatically create any missing parent directories, as in the following command:

```
mkdir -p /cities/Europe/UnitedKingdom/England/London
```

In this example, if the `UnitedKingdom` directory did not exist, it would be created. Then `England` would be created as a subdirectory, and `London` would be created as a subdirectory of `England`.

mkdir allows multiple pathnames, as noted in Table 3.4.

Table 3.4   One Other property of the *mkdir* command:

Property	See page
Allows relative and absolute pathname arguments	70

Tip

The mkdir and rmdir commands under UNIX are similar to those under DOS. UNIX does not allow the shortcuts md or rd.

Removing Existing Directories

Use the rmdir (remove directory) command to delete existing directories, for example:

```
rmdir acme reports/acme
```

rmdir will fail with an error message if any directory specified to be removed contains any files or subdirectories (except for dot [.] and dot-dot [..]):

```
$ rmdir acme
rmdir: acme: Directory not empty
```

If you get the error in the previous example and are sure you really want to delete that directory, use the rm command to delete all the files in that directory first. If there are any subdirectories, they must also be cleared and deleted before the main directory can be deleted.

For a fast (but potentially dangerous) way to remove a directory even if it still contains files or subdirectories, see the next section on how to remove an entire directory subtree. rmdir can remove multiple directories, as noted in Table 3.5.

Table 3.5   One Other Property of the *rmdir* Command:

Property	See page
Allows relative and absolute pathname arguments	70

SEE ALSO

➤ *For more information on deleting files, see page 244*

Removing Entire Directory Subtrees

It is possible to remove a directory and all its existing files and subdirectories (that is, the whole directory subtree) in one command. However, this command is very powerful and hence very dangerous, and it must be typed in very carefully to avoid tragedy.

Warning: Great Disaster Potential

Even experienced UNIX users have accidentally misused the `rm -r` command and deleted the wrong files. This command can obliterate thousands of files in an instant. There is no way to get them back. Beginners should not use this procedure to remove entire directory subtrees. It is too dangerous. Take the slow, safe route of deleting each subdirectory one at a time, as described previously.

Removing Entire Directory Subtrees

1. Make sure you know the exact spelling and full pathname of the directory to be removed. Use the `cd` and `ls` commands to change to that directory and list its contents and the contents of any subdirectories. Make sure that you want to remove all these files and subdirectories. Also make sure that you are deleting a directory created by a user, not a required system directory, especially if you are logged in as root.

2. Enter the following:
   `cd parent-name`

3. Replace `parent-name` with either an absolute or a relative pathname to the parent directory of the directory to be removed.

4. Enter the following to verify that you have arrived in the correct directory:
   `pwd`

Avoid Using `rm -r` While Running as Root

A mistake or typographical error in the `rm -r` command, such as wrong spaces or slashes (/), could wipe out important parts of the UNIX system and make it totally inoperable if you are logged in on the root account. No undelete option exists. Use a non-root account for most operations, and change to root only when absolutely needed.

---

5. Enter the following:
   `ls -dF dirname`

6. Replace *dirname* with the directory to be removed. This command should display the same dirname back to you, followed by a slash (/).

If you see the error message "No such file," something is wrong. Go back to step 1 of this procedure.

7. Enter the following:
```
rm -rf dirname
```

8. Replace *dirname* with the directory to be removed. This command is very dangerous. Double-check that you have spelled everything correctly before you press the Enter key. The rm command normally removes only regular files, not directories. The -r option to rm causes rm to recursively remove the specified directory and its files and all its subdirectories and their files and all their subdirectories and their files, and so on. There is no undelete option.

Increasing Productivity in Accessing Directories

Switching between long directory names can become tiresome and frustrating. The following sections give you some UNIX techniques that can help.

Setting CDPATH for Most-Accessed Directories

In the first chapter, you saw how shell variables can be set to customize how the system operates. The Bourne shell and the Korn shell have a shell variable called CDPATH to enable you to easily get to directories that you use most often, as long as they have distinctive names. After you have set up CDPATH, you can cd to the basename of your common directories as though you were always sitting in the parent directories of those directories.

Setting and Using CDPATH

1. Make a list of the full pathnames of the directories that you cd to most often. The list can be in your head, on scratch paper, in a file, or by some other method. If the basenames of those directories are mostly unique, then this procedure will help you.

2. Make a new list of the full pathnames of the parent directories of the most accessed directories. Call this the CDPATH list.

3. Place the CDPATH list in order so that the parent directories of the directories you cd to most often come first.

4. If any directories you cd to often have the same basename, put the parent directory of the most-used basename before the parent directory of the least-used basename. This procedure enables you to access only the identical basename whose parent comes first in the list. Other identical basenames in other directories must be accessed using a full or relative pathname.

5. Decide whether you want to check for the given basename in the current directory before or after you check all the directories in CDPATH. If before, then the current directory overrides or has higher priority than the CDPATH directories. If after, then CDPATH overrides or has higher priority than the current directory.

   For example, assume that you enter the following:

   ```
   cd docs
   ```

   Now assume that a docs directory exists as a subdirectory of your current directory and also as a subdirectory of one of the directories in CDPATH. You can control whether the current directory has higher or lower priority than the CDPATH directories; hence, you can control which docs directory you end up at.

6. Enter the following:

   ```
   CDPATH=
   ```

   Do not press the Enter key until instructed to. Do not put any spaces around the = sign.

7. If the current directory is to have higher priority than the CDPATH directories, enter the following:

   ```
   .:
   ```

   (That is, period, colon, and no spaces).

8. Enter all the full pathnames in your CDPATH list, using a colon (:) to separate each entry. Do not end your list with a colon (:). Do not enter any spaces.

9. If the current directory is to have lower priority than the CDPATH directories, enter the following:

   ```
   :.
   ```

   (That is, colon, period, and no spaces).

10. Press the Enter key to complete your command. Here is an example of a complete command:

    ```
    CDPATH=.:/usr/fred/reports:/data/acme
    ```

11. Now any time you cd to a basename, the shell will search each of the directories in order in CDPATH until it finds the given basename as a subdirectory of one of these parent directories in CDPATH. It will then take you to that directory.

12. You must re-enter your whole CDPATH= line each time you log in unless you set this shell variable definition in your .profile.

SEE ALSO

➤ *For information on setting up shell variables definitions in* `.profile` *so that they occur automatically each time you log in, see page 410*

➤ *For more information on the different shells, see page 25*

Saving/Accessing Often-Used Directory Names

Sometimes you will find that there are some directories you want to return to several times, but not often enough to warrant updating CDPATH. You can create and use your own temporary shell variables to make it easy to return to directories.

Remembering Directories in Your Own Shell Variables

1. First, `cd` to a directory that you know you want to return to several times.

Make up your own variable names

In this procedure, you can make up your own variable names to remember commonly used directories. They should be in upper case to avoid confusion with lower case UNIX reserved words. They should be short so they are easy to type.

---

2. Enter the following:
   ```
   D1=`pwd`
   ```

   Make sure that you enter backquotes (`` ` ``), not apostrophes ('). Do not enter any spaces in this command. This command will save the full pathname of your current directory in shell variable D1.

3. To return to the directory in D1, enter the following:
   ```
   cd $D1
   ```

   Notice that you must precede the variable with a $ sign to use its contents, but not to set its contents.

4. Following steps 1 through 3, you can set and use other variables such as D2 or D3 to remember and easily change among several directories.

5. You can choose more descriptive variable names, such as the following:
   ```
   CUSTS=`pwd`
   REPORTS=`pwd`
   ```

   You must be sitting in the desired directory before you issue the previous command. You must not choose the name of an existing shell variable. Enter the following to see a list of the existing shell variables:
   ```
   env
   ```

6. If you forget which directory is in a variable, you can display its contents using the echo command, for example:

```
echo $D1
```

7. These definitions will last until you log off. If you want to make some of these shell variables permanent so you don't have to set them up each time you log in, set them up in .profile.

SEE ALSO

➤ *For information on setting up shell variables definitions in* .profile *so they occur automatically each time you log in, see page 410*

chapter

4

Steve "Mor" Moritsugu

Rules for Entering UNIX Commands

Tip for Beginners

This whole chapter has useful rules and trouble-shooting tips for entering UNIX commands to the shell. Read the rules carefully and skim the troubleshooting errors so that you can recognize problems and look up the correct section in this chapter when you encounter that problem. The quoting rules are difficult and involve concepts and commands from later chapters, so put this section off until you have more experience.

A Review of the Shell Prompt

Take a look at what happens when you log in to a UNIX system:

```
login: mori
Password:
Last login: Fri Mar 13 17:33:22 from :0
Sun Microsystems Inc.   SunOS 5.6        Generic August 1997
$ _
```

The messages that appear upon login differ from system to system. In the preceding example, after the login messages are complete, the system displays a dollar sign ($), and the cursor sits next to it, waiting for input. The dollar sign is called a *prompt* because it prompts the user to enter a command.

The program that generates the dollar sign prompt is the *shell*. The shell program is a command-line interpreter that enables the user to enter commands. The purpose of this chapter is to cover the rules for entering UNIX commands to the shell.

Three main shell programs exist, and all are available on most commercial UNIX systems:

- Bourne shell
- C shell
- Korn shell

Root Precautions

If you are logged in as root, a simple typographical error could be disastrous for the whole system. It's a good idea to give the system administrator a regular UNIX account to use most of the time. Then use the **su** command to become root only when necessary.

The syntax of the Korn shell is a superset of the Bourne shell, so the two are very compatible. Both the Bourne and Korn shells use the dollar sign prompt. The only exception to this rule occurs if you log in as root, the system administrator. Because the root account co-owns all files and directories, it can make changes regardless of file or directory permissions. A special shell prompt, the pound sign (#), is presented when you log in as root, to remind you that this is the all-powerful account and that you must take care not to make any mistakes or leave the terminal for anyone to access.

If you see a percent sign (%) as the shell prompt, you are probably in the C shell. The C shell uses different syntax and rules from the Bourne and Korn shells, so it presents a different prompt to the average user. If you log in as root, the C shell uses the pound sign prompt, as the Bourne and Korn shells do.

Other shells you may encounter, especially under Linux, are *tcsh*, which is like the C shell, and *bash*, the GNU Bourne-Again Shell, which incorporates useful features from both the C shell and the Korn shell.

It is possible to customize the shell prompt for a particular user. If you are on a network, you will sometimes see that your shell prompt includes your system name, as in this example:

```
sparcster$ _
```

This is a useful prompt because a network enables you to log in to various UNIX hosts, and it sometimes becomes confusing as to which system you are currently accessing. The shell prompt need not end in the usual shell prompt character, as you can see in this example:

```
[sparcster] _
```

In the Korn shell (but not the Bourne shell), it is possible to add your current directory as part of your shell prompt. Take a look at the following example:

```
/usr/fred > cd /tmp
/tmp > cd /usr/jane/reports
/usr/jane/reports > cd acme/fiscal97/glaccounts
/usr/jane/reports/acme/fiscal97/glaccounts > ls
acme
report6
report7
/usr/jane/reports/acme/fiscal97/glaccounts > _
```

Here, the shell prompt contains the current directory and ends in a greater-than sign (>). Your current directory starts as /usr/fred. When you change to /tmp, you can see that the shell prompt automatically tracks your current directory. Notice also that the current directory can include many subdirectories and can become quite lengthy, leaving you very little room to type in commands. You can still type in long commands because the command automatically wraps to the next line and continues to echo your input. However, this can be difficult to read when you want to look over your previous commands.

As you have seen, the shell prompt can appear in many different guises. When you first log in, take an extra moment to see how your shell prompt appears on that system so that you will recognize it later. As you will see throughout this chapter, one of the skills you must develop to use UNIX is to recognize when you are at the shell prompt versus when you have ended up in some unexpected situation.

SEE ALSO

➤ *For more information on the UNIX shell, see page 25*

UNIX Command-Line Options, Arguments, and Comments

At the shell prompt, you are expected to enter commands to UNIX. A UNIX command can be a simple one-word command, such as this:

```
$ exit
```

Here, the `exit` command enables you to end the shell and go back to a login prompt. If `exit` doesn't work, try the `logout` command or Ctrl+D instead:

```
$ date
Sun Mar 15 07:30:49 PST 1998
$
```

In this example, `date` is another simple one-word UNIX command. Most UNIX commands are all lowercase, although there are exceptions. You must use the proper case (uppercase versus lowercase) when entering commands in UNIX. Be especially wary of handwritten instructions containing UNIX commands. Many people always handwrite certain characters in uppercase or lowercase without remembering that this makes a difference under UNIX.

Some commands require *arguments* (also called *parameters*), which are words telling the command what to act on:

```
$ rm acme peagasus
```

In this example, `acme` and `pegasus` are arguments to the `rm` command, which is the UNIX command to remove files. In this instance, `rm` will delete the `acme` and `pegasus` files. Notice that the first word in the command line must be the UNIX command you want to run. Notice also that multiple arguments are separated by spaces, not commas. In the following example, `/tmp` is an argument to the `cd` command, which you saw in Chapter 3, "UNIX Directories and Pathnames":

```
$ cd /tmp
$
```

The `cd` command lets you change your current directory. Note that in UNIX, no news is good news. You know that the `cd` command was successful in this example because the shell prompt reappears on the next line and no error messages occurred.

It is important to put a space between the command and any arguments. In this next example, you can see that some news is probably bad news:

```
$ cd/tmp
cd/tmp: not found
$
```

Here, the space was accidentally omitted after the `cd` command. First note that you got a message before the next shell prompt. You must read any messages carefully because they usually mean that your command failed (or else UNIX wouldn't have generated any message at all). Beginners often enter a series of commands, ignore the messages, and then wonder why things don't work.

In the previous example, you might think that the `cd` command failed because the system couldn't find the `/tmp` directory, but this is not correct. Look at the error message more carefully. `cd/tmp` wasn't found. Most commands under UNIX are actually compiled or script utilities that reside in separate disk files. The system is telling you that `cd/tmp` is not a valid command—that is, there is no system utility on disk with that name.

Let's summarize the key points so far:

1. At the shell prompt, the first word you enter must be a UNIX command.

2. Most UNIX commands must be typed in lowercase (but there are exceptions).

3. If the command requires a following argument, you must type a space after the command.

4. You may then enter one or more arguments, if required, for that command. Multiple arguments must be separated by spaces.

5. You must enter the proper uppercase and lowercase letters for commands and arguments and all words on the command line.

SEE ALSO

➤ *For more information on the* date *command, see page 156*

➤ *For more information on the* rm *command, see page 244*

➤ *For more information on the* cd *command, see page 62*

Adding Comments to the Command Line

Some of the following examples include comments added to the command lines, so this section introduces you to comments. A *comment* (also called a *remark*) contains explanatory words meant for a human reader. In the UNIX shell, any word that begins with a pound sign (#) is regarded as the beginning of a comment. The comment continues to the end of the line:

Filenames That Start with the Pound Sign (#)
Some system files start with a pound sign so that you must pause and think before handling the file. The shell can't access file `#acme` because it appears to start a comment, but it can access `./#acme`.

```
$ rm acmetmp    # no longer needed so free up the disk space
```

In this example, the `rm` command is followed by a comment. The shell will ignore everything from the pound sign (#) to the end of the line. Comments are used primarily in script programming, where UNIX commands are saved in text files.

The pound sign must be preceded by a space if you want it to begin a comment. Otherwise, it is just a normal character (although I recommend that you avoid using it in filenames).

Entering Options to Commands

Most UNIX commands allow options that modify how the command operates to be specified on the command line. Look at the following example:

```
% ls -l /tmp
```

White Space Separator
UNIX allows any combination of one or more spaces or tabs to separate commands, options, and arguments. These separators are called white space because they form a blank area of separation between the words.

Here, `ls` is a command you have seen earlier to list the files in a directory. `-l` is an option to the `ls` command that causes it to list in long format, showing details about the file as well as the filename. Notice that there is a space after the command, as required. Notice that a dash ([nd]) is used to denote options from arguments. In this example, `-l` is an option that modifies how `ls` operates. `/tmp` is an argument to the `ls` command that tells `ls` which directory to list. Options must follow the command and come before any arguments to the command. Also notice that you are in the C shell, denoted by the percent sign (%) shell prompt.

```
$ ls -l -a /tmp      # case 1
$ ls -a -l /tmp      # case 2
$ ls -la /tmp        # case 3
$ ls -al /tmp        # case 4
```

In these examples, you can see that UNIX allows great flexibility when entering multiple (simple) options. -a is another option to ls (see Appendix A, "UNIX Commands," for more information on ls if you are curious about everything it does).

---

dash dash (- -) Options

Use dash dash (- -) to signify the end of the options section. This is useful if you must specify an argument that begins with a dash, such as rm - - -*filename*.

Linux allows extra command options preceded by - - that are not available on commercial UNIX systems, as in this example:

```
ls --version
```

All four of the preceding cases are different but valid ways to do the same thing. Notice that I used a pound sign on each line to begin a comment, as discussed in the preceding section. The shell ignores all text from the pound sign to the end of the line, allowing me to add explanatory words so that you will know which line I am referring to.

In case 1, I specified each option, preceded by a dash. Notice that a space is required between each option and argument. In case 2, notice that the order of the options doesn't matter. In case 3, notice that simple one-letter options can be combined into a composite option, preceded by one dash. In case 4, notice that the options can be combined in any order within the composite option.

Note that options are not universal. -v to one command can mean something totally different when used with another command. You may find some commands that have the same meaning for one option, but that option might have a totally different meaning for other commands. Also be aware that some options might not be supported on some versions of UNIX, or the option might cause a different result on another version of UNIX.

If options are not single letters, they can't be combined into a composite option, as follows:

```
$ find / -mount -print
```

Here, the `find` command is called with two options, `-mount` and `-print`. These two options can't be combined into a composite option. Also, `find` is an example of a command where the order of the options does make a difference.

One UNIX command doesn't always use a dash before its options:

```
$ tar tv
```

`t` and `v` are options to the `tar` command. This is the one command that usually doesn't use the dash, for historical reasons. Most modern versions of UNIX (including SCO and Solaris) allow a dash before `tar` options, so it doesn't have to be different from other commands in specifying options, as in this example:

```
$ tar -tv
```

Remember that commands must be entered in the following order, separated by spaces:

1. The name of the command.

2. Any desired command options, preceded by a dash.

3. Any desired command arguments.

4. Any desired comments. Put a space and then a pound sign at the start of the comment.

SEE ALSO
➤ *For more information on the* `ls` *command, see page 180*
➤ *For more information on the* `find` *command, see page 187*
➤ *For more information on the* `tar` *command, see page 443*

Entering Arguments to Options

Some options require arguments of their own:

```
$ lp -d laser4 -n3 -s acme pegasus
```

In this example, the following are true:

- `lp` is a command to print files to the printer.

- `-d` is an option to the `lp` command that specifies which printer to use.

- `laser4` is an argument to the `-d` option giving the printer name. It is not an argument to the `lp` command because it is not the name of a file to print.

- `-n` is another option to the `lp` command that specifies the number of copies to print.

- **3** is an argument to the **-n** option, indicating three copies of each file are desired. It is not an argument to the **lp** command.

- **-s** is an option to the **lp** command that suppresses the request id information that normally is displayed. This option takes no arguments of its own.

- **acme** is an argument to the **lp** command that gives a filename to be printed.

- **pegasus** is also an argument to the **lp** command that gives a filename to be printed.

Most commands allow or require a space between an option and the argument to that option. Some commands might not allow any spaces between the option and its argument. Try a space first, because the whole command is a little more legible that way. If you get an error, retry the command without a space. (Hint: Using Korn shell command-line editing makes it easy to edit and submit a previous command.)

When you first learned English grammar, separating a sentence into subject, predicate, prepositions, and objects of prepositions helped you improve your reading and formulate correct sentences. In the same way, analyzing UNIX command lines into commands, options, arguments to options, and arguments to commands helps you better understand the UNIX commands you encounter and also helps you formulate correct UNIX commands.

SEE ALSO

➤ *For more information on the lp command, see page 223*

Commands That Do Not Allow Filename Command Line Arguments

Some commands do not allow filename arguments. Do not assume that you can enter one or more files on the command line of every command. Check the man page for a given command to see if its syntax allows filenames on the command line.

Some commands process only standard input. **tr** is an example of a command that does not allow filename arguments. If you try to add a filename, you get a syntax error:

```
$ tr "[a-z]" "[A-Z]" acme          # wrong
tr: Too many arguments
Usage: tr [-cs] string1 string2
       tr [-c] -s string1
       tr [-c] -d string1
       tr [-c] -ds string1 string2
```

Since **tr** does not accept filename command line arguments, you must use piping or redirection to supply input for **tr** to process:

```
cat acme | tr "[a-z]" "[A-Z]"       # okay
tr "[a-z]" "[A-Z]" < acme           # better
```

In this example, you can use `cat` *filename* to output the contents of the file on standard output. Then you can use piping (|) to feed the contents into the `tr` command for processing. Even better in the previous example is to use < `acme` as shown to provide `stdin` from the `acme` file to the `tr` command without the overhead of a second process like `cat`.

Some commands take in no input at all. For example, the `date` command will output the current date and time. If you pipe data to it or redirect data from a file to it, the `date` command will simply ignore the input like this:

```
$ cat report7 | date            # ignores input
Sun Oct 31 18:16:44 PST 1999
$ date < report7                # ignores input
Sun Oct 31 18:16:51 PST 1999
$
```

Where Can You Get Help?

More than 100 standard UNIX commands and utilities exist. Each one may have options; some commands may have 15 options or more. These options are not universal, so how on earth are you supposed to remember all the options for all the commands? Luckily, you don't have to. UNIX maintains a set of online manuals with information about each command and its options.

Getting Help from the Man Pages

You use the `man` command to access this information:

```
$ man ls
```

This command shows you the online manual pages that describe how to use the `ls` command. This process is called checking the man page on `ls`. Most commercial UNIX systems have similar man pages. As an example, take a look at the man page for `ls` on my Solaris system:

```
User Commands                                          ls(1)


NAME
    ls - list contents of directory


SYNOPSIS
```

```
/usr/bin/ls [ -aAbcCdfFgilLmnopqrRstux1 ] [ file... ]
/usr/xpg4/bin/ls [ -aAbcCdfFgilLmnopqrRstux1 ] [ file... ]
```

Commands Similar to man

Use the man command to see if your system supports additional helpful commands such as `learn`, `tutor`, `help`, or `info`. If your UNIX system has a graphical interface, graphical online UNIX help may be available as well as online manuals.

The SYNOPSIS section is sometimes called SYNTAX or USAGE on other systems. It shows the form required to put together this command. Items in square brackets ([ ]) are optional. Notice that the ls command supports a large number of command options. It also allows one or more filenames to be listed as arguments to the ls command. This example shows that Solaris supports two forms of the ls command. Later in the man page, the differences between the two forms are detailed:

```
DESCRIPTION
    For each file that is a directory, ls lists the contents
    of the  directory;  for  each file that  is an  ordinary
    file,  ls repeats  its  name  and any  other information
    requested.   The   output  is   sorted  alphabetically  by
    default.  When no arguments
    ...
```

The DESCRIPTION section goes on for a while, so let me skip down and show you where the command-line options are covered:

```
OPTIONS
    The following options are supported:

    -a   List all entries, including those that begin with a
         dot (.), which are normally not listed.

    -A   List all entries, including those that begin with a
         dot (.),  with  the  exception of the working
         directory (.) and the parent directory (..).

    -b   Force printing of non-printable characters to be in
         the octal \ddd notation.
```

Because so many options are available in ls, this section also goes on for a while. In fact, the man section on ls would be about seven pages long if you printed it.

> **Setting Up the Man** PAGER
>
> If man on your system doesn't page the output, or if you don't like the paging utility it invokes, set environment variable **PAGER** to your favorite paging utility (for example: PAGER=pg) and then export **PAGER**.

On some UNIX systems, the man pages have so much text that it goes off your screen before you can read it all. In that case, you must pipe the output of man to a page utility:

```
$ man ls | pg
```

On other systems, the man pages automatically pause at the end of each page, but then you must determine which paging utility you are in and issue the correct commands to move around and end your session. This is covered in the section "Displaying Files/Pipelines a Page at a Time (pg/more/less)" in Chapter 8, "Displaying and Printing Files and Pipelines." Here are the basics that will get you around no matter what pager you are in:

- To get to the next page, press the Enter key or the spacebar.
- To end your man session, press the Q key. You may also have to press the Enter key.

For more information on the man command itself, enter this command:

```
$ man man
```

SEE ALSO

➤ *For more information on displaying files or pipelines, see page 211*

Recognizing Man Pages for System Subroutines

The man pages are arranged in sections that cover commands that users can run from the shell, commands for system administration, file formats, system subroutines available when you write C programs under UNIX, and so on. Some commands, such as the kill command, are also the name of C language subroutines, as in this example:

```
System Calls                              kill(2)


NAME
    kill - send a signal to a process or a group of processes


SYNOPSIS
    #include <sys/types.h>
```

```
#include <signal.h>

int kill(pid_t 4mpidm, int 4msigm);
```

```
DESCRIPTION
     kill() sends a signal to a process or group of processes.
     The process or group of processes to which the signal is
...
```

In this example, notice that following the name kill is the man section number in parentheses. Also note the #include statements in the SYNOPSIS section; these always indicate that you are looking at a C language subroutine, not a command that you can enter at the shell prompt. Do a man on man to see how to specify the order of searching the man sections. If you never write C language programs, you want to set up man so that it checks the commands sections of the man pages before it checks system subroutines.

The man command displays only the man page from the first section it encounters. Use the -a option with man to search all the sections. If the first man page is a system subroutine, the second man page displayed may be from the command section you are interested in. There is usually a man option to specify which man section you are interested in, so it will search only that section.

Finding Information in the Man Page Quickly

UNIX beginners go through man pages one page at a time, which is difficult because there is a lot of information to go through on each command. You also might miss an important reference by scanning the pages.

Intermediate UNIX users know how to use the slash (/) command to quickly move the cursor to desired information. For example, if I am checking the man page on the df command, I might want to know whether the size in blocks is based on 512-byte blocks or 1024-byte blocks. Rather than go through page by page, I might enter this command:

```
/512
```

This command tells the paging utility to advance the cursor to the next place it finds the requested string—512, in this case. To find the next occurrence of the same string, enter this:

```
/
```

Advanced UNIX users know that because man pages can contain special control characters that format the output, the slash command in man pages might not find a given string even though you can find that string visually a few pages down. This problem and its solution are explained in the section "Cleaning Up Man Pages (col)," in Chapter 8. This is how advanced UNIX users start the man command so that the slash command will find all strings correctly:

```
$ man ls | col -bx | pg
```

You may replace pg with your favorite pager.

SEE ALSO

➤ *For more information on cleaning up man pages, see page 222*

Finding the Desired Man Page If You Don't Know the Command

To use the man command, you must give it the UNIX command, spelled correctly. But what can you do if you don't know the command? For example, assume that you want to move print jobs currently in one print queue to a different printer. How can you look up the command to do this?

To find UNIX commands on a certain topic, use the -k option to man, as in this example:

```
$ man -k print
accept           accept (1m)      - accept or reject print
requests         acctcom          acctcom (1)      - search and print process
accounting files
asa              asa (1)          - convert FORTRAN carriage-
control output to printable form
cancel           cancel (1)       - cancel print request
curs_printw      curs_printw (3x)   - print formatted output
in curses windows
devinfo          devinfo (1m)     - print device specific
information
...
```

The -k option tells man to search the description of each command to see if it has anything to do with the argument given (which is print, in this example). The output shown here is for my Solaris system. This output went on to show more than 100 commands whose description contains the word *print*.

In Chapter 18, "Searching for Lines in a File or Pipeline," you will see how to use the grep command to filter out lines you don't want and leave the lines you do want. In the following example, grep is used to find out whether any of these 100-plus lines are commands that move printer requests from one printer to another:

```
$ man -k print | grep move
lpmove           lpmove (1m)      - move print requests
```

```
lprm             lprm (1b)      - remove print requests from the print queue
$
```

Aha! There *is* a command to move print requests, called `lpmove`. To find out more about `lpmove`, you can now issue this command:

```
$ man lpmove
```

Of course, you might not find the command you're looking for as easily as in this example. You often have to search for various related keywords and try different filter words before you have any success. For example, if you had looked for "transfer" instead of "move," you wouldn't have found the command you were looking for.

If your system doesn't support the `-k` option to man, try the `apropos` command:

```
$ apropos print
```

Sometimes the `man -k` or `apropos` command will fail, giving you an error message saying that the `whatis` database must be created before they can run. Usually the message will suggest running `catman -w` to create this database. SCO UNIX has a different command, `makewhatis`, to create this database. Refer to the man page on man for information that applies to your system. Root privilege is usually required to create this database.

SEE ALSO
➤ *For more information on the grep command, see page 494*

Using the Permuted Index

The permuted index is a book that ships with some UNIX systems, providing another way to look up topics of interest. To help you understand a permuted index, I have created a permuted index with just two entries: one for `lpmove` and one for `lprm`:

```
                         lpmove (1m)-move print requests_
                         lprm (1b)-remove print request from
                                      the  print queue
lpmove(1m)-              move print requests
lpmove(1m)-move          print requests
lprm(1b)-remove          print requests from the print queue
lprm(1b)-                remove print requests from the print queue
lpmove(1m)-move print    requests
```

Each entry is placed in the permuted index multiple times—once for each of the important words in that line. Note that there is a gap in the middle of all the entries. The permuted index is arranged in alphabetical order based on the word immediately following the gap. Each entry is included multiple times so that each of its keywords can be placed just after the gap. When you want to look up an entry by keyword, find the word you want in alphabetical order just after the gap. Then look at the entire entry to see if it is one you are interested in.

Command Not Found Errors

To execute a UNIX command, utility, or shell script, simply type the command name at the shell prompt, including any options and arguments needed by the command. Some commands are built into the shell program, but most standard UNIX commands are program files stored in directories such as /bin, /usr/bin/, /etc/, /usr/local/bin, /sbin, and so on.

If you try to run a command, you might get an error like this:

```
$ myscript
myscript: not found
$ ./myscript
acme
pegasus
$
```

It's common to see this not found error when you first begin writing your own shell scripts. If the script is in your current directory, run the file as ./scriptname. This might solve the problem.

If you still get a command not found error, check that you have spelled the command properly, that you are using the correct case (uppercase, lowercase, or mixed), and that you have a space after the command to separate it from any options or arguments. Check the man page for that command. If the man page doesn't exist, the version of UNIX on your system might not support that command.

Some UNIX systems offer a series of layered products (extra-cost software). To use certain commands, you must purchase additional packages containing that command. It is now common for the UNIX C compiler to be an extra-cost item. Therefore, you will get a command not found error when you try to run the cc command or the make command until you purchase that software and install it. Sometimes freeware alternatives can be downloaded from the Internet to provide the same or similar functionality. Many of the Web sites for the major UNIX vendors have links to such freeware.

SEE ALSO

➤ *For more information on writing shell scripts, see page 753*

Setting the Path to Your Commands

When you run commands such as ls, cp, and rm, you don't have to worry whether they are in /bin versus /usr/bin. You don't have to type in the full pathname of the command. This is because the shell PATH variable makes it easy to run the standard UNIX commands.

You can display the current contents of the PATH variable using the echo command:

```
$ echo $PATH
/usr/bin:/usr/ucb:/etc:.
$
```

The dollar sign ($) before the shell variable indicates that you are referring to the contents of that variable. PATH contains a series of directory names separated by colons (:). The full pathname of each directory must be specified. The order of the directories is important because it determines how the shell looks for commands that you type in.

The preceding example is from my Solaris 2.x system. PATH on other UNIX systems would include /bin as well as /usr/bin. On Solaris 2.x SVR4, /bin is now just a symbolic link to /usr/bin. In other words, all the system binaries have been collected into one directory, /usr/bin.

My PATH also contains /usr/ucb, which contains many BSD utilities. If I log in as root, my PATH would also contain /usr/sbin, which contains system administration commands.

Let's see what happens when you type in a UNIX command to the shell.

The shell first checks to see whether the command name contains a slash (/). If the name contains a slash, the shell will use that name as a pathname and try to execute that file. Here are some examples of commands that contain a slash:

```
$ /usr/fred/bin/myscript -p acme
$ ./yourscript file1 file2
```

If the command name doesn't contain a slash, the shell checks each of the directories in PATH for an executable file with the correct name and tries to run only the first one it finds. For example, assume that PATH contains /bin:/usr/bin:/usr/local/bin:

```
$ ls /usr/fred
```

This command word is ls, which doesn't contain a slash. Therefore, the shell checks the first directory in PATH, which is /bin in this example. If /bin/ls is an executable file, the shell tries to run that program and doesn't check any more directories in PATH. If /bin/ls doesn't exist or isn't a regular file or isn't executable, the shell then moves to the next directory, which is /usr/bin in this example. If /usr/bin/ls is an executable file, the shell tries to run it and doesn't check any more directories in PATH. When the shell has tried all the directories in PATH and has not found an executable file, it gives up with a command not found error.

Adding Your Current Directory to *PATH*

If your UNIX command doesn't contain a slash, only the directories in PATH will be checked. Some people also want the current directory to be checked. This is usually useful only if you write your own shell scripts and you want to be able to run them easily when you are in the directory where they reside.

To include the current directory in the PATH variable, add either the period directory or an empty directory. I prefer to add the period directory because that is the common way to indicate the current directory. However, you should be able to recognize empty directories in PATH because there are security implications (covered later).

This is an example from the Bourne shell or Korn shell of adding the current directory to PATH using the period (.):

```
PATH=/bin:/usr/bin:.:/usr/local/bin
```

Here, PATH is set up to search the current directory after /bin and /usr/bin but before /usr/local/bin. Here are some more examples using the period:

```
PATH=/bin:/usr/bin:/usr/local/bin:.       # case 1
PATH=.:/bin:/usr/bin:/usr/local/bin       # case 2
PATH=$PATH:.                              # case 3
```

In case 1, the current directory is searched only if the command isn't found in the first three directories. In case 2, the current directory is searched before the other three directories. In case 3, the default value of PATH is retained and the current directory is specified as the last directory to search.

As a shorthand method, you can use an empty directory to indicate the current directory. An empty directory is just like using the period, but an extra colon (:) instead of a period. Look at the following examples:

```
PATH=/bin:/usr/bin::/usr/local/bin        # case 1
PATH=:/bin:/usr/bin:/usr/local/bin        # case 2
PATH=/bin:/usr/bin:/usr/local/bin:        # case 3
PATH=$PATH:                               # case 4
```

In case 1, the current directory is searched after /usr/bin. In case 2, it is searched before the other directories. In cases 3 and 4, it is searched after the other directories in PATH.

Security Implications of *PATH*

In general, you shouldn't specify the current directory at the beginning of PATH. For security reasons, if you're going to add the current directory to PATH, add it at the end. Otherwise, a hacker could create files with common command names such as cp or ls in /tmp or other commonly used directories. If you execute that system command while sitting in the booby-trapped directory, you will run the hacker's program instead of the system command.

For the same reason, any directories in the root's PATH should not have write permission for the average user.

PATH and Add-On Packages

If you add a new software package to your system, that package might want you to add its executable directory to your PATH variable. The installation script for the package might modify PATH in /etc/profile automatically. It requires root privilege to modify /etc/profile. After you add a package as root, log in again and check your PATH variable. Make sure the order of the directories is reasonable, especially if it has been modified by adding that package.

Where Is That Command?

Sometimes it's useful to know the full pathname of commands you run, especially if they aren't working properly and you want to investigate why. PATH can include many directories, so it is fortunate that certain commands will check PATH for you and tell you the full pathname of commands.

The most useful of these is the type command, which works in both the Bourne shell and the Korn shell:

```
$ type ls                  # from the Bourne shell
ls is /usr/bin/ls
$ exec ksh                 # change to the Korn shell
$ type ls
ls is a tracked alias for /usr/bin/ls
$
```

Here, type takes the command you give it and determines the command's full pathname.

If your system doesn't support the type command, use the which command or the whence command to get the full pathname of a command:

```
$ which ls
$ whence ls
```

97

Often the which command works only in the Bourne shell, and the whence command works only in the Korn shell.

Common Errors Users Make When Entering UNIX Commands

UNIX can be frustrating for beginners. At first, it can seem as if UNIX is picky and will object to everything you type. The next sections cover the common errors that beginners make to help you avoid them.

Incorrect Uppercase and Lowercase

UNIX is Case-Sensitive

Case-sensitive means that you must use the same upper- and lowercase letters in a filename or command. If you use the wrong case, you cannot access the file or command.

Under UNIX, the following filenames would refer to different files:

acme	aCme	acMe	acmE
ACME	acME	aCMe	AcMe
AcmE	Acme	aCME	AcME

All these files could be in use in a directory at the same time because, under UNIX, it matters whether the letter is in uppercase or lowercase. At first, your eyes might not even notice a mistaken uppercase letter when it should be lowercase, or vice versa.

Be wary of handwritten instructions to type in UNIX commands, because people often don't pay attention to uppercase and lowercase when writing.

Incorrect Spacing

As mentioned earlier in this chapter, commands, options, and arguments must not be run together; they must be separated by a space. It is equally invalid to insert a space in the middle of a command or pathname.

Misusing the Arrow Insert, Page Up, and Other Special Keys

Avoid using the special keys on the keyboard, such as the arrow keys, the Insert key, the Home key, the End key, and the Page Up and Page Down keys. Linux is the one flavor of UNIX that incorporates these keys well. For most other types of UNIX systems, use of these special keys will simply insert escape sequences into files, email, and even filenames. Once you have inserted this garbage, it can be very tricky to remove.

Why Doesn't UNIX Support Page Up and Page Down?

Windows users are accustomed to PC-style keyboards and PC editing keys. It makes sense for Windows programs to use those special keys because they are always at hand. UNIX runs on a large variety of stations, many with keyboards that do not have these keys. If a UNIX system has 100 stations, it is possible that only the console will have these keys, and the console may be locked away in the computer room. UNIX usually supports these keys on a graphical station, but not on many character-based stations.

If you ever find garbage like this

```
^[[A^[[B^[[C^[[D
```

in a text document, email, or filename, it resulted from the user trying to correct some misspelling by using the arrows keys to reposition the cursor.

To display control characters in a filename, use the ls -b option:

```
$ ls
acme
acme
$ ls -b
acme
abm^[[0^[[0cme
$
```

At first ls seems to show that there are two files named acme in the same directory, which we know can't be true. By adding the -b option to ls, we can see the controls within the second filename. That filename was created by a user who wanted to redirect output to acme but typed abm by mistake. He pressed the left arrow key twice and typed cme over the bm so that the command line would show acme. The user never realized that he made this mistake because everything looked normal.

Correcting Errors Using Backspace Versus Delete

How should you back up and correct typing errors? Well, it depends. There are two primary ways to back up and correct errors:

99

- Use the Backspace key or press Ctrl+H
- Use the Delete key or press Ctrl+?

What makes this complicated is the fact that, on some keyboards, the Delete key sends an ASCII DEL (127) character. On other keyboards, it sends an ESC sequence. The Backspace key will send either a Ctrl+H or an ASCII DEL. Sometimes Backspace is programmable, especially if you use a PC to log in to UNIX. Sometimes Backspace will send Ctrl+H, and Shift+Backspace will send DEL, or vice versa.

To clear up the confusion, enter the following:

```
$ stty -a
speed 38400 baud;
eucw 1:0:0:0, scrw 1:0:0:0
intr = ^c; quit = ^\; erase = ^?; kill = ^u;
eof = ^d; eol = <undef>; eol2 = <undef>; swtch = <undef>;
start = ^q; stop = ^s; susp = ^z; dsusp = ^y;
rprnt = ^r; flush = ^o; werase = ^w; lnext = ^v;
-parenb -parodd cs8 -cstopb -hupcl cread -clocal -loblk -crtscts -crtsxoff -
parext
-ignbrk brkint ignpar -parmrk -inpck istrip -inlcr -igncr icrnl -iuclcixon -
ixany -ixoff imaxbel
isig icanon -xcase echo echoe echok -echonl -noflsh
-tostop echoctl -echoprt echoke -defecho -flusho -pendin iexten
opost -olcuc onlcr -ocrnl -onocr -onlret -ofill -ofdel tab3
$
```

The fourth line tells you how the system expects you to erase characters. You will see erase set to ^H, ^?, or DEL.

To test your erase key, enter this command:

```
$ datex
```

Erase the letter x and press the Enter key. If you see the system date and time, you used the correct key to erase the letter x. Try using Ctrl+H, Delete, Backspace, and Shift+Backspace in separate tests to see if any of these are successful in erasing the letter x. Hopefully you will find an erase character that works with your current setup.

If not, change your erase character to Ctrl+H, as follows:

```
$ stty erase Ctrl+H
```

Here, enter Ctrl+H by holding down the Ctrl key and then pressing the H key. (Do not press C then T then R then L then + then H.) Now you should be able to use

Ctrl+H to backspace and correct input. You can add this `stty` command to your `.profile` if you want to make the change permanent.

Misusing the Three Different Quote Types

UNIX uses all three different quoting characters:

- `"` is the quotation marks key, called the double quote.
- `'` is the apostrophe key, called the single quote.
- `` ` `` is the grave accent, called the backquote.

Each of these quote keys has different uses under UNIX, so you must use the correct one for different situations.

To include spaces in one argument, use the double or single quotes to surround the argument:

```
$ mail -s 'Meeting next week' fred jane harvey   # correct
```

Here, the `mail` command allows an `-s` option to specify a subject for the email being sent. The `-s` option accepts an argument to that option, which is the text of the subject. The single quotes make the phrase "Meeting next week" all one argument. Here is the wrong way:

```
$ mail -s Meeting next week fred jane harvey     # wrong way
```

Here, the single word `Meeting` is the subject of the email, and the phrase `next week` is considered part of the list of users who will receive this mail. Later you will get bounced mail with a message saying that the system can't deliver mail to users `next` and `week`.

Use double quotes when you want to include shell variables:

```
$ mail -s "$PROJECT proposal" fred jane harvey   # correct way
```

Here, the subject of the mail will contain two words: the contents of the shell variable `$PROJECT`, and the word `proposal`.

Use backquotes when you want to use shell command substitution. This allows you to take the output of one command and use it as text within another command:

```
lp `cat flist`
```

Here, the command within the backquotes will be run first, displaying the contents of file flist. That output is then substituted in the original command in place of the backquoted words. Thus, the `lp` command will be followed by a list of filenames as contained within the flist file. The `lp` command will then be executed to print those files to the default system printer.

SEE ALSO

➤ *For more information on backquotes and command substitution, see page 308*

Also see page 759

➤ *For more information on quoting regular expression wildcards, see page 127*

Also see page 507

What Is UNIX Telling Me?

Some UNIX messages are very cryptic. This section tells you how to interpret common error indications so that you can quickly and easily correct what is wrong.

Usage Errors

One kind of error you might receive when entering UNIX commands is a usage error:

```
$ cp abc
Usage: cp [-fip] source_file target_file
       cp [-r|-R][-fip] source_file... target_file
$
```

Usage Means Misusage

I have seen many UNIX beginners ignore usage messages and then wonder why things aren't working. Whenever you see a usage message, remember that it is an *error* message. You messed up the command, so it didn't run properly.

Remembering that no news is good news, this error means that something is wrong and that your command didn't execute. In this case, the error message means all of the following:

- The command didn't execute because you made an error.
- You have misused this command.
- Here is the correct usage (syntax) so that hopefully you will be able to re-enter it correctly.

This usage error is telling you that cp needs both a source_file and a target_file, but you didn't enter both on the command line. The usage statement also shows you valid options that are possible. Because they are shown in square brackets, they are not required (they are optional).

SEE ALSO

➤ *For more information on usage errors, see page 785*

The > Sign (PS2 Prompt)

The greater-than sign (>) is called the PS2 prompt. It appears in cases like this:

```
$ mail -s "meeting tomorrow jane fred
> quit
> exit
> :q!
>
```

The PS2 prompt appears when UNIX thinks you are entering a multiline command. The shell uses this distinctive PS2 prompt on the next line to warn you that what you type is part of the command started on the previous line. In the preceding example, notice that the closing double quote is missing from the `mail` command, so the command is incomplete. The PS2 prompt appears on the next line. In this case, the user didn't recognize the PS2 prompt and became confused because the system had stopped responding to his commands. He couldn't quit or exit to the shell prompt or to a new login. He should abort that command using Ctrl+C or Delete and then enter the whole command again.

There are cases in which the PS2 prompt is valid, as in this example:

```
$ lpstat -t |
> grep '^p104-' |
> awk '{print $1}' |
> while read $RR
> do
>    cancel $RR
> done
p104-143234 canceled
p104-142337 canceled
p104-142338 canceled
$
```

Here, the output from one command is being piped to another command. If one line ends in a pipe sign (|), that signals the shell that the rest of this pipeline command will be entered on the next line. If a pipeline consists of several commands, putting each command on a separate line can improve legibility. Notice that the PS2 prompt appears, confirming that a long multistatement command is being entered.

If you get the PS2 prompt by mistake, press Ctrl+C, Delete, Backspace, or Shift+Backspace to abort the command and get back to the shell prompt. (See the later discussion of the intr key.)

Dropping to the Next Line with No Prompt

When the system is waiting for keyboard input, the cursor will drop to the next line with no prompt, like this:

```
$ grep 'acme' | sort
_
```

The cursor is sitting on the second line. If you don't recognize the problem, you might let the command sit for a while, thinking that maybe it will complete soon. But this command will never complete. Like many UNIX commands, grep can accept a list of filenames after specifying the pattern to look for in those files. If no files are given, grep will read from standard input for lines to process. This example doesn't pipe any output to grep, so it simply waits for keyboard input of the lines to process.

When you recognize that you have this problem, press Ctrl+C, Delete, Backspace, or Shift+Backspace to abort the command and get back to the shell prompt. (See the later discussion of the intr key.)

Can't Stat Filename

The stat subroutine is one way that UNIX utilities determine information about a file or directory. If a command can't stat the filename, it can't get that information. Check to make sure that you have entered your command correctly and that you correctly spelled any filenames or directories within the command. Also check to make sure that expected files exist and are of the correct type (for example, a directory file versus a regular file).

What to Do When Your Session Seems to Be Hung

If you were in vi, it is possible that you are still in insert mode. In that case, all commands you type will echo to the screen but won't execute. Press the Esc key to terminate insert mode. See if you can now use normal vi commands to check your file, and then save and exit, or exit without saving your changes. If that doesn't solve the problem, go on to the next idea.

If you were in a pager program, input would echo to the screen but not be acted on. Press the Q key and then press the Enter key to see if that terminates the pager program and takes you back to the shell prompt. If that doesn't solve the problem, go on to the next idea.

Try aborting whatever command you're in. Press Ctrl+C, Delete, Backspace, Shift+Backspace, and Ctrl+\ to see if any of these take you back to the shell prompt. If that doesn't solve the problem, go on to the next idea.

It's possible that some of your terminal settings have been disturbed. Enter the following, but don't press the Enter key in doing so:

```
Ctrl+J
stty sane
Ctrl+J
stty sane
Ctrl+J
```

Now go back to the beginning of the list of suggestions and try the suggestions again. If that doesn't solve the problem, go on to the next idea.

If you're using a Windows PC or an X terminal to connect to UNIX over a network, it's possible that the UNIX window doesn't have focus. Click inside the window to select it. The outline of the window should be a more intense color when it is selected. After entering the preceding lines of code, go back to the beginning of the list of suggestions and try them again. If that doesn't solve the problem, go on to the next idea.

Make sure that the cable that connects you to the UNIX system is connected securely. Usually cables should be screwed in tightly to avoid connection problems. If you found a loose cable and corrected it, go back to the beginning of the list and try the suggestions again. If that doesn't solve the problem, go on to the next idea.

Your terminal or Windows PC might have lost the correct connection settings. You should record how to set up your terminal or Windows PC program and how to check whether the settings are correct. If you have never done this, check another station nearby using the same terminal or PC program and compare its settings to your own. If you found a bad setting and corrected it, go back to the beginning of the list and try the suggestions again. If that doesn't solve the problem, go on to the next idea.

Some network or device problems can take up to 10 minutes to time out and give control back to your station. If you have been hung up only a few minutes, wait a total of 10 minutes, and then go back to the beginning of the list and try the suggestions again. If that doesn't solve the problem, go on to the next idea.

Newbies: Ask for Help to Avoid Trouble

Don't power anything off, change settings, or kill processes unless you have been shown how to do these safely. Otherwise, you could make things worse or even crash the system.

If you're connected through a terminal, try powering off the terminal, count to 20, and then power the terminal on again. This might allow you to communicate with UNIX again. Warning: Do not power off the UNIX system itself. If you are unsure of the difference, do not proceed. Ask your system administrator for help.

If you are connected through a Windows PC, start another connection to UNIX and see if you can log in. If this is successful, terminate the window that is not responding, and work in the new window.

The UNIX system itself might be down, or the network might be down. Ask other users if they are having the same problem. If so, report the situation to the system or network administrator.

As a last resort, if you are on a terminal and not a Windows station, you might have to kill your process to see if a new login prompt will let you log in using the following procedure.

How to kill your process to get a new login

1. If you're on a Windows station, close the UNIX window to end that session. Start a new UNIX window to begin another session.

2. If you're on a terminal that is hung up, go to another terminal or station and log in on the same ID.

3. Enter this command, replacing `fred` with your login ID:
   ```
   who -u | grep fred
   ```

   You should see output like this:
   ```
   fred    term/a    Mar 15 19:12   .   9476    (10.1.1.7)
   fred    pts/1     Mar 15 20:30   .   0302    (10.1.1.1)
   ```

4. Determine your current working UNIX port by using the `tty` command, as in this example:
   ```
   $ tty
   /dev/term/a
   $
   ```

5. Find the line in the `who -u` output that corresponds to the hung session. The `tty` won't match your current working session. Look for the PID number at or near the end of the line. In the preceding example, PID 9476 is for the working session, so PID 10302 must be the hung session. If your results are unclear, get help. Do not continue.

6. If you have determined the PID of your hung session, kill that session by entering the following two kill commands, replacing `10302` with the PID for the hung session:
   ```
   $ kill 10302
   $ kill -9 10302
   ```

7. Go to the hung session and see if you have a new login prompt. If so, go ahead and log in. If you don't, ask your system administrator for help.

SEE ALSO

➤ *For more information on accessing UNIX from Windows, see page 707*

➤ *For more information on "X terminals," see page 133*

➤ *For more information on ps and processes, see page 420*

➤ *For more information on killing processes, see page 425*

Check Your Intr and Erase Keys in Advance

Earlier, this chapter discussed how to determine your erase character and how to change it, if necessary. You use a similar process to test your character and change it if necessary. Enter this command:

```
$ date
```

Do not press the Enter key. Press Ctrl+C, Delete, Backspace, and Shift+Backspace to see if any of these take you back to the shell prompt. If so, enter date (but don't press the Enter key) and try that same key again. If it takes you back to the shell prompt, it is your intr key. Write down what key it is for this station as it is connected to UNIX. If none of the keys or key combinations worked, press the Enter key to get to a new shell prompt. Enter this command:

```
$ stty intr Ctrl+C
```

Enter Ctrl+C by holding down the Ctrl key and then pressing the C key. Now you should be able to use Ctrl+C to abort commands and terminate the current job. You can add this stty command to your .profile if you want to make the change permanent.

Using a File to Save Command Input or Output (Redirection)

Every UNIX command has access to three standardized channels for doing simple input, output, and error messages:

- I/O channel 0: standard input (stdin)
- I/O channel 1: standard output (stdout)
- I/O channel 2: standard error (stderr)

Usually all UNIX commands display their results using the standard output routine supplied by the system. Commands display any error messages using the standard error routine. They get their input via standard input. These standard output routines are written in such a way that it is easy for the shell to redirect the output to a file or pipeline instead of to the screen. Similarly, it is easy to redirect input to come from a file or pipeline instead of the keyboard.

---

stderr Is Not Just for Errors

Many commands output progress messages on `stderr` so that they will not interfere with data being piped by the same command. Another command might output a heading to `stderr` and then the following data to `stdout`. For commands that use this scheme, the data goes to `stdout`, and everything else (such as headings, progress messages, and summaries) go to `stderr`.

Imagine that a UNIX command is like a submarine. In the submarine you have three port holes labeled `stdin`, `stdout`, and `stderr`. When you want to send some output, you open the stdout port hole and shove the characters through. You have no idea what is on the other side of the port hole. You don't have to worry if the output is going to the screen, to a file, or to a device such as a printer or disk. Why don't you need to be concerned? Because the standard output mechanism takes care of all of that. It gives the command one way to do output that does not change no matter where the output is redirected. Similarly, when you have error messages, you send them out the stderr port hole.

When you need input, you open `stdin` and process the characters that come in. You don't have to worry about where they came from or what type of device generated it.

Not all command output goes to standard output or standard error. Some error messages go directly to the system console. Because they don't go through standard error, they can't be redirected or saved in a file. Similarly, some command output can go directly to a physical device, such as the user's terminal or a physical device. In that case, the output can't be redirected or saved in a file. However, most command output goes to standard output, and most command errors go to standard error.

SEE ALSO

➤ *For more information on understanding standard I/O, see page 47*

Saving Command or Pipeline Output in a File

When in the Bourne shell or the Korn shell, use the greater-than sign (>) to redirect standard output to go to a file instead of the screen:

```
$ cal 1998 > thisyear
```

The `cal` command normally displays a calendar on the screen. In this example, the output of the `cal` command will be put into a file called `thisyear` and will not appear onscreen. The file will be created automatically if it doesn't exist. To save the output in a file in a different directory, use an absolute or relative pathname to specify the file. You may not use filename generation wildcards (as described in Chapter 11, "Generating and Using File Lists") as a shortcut to avoid typing the complete filename.

The shell will give no warning if you are about to overwrite an existing file. Therefore, you should make sure your destination file doesn't have important data before you redirect output to that file.

The shell sets up redirection before it actually starts the command running. The shell then removes all redirection symbols and files from the command, so the command never sees them when it runs. Thus, the redirection symbol and filename can appear anywhere within the command. The following are equivalent to the `cal` command just shown:

```
$ cal > thisyear 1998
$ > thisyear cal 1998
```

`>` is short for `1>`. They are equivalent; hence, these two commands are equivalent:

```
$ cal 1998 > thisyear
$ cal 1998 1> thisyear
```

Standard output is channel 1, which explains the `1` in `1>`.

Making an Empty File

If you are in the Bourne shell or the Korn shell, you can create a new empty file, or you can empty an existing file like this:

```
$ > filename
$
```

If this command gives you the error `Invalid null command`, you are in the C shell, where this command won't work.

On older UNIX systems, you may encounter `cat/dev/null` being used to clear a file as shown in the following example:

```
$ cat/dev/null > filename # old method, now rarely used
$ > filename              # new method
```

The *noclobber* Option in the Korn Shell

You must be careful when you redirect output. If the destination file already exists, it will be overwritten and no warning will be given.

The Korn shell has an option called `noclobber` that prevents you from redirecting on top of an existing file:

```
$ date > junk      # step 1
$ date > junk      # step 2
$ set -o noclobber      # step 3
$ date > junk      # step 4
ksh: junk: file already exists
$ date >| junk      # step 5
$ date > junk      # step 6
ksh: junk: file already exists
$ set +o noclobber      # step 7
$ date > junk      # step 8
$
```

In step 1, you create a file called junk by redirecting the output from the date command to it. In step 2, you overwrite the old junk file with new information. Notice that no error message is generated. In step 3, you turn on the noclobber option in the Korn shell. In step 4, you try to redirect to your junk file again, but it fails, saying that the file already exists. In step 5, notice that you can use greater-than vertical bar (>|) to overwrite an existing file even with noclobber turned on. In step 6, notice that noclobber is still in force for normal redirection. In step 7, you use the +o option to set noclobber. In step 8, notice that you can redirect over your junk file with no errors.

An Input File Cannot Also Be an Output File

Because the shell initializes the output file before the command starts running, you can't use the same file as both the source and the destination of a UNIX command or pipeline.

```
$ grep -v discontinued pricelist > pricelist  # corrupts pricelist
```

In this example, you remove all lines of file pricelist that have the word "discontinued" and save the result to the same file. The file pricelist is initialized for output as an empty file before the grep command starts. Thus, it finds an empty source file and ends immediately, leaving the destination file empty. The same is true if you use a pipeline:

```
$ sort acme | grep -v discontinued > acme      # corrupts acme
```

The way to accomplish this is to use a temporary intermediate file:

```
$ sort acme | grep -v discontinued > /tmp/tmp$$  # step 1
$ mv /tmp/tmp$$ acme                              # step 2
```

Here, you save the output from the pipeline or UNIX command in a temporary file, typically in /tmp if there is sufficient disk space there. I recommend that you use a temporary filename ending in $$, as shown. This appends a unique number to the end of the file so that other users running at the same time and executing the same code won't interfere with your temporary file. In step 2, you overwrite the original source file with the temporary file, completing the procedure.

Commands That Change Only Output, Not the File

Other chapters of this book cover many UNIX commands. In the discussion of a command, I may mention that this command changes only output, not the file. This section covers all that this implies so that I don't have to repeat the explanation.

Many UNIX commands modify a file and output the result to stdout. For example, the sort command will read the contents of a file and display the lines in alphabetical order:

```
sort acme
```

Here, sort represents any command that reads a file, processes its contents, and displays the result to stdout. Other commands like this are sed to make global substitutions, head to display just the start of the file, nl to number the lines of the file, grep to show only lines that contain a pattern, and so on. The acme file itself remains unchanged by all of these.

If you want to change the contents within the file, it is wrong to redirect the result back to the original file:

```
sort acme > acme     # wrong
```

See the previous section, "An Input File Cannot Also Be an Output File," for a discussion of why. That section also shows the correct way to save the results in the original file by using a two-step process:

```
sort acme > /tmp/tmp$$
mv /tmp/tmp$$ acme
```

Saving Errors in a File

You can save error messages totally independent of saving standard output. Because standard error is channel 2, use 2> to save standard error in a file:

```
$ anycommand 2> anycommand.err     # case 1
$ anycommand > log 2> errs          # case 2
$ anycommand 2> errs > log          # case 3
$ anycommand > log                  # case 4
```

In case 1, standard output is not redirected, so it goes to your screen, while any error messages go to a file called anycommand.err and hence are not seen onscreen. In case 2, standard output goes to a file named log, and standard error goes to a different file, named errs. In case 3, you get the same result as case 2 because it makes no difference whether you redirect standard error before standard output or vice versa. In case 4, standard output is redirected to a file. Standard error is not redirected, so any errors will appear onscreen.

Appending Output or Errors to a File

Use the double greater-than sign (>>) to append standard output or standard error to a file. To *append* means to keep the current information in the file and add the new information to the end of the file. If the file doesn't exist, this command will create it:

```
$ anycommand >> outlog 2>> errlog
```

Standard output and standard error are independent, so you can append to one file but not the other, if desired:

```
$ anycommand 2>> errlog > anycommand.out
```

Saving Both Output and Errors in One File

To save standard output and standard error in the same file, redirect standard error using 2>&1:

```
$ anycommand > anycommand.out 2>&1
```

You must not put any spaces within 2>&1, but there must be a space before it. 2>&1 must come after redirecting standard output in the command line. 2>&1 means to redirect standard error to the same place that standard output is going.

Duplicating Output to a File and to the Screen

The tee pipe gets its name from the image of a pipe with flowing liquid that then splits off in two directions, so that half the liquid goes in one direction and half in the other. For UNIX, the tee pipe actually sends duplicate information flowing to two different places: standard output and a file:

```
$ anycommand |tee filename
```

Here, the output of anycommand is stored in the filename specified. That same information also goes to standard output, which goes to your screen because it is not being redirected:

```
$ anycommand | tee file1 | grep -v discontinued | tee file2 | pg
```

This example shows that it is possible to use two tee pipes in one pipeline. The first tee pipe saves the output from anycommand in file1. The same information goes to standard output, where it is piped to grep, which removes any lines containing the word `discontinued`. The output of `grep` is then saved in `file2` and is displayed onscreen one page at a time.

The `-a` option to the `tee` command allows output to be appended to the specified filename:

```
$ anycommand | tee -a filename
```

The `|tee` pipe allows you to keep a transcript for a command:

```
sh |tee logfile  # logs output only
```

This example starts a subshell. The output of any command you run will be saved in `logfile`. This is useful for debugging problems or documenting procedures. When using `cu` or `telnet` to access another system, both the input and the output are saved in the transcript file:

```
cu remotesys |tee logfile      # logs input and output
telnet remotesys |tee logfile  # logs input and output
```

Be aware that hung sessions are more likely when using a tee pipe to keep a transaction log.

Reading Program Input from a File

Assume that at the end of every day, you run a program called nightly. Assume that this program always asks the same two questions and you always type in the same two answers:

```
y
2002
```

Assume that it takes the program 10 minutes of processing before it asks you for these answers. You can use `stdin` to help out here.

First, create a two-line file that has the two answers, each on a separate line (and nothing else). Call this file `nightly.ans`, and then use it like this:

```
nightly < nightly.ans
```

This command redirects `stdin` to come from the keyboard instead from the file. You can walk away as soon as you key in the command. You don't have to wait for 10 minutes for the processing to complete because the nightly program will read its input from `nightly.ans` whenever input is needed.

Input from a Here-Document

This form of input is useful when you write your own shell scripts, as described in Chapter 28, "Writing Bourne Shell Scripts." A script is just a sequence of commands in a text file. A *here-document* allows you to feed input from lines in your script to a command without having to create a separate file to hold that input:

```
cmd <<EOT
y
2002
EOT
```

In this example, the following are true:

- *cmd* represents any UNIX command or program that always asks the same questions and wants the same input.

- *<<* says that you are redirecting input into *cmd* from the following lines of the script.

- *EOT* represents any string that follows *<<*. It is the terminator to look for at the end of the lines to input. This terminator may be replaced by any word or abbreviation, but the exact same string must be found at the end of the here-document as a terminator.

- *y* will be supplied as the answer to the first question asked by *cmd*.

- *2002* will be supplied as the answer to the second question asked by *cmd*.

- *EOT* at the start of a line in the here-document indicates the End of Text terminator. Any further questions asked in *cmd* will receive an empty string as if the user just pressed Enter.

Passing Command Output as Input to Another Command

Redirection of standard output can also be used to feed the output of one command as the input to a second command. This is called *piping*.

The Efficiency of Piping

This is an example of piping:

```
nl acme | lp
```

Here, the `nl` command is used to number each line of the `acme` file. This output is fed to the `lp` command, which prints the numbered output on the system printer. The `acme` file is not modified on disk by this process.

You could accomplish the same thing like this:

```
nl acme > tmpfile
lp tmpfile
```

In this example, you first number each line and save the result in a temporary file. You then print the temporary file. Piping is more efficient because you don't have to create a real temporary file. If acme is a large file, you might not have enough available disk blocks to save a copy of it in its entirety. With piping, the output of the first command is synchronized with the input of the second command so that the first command never gets too far ahead of the second command. Thus, few disk blocks are needed, and most of the time, the data just written is still in a disk buffer when the second command needs it. The data does not have to be written to disk as it would with a temporary file.

Commands That Process Either Filename Arguments or Standard Input

Other chapters of this book cover many UNIX commands. In the discussion of a command, I may mention that this command processes either filenames or piped input. This section covers all that this implies so that I don't have to repeat the explanation.

Many UNIX commands have this capability to process either filenames or piped input. They work like this. If you specify one or more filename arguments, the command processes those filenames and ignores stdin. Otherwise, the command processes stdin.

In the following example, lp represents any command that processes either filenames or stdin, such as sort, grep, pg, and so on. The contents of files report1 and report2 will be processed by the lp command, which prints them to the default system printer:

```
lp report1 report2
```

In the next example, you run the cal command to generate a calendar and pipe its output to the lp command. Because lp has been given no filename arguments, it will print the piped input it receives from the cal command.

```
cal | lp
```

Even though the lp command can process filename arguments or read from Standard Input, it cannot do both of those things in one command:

```
cal | lp report1     # cal output is ignored
```

This example shows that you cannot have it both ways at the same time. The lp command will process only the contents of report1 and will ignore the output of the cal command. If filename arguments are given on the command line, Standard Input is ignored. This is true for all UNIX commands like the lp command that process either filename arguments or Standard Input.

Commands That Allow Output to be Piped or Redirected

Other chapters of this book cover many UNIX commands. In the discussion of a command, I may mention that output from this command may be piped or redirected. This is a mechanism that gives great flexibility and options. This section covers all that this implies so that you don't have to read the explanation over and over.

Assume that *cmd* represents any command being discussed whose output may be piped or redirected. The following syntax will save the output in *filename*. Nothing will appear on the screen:

```
cmd > filename
```

Another option is to use the >> syntax to append the command output to the end of *filename*. It creates the file if it does not exist. Nothing appears on the screen because output is redirected:

```
cmd >> filename
```

You can also use a tee pipe to split the output so you can both save the output in *filename* and also display the same output to the screen:

```
cmd |tee filename
```

The next syntax uses tee -a to append the output to *filename* and also display it on the screen:

```
cmd |tee -a filename
```

The following example shows how to use a pager utility if you have more than one screen of output. The commands for these different pagers are discussed in the section "Displaying Files/Pipelines a Page at a Time (pg/more/less)," in Chapter 8. Three different pagers are shown here in case your system does not offer your favorite pager utility:

```
cmd | pg
cmd | more
cmd | less
```

Remember these basic pager rules:

- To go to next page, press Enter or the spacebar.
- To quit, press q.

The next example shows how to print the output command. The two standard printer commands, `lp` and `lpr`, are covered in more detail in the section "Printing a File or Pipeline," in Chapter 8.

```
cmd | lp
cmd | lpr
```

If you want to specify the destination printer or print more than one copy of the output, use the options in these examples:

```
cmd | lp -d printername -n number-of-copies
cmd | lpr -P printername -# number-of-copies
```

The following shows how to sort the output and then display it, page it, print it, or save and then print it:

```
cmd | sort
cmd | sort | pg
cmd | sort | lp
cmd | sort |tee filename | lp
```

The `sort` command has a number of options that are covered in section "Sorting Files or Pipelines," in Chapter 10, "Modifying, Comparing, Combining, and Splitting Files."

If you don't need to see all the output, you can see just the start of it or just the end of it by using the head or tail command. Options to the `head` and `tail` commands are discussed in Chapter 8. You may want to sort the output and then see the head or tail of the output. That shortened output can be redirected to a file (>) or appended to a file (>>) or printed, as shown in these examples:

```
cmd | head
cmd | tail
cmd | sort | head
cmd | sort | tail
cmd | sort | head > filename
cmd | sort | head >> filename
cmd | sort | head | lp
```

The next syntax shows that you can use `grep`, discussed in Chapter 18, to filter the output and show only lines that refer to `acme in upper or lower case`. You can also page that output, save it in a file, or sort it and append just the beginning lines to another file:

```
cmd | grep -i acme
cmd | grep -i acme | pg
cmd | grep -i acme > filename
cmd | grep -i acme | sort | head >> filename
```

You can use many more utilities, such as sed, awk, and perl, to process the output of any command in other ways. These are discussed in later chapters. You should now have a sense of how powerful the concept of standard output is, giving you almost unlimited flexibility in combining UNIX utilities to customize any desired result.

A Summary of Redirection Symbols

Table 4.1 summarizes the redirection symbols covered.

Table 4.1 Redirection Symbols

`< file`	Redirect stdin from *file*
`0< file`	Same as `< file`
`> file`	Redirect stdout to *file* (overwrite)
`1> file`	Same as `> file`
`>> file`	Append stdout to *file* (add to existing contents)
`1>> file`	Same as `>> file`
`2> file`	Redirect stderr to *file* (overwrite)
`2>> file`	Append stderr to *file*
`> file 2>&1`	Save both stdout and stderr in *file* (overwrite)
`>> file 2>&1`	Append both stdout and stderr in *file*
`cmd1	cmd2`	Pipe stdout of cmd1 to be stdin to *cmd2*
`cmd1 2>&1	cmd2`	Pipe both stdout and stderr of *cmd1* as stdin to *cmd2*
`cmd |tee file`	Save stdout from *cmd* in *file* and display same onscreen
`cmd |tee -a file`	Append stdout from *cmd* to end of *file* and display same onscreen
`cmd1 |tee file	cmd2`	Save stdout from *cmd1* in *file* and pipe same to *cmd2*

The following example shows that multiple file redirections can occur in one command:

```
command < file1 > file2 2> file3
```

In this next example, the first line shows an incorrect combination of symbols:

```
cmd1 > file | cmd2        # wrong
cmd1 |tee file | cmd2     # right
```

If you redirect all the output to a file, there will be nothing left to pipe to cmd2. The correct way is shown in the second line using a tee pipe to duplicate the output so that one copy goes to the file and the other copy of the output goes to cmd2.

When to Use | versus >

If you want to print a calendar on the printer, would this be correct?

```
cal 1999 > lp       # wrong
```

The answer is no. The previous command creates a file named lp that contains the calendar, which is not what you want. The following rules should help you avoid such mistakes:

- **Rule #1**: Use a pipe sign (|) before a UNIX command.
- **Rule #2**: Use file redirection (>, >>, 2>, <, and so on) before a filename.

Because lp is a UNIX command, rule #1 says that you need a pipe sign (|), not a file redirection symbol, before it. Here is the correct command:

```
cal 1999 | lp       # right
```

The command on the right of the pipe sign (|) must be one that reads from stdin. If not, your command won't work.

```
ls | rm       # wrong
```

The previous command follows rule #1 properly. The ls command generates a list of filenames, and you want to pipe them to the rm command to delete them. However, the rm command needs the filenames typed on the command line. It will not read them from standard input, so this command will not work. You will see a solution to this problem in the section "Using xargs to Process a List of Files," in Chapter 11:

```
ls | xargs rm       # right)
```

Quoting Rules

In this chapter, you have encountered these special characters:

- # (comment)
- > (redirection)
- | (piping)

In later chapters, you will encounter other special characters and wildcards. Sometimes it is necessary to turn off the special meaning of these characters and let the character just stand for itself. Turning off the special meaning of a character is called *quoting*, and it can be done with three ways:

- Using the backslash (\)
- Using the single quote (')
- Using the double quote (")

Quoting can be a complex issue, even for experienced UNIX programmers. These next sections give you a series of simple rules to help you understand when quoting is needed and how to do it correctly. Many of these rules are needed by commands in later chapters. If you are not familiar with these commands already, you can skip reading any quoting rule and come back to it when you start using the command it references.

A Backslash Takes Away the Special Meaning of the Following Character

This section uses the echo command to explain first what a special character is. The echo command will be covered in more detail in Chapter 28, but it is a simple command that just displays the arguments it has been given on the command line. For example:

```
echo Hello world
```

will display this on your screen:

```
Hello world
```

Here is a list of most of the shell special characters (also called *metacharacters*):

```
* ? [ ] ' " \ $ ; & ( ) | ^ < > new-line space tab
```

Watch what happens if you add one of them to your echo command:

```
echo Hello; world
```

The screen will now display this error result:

```
Hello
sh: world: Command not found
```

The ; character tells the shell that it has reached the end of one command and that what follows is a new command. This character allows multiple commands on one line. Because world is not a valid command, you get the error shown.

You can resolve the problem by putting a backslash in front of the ; character to take away its special meaning, allowing you to print it as a literal character:

```
echo Hello\; world
```

The backslash causes the ; character to be handled as any other normal character. The resulting output would be this:

```
Hello; world
```

You use the phrase "*escaping* the ; sign" to mean that you are putting a backslash in front of it. To display any shell special character reliably from `echo`, it must be escaped—that is, preceded by a backslash. You can also say that the backslash is quoting the following character, causing it to be used as a literal character. Each of the shell special characters previously listed will cause a different problem symptom if you try to `echo` it without quoting it. This need to quote special characters occurs in many other UNIX commands, as you shall see later.

The Character Doing the Quoting Is Removed Before Command Execution

Notice in the previous example that the quoting character, the backslash, was not displayed in the output. The shell preprocesses the command line, performing variable substitution, command substitution, and filename substitution unless the special character that would normally invoke substitution is quoted. The quoting character is then removed from the command arguments so that the command being run never sees the quoting character. Here is a different example where quoting is needed:

```
echo You owe $1250
```

This seems like a simple `echo` statement, but notice that the output is not what you want because $1 is a special shell variable:

```
You owe 250
```

The $ sign is one of the metacharacters, so it must be quoted to avoid special handling by the shell:

```
echo You owe \$1250
```

Now you get the desired output:

```
You owe $1250
```

Notice that the quoting character (the backslash) is not present in the output.

Single Quotes Remove the Special Meaning of All Enclosed Characters

This is an `echo` command that must be modified because it contains many special shell characters:

```
echo <-$1250.**>; (update?) [y|n]
```

Putting a backslash in front of each special character is tedious and makes the line difficult to read:

```
echo \<-\$1250.\*\*\>\; \(update\?\) \[y\|n\]
```

There is an easy way to quote a large group of characters: Put a single quote (that is, an apostrophe) at the start and at the end of the string:

```
echo '<-$1250.**>; (update?) [y|n]'
```

Any characters within single quotes are quoted just as if you had put a backslash in front of each character. Now this echo command will display properly.

Quoting Regular Characters Is Harmless

In the previous example, you put single quotes around a whole string, quoting both the special characters and the regular letters and digits that need no quoting. It does not hurt to quote regular characters because quoting takes away any special meaning from a character and does not matter if that character had no special meaning to begin with. This is true for the backslash, single quotes, and double quotes.

A Single Quote May Not Appear Within Single Quotes

If a single quote appears within a string to be output, you should not put the whole string within single quotes:

```
echo 'It's Friday'
```

This will fail and output only the following character while the cursor waits for more input:

```
> _
```

The > sign is the secondary shell prompt (as stored in the PS2 shell variable) that indicates that you have entered a multiple-line command: What you have typed so far is incomplete. Single quotes must be entered in pairs, and their effect is to quote all characters that occur between the pairs of single quotes. In case you are wondering, you cannot get around this by putting a backslash before an embedded single quote.

You can correct the previous example by not using single quotes as your method of quoting. Use one of your other quoting characters, such as the backslash:

```
echo It\'s Friday
```

Double Quotes Allow Some Special Characters

Single quotes can sometimes take away too much of the shell's special conveniences. A dollar sign ($) before a word tells you that the word is a shell variable where you can store information that you want to use later. For example, if you use $SHELL in a command, the shell will substitute your current shell in place of $SHELL. This process is called variable or parameter substitution and is covered in Chapter 28.

Another shell convenience is called command substitution, which is covered in Chapter 11:

```
rm `cat zaplist`
```

In this example, cat filelist is a complete UNIX command that is contained within another UNIX command. It displays all the filenames contained within the file zaplist. This command is enclosed in backquotes (`), which causes the output of the inner command to be substituted into the outer command. Therefore, you should remove (rm) all the files contained in the file zaplist.

The following echo statement contains many special characters that you learned previously must be quoted to use them literally:

```
echo '$USER owes <-$1250.**>; [ as of (`date +%m/%d`) ]'
```

The output using single quotes is easy to predict: What you see is what you get:

```
$USER owes <-$1250.**>; [ as of (`date +%m/%d`) ]
```

However, this is not exactly what you want in this case. Single quotes prevent variable substitution, so $USER is not replaced by the specific username stored in that variable. Single quotes also prevent command substitution, so any attempt to insert the current month and day using the date command within backquotes fails.

Double quotes are the answer to this situation.

Double quotes take away the special meaning of all characters except the following:

- $ for parameter substitution
- Backquotes for command substitution
- \$ to allow literal dollar signs
- \` to allow literal backquotes
- \" to allow embedded double quotes
- \\ to allow embedded backslashes
- All other \ characters are literal (not special)

Watch what happens if you use double quotes like this:

```
echo "$USER owes <-$1250.**>; [ as of (`date +%m/%d`) ]"
```

Notice in the following output that the double quotes allow variable substitution to replace $USER and command substitution to replace `date +%m/%d`:

```
Fred owes <-250.**>; [ as of (12/21) ]
```

As you can see, double quotes permit you in this example to output many special characters literally while still allowing $ and backquote substitutions. However, notice that the amount of money owed is incorrect because $1 was substituted (as you saw in a previous example). To correct this, always use a leading backslash to escape any dollar sign within double quotes where substitution is not intended:

```
echo "$USER owes <-\$1250.**>; [ as of (`date +%m/%d`) ]""
```

The escaped dollar sign is no longer a special character, so the dollar amount appears correctly in the output now:

```
Fred owes <-$1250.**>;  [ as of (12/21) ]
```

Now that you have seen all three forms of quoting, read over Table 4.2, which summarizes their usage:

Table 4.2 Three Forms of Quoting

Quoting Character	Effect
Single quote (')	All special characters between these quotes lose their special meaning.
Double quote (")	Most special characters between these quotes lose their special meaning, with these exceptions: $ ` \$ \` \" \\
Backslash (\)	Any character immediately following the backslash loses its special meaning.

This table also shows that double quotes or a backslash may be embedded in a double-quoted string if they are escaped:

```
echo "The DOS directory is \"\\windows\\temp\""
```

The output will look like this:

```
The DOS directory is "\windows\temp"
```

Quoting May Ignore Word Boundaries

In English, you are used to quoting whole words or sentences. In shell programming, the special characters must be quoted, but it does not matter whether the regular characters are quoted in the same word:

```
echo "Hello; world"
```

You can move the quotes off word boundaries as long as any special characters remain quoted. This command produces the same output as the preceding one:

```
echo Hel"lo; w"orld
```

Of course, it is easier to read the line if the quotes are on word boundaries. This point is presented to help you understand quoting and because you will need this knowledge for more complex quoting situations.

Different Types of Quoting May Be Combined in One Command

You may freely switch from one type of quoting to another within the same command. This example contains single quotes, a backslash, and then double quotes:

```
echo The '$USER' variable contains this value \> "|$USER|"
```

This is the output of this command if `fred` is the current contents of `$USER`:

```
The $USER variable contains this value > |fred|
```

Quote Spaces to Embed Them in a Single Argument

To the shell, one or more spaces or tabs form a single command-line argument separator.

The following line:

```
echo Name        Address
```

displays as this:

```
Name Address
```

Even though you put multiple spaces between `Name` and `Address`, the shell regards them as special characters forming one separator. The `echo` command simply prints the arguments it has received separated by a single space.

You can quote the spaces to achieve your desired result:

```
echo "Name        Address"
```

Now the multiple spaces are preserved in your output:

```
Name        Address
```

Spaces must also be quoted to embed them in a single command-line argument:

```
mail -s Meeting tomorrow fred jane < meeting.notice
```

The `mail` command enables you to send mail to a list of users. The `-s` option allows the following argument to be used as the subject of the mail. The word `tomorrow` is supposed to be part of the subject, but it will be taken as one of the users to receive the message and will cause an error. You can solve this by quoting the embedded space within the subject using any of the three types of quoting covered:

```
mail -s Meeting\ tomorrow fred jane < meeting.notice
mail -s 'Meeting tomorrow' fred jane < meeting.notice
mail -s "Meeting tomorrow" fred jane < meeting.notice
```

Quote the Newline to Continue on the Next Line

The newline character is found at the end of each line of a UNIX shell script and is a special character that tells the shell that it has encountered the end of the command line. You insert the newline character by pressing Enter to go to the next line when inserting text in your shell script. Normally you can't see the newline character, but if you are in the `vi` editor, `:set list` will mark each newline character with a dollar sign. You can quote the newline character to allow a long command to extend to the next line:

```
$ cp file1 file2 file3 file4 file5 file6 file7 \
> file8 file9 /tmp
```

Notice that the last character in the first line is a backslash, which is quoting the newline character implied at the end of the line. The shell recognizes this and prints the > sign (the PS2 prompt) as confirmation that you are entering a continuation line or a multiple-line command.

You must not allow any spaces after the final backslash for this to work. A quoted newline is an argument separator just like a space or tab. Here is another example:

```
$ echo 'Line 1
> Line 2'
```

The newline is quoted because it is between a pair of single quotes found on two consecutive lines. Again, the > sign is displayed by the shell and is not something that you enter. Here is the output:

```
Line 1
Line 2
```

Use Quoting to Access Filenames That Contain Special Characters

In Chapter 11, you will learn that any word containing these characters:

```
* ? [ ]
```

will be expanded to a list of files that match the wildcard pattern given. For example, the command

```
rm ch1*
```

removes all files whose names have the prefix of ch1. In this case, the * character is a special character. Most of the time, this is exactly what you want, but here is a case where you need to use quoting to remove its special meaning. Assume that you have these files in a directory:

```
ch1      ch1*      ch1a      ch15
```

Notice that the filename ch1* contains the * character. While this is certainly not recommended, sometimes you will encounter files whose names contain strange characters (usually through some accident or mistake). If you just want to delete the one file ch1*, you should not do so like this:

```
rm ch1*
```

This will delete all your ch1 files. Instead, you should quote the special character using single quotes, double quotes, or the backslash:

```
rm 'ch1*'
```

Quoting the special character takes away its wildcard meaning and allows you to delete just the one file desired.

Avoid Shell Special Characters in Filenames

Here again is the list of special characters:

```
* ? [ ] ' " \ $ ; & ( ) | ^ < > newline space tab
```

Avoid using these characters in filenames, or you will have to remember to quote the special character each time you access that file.

Quoting Regular Expression Wildcards

In Chapter 18, you will learn about another type of wildcards called *regular expressions*. These use some of the same wildcard characters as filename substitution, as you can see in this grep command (which is covered in Chapter 17, "Managing System Resources"):

```
grep '[0-9][0-9]*$' report2 report7
```

The quoted string [0-9][0-9]*$ is a regular expression (wildcard) pattern that grep will search for within the contents of files report2 and report7. Wildcards in the grep pattern must be quoted to prevent the shell from erroneously replacing that pattern with a list of filenames that match the pattern.

Not Quoting Sometimes Works—Why?

You should always quote your regular expressions to protect them from shell filename expansion, but sometimes they work even if you don't quote them. The shell expands the pattern only if it finds existing files whose names match the pattern. If you happen to be in a directory where no matching files are found, the pattern is left alone, and grep works fine. If you move to another directory, though, the exact same command may fail.

Quote the Backslash to Allow *echo* Escape Sequences

In Chapter 28, you will see that echo allows some special characters, such as \n:

```
echo -e "Line 1\nLine 2"
```

This will print the following:

```
Line 1
Line 2
```

The -e option to echo enables it to interpret echo escape sequences as special, not literal, characters. Some versions of UNIX will object to -e as an illegal option to echo. In that case, simply omit -e from your echo command because it is not required on that system to allow these escape sequences.

The \n is called an escape sequence because the preceding backslash causes the following letter *n* to be treated as a special character. How do the quoting rules apply here? If backslash takes away the special meaning of the following character, shouldn't you just see the letter *n* in the output?

Table 4.2 showed that a backslash within double quotes is special only if it precedes these four characters:

- $
- `
- "
- \

\n within double quotes will be treated as two normal characters and will be passed to the echo command as arguments. The echo command allows its own set of special characters, indicated by a preceding backslash. \n passed to echo tells echo to print a newline. In this example, the \n had to be quoted so that the backslash would be passed to echo and not removed before echo could see it. Watch what happens if you don't quote the backslash:

```
echo Line 1\nLine 2
```

This will print:

```
Line 1nLine 2
```

The \n was not quoted, so the shell removed the backslash before echo saw the arguments. Because echo saw the letter *n*, not \n, it simply printed the letter *n*, not a newline, as desired.

Quote Wildcards for *cpio* and *find*

Other commands like echo have their own special characters that must be quoted so that the shell will pass them unaltered to the command. cpio is a command that saves and restores files. It allows shell filename wildcards to select the files to restore. These wildcards must be quoted to prevent shell expansion. This allows them to be passed to cpio for interpretation:

```
cpio -icvdum 'usr2/*' < /dev/rmt0
```

-icvdum includes options to cpio to specify how it should restore files from the tape device /dev/rmt0. usr2/* says to restore all files from directory usr2 on tape. Again, this command will sometimes work correctly even if you forget to quote the wildcards, because shell expansion will not occur if no matching files are found in the current path (in this case, if there is no usr2 subdirectory in the current directory). It is best to quote these cpio wildcards so that you can be sure that the command works properly every time.

The find command is covered in Chapter 7, "Listing and Finding Directories and Files." It supports its own wildcards to look for partial filenames:

```
find / -name 'ch*.doc' -print
```

ch*.doc is wildcard pattern that tells find to display all filenames that start with *ch* and end with a *.doc* suffix. Unlike shell filename expansion, this find command checks all directories on the system for a match. However, the wildcard must be quoted using single quotes, double quotes, or a backslash, so the wildcard is passed to find and is not expanded by the shell.

chapter

5

Steve "Mor" Moritsugu

The UNIX Graphical User Interface (GUI)

> **Tip for Beginners**
>
> If your UNIX system has graphical icons that you can manipulate with a mouse, you can use this graphical user interface (GUI) to copy files, edit text files, and read and send email. A GUI like this is great for beginners and those people who use the UNIX system only occasionally. This chapter covers the CDE, the most common GUI found today on commercial UNIX systems. If your GUI is different, you may still be able to get around by clicking various help choices and by trial and error. (Do not log in as root while you are experimenting!)

Introducing GUI and the X Window System

UNIX can run on inexpensive character-based ASCII terminals that are usually limited to 80 columns by 24 rows of text or limited graphic characters. UNIX can also utilize more expensive bitmapped monitors that can display pictures, images, and graphics and use a mouse to interact with the user. This second method of interaction is called a graphical user interface (GUI).

> **The Proper Name for X**
>
> The X Consortium requests that when referring to this software, you use the names *X*, *X Window System*, *X Version 11*, *Version 11*, or *X11*. X Window System is actually a trademark of the Massachusetts Institute of Technology (MIT).

A GUI screen looks very much like a Windows screen on a PC, with small pictures called *icons* that represent programs and functions. Like Windows, a GUI also uses a mouse to enable the user to make selections by pointing at icons and clicking or double-clicking. A UNIX GUI also usually offers scrollbars, buttons, dialog boxes, and menus. These can make UNIX much easier to use, especially for a Windows user who uses UNIX only occasionally and therefore does not remember the commands, options, and syntax required to enter UNIX shell commands. Even for experienced UNIX users, GUI icons and graphics often give a clearer picture of what is going on. Because the GUI enables you to start a shell command-line session in a window of the screen, it offers the best of both worlds. In fact, a GUI allows multiple command-line windows to run simultaneously, each running independently of the other. The user can use the mouse to interact with these different shell windows and can even cut and paste text from one window to another.

X Windows

Most UNIX GUI implementations are based on the X Window System (also called X11), developed at the Massachusetts Institute of Technology (MIT) and further enhanced by the companies that make up the X Consortium. X11 provides a library of graphics routines that can be used to create applications that use graphics display elements and mouse input. Although many UNIX GUI implementations run on the console of the UNIX system itself, X11 also allows graphics programs to run on stations connected by Ethernet to the host UNIX system. X11 software is also available to run graphics programs on Windows PCs and Macintosh systems connected to a UNIX system.

X Terminals

Low-cost stations called X Terminals also are minimal computer stations with a graphics monitor and mouse. They have a CPU and memory, but typically not a hard disk. They connect to the UNIX host over a network connection and can run X11 applications. The UNIX host computer does the higher-level program computing, and the X Terminal does the lower-level graphics manipulation. This removes overhead from the UNIX host and allows graphics applications without the cost of a full PC.

The Window Manager

A Window Manager is software that utilizes the X Window System to start jobs in windows on the graphic screen, change the size of a window, minimize the window to an icon, maximize the window to the full screen, and so on. One of the most common of these is the Motif Window Manager, developed by the Open Software Foundation (OSF), which is a consortium of companies.

Console GUIs

Most UNIX systems have one special station that is called the system console. Usually this is a bitmapped monitor with a mouse and a keyboard very near to the computer system itself. The console is where any unexpected system warnings display. The console is usually used to interact with the computer when the computer is first powered on or shut down. In large companies, the UNIX computer and its console are often locked away in the computer department, so the average users never see them. On the other hand, there are also UNIX workstations dedicated to a primary user who sits at the console and runs applications such as computer-aided design (CAD) or animation.

Many UNIX systems today provide a GUI to run on the system console. On some UNIX systems, all the terminals are character-based except for the GUI console, which is then the only station that can run graphics applications and display images. If your system is connected to the Internet, a UNIX GUI console may support a

Web browser so that it can surf the Internet. If your system has an application such as WABI, a UNIX GUI console can run Windows applications. If your system network includes X Terminals or PCs running X11, they may also be capable of running the same applications as the graphic UNIX console.

The Solaris Desktop

Solaris 7 is an operating system from SunSoft Inc., which is a subsidiary of Sun Microsystems Inc. Underlying Solaris is Sun's version of UNIX called SunOS (currently version 5.7, which is based on SVR4). Because the previous SunOS version 4.x was based on BSD UNIX, the current SunOS still offers many BSD utilities even though it is a System V (SVR4) type of UNIX. Solaris also includes Sun's networking additions to UNIX and includes two different GUIs that you can choose from when you log on to the system console. These are described in the following sections on OpenWindows and the CDE. Like most UNIX GUIs, they provide graphic mouse-controlled applications to edit a text file, manipulate files and directories, read and send email, and perform system administration functions. In addition to these standard applications, Solaris provides a number of others. Actually, Solaris provides two different versions of most applications: an OpenWindows version and a CDE version.

SEE ALSO

➤ *For more information on BSD and SVR4 UNIX, see page 17*

➤ *For more information on installing the free non-commercial version of Solaris 7 on a home PC, see page 338*

OpenWindows

Older versions of Solaris provided only one GUI, called OpenWindows, based on the Open Look Window Manager. Figure 5.1 shows an example of two windows open on one screen in this GUI format.

Notice that each window has a triangle in the upper-left corner. If you single-click that triangle, you will see the following options (double-clicking has no effect):

- **Close**—This means minimize to an icon.
- **Full Size/Restore Size**—These choices toggle.
- **Move**—This allows the whole window to be moved.
- **Resize**—This allows the window to be changed to a different size.
- **Back**—This moves the window in back of others.

- **Refresh**—This refreshes the window after you have made any changes.
- **Quit**—This means terminate and close this window.

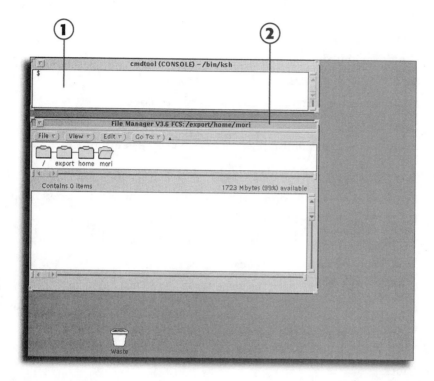

FIGURE 5.1
Solaris' older GUI: OpenWindows.

① A UNIX command-line window (called `cmdtool`).

② A File Manager window.

If you move the cursor to a vacant part of the background and click the right button, you will see these options:

- **Programs**
- **Utilities**
- **Properties**—Sets the color scheme.
- **Workstation Info**—Gives system name and IP address, as well as memory and version information.
- **Help**
- **Exit**—Logs off.

If you select Utilities, you will see these options:

- **Refresh**
- **Reset Input**
- **Function Keys**
- **Window Controls**
- **Save Workspace**—Customize your workspace on logon.
- **Lock Screen**—Enter your logon password to unlock.
- **Suspend**
- **Console**—Start a command session to receive system errors.

If you select Programs rather than Utilities, you will see these options:

- **File Manager**—Create directories, copy files, rename, delete, access floppy.
- **Power Manager**—Set autoshutdown, if inactive.
- **Text Editor**—Edit text files using the mouse.
- **Mail Tool**—Send and receive mail.
- **Calendar Manager**—Schedule appointments and meetings.
- **Command Tool**—View the history, and cut and paste between commands and files.
- **Shell Tool**—Provide shell prompt to enter UNIX commands.
- **Clock**
- **Calculator**
- **Performance Meter**—Monitor CPU usage, disk, and so on.
- **Print Tool**—Print files and manage print queue.
- **Audio Tool**—Record and play back sound files.
- **Tape Tool**—Save, restore, and list tape files.
- **Image Tool**—View and save GIF, JPEG, PostScript, and TIFF files.
- **Snapshot**—Save GUI screen images.
- **Icon Editor**—Create your own icons.
- **Binder**—Connect file type to icon, application, and so on.
- **AnswerBook2**—Access online documentation.
- **Demos**—Learn how to run various applications.

The OpenWindows Text Editor provides a unique split screen option that enables you to edit or cut and paste between two parts of the same file. Note that this capability is not available in the text editor that comes with the other Solaris GUI, called the CDE, described later in this chapter. However, most of these OpenWindows programs can be run from the OpenWindows section of the CDE App Manager. OpenWindows, on the other hand, cannot run the newer CDE applications.

OpenWindows has a feature to keep a desired window from disappearing after you use it. In some OpenWindows menus or windows, a little pushpin icon appears in the upper-left corner. If you click the pushpin, it pins your window or menu in place so that it does not disappear right after you make your selection. You can later make other selections from that window or menu. If you desire no more selections from that window, click the pushpin to unpin the window and allow it to close.

This older OpenWindows GUI is still available on current Solaris systems for those users who don't want to switch to the newer GUI called the CDE, discussed in the following section.

Common Desktop Environment (CDE)

SCO UNIX Adopts the CDE Standard

In its most recent OS release, UnixWare 7, SCO UNIX joins the list of UNIX vendors who provide the CDE GUI as the default. It is worthwhile to learn this GUI because it is becoming available on more UNIX systems from different vendors.

Solaris contains a second GUI called the common desktop environment (CDE), which is based on the X Window System and the Motif Window Manager. Hewlett-Packard, IBM, and Sun jointly contributed to the development of the CDE, so this same GUI is now found on their versions of UNIX: HP-UX, AIX, and Solaris. Other UNIX vendors also offer this GUI, providing a familiar environment on different UNIX platforms.

At the CDE logon screen is a button labeled Options. One of the available options is a Failsafe Session, which is useful in case you have misconfigured your video card or screen resolution. When logging on to the Solaris GUI, you can choose between the older OpenWindows and the newer CDE. On SCO UnixWare 7, you can choose between the newer CDE GUI and a Panorama GUI available on older SCO systems.

Figure 5.2 shows the main panel of the CDE on Solaris 2.x.

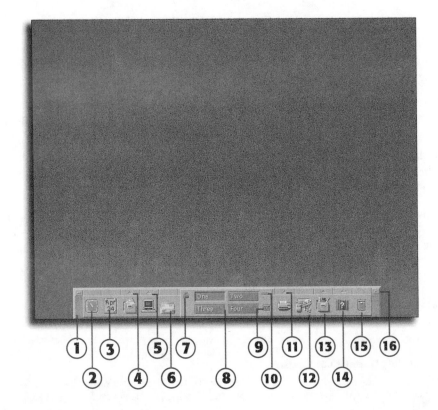

FIGURE 5.2
Main panel of the CDE.

(1) Click this bar to manipulate the CDE main panel.

(2) Shows the current time.

(3) Shows the current month and day.

(4) Click this triangle to see Folders options.

(5) Click this triangle to see Personal Applications options.

(6) Mailer application (send and receive email).

(7) Lock this station (prompts for UNIX password to unlock).

(8) Four separate desktop areas can have windows open.

(9) Exit (log off UNIX).

(10) Flashing LED indicates the GUI is busy servicing your request.

(11) Click this triangle to see Printers options.

(12) Style Manager (configure colors, fonts, backdrops, keyboard, mouse, beep, screen, window, startup).

(13) Click this triangle to see Applications options.

(14) Click this triangle to see Help options (online documentation).

(15) Trash Can icon (drag items to this icon to delete them).

(16) Click here to minimize the main panel.

Busy Screen Savers Hurt Performance

The CDE Style Manager allows you to set up a screen saver to run automatically if the console is inactive. Some screen savers produce fascinating output but remember, all the computation required for that output is at the cost of other jobs on the system. Most servers should use a simple blank screen saver to avoid degrading system performance.

rm Does Not Use the Trash Can

If you delete files in the CDE, you can recover recent files from the trash can. However, you can't do this from the shell command line. Be careful using the UNIX rm command because there is no undelete.

When you click a triangle on the CDE desktop, it opens a set of options. When the options are open, the triangle turns over and points downward as a reminder that, if you click the triangle again, the choices will go away. Beneath each triangle is one icon from the choices in that section. It is a quick start icon because you can click that icon and start it directly from the main panel without having to click the triangle and open all the options.

Change the quick start icon below a triangle in the main panel

1. Click the triangle to open the choices.

2. Place the cursor on the desired icon.

3. Right-click once.

4. Select Copy to Main Panel.

5. Click the triangle to close the choices. Now your desired icon should be in the main panel.

Figure 5.3 shows that the Personal Applications triangle has been clicked to open those selections.

Using Motif Windows

The CDE will run in its own Motif window using the Motif Window Manager and each application you start. Figure 5.4 shows the window controls available on all Motif Window applications.

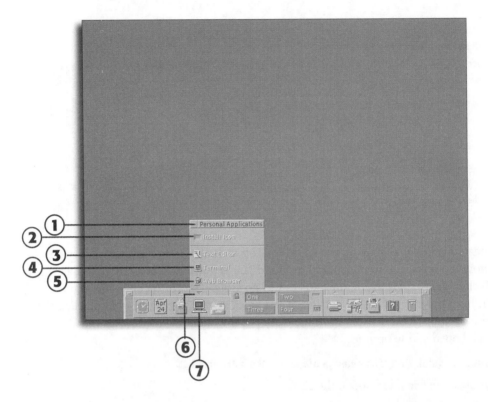

FIGURE 5.3
Personal applications.

① Click this bar for the Move, Lower, or Close options.

② Drag a program or file icon here to the Install icon to add it to this menu. Right-click a menu item if you want to delete it from the menu.

③ Click here for a graphics text editor.

④ Click here for shell command-line window.

⑤ Click here to start the HotJava Web browser.

⑥ Click this downward pointing triangle to close the menu. The triangle will then point upward to indicate that it can be used to open the menu.

⑦ This Main Panel quick access icon allows quick access to one of the items in the menu.

Clicking the top left button will give you access to the following options:

- **Move**—Moves this window.
- **Size**—Resizes this window.
- **Minimize**—Reduces window to an icon.
- **Maximize**—Enlarges window to full screen. Click Restore from this menu to undo this.

- **Lower**—Puts this window underneath any overlapping window.
- **Close**—Terminates application and closes window.
- **Toggle Menu Bar**—Removes or restores the menu bar.

Double-clicking this same menu button is a quick way to invoke Close.

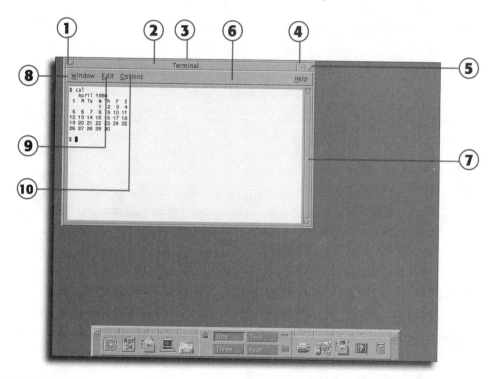

FIGURE 5.4
Window controls.

① Click this menu button for these options.

② Click and drag this title bar to drag the whole window.

③ Name of application running in this window.

④ Minimize button (reduce window to icon).

⑤ Maximize button (enlarge window to full screen; click this again to undo this).

⑥ Menu bar (options depend on the application).

⑦ Scrollbars will appear on the right or at the bottom as needed.

⑧ Window—click here for the New and Close options.

⑨ Edit—click here for the Copy and Paste options.

⑩ Options—click here for the Terminal Characteristics, Window Size, and Font Size options.

If you have started several applications, each one will have its own window. Before you can enter text in that application, you must first select the window by clicking anywhere inside the window. This is called making that window active or giving that window focus. The border around the active window will become darker in color. Selecting one window will automatically deselect the other windows. When a window is not selected, its border becomes a neutral gray color.

In the CDE Style Manager, in the Window section, you can select either of the following:

- Point in Window to Make Active
- Click in Window to Make Active (the default)

Selecting Point in Window to Make Active enables you to select a window just by moving the mouse into that window. I personally don't like this setting because all the windows jump around when I have to go from one end of the screen to another, but different users can have different settings for this option.

You can change the size of a window (resize it) either through the menu button as listed before or by placing the cursor on one corner of the window and dragging it larger or smaller.

You can reposition a window on the screen (that is, move it) either through the menu button as listed before or by placing the cursor within the title bar and dragging the window to its new location.

If one window is behind another, you can lower the top window (that is, put it behind the other) through the menu button, as listed before. Alternatively, you can click any visible part of the lower window to make all of it visible in the foreground.

Transferring Text Between Windows

Motif enables you to easily transfer text between two windows. The windows can be running different applications; so for example, you can transfer text from an email to a text editor, or text from a help document to a UNIX shell command. There is an easy way to transfer text once, as well as a longer way that allows the same text to be remembered and entered multiple times.

How to transfer text once

1. Highlight the desired text by moving the cursor to that text, hold down the left mouse button, and drag the cursor to the end of the text. Then release the left button.

2. Move the mouse cursor to where you want to put the text, either in the same window or a in different window. If the window is running the UNIX vi

command, use vi commands to position the vi cursor and then enter an insert or append command if you have not already done so in this window.

3. Middle-click or right-click to insert the text.

How to save text and paste it one or more times

1. Highlight the desired text by moving the cursor to that text, hold down the left mouse button, and drag the cursor to the end of the text. Then release the left button. If you have a three-button mouse, you can now paste the highlighted text by moving the mouse pointer and clicking the middle button. If you have a two-button mouse, you must perform the following steps.

2. In the menu bar, click Edit and then Copy to save the highlighted text. Alternatively, if Edit also shows a Cut command, you can use it to save the text and remove it from the current application.

3. Move the mouse cursor to where you want to put the text, either in the same window or in a different window. Click one time to set the text cursor. If the window is running the UNIX vi command, use vi commands to position the vi cursor and then enter an insert or append command if you have not already done so in this window.

4. In the menu bar, click Edit and then Paste to insert the saved text at the cursor. If you are in vi, now press Esc manually to Insert mode.

What Applications Does the CDE Support?

The CDE is available on HP-UX, AIX, Solaris, UnixWare 7, and possibly more versions of UNIX. Each of these versions usually supports some basic CDE graphics applications such as the following:

- **File Manager**—Create, copy, move, and delete files and directories
- **Text Editor**—Edit UNIX text files
- **Terminal**—Run UNIX shell commands
- **Mailer**—Send and read email
- **Print Manager**—View the UNIX print spooling
- **Help**—View an online document for this system

Some systems, such as Solaris, have added a number of other applications that can be invoked from the CDE that you will not find on other systems. Under Solaris, you can access these extra applications by moving the cursor to an empty part of the screen, right-clicking, and then clicking Programs.

The following are Solaris 2.6 programs:

- **File Manager**—Create, copy, move, and delete files and directories
- **Text Editor**—Edit UNIX text files
- **Mailer**—Send and read email
- **Calendar**—Schedule appointments and meetings
- **Web Browser**—Surf the Internet using the HotJava web browser
- **Terminal**—Run UNIX shell commands
- **Console**—Works like Terminal, but receives system console errors
- **Clock**—Enables you to use a graphic clock that can be put on the desktop
- **Calculator**—Use a scientific and financial graphical calculator
- **Performance Meter**—Graphically view system usage over time
- **Print Manager**—View UNIX print spooling
- **Audio**—Record and play back audio files
- **Image Viewer**—View and save GIF, JPEG, and TIFF images
- **Snapshot**—Save GUI screen images
- **Icon Editor**—Create your own icons
- **Style Manager**—Customize the look of the CDE
- **App Manager**—Provide access to more programs
- **Desktop Apps**—Run other programs and CDE program development App Builder
- **Desktop Controls**—Use Style Manager and handicap access
- **Desktop Tools**—Use utilities to format floppies, compress files, and so forth
- **Information**—View readme files and Answerbook2
- **OpenWindows**—Use applications from the older OpenWindows GUI
- **System Admin**—Use Admintool, Power Manager, and system configuration utilities
- **Help**—Gain CDE information
- **AnswerBook2**—Gain Solaris and SunOS information

Extensive Help in the CDE

Figure 5.5 shows some of the Help table of contents from the CDE Text Editor application. Each CDE application has helpful information about the screens and options for that application. The Help uses hypertext links (like a Web page) where underlined phrases can be clicked to immediately go to that specific documentation. Hypertext documentation is great because it shows you an overview of each topic in a section and enables you to quickly go to the topics and related topics that you select.

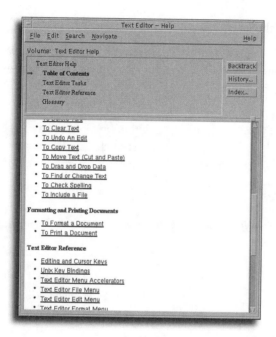

FIGURE 5.5
Extensive help in the CDE.

Running Shell Commands from the CDE

The Terminal application creates a CDE window where you can enter shell commands as if you were on a character-based terminal. You can run this Terminal application in more than one window, so you can run and watch several UNIX commands simultaneously. You can even cut and paste text, as described in the preceding section, between two UNIX terminal sessions or between a CDE application and a UNIX terminal session.

To start the Terminal application, click the Terminal icon, as shown in Figure 5.3. Under the Solaris CDE, you can also start this application by moving to an empty part of the screen, right-clicking, selecting Programs, and then selecting Terminal. (Refer to Figure 5.4 to see the Terminal command-line application and to callout numbers 8, 9, and 10 for options that are specific to the Terminal application.)

When you start a Terminal window, you do not have to log on because you have already logged on at the start of your CDE session. If you type exit in a Terminal window, you will end that window but not your CDE session. To end your CDE session, click the word EXIT (as shown in Figure 5.2).

Editing Text Files from the CDE

The Text Editor is a CDE window application where you can create and modify UNIX text files and system files. You can also cut and paste text, as described earlier, between this Text Editor and other CDE applications such as a UNIX Terminal session.

To start the Text Editor application, click the Text Editor icon, as shown in Figure 5.3. Under the Solaris CDE, you can also start this application by moving to an empty part of the screen, right-clicking, selecting Programs, and then selecting Text Editor.

SEE ALSO

➤ *For information on the StarOffice application suite, which supports full word processing, see page 162*

Opening a File

From the Text Editor, you must first open any UNIX file that you want to edit. Click File, Open. The Open a File dialog box appears (see Figure 5.6).

SEE ALSO

➤ *For more information on regular expression wildcards, see page 502*

Basic Editing

You can move around in the file using the scrollbar or the Page Up and Page Down keys. You can use the Home key to go to the start of the line, and the End key to go to the end of the line.

You have two modes for entering text. In Insert mode, the cursor will be a thin line, and any characters you type in the middle of the line will push the rest of the line to the right. You can change to Overstrike mode by pressing the Insert key or clicking Options and then Overstrike. The cursor will change to a block, and any text you type in the middle of a line will overwrite any existing text there. You can change modes by pressing the Insert key again or by clicking Options and Overstrike again.

The Backspace key deletes the character to the left of the cursor. If the cursor is a block, the Delete key removes the character under the cursor. If the cursor is a line, Delete removes the character to the right of the cursor. You can delete a section of text by dragging over it to highlight it and then pressing the Delete key.

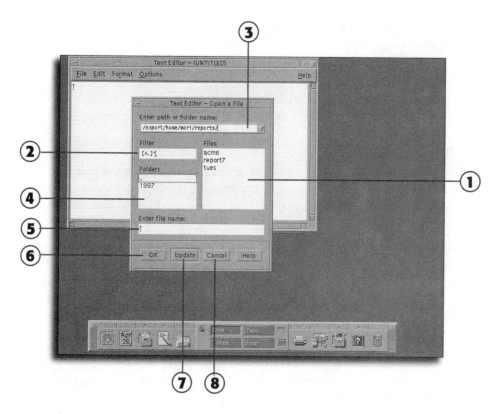

FIGURE 5.6
CDE Text Editor—open a File.

① The Files box shows files that may be opened just by double-clicking the filename.

② The Filter box shows a regular expression wild-card pattern that is used to hide some of the names in the Files box.

③ The path or folder box shows the UNIX directory for the files displayed in the Files box. It begins as your current directory, but you can change this to any desired directory. Click the triangle to the right to get a list of previous and other directories that you can select.

④ The Folders box shows subdirectories of the directory in the path box. Double-click any of

these, and the contents of that new directory will appear in the Files box. You can also click .. to go up one level to the parent directory.

⑤ In the Filename box, you can enter a full pathname for the desired file without having to set any of the other boxes. Press Enter here to open that file.

⑥ Click OK to open the file shown in the filename box.

⑦ Click Update to update the contents of the Files and Folders boxes, including any recent changes.

⑧ Click Cancel to terminate this attempt to open a file.

You can cut and paste or copy and paste within this text file or between windows. See the preceding section on transferring text between windows.

This is a text editor, not a word processor. There are no options for font types or font sizes.

Checking Spelling

To spell-check the current file, click Edit, Check Spelling. This opens the Spelling Checker dialog box (see Figure 5.7).

Formatting Paragraphs

In the UNIX vi command, it can be difficult to format paragraphs. This may leave you with some files that have paragraphs with some lines that are too short and some that are too long. You can use the CDE Text Editor to edit these files and format the problem paragraphs.

Start the CDE Text Editor and open the desired file. Move the cursor to the problem paragraph. Click Format, and then click Settings. You will see the Format Settings dialog box, as shown in Figure 5.8. In this box, set the column numbers for your left and right margins. Then choose your desired paragraph alignment: Left, Right, or Center. You can also choose Justify for both Left and Right alignment, which gives your paragraph a block look. You can then click Paragraph to format just the current paragraph or All to format the whole document.

After you have defined your settings, the next time you want to format, click Format and then click Paragraph or All.

Copying and Moving Files/Directories via the CDE File Manager

To start the File Manager from the CDE main panel, click the icon of a file drawer overflowing with files (see Figure 5.9). On Solaris, it is labeled as Home Folder because it begins showing you your home directory. Figure 5.10 shows the File Manager window that appears.

To rename a file or directory, click it and then change or replace the name as desired.

To move a file to a subdirectory, drag its icon to that directory. To copy the file, press and hold the Control key and then drag the file. To move or copy the file to a different directory, click View, and then click Open New View, which starts another File Manager window. Select the destination directory in that window and drag the file to that directory. To create a symbolic link, press and hold both Shift and Control, and then drag the file icon.

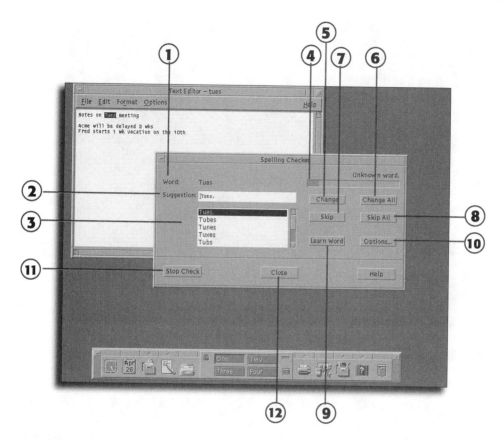

FIGURE 5.7
CDE Text Editor—check spelling.

①   Word is the problem word found in your file.

②   Suggestion is the best alternative found by the spell checker.

③   This shows other alternatives that are valid words. You can double-click one of these to replace your word.

④   This shows how much of the file has been spell checked.

⑤   Change replaces Word with Suggestion once.

⑥   Change All replaces Word with Suggestion throughout the file.

⑦   Skip ignores Word but flags the same Word if found later.

⑧   Skip All ignores this Word throughout the file.

⑨   Learn Word adds this word as a valid word in your personal dictionary so that it will not be questioned any time you run spell check on any file.

⑩   Options enables you to view and remove words from your personal dictionary.

⑪   Stop Check stops the spelling check but leaves the spell check dialog box open so that it can be easily restarted.

⑫   Close closes the Spelling Checker dialog box.

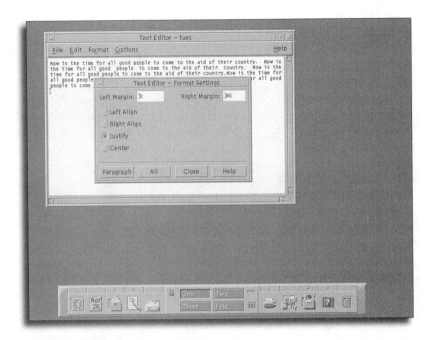

FIGURE 5.8
CDE Text Editor—format paragraphs.

To delete a file, drag it to the Trash Can icon. To permanently delete the file (called shredding it), double-click the Trash Can, select the desired file, click File, and then click Shred. Instead of clicking Shred, you can click Put Back, which undeletes that file.

You can drag a file or folder to the desktop for easy access.

Reading/Sending Email Using the CDE Mailer

The UNIX mail and mailx utilities can be very difficult for UNIX neophytes. The graphic CDE Mailer application makes it much easier to send and receive email. It also handles attachments, which is something the UNIX mail and mailx utilities cannot handle. To start the CDE Mailer application, click the Mail icon in the main panel (refer to callout number 6 in Figure 5.2). You will then see the Mailer window appear (see Figure 5.11).

FIGURE 5.9
Starting the CDE File Manager.

The CDE Mailer enables you to set up your own mail aliases. This is useful if you frequently send mail to a consistent group of people. Click Options, and then click Aliases. Create an alias name for the group, such as salesteam. Enter the list of people under Addresses. Then click Add to add this alias. Now you can send one piece of mail to salesteam, and a copy will go to each member of the group.

There are numerous other capabilities. You can create a signature that contains useful and personal identifying text to add to outgoing mail. You can set up a vacation message that is automatically sent in reply to incoming mail for the days you specify. You can check spelling when composing mail. You can create templates for mail messages. You can create other mailboxes to separate and archive correspondence by project. All these and more are covered in the Help section with hypertext links to quickly get you to the section you need.

SEE ALSO

➤ *For information on the StarOffice application suite which also allows reading and sending email, see page 162*

➤ *For information on reading and sending mail in the* `mailx` *command," see page 700*

➤ *For information on reading and sending UNIX email via Netscape on Windows, see page 725*

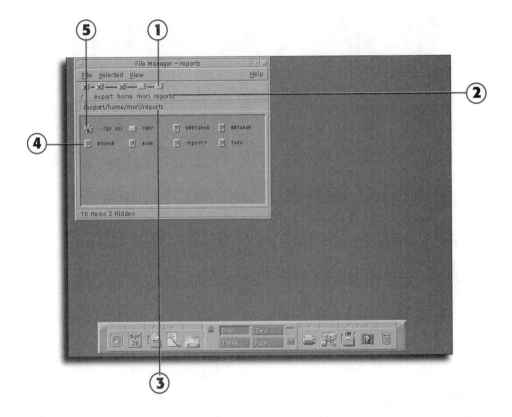

FIGURE 5.10
CDE File Manager.

① Shows how many directories deep your selected directory is. A pencil with a slash through it indicates a directory where you do not have write permission. You can double-click one of these icons to change to that directory.

② Shows the name of each directory.

③ Shows the full pathname of your selected directory. You can use your mouse to edit this and change to a different directory.

④ Shows the files and subdirectories in your selected directory. You can double-click any of the subdirectories to change to that directory.

⑤ You can click this directory to go up one level.

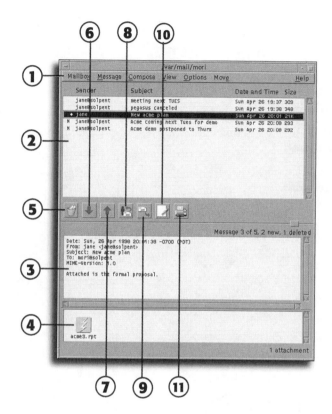

FIGURE 5.11
CDE Mailer.

① Menu bar.

② This window shows one line for each mail item in your mailbox. An N at the start of the line indicates that this item has never been read. A diamond indicates that the mail item contains one or more attachments.

③ This window shows the text of the currently selected mail item in window 1.

④ This window appears only if there are attachments.

⑤ Deletes the current mail item.

⑥ Goes to and displays the next mail item.

⑦ Goes to and displays the previous mail item.

⑧ Replies to sender. This automatically adds the text of the received mail in the reply.

⑨ Forwards a copy of this mail item to another user.

⑩ Click here to compose and send new mail. You can also include attachments.

⑪ Prints mail item.

Steve "Mor" Moritsugu

Miscellaneous UNIX Utilities

Date, time, and calendar

How to count things

How to calculate and do arithmetic

StarOffice: a complete suite of office applications

> **Tip for Beginners**
>
> When beginners get a new UNIX system, they are often surprised at how few office applications come with it. For example, Linux has the `sc` spreadsheet, but that does not begin to compare with the utilities that accompany Excel. The PC store does not sell UNIX applications. Read about custom applications in this chapter to fill in the picture. Read the rest of the sections of this chapter only if you need to use the specific utility discussed.

Custom Applications

The largest, most important group of programs for UNIX systems are custom applications. Programmers choose UNIX for the wide range of languages, compilers, and computer platforms available. These programmers specialize in a particular industry, such as dental offices or petroleum companies. They create software that knows the intimate jargon and requirements of that industry. They then go to trade shows for that industry and demonstrate a turn-key system that can automate that business.

Of course, such software is not sold in PC stores because it is much too specialized for the needs of the general public. Instead, go to the Web sites of the major UNIX vendors to find links to custom applications available for all types of businesses.

Display the Date and Time

The `date` command shows both the current date and time:

```
$ date
Tue Sep 21 22:58:11 PDT 1999
$
```

The output of the `date` command can be customized by adding a format string that begins with a plus sign (+):

```
$ date '+date: %m-%d'
date: 09-21
$
```

In the previous example, `%m` gives the two-digit month, and `%d` gives a two-digit day of the month. These are some of the field descriptors that can be used in a format string:

`%a`	abbreviated weekday, as defined by the locale (for example, Sun to Sat)
`%A`	full weekday name, as defined by the locale
`%b`	abbreviated month name, as defined by the locale
`%B`	full month name, as defined by the locale

%d	day of month, 01 to 31
%D	date as MM/DD/YY
%H	hour, 00 to 23
%I	hour (12-hour clock), 01 to 12
%j	day of the year, 001 to 366
%m	month of year, 01 to 12
%M	minute, 00 to 59
%S	second, 00 to 61
%w	day of the week, with Sunday represented by 0
%W	week number of the year (The first Monday starts week 1)
%y	year (2 digits)
%Y	year (4 digits)

The Calendar Command

The `cal` command prints a calendar of the current month. Some versions of UNIX also include the previous and following months:

```
$ cal
Tue Sep 21 23:15:17 1999
         Aug                    Sep                    Oct
Su Mo Tu We Th Fr Sa   Su Mo Tu We Th Fr Sa   Su Mo Tu We Th Fr Sa
 1  2  3  4  5  6  7             1  2  3  4                   1  2
 8  9 10 11 12 13 14    5  6  7  8  9 10 11     3  4  5  6  7  8  9
15 16 17 18 19 20 21   12 13 14 15 16 17 18    10 11 12 13 14 15 16
22 23 24 25 26 27 28   19 20 21 22 23 24 25    17 18 19 20 21 22 23
29 30 31               26 27 28 29 30          24 25 26 27 28 29 30
                                               31

$
```

You can specify a specific year or a month and year. The following commands all display September 1999:

```
cal 9 1999
cal Sept 1999
cal se 1999
```

The year can range from 1 to 9999 so that you can see what day a particular date fell on in history and in the future, as in the following:

```
cal 99
```

Note that this command displays a 12-month calendar for the year 0099, not 1999.

Counting Lines and Other Things

The wc command displays the number of the following in a file or pipeline:

- Lines (-1)
- Words (-w)
- Characters (-c)

The following is an example of the wc command:

```
$ wc report7
    332    1867  11946 report7
$
```

Add the options -1, -w, or -c to specify if the output should include lines, words, or characters:

```
$ wc -1 report7
    332 report7
$ wc -cw report7
   1867  11946 report7
$
```

This is a very useful command for counting items that can be displayed one per line. In the following example, wc -1 shows that who produced 53 lines, so 53 people must be currently logged into the system:

```
$ who | wc -1
     53
$
```

For more advanced users, wc -c can be used in shell programming to calculate the length of a string:

```
LEN=`echo -n "$STRING" | wc -c`
```

Note the -n option to echo so that wc does not count the newline that echo would otherwise add. In the next section on the expr command, you will see another way to calculate the length of a string.

Arithmetic Integer Calculations

The expr command performs simple integer arithmetic:

```
$ expr 8 / 3
2
$
```

Notice that any fractional result is ignored. The general syntax is as follows:

```
expr integer1 operand integer2
```

Possible operands for this command are given in Table 6.1.

Table 6.1 *expr* Operands

Operand	Description
+	Addition
-	Subtraction
*	Multiplication
/	Integer division (any fraction in the result is dropped)
%	Remainder from a division operation (also called the modulus function)

Notice that the * sign must be enclosed in quotation marks to prevent shell expansion (see the section "Quoting," in Chapter 4, "Rules for Entering UNIX Commands"), but the spaces around the * sign must not be quoted, as in the following example:

```
$ expr 3 \* 5
15
$
```

The remainder or modulus function is what is left over after a division operation:

```
$ expr 19 % 7
5
$
```

Here, 7 goes into 19 two times, with a remainder of 5. The modulus function is often called mod for short. You can say that 19 mod 7 equals 5.

expr requires separate arguments, each separated by a space, or you will not get the expected result:

```
$ expr 3+2
3+2
$
```

expr is often used within backquotes in shell programming to increment a variable:

```
CNT=`expr $CNT + 1`
```

In the previous example, expr adds 1 to the current value in variable CNT, and the backquotes use command substitution to allow the new value to be assigned back to the variable CNT.

expr can also return the number of characters matched by a regular expression (see Chapter 18, "Searching for Lines in a File or Pipeline"):

```
$ expr $ABC : '.*'
7
$
```

.* is a regular expression pattern indicating all characters, so all characters of variable $ABC will be counted. In this case, expr shows that it contains seven characters. Now look at the following code example:

```
$ expr $ABC : '[0-9]*'
4
$
```

[0-9]* is a regular expression pattern that matches any group of digits. In this example, expr counts the number of the digits that occur at the start of the string. Looking at the previous example, you know that there are four digits at the start of variable ABC. Because you knew that there were seven characters total in ABC, you now know that the fifth character is a non-digit.

If part of the regular expression pattern is grouped in escaped parentheses, expr returns the portion of the pattern indicated by the parentheses:

```
$ expr abcdef : '..\(..\)..'
cd
$
```

Each period is a regular expression wildcard that represents one character of the given string. The middle two periods are enclosed in escaped parenthesis, so those two characters, cd, are output. This example also illustrates that the string following expr can be a literal string of characters. However, it is more common in scripts for the string to be generated by variable or command substitution.

A More Powerful Calculator

bc is an arithmetic utility not limited to just integers:

```
$ bc
scale=4
8/3
2.6666
2.5 * 4.1/6.25
1.6400
quit
$
```

In the previous example, you invoke bc and set the scale to 4, meaning that you want it to calculate any fraction to four decimal places. You ask it to calculate 8/3, which gives 2.6666, and then you do a more complex calculation. Note that spaces are optional. Finally, you enter quit to return to the shell prompt. bc can handle addition (+), subtraction (-), multiplication (*), division (/), remainder or modulus (%), and integer exponentiation (^). bc also can accurately compute numbers of any size:

```
9238472938742937 * 29384729347298472
271470026887302339647844620892264
```

In addition, bc can be used within backquotes to assign calculated values to variables, as in the following:

```
AVERAGE=`echo "scale=4; $PRICE/$UNITS" | bc`
```

The echo command is used here to output directives that will be piped to bc. The first directive sets the scale to 4. The second directive is a division operation. Use a semicolon (;) to separate the directives. These directives are piped to bc, which does the calculations and returns the result. The backquotes allow the result from bc to be stored in the variable AVERAGE.

bc allows conversion between different number bases:

```
$ bc
obase=16
ibase=8
400
100

77
3f

10*3
18
quit
$
```

In the previous example, obase=16 sets the output base to hexadecimal; ibase=8 sets the input base to octal. It is important to set the output base first. Enter 400. It shows that an octal 400 is a hex 100. Then enter 77. It shows that an octal 77 is a hex 3f. In the previous example, note that bc allows entering blank lines to make the output more readable. Then you multiply 10*3, which equals 24 because 10 octal is 8 and 8×3 is 24. However, because the output base is hex, you must convert 24 to hex, which gives 18 as the reported result.

SEE ALSO

➤ *For more information on* expr *and* bc, *see page 780*

The StarOffice Application Suite

StarOffice is an integrated set of applications that includes the following:

- **StarOffice Write**—A word processor that also creates Web pages and brochures
- **StarOffice Calc**—A spreadsheet with 3D charts and diagrams
- **StarOffice Draw**—A program that creates illustrations and 3D drawings
- **StarOffice Impress**—A program that creates presentations
- **StarOffice Base**—A database
- **StarOffice Schedule**—An event planner that can synchronize with a Palm Pilot
- **StarOffice Mail**—A program that sends and receives email and attachments
- **StarOffice Discussion**—News postings
- **StarOffice Image**—A program to manipulate images
- **StarOffice Math**—A formula editor
- **StarOffice Basic**—A macro programming language
- **StarOffice Gallery**—Available images, graphics, and sounds

An important component of this package is the filters that allow the import and export of Microsoft Office files. Thus, documents, spreadsheets, and other Microsoft Office files can be easily exchanged with StarOffice.

StarOffice was created by Star Division, in Germany. It was recently acquired by Sun Microsystems, who is currently providing this product "free for personal and commercial use; pay only for services and support." For more information, check the Web site `http://www.sun.com/staroffice`.

Downloading StarOffice

To download StarOffice, follow these steps:

1. Go to the Sun Web page at `www.sun.com` and choose Products & Solutions, StarOffice 5.1, Dot-comming Office Software.

   You will now be at `www.sun.com/dot-com/staroffice.html`. Here you can read more about StarOffice and the dot-com approach to providing free software.

   You can either download the package from this Web page or order it on CD-ROM. Click Download It.

2. Next, you are prompted for type of computer platform. The following are your choices:

   - Solaris SPARC

- Solaris Intel
- Windows 95/98/NT
- Linux
- OS/2

3. At the Choose Language prompt, choose English.

4. Click Download.

5. Click Turn Security On.

6. Click Register.

Case Study: Downloading StarOffice for Solaris

Because the StarOffice interface is similar to existing products and is easy to pick up, I will describe in this chapter how I downloaded and installed StarOffice on my Free Solaris 7 system.

I worked my way through the previous steps until I reached steps 5 and 6. They failed when I was accessing the Internet via the HotJava browser on the Free Solaris 7. To solve this problem, I looked for another Web browser on Solaris.

The CD-ROM Solaris 7 documentation says that Netscape should be included. I ran a `find` command on the whole system, and it reported finding no files whose names contained the letters *etscap*. Therefore I concluded Netscape was not available.

I then tried calling the 800-number listed for Customer Support for Free Solaris on this Web page. Very quickly I was talking to a real person. Alas, I was told that the documentation was in error and that Netscape was not included on the Free Solaris 7 CD-ROMs. The current Sun Web site Solaris 7 documentation does not mention Netscape as included.

I went to a Windows PC and got to the same Web page. I was then able to turn on security and register with no problems. Actually, security is not essential because the product is free and I never had to enter any credit card information.

```
Download from:
    US West
    US Central
    US East
    Europe
```

In the previous Web screen, I chose the closest area to me. Then I clicked the following:

```
Download StarOffice, English 5.1, Intel (72.98 MB)
```

This started a download of a file called so51a_soli_01.tar to my Windows system. It completed after several hours; its size was 72,984,064 bytes.

Moving and Extracting the Files

Before I could move such a large file to my Solaris 7 system, I had to check which filesystems in my Solaris 7 system had enough disk space to hold the file. I ran the following:

```
# df
/proc              (/proc           ):        0 blocks      857 files
/                  (/dev/dsk/c0t0d0s0 ):   168878 blocks    66297 files
/usr               (/dev/dsk/c0t0d0s6 ):   476140 blocks   305147 files
/dev/fd            (fd              ):        0 blocks        0 files
/export/home       (/dev/dsk/c0t0d0s7 ):  2145634 blocks   277878 files
/tmp               (swap            ):   189728 blocks     9443 files
#
```

When I installed Solaris 7, I took the default filesystem layout. The previous output shows that /export/home is the filesystem with the most available space, 2.14GB.

I then had to ftp the file via Ethernet to my Solaris system. I ran the following from the Windows command prompt using the built-in Windows ftp:

```
ftp 200.1.1.244
user: root
password: XXX
ftp> binary
ftp> cd /export/home
ftp> put so51a_soli_01.tar
ftp> quit
```

Because the file ends in .tar, I used the tar command to see if the files had relative or absolute pathnames, as in the following:

```
# tar tvf so51a_soli_01.tar
drwxrwsr-x 4534/310        0 Aug 24 05:25 1999 so51inst/
drwxr-sr-x 4534/310        0 May 11 04:56 1999 so51inst/documentation/
-rw-rw-r— 4706/310 3185043 Aug 24 04:11 1999 so51inst/documentation/setup.pdf
drwxrwxr-x 4780/310        0 Aug 24 05:15 1999 so51inst/office51/
-rw-rw-r— 4780/310 346030 Aug 24 05:12 1999 so51inst/office51/setup.ins
-rwxrwxr-x 4780/310  84016 Aug  9 11:31 1999 so51inst/office51/setup
-rw-rw-r— 4780/310 1765142 Aug  5 04:43 1999 so51inst/office51/f_1_1
...
```

The previous output shows the files have relative pathnames because they do not start with a slash. Relative pathnames will install in my current directory, so I just need to be in the desired directory to run the `tar` command to extract the files.

After I ran the following command to extract the individual files, I found that it had created a subdirectory called `so51inst` and put all the files there:

```
tar xvf so51a_soli_01.tar
```

The following command calculates disk usage in the specified directory, including all subdirectories and files.

```
# du -ks so51inst
71959    so51inst
```

This shows that the total blocks added to the system from the `tar` command was about 71.9MB of disk space. This makes sense. The original tar archive file was 72.98MB. After tar extracts the individual files from this large composite, these individual files take up about the same disk space because the original tar file was not compressed. I have now reduced my total available disk space in this filesystem by the following: 71.9 + 72.98 = 145MB.

I now have no need for the original tar file and can delete it. If I wanted to keep the file around, I could compress it to take up less space until I needed it again. The standard Solaris 7 does not come with the better gzip and bzip2 compression utilities.

Looking around in the files that were extracted, I found two files with documentation:

```
so51inst/documentation/setup.pdf
so51inst/office51/README
```

The README file showed me how to get started, so I did not bother with the setup.pdf file. (I would have had to copy it to Windows and download an Acrobat reader to be able to read the .pdf file.)

Doing the Network Install Once

Two types of StarOffice installations exist:

- **Per user (single-user) install**—Requires that each user who will run StarOffice has a complete copy of all the StarOffice modules in the home directory.
- **Network (multiuser) install**—Requires only one copy of the complete StarOffice modules in a central location and a small set of files (2MB) in the StarOffice user's home directory.

I choose to do the network installation so that many people could share the central StarOffice files. Therefore, this section guides you through installing the central StarOffice files.

I did the first part of the network installation under the root account, to make sure I could create the StarOffice directories to be shared. I invoked setup with the /net option:

```
so51inst/office51/setup  /net
```

> **Performance Graphics**
>
> In Figure 6.1, you will see a small CPU and disk performance monitor on the bottom menu bar. I found that I enjoyed watching these whenever I was waiting for a section to complete. This was confirmation that the system had not died or frozen, so it was easier to wait for completion.

A graphical screen displayed, "Welcome to the installation program." I clicked Next.

The README file you saw earlier was displayed in a window that I could scroll. Again, I clicked Next.

The License Agreement appeared now. I clicked Accept. The following then appeared onscreen:

```
Choose the type of installation.

Standard Installation
Installs the StarOffice 5.1 components optimally. The
installation requires 151.9 MB disk space; temporary 167.7 MB.

Custom Installation
Allows you to select the specific StarOffice 5.1 components.

Minimum Installation
Only installs a minimum of components. The installation
requires 104.4 MB disk space, temporary 111.1 MB.
```

I selected Standard and clicked Next.

Next, I was prompted to select the directory to install the StarOffice 5.1 components. I could accept the default or click the Browse button. I accepted the default /Office51 directory and clicked Next.

Then I got this error:

```
Not enough disk space on the selected drive.
Please choose another drive.
```

I clicked the dot in the upper-right of the window to minimize the installation screen. I was then able to open another command line to look around and create or move directories. I went back to the install screen and chose this directory in my largest filesystem:

```
/export/home/Office51
```

Then I clicked Next. StarOffice prompted me:

```
  Folder '/export/home/Office51' does not exist. Create it now?
```

I clicked Yes. At this point, I had the opportunity to go back and review my previous selections. When I was ready to go on, I clicked Complete.

The installation started. The left panel of the screen showed me what step was being done and the percent complete. At the same time, an automatic slideshow showed me the features of StarOffice 5.1.

This completed in a few minutes. Then I clicked Complete.

Performing an Install for Each User

The previous procedure installed the central StarOffice files that will be shared by all users. A small setup routine must be run for each user who will use StarOffice. Log off as root and log in as a user that you want to be able to run StarOffice. You will have to repeat the following procedure for each user who will run StarOffice, including root, if desired.

Continuing my install of StarOffice, I changed to the bin subdirectory where I just installed StarOffice:

```
cd /export/home/Office51/bin
./setup
```

Note that you should not include /net in this command.

Next a graphical screen displayed, "Welcome to the installation program." I clicked Next.

Next, the README file previously seen was displayed in a window that I could scroll. Again, I clicked Next.

The License Agreement appeared and I clicked Accept.

Next, I entered my User Data for the following information:

- Company
- First and Last Name/initials
- Street

- City/State/Zip code
- Country
- Title/Position
- Tel. (Home)
- Tel. (Work)
- Fax
- Email

If you click Help in the previous screen, it says that the previous fields are used "as default settings when using letter or fax templates, for example." I didn't enter any fields, just to see if the program would complain—it did not.

Next these lines appeared:

```
Choose the type of installation.

Standard Workstation Installation
With this installation, all programs are started from the net directly.
For local files 1.7 MB are required.

Standard Installation (local)
Installs all StarOffice 5.1 components locally to the workstation.
This installation requires 151.9 MB memory; temporary 167.7 MB.
```

I selected the first option (not local) and then clicked Next.

Then, I was prompted to select the directory to install the StarOffice 5.1 local user components. I could choose the default or click the Browse button. I accepted the default in my home directory of /export/home/fred/Office51 and clicked Next.

StarOffice prompted me with the following:

```
Folder '/export/home/fred/Office51' does not exist. Create it now?
```

I clicked Yes. At this point, I had the opportunity to go back and review my previous selections. When I was ready to go on, I clicked Complete.

The following message then appeared:

```
At least one compatible Java Runtime Environment was found which can
be used by StarOffice.
Which environment should be used?
    ( ) No support for Java or JavaScript.
    (*) Use existing system
```

I clicked OK. The installation then started up. The left panel of the screen showed me what step was being done and the percent complete.

> **Troubleshooting Tip**
>
> When I created this user, somehow his home directory was never created. This caused unexpected problems with the StarOffice installation for this user because the system needed to store user-specific files in the user's home directory. Be sure to check that the user's home directory exists before you start the StarOffice user install.

This completed within a minute. Next the following message appeared:

```
During the installation StarOffice was added to the CDE-Frontpanel.
Make sure to restart the workspace manager
in order to complete the integration.
```

I clicked OK and then clicked Complete.

Finally I logged off (click Exit in the menu bar) and logged back in as the same user. When I logged back in, I could start StarOffice from the menu bar (see Figure 6.1).

FIGURE 6.1
Choose StarOffice from the graphical menu.

Alternatively, I could add a line like this to my .profile:

```
PATH=$PATH:/export/home/Office51/bin
```

Then I could start StarOffice from the command line:

```
soffice &
```

When this user started StarOffice, more setup needed to be completed. The following message appeared:

```
Internet Settings - Welcome


Welcome to the Internet setup AutoPilot. It helps you configure
StarOffice to use it with the Internet. You can choose whether you
want to enter the information by yourself or import it from a
different Internet application.
```

I clicked Next. In the previous screen, my network used a proxy server to access the Internet, so I deselected No Proxy Server and entered the following information:

```
(*) No proxy server


    Http proxy server  _____


    Http proxy port    _____
```

Again, I clicked Next and the following screen appeared:

```
[ ] E-mail settings are not required


Account name:
Receiving server (POP3):
Sending server (SMTP):
User name:
Password (optional):
```

I entered my email network settings. (Enter the IP address of the POP3 server system where you pick up your email. Also enter the IP address of the SMTP server where you drop off your outgoing email. If you don't use email, click the top choice that Email Settings Are Not Required.)

In the following screen:

```
[ ] News settings are not required


    Account name:
    News server
```

I selected News Settings Are Not Required.

Next the program gave an overview of what I had selected. I clicked Create.

The program then displayed that it was finished. The result is shown in Figure 6.2.

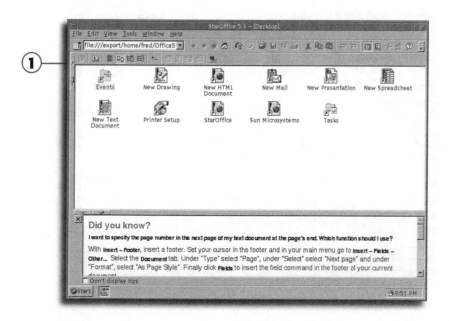

FIGURE 6.2
The StarOffice suite is ready.

① Explorer Show button

Finding Programs

The book *Special Edition Using StarOffice*, published by Que, is devoted entirely to the StarOffice suite. The interface is similar to existing products and is easy to pick up once you find the program you want to run. Some of the programs are hidden in out of the way places, so the next paragraphs help you find them.

You can access most of the StarOffice component programs from the icons shown in Figure 6.2. Once you are done with one StarOffice program, choose File, Close to get back to the screen of icons shown in Figure 6.2.

Some of the StarOffice programs are hidden until you get into the StarOffice Explorer. Follow these steps to get there:

1. Make sure the Explorer Show button is visible, as you see in Figure 6.2. If not, click View in the top menu bar and click Explorer if it is not checked.

2. Click the Explorer Show button. This will open up a column on the left side of the screen with various tabs that you can click.

3. Click the tab that says Explorer. Your screen should now look like Figure 6.3.

FIGURE 6.3
The StarOffice Explorer.

4. To close the Explorer column, find the Hide button near the upper right of the Explorer column. The Hide button points to the left because clicking it will push the dividing wall to the left, thus hiding or closing the whole Explorer column. You can re-open the Explorer column at any time by clicking the Show button as described in step 2.

Figure 6.3 shows that you can use the Explorer to get to the Schedule program and the Gallery of images.

Creating a New Database

Notice that Figure 6.3 also includes an entry for mydata. This is a database that I created and can access from Explorer. You can access more than one database from Explorer.

To create a new database, follow these steps:

1. Click the Tasks tab in the Explorer column.

2. Click Database.

part

II

WORKING WITH UNIX FILES

chapter

7

Listing and Finding Directories and Files

Steve "Mor" Moritsugu

Using *file* to determine the type of file contents

Using *ls* to list file

Using *find* to find filenames or files with properties

Tip for Beginners

Files are important under UNIX, so read the whole section "Introducing UNIX Files." The rest of the chapter is mainly about two commands: `ls` and `find`. Read the beginning of each section because these are useful commands. Don't worry that each command has so many different options. Remember that the `man` command (covered in Chapter 4, "Rules for Entering UNIX Commands") enables you to look up command options online. Come back to this chapter and read about specific options as you need them.

Introducing UNIX Files

You already know a lot about UNIX files from Chapter 3, "UNIX Directories and Pathnames." All UNIX files are organized into a tree-structured directory system. You can then access any file by using an *absolute* or a *relative pathname*.

A filename can contain any letters, digits, or punctuation. Old UNIX systems previously limited filenames to 14 characters, but modem UNIX systems allow them to be as long as several hundred characters.

The most common type of file under UNIX is called a *regular file*. All programs (whether in source code or compiled binary), data files, documents, text files, system utilities, and system configuration tables are regular files. Application languages such as COBOL or BASIC can create sequential files under UNIX (which are read from start to end in sequence) or indexed files (which contain key fields that grant quick access to desired data). To UNIX, these are all regular files.

UNIX does not support contiguous files in which all the blocks of the file are allocated next to each other in one area of the disk. Because UNIX is a *multiuser, multitasking* operating system, the disk services requests from multiple users and multiple jobs and would usually gain little benefit by keeping all the blocks of one file close together. Some applications available for UNIX use raw partitions for storing data. A *raw partition* is a section of a disk that is not organized into UNIX directories and files, so the application can control at the block level how data is stored there.

Directories are the second most common type of file under UNIX. A directory contains the names of all the files and subdirectories that are contained within that directory. Beginners often think that directories and files are two different things, but, in fact, a directory under UNIX is a file with special properties.

Each file under UNIX has a number called an *inode number* that is used in the underlying code to access the desired file. Imagine how difficult it would be if there were no filenames and you had to specify a file number each time you wanted to copy, remove, or print a file. The ability to access files by names instead of numbers is possible only due to directories. A directory contains the list of the filenames within that directory and the associated inode number for each of those files. This directory list may also include subdirectory names, which also have inode numbers just like regular files. (Inodes are also discussed in section "Creating Multiple Names for the Same File (1n)," in Chapter 9, "Copying, Moving, Renaming, Removing, or Linking Files.")

Whenever you type in a UNIX command that refers to a file, you are using a relative or absolute pathname. Based on that pathname, the system looks into the directory that contains the file. From the directory, the UNIX system can determine the inode number for that file. This inode number is then used by the command to access the file.

The next important type of file is the *device file*, which is also called a *device node*. All access to hardware devices, such as tape drives or floppy disks, is done by accessing the device node file for that device. Two types of device nodes exist:

```
character device nodes for raw access to the device
block device nodes for higher level ("cooked") access to the device
```

Some devices can be accessed by both character and block device nodes. Device nodes are also called *special files*.

Another important type of file is the *symbolic link*, which is a pointer to a different file on the system. These are discussed in the section "Using Soft/Symbolic Links," in Chapter 9.

The text has now covered the most common file types. A few other types of UNIX files are used by the system, but the average user almost never needs to know about them.

Hidden Files

A *hidden file* in UNIX is simply any file whose name begins with a period (.). These files are called hidden because they don't appear when listed in the normal method.

In the following example, you first use the 1s command to list the contents of the current directory, which shows three files:

```
$ ls
acme
report6
report7
$ ls -a
.
..
.acmectrl
```

```
acme
report6
report7
$
```

If you add the -a option to ls, you can see all files, including hidden files. In Chapter 11, "Generating and Using File Lists," you will see that wildcard characters can be used to create lists of files; again, hidden files will not appear in those lists unless you specifically include them.

In a directory, most of the files are not hidden and thus will be shown by the ls command and by the wildcards discussed in Chapter 11. Hidden files enable you to put special files that are usually not seen or processed into a directory. These are often system configuration files. Piping and wildcards provide mechanisms for processing lists of files. Hidden files enable you to put special files in a directory that will not be processed with the others unless you specifically include them.

How to Determine the Type of File

You can use the following command to determine the type of file:

```
ls -ld file1 file2
```

In this command the following is true:

- ls is the UNIX command to list files or directory contents.
- -l is an option to tell ls to list in long detailed format.
- -d is an option to show details about a given directory instead of the files within that directory.

This is an example of the previous command showing its output for several common system files:

```
# ls -ld /bin/ls /etc/passwd /tmp /dev/fd0 /dev/rfd0 /usr/bin/uncompress
-r-xr-xr-t   1 bin      bin       43296 May 13  1997 /bin/ls
brw-rw-rw-   2 bin      bin        2, 64 Feb 13 10:11 /dev/fd0
crw-rw-rw-   2 bin      bin        2, 64 Feb 13 10:11 /dev/rfd0
-rw-rw-r--   1 bin      auth       3001 Feb 16 16:01 /etc/passwd
drwxrwxrwt   7 sys      sys        3072 Feb 20 11:16 /tmp
lrwxrwxrwx   1 root     root         40 Feb 13 10:02 /usr/bin/uncompress ->
        /usr/bin/compress
```

In this output, the filename occurs at the end of the line. The first character in each line is a code that gives the type of file, as listed in Table 7.1.

Table 7.1 File Type Letters Used by *ls -l*

File Type Letter	Description
-	Regular file
d	Directory
l	Symbolic or soft link
b	Block special device node file
c	Character special device node file
p, s, m	Other types you might encounter

In this example the following is true:

- `/bin/ls` is a regular file (a system command).
- `/etc/passwd` is a regular file (a text file).
- `/dev/fd0` is a block special file (device node).
- `/dev/rfd0` is a character special file (device node).
- `tmp` is a directory.
- `uncompress` is a symbolic link to the compress program.

SEE ALSO

➤ *For more information on symbolic links, see page 251*

➤ *For more information on block and character special device files, see page 433*

Determining the Nature of the Contents of a File

Use the UNIX `file` command to determine the nature or content type of a file, using this syntax:

```
file file1 file2 ...
```

This is an example:

```
$ file /bin/ls
/bin/ls:        ELF 32-bit MSB executable SPARC Version 1, dynamically
linked, stripped
$
```

In the preceding example, you see that the `/bin/ls` file is a system utility that has been compiled to produce executable code for a SPARC system running Solaris. In the next example, the asterisk (*) Filename Wildcard (which is discussed in Chapter 11) is used to determine the nature of contents of all nonhidden files in the current directory:

```
$ file *
acmetab:     ascii text
report7:     English text
report8:     empty file
runcpio:     executable shell script
cpiofile:    ASCII cpio archive
$
```

Understanding the "Bad Magic Number" Error

If you get this UNIX error, it means that the utility is checking a special word (that is, the magic number) in a file to confirm that the file has the expected type of contents. If a file has a bad magic number, it either is corrupted or is the wrong file type.

In the preceding example, the `file` command makes its best guess as to the type of contents of the file, usually based on analyzing just the beginning of the file. In some cases, the `file` command gets its information from a magic number embedded in the file. It looks up the content type for that magic number in a table of magic numbers (often found in the file `/etc/magic`).

See Table 7.2 for other standard properties of the `file` command.

Table 7.2 Other Properties of the *file* Command

Property	See page
Allows relative and absolute pathname arguments	70
Allows a list of filenames and filename wildcards	292
Allows output to be piped or redirected	116

Listing Files

You can use the `ls` command to list the filenames in either the current directory or a different directory. The following is the general syntax:

`ls options arg1 arg2 ...`

Here, `options` may be `-1` (as you saw earlier) or many other options, as described in later sections. `arg1 arg2` are file or directory names to be listed.

If a directory is given, then the contents of the directory will be shown (unless the -d option is present). If no arguments are given, the contents of the current directory will be shown.

See Table 7.3 for other standard properties of the ls command.

Table 7.3 Other Properties of the *ls* Command

Property	See page
Allows relative and absolute pathname arguments	70
Allows a list of filenames and filename wildcards	292
Allows output to be piped or redirected	116

Listing All Files, Including Hidden Files

Use the -a option to ls to list all files, including hidden files. Hidden files were described earlier in this chapter. In the following example, ls shows only three filenames. ls -a shows an additional three files that were hidden:

```
$ ls
acme
report6
report7
$ ls -a
.
..
.acmectrl
acme
report6
report7
$
```

Listing Files in Columns

Use the -C (capital C) option to ls to list in columns, as in the following:

```
$ ls -C
Main.dt       dtr        lib          proj      trash.dt     var
Personal.dt   etc        lost+found   sbin      u
bin           ghost      mbox         shlib     u2
cdrom         htdocs     mnt          stand     udk
cgi-bin       htlogs     opt          tcb       unix
dev           ibin       pmd          tmp       usr
$
```

On some versions of UNIX, the ls command automatically lists in columns if the listing is not long and if the output is not piped. Some versions of UNIX offer an lc command that is equivalent to ls -C.

Listing Files Appending a Functional Type Indicator

Use the -F (capital F) option to ls to append a character to the end of each filename to denote its function. This can be used with the -C option to list in columns:

```
$ ls -CF
curdoc@      hdnotes/    log         nohup.out   prog2*      xxx
$
```

Table 7.4 shows the suffix character added by the -F option.

Table 7.4   Suffix Added by *ls -F*

/	Denotes a directory
*	Denotes a file with executable permissions
@	Denotes a symbolic link
|	Denotes a named pipe

Listing Files in Long Format Showing Type, Owner, Group, Size, Date, and Time

Use the -l option to ls to list in long format giving details about each file:

```
$ ls -l
total 4
-rw-------  1 lindap   group        552 Feb  1 08:48 acme.linda
-rw-------  1 samw     prog         552 Aug 13  1996 acme.sam
-rw-r--r--  1 stevem   group        420 Feb  1 09:07 report.bak
-rw-r--r--  1 stevem   group        552 Jan 31 18:48 report.sav
$
```

This is a description of each field in the long listing:

```
t perm      ln owner     group        size mon day time filename
```

Here, the following is true:

- *t* is the file type, as given in Table 7.1 earlier in this chapter.
- *perm* is the file permissions, as described in Chapter 14, "File Permissions and System Security."

- *ln* is the hard link count, as described in section "Creating Multiple Names for the Same File (ln)," in Chapter 9. This count is the number of names by which this file is known.

- *owner* is the user who owns this file.

- *group* is the group of the file. Initially, the group of the file matches the primary group of the owner, but it may be changed later to any group.

- *size* is the number of characters within the file. Note that this size does not reflect unused space in the last disk block.

- *mon* is the month when the file was last modified.

- *day* is the day of the month when the file was last modified.

- *time* is the time when the file was last modified. If the file was last modified more than a year ago, time will be replaced by the year when last modified.

- *filename* is the name of the file or directory.

Listing Files in Order of Date Last Modified

Use the -t and -l options to ls to get a long file listing arranged in order from newest to oldest date of last modification:

```
$ ls -lt     # most recently modified are listed first
total 4
-rw-r--r--   1 stevem    group        420 Feb  1 09:07 report.bak
-rw-------   1 lindap    group        552 Feb  1 08:48 acme.linda
-rw-r--r--   1 stevem    group        552 Jan 31 18:48 report.sav
-rw-------   1 samw      prog         552 Aug 13  1996 acme.sam
$
```

This can be useful if you recently changed one or two files and want to find them quickly.

To reverse the sort order from oldest to newest, include the -r option as well:

```
ls -ltr
```

The -r option causes ls to reverse its normal order of listing, whether by date/time or alphabetic order. The option letters l, t, and r can be specified in any order. You should now see output like this:

```
$ ls -ltr    # most recently modified are listed last
total 4
-rw-------   1 samw      prog         552 Aug 13  1996 acme.sam
-rw-r--r--   1 stevem    group        552 Jan 31 18:48 report.sav
-rw-------   1 lindap    group        552 Feb  1 08:48 acme.linda
-rw-r--r--   1 stevem    group        420 Feb  1 09:07 report.bak
```

This can be useful when looking for files that have not changed in a long time.

Listing Files in Order of Date of Last Usage

When you combine the -l and -u options to ls, you get a long listing that shows the date of last usage or access instead of the date of last modification:

```
ls -lu    # alphabetical listing with date last used
```

Access could mean that someone displayed the file, copied it, printed it, and so on. Access or usage includes both reading and writing to the file.

Note that many backup programs access all files nightly. Some backup programs have the capability to reset the last access date of the files so that utilities such as ls -lu can show when a user last accessed the file.

As before, it is possible to list the files from most recently accessed to least recently accessed. Add the -t option to list the files in order of date/time usage:

```
ls -ltu   # most recently used files are listed first
```

Add the -r option to reverse the order so that the oldest accessed files are listed first. This can be useful when you are low on disk space and you want to archive and purge files in this directory that no one uses anymore.

```
ls -lutr    # most recently used files are listed last
```

Remember that the option letters to the ls command can be specified in any order.

Listing Files in Order of Date of Last Inode Change

Add the -c and -l options to ls to replace the date of last modification with the last date when the inode was changed. Some people mistakenly think that the -c option gives you the file creation date, but this is incorrect. UNIX does not keep that date. The inode is updated when you first create the file but also when you change the file owner, group, permissions, and so on.

```
ls -lc    # alphabetical listing with last inode change date
ls -ltc   # most recently changed inode is listed first
ls -ltcr  # most recently changed inode is listed last
```

Listing Files Recursively

The -R option to ls shows not only the files in the selected directory(s), but also each of the subdirectories and their contents:

```
$ ls -R
99Feb
```

```
99Jan
report23
report7

./99Feb:
gl.acme

./99Jan:
gl.acme
inv.acme
$
```

In the previous example, 99Jan and 99Feb are directories. That fact is clearer if you use both the -R and -F options together so that a slash (/) is appended to directories.

```
$ ls -RF
99Feb/
99Jan/
report23
report7

./99Feb:
gl.acme

./99Jan:
gl.acme
inv.acme
$
```

You can also combine the -R and -l options for a long recursive listing:

```
$ ls -lR
total 10
drwxrwx---   2 mori     group          512 Sep  6 20:49 99Feb
drwxrwx---   2 mori     group          512 Sep  6 20:49 99Jan
-rw-rw----   1 mori     group         1897 Sep  6 20:36 report23
-rw-rw----   1 mori     group          536 Sep  6 20:36 report7

./99Feb:
total 2
-rw-rw----   1 mori     group           29 Sep  6 20:49 gl.acme

./99Jan:
total 90
-rw-rw----   1 mori     group        43640 Sep  6 20:49 gl.acme
```

```
-rw-rw----    1 mori       group            29 Sep  6 20:48 inv.acme
$
```

Listing Information About a Directory

If you try to list information about a specific directory, you will get information about the contents of the directory, not the directory itself:

```
$ ls -l /tmp
total 166
-rw-r--r--    1 stull      group             0 Sep  3 10:55 27753
-rw-r--r--    1 stull      group             0 Aug 31 09:53 6553
-rw-r--r--    1 stull      group         27202 Sep  1 13:41 8167
-rw-------    1 mori       group         13312 Sep  1 04:58 Ex10905
...
```

Use the -d option to ls when you want information about the directory itself, not its contents:

```
$ ls -ld /tmp
drwxrwxrwt    7 sys        sys            3584 Sep  6 21:00 /tmp
$
```

Listing Files Showing Any Control Characters in the Name

Use the -b option to ls to show any control characters within the filenames. The following example appears to show two files with the same name in the same directory, but that should be impossible.

```
$ ls
acme
acme
$
```

ls -b shows the real story. The second acme file contains control characters from a user trying to correct a mistake by using the arrow keys instead of the Backspace key.

```
$ ls -b
acme
ad\033[Dcme
$
```

\033 indicates the Escape character. In general, \0XX indicates a control character whose octal value is XX.

Using the *find* Command

The `find` command is a powerful, flexible way to create a list of files based on filename or part of a name, size, owner, or many other characteristics and combinations of characteristics. The `find` command not only searches the requested directory, but it also searches all subdirectories. The basic syntax is as follows:

```
find starting-dir(s) options
```

See Table 7.5 for other standard properties of the `find` command:

Table 7.5 Other Properties of the *find* Command

Property	See page
Allows output to be piped or redirected	116
For the starting directory:	
Allows relative and absolute pathname arguments	70
Allows a list of filenames and filename wildcards	292

Finding All the Directories That Contain a Given Filename

Start with a simple, commonly used application of the `find` command. Assume that you created a filename `alpha` several days ago, but you cannot remember what directory the file resides in. You can use the `-name` option of the `find` command to find and display the full pathnames of all files named `alpha`:

```
$ find / -name alpha -print
/reports/1998/alpha
/reports/1998/region2/alpha
/tmp/alpha
$
```

The previous example found a file named `alpha` in three different directories. The `find` command looks only for matching file basenames; this means it does not check the directory portion of the filename for a match, so the previous find command would not list a name such as this:

```
/data/alpha/report7       (would not be listed)
```

The `-name` option looks for any type of file (including directory names) with the requested name. Some of the `alpha` files found in the previous example might actually be directories that contain other files. If you want to restrict `find` to report only certain file types, add the `-type` option as described later.

Here is the general syntax of the `-name` find option:

```
find starting-dir(s) -name filename-to-find -print
```

Specifying a Starting Directory to Speed Up the *find* Command

A UNIX system can contain a huge number of files, often so many that the `find` command can take 10 minutes or more to complete. For this reason, `find` allows you to specify a starting directory to narrow down the number of files it must search for. Only files in this starting directory and all its subdirectories will be checked.

```
$ find /reports -name alpha -print
/reports/1998/alpha
/reports/1998/region2/alpha
$
```

This `find` command checks only the directory `/reports` and its subdirectories. This not only gives results more quickly, but it also reduces system overhead for other users. What should you do if you don't know the starting directory? Try guessing. If you have one or two directory names where the file might be, use the `find` command to check those directories first. If you don't locate the desired file in those directories, then use `/` as the starting directory to check the whole system.

Using *find* with Relative Pathnames

The `find` command can take either an absolute or a relative pathname as the starting directory. Here `find` is given an absolute starting directory:

```
$ find /reports -name alpha -print
/reports/1998/alpha
/reports/1998/region2/alpha
$
```

In the previous example, notice that all the files found are also reported as absolute pathnames. In the following example, you search for the same name but use dot (that is, a period) as a relative pathname for the current directory:

```
$ cd /reports
$ find . -name alpha -print
./1998/alpha
./1998/region2/alpha
$
```

Notice in the previous example that the pathnames found are reported relative to the current directory `/reports`, as in this example:

```
./1998/alpha
```

The previous filename found by `find` is a relative pathname. The beginning dot (that is, period) indicates that it is relative to the current directory, which is `/reports`. Thus, in this case, it is equivalent to this full pathname:

```
/reports/1998/alpha
```

This is another example of the same `find` command, but starting in the root directory:

```
$ cd /
$ find ./reports -name alpha -print
./reports/1998/alpha
./reports/1998/region2/alpha
$
```

Should you use absolute or relative pathnames when you use the `find` command? If you do use relative pathnames, what directory should you change to before you run the `find` command? Most people use absolute pathnames when running the `find` command at the shell prompt because it is simpler. Then it does not matter what your current directory is. When using the `find` command in a pipeline or script programming, the files listed by `find` are often fed to other commands for processing. You will find that choosing relative pathnames and changing to a convenient directory before you run `find` can facilitate copying, storing, or retrieving files.

The remaining section on `find` uses absolute pathnames in some examples and relative pathnames in others. Because you will not be piping these `find` commands to other commands, you can use either absolute or relative pathnames. The examples use both so that UNIX users will not see only absolute pathname examples and become disoriented when faced with relative pathnames in `find`.

Using *find* with Multiple Starting Directories

On older versions of UNIX, the `find` command allowed only a single starting directory. If you wanted to check three different directories, you had to run the `find` command three times.

Newer UNIX systems allow `find` to check several starting directories:

```
find /reports /data/archives/1999 /u/acme -name alpha -print
```

In the previous example, `find` checks these three directories and all their subdirectories for a file (or directory) named `alpha`:

```
/reports
/data/archives/1999
/u/acme
```

If `find` complains that the second directory—`/data/archives/1999`, in this case—is an illegal option, then your version of `find` does not allow multiple starting directories. You can determine whether your version of `find` allows multiple starting directories by checking its man page:

```
man find
```

Under Syntax, Synopsis, or Usage (depending on your brand of UNIX), see if more than one starting directory is indicated.

```
find [path...] [expression]
```

In the previous example, the three dots after `path` indicate that one or more starting directories may be specified. Multiple directories may also be indicated in the man page by using the plural (such as `paths`), or by adding the word list (as in `pathlist`).

Searching the Whole System with *find*

To search the whole system, specify `/` as the starting directory. This `/` indicates the system root directory, which includes all other files and directories:

```
$ find / -name alpha -print
/reports/1998/alpha
/reports/1998/region2/alpha
/tmp/alpha
$
```

To search the entire system and display all found files as relative pathnames, `cd` to the root directory and specify the `find` starting directory as a period, which indicates the current directory.

```
$ cd /
$ find . -name alpha -print
./reports/1998/alpha
./reports/1998/region2/alpha
./tmp/alpha
$
```

Suppressing *find* Errors: Cannot Access Some Directories

If you run the `find` command as a non-root user, you may encounter error messages like this:

```
$ find / -name alpha -print
find: /var/spool/cron: Permission denied
find: /var/spool/atjobs: Permission denied
find: /var/spool/atspool: Permission denied
```

A number of system directories can be read only by the system administrator (root). If a non-root user uses `find` to check these restricted directories, an error message will be displayed for each restricted directory, indicating that access was denied. There can be hundreds or thousands of these restricted directories, and the files found by the `find` command can be hard to spot amid all the error lines flashing by.

To resolve this problem, you can suppress all error messages from `find` by redirecting standard error to `/dev/null`.

```
$ find / -name alpha -print 2> /dev/null
```

No space is allowed between the 2 and the > sign. 2> redirects standard output to be processed by device `/dev/null`, which simply discards everything you send it so that no error messages appear on the screen.

Although this solution is commonly used, it has the disadvantage that all error messages will be suppressed, even if they warn of a different type of problem, such as a syntax error in your `find` command. A better solution is to discard just the `Permission denied` error messages, like this:

```
$ find / -name alpha -print 2>&1 | grep -vi 'Permission denied'
```

No spaces are allowed within 2>&1. 2>&1 redirects standard error to standard output, where it can be piped to `grep` to ignore all lines that contain the `Permission denied` error message, while still allowing other errors to be seen. Your brand of UNIX may use other words than `Permission denied`, so customize this `grep` command to use words that you find in your error message. Choose at least two words of the error message to prevent `grep` from suppressing filenames that contain words such as *Permission* or *denied*.

Surveying Types of *find* Options

Unlike most other UNIX commands, each `find` option is always a complete word beginning with a dash, such as `-name` or `-type`. `find` allows an almost bewildering assortment of such options. To help make sense of them, these commands have been grouped into the following categories:

- File selection options:
  - Options that aøllow wildcards
  - Options requiring a simple argument
  - Options requiring +n, n, or -n
  - Options that take no argument
- Controlling options (includes logical "OR" and grouping)
- Action options

191

File selection options enable you to specify criteria for choosing files. Controlling options affect how find does its job. Action options enable you to define what to do with the files that match the previous selection criteria. Note that some UNIX systems do not support all find options covered here. Check the man page on find on your system to see which options your version supports.

Finding Files When You Know Only Part of the Name

The -name option can be used with wildcards when you are sure of only part of the filename to find.

To specify a partial pathname, use filename substitution wildcards, covered in Chapter 8, "Displaying and Printing Files and Pipelines." For instance, look over this code:

```
$ find / -name '*alpha*' -print
/reports/1998/alpha
/reports/1998/alpha2
/reports/1998/old-alpha
/reports/1998/region2/alpha
/tmp/alpha
/usr/fredp/ralphadams
$
```

This displays all files that contain *alpha* anywhere within the base filename. All the wildcards covered in Chapter 11 can be used:

```
* ? [characters] [!characters]
```

You must quote the filename containing these wildcards (see Chapter 11); otherwise, your find command will not always give you the desired results. Here are two more examples:

```
find /prog -name '*.c' -print
```

This command displays (as absolute pathnames) all files in /prog and its subdirectories whose base filenames end in .c:

```
cd /data/reports
find . -name '*acme*' -name '*98' -print
```

In this example, files must match two conditions to be selected:

- The base filename must contain the word *acme*.
- The base filename must end in *98*.

Here are some base filenames that match both criteria:

```
acme98
acmereport.1998
report.acme.12-98
```

This example prints relative pathnames that are relative to the directory `/data/reports`. In other words, if `./tmp/acme98` is printed by this `find` command, it indicates that a file exists whose absolute pathname is `/data/reports/tmp/acme98`.

The next group of `find` options all take some sort of argument. These options are additional file selection criteria that you can use in your `find` commands to eliminate files in which you have no interest.

Finding Only Files of a Certain Type

The `-type` option enables you to specify the type of file to search for, as indicated by a single letter argument to `-type`:

```
find / -type d -print
```

Here, `-type d` indicates directories, so only files that are directories will be displayed. In this example, all directories in the whole system will be displayed. Notice that no `-name` option has been given, so `find` displays all directories regardless of their names. Table 7.6 lists other types that are available.

Table 7.6 Types Available for the *find* Command

Type	Description
f	Regular or normal file
d	Directory
b	Block special device file
c	Character special device file (raw)
l	Symbolic link
p	Named pipe

Here is an example using the `-type` option:

```
find /dev -type f -print
```

The `/dev` directory usually holds only block and character special devices files. Sometimes a user will make a mistake and redirect output to a misspelled device name, which creates a regular file with that misspelled name in the `/dev` directory. If this is a backup operation, the file created can be large and can consume an excessive number of disk blocks. This `find` command shows you any regular files in `/dev` so that you can manually check to see if they are misspelled device names that should be deleted.

Finding Only Files Owned by a Specified User

The `-user` option enables you to select only files belonging to a particular user. This example prints only files owned by user fred:

```
find / -user fred -print
```

Each user has a numeric user ID number that can also be used as the argument to `-user`:

```
find / -user 127 -print
```

Finding Only Files That Belong to a Specified Group

Files can also be selected by the group to which they belong. This example prints only files belonging to group acme:

```
find / -group acme -print
```

Each group has a numeric group ID number that also can be used as the argument to `-group`:

```
find / -group 402 -print
```

Finding Files That Have a Specified Inode Number

Hard links allow UNIX to have multiple names for the same file. All the UNIX file information (except for the filename) is kept in a structure called the *inode*. This includes the file contents, its owner, its group, the last modification date, and so forth. Inodes are numbered sequentially and are accessed by inode number. A UNIX directory is a table that associates a filename with the inode that contains all the information about that file. If two different filenames map to the same inode number, they are two different names for the same file. You can determine a file's inode number by using the `ls -i` command:

```
$ ls -i
 4703 report3
16242 acme
$
```

If you want to know whether there are any other names for report3, you can use the find `-inum` option:

```
$ find / -inum 4703 -print
/usr/fred/report3
/tmp/acmereport
/data/inventory
$
```

This command found three files whose inode number is 4703. There is one complication: Your disk space may be divided into separate areas called *filesystems*. Each filesystem has its own set of inodes and inode numbers. If several files in the same filesystem have the same inode number, they are multiple names for the same file. If two files in different filesystems (coincidentally) have the same inode number, they are not the same file because they reference different sets of inodes and different file contents.

`-inum` allows `find` to print files with the same inode number. To interpret the results, however, you must check whether the files are in the same filesystem. To do that, see the section "How to Determine Which Filesystem a File Is In," in Chapter 17, "Managing System Resources."

Finding Files with Newer Contents Than a Specified File

The `find` `-newer` option takes a filename argument. It prints all files that were modified more recently than the given file, for example:

```
find / -newer /data/last.backup -print
```

This command displays the absolute pathname of any files modified later than `/data/last.backup`. This option to `find` is useful in conjunction with `cpio` for doing an incremental backup, which backs up only files that have changed since the last backup:

```
cd /
  touch /data/next.backup
  find . -newer /data/last.backup -print |
        cpio -ocvaB > /dev/ctape0
  mv /data/next.backup /data/last.backup
```

This code first changes to the root directory (/) so that `find` can process all files on the system using relative pathnames. Then the `touch` command is used on file `/data/next.backup` so that the starting time and date of the backup is recorded. `find` uses its `-newer` option to generate a list of all files that were modified after the start of the last backup. This list is piped to cpio, which backs up these files to the system's tape drive. Then `next.backup` is renamed as `last.backup` in order to be ready for the next night's backup.

Finding Files with Specified Permissions

The `find` `-perm` option takes a numeric argument. It selects files that have the desired permissions, for example:

```
find / -perm 777 -print
```

This command displays all files with permission 777. An explanation of the permission digits is covered in Chapter 14. This form of the `-perm` option looks for an exact permission match.

If the -perm option is given a negative argument, the given permission digits become a mask instead of an exact match, for example:

```
find / -perm -020 -print
```

This find command displays files that contain the 020 permission bit, which means that write permission is enabled for any user whose group matches the group of the file. It does not matter how the other permission bits are set. You might use this type of -perm in conjunction with the -group option:

```
find / -perm -020 -group guest -print
```

A file must meet two conditions to be displayed by this command: It must be writable by group, and it must also belong to group guest. This example enables you to find all files that can be modified specifically by all members of group guest as long as they are not the file owner.

The negative permission mask enables you to search for three special permission bits:

-perm -4000	Checks for the setuid bit
-perm -2000	Checks for the setgid bit
-perm -1000	Checks for the sticky bit

If the setuid bit is set for an executable binary program, any user who executes the program becomes the user who owns the file for the duration of the program. If the program file is owned by root, if you have permission to run the program; if the program has the setuid bit set, you have root permission while you run the program. Of course, this can be a dangerous feature if misused. The -perm -4000 option is useful because it enables you to find all files with the setuid bit set:

```
find / -perm -4000 -user root -mtime -90 -print
```

This find command displays any files with the setuid bit set that are owned by root and that have been modified within the last 90 days. (The topic of -mtime is covered later in this chapter.) Most setuid programs are set up when the system is installed and never change. If there are any new setuid programs or newly modified setuid programs, they should be checked to see whether a hacker is compromising your system.

If the setgid bit is set for an executable binary program, any user who executes the program becomes a member of the group of the file for the duration of the program. Again, misuse of the setgid feature can be a security issue, and the find command is useful because it can list all files with this bit set.

> **Note**
>
> Note that the `setuid` and `setgid` bits affect only binary-compiled programs. They do not work with shell scripts.

On modern UNIX systems, the sticky bit is no longer used to force programs to stay resident in memory; the bit is simply ignored for programs. However, if the sticky bit is set for a directory, it tightens up the security for that directory. Normally, any user who can create files in the directory can delete files belonging to other users. With the sticky bit set for the directory, only the file owner or root can delete a file. The `-perm -1000` option enables you to list all directories with the sticky bit set.

SEE ALSO

➤ *For more information on file permissions,* setuid, *and* setgid, *see page 377*

Finding Files to a Specified Level

You can control how many directories deep `find` will go by using the `-level` option:

- `-level 0`—Don't check any subdirectories.
- `-level 1`—Check one level of subdirectories deep.
- `-level 2`—Check two levels of subdirectories deep.

In the following example, find `-level 0` only shows directory eq. find `-level 1` shows that 99Jan is contained in eq but does not go further. find `-level 2` shows that inv.acme is contained in 99Jan, but it also does not go further:

```
$ find . -level 0
.
./hdnotes
./log
./eg
$ find . -level 1
.
./hdnotes
./log
./eg
./eg/report7
./eg/report23
./eg/99Jan
```

```
./eg/99Feb
$ find . -level 2
.
./hdnotes
./log
./eg
./eg/report7
./eg/report23
./eg/99Jan
./eg/99Jan/inv.acme
./eg/99Jan/gl.acme
./eg/99Feb
./eg/99Feb/gl.acme
$ -
```

Using *find* Options That Require *+n*, *n*, or *-n*

The next group of find options requires an integer argument. This value can be preceded by an optional plus or minus sign:

- +n matches some file property whose value is greater than *n*.
- +n matches some file property whose value is less than *n*.
- n matches some file property whose value is exactly equal to *n*.

There are several find options that take an integer +n, n, or -n argument. The next section on find -size is a good example.

Finding Files Above, Below, or At a Specified Size

The find -size option enables you to locate files based on the number of blocks in the file. A block is usually 512 bytes, but check the man page on find on your system to be sure.

```
find / -size +2000 -print
```

This find command prints the names of all files that contain more than 2,000 blocks. This is useful when you want to find the largest files that are consuming disk space.

Following -size, you must specify a number:

+n	Finds only files that contain more than *n* blocks
n	Finds only files that contain exactly *n* blocks
-n	Finds only files that contain fewer than *n* blocks

Plus or Minus Is Usually Needed

Rarely will you need to search for files that contain an exact number of blocks. Usually, you will look for files that contain more than *n* blocks or fewer than *n* blocks. UNIX neophytes often forget the plus or minus sign for these types of `find` options and then wonder why `find` did not locate the expected files.

Finding Files Based on Date/Time of Last Modification, Access, or Inode Change

The `find -mtime` option enables you to locate files that were last modified recently or that have not been modified in a long time:

```
find / -mtime -5 -print
```

`-mtime` takes an integer argument that is measured in days. This `find` command locates files that were last modified less than five days ago. This is a useful option when you are sure that you modified a file recently, but you can't remember its name or directory.

Following `-mtime`, you must specify an integer value:

+n	Find only files last modified more than *n* days ago
n	Find only files last modified exactly *n* days ago
-n	Find only files last modified less than *n* days ago

To find files that have not been modified in the last *n* days, look for files that were last modified more than *n* days ago:

```
find / -mtime +90 -print
```

This shows all files that were last modified more than 90 days ago. This means that they have not been modified in the last 90 days.

There are three forms of date checking, and each takes +n, n, or -n as an argument:

-mtime	Find files last modified (more than, exactly, or less than) *n* days ago.
-atime	Find files last accessed (more than, exactly, or less than) *n* days ago.
-ctime	Find files whose inode was last changed (more than, exactly, or less than) *n* days ago. The inode is changed when the file is first created, and also later if the owner, group, or permissions are changed.

Finding Files Based on Number of Linked Names

The `find -links` option enables you to locate files based on number of hard links. Most files have only one hard link, which means that only one filename exists for that file. As mentioned earlier in this chapter, if more than one filename in the same filesystem references the same inode number, these will be multiple names for the same file. If you change the file contents, owner, group, or permissions for one of the filenames, all the other filenames for that file will automatically reflect that change. Each filename for the same file is a hard link to that file's inode. Thus, the hard link count is the number of different names by which one file can be accessed.

-atime Is Often Defeated by Nightly Backups

In theory, find's -atime option is useful if you are short on disk space and want to find files that have not been accessed in a long time so that you can archive them and delete them. However, some backup programs, such as tar, prevent -atime from being useful because all files are accessed nightly during the system backup. cpio provides the -a option, which remembers each file's last access date and time and restores it after the file has been backed up so that find's -atime option will still be useful.

UNIX Does Not Keep Track of the File Creation Date

UNIX maintains a third date and time for each file: the last inode change, which can be displayed by adding the -c option to ls -l. Erroneous references to this option sometimes show the file creation date. The inode (see the glossary) is changed when the file is created, but also when you change its owner, group, or permissions.

A file that can be accessed by many different filenames may cause some unexpected results. The find -links option enables you to locate files based on how many hard links or filenames they have.

Following -links, you must specify a numeric argument:

+n	Finds only files that contain more than n hard links
n	Finds only files that contain exactly n hard links
-n	Finds only files that contain fewer than n hard links

```
find /data -links +1 -type f -print
```

This find command searches /data and its subdirectories for any files that have more than one filename. Note that a directory will have one hard link from every subdirectory, so you can add the -type f option to exclude directories from your search. If any filename is printed, you can then do further research to see whether multiple hard links are reasonable for that file.

Test Your UNIX Skills

Assume that your system has suddenly lost most of its available disk space. Compose a UNIX command to display the full pathnames of all files larger than 5,000 blocks that were modified less than 24 hours ago. You can then visually scan this list for log files and data files that seem too large. (Answer on bottom of page.)

Finding Files with No Local Owner or Group

Two file selection options take no argument:

-nouser	Finds files whose owner is not a user on this system
-nogroup	Finds files whose group is not a group on this system

If you transfer a group of files from another system, it is possible that the files' owners and groups do not exist on your system. In that case, `ls -l` shows the user ID and group ID numbers instead of names:

```
-rw-r--r-- 2   427      104      6273 Dec 19 13:11 report6
```

This file, `report6`, was owned by user ID 427 and had group ID 104 on its original system. That user ID and group ID do not exist on this system, so `ls` cannot resolve the ID numbers to a username and group name. Because permissions are based on the file owner and group, this file may not have the correct access permissions for your system.

Use the `-nouser` and `-nogroup` options so that `find` can locate files with an invalid owner or group. Then manually assign these files to a valid owner and group, and set the permissions as desired. See the section that follows on combining `find` options to see how to use both `-nouser` and `-nogroup` in one `find` command.

Using *find* Controlling Options (Includes Logical *OR* and Grouping)

This chapter has now covered all the `find` file selection options. The next group of `find` options enables you to control how `find` does it job.

Answer to Test on Top of Page
```
find / -size +5000 -mtime -1 -print
```

Restricting *find* to Search Only the Current Filesystem

The `-mount` option prevents `find` from searching in a different filesystem from the starting directory:

```
find / -mount -print
```

This command displays all files in the root filesystem. The -mount option prevents it from printing files in other filesystems.

```
cd /data
find . -mount -name acme -print
```

This command locates all files named acme in the /data directory and all its subdirectories. It displays the matching files as pathnames relative to the /data directory. If any filesystems are mounted on directories under /data, they will not be searched due to the -mount option.

Instructing *find* to List the Contents of a Directory Before the Directory Itself

The -depth option causes find to process the contents of a directory before it processes the directory itself. For example:

```
$ find . -print
.
./reports
./reports/report7
./reports/report8
$
```

In this example, notice that find lists the reports subdirectory before it lists the two files that are in that directory. Now add the -depth option:

```
$ find . -depth -print
./reports/report7
./reports/report8
./reports
.
$
```

The -depth option causes the filenames within the reports directory to be listed before the directory itself is listed. This find option is often used with cpio when backing up files to tape. -depth for the backup is useful when a non-root user wants to restore these files. Without -depth, the directory will be restored first and then its contents. If the non-root user does not have write permission in that directory, that user will get a permission error and will fail to restore the contents of the directory. -depth solves that problem by presenting the files within the directory before it lists the directory itself.

Assuming that the cpio -d option is used during the restore, a dummy directory will be created where the user can successfully restore the files within the directory. Then the directory itself will be encountered on the tape; it will be restored, overwriting the dummy directory and its permissions. Now the restored permissions prevent that user from writing to that directory anymore, but it does not matter because the user has already successfully restored the contents of that directory.

Instructing *find* to Follow Symbolic Links

A *symbolic link*, also called a *soft link*, is a small file that points to another file or directory. If you access the symbolic link, it is usually the same as accessing the file to which it points. In other words, a symbolic link creates another name for a file so that it can be accessed by either name.

Some UNIX commands operate on the link file itself. Other commands operate on the file to which it points; you could say that they follow the link to operate on the destination file. For example, vi follows the symbolic link and enables you to edit the destination file. rm does not follow the symbolic link, so the link itself is deleted, not the destination file.

Normally, find does not follow symbolic links. Even if the symbolic link points to another directory, find will not search that directory because it does not follow symbolic links. However, if you use the find -follow option, find will follow the symbolic link to other directories and will search those directories and their subdirectories.

If you are using find and cpio to transfer selected files and directories via tape to another system, -follow is useful so that the tape will contain all necessary directories, not just pointers to them. On the other hand, if there are many symbolic links to the same directory, you risk backing up that one directory many times, which could needlessly exhaust your tape capacity.

Finding Files That Do Not Match an Option

You can use a ! sign to select files that do not match an option:

```
find / ! -type f -print
```

This locates all files that are not type f regular files.

Earlier in this chapter, you learned about the -perm option that searches for files that match a specific set of permissions.

```
find / ! -perm 644 -print
```

The ! sign says to select all files that do not have permission 644. This is useful if you have just delivered a set of files that should all have the same permissions, and you want to check whether any of the files have the wrong permission. Any of the file selection options can be negated in this way.

Finding Files That Match Several Options

If you specify more than one option, the file must match all options to be displayed:

```
find / -name alpha -size +50 -mtime -3 -print
```

Here find displays only files in which all the following are true:

- The name is alpha.
- The size is greater than 50 blocks.
- The file was last modified less than three days ago.

You can specify a logical OR condition using -o:

```
find / -nouser -o -nogroup -print
```

Earlier, this chapter covered the -nouser and -nogroup options. You saw that these are useful for finding files that may have owner, group, or permission problems. You can combine both tests into one find command by using the -o option, as shown previously. This prints files that either have no valid owner or have no valid group. Note that the following is not the correct way to combine both options:

```
find / -nouser -nogroup -print     # not what we want
```

Multiple options such as this form a logical AND condition. Only files that lack both a valid user and a valid group would be displayed, but this is not what you want.

For more control in combining options, you can group them within escaped parentheses—that is, where each parenthesis is preceded by a backslash:

```
find / ! -name '*acme*' \( -size +4000 -o -atime +90 \) -print
```

Why Escaped Parentheses?

On the UNIX command line, parentheses tell the shell to run the enclosed commands in a subshell. You can escape the parentheses (that is, put a backslash [\] in front) to tell the shell to ignore them and simply pass them on to the find command.

This find command selects files only if both of the following are true:

- The filename does not contain acme.
- The file either has more than 4,000 blocks, or it has not been accessed in the last three months (90 days).

Note that spaces are required on either side of the ! sign, the escaped parentheses, and each option and argument.

find Action Options

This section now looks at the last group of `find` options, which enable you to specify what action to take on the files that match your stated selection criteria. You may think that `find` can print only a list of files, but you will see that it can take a wide variety of actions upon those files.

Instructing *find* to Display Just the File Pathnames Found

`-print` is an action option that tells `find` to display the pathnames of all files that match the options given before `-print`. If you put the `-print` action before other options in the command line, those options will not be used in the selection process:

```
find / -size -20 -print -mtime +30
```

This command prints all files that contain fewer than 20 blocks. The `-mtime` option is ignored because it comes after the `-print` action on the command line.

It is possible to place more than one `find` action on the command line:

```
find / -size -20 -print -mtime +30 -print
```

This command prints all files that contain fewer than 20 blocks. Within that list, any file that contains fewer than 20 blocks and that was last modified more than 30 days ago will be printed a second time.

If no action is specified on the command line, `-print` is usually done by default. On older versions of UNIX, however, you must remember to include `-print`, or no output will be generated. It can be frustrating to wait a long time for `find` to complete and then notice that you forgot the `-print` option, so `find` will not show you the information it worked so hard to discover.

Instructing *find* to Display Details About Each File Found

The `-ls` option provides much more information about each file than the `-print` option. The output looks much like the output of `ls -lis`:

```
$ find . -ls
 3889   2 drwxrwxrwt 3 root   root    2048 Dec 27 21:30 .
 4348  35 -rw-r--r-- 1 root   root   34989 Dec 26 19:11 ./rjunk
 4741   1 -rw-r--r-- 1 fred   users    253 Dec 27 11:22 ./junk
 4740   1 -rwx------ 1 fred   users     68 Dec 22 07:04 ./tst
 4742   1 -rw-r--r-- 1 fred   users    314 Dec 27 11:22 ./junk1
16204   1 drwxr-xr-x 4 fred   users   1024 Dec 27 19:42 ./tstdir
16264  35 -rw-r--r-- 1 fred   users  34989 Dec 27 19:42 ./tstdir/rjunk
  411   1 drwxr-xr-x 2 fred   users   1024 Feb 22  1998 ./tstdir/dir1
  412   1 drwxr-xr-x 2 fred   users   1024 Feb 22  1998 ./tstdir/dir2
 4743   1 lrwxrwxrwx 1 fred   users     12 Dec 27 19:42 ./ptr -> tstdir/rjunk
```

```
    4746  1 lrwxrwxrwx 1 fred   users      6 Dec 27 19:45 ./ptrdir -> tstdir
$
```

The following information is displayed about each file selected: inode number, size in blocks, file type, permissions, hard link count, owner, group, size in bytes, date/time of last modification, filename, and whether the file pointed to a symbolic link.

Instructing *find* to Execute a UNIX Command on Each File Found

-exec is an action that enables you to specify a UNIX command to run on each of the files that match the options given:

```
find / -name alpha -exec chmod a+r {} \;
```

Following -exec, you should specify a complete UNIX command and put {} where the filename will be inserted. Add \; at the end of the command to complete the required syntax. In the previous example, chmod will run on every file named alpha so that everyone can read the file.

```
find / -name core -exec rm -f {} \;
```

This example finds all files on the system named core and executes the rm command to delete them. The -f option to rm is specified so that rm will not ask for confirmation if you don't own the file and don't have write permission to the file. This is a useful command for root to run periodically because, if a process aborts, it may leave a debugging file named core in the current directory. After a while, these core files, which are not small, may collectively consume an unreasonable amount of disk space. This find command will restore that disk space by finding and deleting those core files.

> **Note**
>
> If you have thousands of files to process, xargs (covered in Chapter 11) is more efficient than -exec. For example:
>
> ```
> find / -name core -print | xargs rm -f
> ```
>
> This command also deletes all core files much more quickly and with less overhead than the -exec option, which calls rm once for each file.

Waiting for Confirmation before Running a Command on Each File Found

The -ok option has a format exactly the same as that of -exec. Unlike -exec, -ok asks for confirmation for each selected file before it executes the given command:

```
$ find / -name core -ok rm -f {} \;
<rm ... /usr/fred/core>? y
<rm ... /tmp/docs/core>? n
$
```

-ok displays one line for each selected file, containing the command it will execute and the selected filename within angle brackets, followed by a question mark. Enter y to execute the command or n to ignore this file. This is a useful option if you are not sure that you specified your find options correctly and want to confirm each file before it is processed. This option is not usable if thousands of files match the criteria.

Running Multiple Commands on Each File Found

It is useful in a shell script to be able to process all the files in a directory and its subdirectories. If multiple UNIX commands must be done to each file, find can be used with a shell loop:

```
for FILE in `find / -name '*acme*' -user fred -print`
do
        echo Processing $FILE ...
        chmod a+r $FILE
        chown jane $FILE
        CHECK=`grep -i merger $FILE`
        [ "$CHECK" ] && lp $FILE
done
```

This example uses a for loop (covered in Chapter 28), where backquotes invoke find to list the desired files. The loop between do and done executes once for each file. For all filenames containing acme and owned by fred, the following is done:

1. Use chmod to allow everyone to read the file.

2. Use chown to make jane the owner of the file.

3. Use grep to check whether the file contains the word *merger*. If so, use the lp command to print a hard copy of that file.

chapter

8

Steve "Mor" Moritsugu

Displaying and Printing Files and Pipelines

Displaying files

Displaying output one screen at a time

Displaying just the beginning or ending lines of output

Adding line numbers to output

Displaying output that contains control characters

Displaying a banner

Displaying DOS files

Printing files and pipelines

Checking the print queue

Canceling print jobs

Tip for Beginners

As you read this chapter, you will quickly get to the section on displaying text one page at a time using either the `pg`, `more`, or `less` commands. Stop reading at that point, and test the `man` command as covered in Chapter 4, "Rules for Entering UNIX Commands." Follow this chapter to determine which pager the `man` command on your system is using, and concentrate on learning and practicing that particular pager for now. Don't learn all three pagers at one time. Then go on to read the section in this chapter on printing files. Come back later and cover the remaining commands in this chapter as needed.

Displaying Files and Pipelines

UNIX provides a number of utilities that enable you to view the contents of text files and control how you are shown the output. Many of these utilities can also be used as part of a pipeline sequence, in which output is fed from one command directly to another.

This chapter does not cover text editors, which are another way to view the contents of a file (and also make modifications). Text editors are covered in the following chapters:

- vi and view (Chapters 20, "Using vi to Edit a Text File," and 21, "Letting the vi Editor Work for You")
- Emacs (Chapter 23, "Introducing the Emacs Editor")

To display only lines that contain a specific string pattern, see Chapter 18, "Searching for Lines in a File or Pipeline." To modify strings in the output, see Chapter 19, "Replacing or Removing Text from a File or Pipeline."

Displaying a Small File

The standard way to display a small file is to use the `cat` command:

`cat` *filename*

In UNIX, the word *cat* is synonymous with *display*, so directions may ask you to *cat* a file or may refer to *catting* file. See Table 8.1 for other properties of the `cat` command and where to read more about those properties.

`cat` is short for concatenate

The `cat` command gets its name from the word *concatenate*, which means to combine things together. We will see in Chapter 10 how `cat` can combine several files into one big file.

Table 8.1   Other Properties of the *cat* Command

Property	See page
Allows relative and absolute pathname arguments	71
Processes either filename arguments OR standard input	115
Changes only the output, not the file	111
Allows a list of filenames and filename wildcards	292
Allows output to be piped or redirected	116

Tip for Advanced Users

The `cat` command can be used to send any size of file directly to a device, such as a printer. Because this bypasses normal system printing, it is not standard usage, and you must first make sure that the device is available.

```
(stty 19200 cs7 parenb -parodd; cat filename) < /dev/tty46 > /dev/tty46
```

The preceding example illustrates using the `stty` command to initialize the port before each direct print.

Displaying Files and Pipelines a Page at a Time

If a UNIX command has more than 24 lines of output, you will see the output whiz by, too fast to be read. Only the last lines will remain on the screen, and the beginning lines will be lost. You might wonder why all commands do not automatically page their output, which means that they would wait for you to finish reading the current screen page before displaying the next one. The reason paging is not automatic is because, in UNIX, you often pipe the output of the command to another command for processing, so there is no need to wait for a human to read it page by page. A UNIX user is expected to know that you can always pipe output to your favorite pager utility and let it show you the output one page at a time. Three common pager utilities exist under UNIX:

- pg
- more
- less

In general, commercial UNIX systems usually offer pg and more but not the less command. The pg command has the most functionality, but the traditional more command is often the default pager. Linux/GNU systems usually provide the less pager, but often not pg or more. If you use a variety of UNIX systems and commands, you need to learn the basics of all three of these pagers.

Several UNIX commands, such as man or mail, automatically invoke one of these pagers so that you can see the output one page at a time. Look at the bottom of the screen for a clue as to what pager is being used. If the last line is a colon, then you are in the pg utility. If you are at the end of output, pg will show this on the last line:

```
(EOF):
```

If you see a line number such as this on the last line, then you are in the less utility:

```
line 203
```

If you are in the more utility, your last line might look like any of these:

```
stdin
--More--
--More--(34%)
report7 (34%)
```

You should learn how to operate all three of these pager utilities, because you sometimes have no control over which pager is invoked. This is not difficult because you only need to remember three basic pager commands to handle most situations. Table 8.2 lists these three commands.

Remember q to Quit

The more and less commands will not let you exit from the pager, even if you get to the end of the file. You will be stuck in the pager utility unless you remember to enter q to Quit. Alternatively, you could enter Ctrl+C or DELETE to interrupt and abort the current command.

Table 8.2 Three Basic Pager Commands to Remember

Command Description	pg	more	less
Go to next page:	Enter	space	space
Quit or exit:	q	q	q
Help menu:	h	h	h

Table 8.3 shows that pagers can do a lot more than just show one page at a time. The more command is typically the weakest of the three pagers and may not be able to do some of the commands shown.

Table 8.3 Other Pager Commands

Command Description	pg	more**	less
Go to previous page	-	Ctrl+B	Ctrl+B

Command Description	pg	more**	less
Go to end of output	$	G	G
Go back to start of output	1	1G	1G
Redisplay current page	.	Ctrl+L	Ctrl+L
Go to *STRING*	*/STRING*	*/STRING*	*/STRING*
Go down a half page	d	d	d

** *The commands shown are often not available when using the* more *command.*

Use the commands in the previous Table 8.3 to go from page to page, forwards or backwards. You usually will not have to press the Enter key after your command except for searching ahead via */STRING*. Table 8.4 gives other properties of these pagers and lists where to read about those properties.

Table 8.4   Other Properties of the *pg, more,* and *less* Commands

Property	See page
Allows relative and absolute pathname arguments	72
Processes either filename arguments OR standard input	115
Allows a list of filenames and filename wildcards	292

Beware of using pg on a huge pipeline. When you use the pg $ sign command when displaying piped output, it can take a long time to complete because the system is saving in a temporary file all the text encountered to allow you to go back to the first page, if desired. Some systems do not have enough temporary disk space to store huge files. When that disk space is exhausted, all user tasks can be disrupted and the system can crash.

How Large Is Huge?

When do you have to start worrying about crashing the system by using pg of a pipeline? The pg pager usually builds its temporary file in /tmp. Use the df command to check how many free blocks you have in /tmp, or in root (/) if df does not show /tmp. That free block count is your limit, but you should not even come close to that for safety. (For more information on df, see Chapter 17, "Managing System Resources.")

The pg option has a feature that is useful when you want to locate and consider each occurrence of some word in the file. Usually this is difficult because the slash (/) command to locate a word begins its next search at the end of the current screen. If there are multiple occurrences on one screen, you might miss some of them.

Using *pg* to Find All Occurrences of a String

1. Use pg to view a file or pipeline.

2. While running pg, enter this line:

   /*string*/b

   Replace *string* with the text you want to find. Without /b, the found string would be placed on the top line of the screen. The /b tells pg to put the found line at the bottom of the screen for this and future searches.

3. To find the next occurrence of the same string, enter this line:

   /

   The system uses the previous string given. Because /b was given in step 2, the next occurrence of the string will be positioned on the bottom line. Without the /b in step 2, you might miss some occurrences of the string because / assumes that you have visually found all matches anywhere on the current screen, and it starts searching from the bottom line of the screen.

4. Repeat step 3 as desired or until the end of the file.

Displaying Just the Starting Lines of a File or Pipeline

To display just the first lines of a file, use the head command, as shown here:

```
head groceries friends
```

The head command accepts a list of files on the command line. When more than one file is given, head identifies the start of each one with a small banner, as follows:

```
==> groceries <==
5 apples
3 grapes
2 melons

==> friends <==
James B. Nguyen, Los Angeles
Henry H. Nguyen, Yuba City
William A. Smith, St. Louis
Mary K. Zornan, Cleveland
Mary A. Zornan, Pittsburgh
```

Multiple File Arguments Change the Output

Output from the head and grep commands will indicate the filename if multiple files were given on the command line. The filename is omitted from the output if only one file was given in the command line.

head normally displays a maximum of 10 lines of output from each file. This can be useful when you want to see just a few lines from several files. To display more or fewer lines, use the –n option to head, as follows:

```
/acme/salestotal | head -20
```

In this example, the –20 option causes the head command to display a maximum of 20 lines. Also in the preceding example, you can see that if no files are specified as arguments on the command line, head will read from standard input. /acme/salestotal represents any program that generates output. When the head command in this example receives and displays 20 lines of output, it will cause the salestotal program to terminate because no more output is needed. Table 8.5 shows other properties of the head command and page references where those properties are covered.

Table 8.5 Other Properties of the *head* Command

Property	See page
Allows relative and absolute pathname arguments	72
Processes either filename arguments OR standard input	115
Changes only the output, not the file	111
Allows a list of filenames and filename wildcards	292
Allows output to be piped or redirected	116

If the head command is not available on your system, you can use the sed command in this way:

```
sed nq filename
```

Replace n with the number of beginning lines to display, as shown here:

```
/acme/salestotal | sed 5q
```

This example displays only the first five lines. The preceding example also illustrates that seq will read from standard input if no files are specified on the command line, so it can also be used in pipelines. If multiple files are given on the command line, sed nq will display the first *n* lines of those files, but it will not identify the filenames as head does.

Displaying Just the Ending Lines of a File or Pipeline

To display just the ending lines of a file, use the tail command, as shown here:

```
tail filename
```

The `tail` command usually accepts only one filename on the command line, and `tail` normally displays just the last 10 lines of the file. To specify how many of the last lines to display, use the –n option to `tail`, as follows:

```
/acme/salestotal | tail -25
```

In this example, `/acme/salestotal` represents any program that generates output. The `tail` command will accept all output from the salestotal program, but it will not display anything until salestotal completes. Then it will show only the last 25 lines of output.

`tail` Output Is Limited

On many versions of UNIX, `tail` –n is limited to a maximum of several hundred lines (or several thousand, on newer UNIX systems). If you exceed this limit, you will not see an error. You will just get fewer lines of output than you requested.

To display the end of the file by starting at line n of the file, use `tail` with the +n option, as in the following:

```
tail +350 filename
```

The preceding example starts at line 350 of the file and displays all lines until the end of the file.

Press DEL to Stop Viewing

You might have run `tail` -f before without realizing it. Some system processes will run in the background and output progress messages and errors to a log file. To allow you to see the errors as they occur, the process may invoke `tail` -f of the log file so your screen is updated as soon as a new line is put in the file. The process may remind you to press DEL or Ctrl+C to interrupt and abort the `tail` -f viewing process when desired or when done.

To watch lines being added to a file, such as a log file, enter this:

```
tail -f filename
```

`tail` will first display the last 10 lines of the file. The command will not stop there, though: It will continue to follow the file, and as new lines are added to the end of the file, `tail` will display them on your screen. This continues until you press the INTR key, which is usually Ctrl+C or Delete. Table 8.6 shows other properties of the `tail` command and where to read about them.

Table 8.6 Other Properties of the *tail* Command	
Property	See page
Allows only one relative or absolute pathname	70
Processes either filename argument OR standard input	115
Changes only the output, not the file	111
Allows output to be piped or redirected	116

Adding Line Numbers to the Output

You can add line numbering to the display of a file or pipeline using either nl (number lines) or cat –n. If your UNIX system does not support nl, use cat –n, and vice versa. In the following examples, the cat command is used as a simple example of adding line numbers to output that normally does not have line numbers:

```
$ cal | nl
     1          February 2009
     2     S   M Tu  W Th   F   S
     3     1   2   3   4   5   6   7
     4     8   9  10  11  12  13  14
     5    15  16  17  18  19  20  21
     6    22  23  24  25  26  27  28
$ cal | cat -n
     1          February 2009
     2     S   M Tu  W Th   F   S
     3     1   2   3   4   5   6   7
     4     8   9  10  11  12  13  14
     5    15  16  17  18  19  20  21
     6    22  23  24  25  26  27  28
     7
     8
$
```

Notice that cat –n numbers all lines, including blank lines. The nl command does not number the blank lines. Command options can be added to change this default behavior.

To number all lines, including blank lines, use these options:

```
cat -n
nl -ba
```

To number only the lines that aren't blank, use these options:

```
cat -nb
nl
```

Seeing line numbers is useful to programmers when errors are reported by source code line number. Alternatively, you can see line numbers while editing a file using vi. (See the section "Turning on Line Numbering," in Chapter 21.)

Other properties of the cat command were given in Table 8.1 at the start of this chapter. Table 8.7 gives other properties of the nl command and page references for futher information.

Table 8.7 Other Properties of the *nl* Command

Property	See page
Allows only one relative or absolute pathname	70
Processes either filename arguments OR standard input	115
Changes only the output, not the file	111
Allows output to be piped or redirected	116

Displaying Files Containing Control Characters

Text files contain only printable characters, whereas binary files can contain all possible character values, including the range called *control characters*. If you display a binary file to your screen, the control characters within the file can set undesirable modes for your station, can cause all further output to appear as garbage or gibberish, and can even make your station stop responding altogether.

Before you display an unknown file, use the file command (see Chapter 7, "Listing and Finding Files") to see whether it is a text file. If it is not a text file, then it is not safe to simply display it to your screen. Some safe ways to look at the text within binary files do exist, as you shall see in this section.

Finding Text Clues in Binary Files

Finding printable text in binary programs can be useful in solving problems when the program is not working. You cannot read the source code, but sometimes text error messages, usage messages, and file and directory names contained within the binary file offer just the clue needed to set up the environment so that the program will start working.

The cat –v option will make control characters visible in a safe way and won't put your screen into any strange modes:

```
$ cat -v binfile
^?ELF^A^A^A^@^@^@^@^@^@^@^@^@^@/usr/lib/libc.so.1^@^@M- M-&^@
$
```

cat −v represents each control character by a caret (^) and the corresponding printable character. You may find that the output does not contain enough linebreaks, so
you cannot easily view or page the output. Try some of the following commands in
that case.

The od command stands for octal dump. This command displays every word of a file
or pipeline in octal (that is, using the base 8 numbering system), as in this example:

```
# od /bin/ls | head -5
0000000 077505 046106 000402 000400 000000 000000 000000 000000
0000020 000002 000002 000000 000001 000001 007374 000000 000064
0000040 000000 040140 000000 000000 000064 000040 000005 000050
0000060 000030 000027 000000 000006 000000 000064 000001 000064
0000100 000000 000000 000000 000240 000000 000240 000000 000005
#
```

The −b option to od breaks each word into 2 bytes or characters, as in this example:

```
# od -b /bin/ls | head -5
0000000 177 105 114 106 001 002 001 000 000 000 000 000 000 000 000 000
0000020 000 002 000 002 000 000 000 001 000 001 016 374 000 000 000 064
0000040 000 000 100 140 000 000 000 000 000 064 000 040 000 005 000 050
0000060 000 030 000 027 000 000 000 006 000 000 000 064 000 001 000 064
0000100 000 000 000 000 000 000 000 240 000 000 000 240 000 000 000 005
#
```

The −c option to od shows you any printable characters within the output, as in this
example:

```
# od -c /bin/ls | head -5
0000000 177   E   L   F 001 002 001  \0  \0  \0  \0  \0  \0  \0  \0  \0
0000020  \0 002  \0 002  \0  \0  \0 001  \0 001 016 374  \0  \0  \0   4
0000040  \0  \0   @   `  \0  \0  \0  \0  \0   4  \0       \0 005  \0   (
0000060  \0 030  \0 027  \0  \0  \0 006  \0  \0  \0   4  \0 001  \0   4
0000220  \0 001  \0  \0  \0  \0  \0 001  \0  \0   : 250  \0 002   : 250
#
```

Here, strings is the command that shows any strings of printable characters with a
length of about four characters or longer. Notice in the preceding example that the
printable letters ELF occur near the beginning of the file, but strings does not
report it because four printable characters do not exist in that section.

```
# strings /bin/ls | head -5
SUNW_OST_OSCMD
```

```
RaAdC1xmnlogrtucpFbqisfL
usage: ls -1RaAdCxmnlogrtucpFbqisfL [files]
COLUMNS
total %llu
```

You can use the –n option to strings to set the minimum length of printable string to display.

Other properties of the cat command were given in Table 8.1 early in this chapter. Table 8.8 gives properties that apply to both od and strings and where you can read about these properties.

Table 8.8 Other Properties of the *strings* and *od* Commands

Property	See page
Allows relative and absolute pathname arguments	70
Processes either filename arguments OR standard input	115
Changes only the output, not the file	111
Allows a list of filenames and filename wildcards	292
Allows output to be piped or redirected	116

SEE ALSO
➤ *For an example of using* strings *to identify an unknown file, see page 480*

Displaying Text in Large Banner Letters

The banner command can be used to display short messages using large-scale letters, as in this example:

```
# banner hello
```

```
   #     #  ######  #        #          ####
   #     #  #       #        #         #    #
   ######  #####   #        #         #    #
   #     #  #       #        #         #    #
   #     #  #       #        #         #    #
   #     #  ######  ######  ######     ####


   #
```

This technique is useful in creating separator pages between printer jobs because it generates readable text that stands out. You can redirect the output of `banner` when you want the output in a file.

The `banner` command puts separate words on separate lines. If you want these on the same line, escape any spaces between the words by preceding each space with a backslash (\), or enclose any spaces in single or double quotes, as in this example:

```
banner "Acme Corp."
```

The maximum line for `banner` is 10 characters. The command truncates any characters after that. This command does not allow any file arguments, as shown in Table 8.9.

Table 8.9 Other Properties of the *banner* Command

Property	See page
Does not allow filename command line arguments	87
Allows output to be piped or redirected	116

Displaying DOS Files

Text files under DOS/Windows end each line with both a carriage return and a linefeed. UNIX text files end with just the linefeed, which UNIX calls the *newline character*. If you bring a DOS text file to UNIX and try to edit it with `vi`, you might see that the file looks like this:

```
This is a text file^M
that came from a DOS^M
system via disk or^M
download via network.^M
```

The `Ctrl+M` at the end of each line is the carriage return. There are a number of ways to remove the `Ctrl+M` by using the `col` command, which is a utility to filter control characters.

To create a UNIX text file from an existing DOS text file, enter this line:

```
col -bx < dosfile > unixfile
```

If you are in `vi` and find that each line ends with `^M`, enter this line:

```
:%! col -bx
```

The preceding command causes `vi` to apply `col –bx` to every line in the file, removing the `^M` at the end of each line. You can now continue your editing. Table 8.10

shows that col does not allow filename arguments, but output can be piped or redirected.

Table 8.10   Other Properties of the *col* Command

Property	See page
Does not allow filename command line arguments	87
Allows output to be piped or redirected	116

Cleaning Up Man Pages

If you save a man page to a file, you are likely to find ^H or backspace characters interspersed inside important words. The ^H is a directive to the printer to go back and reprint the previous character again as bold or to underline the character. The following is an example of a saved man page showing the ^H instances:

```
NAME
     ls - list contents of directory


SYNOPSIS
     /usr/bin/ls [ -aAbcCdfFgilLmnopqrRstux1 ] [ _^Hf_^Hi_^Hl_^He... ]
     /usr/xpg4/bin/ls [ -aAbcCdfFgilLmnopqrRstux1 ] [ ^Hf_^Hi_^Hl_^He... ]


DESCRIPTION
     For each _^Hf_^Hi_^Hl_^He that is a directory, ls lists the contents of
     the  directory;  for  each _^Hf_^Hi_^Hl_^He that is an ordinary file, ls
     repeats its name and any other information  requested. The
```

You can run col −bx from either the command line or in vi, as shown in the previous section. The following is the same man page file after col −bx has been run:

```
NAME
     ls - list contents of directory


SYNOPSIS
     /usr/bin/ls [ -aAbcCdfFgilLmnopqrRstux1 ] [ file... ]
     /usr/xpg4/bin/ls [ -aAbcCdfFgilLmnopqrRstux1 ] [ file... ]


DESCRIPTION
     For each file that is a directory, ls lists the contents of
     the  directory;  for  each file that is an ordinary file, ls
     repeats its name and any other information  requested. The
```

This also explains why sometimes in a man page you use slash (/) to search for a string and man says that it is not there—yet you find that string later in the man page. Why didn't slash (/) find it? The answer is likely to be that it is an important word, hence it contains some ^H instances. You can improve your ability to search the man pages by entering your man commands like this:

```
man ls | col -bx | pg
```

The col –bx removes the ^H instances from key words, which enables slash (/) to find them in searches.

SEE ALSO

➤ *For more information on man pages, see page 88*

Printing Files and Pipelines

Usually one or more printers exist on a UNIX system. The system administrator gives each printer a name so that users can specify the printer or group of printers to which they want their output to go. Users use the lp or lpr commands to print to the desired printer.

Introducing the UNIX Spooling System

What actually happens is that the text to be printed is saved in a system disk file, called a *spool file*. Each different print job gets its own spool file. The lp/lpr command actually completes very quickly because it does not take long to save all the text in a disk file. This process is called queuing up a printer request. A print scheduler program, which runs in the background, waits for the desired printer to become available and then prints the next job in the queue for that printer.

Spooling provides a number of benefits. With spooling, printing does not tie up your station while the printer prints your job (this can be a slow process for large print jobs). All jobs go through one printer scheduler program, so there is no danger that two users printing to the same printer at the same time will get their output interspersed.

Spooling Limitations

Standard UNIX spooling does not offer the capability to reprint a previously completed job or to restart a currently printing job on an earlier page number. These would be desirable if you encounter a paper jam or a faint ribbon. Sometimes third-party print spooling packages may be found or purchased that provide these additional capabilities.

Spooling has some disadvantages. A spool job does not start printing until the spooling program has terminated. This fact offers a distinct advantage, in that the printer can always run at full speed because it does not have to wait for program computation and disk access to generate the next line of printer output. The disadvantage occurs when a job takes a long time, say six hours, to generate the output. After the six-hour job completes, the printing begins, so the user must wait even longer for the printed output.

It is possible for applications to open and output directly to a printer device. For the example in the previous paragraph, a direct printer would allow printing to be done throughout the full six hours of program time, so most of the printing would be completed with a direct printer just when a spooled printer would be starting the output.

A direct printer is also more useful when you have checks and forms on the printer and want to control the proper centering of the form from the application. Often the application will print some test forms and ask the user to check the form alignment before printing the batch of forms. A spooler cannot print a test form unless the application closes the output channel, which leaves the printer open to jobs that will waste the forms just loaded.

A direct printer has difficulty keeping users from interspersing their output. Often an application will lock the printer while it is in use, forcing all other users to wait until the job is done. Different applications often use different locking mechanisms, so output from one application can intersperse with another application. If more than one application uses the same printer, spooling is usually required to keep the output from interspersing.

Whenever UNIX documentation refers to printing, it usually means the print queuing/spooling system. The rest of this section refers to the print queuing/spooling system.

Determining Your System Printer Names

To get a list of the printer names on your system, enter this line:

```
lpstat -p -D
```

The lpstat command shows the printer status. The -p option to lpstat limits the output to show the printers and their availability. The –D option to lpstat displays the description, if any, for that printer. You should see output that looks like this:

```
printer p104 is idle. enabled since Sat Aug 23 16:32:49
  1998. available. Description:
printer p108 is idle. enabled since Thu Aug 21 16:28:28
  1998. available. Description: Laser III by copy room
```

```
printer p206 is idle. enabled since Sat Feb 14 16:50:49
  1999. available. Description: HP LaserJet in Accting
```

Enable versus Accept

Each print spooler or print queue can be set by the System Administrator to accept or reject requests from users. A spooler would be set to reject if it will be out of service for a long time. The Administrator can set a physical printer device to enable printing or disable. A device would be disabled, for example, to stop printing in order to fix a paper jam. The spooler can still accept user requests, to be printed once the printer is enabled again.

The preceding example shows that three printer names are available: p104, p108, and p206. All are currently idle, which means they're not printing any jobs. None has been disabled (for example, none is out for repair). There is no way to determine where printer p104 is located in the building, though; it might be in room 104, but it might also be the printer that started in room 104 but was later moved to room 237.

Printing a File or Pipeline

Two general commands under UNIX handle printing a file or pipeline:

- lp (a System V utility)
- lpr (a BSD utility)

You should learn both styles of print commands so that you can function on a UNIX system that offers only one of them.

UNIX Spooling Also Works with Network Printers

You can use the lp or lpr commands in this section to print to printers on other systems in the network or to printers with their own network cards. The system administrator must first configure those printers under UNIX so that they appear in lpstat. This configuration process is different for each type of UNIX.

In the simplest case, you can simply give lp or lpr a list of files to print, as in the following:

```
lp file1 file2
lpr file1 file2
```

In these examples, the files will be printed on whatever printer the system administrator has set up as the system default printer. If no system default printer is set up, both commands will fail with an error that no system default is defined.

Two important options exist for these print commands:

```
lp -dlaser2 -n3 file1 file2
lpr -Plaser2 -#3 file1 file2
```

In the preceding example, the `lp` —d option and `lpr` —P option allow specifying the destination printer. You saw in the previous section how to list the available printer names.

Also in the previous example, you can see an example of using the `lp` -n option and the `lpr` -# option to specify how many copies to print of each file. The spooling system uses an interface script to pass the output to the printer. Each different print script may allow other option letters and arguments that are unique to that script. On System V UNIX, you can often find the interface scripts in the following directory:

```
/usr/spool/lp/admins/lp/interfaces
```

Each script has the same name as the printer it controls. Read the script to see if there are any useful options to try out. For example, you might find that your printer script supports some of these options:

- —o landscape

- —o nobanner

- —o nb (*no banner*)

- —o raw (send output unmodified)

Your `lp` or `lpr` command will queue up an output request. You should see one request id displayed for your (combined) output so that you can track whether your job has printed yet and so that you can abort the printing, if desired, as in this example:

```
$ ls -l | lp  -n2
request id is hp-85 (standard input)
$
```

The System V `lp` command has a —c option that you must be aware of if you print a file and then modify it immediately or delete it. The `lp` command usually just queues up the name of the file. If there are several jobs to print before your job prints, it could take a while to start your job printing. If you modify or delete the file before it prints, this will affect what is printed. Add the —c option to force `lp` to copy the file when `lp` is run so that subsequent changes to the file do not affect the output:

```
lp -c file1
```

Table 8.11 shows other properties of both the `lp` and `lpr` commands.

Table 8.11 Other Properties of the *lp* and *lpr* Commands

Property	See page
Allows relative and absolute pathname arguments	70
Processes either filename arguments OR standard input	115
Allows a list of filenames and filename wildcards	292

Checking the Print Queue

On System V UNIX, you can check the requests in the print queue by entering lpstat with no options, as in this example:

```
$ lpstat
hp-85     mori     111946   Feb 23    22:03 on hp
hp-86     fred        203   Feb 23    22:04
$
```

lpstat limited to your requests

On some UNIX systems, lpstat will only show you your own printer jobs that are queued. If you only see your own jobs in the queue, remember that there may be large print jobs ahead of you that you are not seeing.

Each line output by lpstat begins with the print job request id, which starts with the printer name. In the preceding example, both Fred and Mori queued up print jobs for printer hp at about the same time. Because Mori got there first, his job is currently printing on hp. Even though Fred's job is quite small (only 203 characters), his job won't print until Mori's job is done.

If lpstat is not supported on your system, try lpq to get a list of queued print jobs for a specific printer. In the following example, you specify the desired printer after the –P option and add –l for longer output:

```
$ lpq -P sp7 -l
 Queue Dev Status  Job   Name         From       To
                         Submitted    Rnk Pri  Blks  Cp
 ..... ... ......  ..........        ... ...   .....
 sp7   lp7 RUNNING 713   STDIN.41278 doreen     doreen
                         07/19/99 11:32:18  1   15     2    1
                           /var/spool/qdaemon/t5pEtUa
          QUEUED   717   STDIN.37282 dick       dick
                         07/19/99 11:33:22  2   15     2    1
                           /var/spool/qdaemon/tbnA1ia
```

If lpq is not on your system, try lpc. After you're in lpc, useful commands are help, status, and quit:

```
$ lpc
lpc> help
Commands may be abbreviated. Commands are:

abort   enable  disable help    restart status  topq    ?
clean   exit    down    quit    start   stop    up
lpc> status
lp:
        queuing is enabled
        printing is enabled
        no entries
        no daemon present
lpc> quit
$
```

Cancelling a Print Job

On System V UNIX, you can cancel a print job by its request id number. Use the lpstat, lpq, or lpc command, as shown in the previous section, to determine which current print request you want to cancel, as in this example:

```
$ lpstat
hp-85           mori    111946  Feb 23  22:03 on hp
hp-86           fred       203  Feb 23  22:04
$ cancel hp-85
request "hp-85" canceled
$ lpstat
hp-86           fred       203  Feb 23  22:04 on hp
$
```

On BSD UNIX, use lprm with a job number to remove (that is, cancel) a current print request.

On AIX UNIX, use qcan to cancel a print request, as in this example:

```
qcan -P printername -x jobid
```

On all systems, non-root users can cancel only jobs they submitted; root can cancel any print job.

Moving Print Requests from a Down Printer

If a printer is broken, the system administrator (root) can move some or all pending print requests for that printer to another printer by using the lpmove command.

To move one or more specific print jobs to another printer, root can use this syntax:

```
lpmove list-of-req-ids new-printer
```

To display all pending print job request ids from all users for a given printer, root can enter this syntax:

```
lpstat -p printer-name
```

To move all print jobs from a broken printer to another printer, root can enter this syntax:

```
lpmove broken-printer new-printer
```

This will also take the broken printer out of service so that it no longer accepts new print jobs.

Formatting Output for Printing

If you print output on a dot matrix continuous-feed printer, the most unsatisfactory part of the output will be the fact that the printing does not leave any margins at the top and bottom of each page. If you print output on a laser printer, you will notice that all the output starts at the very left margin and gives you no room to bind the pages or three-hole punch them. These types of problems can be solved by processing your output through the pr command before printing it.

By default, pr puts a five-line header and trailer at the top and bottom of each page. The header includes the page number, date/time, and filename (if not piped). The pr command accepts a list of files on the command line. If no list of files is given, you can pipe your output to pr. You can then pipe the output of pr directly to the printer, as in these two examples:

```
pr file1 acme* | lp
```

```
prog2 | pr | lpr -Paccting
```

The main problem in using pr is to determine the number of lines per page on your printer. By default, pr assumes 66 lines per page, which does not work on many printers—you end up with page breaks in the middle of pages. To set the number of lines per page, use the length option -l, as in this example:

```
pr -l60 file
```

Because pr does not usually send a form feed at the end of each page, you must set the length to the exact value required; otherwise, you will find page breaks in the middle of later pages of output. Previously, this chapter discussed how to number each line of output. Printing the output with line numbers will help you determine the value to use for your printer. Print at least 10 pages of output to make sure you are using the correct value.

You can tell pr to send a formfeed at the end of each page by using the ·f option, as in this example:

```
pr -f file
```

This method can be useful if page breaks drift on the page on very long outputs. This will be more efficient if you are printing only a small number of lines per page on normal-size paper. If the output is going to your screen (that is, if it is not redirected) then the –f will cause a beep and will wait for you to press the Enter key at the beginning of the first page. This is useful if you are running on a printing terminal so that you can adjust the top of form.

If you are running on a sheet-feed terminal, use the –p option to pr so that it will beep and wait for the Enter key at the start of each page.

To set a left margin for output, use the –o option to offset printing, as in this example:

```
pr ·o5 file
```

In the preceding example, pr prints five spaces at the start of each line of output. The default (if no –o option is given) is offset 0.

To set your own heading at the top of each page instead of the filename, use the –h option. To include spaces in your new header, enclose the whole header in double or single quotes. Warning: You must include a space after –h, or your whole output will be garbage, as in this example:

```
pr -h "    Acme Proposal    " acmeprop | lp
```

To double-space your output, use the –d option to pr.

To number each line of output, use the –n option. Follow –n with an optional number of characters to use for the line number. If no value is given, the default is to use five characters, as in this example:

```
pr -n file
```

```
pr -n4 file
```

Although pr will number all lines (even blank lines) in the body, it will not number the lines in the header and trailer on each page. Line numbering starts at 1 and increases constantly throughout the document—that is, it never resets back to 1.

To expand tabs in the output to the corresponding number of spaces, use the –e option. To change the default tab setting from every eight columns, follow –e with a new value, as in this example:

```
pr -e file

pr -e12 file
```

This can be useful when printing tab-separated columns that are longer than eight characters.

Then pr can display your output in columns, as in this example:

```
pr -3 file
```

In the preceding example, –3 tells pr to compose the output into three equal-size columns across the page. Note that pr does not take normal line length output and transform it into columns. You must first manually compose your output so that no one line exceeds the column size (1/3 of a page for three columns, 1/4 of a page for four columns, and so on). Any text that is longer than the column size is truncated— that is, lost.

Table 8.12 shows other properties of the pr command and where you can read about them.

Table 8.12   Other Properties of the *pr* Command

Property	See page
Allows relative and absolute pathname arguments	70
Processes either filename arguments OR standard input	115
Changes only the output, not the file	111
Allows a list of filenames and filename wildcards	292
Allows output to be piped or redirected	116

chapter

9

Copying, Moving, Renaming, Removing, or Linking Files

Steve "Mor" Moritsugu

Copying files

Moving files

Renaming files

Removing files

Creating multiple names for the
same file

Tip for Beginners

This chapter covers the important basic file operations of copying, moving, renaming, and removing files. Make sure that you have thoroughly mastered Chapter 3, "UNIX Directories and Pathnames," before you start this chapter. Commands in this chapter are more difficult when the source and destination are in different directories, and that is why you must master Chapter 3 first. Stop reading when you get to the final section of this chapter on linking files, which is for more advanced users. Come back to that section only after you have gained some experience with the basic file operations.

Choosing the Destination

In this chapter, the concepts of *absolute* and *relative pathnames* are very important. You can review them in Chapter 3, if needed. That chapter also discusses standard directories found on most UNIX systems. In that discussion, /tmp was mentioned as a directory for temporary files. This is a good directory for users to use when they want to build a few small temporary files (also called *scratch files*).

Because all users can build files in /tmp, choose a name for your file that is not likely to be used by other users—include your logon ID as part of the name, for example. I usually add the word junk or tmp to such files. Whenever I later encounter files that I created with junk or tmp in the name, I can freely delete them without having to take time to evaluate their contents.

Chapter 3 also mentioned the fact that every user has a home directory. Some systems make a group of users share the same home directory, but usually you have a home directory all to yourself. Therefore, this is a good place to store files that you want to keep for a while.

It is a good idea to create subdirectories within your home directory so that you can organize your files. One of the traditional ways to organize files is by file type or function. You might create a directory for text files, for example, and another for executable programs. (Traditionally, executables would be put in a bin directory.) The advantage of having one bin directory is that you can then add it to your PATH to make it easy to execute any program in that directory no matter what your current directory is.

One way to organize your home directory by projects. Create a directory for each project, and put all files associated with that project into the one directory. You can create subdirectories if it is a complex project. You will realize the benefit of this organization when you need to purge old unneeded files to clean up your disk usage. Many projects are no longer needed six months or a year later. Organizing by project enables you to easily remove all the files associated with that project.

If you need to build any huge files or create thousands of files, you should consult your system administrator first. If you use up all the disk space or inodes in a file system, you can cause serious system problems. The df command can show you the free disk space and free inodes in each file system. If you need a large amount of disk space, the system administrator might create a directory in another file system for you to use.

SEE ALSO

➤ *For more information on absolute and relative pathnames, see page 70*

➤ *For more information on standard UNIX directories, see page 60*

➤ *For more information on home directories, see page 65*

Handling Permission-Denied Errors

Where can you save files?

On any UNIX system, there are usually only two standard directories where you can save files: your home directory and the /tmp directory. All other system directories are usually tightly controlled to make sure that users do not delete any files or create new files. If you are setup to run an application, you may have write permission to some application directories, but you should always use the application menus to access those directories.

To create files and subdirectories within a directory, you need write permission to that directory. If you created the directory, you normally have write permission for that directory. If the directory belongs to someone else, you may need to ask that person to open up write permission to the directory. The traditional UNIX approach is to create a new group for users who need to share files and directories, assign those files and directories to the new group, and allow write permission for group members but not the whole world. You must then ask root (the system administrator) to add you to the group.

SEE ALSO

➤ *For more information on file and directory permissions, see page 385*

Copying, Moving, or Renaming Files

In many instances you will need to rework a file's name or location, and you may have special concerns for each action. UNIX has a number of commands and options for these procedures; the following sections detail the available commands and options.

Copying a File Within the Current Directory

Use the cp command to copy a file, which means to create a second identical file with a different name.

Signs your UNIX is too Old

ls -i an illegal option to cp or mv on your UNIX system? Are you restricted to only 14 characters in a filename? Is the Korn or Bash shell not available on your system? If you answered yes to any of these questions, you should consider upgrading to a more modern version of UNIX.

This is one way to make a backup copy of a file:

```
cp -ip report7 report7.bu
```

The cp-i option (not available on older UNIX systems) will give a warning if the destination file already exists:

```
$ cp -i report2 /tmp/report
cp: overwrite '/tmp/report'?
```

Enter y to overwrite or no to abort the copy. Warning: If you omit the-i option, cp will overwrite an existing file without any warning or notice.

The cp-p option (not available on older UNIX systems) will preserve the file's owner, group, and permissions. Note that you may not be able to modify the file if you use this option, even though you created it.

Renaming a File Within the Current Directory

Use the mv command to rename a file in the current directory, for example:

```
mv -i report71899 report07181999
```

The mv -i option (not available on older UNIX systems) will give a warning if the destination file already exists:

```
$ mv -i report71899 report07181999
cp: overwrite 'report07181999'?
```

Enter y to overwrite or no to abort the operation. Warning: If you omit the -i option, mv will overwrite an existing file without any warning or notice.

cp and *mv* Errors

If you get a Usage error complaining that −i is not a valid option, your UNIX system does not allow that option. In that case, you must manually check whether the destination already exists before doing any `mv` or `cp` commands because they will not warn you before overwriting a file.

−i Option and Automatic Headlights

Under the C shell or Korn shell, it is possible to set up an alias for your logon ID so that the `−i` option is automatically added to any `cp` and `mv` commands that you enter. I personally don't do this for the same reason I don't like car headlights that turn off automatically. If you work on a number of UNIX systems or drive different cars, you want to get into the habit of using `−i` with `cp` and `mv` and turning off your own headlights.

You will also get a Usage error if −p is a not a valid option for `cp` on your system.

If you get a permission denied type of error, you either don't have permission to read the source file, or you don't have permission to write to the directory and create a new file there. See the preceding section on handling permission-denied errors.

No news is good news. If no message is generated and you just return to the shell prompt, your copy or move was successful.

Copying, Moving, or Renaming to a Different Directory

If the destination filename is to be the same as the source filename, you can specify just the destination directory without specifying a filename. The following are your options:

- **Option #1** is to use absolute pathnames for both the source and the destination of your copy or move. Then it does not matter what your current directory is. The drawback to this approach is that it requires more typing, so it is rarely used. The following example illustrates using an absolute pathname for both the source and destination:
  ```
  cp -i /usr/fred/doc/acme/rep7  /usr/fred/doc/98/rep7
  ```

- **Option #2** is to sit in the source directory when you do the command (which means that it is your current directory). Then you can specify the source file as a basename. You must specify the destination file as either an absolute or a relative pathname. This option is useful when you have further commands to do in the source directory. This is shown in the following code, which is equivalent to the copy done in the previous example:
  ```
  cd /usr/fred/doc/acme
  cp -i rep7  /usr/fred/doc/98/rep7
  ```

- **Option #3** is to sit in the destination directory, specify the source file as either an absolute or a relative pathname, and specify the destination file as a basename.

This option is useful when you have further commands to do in the destination directory. This is shown in the following code, which is equivalent to the copies done in the previous examples:

```
cd /usr/fred/doc/98
cp -i /usr/fred/doc/acme/rep7   rep7
```

- **Option #4** is to sit in some nearby directory that can access both the source and the destination directories conveniently.

  In our previous copy examples, notice that /usr/fred/doc is common to both the source and the destination directories, so you can sit there and access both the source and destination files using convenient relative pathnames, as shown here:

```
cd /usr/fred/doc
cp acme/rep7  98/rep7
```

  You will see the advantage of using the relative pathnames over absolute pathnames if you have a number of files to copy from the same source to the same destination directory.

- **Option #5** is to use your own shell variables when you want to copy several different files between the same two directories, as described next.

Setting shell variables for two directories

1. First, cd to the source directory, for example:

```
cd /usr/fred/doc/acme
```

Make up Your Own Variable Names

I chose SD for Source Directory and DD for Destination Directory. These are not standard UNIX names and you may choose any other names that you will remember. For example, you might choose INV to hold the pathname for an inventory directory. You also might choose II for that same directory, because repeated letters are easier to type than different letters.

---

2. Enter: SD=`pwd`

In the preceding command, you take the current directory as reported by pwd and use backquotes to save that directory name in variable SD. You can choose your own variable names; I chose SD for source directory in capital letters to avoid confusion with UNIX commands, which are usually lowercase.

3. Next, cd to the destination directory, for example:

```
cd /usr/fred/doc/98
```

4. Enter DD=`pwd`

5. Now it is easy to copy or move files between the two directories. SD and DD contain absolute pathnames, so it does not matter what the current directory is. To copy a file from the source directory to the destination directory, enter the following:

```
cp -i $SD/filename $DD/.
```

To copy the rep7 file from our previous example, enter:

```
cp -i $SD/rep7 $DD/.
```

Notice that you do not have to specify the destination filename if it is to be the same as the source filename. Notice that slash period (/.) was added after the directory name, as recommended in the next section.

6. You can repeat step 2 to change the directory in $SD any time you like. Similarly, you can repeat step 4 to change $DD. These variables will retain the last directory name set, until you log out. If you want to automatically set a variable to a value each time you login, add the variable definition to your .profile.

Table 9.1 shows other useful properties of cp and mv and pages where those properties are described.

Table 9.1 Other Properties of the *cp* and *mv* Commands

Property	See page
Allows relative and absolute pathname arguments	70
Allows a list of filenames and filename wildcards	292

SEE ALSO

➤ *For more information on shell variables, see page 35*

➤ *For more information on .profile, see page 410*

Determining Where Your File Is Going

It is not always so easy to predict what destination file will be created by cp or mv. This is because the results differ depending on whether the destination specified is an existing directory. For example, consider this line:

```
mv /usr/jane/acme  /usr/fred/reports
```

If reports (in /usr/fred) is a directory, mv (or cp) will take the source file acme and move it (or copy it) into the reports directory. Therefore, the resultant filename will be this:

```
/usr/fred/reports/acme
```

Notice that the source `dirname`—/usr/jane, in this case—tells only where to find the source basename. It is just the source basename that is moved or copied; none of the source dirname directories are ever brought along.

If the specified destination `/usr/fred/reports` does not exist, `mv` (or `cp`) will create it and put the contents of `acme` into it. Therefore, the resultant file will be a regular file named the following:

```
/usr/fred/reports
```

If `reports` existed as a regular file in `/usr/fred`, this would produce the same result. The old `reports` file would be lost, and the contents of file `acme` would be put in its place. There would be no warning that the old contents of reports had been over-written because the –i option was not used in this example.

Here is the summary of the possible results from cp or mv:

If the destination given is a directory the source file will be copied into the destination directory and will retain the same name as the source.

If the destination is a regular file or does not exist a file with the destination name will be created as a copy of the source file.

None of the source directories are copied to the destination. Only the source file is copied.

Whenever you copy or move a file into a directory, I recommend that you add slash period (/.) to the directory name, as in the following:

```
mv acme   /usr/fred/reports/.
```

The slash period (/.) tells the system that you are expecting `/usr/fred/reports` to be a directory and to move the `acme` file into that directory. If reports was not an existing directory, the command would fail with an error message, and you would be alerted that something went wrong. If `reports` happened to be an existing filename, adding slash period (/.) in the preceding command would prevent overwriting the `reports` file and losing its data.

Another attempt to do the same thing is to add just a slash (/):

```
mv acme   /usr/fred/reports/      # can get a syntax error
```

I don't recommend just adding slash (/) because it is an illegal syntax on many UNIX systems.

This is an example where using slash period (/.) would have prevented loss of data:

```
mv file1 /usr/fred/reports
mv file2 /usr/fred/reports
mv acme /usr/fred/reports
```

In the preceding example, the user expected that /usr/fred/reports is an existing directory; however, this was not true. Therefore, the first command created a regular file in /usr/fred called reports, containing all the data from file1. The second command overwrote the reports file with the contents of file2. The contents of file1 are now totally gone from the system and irretrievable. (Notice that the –i option would have given a life-saving warning here.) The third command will again overwrite reports, so the contents of file2 will also be lost and irretrievable. Here is the same sequence done as recommended:

```
mv -i file1 /usr/fred/reports/.
mv -i file2 /usr/fred/reports/.
mv -i acme /usr/fred/reports/.
```

The very first command will fail with an error message if /usr/fred/reports is not a directory.

Adding slash period (/.) to destination directories also makes it easier to understand what result to expect from mv or cp. This is true for both written instructions and when commands are inserted in shell scripts (as covered in Chapter 28).

Copying/Moving a List of Files to a Directory

If the destination for cp or mv is a directory, the source can include one or more regular files—that is, a list of files, for example:

```
cp -i file1 file2 file3 /data/acme/.
```

In this example, file1 and file2 and file3 will be copied to the /data/acme directory. If there are two or more source files, the destination file must be a directory; otherwise, you will get an error.

In a later chapter, you will see that file lists can be created using filename generation wildcards, which can be used with cp and mv if the destination is a directory. The following is an example:

```
cp -i *acme* /usr/fred/acmefiles/.
```

SEE ALSO

➤ *For more information on filename generation wildcards, see page 292*

Handling Confirmation Requests

If mv or rm is about to overwrite or delete an existing file, these commands will check to see whether you have permission to write to the file. If not, you will be asked for confirmation like this:

```
mv: dest-file: override protection 400 (yes/no)?
```

On some systems, the confirmation message is very terse, such as the following:

`400?`

The short message `400?` and the previous longer message both convey all of the following information.

Your command (`mv` or `cp`) is about to overwrite another user's file and the owner of that file has not given you permission to write to or modify this file. You have administrative control over the directory, however, so you can override the permissions. The three permission digits for this file are 400 (in this example). Do you want to overwrite this file anyway? Enter y for yes or n for no.

Moving or Renaming a Directory

You can use the `mv` command to move or rename directories. In this way, directories can be removed from the UNIX directory tree structure and can be reattached to a different part of the tree. All the subdirectories of that directory will go along with it.

Assume that this file exists on a system:

`/usr/fred/reports/compsys/pegasus`

Note that the file `pegasus` is in the `compsys` directory. Now assume that you execute this command:

`mv /usr/fred/reports/compsys /usr/fred`

For both `mv` and `cp`, if the specified destination is an existing directory, the destination will be created within that directory. You know that `/usr/fred` does exist as a directory in this example. From the previous part of this chapter, you know that `mv` (and `cp`) takes only the source basename and places it into the existing destination directory. Therefore, the new absolute pathname for `compsys` will be as follows:

`/usr/fred/compsys-`

The new absolute pathname of the `pegasus` file will be this:

`/usr/fred/compsys/pegasus`

In the preceding example, the `mv` command removed directory `compsys` and all its files and subdirectories from the UNIX directory tree structure and reattached `comp-sys` and all its files and subdirectories in a new place.

Older versions of UNIX aborted with an error if you tried to move a directory into a different file system. Many modern UNIX systems can do this without any problems.

Copying a Whole Directory Subtree

Sometimes you may want to copy a directory and all its subdirectories and files to some destination directory. You cannot accomplish this using the cp command with wildcards because it will not access all the subdirectories.

Some UNIX systems offer a copy command that can do this if you use the –r option to copy subdirectories recursively which means: copy all the subdirectories no matter how many levels deep. (I recommend using copy -rom if your UNIX supports this command.) Other UNIX systems may offer a –R or -r option to cp to allow recursive copying of directories. It is also possible to use tar to read all the source directories and files and then pipe the output to another tar command to restore them.

You also can copy directory subtrees by using the cpio command. It works on all UNIX systems, even old ones that do not offer the copy command or the cp -R option. The cpio command also offers more versatility than the tar method, such as excluding some directories from being copied.

To copy a whole directory subtree, follow these steps:

1. If the source directory contains files owned by several users, and if you want the destination directory to accurately mirror the ownership and permissions of the source, you must be logged on as root to do this procedure.

2. Determine the exact absolute pathname of the source directory. Every file and subdirectory of this source directory is to be copied to the destination.

3. Determine the exact absolute pathname of the destination directory. A copy of each subdirectory and file of the source directory (and its subdirectories) will be made in the destination directory.

4. Now cd to the source directory.

5. Enter pwd to make sure that you are sitting in the source directory.

6. Enter the following:

   ```
   find . -print | cpio -pvdum dest-dir
   ```

   Replace dest-dir with the desired destination directory. You may express the dest-dir as either an absolute or a relative pathname. When you run this command, cpio will display each filename as it copies the whole directory subtree.

7. In step 6, the following cpio command options are optional, and one or more of them may be added or left out as desired:

   a   Means to reset date/time of last access for each file to what it was before cpio accessed the file. This may not be used if the –m option is included.

continues...   **243**

...continued

d	Means to create destination directories as needed.
L	Means to follow soft links (see the next section) so that the file pointed to is copied rather than the pointer file.
m	Means to keep the same date/time of the last modification for each destination file as in the source directory. This may not be used if the –a option is included.
u	Means to unconditionally overwrite any existing destination files, or an older file will not overwrite a newer one.
v	Means verbose output, which lists each file as it is copied.

For advanced users who are familiar with the grep command (see Chapter 18, "Searching for Lines in a File or Pipeline"), you can modify step 6 to exclude directories from being copied, like this:

```
cd source-dir
find . -print |
   grep -v '^./dir1/' |
   grep -v '^./dir2/dir3/' |
   cpio -pvdum dest-dir
```

In the preceding example (for advanced users), notice that you can press the Enter key after each pipe sign (|) for greater readability as you enter the command. grep -v will exclude the specified directory and all its subdirectories from being copied. The grep -v pattern of '^./dir1/' says to exclude all files and directories generated by the find command that start with ./dir1/.

SEE ALSO

➤ *For more information on cpio, see page 455*

Removing Files

Use the rm command to remove (delete) one or more files, for example:

```
rm acme doc/report7 /data/acme
```

The rm command cannot remove directories:

```
$ rm /tmp
rm: /tmp: is a directory
$
```

Previously, the text discussed confirmation requests for rm and mv. If you want to prevent getting a confirmation request when you delete another user's file that you don't have permission to modify, use the rm -f option to force the removal without asking for confirmation. This is useful when you are deleting a group of files belonging to several users that you are sure you want to delete. This option will also suppress any error message if the file does not exist.

If you are deleting a group of files, you can use the rm -i option to display each filename to be deleted and ask for confirmation. This interactive option is useful when you are using a wildcard pattern to specify the list of files to delete to make sure that you do not delete more files than you intended.

Removing a List of Files

Be Careful with Wildcards!

In UNIX, there is no undelete capability. If you delete the wrong files, they are gone forever. The best you can do is to restore previous versions of those files from your last backup. Wildcards enable you to delete hundreds or thousands of files in one command. Make sure your are in the correct directory and use the proper wildcard.

The rm command does allow a list of files to be specified. This list can be generated by filename generation wildcards. For example, the following command will delete all files in the current directory whose names start with acme:

```
rm acme*
```

If you want to delete a directory, you first must remove all the files in that directory. If you change to that directory, the following commands will remove all the non-hidden files there:

```
cd dir-to-remove
rm *
```

In this example, *dir-to-remove* can be any desired directory, expressed as a relative or absolute pathname. You must then delete any hidden files (files whose name starts with a period) and any subdirectories. Then change to the parent of the directory to be removed and issue the rmdir command, like this:

```
cd ..
rmdir dir-to-remove
```

SEE ALSO

➤ *For more information on filename generation wildcards, see page 292*

Table 9.2 shows other useful properties of the rm command.

Table 9.2   Other Properties of the *rm* Command

Property	See page
Allows relative and absolute pathname arguments	70
Allows a list of filenames and filename wildcards	292

Filenames That are Difficult to Remove

There are three types of filenames that require special handling to remove them:

- filenames that begin with dash (-)
- filenames that contain special characters
- filenames that contain control characters

If there is a file named -abc, notice that the rm command gives an error and will not remove that file:

```
$ rm -abc
rm: ERROR: Illegal option -- a
usage: rm [-fiRr] file...
$
```

The leading dash (-) confuses the rm command, which expects a dash (-) to indicate options to the command, not a filename to be removed. To fix this, use dash dash (--), which indicates the end of any command options. The file is successfully removed like this:

```
$ rm -- -abc       # rm <dash><dash> <dash>abc
$
```

The second type of filenames that are troublesome to remove contain one or more of the following special characters:

```
* ? [ ] ' " \ $  ; & ( ) | ^ < > new-line space tab
```

Filenames that contain these special characters will cause problems for any UNIX command. Often these files are not created intentionally but are simply found mysteriously after a bad connection, a burst of line noise, or wrong key strokes. To avoid problems when removing such files, follow this simple rule:

Put single quotes around any filename to be removed that contains any punctuation.

Here are two examples that follow this rule:

```
rm 'abc*xyz'
rm 'a;$*(x)>b'
```

SEE ALSO

➤ *For more information on accessing filenames that contain special characters, see page 127*

Filenames that contain control characters are the most challenging and dangerous to remove. In the following example, it looks like the same filename is found twice in the current directory, which should be impossible. Using the -b option to ls shows that the second file contains the ESCAPE character, whose octal ASCII value is 33. The ESCAPE character causes the cursor to reposition while displaying the filename so it looks like the same name is there twice:

```
$ ls
acme
acme
$ ls -b
acme
ad\033[Dcme
$
```

If the filename contains control characters such as carriage returns or new lines, one name may appear on several lines as if there were several files.

There are many ways to remove the bad acme file in the previous example. One method is to rename the good acme file so it is protected and then use filename wildcards to remove the bad acme file:

```
$ mv -i acme xxx
$ ls -b *cme
ad\033[Dcme
$ rm *cme
$ mv xxx acme
$
```

In the preceding example, note that ls -b is used to check that the wildcard pattern only matches the bad file and no others. Then the rm command is used with that same tested wildcard pattern to delete the bad file. Finally the good acme file is restored to its correct name.

SEE ALSO

➤ *For more information on filename wildcards, see page 292*

Removing a Whole Directory Subtree

To remove a directory, it must be entirely empty except for a dot (.) and dot-dot (..) entry. If you are sure that you want to delete a directory, all its files and subdirectories, and all their subdirectories, you can accomplish this in one simple command. You must be very careful when you use this command because there is no way to bring files back if you make a mistake.

SEE ALSO

➤ *For more information on deleting a whole directory tree, see page 73*

Creating Multiple Names for the Same File

UNIX refers to all files and directories by an inode number. This inode number is actually an entry number in an inode table. Each file system has its own inode table, and each inode entry in use contains information about one file in that file system. An inode entry contains most of the information about a file, such as the owner, group, permissions, type of file, date/time of last access, date/time of last modification, and so on. You might be surprised to learn that the inode table entry contains everything about the file except for the filename.

A directory is a file under UNIX that has two purposes:

- To keep track of the filenames and subdirectory names contained in that directory
- To keep track of the inode number for each of those filenames

When you access a filename under UNIX, the system determines which inode table entry to use from the directory entry for that filename. UNIX allows more than one filename to reference a given inode number, which in effect allows multiple names for the same file. Because the filename is not part of the inode information, each of the names for a file are equally valid; it does not matter which name came first.

It would be incorrect to think of these names as copies of the file because there is only one inode being referenced. This means that if you change the file using one name, that change will be visible when you access the file under its other names.

When you have multiple names for the same file, each name is called a hard link to the file. Allowing multiple names or hard links for a file can be useful in UNIX's hierarchical directory system when you want to put the same file into two different directories. Let's say, for example, that you have a customer directory with one file for each of your customers that contains their name, address, phone number, and transaction history. Let's say you also have a vendor directory for companies that you purchase products from, and each file in the vendor directory has the vendor name, address, phone number, and transaction history.

Now imagine that some companies buy things from you, so they should be in the customer directory; but you also buy things from them, so they should be in the vendor directory. You can solve this problem by creating two hard links. That is, you can create a file in the customer directory and also put that same file in the vendor directory. By using hard links, these files are not copies of each other; they are two names for the same file. Therefore, if you update the phone number for that company in the customer directory, that change is automatically reflected for that company in the vendor directory.

If you have a large file, hard links take up much less space than making copies of the file. No matter how many hard links there are, there is only one copy of the file.

Creating Multiple Names Using Hard Links

Use the `ln` command to create a hard link, as in the following:

```
ln existing-file new-link
```

Here, *existing-file* is the relative or absolute pathname of an existing file, and *new-link* is a relative or absolute new pathname by which you can access the existing file. The *existing-file* may not be directory. Both *existing-file* and *new-link* must be within the same file system. (For more information on file systems, see Chapter 17, "Managing System Resources.")

The following command creates a hard link in the `/customers` directory called `acme` that accesses the same data found in `/vendors/acme`:

```
ln /vendors/acme /customers/acme
```

This is not a separate copy of that file. Any changes made to /customers/acme are immediately and automatically reflected in /vendors/acme.

Finding All the Hard Links to a File

To determine how many hard links there are to a file, enter the following:

```
ls -l filename
```

This is an example output:

```
-r-xr-xr-x  3 bin   bin    15176 Jul 15  1997_compress
```

After the permissions, and before the owner and group, is a field called the `link` `count`, which has a `3` in the preceding example. This means that the `compress` command (which is in the `/bin` directory) has a total of three names to reference the same file. One of the names is compress, so there are two other names for the file that you don't know.

To determine whether there are more hard links for the file in the same directory, enter the following:

```
ls -li | sort | pg
```

This is an example output:

```
5527 -r-xr-xr-x  1 bin  bin    10832 Jul 15 1997 col
5528 -r-xr-xr-x  1 bin  bin     6344 Jul 15 1997 comm
5529 -r-xr-xr-x  3 bin  bin    15176 Jul 15 1997 compress
5529 -r-xr-xr-x  3 bin  bin    15176 Jul 15 1997 uncompress
5529 -r-xr-xr-x  3 bin  bin    15176 Jul 15 1997 zcat
5530 -r-xr-xr-x  1 bin  bin    30596 Jul 15 1997 csplit
5531 -r-xr-xr-x  1 bin  bin    39916 Jul 15 1997 dc
```

The –i option to ls causes ls to display the inode number at the start of the line, where it is in perfect position to apply the sort command so that lines that start with the same inode number will be together. Notice in the preceding example that compress, uncompress, and zcat all have the same inode number (5529), the same permissions (r-xr-xr-x), and the same owner, group, size (15176), and date of last modification. Because they have the same inode number and are in the same directory, they are hard links to the same file—that is, they are different names for the same file.

If all the hard links are not found, some of them must exist in other directories. To find all filenames that match a given inode number, enter the following:

```
find /STARTDIR -inum INODE -print
```

Replace *INODE* with the inode number that you want to look up. Replace /*STARTDIR* with the desired file system directory from the df command, as you saw in step 2. For example:

```
# find / -inum 17248736 -print
/usr/fred/acme
/usr/jane/acme
/acmeproject/report7
/data7/pegasus3
#
```

In step 2 of the preceding procedure, you saw how to determine whether two pathnames were in the same file system. Inode numbers are re-used in other file systems for other totally unrelated files. Filenames with the same inode number are only hard links to the same file if they are in the same file system. Use this knowledge to ignore files reported by Find that are not in the correct file system.

SEE ALSO

➤ *For more information on other options for the* ls *command, see page 180*

➤ *For more information on the find command, see page 187*

➤ *For more information on how to determine which file system a file is in, see page 478*

Deleting a Hard Link

If a file has multiple hard links, it has multiple names. If you use the rm command to delete one of those names, the rest of the names and the file contents are not affected, but the total link count for the file is reduced by one. If you delete a file-name with a link count of 1, the link count for the inode will go to 0, which means that there are no names left to access this file. After the link count goes to 0, that file will be deleted from the system. After a file has been deleted, there is no way to bring it back.

Using Soft/Symbolic Links

There is another way to create multiple names for the same file. You can create a soft link, also called a symbolic link, to an existing file. Soft links have three advantages over hard links:

- You can create a soft link to a directory as well as to a file.

- You can create a soft link to a file or a directory in another file system.

- ls -l shows the filename that a soft link points to. Thus, given a soft link name, it is easy to determine the other filename to which the link points. It is more difficult to determine the other filename(s) given one hard link to the file. See the section "Finding All the Hard Links to a File (ls, find)," earlier in the chapter.

A soft link is a small pointer file, indicated with a small arrow (->) in ls -l output, as in the following:

```
$ ls -l /usr/spool
lrwxrwxrwx 1 root root 10 Feb 13 09:19 /usr/spool->/var/spool
$
```

In the preceding example, /usr/spool is a soft link to directory /var/spool. One of the changes introduced in SVR4 was to move the spool directory from /usr to /var. SVR4 usually creates /usr/spool as a soft link to /var/spool. This enables users and programs to continue to access /usr/spool, and the soft link causes them to actually access /var/spool. In the preceding example, notice that /usr/spool is a file whose size is only 10 characters; that is, its only contents is /var/spool, which is 10 characters. Notice that at the beginning of the line, the type is l, which indicates a soft link. Notice that the permissions are rwx for all users. This enables all users to access the soft link. However, read/write/execute permissions are then determined by the file being pointed to.

Creating Soft/Symbolic Links

Use the ln -s option to create a soft link, also known as a symbolic link:

```
ln -s real-file ptr-file
```

Here, `real-file` is the name of a real directory or file. It can be relative or absolute; it does not have to exist. `ptr-file` is a relative or absolute soft link or pointer file to be created. For example, the following command creates a soft link in the root directory whose name is currpt:

```
ln -s /data/reports/acme7 /currpt
```

If you attempt to edit or print /currpt, the actual file accessed will be /data/reports/acme7. If you get an error that the file does not exist or that you don't have permission to access it, it means that /data/reports/acme7 does not exist or has permissions that do not allow your access.

Don't Link a Directory to Itself

A command such as this can link a directory to itself:

```
ln -s dir2 dir2
```

The cd command on modern UNIX systems will detect this error and immediately report **Bad Directory**. Very old UNIX systems might get into an endless loop.

In the preceding example, /currpt points to another file. Consider why this symbolic link is useful. Imagine that every month, you must create and maintain a report whose directory and filename change each month. Rather than memorizing a new pathname each month, you simply create /currpt as a soft link to the current report file for this month. Now you just have to remember /currpt, whose name does not change.

Determining Whether a Command Follows a Soft Link

With hard links, every name for the file is indistinguishable from every other name for that file. On the other hand, a soft link is quite different from the file to which it refers. Most commands will follow the soft link, which means that when you ask them to access a soft link, they will instead access the file pointed to by the soft link.

If you use vi to edit a soft link, for example, it will edit instead the file pointed to by the soft link. If that file does not exist, you have a stale soft link—that is, a link that goes nowhere. In that case, vi will give a "No Such File" error, even though the soft link itself does exist.

Some UNIX commands will not follow the soft link, which means that they operate on the soft link itself. For example, mv and rm normally do not follow the link, enabling you to rename or delete the soft link itself. Check the man pages for individual commands to see whether they follow the soft link and operate on the pointed-to file.

The following is an excerpt from man rm on a Solaris system:

```
If file is a symbolic link, the link will be removed, but
the file or directory to which it refers will not be
deleted. Users do not need write permission to remove a
symbolic link, provided they have write permissions in
the directory.
```

The preceding excerpt indicates that rm does not follow the link. It operates on the soft link itself.

This is an excerpt from man ls on a Solaris system:

```
-L   If an argument is a symbolic link, list the file
     or directory the ink references rather than the
     link itself.
```

This excerpt reveals that ls normally does not follow the link; it normally gives information about the soft link itself. If the –L option is added to ls, it will follow the link and display the pointed-to file.

This is an excerpt from man file on a Solaris system:

```
If file is a symbolic link, by default the link is
followed and file tests the file to which the
symbolic link refers.
```

SEE ALSO

➤ *For more information on the man command, see page 88*

chapter

10

Steve "Mor" Moritsugu

Comparing, Sorting, Modifying, Combining, and Splitting Files

Comparing text files, nontext files, and
files on different systems

Sorting output and using sort fields

Encrypting, compressing, and encoding
files

Combining files in various ways

Splitting a file into equal-size segments
or by sections

> **Tip for Beginners**
>
> Skim this chapter to get a feel for the various commands that are available in each section. Learn to use `diff` and `cmp` to compare files. Then go on to the `sort` command and learn the first options, which are covered in order of most usefulness. Primary and secondary sort keys are very powerful sort capabilities for more advanced users. Postpone the rest of the chapter until you need to use a particular command.

Comparing Files

UNIX uses simple text files in a variety of important roles, including system configuration tables, C program source code, HTML Web pages, and user data. Because text files have so many important uses under UNIX, several different UNIX utilities enable you to compare text files and see their differences. To compare binary, non-text files, other commands can be used.

Showing Differences Between Two Files

To show the differences between two text files, use this command:

```
diff file1 file2
```

> **287c287 in `diff` Output**
>
> For the beginner, remember no news is good news. If `diff` shows no output, the files are identical. Any `diff` output means the files are different. The more output, the more lines that are different. In the example, you see **287c287**. The first **287** indicates the line number in the first file that differs from his counterpart, also at line **287** in the second file. **c** means that the numbered lines in the first file require a change to become the numbered lines in the second file. The letter **a** means lines that must be added, and **d** means lines that must be deleted to transform the first file into the second.

You should see output similar to this:

```
287c287
<        Now is the time for all good men to come to the
---
>        Now is the time for all good men to go to the
```

Because there is little output from `diff` in this example, the two files must be very similar. A lot of output from `diff` would indicate that the files are very different. No output before the next shell prompt would indicate that the files are identical.

After `diff` finds any differences between the two files, it looks ahead in both files to find whether any later lines in one file match later lines in the other. In this way, it can identify added lines, deleted lines, and changed lines. Output lines that begin with the < sign are from the first file. The sign>> sign indicates lines from the second file that differ. Only lines that are different are displayed. The preceding example shows the only difference between the two files is that the word *come* in the first file has been changed to *go* in the second file.

In the preceding output, 287c287 indicates directives to change the first file into the second file. In this case, the c indicates that line 287 of the first file must be changed to match line 287 of the second file. Other possible directives are a for append line(s) and d for delete line(s). In practice, most UNIX users look at the line differences that are displayed and ignore the directives except for the line-number information.

Use the −b option to diff to cause it to ignore trailing spaces and tabs in the line. This option also regards any collection of consecutive spaces and tabs as one space. This can be useful if you want to compare two text files but want to ignore the fact that one has a larger left margin (that is, more leading spaces) than the other.

Sometimes it is useful to see the context that surrounds the changed lines. The −c option to diff causes three lines before and after each difference to be included in the output. An exclamation point (!) at the start of a line marks the lines that are different:

```
$ diff -c report2 report6
*** report2 Thu Oct  7 21:49:23 1999
--- report6 Thu Oct  7 21:56:23 1999
***************
*** 3,9 ****
        my $hdrealname = $hdrealhash{$flnameuc};

        if ($hdmodhash{$flnameuc} > $flmod) {
!           print "$hdrealname was newer on hard disk than floppy\n";
            $cmds[$cmdcnt++] =
                "copy \"$hddir\\$hdrealname\" \"$fldir\\$hdrealname\"";
        }
--- 3,9 ----
        my $hdrealname = $hdrealhash{$flnameuc};

        if ($hdmodhash{$flnameuc} > $flmod) {
!           print "$hdrealname was newer on hard disk than diskette\n";
            $cmds[$cmdcnt++] =
                "copy \"$hddir\\$hdrealname\" \"$fldir\\$hdrealname\"";
        }
$
```

In the preceding example, the initial heading shows that lines from the first file, report2 in this case, will be indicated by three asterisks (***). Lines from the second file, report6, will be shown by three dashes (- - -). Here is the heading from the previous example. It also includes the date and time each file was last modified:

```
*** report2 Thu Oct  7 21:49:23 1999
--- report6 Thu Oct  7 21:56:23 1999
***************
```

Table 10.1 shows other properties of the diff command.

Table 10.1 Other Properties of the *diff* Command

Property	See Page
Allows relative and absolute pathname arguments	70
Allows output to be piped or redirected	116

Commands that Allow Dash (-) for Standard Input

Some UNIX commands, especially those in this chapter, allow a dash (-) in the filename list to cause the command to read data from Standard Input. In the following example, a user script called myprog generates some output, which is piped to the diff command. This command normally compares two disk files. In the example, a dash (-) is given to diff instead of a filename, so diff will read from standard input the data piped from myprog and compare it to the contents of file exptxt. The diff command will then display any differences in its normal fashion.

```
myprog | diff - exptxt
```

> **Using the Dash for Standard Input**
>
> Some UNIX commands allow a dash (-) in place of a filename. Older versions of some commands, like the cmp command, only allowed the dash in place of the first file. The cmp command on newer UNIX systems allows the dash either for *file1* or *file2* being compared. You must use the dash for standard input only once on any command line.

In the next example, flist is a text file containing a list of filenames, converted to all upper case. To determine if that list matches the files in the current directory, use ls to generate the list of files in the current directory and use tr to convert that list to upper case. Pipe this list to diff using a dash (-) argument to read from standard input. It will display any differences between the list of files in flist versus standard input.

```
ls | tr "[a-z]" "[A-Z]" | diff - flist
```

Many commands that allow filename arguments do not allow a dash (-) in place of a filename. Check the man page for any particular command to see if it allows a dash (-) to read from standard input.

Showing Differences Side by Side

To show the differences between two text files side by side, use this command:

```
sdiff file1 file2
```

You should see output similar to this:

```
report02                        report02
report07                        | report05
report09                        <
report04                        report04
report03                        report03
                              > report01
```

The left column shows lines in the first file. The column on the right shows lines in the second file. The < sign shows lines that occur in the first file but not the second. The sign>> sign shows lines that occur in the second file but not the first. The ¦ sign shows lines that are different between the two files.

sdiff works well to compare lists of short words or filenames, but it can be very difficult to read with longer lines.

Table 10.2 shows other standard properties of the sdiff command.

Table 10.2 Other Properties of the *sdiff* Command

Property	See page
Allows relative and absolute pathname arguments	70
Allows output to be piped or redirected	116

Showing Differences Among Three Files

To show the differences among three text files, use this command:

```
diff3 file1 file2 file3
```

The contents of three example files are shown in Table 10.3.

Table 10.3 Contents of Three Example Files

file1	file2	file3
green	green	yellow
blue	blue	blue
red	red	green
yellow	yellow	brown
blue	blue	tan
green	green	red
brown	brown	orange
pink	azure	black
red	red	gray
orange	orange	
black	black	
gray	gray	

Here is the diff3 command entered and its output:

```
$ diff3 file1 file2 file3
====3
1:1,3c
2:1,3c
   green
   blue
   red
3:0a
====
1:8c
   pink
2:8c
   azure
3:5c
   tan
$
```

In this code, ==== separates each section of differences found in the three files. If the ==== is followed by the number X, it means that file x differs from the other two, which match each other. The following example line indicates the start of a section of differences where files 1 and 2 match each other but file 3 has lines that do not match them:

```
====3
```

If no number follows ====, it means that all three files differ in this section.

The following is a commentary on the preceding output from diff3:

```
====3       means file 3 differs from the other two
1:1,3c      means file 1, lines 1 thru 3 contain the
            same contents as the following file:
2:1,3c      means file 2, lines 1 thru 3 contain these
            3 lines as listed here:
  green
  blue
  red
3:0a        means file 3 would have to add the preceding 3 lines
            after line 0 in order to become the same
            as the other two files.
====        means all three files differ in this next area:
1:8c        means file 1, line 8 contains: pink
  pink
2:8c        whereas file 2, line 8 contains: azure
  azure
3:5c        whereas file 3, line 5 contains: tan
  tan
```

Table 10.4 shows other standard properties of the diff3 command.

Table 10.4 Other Properties of the diff3 Command

Property	See page
Allows relative and absolute pathname arguments	70
Allows output to be piped or redirected	116

Finding Common and Unique Lines in Sorted Text Files

If two text files are in sorted (that is, alphabetic) order, the comm command can show easily the lines common between the two files and the lines that are unique. To do this, enter the following command:

```
comm file1 file2
```

You should see output similar to this:

```
                report21
report23
        report29
                report33
report34
                report35
        report37
report91
```

The leftmost column shows lines unique to the first file; therefore, report23, report34, and report91 exist only in the first file. The middle column shows lines unique to the second file; so report29 and report37 exist only in the second file. The third column shows lines common to both files. In this case, report21, report33, and report35 exist in both files.

Don't Use comm If There Are Leading Tabs
comm uses one tab character to start lines in the middle column and two tabs to start lines in the right column. If your two files start with one or more tabs, the comm output will be misleading.

You can add options to comm to suppress one or more of the columns, as follows:

```
comm -1 file1 file2    # suppress column 1, so we show
                       # only columns 2 and 3
comm -23 file1 file2   # show only lines unique to file1
comm -13 file1 file2   # show only lines unique to file2
comm -12 file1 file2   # show only lines in common
```

Remember that the files must be in sorted order for comm to work. If you have two files to compare that are not sorted, you can use the sort command to create sorted versions of those files and then use the comm command on the sorted versions.

Table 10.5 shows other standard properties of the comm command.

Table 10.5 Other Properties of the comm Command

Property	See page
Allows relative and absolute pathname arguments	70
Allows output to be piped or redirected	116

SEE ALSO

➤ *For more information on the* sort *command, see page 266*

Comparing Any File Type by Contents

To compare any type of files, even if they are not text files, use this command:

```
cmp file1 file2
```

You should see output similar to this:

```
file1 file2 differ: char 26, line 3
```

If cmp goes back to the shell prompt without displaying any messages, the files are identical. cmp stops after the first difference is found, so it does not tell you how similar the two files are. Use the -1 option to cmp to list all the differences between the two files.

---

cmp Versus diff

If you want to know only whether two files are identical, cmp is faster than diff because it stops on the first difference. cmp works with all types of files; diff handles only text files. However, diff shows the actual line differences. This enables you to pinpoint added or deleted characters or lines.

Use cmp to compare nontext files because it does not try to output the differences. Using diff, sdiff, diff3, or comm on binary files can cause misleading output because control characters from the binary files can leave your screen in an unknown state.

Table 10.6 shows other standard properties of the cmp command.

Table 10.6 Other Properties of the *cmp* Command

Property	See page
Allows relative and absolute pathname arguments	70
Allows output to be piped or redirected	116

Comparing Files on Different Systems

If you transfer a file to another system, you may want to verify that the file arrived intact. diff, sdiff, diff3, comm, and cmp can compare only files on the same system.

To compare two files that exist on different systems, use this command on each system:

```
sum -r filename
```

You should see output similar to this:

```
35424    14    filename
```

The `sum` command calculates a checksum on the full contents of the file. In the preceding output, `35424` is the checksum for the file, and `14` is the size in blocks. If the checksums for the two files do not match, the two files are not identical. If the checksums match, there is a very high probability that the two files are identical. The checksum algorithm (that is, calculation) is the same on almost every type of UNIX system, allowing remote files to be compared even if the UNIX system is a different type.

Note that the size in blocks reported by `sum` may differ by a factor of 2 between two different types of UNIX systems. This is because some UNIX systems compute file size using 512 bytes per block, and others use 1024 bytes per block. SunOS Version 4 (based on BSD) uses 1024 bytes per block, for example, whereas Solaris 2.x using SunOS Version 5 (based on System V) uses 512 bytes per block. Note that the block size in bytes used by the `sum` command may not be the internal logical block size used when adding additional blocks to the file.

What Are the Odds?

`sum` produces a checksum that can range up to about 65,000. In general, if two files have randomly selected data and give the same checksum, there is only about one chance in 65,000 that they could still have different contents.

Here is another way to think about the odds. If you have millions of diverse files, you are sure to have hundreds of files with different contents that give the same checksum.

The `-r` option to `sum` causes it to use a better (rotating) checksum calculation that can better detect differences in the order as well as the contents of the files. If you want to be extra sure that two files are identical, take advantage of these two different calculations, as follows:

Taking an extra step to ensure that files are the same

1. On the first system, run the `sum` command and then `sum -r` on the file in question. In the following example, it is called file1.

```
$ sum file1
10308 73 file1
$ sum -r file1
12112    73 file1
$
```

2. On the second system, run sum and sum -r on the file to compare on that system. It is called file2 in the following example:

```
$ sum file2
10308 73 file2
$ sum -r file2
12112    73 file2
$
```

3. Check whether the results of the two sum calculations are the same. Check whether the results of the two sum -r calculations are the same. In step 1, sum of file1 produced 10308 73, which matches the sum of file2 in step 2. Similarly, sum -r of file1 matches sum -r of file2.

4. If the two types of checksums match (as they do in the steps 1 and 2), the files are the same (to a very high degree of probability). If either the sum or the sum -r does not match, it is 100% certain that the files are not identical.

There is a slim chance that two files can be different and still produce the same checksum, but it is extremely unlikely that two different files would match using both checksum methods.

See Table 10.7 for other standard properties of the sum command.

Table 10.7   Other Properties of the *sum* Command

Property	See page
Allows relative and absolute pathname arguments	70
Processes either filename arguments OR standard input	115
Allows a list of filenames and filename wildcards	292
Allows output to be piped or redirected	116

Finding Identical Files Under Different Names

To quickly determine which files in a directory are identical, use this command:

```
sum -r * | sort
```

You should see output similar to this:

```
06948    21 report02
14252    15 report04
22792   192 acme.980201
22792   192 report05
```

If the output goes off the screen, rerun the command and pipe the output to pg or more or less. In the preceding example, acme.980201 and report05 have the same checksum and size in blocks. Therefore, it is highly probable that they are identical. You could then use `diff` or `cmp` on those two files if you needed to be 100 percent certain. `report02` and `report04` have different checksums from the others, so they cannot match `acme.980201` and `report05` or each other.

In the previous example, you could use other filename generation wildcards to produce a smaller list of only the files you want to see.

Sorting Files or Pipelines

Sorting means to arrange lines in alphabetical order. To sort one or more files, use the `sort` command, as in the following:

```
sort file1 file2 file3
```

`sort` will merge all the specified files into its workspace, sort the workspace, and then display the result. The `sort` command offers many features to enable you to control what characters or fields are used to order the lines.

Why Don't UNIX Commands Have Built-in Sort or Paging Options?

If a user wants sorted output, or paged output, or sorted output one page at a time from any UNIX command, it is expected that the user will just pipe to `sort`, or pipe to `pg`, or pipe to `sort` and then to `pg`. In this way, UNIX utilities don't duplicate efforts and can be more efficient.

See Table 10.8 for other standard properties of the `sort` command.

Table 10.8 Other Properties of the *sort* Command

Property	See page
Allows relative and absolute pathname arguments	70
Processes either filename arguments OR standard input	115
Changes only the output, not the file	111
Allows a list of filenames and filename wildcards	292
Allows output to be piped or redirected	116

Determining How Lines Will Be Sorted (ASCII)

`sort` arranges lines based on the ASCII values of the characters within the lines. You can usually look up the ASCII sequence by entering this command:

```
man ascii
```

This is a sample ASCII table that man might show (modified slightly to fit the margins of this book):

```
|000 NUL|001 SOH|002 STX|003 ETX|
|004 EOT|005 ENQ|006 ACK|007 BEL|
|010 BS |011 HT |012 NL |013 VT |
|014 NP |015 CR |016 SO |017 SI |
|020 DLE|021 DC1|022 DC2|023 DC3|
|024 DC4|025 NAK|026 SYN|027 ETB|
|030 CAN|031 EM |032 SUB|033 ESC|
|034 FS |035 GS |036 RS |037 US |
|040 SP |041 ! |042 " |043 # |044 $ |045 % |046 & |047 ' |
|050 ( |051 ) |052 * |053 + |054 , |055 - |056 . |057 / |
|060 0 |061 1 |062 2 |063 3 |064 4 |065 5 |066 6 |067 7 |
|070 8 |071 9 |072 : |073 ; |074 < |075 = |076 > |077 ? |
|100 @ |101 A |102 B |103 C |104 D |105 E |106 F |107 G |
|110 H |111 I |112 J |113 K |114 L |115 M |116 N |117 O |
|120 P |121 Q |122 R |123 S |124 T |125 U |126 V |127 W |
|130 X |131 Y |132 Z |133 [ |134 \ |135 ] |136 ^ |137 _ |
|140 ` |141 a |142 b |143 c |144 d |145 e |146 f |147 g |
|150 h |151 i |152 j |153 k |154 l |155 m |156 n |157 o |
|160 p |161 q |162 r |163 s |164 t |165 u |166 v |167 w |
|170 x |171 y |172 z |173 { |174 | |175 } |176 ~ |177DEL|
```

The preceding table shows that each ASCII character has a value, often given in octal or base 8 numbering. A capital A has the value 101, for example, whereas a lowercase a has the value 141. Lines that start with capital letters come before all lines that start with lowercase letters. Notice that the digits sort before any letters. Punctuation characters also have values; hence, lines that begin with punctuation will be sorted based on the ASCII value of the punctuation characters. Notice that the bang sign (!) has the smallest ASCII value for any printing character (except for a space). Sometimes you will find headings that begin with a bang sign (!) so that they will still be at the start of the output even if the output is sorted.

The order in which characters are sorted is called a *collation sequence*. Although ASCII is the normal sort order in the United States, other countries sometimes have special keyboards and special alphabets. Therefore, you may encounter a different collation sequence.

SEE ALSO

➤ *For more information on man pages, see page 88*

Ignoring Leading Blanks When Sorting

-b Versus +0b

Linux and some older versions of UNIX allow -b as a simple `sort` option to ignore leading blanks. Newer versions of commercial UNIX such as Solaris 7, SCO UnixWare 7, and SCO OpenServer 5 consider -b to be an incorrect usage and ignore it. They follow the man page description of sort options where -b is not listed with the other global options, but is put in a special section of field options. As a field option, described later in this chapter, the -b functionality can be invoked by using the +0b option or -b +0 option but not by a -b option. Other sort options in this chapter can be simple sort options, but I recommend you always enter the -b as a field option because this is compatible on all types of UNIX systems. .

If lines begin with the same character, their order will be determined by the first character in the lines that are different. For example, long lines that start with many spaces will sort before long lines that start with fewer or no spaces because a space sorts before any nonspace character based on the ASCII chart. For example:

```
$ sort tstfile
    zebra
  monkey
  apple
$
```

To ignore leading spaces in the line when sorting, use the +0b option, as shown here:

```
$ sort +0b tstfile
  apple
   monkey
     zebra
$
```

Sorting Numbers by Magnitude

This left-to-right principle also applies to lines that start with numbers. For example:

```
$ sort numfile
10 oranges
5 apples
66 grapes
$
```

The preceding lines are in sorted order because 1 comes before 5, which comes before 6. To sort lines based on the magnitude of numbers at the start of the lines, use the -n option, as shown in the following:

```
$ sort -n numfile
5 apples
10 oranges
66 grapes
$
```

The sort -n option handles negative numbers and decimal fractions as well. For example:

```
$ sort -n numfile3
-30 bananas
-2 pineapples
5.44 apples
5.5 apples
10 oranges
66 grapes
$
```

In the next example, the numbers are right-justified, which means that the numbers may start in different columns, but they all end in the same column position.

```
$ cat numfile2
      5 pencils
   2032 crayons
    153 erasers
$
```

In the preceding case, and whenever you have lines that start with right-justified numbers, the -n is not needed because a regular sort will arrange them by magnitude, as follows:

```
$ sort numfile2
      5 pencils
    153 erasers
   2032 crayons
$
```

When the -n option is used, it ignores all leading blanks in the line as if a b option had also been given. If any lines do not start with a number, -n will regard those lines as having a zero value and will sort them before lines that do start with a number greater than zero.

Folding Lower/Uppercase Together

In the ASCII sequence, all lines beginning with any capital letters will sort before any lines beginning with lowercase letters. To sort ignoring upper- or lowercase, add the -f option to sort. This is called folding the upper- and lowercase letters together. For example:

```
$ sort tstfile
APPLE
Orange
banana
grape
$ sort -f tstfile
APPLE
banana
grape
Orange
$
```

Sorting in Reverse Order

To sort the lines in reverse order, add the –r option to sort. This can be especially useful with the -n option to sort when you want to see the largest values first. For example, ls -s will list the files in the current directory, preceded by the size of the file in blocks:

```
$ ls -s
total 660
  15 acme
625 pegasus
  20 report7
$
```

When there are a lot of files, it can be difficult to visually pick out the large files. You can pipe the output to sort and let sort arrange the files from largest to smallest:

```
$ ls -s | sort -rn
625 pegasus
  20 report7
  15 acme
total 660
$
```

In this example, notice how the –r and -n options to sort were combined. Actually, the -n option to sort was not really needed because the numbers are right-justified. Notice that the total line comes at the end. Because it does not start with a number, –n sorts it as a zero value.

In the preceding example, why does 660 in the total line come at the end? This is because sort -n is looking for a number at the start of the line (after any leading spaces). Any line that starts with a nonletter (such as the total line) is regarded as having a zero value.

Ignoring Punctuation When Sorting

As you have seen, punctuation is scattered throughout the ASCII table and will therefore affect the sort order of lines that begin with punctuation, as in the following:

```
$ sort tstfile3
"orange"
'grape'
<apple>
melon
{banana}
$
```

To ignore punctuation and sort only on letters, digits, spaces, and tabs, use the –d option to sort in dictionary order, as shown here:

```
$ sort -d tstfile3
<apple>
{banana}
'grape'
melon
"orange"
$
```

The -d option to sort cannot be combined with the -n option, so there is no way, using only sort options, to sort numbers by magnitude if the lines start with punctuation.

Combining *sort* Options

sort options may be combined, as described in the section "Command-Line Options," in Chapter 4, "Rules for Entering UNIX Commands." For example, the following commands are equivalent:

```
sort -d -f -r filename
sort -f -r -d filename
sort -rf -d filename
sort -dfr filename
sort -rdf filename
```

If you want to include the –b option, on most newer versions of UNIX, you must add +0 after all the options have been specified. This works on all versions of UNIX, so it is a good habit to add the +0 even if it is not necessary.

```
sort -d -f -b -r +0 filename
sort -bdrf +0 filename
```

Sorting Based on Fields Within the Line

The `sort` command regards any sequence of spaces or tabs as the start of a new field. You can use the `sort +n` option to skip (ignore) n fields and sort based on the remaining characters in the line. For example, `ls -l` produces nine fields:

```
$ ls -l
total 3
-rw-r--r--  1 william  mgr         17157 Feb 1 11:31 acme
-rw-r--r--  1 janepf   accnting   1972 Feb 1 11:31 rep04
-rw-r--r--  1 mori     group    196484 Feb 1 11:33 rep07
-rw-r--r--  1 janepf   accnting     25 Feb 1 11:33 rep08
(field 1   f2    f3        f4        f5  f6 f7  f8      f9)
```

The fields in this example are numbered just so that you can refer to them. Field 3 is the owner of each file. To sort the output in order of owner name, you want to `sort` on field 3, so you must skip two fields (namely, field 1 and field 2):

```
$ ls -l | sort +2
total 3
-rw-r--r--  1 janepf   accnting   1972 Feb 1 11:31 rep04
-rw-r--r--  1 janepf   accnting     25 Feb 1 11:33 rep08
-rw-r--r--  1 mori     group    196484 Feb 1 11:33 rep07
-rw-r--r--  1 william  mgr         17157 Feb 1 11:31 acme
(field 1   f2    f3        f4        f5  f6 f7  f8      f9)
```

The preceding example shows lines that are in order of owner: `janepf`, `mori`, then `william`. This sort was easy because there was the same number of spaces before each owner name. Sorting on field 4, the `group`, is more difficult due to the fact that `sort` regards each field as starting with the leading spaces in that field. To illustrate the problem, consider these lines:

```
$ ls -l | sort +3
total 3
-rw-r--r--  1 mori     group    196484 Feb 1 11:33 rep07
-rw-r--r--  1 janepf   accnting   1972 Feb 1 11:31 rep04
-rw-r--r--  1 janepf   accnting     25 Feb 1 11:33 rep08
-rw-r--r--  1 william  mgr         17157 Feb 1 11:31 acme
(field 1   f2    f3        f4        f5  f6 f7  f8      f9)
```

The preceding output is sorted by field 4 (because you skip three fields), and yet it puts group before accnting. This makes sense when you consider that field 4 really looks like this:

```
<space><space><space><space>group
<space><space>accnting
<space><space>accnting
<space>mgr
```

You can solve this problem by using sort +3b, which means skip three fields and ignore leading blanks when sorting. You are actually using the -b option following the +3 field specifier. -b will work on all UNIX systems as long as there is a preceding or following field specifier:

```
$ ls -l | sort +3b
total 3
-rw-r--r--  1 janepf   accnting 1972 Feb 1 11:31 rep04
-rw-r--r--  1 janepf   accnting   25 Feb 1 11:33 rep08
-rw-r--r--  1 mori     group   196484 Feb 1 11:33 rep07
-rw-r--r--  1 william  mgr       17157 Feb 1 11:31 acme
(field 1    f2  f3       f4       f5  f6 f7  f8     f9)
```

The preceding example shows that you succeeded in sorting by group: accnting, then group, then mgr. If you want to sort the same output by file size in field 5, you will have a similar problem that requires a different solution. Even though the file size numbers appear to be right-justified (and therefore sortable without any problems), the previous field 4 does not end in the same column for each line. Each field 5 begins with a random number of leading spaces that will prevent sorting in the desired order. If you simply ignore leading spaces as before, you get this result:

```
$ ls -l | sort +4b
total 3
-rw-r--r--  1 william  mgr       17157 Feb 1 11:31 acme
-rw-r--r--  1 mori     group   196484 Feb 1 11:33 rep07
-rw-r--r--  1 janepf   accnting 1972 Feb 1 11:31 rep04
-rw-r--r--  1 janepf   accnting   25 Feb 1 11:33 rep08
 (field 1    f2  f3       f4       f5  f6 f7  f8     f9)
```

In the preceding output, notice that the numbers are sorted in correct ASCII order:

```
171
196
197
25
```

ASCII order does not sort the numbers by size. You want the file sizes sorted by magnitude, not by ASCII order. When you use sort -n to sort by magnitude, it automatically ignores leading spaces:

```
$ ls -l | sort +4n
total 3
-rw-r--r--  1 janepf  accnting     25 Feb 1 11:33 rep08
-rw-r--r--  1 janepf  accnting 1972 Feb 1 11:31 rep04
-rw-r--r--  1 william mgr       17157 Feb 1 11:31 acme
-rw-r--r--  1 mori    group   196484 Feb 1 11:33 rep07
 (field 1   f2   f3      f4        f5  f6 f7  f8     f9)
```

Sorting Based on Primary and Secondary Sort Keys

Assume that you have a `friends` file that lists the first name, middle initial, last name, and city for several friends. Notice what happens if you sort by the last name:

```
$ sort +2 friends     # this is not what we want
William A.  Smith, St. Louis
James B. Nguyen, Los Angeles
Henry H. Nguyen, Yuba City
Mary K. Zornan, Cleveland
Mary A. Zornan, Pittsburgh
$
```

Notice that Smith comes first because there happens to be two spaces before Smith in that entry, and space-space comes before space-letter, just as aa comes before ab. You can ignore leading spaces by adding the `-b` option, as shown here:

```
$ sort -b +2 friends     # this is closer to what we want
James B. Nguyen, Los Angeles
Henry H. Nguyen, Yuba City
William A.  Smith, St. Louis
Mary K. Zornan, Cleveland
Mary A. Zornan, Pittsburgh
$
```

Now notice that the two Nguyen entries are in order by city. This is understandable because you are skipping the first two fields and sorting the rest of the line. What if you want to sort first by last name and, if the last names are the same, then by the first name? This process is called using a primary and secondary sort key. Here is the general format of a sort key:

```
+m -n
```

`+m` specifies how many fields to skip to reach the start of the key. `-n` specifies the last field in the key.

In the previous example, here are some possible sort keys you could use:

- `+0 -1` specifies field 1: first name
- `+1 -2` specifies field 2: middle initial
- `+0 -2` specifies fields 1 and 2: first name and middle initial
- `+2 -3` specifies field 3: last name
- `+3` specifies field 4 and all remaining fields to the end of the line: city

The following command will use field 3, the last name, as the primary sort key:

```
sort +2 -3 +0 -2 friends
```

This means that most lines will be sorted based on that field. Fields 1 and 2, the first name and middle initial, will be the secondary sort key. The secondary sort key is used to sort only lines that have identical primary keys; so, if the last names are identical, those lines will be sorted by first name and middle initial.

You can ignore characters at the start of the sort field and include characters from the next field, like this:

```
+m.x -n.y
```

`+m.x` specifies how many fields to skip; then skip x characters to reach the start of the key. `-n.y` specifies the last field in the key, augmented by y characters in the next field.

Global *sort* Options

The `sort` options in this chapter—`-b`, `-d`, `-f`, `-n`, and `-r`—may be specified before any sort key specifiers (`+m`). In that case, they apply to all the sort keys, unless overridden by field `sort` options.

Field *sort* Options

All of the `sort` options discussed previously in this chapter—(except for `-b`) may be specified after any sort key specifier of the form +m. In that case, they apply only to that sort key and turn off all the global `sort` options for that sort key.

```
sort -bdf +3 -5 +2n -3 +7 filename
```

In the previous example, there are three sort keys, some global `sort` options, and one field `sort` option:

- `-bdf` is a global `sort` option because it occurs before any sort key specifiers.
- `+3 -5` means that fields 4 and 5 make up the primary sort key. The global `sort` options will apply when sorting on this field.

- +2n -3 means that field 3 is the secondary sort key, which is used to sort only lines that have identical primary sort keys. This field uses only the -n option. Because of this field option, none of the global options apply to this field.

- +7 means that the third sort key is field 8 to the end of the line. It is used to sort only lines with identical primary and secondary sort keys. It has no field options, so the global sort options apply to it.

Now you can complete the example started earlier and sort the friends file by last name. If the last names are the same, sort by first name and middle initial. If that is the same, sort by city to the end of the line. Here is the sort command that accomplishes all that:

```
$ sort -b +2 -3 +0 -2 +3 friends
Henry H. Nguyen, Yuba City
James B. Nguyen, Los Angeles
William A.  Smith, St. Louis
Mary A. Zornan, Pittsburgh
Mary K. Zornan, Cleveland
$
```

Sometimes you will encounter a -k option to sort, which allows specifying the sort keys using a newer method. Most UNIX systems today support both the newer method and the older method. The older method was covered earlier because it is supported on older and newer UNIX systems. Here is the equivalent command for the friends file, using the newer -k method:

```
sort -b -k 3,3 -k 1,2 -k 4 friends
```

Use -k to specify each sort key using this general, simplified format:

```
-k aOPTS,b
```

In this code, a is the starting field number (not the fields to skip) for this sort key. OPTS can be b, d, f, n, or r and will apply only to this key. b is the ending field number for this key.

Modifying Files or Pipelines

Several commands let you modify or transform the contents of files or pipelines. The crypt command scrambles the contents of sensitive files so that no one else can read them unless they have the key to unscramble them. This command has not kept pace with hackers because of government regulations on encryption software. In a similar fashion, the standard UNIX compress command is behind the times. The government, however, is not worried about compression software falling into the wrong hands, so there are newer better compression commands (gzip and bzip2) that will be presented. Finally a third modification command will be discussed. uuencode was once the standard method to transform a binary file into printable text so that it could be emailed or transmitted to another system. Today email has no problems with binary attachments, but occasionally uuencode still comes in handy.

Encrypting a File or Pipeline

If you have confidential text information or data, you can use the crypt command to encrypt or scramble the information so that only someone who knows the proper password or key can decrypt—that is, unscramble—the information and use it. Be aware that encryption has come a long way since the crypt command, and today there are reportedly several programs that can break this security. For better encryption, look into pgp or des, available from some UNIX vendors, technical bookstores, and via the Internet.

Encryption Software Is Often Not Included

You don't always get encryption software because the U.S. government has rules that prevent the export of this type of security technology to outside countries. If encryption is not included on your commercial UNIX system, you may find that it is available for domestic use. Ask the vendor of your specific type of UNIX.

How to encrypt a file using crypt

1. Make sure you know the full pathname of the file that you want to encrypt. That file can either be a text file or a data file.

2. cd to the directory that contains the file to encrypt.

3. Enter crypt < *EXISTING-FILE* > tmpfile$$.

   Replace *EXISTING-FILE* with the basename of the file to encrypt. tmpfile$$ is a temporary file used in this procedure. Enter that name exactly as shown, but be aware that the shell will replace $$ with some digits to make the name unique so that a conflict will not arise if other users are doing this same procedure at the same time in the same directory.

4. After you enter the command in step 3, you will see this prompt:
   Enter key:

   Enter one or more characters or words to be the encryption key. What you type in will not echo to the screen as a security measure, so enter your key slowly and carefully.

> **Warning**
>
> You will need to know the exact spelling of this key to decrypt and use your file later. There is no back door around this key, so if you can't remember this key, you can't decrypt your file.

5. After you enter the key in step 4, `tmpfile$$` will hold the encrypted information.

6. Test `tmpfile$$` by entering this command:

```
crypt < tmpfile$$ > tmp2$$
```

Again, you will see this prompt:

```
Enter key:
```

7. Enter the same key used to encrypt this file. Note that the same key is used to encrypt and decrypt the information.

8. Enter `cmp EXISTING-FILE tmp2$$`.

Replace `EXISTING-FILE` with the original filename you want to encrypt. This `cmp` command should just return to the shell prompt with no other output, indicating that the two files are the same. If not, something went wrong.

Do not proceed with this procedure. Perhaps you entered the key incorrectly. Try going back to step 6 again. If step 7 still shows that the files are not the same, delete the temporary files, as follows:

```
rm tmpfile$$ tmp2$$
```

Then go back to step 1 of this procedure.

9. Enter `mv tmpfile$$ EXISTING-FILE`.

Replace `EXISTING-FILE` with the original filename you want to encrypt. This replaces the original file with the encrypted version.

10. Enter `rm tmp2$$`.

This removes the other temporary file that you don't need anymore.

To decrypt the file, enter the following:

```
crypt < ENCRYPTED-FILE > DECRYPTED-FILE
```

Replace `ENCRYPTED-FILE` with the filename to decrypt. Replace `DECRYPTED-FILE` with any new name that you want to create. Make sure that that name does not already exist, because that name will be overwritten by this command. `crypt` will output this prompt message:

```
Enter key:
```

Then enter the same key used to encrypt the file.

You can also supply the key on the command line, for example:

```
crypt "Mary had a little lamb" < file1 > file2
```

This can be useful when you want to use crypt within a shell script and you don't want to be prompted to enter the key from the keyboard. Be aware, however, that anyone who reads the shell script will see what the key is; thus, this is not very good security.

See Table 10.9 for other standard properties of the crypt command.

Table 10.9 Other Properties of the *crypt* Command

Property	See page
Does not allow filename command line arguments	765
Allows output to be piped or redirected	116

Compressing Files

Compressing a file means to encode its contents so that it becomes smaller in size and yet can be restored to its original size and contents later when desired. How small you can make the file depends on the data within the file. Text files with many repeated characters can be compressed to a much smaller size than binary files with random data.

Don't Compress a Compressed File

You might think that compressing a file a second time should make it even smaller. Often just the opposite is true. The first compression took advantage of all the repeated sequences. The second compression may actually make the result slightly larger.

Files are usually compressed for two reasons:

- They take up less disk space. For example, you might compress a group of archive files that are rarely used but must be kept accessible.

- They can be transferred to another system in a shorter amount of time. This can be an important factor if you are downloading the file by a slow connection.

Under UNIX, three commands are available to compress a file and then uncompress it, which means restore it back to its original size and contents. Table 10.10 shows the three commands in order from least efficient to most efficient, where more efficient means it produces better compression and a smaller resultant file. The Suffix

Appended column shows the suffix each command adds to the filename to show the file is now compressed.

Table 10.10 Comparison of Three Compression Utilities

Command to Compress	Command to Uncompress	Suffix Appended	Example Size
compress	uncompress	.Z	179370
gzip	gunzip	.gz	113092
bzip2	bunzip2	.bz2	107012

In the preceding table, the Example Size shows how small each utility made a 1.44 MB test file. The amount of compression you get will depend on the type and arrangement of data in your file. If your file contains purely random binary data, you will be lucky if any compression utility can reduce the file size by 50%. If your file contains large stretches of repeated patterns, you may reduce the size by 80% or more.

compress is available on most UNIX systems. gzip usually performs better compression but is often not part of a standard commercial UNIX distribution. bzip2 is a newer utility that compresses even better than gzip, but it is found on fewer versions of UNIX than gzip or compress.

---

gzip or bzip2 Is Often Downloadable

gzip or bzip2 is usually not supplied with commercial UNIX systems but is often available through the Internet from Web sites that specialize in shareware or nonsupported free utilities for the UNIX platform you are running (www.sun.com, www.ibm.com, or www.sco.com, for example) Look for downloadable operating system software.

To compress a file with the compress command, enter the following:

```
compress filename
```

Replace *filename* with the file to be compressed. compress creates a compressed file with the same name, ending in .z, and removes the original file. To reverse the process, enter this:

```
uncompress filename.Z
```

uncompress will restore the file to its original size, contents, and filename. It will also remove the .Z suffix.

You can display the original contents of a compressed file, without uncompressing it to a disk file, by using the zcat command to display the uncompressed text:

```
zcat filename.Z | pg
```

The preceding command shows the readable contents of the compressed file one page at a time. You could also pipe the output of zcat to lp or lpr instead of pg if you wanted a printout.

On SCO UNIX OpenServer 5 only, the –H option to compress causes it to use a better compression method and produce smaller files. You cannot uncompress such a file on any other type of UNIX system because this option is found only on SCO OpenServer 5. To compress a file using gzip, enter the following command:

```
gzip filename
```

gzip adds .gz to the filename. The following command uncompresses that file:

```
gunzip filename.gz
```

To get the best compression in gzip, add the -9 option, as shown here:

```
gzip -9 filename
```

Nine options, from -1 to -9 are available. Use -1 when your main concern is to finish the compression quickly even if the file is not as small as possible. Use -9 when your main concern is to make the result as small as possible, which will take more time to complete. Use any number in between as a trade-off between speed versus smallness. -6 is the default if no value is given.

To compress a file using bzip2, enter the following:

```
bzip2 filename
```

To uncompress a file using bzip2, enter the following:

```
bunzip2 filename.bz2
```

See Table 10.11 for other standard properties of the compress, gzip, and bzip2 commands.

Table 10.11 Other Properties of the *compress, gzip,* and *bzip2* Commands

Property	See page
Allows relative and absolute pathname arguments	70
Processes either filename arguments OR standard input	115
Allows a list of filenames and filename wildcards	292
Allows output to be piped or redirected	116

Encoding Files as Transmittable Simple Text

To send information in the body of an email, it is necessary that the information be simple, printable text characters. When you use the UNIX `mailx` command from the command line, you cannot include attachments, so any binary files to be sent must be converted or encoded into a string of simple text characters. This process is called *uuencoding*, where *uu* is a standard UNIX prefix used for utilities that involve UNIX-to-UNIX transfers.

This process of uuencoding is also useful if you are dialed in to another UNIX system using `cu` and you want to download or upload a binary file. The `~%put` and `~%take` commands in `cu` can download or upload only text files. Binary files can first be uuencoded into text files. These files can be transferred and then uudecoded back to their original binary form.

> #### uuencode/uudecode Under Windows Email
>
> Some email programs under Windows support **uuencode/uudecode**. This is useful if you want to email a binary file from Windows to UNIX. Click **uuencode** to insert a text version of the binary file directly into your email. This is not an attachment! If you receive uuencoded data in email on Windows, click **uudecode** to save the data in a file. You may have to adjust the destination filename in the uuencoded text.

To uuencode a file, at the shell prompt, enter the following:

```
uuencode BINFILE DESTFILE > TEXTFILE
```

Replace *BINFILE* with the binary filename to encode. Replace *DESTFILE* with the desired filename to create on the destination system. Replace *TEXTFILE* with the filename to create on your system with the uuencoded text information.

To uuencode the output of another UNIX command or pipeline, enter this:

```
CMD | uuencode DESTFILE > TEXTFILE
```

Replace *CMD* with the desired UNIX command or pipeline to generate the output to be uuencoded.

After the *TEXTFILE* has been transmitted to the other UNIX system, you can restore it to its original form by entering the following:

```
uudecode TEXTFILE
```

The preceding command creates the binary file and gives it the name *DESTFILE*, which was specified when uuencode was run.

Check the Destination Name First

Before you uudecode a file, check the destination that it will use. Make sure that all the directories needed exist. More importantly, make sure the destination name does not contain any important data since it will be overwritten! A safer way to uudecode is the use the -s option as described in this section so you can select your own destination filename.

To determine what *DESTFILE* will be created before you run uudecode, enter this:

```
head TEXTFILE
```

You should see output like this:

```
begin 660 /usr/fred/acme
M?T5,1@$! 0            (  P !    <)T$"#0   !0I@     #0 ( &
M "@ $@ 0  8    T  -( $""    #   P     4      P  /0
M              !,          !      !    -   #2 ! @    9'X
M &1^    %    $    $    "8?@ F F  F    #@)@ 5$$@  <      &
```

In the first line, you can see that when this file is uudecoded, it will try to create a file called /usr/fred/acme. You can edit the name in this file if you want to change the destination file before you uudecode it. This is especially true if sending uuencoded files between UNIX and Windows. Notice that the rest of the lines begin with the letter M. A begin line followed by many M lines usually indicates a uuencoded file.

A safer way to run uudecode is to add the -s option to write to standard output rather than use the destination name contained in the body of the text. After all, the sender may not know what directories and files should be used on your system. The following command will uudecode whatever filename you use for *TEXTFILE* and it will save the output in whatever name you give for *YOURDEST*:

```
uudecode -s TEXTFILE > YOURDEST
```

If you receive email with a uuencoded file in the middle, you can save this email and uudecode it without stripping off the mail lines that come before or after the uuencoded lines.

SEE ALSO

➤ *For more information on using cu, see page 661*

Combining Files

Several commands that can combine file contents for various purposes will be covered in this section. The files can be combined and intertwined in sorted order. They can be concatenated one after the other. They can be pasted side by side on each line or joined side by side where a line in one file is paired with the corresponding line in a second file. These combinations do not affect the original files. The results can be redirected and saved in another file, if desired.

Sorting Multiple Files Together

You looked at sort at the beginning of this chapter. If sort is called with a list of files on the command line, sort first merges their contents and then displays the combined contents in sorted order, as shown here:

```
sort file1 file2 file3 > bigsort
```

Concatenating Files One After the Other

To combine files one after the other, use the cat command:

```
cat file1 file2 file3 > bigfile
```

The cat command gets its name from *concatenation*.

Pasting Files Together Side by Side

The cat command combines files one after the other. The paste command combines files side by side. Line 1 of the paste output contains line 1 of file1, then a tab, then line 1 of file2, then a tab, then line 1 of file3, and so on. Similarly, line 2 contains line 2 from each of the files. To paste files together in this way, enter the following:

```
paste file1 file2 file3 ...
```

If the colors file contains one color per line and the fruits file contains one fruit per line, pasting them together would produce output like this:

```
$ paste colors fruits
red     grape
green   apple
blue    banana
yellow  melon
$
```

See Table 10.12 for other standard properties of the paste command.

Table 10.12 Other Properties of the *paste* Command

Property	See page
Allows relative and absolute pathname arguments	70
Changes only the output, not the file	111

Property	See page
Allows a list of filenames and filename wildcards	292
Allows output to be piped or redirected	116

Merging Sorted Files Based on a Join Field

The join command enables you to merge data from a line in one file with data from a corresponding line in a second file. The corresponding line is determined by finding a line with a matching *join* field. Both files must be in sorted order. You can designate which field is the join field, and that field number can be different between the two files. You can designate what data will be extracted from each file. Here is an example.

How Useful Is join?

Some UNIX books imply that you can implement a whole relational database with join. Other UNIX books don't mention join at all. I find that join is useful in some cases for merging data from different files. Because join is very limited, however, I would use awk or perl to query and write reports from data files.

A friend of mine was studying the stock market. He joined a service that would send him the average stock prices each day in a file. He wanted to put these small files together into one large history file that would show him at a glance whether a particular stock value was rising or falling over time. Here is an example file for day1. It just has three made-up stocks:

```
ABC     2 1/8
DEF    24 5/8
GHI     6 3/8
```

This is the file for day2:

```
ABC     2 3/8
BCD    12 2/8
DEF    22 7/8
GHI     6 5/8
```

This is the file for day3:

```
ABC     2 5/8
BCD    14 3/8
DEF    22 5/8
```

You can see that in day2, my friend gained a new stock, BCD. In day3, he lost stock GHI. Line 3 of each file is not always the same stock; therefore, the paste command cannot be used to combine these files. This is a job for the UNIX join command. In this example, the stock name was used as the join field:

```
$ join -t'   ' -a1 -a2 day1 day2
ABC    2 1/8    2 3/8
BCD   12 2/8
DEF   24 5/8   22 7/8
GHI    6 3/8    6 5/8
$
```

In the preceding example, -t enabled my friend to specify the field separator. In this case, a tab separates the stock name from its average value in each file. Therefore, a tab has been indicated after the -t option to join. -a1 and -a2 mean to include all lines from file 1 and from file 2. Otherwise, only lines whose join field value appears in both files will be listed. In this example, stock BCD is listed only in file 2, so it would not have been included in the join output if -a2 was not specified:

```
$ join -t'   ' -a1 -a2 day1 day2 | join -t'   ' -a1 -a2 - Âday3
ABC    2 1/8    2 3/8    2 5/8
BCD   12 2/8   14 3/8
DEF   24 5/8   22 7/8   22 5/8
GHI    6 3/8    6 5/8
$
```

In the preceding example, the joined output of day1 and day2 was joined to day3. Notice how the output of one join command can be piped to another join command if that join command lists dash (-) as one of its filenames to indicate standard input.

To handle cases in which the join field is not the first field on each line, add the -j option to join. Follow -j with the field number of the join field in each file. For example:

```
join -j 3 file1 file2
```

To handle files where the join field is not the same field number between the two files, use -j followed by *n m*—where *n* is 1 or 2 for files 1 or 2, and *m* is the field within that file to use as the join field—as shown here:

```
join -j1 2 -j2 4 file1 file2
```

In this example, the join field is field 2 in file 1, but it is field 4 in file 2.

To display only certain fields for each line of output from join, use the -o option, followed by a space separated list of n.m entries, where n is 1 or 2 for file1 or file2, and where .m specifies the mth field in that file, as follows:

```
join -j1 2 -j2 4 -o 1.1 2.3 2.5 file1 file2
```

The preceding example displays only three fields per line of output, as controlled by the -o option:

```
1.1 means display field 1 in file1 first.
2.3 means display field 3 in file2 next.
means display field 5 in file2 next (and last).
```

Splitting a File into Multiple Smaller Files

Sometimes it is useful to be able to split a file into smaller files. If a file will not fit on a disk, for example, you could split the file into smaller files that would each fit on a disk. As another example, when using cu to dial into another UNIX system, you can put and take text files between systems. Because there is no error checking, noisy phone lines can result in the destination file being corrupted. In this situation, I have had good success by splitting the file into several smaller files and then transmitting them separately. Using the cat command, it is simple to reconstitute the original file by concatenating the smaller files.

Splitting a File into Equal-Length Pieces

To split one text file into a group of files, each containing 1000 lines from the original file, enter the following:

```
split filename
```

For example, the following code:

```
$ split report7
```

would create the following files:

```
xaa   xab   xac   xad
```

The first three files, xaa through xac, would each contain 1,000 lines from the original file. The last file, xad, would probably contain less than 1,000 lines because it gets whatever lines are left over.

You can also specify the number of lines to put into each segment and a prefix to use for the segment name:

```
split -1500 report7 report7-
```

This command would create the following:

```
report7-aa   report7-ab   report7-ac
```

report7-aa and report7-ab would each contain 1,500 lines, and report7-ac would contain the lines left.

To re-create the original file from the segments, use the `cat` command with the asterisk (*) filename generation wildcard, covered in Chapter 11, "Generating and Using File Lists." For example:

```
cat report7-* > bigfile
```

The preceding command concatenates—that is, combines—all files whose names start with `report7-` and saves the reconstituted result in a file called `bigfile`. If other files begin with the prefix `report7-` but are not segments of the large file, you can use a more specific wildcard pattern to avoid them, such as the following:

```
cat report7-a[a-c] > bigfile
```

This command concatenates only these three files, even if other `report7-` files exist in the directory:

```
report7-aa    report7-ab    report7-ac
```

Splitting a File by Section Headings

The `csplit` command enables you to split a file into segments based on a keyword found at the start of each segment:

```
csplit -f parts report7 '/Research/' '/Proposal/' '/Summary/'
```

This command reads from file `report7` and creates these subfiles of different lengths:

- `parts00`: Text in `report7` before "`Research`"
- `parts01`: Text starting at "`Research`" and ending just before "`Proposal`"
- `parts02`: Text starting at "`Proposal`" and ending just before "`Summary`"
- `parts03`: Text starting at "`Summary`" to the end of the file

Some versions of UNIX support a `split -b` option to split a binary file into sections whose size you specify as an argument to the -b option. -b400 would create 400 byte sections. -b400k would create sections of 400 kb, which equals 400*1024 bytes. -b400m would create sections of 400 mb or 400*1024*1024 bytes.

You may use regular expression wildcards (as described in Chapter 18, "Searching for Lines in a File or Pipeline") as part of your keyword. The −f option enables you to define the prefix for each subfile name. Note that the suffixes are numeric (00, 01, 02) in contrast to the split command, where they are letters. If the -f and prefix are omitted, the default file prefix will be the letter *x*.

If each section starts with the same keyword, you can add a repeat count in braces ({}), like this:

```
$ csplit -k report7 '/Chapter/' '{99}'
{99} - out of range
$
```

Because -f was not used to specify a segment prefix, the following files will be created by the previous command:

- x00: Text in report7 before the first chapter
- x01: Text from first chapter, ending just before the second chapter
- x02: Text from second chapter, ending just before the third chapter

And so on.

In the previous example, replace report7 with your desired filename. Replace "Chapter" with the keyword found in your file in the first line of each section. You may use regular expression wildcards (as described in Chapter 18) as part of your keyword.

{99} says to use the previous keyword to look for 99 segments. Use a number larger than the real number of sections so that you don't have to determine the exact number before you run this command. In that case, ignore the out of range error that will result because 99 sections are not found. Use the -k option to keep the subfiles, even though 99 segments were not found.

chapter

11

Generating and Using File Lists

Steve "Mor" Moritsugu

Tip for Beginners

Don't start this chapter until you are comfortable with the basic file commands in Chapters 7, "Listing and Finding Directories and Files"; 8, "Displaying and Printing Files and Pipelines"; and 9, "Copying, Moving, Renaming, Removing, or Linking Files." This chapter augments those file commands by teaching you how to easily specify lists of files to process. This chapter gives rules to help you understand and use wildcards to generate these file lists. The rules are given in order of usefulness. Stop reading just before you reach the section "Allowing Any Characters in Certain Pattern Positions (?)." At that point, you will have learned many rules for handling the asterisk (*) wildcard, which is the most powerful and most useful one. After you have gained some practical experience with those rules, then come back to this chapter and learn the question mark (?) and the remaining wildcards in this chapter, as needed.

Using Filename Generation Wildcards

Most of the file commands can work with one or more files. For example, file commands can work with the following:

- Single files
- Several files
- Hundreds of files
- Tens of thousands of files (This is, of course, more difficult.)

As always, UNIX can increase productivity. In this case, UNIX provides a way to enter a very long series of filenames to a command by using a very short sequence of keystrokes. The user can enter within any command one or more pattern words, and the shell will replace each pattern with a list of all filenames that match that pattern. A pattern word is any word that contains one of the wildcard characters shown in Table 11.1. Each of these wildcards will be covered in the following sections.

Table 11.1 Filename Generation Wildcard Characters

Character	Description
*	Matches zero or more of any characters
?	Matches any one character
[. . .]	Matches a single occurrence of any of the alternative characters enclosed in brackets
[! . . .]	Matches any one character except those enclosed in brackets
Exception:	None of the above wildcards will match a slash (/) or a leading period

Generating Names That Start with, End with, or Contain a Pattern

For starters, this chapter examines the asterisk (*) wildcard, which is both the most powerful and the easiest to understand of the wildcards—and hence the one most commonly used. Consider this example:

```
rm report*
```

Here, `rm` is the UNIX command to remove (that is, delete) one or more files. `report*` is a pattern word because it contains one of the three possible wildcard characters given in Table 11.1. Before the command begins to execute, the shell recomposes the command, replacing the pattern word with a list of all existing filenames that match the pattern.

Where Does the Term *Wildcard* Come From?

In card games, if deuces happen to be wild and you are dealt a deuce, you can use that wildcard as if it were any card in the deck. A wildcard has a special meaning beyond its face value. In the UNIX shell, the same applies—some characters have a special meaning beyond their face value. These are called *metacharacters* or *wildcards*.

From Table 11.1, you can see that asterisk (*) matches zero or more of any characters. Therefore, `report*` is a pattern that matches all existing filenames that begin with `report` and are followed by zero or more of any characters. Table 11.2 shows filenames that do match this pattern and would be removed. It also shows files that do not match the pattern and explains why the pattern does not apply.

Table 11.2 Using *rm report*

Files That Would Be Removed by `rm report*`

report	report2	reports	reporters
reportacme	report.acme	report-98.01.15	

Files That Would Not Be Removed by `rm report*`

Filename	Reason Pattern Does Not Apply
Report	Uppercase *R* does not match the pattern
98report	Filename does not start with the word *report*
reprot.acme	Report is misspelled in this name

Take a look at another example:

```
rm acme*
```

This command removes all files whose name starts with *acme*. Here is how the shell processes that command:

1. The shell sees the asterisk (*) wildcard. It removes the word that contains the wildcard and replaces it with a list of files that match the pattern. This process is called shell substitution. It is also called preprocessing because it is done by the shell before the command is processed and executed.

2. If no files match the pattern, the shell leaves the wildcard pattern in the command.

3. The shell starts the rm command running as a process. The rm command finds the list of files substituted in step 1 as the arguments it is supposed to remove, and it then does so. The rm command never sees the wildcard pattern unless no files are found to match the pattern, as in step 2.

UNIX Avoids Using the Word *Wildcard*

Standard UNIX documentation often goes to great lengths to avoid the word *wildcard*. The documentation calls these things such as filename generation pattern characters, normal shell argument syntax, or shell pattern metacharacters. I think the term *wildcard* is apt and easier to grasp, so I use it in this book.

The preceding procedure can be modified slightly to remove all files that end with a pattern or that contain a pattern. To use the asterisk wildcard as shown in Table 11.3, you should learn three useful phrases. The wording of the phrase tells you whether the asterisk (*) should come before, after, or on both sides of the pattern.

Table 11.3 Asterisk (*) Filename Wildcard Useful Phrases

Useful Phrase	Example	Description
Start with	rm acme*	Removes all filenames that start with the word *acme*
End with	rm *acme	Removes all filenames that end with the word *acme*
Contain	rm *acme*	Removes all filenames that contain the word *acme*

Checking Man Pages to See Whether File Lists and Wildcards Are Allowed

The shell preprocesses and expands all filename wildcard patterns into a list of matching files; however, not all commands can accept a list of files. For example, the following:

```
pwd report*
```

does not make any sense because pwd just displays the current directory and does not expect any following arguments on the command line. Similarly,

```
cd report*
```

does not make any sense if several directories all start with the word *report* because you can change to only one directory at a time.

The UNIX man command (online manual) gives extensive information on how to use each UNIX command, including syntax (that is, how to correctly put together the elements of the command). Table 11.4 lists the syntax for several commands to illustrate how file lists are documented in the man pages.

Table 11.4   How Man Pages Indicate File Lists

Command Syntax from Man	Description (Not in Man Page)
head [-count] [file ...]	Displays the beginning lines of a list of files
sort [-cmu] ... [files]	Sorts the contents of a list of files
tail [+/-[number][lbc] [-f]] [file]	Displays the ending lines of the given single file
tr [-cds] [string1 [string2]]	Translates characters from std input to std output
cp file1 file2	Copies file1 to file2
cp files directory	Copies list of files to a directory

In this table, ignore the command options such as -count or -cmu, and focus for now on how filenames are specified to these commands. Notice that the head and sort commands both allow a list of files to be specified, but one case uses *file* and the other case uses *files* to indicate that one or more files are allowed. The tail command shown allows only a single file. The tr command does not allow any filenames at all. The cp command has two modes: The first mode copies a single file to another name; the second mode shown copies a list of files to a directory. Commands can vary in this regard from one type of UNIX system to another. Therefore, check the man pages for the system you are using to see whether a particular command allows a file list, a single file, or no files at all.

SEE ALSO

➤ *For more information on man pages, see page 88*

Appendix A, "UNIX Commands," contains a capsule summary of how to use each command and where information about aspects of that command are described in this book. From the appendix, here are the first two lines of the sdiff and sort commands:

`sdiff`: Show text file differences side by side

usage: `sdiff file1 file2`

`sort`: Sort file or datastream

usage: `sort options [list-of-files]`

Notice that `sdiff` does not allow a list of files, so wildcard patterns would not be used in an `sdiff` command. Notice that `sort` does allow a list of files, which could be composed by using one or more wildcard patterns. The brackets (`[...]`) under `sort` usage indicates that the list of files is optional, meaning that zero or more filenames may be supplied.

Reducing Typing of Long Filenames

The asterisk (*) wildcards can be useful when you encounter very long filenames. Older versions of UNIX were often limited to 14 character filenames, but current versions of UNIX generally allow filenames to be hundreds of characters long. Assume, for example, that the current directory contains these five files:

- `inventory-after-special-order`

- `pricelist`

- `reports-in-old-format`

- `sales-Jan-1997-to-Dec-1997-adjusted-for-commissions`

- `security.memo`

Test Your Wildcard Pattern First

Before you use a wildcard pattern to delete or take any action on a file or group of files, test your pattern first like this:

`echo sales*`

The `echo` command will display the matching filenames so you can check if the correct files are matched. If you test your pattern using `ls` instead of `echo`, here are some useful `ls` options to include:

`ls -dCF sales*`

`-d` prevents useless output in case you match a directory name. `-C` outputs in columns and `-F` appends a character to show you the function of each file.

If you want to remove the sales file, the asterisk (*) wildcard can save you a lot of typing, as in the following:

`rm sales*`

However, you cannot shorten the command to this:

```
rm s*
```

This would remove more than just the sales file.

You can use any wildcards as a shortcut for a long filename, even wildcards that will be introduced in the following sections.

Filename Wildcards Not Allowed in Bourne Shell Redirection

In the Bourne shell, you cannot use wildcards as a shortcut for filenames used in redirecting standard input, standard output, or standard error.

In the following example, there is already a long filename that ends in *list*, so you attempt to use the asterisk (*) wildcard to avoid typing the whole name:

```
ls > *list      # bad idea
```

This is a bad idea because the Bourne shell will not substitute wildcard patterns after redirection symbols such as the following:

```
> filename       >> filename    2> filename     2>> filename
< filename
```

The previous example saves the output of ls in a file called *list, which is not desirable. Any filenames that contain special characters, such as an asterisk, are very difficult to access and very dangerous to delete.

The Korn shell does not have this problem, so wildcards can be used to reduce typing in redirection.

SEE ALSO

➤ *For more information on redirection, see page 112*

➤ *For more information on how to use quoting to access filenames that contain special characters, see page 127*

Ignoring Directories in Your File List

File lists generated by the asterisk (*) wildcard (and the other wildcards discussed in this chapter) can include regular files, directories, device node files, and so on. All filenames that match the pattern are included in the list, regardless of the type of file. If the command cannot process that type of file, it will report an error for that file and will continue processing the list:

```
$ rm abc*
rm: abcrdr: is a directory
rm: abc25: is a directory
$
```

In the preceding example, the asterisk-generated list included two directory names. rm deleted all the regular files whose filenames matched the pattern given. rm also output error messages for the two directories, indicating that it did not process them. In general, I just ignore these directory errors because I usually use wildcard patterns to process a list of text or data files. The error messages simply tell me what was not processed in case I want to take further action on them.

Making One File List from Multiple Patterns

One file list can be generated by more than one wildcard pattern, as shown here:

```
rm acme* report*
```

In this example, two wildcard patterns are separated by a space, making up one list of files to be removed. Any filenames that start with the word *acme* and any filenames that start with the word *report* will be in the one list to be removed.

Be aware that multiple lists may generate the same filename more than once, such as the following:

```
lp acme* *.c
```

In the preceding example, the lp command is used to print on the system printer. This command is given a list of files made by two wildcard patterns: all files that start with *acme* and all files that end in *.c*. Note that any files that both start with *acme* and end in *.c* will be in the lp file list twice and thus will be printed twice. (Later in this chapter, you learn how backquotes [`] can resolve this problem.)

In a later section, as you encounter backquotes (`) and other wildcards, such as question mark (?) and brackets ([]), keep in mind that one file list can be made by combining smaller lists generated by any of these techniques.

SEE ALSO
➤ *For more information on the* lp *command, see page 223*

Including Hidden Files in File Lists

Filenames that begin with a period are called hidden files because the ls command normally hides them (that is, ignores them) unless you add the -a option to ls to show all files. Hidden files are usually system files and are hidden so that they will not be displayed or affected when the user lists or processes data and application files.

Wildcards also follow this convention by ignoring hidden files unless they are specifically indicated in the wildcard pattern, for example:

```
rm *-sav
```

This command would remove any nonhidden files that end in -sav. However, . acme-sav ends in -sav but would not be removed because a leading asterisk (*) cannot match a leading period in the filename.

To remove all hidden files that end in -sav, use this command:

```
rm .*-sav
```

This command removes only files that start with a period (.) and end in -sav. To remove both hidden and nonhidden files that end in -sav, use this command:

```
rm   *-sav   .*-sav
```

This command uses two wildcard patterns to create one list of files to be removed. The extra spaces have been added just for clarity.

Generating Lists of Files in Other Directories

You have seen that the asterisk can match zero or more of any character except for a leading period. There is a second exception: The asterisk cannot match a slash (/) directory separator. This is a good rule; otherwise commands such as the following

```
rm *-sav
```

would comb the whole system, looking for files ending in -sav to remove. Because asterisk (*) cannot match a slash (/), the list is restricted to just files in the current directory that match the pattern.

You can explicitly generate filenames in directories other than the current directory by using either absolute or relative pathnames (see Table 11.5)

Table 11.5 Using File Lists Not Necessarily in Current Directory

UNIX Command	Description
rm *-sav	Removes any files in the current directory ending in -sav
rm /tmp/*-sav	Removes any files in /tmp ending in -sav
rm /tmp/*/*-sav	Removes any files in any subdirectory of /tmp ending in -sav
rm /*-sav	Removes any files in the root directory ending in -sav
rm */*-sav	Removes any files in any subdirectory of the current directory ending in -sav
rm *-sav */*-sav	Removes any files in the current directory or any subdirectory of the current directory ending in -sav

Later in this chapter, as you encounter other wildcards such as the question mark (?) and brackets ([]), keep in mind that they can generate file lists in other directories just as the asterisk (*) does.

Allowing Any Characters in Certain Pattern Positions

The question mark (?) wildcard matches any single character except for a leading period (.) or a slash (/). It enables you to specify exactly how many character positions to allow before, after, or in between other pattern elements. For example:

```
rm report-?
```

This command removes any filenames that begin with *report-* and that are followed by exactly one character (see Table 11.6).

Table 11.6 *rm report-?*

Files That Would Be Removed by rm report-?

report-3

report-7

report-d

report-M

report-:

Files That Would Not Be Removed by rm report-?

Filename	Reason Pattern Does Not Apply
report	No dash (-) after report
report-	No character after dash
report-33	Too many characters after dash
acme.report-4	Does not start with report

As with the asterisk (*), the ? wildcard cannot match a leading period or a slash (/).

Specifying Fixed-Length Filenames

The question mark wildcard is also useful for situations in which you want to access all files whose names are an exact number of characters. For example, the following command deletes all three-character filenames that start with the letter *x*:

```
rm x??
```

The following command deletes all filenames that start with the word report and are followed by any two-character suffix:

```
rm report??
```

Specifying Patterns at Certain Positions in the Filename

Use the question mark filename wildcard to specify that a pattern occurs at a specific position within the filename. The positions or column numbers can be counted from the start or end of the filename or can be relative to a pattern:

```
rm ?a*    # remove all non-hidden files in the current directory where
          # the letter a is the second character
rm ??x*   # remove all non-hidden files in the current directory where
          # the letter x is the third character
rm ??x    # remove all non-hidden files in the current directory where
          # the letter x is the third and last character
rm *k?    # remove all non-hidden files in the current directory where the
          # letter k is the second to the last character
rm *k??*  # remove all non-hidden files in the current directory where the
          # letter k is followed by at least two more characters
```

Specifying Allowed Characters in Pattern Positions

Square brackets enable you to specify a range of alternatives for that character position within the filename, except for a leading period (.) or a slash (/). Assume, for example, that more than 20 filenames begin with report-, followed by a single character, and you want to remove just the following seven files:

```
report-1  report-2  report-3  report-4  report-5  report-m  report-v
```

You can accomplish that by using the bracket wildcard ([ ]) as in this example:

```
rm report-[1-5mv]
```

The square brackets enable you to specify the character alternatives you want to allow for this position within the filename. A dash between two characters within the brackets allows all characters in that inclusive range. Do not include any spaces or commas within the brackets unless they are character alternatives in the filename itself.

Ranges

Within square brackets, a dash between two characters indicates a range. Ranges should always go from smaller to larger: [a-z] and not [z-a]. Ranges should always stay within the following three types: lowercase letters, uppercase letters, or digits. Don't mix these types in one range. Don't use these: [0-z] [:-9].

Test Your UNIX Skills

Compose a UNIX command to delete all files with names that start with *acme* followed by only two digits, where those two digits fall in the range from 23 to 67 inclusive.

Answer on next page.

What if `report-3` did not exist? There is no problem, and no error message would be generated by the preceding command. These wildcard patterns select from the existing files just those filenames that match the wildcard pattern, as in the following.

```
rm report-[4m51-3v]
```

The preceding example is equivalent to the previous example. It is not good practice to jumble up your alternatives in this way, but it does illustrate that the alternatives can be listed in any order. Ranges using dash (-) must be specified from low to high. For example, specify `b-g`, not `g-b`. Notice that 51 in the brackets in the preceding example means that both a 5 and a 1 are alternatives for this character position in the filename. This pattern would *not* match `report-51` because the square brackets match only a single character from the alternatives, not multiple characters (see Table 11.7).

Table 11.7 *rm report-[1-5mv]*

Files That Would Be Removed by `rm report-[1-5mv]`

```
report-1
```

```
report-2
```

```
report-3
```

```
report-4
```

```
report-5
```

```
report-m
```

```
report-v
```

Files That Would Not Be Removed by `rm report-[1-5mv]`

Filename	Reason Pattern Does Not Apply
`report`	No dash after `report`
`report-`	No character after dash
`report-33`	Too many characters after dash
`report-6`	Number 6 is not one of the allowed alternatives
`report-x`	Character x is not one of the allowed alternatives
`acme.report-4`	Does not start with the word `report`

Answer to Test on Previous Page
```
rm acme2[3-9] acme[3-5][0-9] acme6[0-7]
```

An asterisk or question mark within square brackets would not be treated as wild-cards. It is not a good idea, however, to include asterisks or question marks as char-acters within filenames; therefore, you will usually never include them within square brackets.

If you want to include a dash as one of the alternatives, include it as the first or last character within the square brackets, as in the following. See Table 11.8 for other examples.

```
rm report-[a-g-]
```

Table 11.8 More Examples of the *[]* Wildcard

Wildcard Pattern	Description
`report[0-9]`	Matches `report` followed by one digit
`report[0-9][0-9]`	Matches `report` followed by two digits
`[A-Z]*`	Matches all files that start with a capital letter
`report[0-9][a-zA-Z]`	Matches `report` followed by a digit, followed by a letter in upper- or lowercase

As with the asterisk, the bracket wildcard cannot match a leading period or a slash.

Specifying Disallowed Characters in Pattern Positions

If the list of characters inside the square brackets begins with an exclamation point (!), any one character will match that wildcard except for the characters within the bracket list. For example:

```
rm acme[!2-5x].c
```

The pattern in this example removes any seven character filenames where all of the following are true:

- The first 4 characters are: acme
- The 5th character is anything except 2, 3, 4, 5, or x
- The 6th character is a period
- The 7th and last character is the letter c

See Table 11.9 for examples of filenames that do and do not match this pattern.

Table 11.9 *rm acme[!2-5x].c*

Files That Would Be Removed by `rm acme[!2-5x].c`

`acme1.c`

`acme6.c`

`acme9.c`

`acme-.c`

`acmea.c`

`acmeB.c`

`acmeX.c`

Files That Would Not Be Removed by `rm acme[!2-5x].c`

Filename	Reason Pattern Does Not Apply
`acme.c`	Needs one character after *acme* and before *.c*
`acme2.c`	Number 2 is specifically disallowed
`acme77.c`	Only one character is allowed between *acme* and *.c*
`acmex.c`	Character *x* is disallowed, but *X* (uppercase) is allowed
`acmeb.m`	Does not end in *.c*
`f-acme9.c`	Does not start with *acme*

Matching Hidden Versus Non-Hidden Files

Wildcards cannot match a leading period. The phrase "nonhidden" applies whenever a filename wildcard is found at the beginning of a pattern. The following command will delete all non-hidden files in the current directory whose filename ends with a 7:

```
rm *7
```

To delete all hidden files in the current directory whose filename ends with a 7, use this command:

```
rm .*7
```

To delete all files (both hidden and non-hidden) in the current directory whose filename ends with a 7, use two patterns to make one list:

```
rm *7 .*7     # extra spaces may be added for readability
```

If the wildcard is not at the start of the pattern, there is little need to specify hidden or non-hidden. The following command will delete all files whose filename starts with acme:

```
rm acme*
```

When describing this example, you do not need to specify hidden or non-hidden because only there are no hidden files that start with acme. Hidden files start with a period.

Wildcard Phrases: "Or More" or "At Least"

Any time you have an asterisk wildcard next to a pattern, you should add the words "at least" or "or more" to describe the pattern, as shown in these examples:

```
rm 7*    # delete all files that start with at least one seven
rm 7*    # delete all files that start with one or more sevens
rm *77   # delete all non-hidden files that end with at least two sevens
rm *77   # delete all non-hidden files that end with two or more sevens
```

In these examples, you should use the terms "or more" or "at least" because the asterisk wildcard can match more occurrences of the pattern. It would be incorrect to say that the first example just removes files that start with a single 7. Here is another example:

```
rm [0-9][0-9]*
    # delete all files that start with at least 2 digits
    # It is equally valid to say:
    # delete all files that start with 2 or more digits
```

In these examples, you do not need to add the term "nonhidden" because there are no hidden files that start with a digit. All hidden filenames start with a period (.).

Wildcard Phrases: In the Current Directory

If the wildcard pattern does not contain a slash (/), you should, when describing the files matched, include the phrase: in the current directory.

```
rm *77 # delete all non-hidden files in the current directory that
       # end with two or more sevens
```

Wildcards do not match a slash so directories must be specified explicitly if desired. In the following example, /tmp/doc is added to the wildcard pattern:

```
rm /tmp/doc/*77 # delete all non-hidden files in the /tmp/doc directory
                # that end with two or more sevens
```

Any absolute or relative directory can be included in the wildcard pattern:

```
rm /*77          # delete all non-hidden files in the root directory
                 # that end with two or more sevens
rm report/*77    # delete all non-hidden files in the report subdirectory
                 # of the current directory that end with two or more sevens
rm ../*77        # delete all non-hidden files in the parent directory
                 # of the current directory that end with two or more sevens
```

Matching Fixed Versus Variable Length Filenames

If the wildcard pattern does not contain an asterisk, it matches only filenames of a fixed length. You can calculate the length of filename a pattern will match by adding the number of characters in the pattern plus one for each ? wildcard or square bracket list:

```
lpr abc???       # matches only 6 character filenames
lpr m[a-z]?[0-9] # matches only 4 character filenames
```

The presence of one or more asterisks in the pattern indicates it will match variable length filenames, which means filenames of various lengths. You can calculate the minimum filename length matched by adding the number of characters in the pattern plus one for each ? or square bracket wildcard. This is the same formula given in the previous paragraph but it now computes the minimum length filename matched:

```
lpr *abc???       # matches filenames with 6 or more characters
lpr m[a-z]?[0-9]* # matches filenames with 4 or more characters
```

Turning Off Filename Generation

It is possible to turn off filename generation. This is usually needed only if you encounter filenames that actually contain an asterisk, a question mark, or brackets. You must be careful how you handle these files so that you don't process the filename as a wildcard pattern. You are strongly recommended not to create filenames that contain these characters, but you might encounter this situation anyway. For example, the following command creates a file named acme* if no files are found that start with acme:

```
vi acme*
```

Later, you may want to delete this file:

```
rm acme*    # no don't do this.
```

This example shows the wrong way to handle a filename with an imbedded wildcard. If you created any filenames that start with *acme*, they will also be deleted. You can turn off the wildcard by escaping it or quoting it (as covered in Chapter 4).

Any of the following commands will safely delete the file:

```
rm acme\*
rm "acme*"
rm 'acme*'
```

You can also turn off filename generation in the Bourne shell or Korn shell like this:

```
set -f
```

You can later turn it back on with this command:

```
set +f
```

Globbing and `noglob`

The capability of the shell to substitute a list of files in place of a filename generation wildcard pattern can be referred to as globbing. The C shell has an option called `noglob` that turns off this feature.

Handling the Error *arg list too long*

The shell processes the command line in a buffer that was several hundred characters long on older UNIX systems and that is several thousand characters long—or longer—on newer UNIX systems. If the wildcard pattern generates a file list that overflows the command-line buffer, it would be dangerous to execute this partial command or use a partial filename, so the shell aborts immediately, as in this example:

```
$ rm report*
rm: arg list too long
$
```

The UNIX standard is, "No news is good news," so the message from the `rm` command indicates a problem. In the preceding example, too many filenames begin with *report* and the shell's command-line buffer has overflowed; therefore, the shell will not allow the command to start. Some users mistakenly might think that the `rm` command removed some of the files that start with *report* before it got the error. They keep repeating the same command in hopes that the list will keep getting smaller and smaller until the command eventually succeeds, but it never does.

One workaround for this problem is to divide up the one command into several commands, each specifying a smaller group of files. For example:

```
rm report[a-m]*
rm report[n-z]*
rm report[!a-z]*
rm report
```

The remainder of this chapter discusses other ways of using file lists that do not use filename wildcards and therefore can be used whenever you get the `arg list too long` error.

Using Backquotes to Generate a List of Files

In addition to filename generation wildcards, backquotes are another (different) mechanism that you can use for many purposes, including generating a list of files for a command to use. The backquote (`` ` ``) is the "other" single quote and is more correctly called the grave accent.

Finding the Backquote (`` ` ``) Key on the Keyboard

The backquote is usually located on the same key as the tilde. The backquote (`` ` ``) slants from upper left down to lower right but is not as long as a backslash (\). Don't confuse it with the single quotation mark, also known as the apostrophe ('), which slants from upper right down to lower left, or that sometimes has no slant at all.

Use backquotes to use the standard output of a UNIX command or command sequence as part of another command. This technique is called *shell command substitution*. If you have a file called `flist` that contains a list of files that you want to remove, for example, you can remove all those files as follows:

```
rm `cat flist`
```

In this example, the list of files to remove is generated by the `cat` command in backquotes. It is essential that the command inside the backquotes output the list of files to standard output, as `cat` does in the example. If the files are not in the current directory, the list should contain a proper relative or absolute pathname for each file, for example, not just a basename.

These backquotes are another example of shell command-line substitution. The backquoted command is removed from the command line and is replaced by the output of the command within the backquotes. When the substitution is complete, the command (`rm`, in this case) is started to process its new command list.

Note that the following will not work:

```
cat flist | rm        # this won't work
```

`rm` does not read filenames from standard input; it works only with command-line argument filenames.

Multiple filenames generated by backquotes may be separated by a space or tab, or may even be output on separate lines, as the backquotes will convert each new line to a space. Backquotes can also solve the printing problem that could not be solved earlier by using just wildcard patterns. Assume that you want to print all files that either start with *acme* or end in a *.c*. Using multiple wildcard patterns—for example, lp acme* *.c—you saw that any files that started with *acme* and that ended in *.c* would be printed twice. That problem now can be solved by using backquotes:

```
lp `echo acme* *.c | sort | uniq`
```

In the preceding example, the echo command generates a list of files that start with *acme* or end in *.c*. This list is then piped to sort so that any duplicates will be put on adjoining lines. That result is then piped to uniq, which ignores any lines identical to a previous line—that is, it removes the duplicate lines. The backquotes then cause that list to become part of the lp command line, so the files will be printed with no duplicates.

Backquotes give you finer control over the file list generated than filename wildcards alone could do. Here is a command to remove all files that start with *acme* except for those acme files that end in -sav:

```
rm `echo acme* | grep -v '-sav$'`
```

Now analyze the parts of this command. echo acme* generates the list of all files that start with *acme*. grep -v '-sav$' uses regular expression syntax to display only lines that do not end in –sav; hence, grep removes any files from the file list that end in –sav. The backquotes then provide this generated list to the remove command.

SEE ALSO
➤ *For more information on the* cat *command, see page 210*
➤ *For more information on the* grep *command and regular expressions, see page 494*

If you are using the Korn shell, backquotes may be replaced by $(...), as in the following:

```
lp $(cat filelist)     # Korn shell only
```

For advanced users, this Korn shell syntax offers the ability to nest, which is difficult and limited using backquotes:

```
lp $(cat $(cat ptrfile))    # Korn shell only
```

This example will first cat ptrfile to get the filename that contains the list of files. It will then substitute those filenames on the lp command line so that they will be printed.

Handling the Backquotes Error *No Space*

If the backquotes generate a file list that is too long, the command can fail with error messages such as one of the following:

```
sh: no stack space
ksh: no space
```

Newer versions of UNIX seem to be capable of processing much longer backquotes lists than earlier UNIX versions. If using backquotes gets this No Space error, your list is too long. To solve the problem, go to the section "Using xargs to Process a List of Items (xargs)," later in this chapter.

Commands that Allow a List of Filenames and Filename Wildcards

An earlier section in this chapter showed how to interpret the man page for any UNIX command to see if the command allows:

- a list of filenames
- just two filenames
- just one filename
- no filenames

Filename generation wildcards, the main topic of this chapter, are usually only used with commands that allow a list of filename arguments on the command line.

An earlier section showed how to use a wildcard pattern as a short cut for a single long filename. This is useful, even if the command only accepts one or two filenames.

If the command does not accept any filenames on the command line, then you should not use any filename wildcards with this command.

The following example shows that several wildcard patterns and backquotes can be combined in one command:

```
lpr abc* `cat /tmp/flist` /data/archive/*acme[0-9] reports/*/[0-9]*
```

This example shows that one file list can be generated by several mechanisms (which are all covered earlier in this chapter):

- abc* generates all filenames that start with abc in the current directory.
- `cat /tmp/flist` adds to the list the contents of file /tmp/flist.
- /data/archive/*acme[0-9] adds to the list all nonhidden files in /data/archive whose filenames contain acme followed by a single digit. Notice how absolute and relative pathnames can be mixed in one list.
- reports/*/[0-9]* adds to the list any file whose name starts with a digit if found in any subdirectory of the reports subdirectory of the current directory. Here you are adding partial pathnames to the list.

Using *xargs* to Process a List of Items

So far in this chapter, you have used filename wildcards to generate file lists on the command line, but that technique can fail (remember the error arg list too long) if there are too many files that match the pattern. Backquotes can be used to generate file lists from a pipeline of UNIX commands, giving you much more control over the files in the list. However, backquotes also can fail if too many filenames are generated, especially on older UNIX systems. The xargs command can succeed where these other techniques failed.

Test Your UNIX Skills

lp *[0-9][0-9]

Use this command to print all (nonhidden) files whose name ends in two or more digits. Assume that this command fails with the error arg list too long. Compose an equivalent xargs command that will succeed. (Answer on next page.)

The xargs command can be used to process a list of files. It offers the same degree of control over the list that backquotes offer, and there is no limitation on the number of files it can process. When you have tens of thousands or millions of files to process, xargs can do the job.

This is the general syntax for using xargs to process a large number of files:

cmd1 | xargs cmd2

cmd1 is a complete UNIX command or pipeline that generates a list of files. These may be relative or absolute pathnames.

cmd2 is a partial UNIX command that expects a list of files to be entered on the command line. Enter the command name and any needed options, but omit the list of files. xargs will cause the command cmd2 to process all the files generated by cmd1.

Here is a simple example:

ls gl* | xargs lp

Here, the ls command will pipe a list of files whose names start with the letters gl. xargs will create and run one or more lp commands with the filenames it receives, like this:

```
lp gl101 gl102 gl103 gl104 gl105 gl106 gl107 gl108 gl109 gl110
lp gl111 gl112 gl113 gl120 gl121 gl122 gl123 gl125 gl130 gl138
lp gl206 gl207 gl315 gl317 gl527
```

> **Answer to Test on Previous Page**
> ```
> ls | grep '[0-9][0-9]$' | xargs lp
> ```

The xargs command creates and runs multiple lp commands so that there is no danger of creating a command line that is too long.

> **Use echo * Instead of ls on Linux**
> The ls command on Linux appends an asterisk to denote executable files and other such indicators to the filenames it outputs. If you pipe the output of ls to another command, these indicator letters will be taken as part of the filename and will prevent you from processing the files. You can use echo instead of ls to generate clean filenames on Linux or UNIX:
>
> echo * *is equivalent to* ls *
> echo gl* *is equivalent to* ls gl*

Here is an example of using xargs to solve the arg list too long problem:

```
$ cd /usr/fred
$ chmod a+r gl*
chmod:arg list too long
$ ls | grep '^gl' | xargs chmod a+r
```

In this example, you want to add read permission for everyone to all files in directory /usr/fred that start with gl. First, try using a filename generation wildcard (gl*). Because too many files match that pattern, you get the error arg list too long. The xargs command shown accomplishes the same objective and will never get the arg list too long error.

If you get the error arg list too long when using xargs in the preceding procedure, change xargs to the following:

```
xargs -n 20
```

This forces xargs to issue multiple commands if any one command uses a maximum of 20 arguments from standard input. This is usually needed only on Linux systems. The xargs command on commercial UNIX systems usually does not need the -n option because xargs automatically adjusts the number of arguments placed on the command line so that no one command ever gets the error arg list too long.

The difficult part of using xargs to solve the arg list too long problem is to use grep and regular expression wildcards (covered earlier in this chapter) to produce the same output as a filename generation wildcard. Table 11.10 shows some common filename wildcards and how to translate that to the equivalent `grep` with regular expressions.

Table 11.10 Filename Wildcard to Regular Expression Wildcard Conversion

Filename Wildcard	Equivalent Regular Expression Sequence
abc*	ls | grep '^abc'
*abc	ls | grep 'abc$'
abc	ls | grep 'abc'
abc[0-9]	ls | grep '^abc[0-9]$'
[!A-Z]??.c	ls | grep '^[^A-Z]..\.c'

The `xargs` `-n` option also enables you to accept commands that allow only a single filename argument, such as `tail` or `compress` (on some versions of UNIX).

In the first example that follows, `xargs` with `tail` enables you to see the ending lines of a number of files. In the second example, you can `compress` a group of files, even if `compress` allows only a single filename on your version of UNIX:

```
ls gl* | xargs -n 1 tail | less
ls gl* | xargs -n 1 compress
```

xargs can be used for lists of things other than filenames. In the next example, xargs is used to handle a list of user names. Assume that userlist is a file that contains the names of users. Some of those names might be email addresses. Also assume that sendusers is a script that sends email to each user listed on the command line. xargs can be used (as shown here) to receive the list of users on standard input and will then generate and execute one or more sendusers commands with usernames on the command line.

```
cat userlist | xargs sendusers
```

SEE ALSO

➤ *For more information on piping, see page 114*

➤ *For more information on command-line arguments, see page 82*

part

III

SYSTEM ADMINISTRATION

chapter

12

Steve "Mor" Moritsugu

Installing UNIX at Home

General UNIX installation issues

Installing SCO UnixWare 7 at home

Installing Sun Solaris 7 at home

Tip for Beginners

Two of the most advanced, sophisticated UNIX operating systems available today (UnixWare 7 and Solaris 7) are very inexpensive for you to load on a home PC for non-commercial purposes. There is no better way to become a UNIX expert than to install, administer, and use your own UNIX or Linux system. This is not an easy job but this chapter will help you understand the installation issues, obtain the software, and install it.

Understanding General UNIX Installation Issues

Installing UNIX on a computer is a complex process. In the old days (through the mid 1990s), UNIX would be installed only by system administrators in the computer department with years of UNIX experience. The advent of powerful home PCs and Linux has changed all that. Thousands of enthusiasts have installed Linux by themselves on home computers. Today, even the foremost versions of commercial UNIX can be installed on a home PC.

This chapter shows you how to install these two versions of commercial UNIX on a home PC:

- UnixWare 7 from SCO
- Solaris 7 from Sun Microsystems

Installing Linux Is Not Covered

Although I have installed a number of Linux systems and think this is a great product that has re-energized traditional UNIX, the focus of this book is UNIX. Other books focus on Linux, so I have left Linux installation to them.

Both these versions of commercial UNIX can be ordered for noncommercial home use. There is usually a charge for the media, ranging from $20 to $60. Both are called "free UNIX" because the license fee (which is often $1,000 and up) has been totally waived. It may sound incongruous to pay $20 for something that is free, but it is more correct to say that you pay $20 for the media and also get a free UNIX license.

This chapter shows you some of the problems that I ran into and how I solved them, but I cannot cover every situation that you might run into. Many users will find that commercial UNIX cannot be installed on a home computer because it is incompatible with one or more components. Sometimes the install will fail without giving any clue as to the problem. Yet the same machine will run Windows or Linux successfully.

Be prepared for a difficult road when you install UNIX, but you will certainly learn a lot, even if you are not successful.

Who Should Not Install UNIX

If you meet the following criteria, you should not try to install UNIX at home:

- You have only one computer, and it was a major investment.
- You did not get any media with your computer, so you cannot reinstall Windows or any applications.
- You have never unscrewed the case of your computer and looked inside.

Warning: Be Ready to Reinstall Everything

Do not try to install UNIX on your computer unless you are capable of reinstalling Windows and all your programs and data. You must have good backups that are not on the hard disk and the media needed to reinstall Windows, Office, and other programs.

It is very difficult to run both Windows and UNIX on the same computer. There is a good chance that you will have to totally reload both Windows and UNIX more than once before you get everything working. The profile just given shows someone who should definitely not try to install UNIX at home.

On the other hand, this is the perfect candidate to load UNIX at home:

- You have several computers and spare parts that you put together in different combinations.
- You have upgraded components in your computer.
- You have reloaded Windows more than once.

PC Partitions

The PC architecture allows the hard disk to be divided into areas called *partitions*. There can be up to four of these partitions, and each partition can hold a different operating system. Here is an example 4GB disk drive with four different partitions, each with a different operating system:

- Partition 1: Windows 98 (C:)
- Partition 2: Extended partition with logical Windows NT drives D: and E:
- Partition 3: UnixWare 7 UNIX
- Partition 4: Solaris 7 UNIX

UNIX-only Systems Can Ignore Partitions

If you want only UNIX on your system and not Windows, you can skip all this partition stuff. UNIX will happily install itself on the entire disk, overwriting what was there before. If you want both Windows and UNIX on the same system, then make sure you read about partitions carefully!

UNIX partitions do not have drive letters as Windows partitions do. The previous disk contains four different operating systems, but only one operating system can run at any time. The partition containing the running operating system is called the Active partition.

If you want to run a different operating system, make its partition the Active partition and then shut down. When you reboot, the operating system in the new Active partition will come up and run.

Windows 95 contains a utility called fdisk that enables you to view and change these disk partitions. When you run it, you will see these options:

1. Create DOS partition or Logical DOS drive

2. Set active partition

3. Delete partition or Logical DOS Drive

4. Display partition information

If you run option 4, you will usually see that the Windows partition(s) take up the entire drive:

```
                Display Partition Information


Current fixed disk drive: 1


Partition  Status   Type    Volume Label   Mbytes   System   Usage
  C: 1              PRI DOS                  4134    FAT16    100%



Total disk space is  4134 Mbytes (1 Mbyte = 1048576 bytes)
```

Notice in this fdisk output that the Windows partition 1 contains 4134MB, which matches the total disk space. The Usage column shows that 100% of the disk space is in this partition. There may be plenty of available blocks within the partition to create new Windows files. The 100% usage indicates that Windows controls 100% of the disk space, whether the blocks are in use or available. Therefore, this system has no available partition space to load UNIX.

Take a look at this fdisk output that you need before you can load UNIX:

```
                    Display Partition Information

Current fixed disk drive: 1


Partition  Status   Type     Volume Label  Mbytes   System   Usage
  C: 1              PRI DOS                  2047    FAT16     50%



Total disk space is  4134 Mbytes (1 Mbyte = 1048576 bytes)
```

In this example, partition 1 uses only 50% of the total disk capacity. The remaining half of the drive is unallocated. This is what you need to install UNIX. UNIX will create its own partition in the unallocated disk space.

Getting Windows to Give Up Disk Space

When you purchase a Windows system, 100% of the partition space is allocated—otherwise, it would be wasted. Getting Windows to give up disk space is very difficult.

One way to have Windows use only part of the disk is to totally reinstall it from scratch. You must have all the necessary media to install Windows and any applications, such as Office. You also must have the required license certificates.

These are the steps needed to install Windows so that it does not use the entire disk:

Warning: Format Wipes Out Everything

This is a drastic procedure. Everything will be wiped out and then everything must be reloaded again. You may find that you don't have the correct media or that it has gone bad. You may not be able to find your licenses. You may not be able to restore your programs and data. There is great risk in this procedure!

1. Back up all programs and data.
2. Run fdisk and create a Windows partition that does not use the entire disk. Make that partition active.
3. Use the format program to format that partition. (This must be done before you install Windows.)
4. Install Windows. If it gives you a choice between installing in the Active partition or using the whole disk, choose just the Active partition.

5. Reinstall all applications. Reload all data and programs.

This procedure is quite drastic and difficult. Fortunately, there are alternatives. You can buy a product called Partition Magic that will enable you to reduce the size of the Windows partition so that you can install UNIX. This does not require that you reinstall Windows. Another freely available utility, called FIPS, also allows you to reduce an existing disk partition. Still, take suitable precautions when using such products.

1024-Cylinder Limit

The PC architecture will have problems if you want to boot up and run an operating system whose partition resides above cylinder 1024. The standard way to solve this is to pretend that your disk has fewer cylinders than it really does and more heads. As you saw, you are mapping the cylinders to logical cylinders that are much larger; hence, there will be fewer than 1024 of them, even on a large disk drive.

> **Warning: Turning These on Wipes Out Your System!**
> If you turn on LBA or the greater than 1GB SCSI option, you change how the disk is laid out into cylinders, as well as all the block addressing. This can cause irreparable damage to any programs and data on the system. Plan to reinstall everything if you change these options.

On IDE disks, make sure that the LBA option is on to do this mapping.

On SCSI disks, turn on Extended BIOS Translation for DOS Drives greater than 1GB. This is usually an option in the SCSI setup utility.

If these are not on, you might load UNIX into the partition and then find that it will not boot up.

If these options are not on, you must format your disk after turning them on. If Windows was on the system, you must then create the Windows partition and reinstall Windows. Then install UNIX into the unallocated partition space.

Open Your Machine and Write Down Any Markings

Before you install UNIX, you must know something about each of the devices in your computer, especially these:

- Video graphics card
- Ethernet card (if any)

- Modem card (if any)
- Sound card (if any)

The Dangers of Opening the Box

The plastic outside box of your computer is called the chassis. Follow the documentation that came with your machine to open it up. Make sure the system is shutdown and all power cords are disconnected before you open the box. Don't touch the computer if the air is dry and you feel static shocks when you touch any metal object because a static shock can damage your computer. If you have never opened a computer before, ask someone who is knowledgeable to help you.

Shutdown, power off, and open up the machine and check these cards carefully for vendor names and model numbers, and write down all chip numbers that you see. You will see an example of where this is useful in the Solaris install section where I had to choose the type of video graphics card from a list.

Avoid CD-ROM Drives Through Sound Cards

To install UNIX at home, you must have a CD-ROM drive. You can either use one of the following:

- IDE CD-ROM (ATAPI)
- SCSI CD-ROM

Avoid CD-ROM drives that connect through a sound card to your system.

UNIX Versus Linux

If you are going to do all this work to load another operating system on your home computer, should it be commercial UNIX or Linux?

First, remember that you do not have to limit yourself to one or the other. You can create multiple partitions and load both on the same computer.

If you use Solaris or UnixWare 7 at work, you have a strong reason to load the same operating system at home. You will learn a great deal that will directly benefit you at work, and you will be able to run programs at home in exactly the same environment as at work.

You may find that having experience with commercial UNIX gives you an added plus on your resumé when job hunting.

That being said, remember that the primary thrust of commercial UNIX is not the home/hobbyist market. For example, Zip drives are quite useful at home. Commercial UNIX systems need to back up gigabytes of data, so you often find that they offer no built-in support for 100MB or 250MB Zip drives. Linux is more oriented to home low-cost computer equipment, and it supports Zip drives quite nicely.

Take a look at some comparisons between Solaris 7 and UnixWare 7. You can download StarOffice from the Sun Web site to run on Solaris 7. This provides Microsoft-compatible word processing, spreadsheet, presentations, and so on. UnixWare 7 runs on both IDE and SCSI and is capable of autodetecting and using a wider variety of video graphics cards than Solaris 7.

Installing SCO UnixWare 7 at Home

Santa Cruz Operation (SCO) now owns the rights to the UNIX source code. The company has modified AT&T SVR4 UNIX to produce SVR5, which has been released as UnixWare 7. SCO is working closely with IBM to add AIX features to this system. The company plans for this operating system to be one of the first that can run on the new Intel 64 bit processors.

SCO also created and maintains an earlier version of UNIX called OpenServer 5. This version of UNIX runs on large numbers of Pentium PCs in businesses today.

Both OpenServer 5 UNIX and UnixWare 7 are available from SCO's Web site for home, educational, and noncommercial use. The license is free, although there is a charge for the CD-ROM media.

Ordering UnixWare 7

To order UnixWare 7, first go to the SCO Web site: `http://www.sco.com`. As you connect to the home page, the tag says "SCO: Defining the Future of UNIX."

This reminds you that SCO controls the future changes to the UNIX source code. Click the Buy or Register link and then the Special Offers link, in that order.

If you want to read more about the features of SCO UnixWare 7.1, you can click the Fact Sheet (new) Release 7.1 link. Also on this page, you can read about technical support available for the free UNIX by clicking the Special Support Offer for Free UNIX Customers $99 for 99 Days! link.

Next click the Obtain Your Personal/Noncommercial License at Any Time Free of Charge link. This takes you to a page where you are asked to choose a product to license:

- UnixWare 7
- Free SCO UnixWare (2)
- SCO OpenServer Release 5.0.5
- SCO OpenServer Release 5.0.4
- SCO Merge 4.0

Select UnixWare 7 and click Continue.

Next you will be asked to fill out your name, address, and other information. Click Submit when you are finished.

Very quickly, your noncommercial license information will be displayed like this:

```
SCO CERTIFICATE OF LICENSE
Steve:


Your License Numbers and License Information for your single-user copy are
displayed below. You will need to enter all of the license information below
during your installation.
```

This Is Not a Valid License

This chapter uses the same license number, code, and data format as a valid license just so that you will recognize one. You must get your own license from the SCO Web site.

```
SCO UnixWare 7


License Number: 7AB123456
License Code:   abcdefgh
License Data:   a1;b2;c345


SCO Vision2K


License Number: 62738-12345-12345-12345
```

Print the license information that you receive. Then click Return to SCO Offers and then Shopping Cart.

This are the options and prices as of July 1999:

```
SCO Free Products Order Specification
```

```
Free SCO OpenServer 5.0.5
CB200-UX74-5.0.5
32.00 UK Sterling
or $49.00 US Dollars


Free UnixWare 7.1
CA400-UW74-7.1
32.00 UK Sterling
or $49.00 US Dollars


Free UnixWare 7.0.1-Promotional Edition
CA480-UW79-7.0
12.26 UK Sterling
or $19.95 US Dollars


Free SCO Skunkware 98
SA901-XX79-98
6.42 UK Sterling
or $9.95 US Dollars
```

I chose to order the 7.0.1-Promotional Edition because it was less expensive. The 7.1 was more expensive, not because it was the newer release but because it contained the full software distribution that takes about 6 CD-ROMs. I have heard that SCO will soon have a less-expensive version of the 7.1 distribution that comes on fewer CD-ROMs.

In general, you should always choose the newest version of the operating system. You don't have to worry about getting beta (non-released) software because SCO does not post such software in this section. If the cost is not a problem, order the set with more CD-ROMs so that you have access to all the software packages.

I entered my credit card information. The total price was $24.50, including shipping and tax. Then I received the following message:

```
Thank you for ordering from SCO!
```

I received my order quite promptly.

While you are on the SCO Web site, check the hardware compatibility guide and make sure that the components in your home PC will work with UnixWare 7.

UnixWare 7.0.1 Components

I ordered the lower-cost UnixWare 7.0.1 Promotional edition, which contained the following:

- Two CD-ROMs:
- UnixWare 7 Release 7.0.1, Installation CD-ROM
- UnixWare and OpenServer Development Kit
- One 20 page booklet:
- Basic Installation Guide

The booklet has a nice overview of the whole procedure and the specific commands you will need.

Making the Required Disks

You must make three disks before you can start. The image files to make the disks are found on the first CD-ROM. If you have access to an existing SCO OpenServer or UnixWare system, the booklet gives you specific commands to create the disks from the image files.

Otherwise, the booklet instructs you to go to the SCO Web site and download a utility called floppycp.exe. This utility creates a binary disks directly from the image file while running under Windows. This is similar to rawrite.exe but has the advantage that it can run under Windows NT.

Starting the Installation

Warning: You May Lose Everything

If your computer already has Windows—and programs and data—you may lose all of those by trying to install UNIX on the same machine. Don't attempt to install UNIX unless you are sure that you can reinstall Windows and all programs and data, if needed.

Insert the first installation disk, made from image file boot_ima.1. Power up or reset your machine.

You will see a large colorful UnixWare 7 logo screen and then the following:

```
+ Proceed with installation in English
  Proceder a l'installation en Francais

  ...

  Press <Enter> to continue...
```

In the previous screen, English should already be selected, so press Enter. Then you should see the following:

```
insert the disk labeled "UnixWare 7 Installation Diskette 2 of 2"
```

When you see this message, insert the second boot disk that you made. Then you will see the following:

```
Extracting files from diskette.
Please wait.


Welcome to UnixWare 7
You will now be prompted for the information needed
to install your system. Default values are provided
where useful.
...
<F1>=Help   <F3>=Read Response Diskette   <F9>=Back   <F10>=Next
```

When you see this screen, just press F10. Then you should see the following:

```
Choose a zone for this system and press <F10>.


   (*) Americas
   ( ) Eastern Europe
   ...
<F1>=Help   <F9>=Back   <F10>=Next   Arrow keys or <Tab>=Select
```

If you are in North or South America, leave Americas selected, and press F10. The following appears:

```
Choose a locale for this system and press <F10>.


   (*) C (English)
   ( ) POSIX (English)
   ( ) English for Canada
   ( ) English for USA
   ...
<F1>=Help   <F9>=Back   <F10>=Next   Arrow keys or <Tab>=Select
```

In the previous screen, it is very important to leave the default C selected. English for USA is tempting, but this choice will change your collation sequence to non-ASCII, which can cause scripts that convert between upper- and lowercase to fail. The following then appears:

```
Keyboard


   (*) United States
   ( ) Japanese A01
   ...
<F1>=Help   <F9>=Back   <F10>=Next   Arrow keys or <Tab>=Select
```

In the previous screen, leave United States keyboard selected, and press F10. Next, this appears:

```
License Number  _____
License Code    _____
License Data    _____


<F1>=Help <F8>=Defer <F9>=Back <F10>=Next  Arrow or<Tab>=Select
```

Here, enter the free noncommercial license that you got from SCO Web site. If you have lost it, go out to www.sco.com and get another license instantly. The following then appears:

```
If you do not have an HBA diskette, press <F10> to continue.
If you have one or more HBA diskettes, insert one, select
"Install HBA diskette", and press <F10>. ...


   (*) Install HBA diskette
   ( ) Proceed with installation


<F1>=Help        <F9>=Back        <F10>=Next
```

In the previous screen, select the first option, insert your HBA disk, and press F10. Then the following appears:

```
Please wait while the HBA
hardware modules are installed.
```

When you are done, you will have a chance to read in more HBA disks:

```
If you do not have an HBA diskette, press <F10> to continue.
If you have one or more HBA diskettes, insert one, select
"Install HBA diskette", and press <F10>. ...


   ( ) Install HBA diskette
   (*) Proceed with installation


<F1>=Help        <F9>=Back        <F10>=Next
```

At this screen, press F10 because only one HBA disk is part of the free UnixWare 7.0.1 package. The following then appears:

```
( ) Enter the DCU (manually configure drivers)
(*) Do not enter the DCU (auto-configure drivers)

<F1>=Help   <F9>=Back   <F10>=Next   Arrow keys or <Tab>=Select
```

In the previous screen, do not enter the DCU. Press F10. Actually, if you are having hardware problems that prevent the install, you can enter the DCU to adjust hardware settings, but that is beyond the scope of this book. Then you receive the following message:

```
Please wait while the system hardware drivers are loaded.
```

Next you will see this:

```
Name: _____


Enter the node name for your system and press <F10>.


<F1>=Help       <F9>=Back       <F10>=Next
```

At this screen, enter a unique name for your system. Make sure that the name is not already in use by any other system in your local network. Then press F10. The following appears:

```
Installation Method


  Install from cartridge tape
+ Install from CD-ROM
  Install from TCP network server
  Install from SPX network server
  Cancel installation and shut down


 <F1>=Help   <F9>=Back   <F10>=Next   Arrow keys or <Tab>=Select
```

In the previous screen, leave CD-ROM selected. Insert the first UnixWare 7.0.1 CD-ROM and press F10. If that CD-ROM is not in, the system will prompt you to insert it. Then the following appears:

```
Disk Configuration
Disk No.   Character Node        Action
==========  ====================  ====================
1           /dev/rdsk/c0b0t0d0s0  Customize partitions


 <F1>=Help <F2>=Choices <F9>=Back <F10>=Next  Arrow or<Tab>=Select
```

Here, the Customize Partitions option enables you to preserve any existing DOS/Windows partitions. If you do not need to save those other partitions, press F2 and select Use the Whole Disk for UNIX.

Press F10. Here is what I saw next (because I selected Customize partitions):

```
Disk 1 Partitions (4133MB)
    Type       Status Start    End     %  Cylinders Size (MB)
 =  ========   ====== =====    =====   === ========= =========
```

```
1  DOS         Active 0      260     50 261      2047
2  unused
3  unused
4  unused


      Number of cylinders: 527    Currently used: 261


  <F1>=Help <F2>=Choices <F9>=Back <F10>=Next  Arrow or<Tab>=Select
```

The previous screen shows that DOS/Windows is taking up roughly half of the disk drive: 261 cylinders out of a total of 527 cylinders.

Use the arrow keys and the Tab key to move to the line for partition 2. Use F2 to display choices for each field. Set up a UNIX partition to use the rest of the disk, as shown. Make sure that the number of currently used cylinders at the bottom exactly matches the (total) number of cylinders listed to the left. Check that the start of partition 2 is exactly 1 greater than the end of partition 1. Check that the end of partition 2 is exactly 1 less than the (total) number of cylinders:

```
Disk 1 Partitions (4133MB)
     Type        Status Start    End    %  Cylinders Size (MB)
=  ========    ====== =====    =====   === ========= =========
1  DOS                   0      260     50 261        2066
2  UNIX System Active 261       526     50 266        2066
3  unused
4  unused


      Number of cylinders: 527    Currently used: 527


  <F1>=Help <F2>=Choices <F9>=Back <F10>=Next  Arrow or<Tab>=Select
```

This shows how my system looked after adding the UnixWare 7 partition 2. In the previous screen, make sure that the (total) number of cylinders on the drive is less than 1024. If this is greater than 1024, partition 2 may have trouble booting. This was discussed earlier in this chapter in the section "1024 Cylinder Limit." The following then appears:

```
(*) Use default filesystem sizes and types
( ) Customize filesystems and slices


  <F1>=Help    <F9>=Back    <F10>=Next   Arrow keys or <Tab>=Select
```

In the previous screen, leave the default filesystems and press F10. More experienced users can customize these, if desired. Next, this appears:

```
(*) Use default disk options
```

```
( ) Customize disk options


<F1>=Help    <F9>=Back    <F10>=Next    Arrow keys or <Tab>=Select
```

Warning: In the previous screen, if you change your disk options, it could make your DOS/Windows partition unusable. Press F10 to use the defaults and get to this screen:

```
+ License-Based Defaults              378.19 MB
  Small Footprint Server               97.76 MB
  Full (All Packages)                 384.61 MB
  Customize Installation of Packages  378.19 MB


<F1>=Help    <F9>=Back    <F10>=Next    Arrow keys or <Tab>=Select
```

The first option, License-Based Defaults, includes all the software that your license can run. If you are tight on disk space, choose the Small Footprint Server, which bypasses much of the software to install a minimal compact system. Then press F10 to get to the following screen.

```
The following network interface adapter(s) were detected:

Bus   BusNum  Slot  Network Adapter Name
....  ......  ....  ..............................
PCI     0       2   3Com EtherLink XL

    (*) Use the detected adapter shown above.
    ( ) Select from the full list of supported adapters.
    ( ) Defer network configuration.


<F1>=Help    <F9>=Back    <F10>=Next    Arrow keys or <Tab>=Select
```

This screen shows that my 3Com 905B-TX Ethernet card was auto-detected. Press F10. The following then appears:

```
  System IP Address
     System Netmask
  Broadcast Address
     Default Router


        Domain Name
Primary DNS Address
  Other DNS Address
  Other DNS Address


     Frame Format   ETHERNET_II
```

```
<F1>=Help <F2>=Choices <F8>=Defer <F9>=Back <F10>=Next <Tab>=Select
```

In the previous screen, I filled in my system's IP address. If you are not sure, get a unique IP address from your network administrator. Pressing Tab then calculated the standard netmask and broadcast, which I accepted. I left the rest of the fields blank and then pressed F10:

```
Configure IPX Networking Protocol


IPX Net Number    0
Frame Format      AUTO_DISCOVER


<F1>=Help <F2>=Choices <F8>=Defer <F9>=Back <F10>=Next <Tab>=Select
```

Always press F8 to defer Novell setup in the previous screen, unless you know how to set up IPX/SPX and want to do so:

```
NIS Configuration


NIS Type           client
NIS Domain
Optional NIS Server
Optional NIS Server
Optional NIS Server


<F1>=Help <F2>=Choices <F8>=Defer <F9>=Back <F10>=Next <Tab>=Select
```

Again, press F8 in this screen to defer NIS setup, unless you know how to do this and want to do so. The following then appears:

```
Date and Time


<F1>=Help    <F9>=Back    <F10>=Next   Arrow keys or <Tab>=Select
```

In the previous screen (not all shown), enter the correct date, time, and time zone. F2 gives time zone choices when you tab down to the time zone entry:

```
Choose the desired security level.


  Low
+ Traditional
  Improved (C2)
  High (Above C2)


<F1>=Help    <F9>=Back    <F10>=Next   Arrow keys or <Tab>=Select
```

Locked Account or Terminal Hassle

I tried C2 security on one system, but I went back to traditional because I spent too much unlocking user accounts and terminals after users keyed in their username or password incorrectly several times. Typing a correct login and password did not reset the error count.

In the previous screen, press F1 for more info about these system security settings. Press F10 to leave traditional security. At higher security levels, the system will lock a user's account and/or terminal if there are too many invalid login attempts:

```
System owner name:
System owner login name:
System owner user ID number: 101
System owner password:
Repeat password:


<F1>=Help    <F9>=Back    <F10>=Next    Arrow keys or <Tab>=Select
```

In this screen, press F1 for more information about the owner account. Enter a name and password you will remember, and press F10:

```
Root password:
Repeat root password:


<F1>=Help    <F9>=Back    <F10>=Next    Arrow keys or <Tab>=Select
```

Root Account Versus Root Directory

Don't confuse the root account with the root directory. The root account is the all-powerful system administrator account, also called the superuser. The root directory is the main system directory that contains all other files and subdirectories within it.

In the previous screen, it is very important to restrict access to the root account. Enter a password you will remember. Press F10 to get the following:

```
Optional Services
```

This screen does not install anything. Press F1 if you want to display information about various optional services from SCO. Press F10 to go on with the installation:

```
License Agreement


(*)  Accept
( )  Do not accept
( )  Display Licenses
```

Press F10 to accept the license agreement. The following appears:

```
WARNING: This is your last chance to exit the
installation before potentially erasing data on your
hard disk. ...


If you want to save the responses you gave to the
installation prompts, to use as defaults for another
installation, insert a blank, formatted diskette
into the diskette drive and press <F3>.


If you are ready to install the system, press <F10>.


<F1>=Help <F3>=Save answers to disk  <F9>=Back <F10>=Install software
```

Press F10 to start installing UnixWare 7 to the hard disk. Later you will see the following:

```
You must now reinsert the HBA diskette labeled
UnixWare 7.0.1a HBA Drivers
```

Insert that disk if it is not already still in the floppy drive, and press Enter:

```
UnixWare 7 installation is complete. ...


*** Make sure that the CD-ROM and floppy disk drives are empty ***


When you press <Enter>, the system will shut down and restart.
```

Remove the CD-ROM and floppy, and press Enter. You will see a large, colorful UnixWare 7 logo screen and then the following:

```
The system is coming up.  Please wait.
```

Now post-installation configuration will be started automatically:

```
(*) Serial Mouse
( ) Bus Mouse
( ) PS/2-compatible Mouse
( ) No Mouse


<F10>=Next     Arrow keys or <Tab>=Move
```

My system has a PS/2 mouse, so I selected that option and pressed F10:

```
PS/2 Mouse


Number of buttons 2


<F2>=Choices    <F10>=Next    Arrow or<Tab>=Select
```

My mouse has just two buttons, so I just pressed F10 to get the following:

```
Your mouse selection is ready to be tested. After
you press any key, you have 15 seconds to test
the mouse.  Make sure it moves as you expect, then
press a mouse button to end the test.  If you do not
press a button within 15 seconds, the test will
appear to fail.


Press any key to continue...
```

After I pressed a key, the mouse test began. The cursor on the screen moved as I moved the mouse. When I clicked, it ended the test, so my mouse checked out okay:

```
To continue installing the system, please insert
CD-ROM #2 and press <F10>.


To defer installing this CD-ROM, press <F8>.


<F8>=Defer                    <F10>=Continue
```

The second CD-ROM that comes with the two CD-ROM UnixWare 7.0.1 Promotional edition package is not what this question is looking for, so press F8 to defer:

```
To continue installing the system, please insert
CD-ROM #3 and press <F10>.


To defer installing this CD-ROM, press <F8>.


<F8>=Defer                    <F10>=Continue
```

Again, the second CD-ROM that comes with the two CD-ROM UnixWare 7.0.1 package is not what this question is looking for, so press F8 to defer:

```
The system is coming up.


...
Welcome to systemname
 UnixWare 7 CDE


Please enter your user name
```

At this point, you can log in as root or as owner. UnixWare 7 uses the CDE GUI as described in Chapter 5, "The UNIX Graphical User Interface (GUI)." Figure 12.1

shows the UnixWare 7 graphical screen with a command-line session (dtterm) and
SCO Help running.

FIGURE 12.1
UnixWare 7 graphical login.

Getting Help with SCO UNIX

SCO's Web site, www.sco.com, has a large set of technical articles in the support section that you can search by key word. Use the key word "free" to search for helpful
articles about loading the free versions of SCO UNIX. Use the largest words in any
error message to look for articles about that particular error.

Go to www.sco.com/skunkware and you will find a large selection of open source and
GNU software that has already been compiled to run on SCO UNIX.

Shut Down Before You Power Off UnixWare 7

Before you power off any UNIX system, it is important to do a proper shut down.
First make sure that you shut down any databases that you may be running. Check
your database documentation for the proper procedure. Then make sure that no
important user programs are still running. The who and ps commands are useful
for this.

Log in as root and do the following:

```
cd /
shutdown -g0 -i0 -y
```

Change the `-g0` to `-g5` if you want to give all users a 5-minute warning or delay before the system shuts down. When the shutdown process begins, expect a number of messages as system processes are terminated. Eventually you will see this message:

```
The system has halted and may be powered off (Press any key to reboot)
```

Booting Up UnixWare 7 or Windows

If your disk has both a UnixWare7 UNIX partition and a Windows partition, you can bring up either operating system, but you cannot run them both at the same time. From UnixWare 7, you can run fdisk. If you make the Windows partition active, then the system will always boot to Windows, and vice versa.

Installing Sun Solaris 7 at Home

Solaris is a UNIX-based operating system from Sun Microsystems, a well-known UNIX and Internet company. Solaris is based on Sun's version of UNIX, called SunOS. Solaris runs on both Sun SPARC computers and also on Intel computers. These different types of computers are also referred to as platforms.

Solaris Skipped from 2.6 to 7

Why did the Solaris revision level jump from 2.6 to 7? At one point in the Solaris 7 installation, it referred to itself as Solaris 2.7. Maybe Solaris 2.7 was changed to Solaris 7 to match SCO UnixWare, which also jumped from rev 2 directly to rev 7.

When I first wrote Chapter 5 of this book in 1998, the current release of SunOS was 5.6 and Solaris was 2.6. Today, in late 1999, SunOS is 5.7, but Solaris has jumped from 2.6 to 7. Solaris 7 provides a 64-bit operating system for the SPARC platform, but not for the Intel platform.

Ordering Solaris 7

Go to the Sun Web site at `www.sun.com`.

Search for the word *free*, and you will find an article on how to order Solaris 7. This is some information from the Web site as of September 1999:

Pricing & Availability

For the price of media, shipping and handling, non-commercial developers
worldwide can register for free membership in the Sun Developer Connection
program and place an order for a copy of the Solaris 7 operating environment
for non-commercial use. This offer is available for a limited time only. Use of
the Solaris operating environment secured through this offer is limited to
non-commercial use only. Participants are free to develop and test
applications, but in order to deploy them for commercial use, they must upgrade
their software to a commercial license. Developers can access installation
support by calling: 1-800-786-7638, prompt 4. StarOffice 5.0 Personal Edition
can be downloaded for free to individual non-commercial users by following the
links on the Solaris Website at
http://www.sun.com/solaris/.

Solaris 7 Components

The Solaris 7 (free license) package comes with the following components:

- Diskette: Solaris 7 Device Configuration Assistant
- CD-ROM: Solaris 7 Software, Intel Platform Edition
- CD-ROM: Solaris 7 Software, SPARC Platform Edition
- CD-ROM: Solaris 7 Documentation
- booklet: Start Here, Solaris 7

The Start Here booklet briefly lists the six major steps to install Solaris 7 on your
computer in six different languages. It shows these two minimum requirements for
installation:

- 32MB of memory
- 700MB of disk space

Installation Documentation

For more documentation, the booklet points you to two places:

- README.html on the Documentation CD-ROM
- http://docs.sun.com on the Internet

The Documentation CD-ROM has some problems, but they are easy to work
around. There is no README.html file, there is a file with English documentation
called README_1.HTM.

You can view this HTML documentation file using a browser under Windows. In that page, you will find a section like this:

```
To read complete Solaris installation information, see:


Solaris 7 (SPARC Platform Edition) Installation Library
Solaris 7 (Intel Platform Edition) Installation Library
Solaris 7 (Intel Platform Edition) Device Configuration Guide
Solaris 7 (Intel Platform Edition) Hardware Compatibility List
```

Unfortunately, these links don't exactly match the directories and files on the CD-ROM, but luckily they are close. To see the Intel Installation Library, use your browser to access this file on the CD-ROM:

`Solaris_\Common\Html_En\Intel_In\Book01.htm.`

Here you will find useful topics such as "Planning and Starting Your Installation." This covers what's new in Solaris 7. There is also a section called "Preserving Existing Operating Systems and User Data," which covers how to put Solaris and Windows on the same disk drive.

You will find the Device Configuration Guide on the CD-ROM as `Solaris_\Common\Html_En\Device_c\Book.htm`. You will find tips here on troubleshooting resource conflicts and setting up devices.

Hardware Compatibility

Hardware Compatibility Is No Guarantee

Even if your device is found in the compatibility table, you may still have problems with it because of the other hardware in your computer. If your device is not in the table, it still might work because it emulates another device that is in the table. The table is good general indicator of what hardware will work, but there will be some exceptions.

Before you start to install Solaris 7, you should check the hardware compatibility information on the Documentation CD-ROM to make sure that Solaris 7 will install and run on your computer. Here is the correct path for this information:

`Solaris_\Common\Html_En\Hardware\Book.htm.`

You will find hardware that has been tested under Solaris 7 listed in various categories, such as System Platforms (computer vendor and type of CPU) and Devices such as SCSI controllers and RAID controllers.

The Advantage of Alternatives

When loading any type of operating system, it is useful if you have access to more than one type of controller card for disk, video, network, and other adapters. If one brand or style of card is not successful, another type might be.

Starting the Solaris 7 Installation

Warning: You May Lose Everything

If your computer already has Windows and programs and data, you may lose all those by trying to install UNIX on the same machine. Don't attempt to install UNIX unless you are sure that you can reinstall Windows and all programs and data, if needed..

Before you start to install Solaris 7, be warned that any programs and data currently on your machine might be overwritten. Trying to keep Windows and install UNIX on the same machine is very complex. You may have to totally reinstall Windows and UNIX several times before you are successful.

If you want to have both Windows and Solaris UNIX on your computer, you must have at least 1GB of unallocated disk space. See the earlier section "How to Get Windows to Give Up Disk Space."

Before starting to install Solaris 7, you must either:

- Have 1GB of unallocated disk space.
- Plan to run only Solaris UNIX on this computer and lose all current Windows and programs and data.

If you meet one of these two conditions, you are ready to begin. Insert the disk that came in the Solaris 7 package and has this label:

```
Solaris 7
Device Configuration
Assistant
3/99
Intel Platform Edition
```

Power up or press Reset. You will then see various boot messages and then this screen:

```
The Solaris(TM) (Intel Platform Edition) Device Configuration Assistant
scans to identify system hardware, lists identified devices, and can
boot the Solaris software from a specified device. This program must be
```

used to install the Solaris operating environment, add a driver, or
change the hardware on the system.

> To perform a full scan to identify all system hardware, choose Continue.

> To diagnose possible full scan failures, choose Specific Scan.

> To add new or updated device drivers, choose Add Driver.

...

- The mouse cannot be used.
- If the keyboard does not have function keys or they do not respond,
  press ESC. The legend at the bottom of the screen will change to show
  the ESC keys to use for navigation.

```
F2_Continue    F3_Specific Scan    F4_Add Driver    F6_Help
```

Press F2 and you should see this:

Determining bus types and gathering hardware configuration data ...

Then you will see these lines:

The system is being scanned to identify system hardware.

If the scanning stalls, press the system's reset button. When the
system reboots, choose Specific Scan or Help.

The next screen shows the hardware that was detected.

The following devices have been identified on this system. To identify
devices not on this list or to modify device characteristics, such as
keyboard configuration, choose Device Tasks. Platform types may be
included in this list.

```
        ISA: Floppy DISK CONTROLLER
        ISA: Motherboard
        ISA: PS/2 mouse
        ISA: PnP bios: 16550-compatible serial controller
        ISA: PnP bios: 16550-compatible serial controller
        ISA: PnP bios: Parallel port
        ISA: System keyboard (US-English)
        PCI: 3Com 3C905B-TX Fast Etherlink XL 10/100
        PCI: Adaptec AHA-2940W/2940UW Rev B Ultra SCSI Adapter
        PCI: Bus Mastering IDE controller
```

```
PCI: Universal Serial Bus
PCI: VGA compatible controller
```

```
F2_Continue    F3_Back    F4_Device Tasks    F6_Help
```

Notice that my disk and CD-ROM controller (Adaptec), my PCI video card, and my 3Com Ethernet card were all autodetected in the previous screen. If any of these four elements are in your computer but are not detected here, you should abort the installation and make sure that the hardware is properly installed. If you have a Windows partition, bring up Windows and make sure that the missing hardware is usable by Windows. For the beginner, it is much easier to install Solaris if you resolve any hardware or connection problems now so that these four important components are seen and configured during the initial Solaris install.

F4 enables you to view and edit devices so that you can check for device conflicts, I/O addresses, and IRQs; remove devices; and add them back with different settings. These steps require some PC expertise, but luckily they are needed only if there are problems.

Because I did not anticipate any problems, I pressed F2 to continue. You will see some messages like this:

```
Loading Driver xxx
```

Then you will see this screen:

```
Select one of the identified devices to boot the Solaris kernel and
choose Continue.


To perform optional features, such as modifying the autoboot and property
settings, choose Boot Tasks.


> To make a selection use the arrow keys, and press Enter to mark it [X].

  [ ] NET : 3Com 3C905B-TX Fast Etherlink XL 10/100
          in PCI bus 0, Slot 2
  [ ] DISK: Target 0, IBM DCAS-34330 S65A
          on Adaptec AHA-2940W/2940UW Rev B Ultra SCSI Adpater in PCI  bus
  [ ] DISK: Target 1, IBM DCAS-34330 S65A
          on Adaptec AHA-2940W/2940UW Rev B Ultra SCSI Adpater in PCI  bus
  [X] CD  : Target 5, TOSHIBA CD-ROM
          on Adaptec AHA-2940W/2940UW Rev B Ultra SCSI Adpater in PCI  bus



F2_Continue    F3_Back    F4_Boot Tasks    F6_help
```

Arrow to CD and press Enter to insert an X, as shown. The Solaris kernel mentioned at the top of the previous screen is contained on the CD-ROM from the Solaris 7 package that has the following label:

```
Solaris 7
Software
Deutsch, English, Espanol,
Francais, Italiano, Svenska
Intel Platform Edition
```

Insert the previously mentioned CD-ROM and press F2 to continue. Some information will be read from the CD-ROM and then you will see this:

```
Select the type of installation you want to perform:


1 Solaris Interactive
2 Custom JumpStart
3 Solaris Web Start
```

Option 1 is the default, which is chosen automatically after 30 seconds. The Web Start offers a simplified way to load all the components at once, but it will automatically use the entire disk, which will totally wipe out any existing Windows partition. This example uses the Solaris Interactive install option. This should preserve any Windows partition and its Windows files and programs. You will then see messages like this:

```
<<< starting interactive installation >>>


Booting Kernel/unix...
SunOS Release 5.7 Version Generic_106542-02 [UNIX(R) System V Release 4.0]
Copyright  1983-1998, Sun Microsystems, Inc.
...
Select a language


0) English
1) German
...
```

Select 0 for English/American at this prompt.

```
Select a locale


0) USA (ASCII)
1) Bulgaria
...
42) Go back to Previous Screen
```

Next select your geographical locale. There are so many choices in the list that the first lines will go off the screen. The last option, 42, to go back to see the previous screen is no help because the initial lines of this screen go by too quickly to be read. Option 0 is the default and will select USA, even if that item is off the screen.

```
The Solaris Installation Program
You are now interacting with the Solaris installation program.  The
program is divided into a series of short sections.  At the end of each
section, you will see a summary of the choices you've made, and be given
the opportunity to make changes.

As you work with the program, you will complete one or more of the
following tasks:

   1 - Identify peripheral devices
   2 - Identify your system
   3 - Install Solaris software

About navigation...

   - The mouse cannot be used

   - If your keyboard does not have function keys, or they do not respond,
     press ESC; the legend at the bottom of the screen will change to show
     the ESC keys to use for navigation.


F2_Continue    F6_Help
```

Read the previous overview of the next steps, and then press F2. In the next screen, you will see an overview of kdmconfig, which will set up graphical windowing under Solaris UNIX.

```
kdmconfig - Introduction

kdmconfig has attempted to identify the devices necessary for
the window system.  If the configuration is incorrect or
incomplete, you will not be able to use the window system.

Press F2 to view and edit the current configuration.

Press F4 to bypass viewing and editing.  If you choose this
option, you can subsequently review and edit the window system
configuration by rebooting the system or running kdmconfig
from the command line.
```

```
Note: If you are installing Solaris, you do not have to configure
the window system at this time.  Choosing this option will cause
the installation to run in non-window-system mdoe.

Press F6 or <ESC>-6 for Help.  The Help information covers
kdmconfig screens as well as screen navigation and how to
substitute Escape key sequences for function keys.

F2_Continue    F4_Bypass    F6_Help
```

The previous screen offers an overview for configuring the video for X Windows.
This can be a tricky process. Your video card and monitor may not be compatible
with any of the choices. The previous screen shows you that if you eventually give up
on trying to get the graphical windowing working, you can get back to the screen
and press F4 to bypass the X Windows setup, which allows you to run all the Solaris
UNIX commands from the command line.

```
kdmconfig - View and Edit Window System Configuration

Current Window System Configuration:

   Graphics Device: Unknown

      Monitor Type: Plug and Play Mfreq 13 Inch CTX1451 (up to 1024x768 @ 6)

    Keyboard Type: Generic US-English

  Pointing Device: Built-in PS/2 Mouse (2 button)

   Configure Devices
   -----------------------------------------
   [ ] No changes needed - Test/Save and Exit
   [X] Change Graphics Device/Monitor
   [ ] Change Keyboard
   [ ] Change Pointing Device

  F2_Continue    F3_Quit Without Save    F6_Help
```

In the previous screen, the kdmconfig module of the Solaris 7 installation process
has correctly identified the type of monitor that I am using, my keyboard, and my
mouse. It did not detect my graphics card, so I will select Change Graphics
Device/Monitor and press F2 to go to that section.

Graphics Device Selection

You must select the graphics device that is installed in your machine.

```
    Graphics Device
    ------------------------------------------------
    [ ] 16 color Standard VGA 640x480 (256K)
    [ ] 16 color Standard VGA with panning @800x600 (256K)
    [ ] ALR FLYER VL with WD90C33 (60Hz) (1MB)
    ...
    [ ] Trident Trident 9440 (1MB)
    [ ] Trident Trident 9680 (2MB)
    [ ] Trident Trident 9680 (4MB)
    ...
```

In the previous screen, enter T and then R to get to the Trident entries quickly.

You might wonder how I knew that my video card was a Trident. Sometimes the initial system bootup messages identify that type of video card, but that was not true in my case. Before I started to install Solaris, I opened my machine and looked at my graphics (video) card. I found these markings on the card that are similar to the Trident entries in the previous table.

```
Trident TGUI 9680-1
U-T9680 1M
```

Notice that my Trident 9680 card with only 1MB of memory is not listed in the Solaris list. I selected the Trident 9680 (2MB) choice in the list, but it failed the video test that comes up later. I went back here and tried the Trident 9440 (1MB) choice, but that did not work either.

Warning: Video Mismatch Can Damage Hardware

If you can't find your video card in the Solaris list, beware of trying other entries that sound similar. Some mismatches might damage your video card or monitor permanently.

New video cards are replacing old cards all the time. Sometimes you can find a different entry in the Solaris list that will work for your card. You can also try the generic entry of Standard VGA, but this may not support the degree of resolution and number of colors needed for effective graphics.

I was not able to get my 1MB Trident card to work with Solaris. I changed to a 2MB Trident 9680 card, and it worked just fine.

Having selected a video graphics card, press F2 to go to monitor choices. The type that it autoselected for my system was correct.

```
[ ] IBM VGA (31.5kHz)
...
[ ] MultiFrequency 100kHz (up to 1600x1200 @ 80Hz)
[ ] MultiFrequency 105kHz (up to 1600x1200 @ 85Hz)
[ ] MultiFrequency 110kHz (up to 1600x1200 @ 90Hz)
[ ] MultiFrequency 115kHz (up to 1600x1200 @ 95Hz)
[ ] MultiFrequency 38kHz (up to 1024x768 interlaced)
[ ] MultiFrequency 48kHz (up to 1152x900 interlaced)
[ ] MultiFrequency 56kHz (up to 1280x1024 interlaced)
[ ] MultiFrequency 64kHz (up to 1600x1200 interlaced)
...
[X] Plug and Play Mfreq 13 Inch CTX1451 (up to 1024x768 @ 6)
...
[ ] Super VGA 35.5 kHz (800x600 @ 56Hz and 1024x768 Interlaced)
```

Not a lot of monitor choices are available. If you have the manual or specifications for your monitor, you might be able to pick a compatible generic multifrequency choice.

Pressing F2 brings you to options for selecting resolution and colors. You want at least 800×600 resolution and 256 colors. If you can get higher resolution and more colors, that is better. Be aware that the higher the resolution, the smaller everything will look on the screen. This is valuable if you want to see more things all at once. If you have poor eyesight, choose lower resolution so that images will be larger.

```
Resolution/Colors/Refresh Rate
- - - - - - - - - - - - - - - - - - - - - - - - - - - - - - - - - - -
[ ] 640x480 - 256 colors @ 72 HMz
[X] 800x600 - 256 colors @ 72 HMz
[ ] 1024x768 - 256 colors @ 60 HMz
```

I chose 800×600 as a good compromise between screen coverage versus eye strain.

Now I'm back to the Configure Devices screen we saw earlier. I've made all my changes, so I'm ready to Test/Save and Exit:

```
Configure Devices
- - - - - - - - - - - - - - - - - - - - - - - - - - - - - - - - - -
[X] No changes needed - Test/Save and Exit
[ ] Change Graphics Device/Monitor
[ ] Change Keyboard
[ ] Change Pointing Device
```

The next screen allows me to test whether my choices for the video graphics card and the type of monitor really match my hardware. If I can't run Solaris in Graphical mode, I can always bypass the graphics and run Solaris purely in character mode.

```
kdmconfig Window System Configuration Test


You can test the current window system configuration now by
pressing F2. If the configuration is correct, you will see
the sample image, be able to move the pointer, and click on
a button.  If you see a blank screen and kdmconfig does not
regain control within a minute or two, you will have to reboot
your system.


Press F4 to bypass the test.  If you bypass the test and you
have an incorrect or incomplete configuration, you will not be
able to use the windowing systems.


F2_Continue    F4_Bypass    F6_Help
```

When you press F2, there will be some delays, the screen will go dark for less than 60 seconds, and then it will display a test pattern with different colors and their names. It will ask if this screen is acceptable. You can then click on Yes or No. Move the mouse to the correct choice, and left-click.

You will next see a graphical Solaris logo. The screen will clear for about 20 seconds. Then you see this in a graphical window:

```
The system is coming up. Please wait.
```

This message does not refer to the real Solaris system, but to a temporary system that will complete the rest of the installation. Nothing has been installed on the hard disk yet. Soon you will see the following:

```
On the next screens, you must identify this system as networked or
non-networked, and set the default time zone and date/time.


...
Continue               Help
```

Next you are prompted to enter the hostname for this system. The prompt describes how long and what characters you can use. The name must not match any other system in the local network.

```
Host name: _____
```

Answer yes to the next question that asks if your system has a Ethernet or another LAN card. Answer no to the following question if your only connection to another computer is by dial-up modem.

```
Networked: Yes
           No
```

If you answer yes to this question, you will then be prompted to choose an IP address, a type of name service, and subnet information so that your system can communicate in the network without interfering with other systems.

Next enter the IP address for this system. You must choose an address that is not currently in use. The beginning part of this IP address must match the other systems in your network, and the ending part must be unique. Ask your network administrator for an available IP address for your system.

```
IP address: _____
```

Next select the type of name service used in your network:

```
Name service: NIS+
              NIS (formerly yp)
              Other
              None
```

In the previous screen, choose Other if you are using DNS. Ask your network administrator if you are not sure, or simply enter None for now.

```
System part of a subnet: Yes
                         No
```

Ask your network administrator the previous question. The answer will be used in calculating your netmask and broadcast address.

```
Specify timezone by: Geographic region
                     Offset from GMT
                     Time zone file
```

Choose Geographic Region in the previous screen, and then select your time zone in the following screen. Then enter the correct date and time when prompted.

So far, you have not actually installed any software on the hard disk.

```
On the following screens, you can accept the defaults or you can customize
how Solaris software will be installed by:

  -Allocating space for diskless clients or AutoClient systems
  -Selecting the type of Solaris software to install
  -Selecting disks to hold software you've selected
  -Specifying how file systems are laid out on the disks
```

The previous screen indicates that you are about to allocate some or all of the hard disk space for Solaris. Select Continue to go on.

```
Do you want to allocate space for diskless clients and/or AutoClient
systems?
```

```
Continue   Go Back   Allocate...   Exit   Help
```

Select Continue to bypass the previous option. The next screen enables you to select
a language besides English. Select Continue to use English.

```
Select the Solaris software to install on the system.
```

```
Entire Distribution          710 MB
Developer System Support     663 MB
End User System Support      353 MB
Core System Support          138 MB
```

```
Continue   Go Back   Customize...   Exit   Help
```

You may select Help in the previous screen to read more about these options.
Choose Entire Distribution if you are not tight on disk space.

```
Select the disks for installing Solaris software. ...
```

```
Available Disks                Selected Disks
c0t0d0 (boot disk) 4133 MB
c0t1d0             4133 MB
```

The previous screen shows that Solaris detected two disk drives in my system, both
about 4GB in size. When I select the first disk (c0t0d0—controller 0, target scsi id
0), the > button becomes available. When I click that > button, the drive is moved to
the Selected Disks column:

```
Available Disks                Selected Disks
c0t1d0             4133 MB     c0t0d0 (boot disk) 2083 MB
```

Notice in this screen that the capacity of the boot disk went down from 4133MB to
2083MB. This is because Solaris detected that part of the disk was used by
Windows, so it used the unallocated space left on that disk.

If I click the second disk, c0t1d0, and then the > button, I get this message:

```
There is no Solaris fdisk partition on this disk. You must create a
Solaris fdisk partition if you want to use this disk to install
Solaris software.
```

It then gives me two or three options for this second disk. The middle option that
follows is given only if there is unallocated disk space on that drive.

```
Auto-layout Solaris partition to fill entire disk
    (which will overwrite any existing fdisk partitions)
```

```
Auto-layout Solaris partition to fill the remainder of the disk
   (which will layout ... around existing fdisk partitions)
Manually create Solaris fdisk partition
```

```
Do you want to use auto-layout to automatically layout the file systems?
Manually laying out the file systems requires advanced system administration
skills.
```

```
   Auto Layout    Go Back    Manual Layout    Exit    Help
```

Select Auto Layout in the previous screen. You will then be shown some optional file systems that can also be created. You do not have to select any of these. Press Continue to go on. You will then be shown a summary of your disk selections. You can go back or make new selections. Select Continue to go on. The following question appears:

```
Do you want to mount software from a remote file server?
```

Select Continue to bypass the previous option. You will then be shown a profile of your installation choices followed by these options:

```
Begin Installation    Change    Exit    Help
```

I selected Begin Installation, but it stopped with an immediate error.

I had tried to preserve a 2GB Windows partition on the disk drive and install Solaris in the last 2GB of a 4 GB disk. At this point, Solaris detected that its boot code would be above cylinder 1024, which is not allowed on PCs. I think I might have prevented this problem by initially setting logical block addressing (LBA) for IDE disk drives in the BIOS or Extended BIOS Translation for DOS Drives > 1 GByte for SCSI disk drives.

```
Auto Reboot         Manual Reboot
```

In the previous screen, select Auto Reboot when installation is done. The system then prompts you to remove the disk. The installation will proceed on its own. After a while, it will ask you for the following:

```
Root password: _____
```

What you type will not echo to the screen. The system will ask you to re-enter it to make sure that you have typed what you intended.

Next log in as root. You will be prompted to select a GUI.

```
Common Desktop Environment (CDE)
OpenWindows Desktop
```

Choose the CDE because you will find this on many commercial UNIX systems. Both of these graphical interfaces are described in Chapter 5.

Congratulations! You have now loaded Solaris 7 on your computer. Next you should create a non-root account to use, as described in Chapter 13, "Users, Logins, and Groups."

CDE 1.3 in Solaris 7

The CDE 1.3 GUI in Solaris 7 is slightly different than the older CDE covered in Chapter 5.

To bring up a Web browser, find the earth globe on the far left of the bottom main panel (see Figure 12.2). Click the triangle above the globe to display a list of options. Click Web Browser in that list, which invokes the HotJava browser. This browser starts up and gives you several configuration options. If you go through a proxy server to get to the Internet, click Proxies and enter the IP address and port to access. Now you should be able to surf the Net.

To get a command-line prompt, find the CPU and Disk Performance Monitor on the right of the bottom main panel (see Figure 12.2). Click the triangle to display a list of options. Click This Host in that list to start a window with a UNIX command line to run commands on this host.

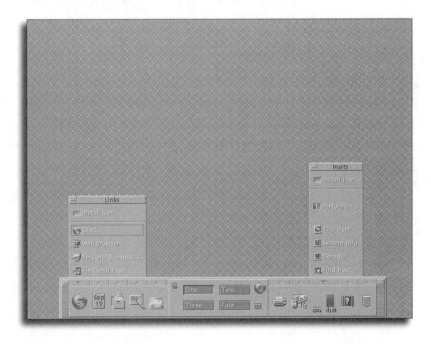

FIGURE 12.2
CDE 1.3 in Solaris 7.

Shut Down Before You Power Off Solaris 7

Before you power off any UNIX system, it is important to do a proper shutdown. First make sure that you shut down any databases that you may be running. Check your database documentation for the proper procedure. Then make sure that no important user programs are still running. The who and ps commands are useful for this.

Log in as root and do the following:

```
cd /
/usr/sbin/shutdown -g0 -i0 -y
```

Change the -g0 to -g5 if you want to give all users a five-minute warning or delay before the system shuts down. When the shutdown process begins, expect a number of messages as system processes are terminated. Eventually you will see these messages:

```
The system is down.
syncing file systems... done
Type any key to continue
```

Now it is safe for you to power off the system, or you may press any key as prompted to boot up the system again.

Booting Up Solaris or Windows

If your disk has both a Solaris UNIX partition and a Windows partition, you can bring up either operating system, but you cannot run them both at the same time.

If Solaris was the last operating system to be loaded, it installs a nice boot program that gives you the option of running Solaris or Windows. When you first power up, you will soon see a screen like this:

```
SunOS - Intel Platform Edition

    Current Disk Partition Information

    Part# Status  Type      Start     Length
    ===========================================
      1            BIGDOS        63    4192902
      2    Active  SOLARIS  4192965    4257225
      3
      4

    Select the partition you wish to boot:
```

This screen shows that you can enter 2 to run Solaris or 1 to run DOS/Windows. The system will wait for 30 seconds. If you don't make a selection, it brings up Solaris. As Solaris comes up, you will be given options to interrupt the normal boot up sequence. Just ignore these and let the system come up on its own:

Let Solaris Come Up on Its Own

The easiest way to bring up Solaris is to power up and walk away; it will come up on its own. While it's coming up, you will see many opportunities to interrupt the bootup. Don't do this unless you know what you are doing.

```
If the system hardware has changed, or to boot from a different
device, interrupt the autoboot process by pressing ESC.

Press ESC to interrupt autoboot in 5 seconds.

Initializing system
Please wait...

Type    b [file-name] [boot-flags] <ENTER>    to boot with options
or      i <ENTER>                             to enter boot interpreter
or      <ENTER>                               to boot with defaults

        <<< timeout in 5 seconds >>>

Select (b)oot or (i)nterpreter:

SunOS Release 5.7 Version Generic_106542-02 [UNIX(R) System V Release 4.0]
Copyright  1983-1998, Sun Microsystems, Inc.
configuring network interfaces: elx10.
Hostname: morisol
The system is coming up. Please wait.
checking ufs filesystems
/dev/rdsk/c0t0d0s7: is clean.
starting routing daemon.
...
```

After a number of other bootup messages, you will see a login prompt. The system is now up and ready for you to log in.

Hiding Solaris

If you want to prevent other Windows users from being confused by the Solaris bootup options, you can hide Solaris by running fdisk from either Windows or Solaris and then making the DOS/Windows partition the Active partition. Once you do that, the system will only boot to DOS/Windows. If you later want to boot Solaris, run fdisk from Windows and make the Solaris partition active. Then reboot, and Solaris will come up.

To run fdisk from Solaris on SCSI disk 0, enter this:

```
fdisk /dev/rdsk/c0t0d0p0
```

You will see a screen like this:

```
Total disk size is 527 cylinders
        Cylinder size is 16065 (512 byte) blocks
```

				Cylinders		
Partition	Status	Type	Start	End	Length	%
=========	======	============	=====	===	======	===
1		DOS-BIG	0	260	261	50
2	Active	Solaris	261	525	265	50

```
SELECT ONE OF THE FOLLOWING:

   1. Create a partition
   2. Specify the active partition
   3. Delete a partition
   4. Exit (update disk configuration and exit)
   5. Cancel (exit without updating disk configuration)
Enter Selection:
```

Enter option 2 and then select partition 1 to make the DOS/Windows partition active. Then enter option 4 to update and exit. Shut down Solaris as described in the previous section. When you reboot, only Windows will come up.

# chapter 13

Users, Groups, and Logins

Steve "Mor" Moritsugu
and Dan Wilson

User information

The home directory

Passwords

Groups

The login environment

Creating a user on three different
types of UNIX

> **Tip for Beginners**
>
> This chapter discusses UNIX users, groups, logins and related commands. At the end, it shows how to create a new user account on three different commercial versions of UNIX, to give you a sense of how different these types of UNIX are and yet how similar administrative menus can be. If you install UNIX at home, you should definitely create a non-root user, as recommended in this chapter. Use the root account only when absolutely necessary.

UNIX User Accounts

In the last section of this chapter, you will see how to create a new user and assign that user to one or more groups. Users can create directories and files of their own. In Chapter 14, "File Permissions and System Security," you will see how users can set access permissions on their directories and files so that some other users can access those directories and files, while other users cannot.

Check out the following example:

```
-rw-rw----   1 mori      dbhelp      948 Jul 17  1996 mp4.1.2
-rw-rw----   1 lazar     integ       948 Jul 29  1996 mp4.1.3
-rw-rw----   1 stull     dbhelp      951 Mar 24  1998 mp4.1.3a
```

In this example, the following is true:

- File mp4.1.2 belongs to user mori and to group dbhelp.
- File mp4.1.3 belongs to user lazar and to group integ.
- File mp4.1.3a belongs to user stull and to group dbhelp.

The following is true about each user:

- Each user has a unique user number (UID).
- Each user has one login or primary group.
- Each group has a unique group number (GID).
- A new file is owned by the user who creates the file and belongs to that user's login group.
- A user may belong to several groups as well as the login group.
- Each user has a home directory that is usually unique but may be shared among more than one user.

The *id* Command

The id command displays the following information about a user:

```
$ id
```

```
uid=418(mori) gid=50(group) groups=50(group),102(maintm),103(customer),104(mtcop
y),108(dtrlib),109(mtbackup),110(dbhelp),114(suppltd)
$
```

In this example, the id command shows the following:

- The username is mori.
- The user ID number (UID) is 418.
- The primary group is called group.
- Group's group ID number (GID) is 50.
- The user belongs to these groups: group, maintm, customer, mtcopy, dtrlib, mtbackup, dbhelp, and suppltd.
- The id command shows the GID number for each group the user belongs to.

The Home Directory

/home Is Probably Not Your Home Directory

Many UNIX systems have a system directory called /home. Don't confuse this with your home directory. The /home directory might contain your home directory, such as /home/fred.

The system administrator can assign any directory to be a user's home directory. If you do not know your home directory, run these two commands:

```
$ cd
$ pwd
/u/mori
$
```

The cd command without an argument takes you to your home directory. pwd then displays where you ended up. In the previous example, the home directory is /u/mori.

These files are often found in your home directory:

- **.profile**—This file is executed automatically when you log in (if your default shell is the Bourne shell or Korn shell), so it often contains initialization code.
- **.cshrc**—This is executed automatically on login if you use the C shell.
- **.login**—This is another file that is executed automatically on login if you use the C shell.
- **.exrc**—You can put your favorite vi set commands into this file so that they are automatically established each time you invoke the vi editor.

359

- .forward—If this file exists, it will cause your email to be forwarded to the user named in the file. If several names are listed, separated by a comma, your email will be duplicated and sent to each name.

- .rhosts—This file enables you to specify which users on other systems in the network can run rlogin to log in to your account on this system without giving a password. This file also lets other users on other systems run rcp to copy your files without having to enter a password.

- .plan—This file can be seen via the finger command so that other users can read any plans you put there, such as being on vacation in September.

- .project—Similar to .plan, this allows whatever project information you include to be available by using the finger command.

The *finger* Command

The finger command with a username argument displays the following type of information about that user:

```
dtr> finger mori
Login: mori                        Name: Steve Moritsugu
Directory: /u/mori                  Shell: /bin/ksh
On since Mon Sep 20 08:35 on ttyp1 (messages off) from sm
On since Mon Sep 20 08:59 on ttyp14, idle 0:06, (messages off) from sm
No unread mail
Project:
Will be at BIS Oct 15, 2000 teaching a seminar.
Plan:
I will be on vacation Oct 16-17, 2000.
dtr>
```

The following is the finger command without an argument displaying one line for each user currently logged in:

```
dtr> finger
Login     Name                 Tty    Idle  Login Time      Where
beltran   Rene Beltran         *p0    4:44  Mon Sep 20 15:39 10.1.1.101
dbhelp    dbhelp System        *p20   7:42  Mon Sep 20 12:53 sm
ingrid    Ingrid Van Zalingen  *p2    9:54  Mon Sep 20 07:10 iv
mori      Steve Moritsugu      *p1    1     Mon Sep 20 08:35 sm
mori      Steve Moritsugu      *p14   8     Mon Sep 20 08:59 sm
sisler    Shawn Sisler         *01    4:43  Mon Sep 20 16:11
sisler    Shawn Sisler         *p15         Mon Sep 20 09:19 ss
sisler    Shawn Sisler         *p16   2     Mon Sep 20 09:20 ss
sisler    Shawn Sisler         *p21   1     Mon Sep 20 15:02 comm
```

```
sloan    Bill Sloan         *p4    4:04  Mon Sep 20 16:51 10.1.1.106
stull    Michael Stull      *p9    3:56  Mon Sep 20 08:03 ms
stull    Michael Stull      *p10   4:31  Mon Sep 20 08:04 ms
stull    Michael Stull      *p11   9:27  Mon Sep 20 08:04 ms
stull    Michael Stull      *p12   3:56  Mon Sep 20 16:22 ms
dtr>
```

Displaying Information About the UNIX Password File

As with most secure systems, UNIX requires users not only to be registered with the system, but also to validate their login by supplying a user ID and a password. It's not completely foolproof, though, because users sometimes share their passwords with others, or someone uses another user's password.

First, take a look at the UNIX password file (passwd). The following is an example password file that resides in the /etc directory:

```
root:Thisisasecret:0:3::/:/sbin/sh
daemon:*:1:5::/:/sbin/sh
bin:*:2:2::/usr/bin:/sbin/sh
sys:*:3:3::/:
adm:*:4:4::/var/adm:/sbin/sh
uucp:*:5:3::/var/spool/uucppublic:/usr/lbin/uucp/uucico
lp:*:9:7::/var/spool/lp:/sbin/sh
nuucp:*:11:11::/var/spool/uucppublic:/usr/lbin/uucp/uucico
hpdb:*:20:1:ALLBASE:/:/sbin/sh
nobody:*:-2:-24::/:
oracle:BJXXXX3HTWSls:201:200:,,,:/home/oracle:/usr/bin/sh
cfliss:XXXXXXXXXXXXX:100:200:,,,:/home/cfliss:/usr/bin/sh
dwilson:Can'tguessme!:101:200:DanWilson,Indy,_317.555.5555,:/home/dwilson:/usr/
➥bin/sh
```

Each line in the passwd file identifies a single user to the system. Each field is separated by a colon (:). You can break down each entry as follows:

- Login name
- Encrypted password
- Numerical user identification
- Numerical group identification
- User information field

- User's home directory
- Shell program to use at sign-on

In the preceding example of passwd, you'll notice that some accounts have an asterisk (*) in their encrypted password field. This instructs the operating system to prevent anyone from directly logging into these accounts.

Notice the root (userid 0) account. This account is the superuser account. Persons logging onto this account are usually systems administrators because this account enables them to execute any command in the system, as well as start up and shut down the machine.

Also take a look at the nobody account. Notice that its user ID is -2. This account is reserved for remote root access, specifically NFS. NFS is a Network File System that enables you to mount directories (through a remote file system) onto your host machine.

Most versions of UNIX support shadow passwords. As you'll notice in the previous passwd file example, you can see the encrypted password for each user who has a password (it is possible but inadvisable to have user accounts without passwords). This is somewhat of a security issue because users can use this information to break other user's passwords. To prevent this, the UNIX vendors started implementing a shadow password system. This system places the encrypted password information into a special shadow password file located in another directory that only privileged users can access. Some systems have an /etc/shadow file that only privileged users can access. Either way, the goal is to keep ordinary users from reading the encrypted password.

Changing Your Password

Now is a good time to take a look at how you can change your password with the passwd command.

If You Forget Your Password

Even the system administrator (root) cannot look up someone's password because passwords are encrypted before they are saved. When you type in your password, it is validated by first encrypting it and then comparing it to your saved encrypted password. Thus, the system does not have to know your actual password, just your encrypted password. If you forget your password, the system administrator can give you a new one but cannot determine what your current password is.

At the shell prompt, type `passwd`:

```
$ passwd
Changing password for mschick
Old password: <Enter Old Password Here>
New password: <Enter New Password Here>
Re-enter new password: <Re-Enter New Password Here>
$
```

The `passwd` command interactively steps you through changing your password.

Groups

Another system file worth mentioning is the `group` file. This file also resides in the `/etc` directory and maintains a list of the primary and associated groups to which you belong. Take a look at an example of a `group` file and identify the components that comprise it:

```
root::0:root
other::1:root,hpdb
bin::2:root,bin
sys::3:root,uucp
adm::4:root,adm
daemon::5:root,daemon
mail::6:root
lp::7:root,lp
tty::10:
developer::99:dwilson,ssmith,cfliss
nuucp::11:nuucp
users::20:root,dwilson,ssmith,cfliss
nogroup:*:-2:
dba::200:oracle,dwilson,ssmith,cfliss
```

Notice that a user can exist in more than one group. Your entry in the `passwd` file determines your primary group membership. The `cfliss` account's primary group is

200 (dba). But this user also is a member of the developer (99) and user (20) groups as well.

The Login Session

When you log in and your password is verified, you are now a user on the system. Several commands give you information about your session.

The *tty* Command

Another command you should examine is the tty command. This command tells you the terminal or, if you are logging in across the network, the pseudo-terminal with which you are connected. The term *pseudo-terminal* means that you are not directly connected to the machine through a physical connection; you are connected through the network. Take a look at an example:

1. At the shell prompt, type tty.

2. You should see something close to the following:

```
$ tty
/dev/ttyp1
$
```

3. The system returns the device name that your terminal uses to connect to the system.

   Take note that the output /dev/ttyp1 contains a p before the device number. This indicates that the device is a pseudo-terminal. If you logged directly into the machine via your system console, you might see the following:

```
$ tty
/dev/console
$
```

The *$TERM* Variable

The $TERM environment variable tells the system the terminal type you want to emulate. Depending upon the system and terminal you are on, you can emulate either a character terminal or an X-Windows terminal. The X-Windows[nd]type terminal grants you graphics capabilities, whereas the character-based terminal does not. You can check with your systems administrator to determine your type of terminal. Chances are, the system administrator has already set your environment variables, which are active as soon as you log into the machine.

Take a look at how you view your $TERM setting and how you would change it if you needed to:

1. At the shell prompt, type echo $TERM.

2. The system echoes the value of TERM to the screen.

```
$ echo $TERM
vt100
$
```

If you are in the ksh (Korn shell) or the sh (posix shell) and you want to change the value of TERM, you would perform the following steps:

1. At the shell prompt, type TERM=vt220;export $TERM.

2. To check whether TERM changed, type echo $TERM.

3. You now see that TERM is set to vt220.

In the csh (C shell), perform these steps to change TERM:

1. At the shell prompt, type set term=vt220.

2. To check whether TERM changed, type set.

```
% set
```

3. You should see *all* your environment variable settings. In the output, you should see a line similar to this one:

```
term    vt220
```

The Set/View *tty* Settings

The stty command sets or displays the current settings of I/O options for your terminal. You use stty to set useful functions, such as your Backspace or process interrupt keys. Take a look at an example of this:

1. At the prompt, type stty -a:

```
$ stty -a

    speed 9600 baud; line = 0;
    rows = 0; columns = 0
    min = 4; time = 0;
    intr = ^C; quit = ^\; erase <undef>; kill = ^U
    eof = ^D; eol = ^@; eol2 <undef>; swtch <undef>
    stop = ^S; start = ^Q; susp <undef>; dsusp <undef>
    werase <undef>; lnext <undef>
    parenb -parodd cs7 -cstopb hupcl -cread -clocal -loblk -crts
    -ignbrk brkint ignpar -parmrk -inpck istrip -inlcr -igncr icrnl -iuclc
    ixon -ixany ixoff -imaxbel -rtsxoff -ctsxon -ienqak
    isig icanon -iexten -xcase echo echoe echok -echonl -noflsh
    -echoctl -echoprt -echoke -flusho -pendin
    opost -olcuc onlcr -ocrnl -onocr -onlret -ofill -ofdel -tostop
$
```

2. From the preceding output, you see that there are numerous settings. For the most part, you'll have to alter only a few of these. Notice in the output that the erase setting is undefined (<undef>). Set this to work for the Backspace (<Backspace>) key. (CTRL+H is the key combination for the Control key and the H key. CTRL+H is the default value for the Backspace key.) You use the stty command to tell the system to use this key sequence to perform the backspace function.

At the shell prompt, type stty erase ^H:

```
$ stty erase ^H
```

3. Now look at the results of typing stty -a:

```
$ stty -a
  speed 9600 baud; line = 0;
  rows = 0; columns = 0
  min = 4; time = 0;
  intr = ^C; quit = ^\; erase = ^H; kill = ^U
  eof = ^D; eol = ^@; eol2 <undef>; swtch <undef>
  stop = ^S; start = ^Q; susp <undef>; dsusp <undef>
  werase = ^K; lnext <undef>
  parenb -parodd cs7 -cstopb hupcl -cread -clocal -loblk -crts
  -ignbrk brkint ignpar -parmrk -inpck istrip -inlcr -igncr icrnl -iuclc
  ixon -ixany ixoff -imaxbel -rtsxoff -ctsxon -ienqak
  isig icanon -iexten -xcase echo echoe echok -echonl -noflsh
  -echoctl -echoprt -echoke -flusho -pendin
  opost -olcuc onlcr -ocrnl -onocr -onlret -ofill -ofdel -tostop
$
```

As you can see here, the Backspace key is set.

4. In the previous output, note one other important stty value: the intr or interrupt key. Press the interrupt key to break out of a UNIX command (it is usually Ctrl+C or Delete). Use the stty command to look up its value. In the previous example, Ctrl+C is the interrupt key.

Commands to See Who Is Logged In

You're now ready to learn commands that tell about the other users logged into the system. Earlier in the chapter, you saw that the finger command shows one line for each user currently logged in, as in the following:

```
dtr> finger
Login    Name               Tty   Idle  Login Time       Where
beltran  Rene Beltran       *p0   4:44  Mon Sep 20 15:39 10.1.1.101
dbhelp   dbhelp System      *p20  7:42  Mon Sep 20 12:53 sm
ingrid   Ingrid Van Zalingen *p2  9:54  Mon Sep 20 07:10 iv
mori     Steve Moritsugu    *p1   1     Mon Sep 20 08:35 sm
```

The who command gives similar information:

```
$ who
    Tim_Wilson          ttyp1       Mar 19 18:27
    Emily_Wilson        tty10       Mar 19 18:30
    oracle              ttyp2       Mar 19 15:27
    Taylor_Klausner     ttypd5      Mar 19 10:20
    Marissa_Klausner    ttypd1      Mar 18 06:00
    BPierce             ttyp7       Mar 19 19:17
    BWood               ttyp47      Mar 19 14:00
    CSarjent            ttyp10      Mar 19 11:27
    PSingleton          ttyp19      Mar 19 08:27
    Zach_Wilson         ttyp15      Mar 19 09:27
    Travis_Wilson       ttyp17      Mar 19 12:27
    JBerglund           ttyp19      Mar 19 08:27
    Rich_Blum           tty21       Mar 19 12:12
    Ed_Lewis            tty35       Mar 19 12:13
    Tony_Amico          console     Mar 19 12:00
$
```

As you can see from the output from who, a number of users are on the system. Notice that some of the users are directly connected (tty terminal ids), and others are connected through the network (ttyp terminal ids). Also notice that terminal ids ttypd1 and ttypd5 are different from the others. That's because these users are logged in through a modem.

You can also see that someone other than the system administrator has logged onto the system console. This is potentially dangerous because on some systems it is easier to gain privileged access by logging into the system console. You can use this one simple command to see who is logged on, how they are coming into the system, and when they logged in.

Take a look at another use for the who command. This time you use the command to show some information about your UNIX machine.

At the shell prompt, type who -b:

```
$ who -b
            system boot  Oct 28 13:35
```

This output tells you the date and time that the machine was booted (or restarted). This is useful to know if you had started a job prior to leaving work and came in the next day to find that the computer had crashed. Any information you find out before you talk to your system administrator will help in solving any problems you encounter.

The *uptime* Command

Another command that shows you information about users and the system is the uptime command. Here's an example of its use.

At the shell prompt, type uptime:

```
$ uptime
8:00pm up 142 days, 6:25, 2 users, load average: 0.51, 0.52, 0.52
$
```

The output tells you that the current time is 8:00 PM and that the system has been up for 142 days, 6 hours, and 25 minutes. Two users are currently logged onto the system. The load average is used by the system administrator to help gauge the performance of the system.

Now take a look at how you can use the uptime command with a special option to see output identical to the w command.

At the shell prompt, type uptime -w:

```
dtr> uptime -w
  9:45pm  up 1 day, 17:31,  14 users,  load average: 0.00, 0.00, 0.00
User     Tty       Login@   Idle   JCPU   PCPU   What
sisler   tty01     4:11pm   5:31    2      -     -sh
beltran  ttyp0     3:39pm   5:32    1      1     unibasic -f ml.mnt
mori     ttyp1     8:35am   31     13      -     uptime -w
ingrid   ttyp2     7:10am   10:42   3      -     -sh
```

The *w* Command

Now enter the w command:

```
dtr> w
  9:46pm  up 1 day, 17:32,  14 users,  load average: 0.00, 0.00, 0.00
User     Tty       Login@   Idle   JCPU   PCPU   What
sisler   tty01     4:11pm   5:32    2      -     -sh
beltran  ttyp0     3:39pm   5:33    1      1     unibasic -f ml.mnt
mori     ttyp1     8:35am   1      13      -     w
ingrid   ttyp2     7:10am   10:43   3      -     -sh
$
```

As you can see, w produced the same output as uptime -w. Using the w command, however, is a bit easier than remembering the options to the uptime command.

Writing A Message to All Users

The wall command is used by the root account to warn all users about some impending event:

```
# wall
Please log off in 5 minutes for system maintenance.
The system will be down for 2 hours.
Ctrl+D
#
```

After you type wall, you enter one or more messages lines. At the start of any line, press your EOT key (usually Ctrl+D) to indicate the end of the message.

All local users who are logged in will immediately see a message like this on their screens:

```
Broadcast Message from root (ttyp1) on dtr   Sep 20 21:53 1999...
Please log off in 5 minutes for system maintenance.
The system will be down for 2 hours.
```

The previous message will also beep to get their attention.

Writing Messages to All Remote Users

rwall is similar to the wall command except that it writes to all users in the local network, not just to users on your system:

```
# rwall
Please log off in 5 minutes for system maintenance.
All systems in the network will be down for 2 hours.
Ctrl+D
#
```

Remote systems must be running rwalld (the rwall daemon) to pick up and broadcast rwall messages.

User Account Administration

Most versions of UNIX provide menu programs to create new users, modify users, retire users, or delete users.

Delete versus Retire

In early UNIX systems, you could not ever delete a user due to security reasons. The fear was that many system tables provide special capabilities by username, not

UID number. Thus, if you deleted a user and later added the same name again, that name would still have the old user's special privileges.

Instead of a delete user option, you sometimes had a retire option. This put the account out of action so that it could not be used, and it also kept the name reserved so that it could not be used for a new user.

Today, it is common to be able to delete a username and later add that username back into the system. Be aware, though, that the old user might still be in system tables such as `cron.allow`, `cron.deny`, `.rhosts`, `/etc/hosts.equiv`, and so on.

Even today, it is difficult to change a username you have created, so make sure you spell it properly when you first create the account.

Becoming a Superuser

When you first install UNIX, it is important to create a non-root account to use. Don't work as the root account most of the time; if you make a mistake as root, it can damage the whole system much more than if you make the same mistake from a non-root account. Become root only when needed. (Remember, Superman spent most of his time as Clark Kent.)

An easy way to become the superuser (root) from a non-root account is to use the `su` command:

```
dtr> su
Password:
#
```

The previous example shows how you will be prompted for the root password when you run the `su` command. In the following example, a dash (-) is added to the `su` command:

```
dtr> su -
Password:
Last    successful real login for root: Mon Sep 20 22:23:10 1999 on ttyp0
Last unsuccessful real login for root: Mon Sep 20 11:20:30 1999 on ttyR029
TERM = (vt100)
#
```

This causes the `.profile` script to run to set up your environment just as if you had logged in as root. If you omit the dash, some administration commands might fail because you do not have the regular root environment.

The following example shows that users can use the `su` command to become other non-root users:

```
# su - stevemor
Last    successful real login for mori: Mon Sep 20 08:59:24 1999 on ttyp14
Last unsuccessful real login for mori: Fri Aug 13 17:28:00 1999 on ttyp1
TERM = (vt100)
$
```

If root runs the command, no password is needed, but other users must enter your password to become you. As before, include the dash after su so that the complete environment is set up.

Creating a New User Under IBM's AIX UNIX

Different brands of UNIX differ considerably in how you configure users, printers, networking, and so on. There are no standards in the area of UNIX system administration, so each type of UNIX can do things quite differently than any other UNIX does it. The next sections show you how to create a new user account under several versions of UNIX so that you can see how different the approaches are and yet the end results are the same.

To create a new user under AIX, follow these steps:

1. Log in as root and run the administrative menu program called smit:
   ```
   # smit
   ```

   You will see the following top menu options:
   - Software Installation and Maintenance
   - Software License Management
   - Devices
   - System Storage Management (Physical & Logical Storage)
   - Security & Users
   - Communications Applications and Services
   - Print Spooling
   - Problem Determination
   - Performance & Resource Scheduling
   - System Environments
   - Processes & Subsystems
   - Applications
   - Using SMIT (information only)

2. Select Security & Users. You will see the following options:

- Users
- Groups
- Passwords
- Login Controls

3. Select Users. You will see the following options:

- Add a User
- Change a User's Password
- Change/Show Characteristics of a User
- Lock/Unlock a User's Account
- Reset User's Failed Login Count
- Remove a User
- List All Users

4. Select Add a User. You will see the following screen:

```
* User NAME                              []
  User ID                                []
  ADMINISTRATIVE USER?                    false
  Primary GROUP                          []
  Group SET                              []
  ADMINISTRATIVE GROUPS                  []
  Another user can SU TO USER?            true
  SU GROUPS                              [ALL]
  HOME directory                         []
  Initial PROGRAM                        []
  User INFORMATION                       []
  EXPIRATION date (MMDDhhmmyy)           [0]
  Is this user ACCOUNT LOCKED?            false
  User can LOGIN?
```

5. In the above screen, there are 30 additional lines of user options not shown that you can set when you create this user. Notice that User NAME at the top is the only option with an asterisk (*), so it is the only option that must be entered to create a user.

Creating a New User Under Solaris 7

To create a new user under Solaris 7, follow these steps:

1. Click This Host to get a command-line window.

2. Enter admintool. The Admintool Users menu window should appear. If not, click Browse and then Users.

3. Click Edit.

4. Click Add. You should see a screen like the one shown in Figure 13.1.

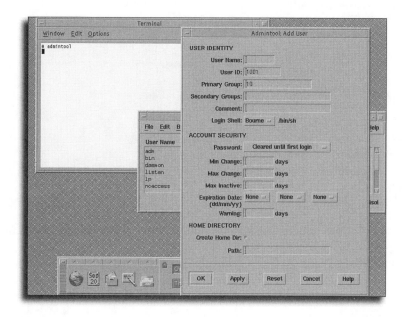

FIGURE 13.1
Add User under Solaris 7.

5. Only the name and the home directory are required to be filled in. Then click OK to create the user.

Creating a New User Under SCO UNIX

The procedure to create a new user under SCO UnixWare 7 is almost exactly the same as that for SCO OpenServer 5, which follows:

1. Log in as root.

2. Run scoadmin. The following screen appears.

This Example Is Character-Based

You can also run SCO Admin from the GUI, which gives a nice graphical display and enables you to use the mouse to make selections.

```
|| File   View   Options                                          Help ||
|+..........................................................+|
|+..........................................................+ |
||*   Account Manager                                          ^ |
||    Backup Manager                                           * |
||    BackupEDGE                                               * |
||    Hardware/Kernel Manager                                  * |
||    Internet Configuration                                   * |
||    License Manager                                          * |
||    Process Manager                                          * |
||    SendMail Configuration                                   * |
||    Software Manager                                         * |
||    Video Configuration Manager                              | |
|| > Filesystems                                               | |
|| > Mail                                                      | |
|| > Netscape
```

3. In the previous screen, arrow to Account Manger as shown and press Enter to get the following:

```
|| Host   Users   Groups   View   Options                      Help ||
|+...........................................................+|
| User accounts on dtr.dtrbus.COM:                             |
|                                                              |
| Status  User       ID       Comment                          |
|+..........................................................+ |
||*       root       0        Superuser                        ^ |
||        daemon     1        System daemons                   * |
||        bin        2        Owner of system commands         * |
||        sys        3        Owner of system files            | |
||        adm        4        System accounting                | |
||        uucp       5        UUCP administrator                | |
||        nuucp      6        Anonymous UUCP site              | |
||        auth       7        Authentication administrator     | |
||        asg        8        Assignable devices               | |
||        cron       9        Cron daemon                      | |
||        sysinfo    11       System information                | |
||        dos        16       DOS device
```

4. In this screen, tab to Users and press Enter. You will see options like this:

- Add New User

- Modify

- Delete

- Retire
- Change Password
- Password Restrictions
- Login Controls
- Authorizations
- Privileges

5. Select Add New User. You will see a screen like this:

```
+------------------------ dtr: Add New User ----------------------+
|                                                                 |
|             Login:  | _____ |                                |
|           User ID:  |477___|                                    |
|           Comment:  |_____||
|                     +---------------------------------------------+  |
|          Password:  |<*> Set password now   < > Set password later |  |
|                     +---------------------------------------------+  |
| --------------------------------------------------------------- |
|                                                                 |
|       Login Shell:  |sh_____|    [(Change Login Shell...)]  |
|      Networked Via: |_____|    [(Change Distribution...)] |
|   Home Directory:   |/usr_____|    [(Change Home Directory...)]  |
|      Login Group:   |group_____|    [(Change Group Membership...)] |
|---------------------------------------------------------------|
|[   OK   ]                   [ Cancel ]            [  Help  ]|
```

6. Fill in the details about the new user, and select OK to create the new user.

chapter

14

Jesper Pedersen and
Steve "Mor" Moritsugu

File Permissions and System Security

Login security

Planning groups for a system

Understanding file modes

Changing permissions/owner/group

Setting default permissions for new files

Watching the dangerous *setuid* and *setgid* permissions

> **Tip for Beginners**
>
> If you are planning to share files or programs with any other user on UNIX, you need to understand file and directory permissions as covered in this chapter. Beginners should not stay in the root account and should not change the owner, group, or permissions of any system files because a mistake in this area can crash or corrupt your whole system.

Login Security

When you want to log on to a UNIX system, you are queried for a login name and a password. The login name is your unique name on the given UNIX system. The password is your secret key to the account, which, when selected carefully, is your guarantee that no one else (except root) can access your personal files.

> **Changing Your Login Name**
>
> For maximum security, some UNIX systems never allow your login name to change. Your name can be retired, but then it can never be used again. To get a new name, a totally new account must be created. Even on UNIX systems that allow the administrator to change the login name, choose the name carefully so that you won't have to ask for a change later.

You can change your password yourself, but your login name will be the same forever. If you changed your login name, your email address would change, too, and people would not know how to contact you on the computer. You can think about your login name as your personal name and your password as the key to your home.

Delays After Invalid Login

If you mistype your password, you get a message saying that the login is invalid. After a few seconds of delay, the computer will ask you for a login name and password once again.

This delay is imposed to avoid the instance when someone may try to log into your account repeatedly, with a different password each time. With a delay, a program can try only about 500 different passwords per hour. Without the delay, such a program may try above a hundred thousand passwords per hour.

Secondary Passwords

On some systems, you may encounter additional passwords when you want to use a modem, a fax, or another external device. You may also encounter passwords when you want to start a program that is licensed and thus restricted.

The reason for passwords on devices may be to restrict the devices to a certain group of people. For example, it is possible to restrict the use of a modem to only employees at a university and not the student users.

Such restrictions can be obtained by setting up a group in which the given device was located. This way, only the members of this group have read/write/execute permissions to the device in question. Password restriction on the device has one major advantage over the group solution: If someone guesses your login password, he still must guess your password to the device as well before using it. The moral of this: Do not use your login password as the same password for such secondary passwords. If you do, the security will be compromised.

Password Aging

On some systems, you may have your password for only a maximum amount of time before the system requires you to change it. This is designed to increase the level of security in the system, which occurs in two ways:

- When your password is periodically changed, the chance that someone may learn your password (over your shoulder) decreases. It may take several attempts for someone to steal the whole password, so the fact that it is changed periodically lessens the chance of a complete password theft.

- If someone has gotten his hands on the encrypted version of your password (a description of the encrypted password appears later in this chapter), he may systematically try to crack your password by encrypting words and comparing the encrypted version with the encrypted version of your password. The shorter a period you have for each password, the less the chance that someone will crack your password this way as well.

In addition to restricting the maximum time you may have a password, some systems also restrict the *minimum* time you may have one. This is to ensure that you do not have one favorite password that you insist on using all the time. This prevents you from using a dummy password when the system prompts you to change your password, and then promptly returning to your favorite one.

If you use the recipes for choosing passwords described in the next section, it should not be hard to select a new password each time the system asks you to do so. Proper use of passwords increases the security that no one else can access your personal files, your email account, and so forth.

Changing Your Password

Several reasons exist as to why you may want to change your password:

- Because you suspect that someone has guessed your password or has seen you type it.

- Because the system demands that you change it once in a while.

- Because the initial password given to you is hard to remember, or the password is required to be changed at first login.

Different UNIX systems have different restrictions on which passwords you may choose. If you choose a password that fulfills the following recommendations, however, you should be on safe ground:

- Choose a password with at least eight characters (only the first eight characters matter, but if it is easier for you to remember a longer password, you are welcome to use more than eight characters.)

- Use lowercase and uppercase letters.

- Use characters from the keyboard that are not letters. For instance, numbers or some of the special characters such as the dollar sign, the quotation mark, or the less-than sign make good additions to a password.

- Choose a password that is not available in a dictionary, a book, or any other text that might be electronically available.

Avoid Short Passwords and Dictionary Words

A hacker, trying to break into a UNIX system, will often set up a program that attempts to log in as root by trying all possible short passwords and encrypted dictionary words. Short passwords and common dictionary words will let an intruder in much more readily than long passwords with upper- and lowercase and punctuation.

Several good rules exist for choosing a password that is easy to remember.

- Choose the first letter from each word of a poem, a saying, or a song, and capitalize some of the letters (maybe include a non-letter somewhere in between). An example might be the phrase "There is more to love than boy meets girl," which might give you the password TimtlTbmg. (Note that this password is nine character long, so the final g may be omitted, but it might be easier to remember if you include it.)

- Choose two words that have something to do with each other, and combine them with a non-letter). An example might be *dog* and *capital*, which might give the passwords cApI dOg, DOG=capi, or dog&capital. It might be easier if you choose two words that have some kind of connection for you (but which no one else knows about). Using the previous example, you might have bought a dog the weekend after you had visited someone in the capital!

After you've chosen a good password, it is time to actually change your login password. Depending on your system, you should use either `yppasswd`, `nispasswd`, or `passwd`. If you do not know which one to use, try `yppasswd` and `nispasswd` first; if the result of both commands is `command not found`, try `passwd`.

When you have invoked the appropriate command, the system asks you for your old password. (By first asking for your old password, nobody can change your password if they find a terminal where you have forgotten to log out.) Next, the system asks you for the new password. Finally, you are asked to retype your new password to make sure you have not made a typing error.

Who Can See Your Password?

To fully understand how secret (or nonsecret) your password is, you need to understand how the password mechanism works. When you select a new password, it is encrypted to a text string, which is saved on the system. It is not possible to do the inverse function—that is, given an encrypted password, you cannot find the nonencrypted version. (Technically, it is possible, but it is *very* unlikely. Such a process might take thousands of years on even the fastest computers.) When you want to log on to the system, the unencrypted password (which you type to log on) is encrypted, and the result is matched against the version that was computed when you first selected the password.

If someone wants to crack your password and has the encrypted version, that person may take a word, encrypt it, and compare it with your encrypted password. However, this is not as simple as it sounds because there are so many words to try. Imagine that you choose between 90 different keys on your keyboard (including capital letters) and that you use the full length of eight characters for your password. Then, it takes a computer that has the capability to test 1,000 words per second more than 200,000 years to try all combinations; said in another way, it will take all computers in a large city one year to crack just one password.

If your password can be found in a dictionary, however, it may be cracked this way within a few seconds by a powerful computer.

One conclusion you can draw from the preceding information is that not even root may see your nonencrypted password!

In older UNIX systems, the encrypted password was located in the /etc/passwd file, and this file could be read by everybody. This produced a possible security hole; a user with access to the system could crack other users' password by the method described earlier. A new method was developed, which many systems use today, called *shadow passwords*. The idea is to remove the encrypted password from the /etc/passwd file and hide it in a file that is readable only by root and the login programs (which is to say, setuid root programs).

To see whether your system uses shadow passwords, you can check the /etc/passwd file. If the second field contains 13 letters (which seem random), then it doesn't. (These 13 letters are, in fact, your encrypted password.)

Permitting Users to Become Another User or root

Occasionally, you want to access another user's files or run a program in the name of another user. One way you can do that is to log out and let the user log in on your terminal. However, there is an easier way! Using the command su (*substitute user*), you can change the owner of the shell to another user.

Typing su username changes the owner of the shell to the user username. If you don't give a username, you will change to root. After typing the su command, you will, of course, have to give the password for the given user.

When you change the ownership of the shell using su, the shell still knows who the original user was (due to environment variables). This might sometimes be a desirable effect, and sometimes not. If you want every environment variable to be reset when using su, you should give it a dash as argument su - username.

Planning Groups for a System

Each file on a UNIX system belongs to exactly one user and one group. This ownership dictates who may read and edit the file and, in case the file is an executable file, who might execute it. Directories have similar permissions, which you'll see later.

Ownership information can be seen by using the command ls, if you give it the appropriate set of options:

```
ls -ldg security.html
-rw-r--r--   1 blackie   users       12383 Mar 15 10:27 security.html
```

Finding the Names for a File

The second column of long listing is the number of names for the given file. This is the number of hard links for the given file if it is a plain file. For directories, this is 2 plus the number of subdirectories: Each subdirectory has a link to the directory with .., the directory has a reference to itself with ., and the directory in which it is placed has a reference to it with the name of the directory.

In the first column you can see the permissions for the file, in the third column you can see the owner of the file (blackie—that's me), and in the fourth column you can see the group to which the file belongs.

If several people have to work together on a set of files, they do not have to log in as the same user. Instead, a group should be created, and the set of files should be placed in this group with appropriate permissions. For example, you would need read and write permissions for the user and the group.

Groups cannot be maintained by an ordinary user, but they must be administered by the superuser (root). As an ordinary user, however, you may be in several groups at one time. To see the groups in which you are located, type groups.

Understanding File Modes (Permissions)

The following section uses the word *file* to mean both files and directories, and the word *plain*, or *regular*, *file* to refer to a file (not a directory).

In the previous section, you saw that ls could tell you permission information about files:

```
ls -ldg security.html
-rwxr-xr--   1 blackie   users 12383 Mar 15 10:27 security.html
```

The following file modes (permission information) are given in the first 10 characters of each output line from a long listing (see Figure 14.1):

- 1 character: file type
- 3 characters: permissions for the user who is the file owner
- 3 characters: permissions if not owner but in same group
- 3 characters: permissions if not owner nor in same group

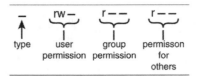

FIGURE 14.1
File mode is one file type bit and nine file permission bits.

The first character (file type) is usually one of the following:

- - (dash) for a regular file
- d for a directory

SEE ALSO

➤ *For a more complete list of file type characters, see page 178*

These are the possible three-character permission settings:

- Character 1: Read permission allowed (r) or not allowed (-)
- Character 2: Write permission allowed (w) or not allowed (-)
- Character 3: Execute permission allowed (x) or not allowed (-)

In the previous example, you saw these example permissions:

rwxr-xr--

In this code, the following is the summary:

- rwx in the first set of three describes the user who is the file owner. rwx says that the owner can read, write, and execute the file (if it is a program).
- r-x in the second set of three describes any user who is not the owner but who belongs to the same group as the file. r-x says that group members can read and execute but not write or modify the file.

- r-- in the third set of three describes other users (who are not the owner and not in the group). r-- says that others may read the file but not write to it or execute it.

Permissions should always be read as three groups of three. If the file permissions are

r w x r- xr--

you would say them aloud as this:

rwx, r-x, r - -   (correct)

You would pause for each comma (,) and say "dash" for the - sign. Do not read it like this:

rw, xr-, xr-, -   (incorrect)

This is a summary of the key points about file permissions:

- Every file has an owner.

- Every file belongs to one group. Initially, this is the primary group of the owner, but the group can be changed later.

- Every user belongs to one or more groups simultaneously. The system administrator can add or remove users from groups or create new groups.

- Only one of the three sets of file permissions applies to you. If you are both the file owner and in the same group as the file, only the owner permissions apply to you, not the group permissions.

- The owner of a file can be denied read, write, or execute permission. For example, I might turn off write permission on my file so that I don't modify it by accident.

Directory Permissions

Directory permissions are not intuitive:

- **Read** permission to a directory is needed to list the files in the directory. If you lack read permission, you may still be able to access files there if you already know their exact spelling.

- **Write** permission to a directory gives you what I call administrative control over the directory. It allows you to add, remove, or change names in the directory. This gives you the ability to create new files, delete existing files, and rename existing files, even if you don't have permission to write to the existing files.

- **Execute** permission to a directory allows you to use the cd command to change to a directory. Lack of execute permission prevents you from accessing any file in the directory and any of its subdirectories.

Sometimes you may encounter a letter other than x or dash (-) in the third position. This is described in Table 14.1.

Table 14.1 Additional Options for the Execute Bit

User	Group	Other	
Execute Permissions Files			
s:			1) The file has x permission for the user.
			2) The file is a setuid program (see "setuid / segid Programs" section).
S:			1) The file does not have x permissions for the user.
			2) The file is a setuid program (see "setuid / segid Programs" section).
	s:		1) The file has x permission for the group.
			2) The file is a setgid program (see "setuid / segid Programs" section).
	S:		1) The file does not have x permissions for the group.
			2) The file is a setgid program (see "setuid / segid Programs" section).
Execute Permissions for Directories			
	s:		1) The directory has x permission for the group.
			2) New files in this directory will be created with the group ownership as the directory not the user's default group (see "setuid / segid Programs" section).
	S:		1) The directory has no x permission for the group.
			2) New files in this directory will be created with the group ownership as the directory; that is, not the user's default group (see "setuid / segid Programs" section).
		t:	1) The directory has x permissions for others.
			2) Others may create new files in the directory, but they may not delete each other's files (see "setuid / segid Programs" section).
		T:	1) The directory has no x permissions for others.
			2) Others may create new files in the directory, but they may not delete each other's files (see the following section).

setuid/setgid Programs

As you saw earlier with the su command, you can change the identity of the shell to another user. However, this requires that you know the password of the other user, unless you are already the root. This restriction is not acceptable in certain specific situations, as the following example shows.

The password file called /etc/passwd is writable only by root (that is, only root may edit this file). When you want to change your password, you must change the content of this file. This is achieved by the passwd program, which is a setuid program (Set User ID). When this program is executed, the identity of the process changes from you to root. This shift of identity happens without querying you for a password.

The passwd program has been made a setuid program by the chmod program.

Likewise, a program may shift group on execution. This means that the user becomes a member of the group of the program file while running that file. Such programs are called setgid programs.

Directory Sticky Bit

Users who have write permission to a directory have effective administrative control over that directory. In addition to creating files, these users can delete and rename files of other users, even if they don't have permission to modify those files.

This may be a problem, for example, if you are an instructor at a university and want to create a directory in which your students can place their assignments. The problem is that if you give the students write permission to the directory, they will also get administrative control over that directory and thus have the capability of removing the assignments of other students!

A solution to this problem is to set the sticky bit on the directory. This gives the student write permissions to the directory but not administrative control over the directory.

In this case, you would set the permissions as follows:

```
chmod u=rwx,og=wxt directory
```

This gives the permission drwx-wx-wt. I have purposely left out the read permission for the group and others. This way, the student cannot see the files in the directory and thus cannot tell who has returned the assignments.

setgid Bit Sets Group on New Files

After you have a group set up for a given assignment, files for this assignment should be created with the group identity of group. This can be achieved in three ways:

1. You could create the files and use the chgrp command to change their group identity afterward.

2. You could change the default group in which the new files you create belong. This can be done with the command newgrp, but it will have effect only in the shell in which you invoke the newgrp command. To change the group this way, just invoke the command newgrp group.

3. You could set the setgid bit on the directory. With this method, new files created in this directory have the same group identity as the directory; thus, they don't share the group identity of the one who creates them.

To set the setgid bit for a directory, type chmod g+s directory.

Read and Execute Permission on Directories

Many people get confused by the use of the read permission and the execute permission on directories. Take a close look at the following four situations:

- **No read permission and no execute permission**

  In this case, the directory is closed.

- **Read permission and execute permission**

  In this case, the directory is open for listing the content of files, listing the content of the directory, and accessing subdirectories (if the subdirectories allow this).

- **Read permission and no execute permission**

  This is an odd case that seldom occurs. A user can see the filenames but cannot access them, get information about their attributes, or traverse into subdirectories.

- **No read permission and execute permission**

  In this situation, a user may not list the content of the directory but may access files, if he knows their names. This is a very convenient permission to set on your home directory, for example. With this permission, people might eventually go into a directory and see your emacs file (if it has the permission for it), but they may not see any other files you have. In other words, the users may see only the files that you tell them you have and that the users have the permission to see.

Changing Permissions/Owner/Group

Permissions of files and directories can be changed using the command chmod (change mode). This command can either be used with a numerical argument, which states exactly what the permission should be, or with a symbolic argument, which may change only part of the permissions (such as only the permissions for the user). Here is the general syntax of the chmod command:

```
chmod perm-changes file1 file2 ...
```

perm-changes specifies what permissions to change and may be specified in either numeric or symbolic mode, as you shall see shortly.

Only the user who owns a given file may change the permissions for this file. (An exception to this rule is, of course, the superuser, who may do anything!)

The chmod program changes permission for all files in a directory hierarchy by using the -R options (R stands for *recursive*).

See Table 14.2 for other standard properties of the chmod command.

Table 14.2   Other Properties of the *chmod* Command

Property	See page
Allows relative and absolute pathname arguments	70
Allows a list of filenames and filename wildcards	292

Setting Permissions by Using Numeric Mode

The chmod command changes the permission for files and directories using a number. This is a very convenient (and fast) way to set all the permissions for a file or directory.

The idea is that you describe the permission with three or four digits, where each digit describes one of the following permissions (see Table 14.3):

1. The setuid, setgid, and sticky bit (optional)
2. Permission for the user who is the owner of the file
3. Permission for the group
4. Permission for others

Table 14.3 Permission Figures for the *chmod* Command

Digit	Corresponding Permissions
0	- - -
1	- - x
2	- w -
3	- w x
4	r - -
5	r - x
6	r w -
7	r w x

Table 14.3 shows that if you want this permission for file `acme`:

`r w x r-x r--`

you should run this command:

```
chmod 754 acme
```

You can derive the digits in Table 14.3 if you pretend that the individual permission letters have these point values:

- `r = 4`
- `w = 2`
- `x = 1`

The special permissions have similar values

- The `setuid` bit = 4
- The `setgid` bit = 2
- The directory sticky bit = 1

Thus, if you want the file to be `setuid` and `setgid`, you should use the number 6 (that is, 4 + 2.) If you do not want any of the three options selected, you should use 0.

Test Your UNIX Skills

Assume that file **pegasus** has these permissions (mode):

r w - r w - r w -

What will be the resulting permissions after running this command:

chmod 751 pegasus

Answer at the bottom of this page.

Here is another example. If you want read and write permissions for the user and only read permissions for the group and others on a file called myfile, you should execute this command:

chmod 0644 myfile.

Leading zeros may be omitted, so the following command is equal to the previous one:

chmod 644 myfile.

Setting Permissions by Using Symbolic Mode

In the previous section, you saw how to set the permission for files using numerical mode. The major drawback of this is that you do not have the ability to change selected permissions while leaving the rest as they were.

Using chmod in symbolic mode, you can alter only part of the permission for files and directories.

The syntax for the permission changes in symbolic mode is given in the following form:

<who><operator><permission>,<who><operator><permission>,...

Here, <who> is zero or more of the characters u, g, o, and a:

- u is the user who is the owner of the file.

- g is any nonowner in the same group as the file.

- o is other users, not owner, not in same group.

Answer to test at top of page:

rwxr-x--x

- a is all users. If *<who>* is omitted, it defaults to a, but the value of the file mode creation mask is taken into account (see the following section for information on the file mode creation mask, called umask).

- *<operator>* is either +, - or =.

- + means add the following permissions.

- - means remove the following permissions.

- = means add the following permissions and remove any permissions not specified.

<permission> is one or more of r, w, x, s, t:

- r = read permission

- w = write permission

- x = execute permission

- s = setuid if *<who>* is u and setgid if *<who>* is g

- t = sticky bit if *<who>* is o

- u,g,o = permission is to be taken from the current user, group, or other mode, respectively

Several permissions may be changed at a time by repeating the *<who>*, *<operator>*, or *<permission>* commands with a comma in between. No spaces are allowed within this permission specification to chmod.

A Few Examples

Test your UNIX Skills

Assume that file **pegasus** has these permissions (mode):

```
r w - r w - - - -
```

What will be the resulting permissions after running this command:

```
chmod g+r-w,a+rx,o=x pegasus
```

Answer on next page.

To add read permission for the group and others on a file called `myfile`, type this line:

```
chmod go+r myfile
```

To add read permission for the group and others on all files and directories in a given directory, type this line:

```
chmod go+r *
```

To add read permission for the group and others on all files and directories in a given directory and on directories below, type this line:

```
chmod -R go+r *
```

To enable users to access files in your home directory only if they know the name of the file they want to access, type this line:

```
chmod go=r /home/user/
```

To be a bit less restrictive and give the group the possibility to see which files you have but to withhold this option from others, type this line:

```
chmod g=rx,o=r /home/user/
```

To open all your files in a directory for the group in a given directory, type this line:

```
chmod g+rX *
```

This has the following effects:

- Read permission will be added on all files and directories.
- Execute permission will be added on all directories.
- Execute permission will be added on files that already have execute permission for one of user group or other.

Changing the Group of a File

Using the `chgrp` command, you can change the group of a file, a directory, or a whole directory hierarchy.

To change the group for specific files, use this syntax:

```
chgrp new-group file1 file2 ...
```

This command may include directory names. If so, only the group of the directory will be changed, but not the files within the directory.

Add the -R option to change the group recursively, which means that if any directories are given, it will also change the group of all subdirectories and files within the given directory. For example:

```
chgrp -R accting acme /usr/fred/finance
```

In this example, acme is a regular file that will be changed to group accting. /usr/fred/finance is a directory, so it and all its subdirectories and all their files will be changed to group accting.

You must be the owner of the file to run chgrp to change its group. You do not have to be a member of the new group. To see the groups of which you are a member, use the either the groups or id command. Note that root, the system administrator account, is the virtual co-owner of all files on the system and thus can change the group of any file.

See Table 14.4 for other standard properties of the chgrp command.

Table 14.4 Other Properties of the *chgrp* Command

Property	See page
Allows relative and absolute pathname arguments	70
Allows a list of filenames and filename wildcards	292

Changing the Owner of a File

If you are the owner of a file, you can give the file to someone else by using the chown command, which has this syntax:

```
chown new-owner file1 file2 ...
```

Make sure you really want to do this, because once you make someone else the owner, you cannot run chown to take the file back if you change your mind. You must ask the new owner to run chown to give the file back to you. Note that root, the system administrator account, is the virtual (invisible) co-owner of all files on the system and thus can run chown to change the owner of any file.

See Table 14.5 for other standard properties of the chown command.

Table 14.5 Other Properties of the *chown* Command	
Property	See page
Allows relative and absolute pathname arguments	70
Allows a list of filenames and filename wildcards	292

Setting Default Permissions for New Files

With the umask command, you can control the permissions of newly created files and directories. To view your current umask value, enter umask with no argument:

```
$ umask
077
$
```

To change your umask value, enter the new value as an argument:

```
$ umask 27
```

Don't confuse the umask value with chmod in numeric mode. Here is how umask works.

UNIX wants to create any new file with read/write permission for everyone:

```
rw-rw-rw-    # default new file permission
```

It wants to create the same for directories but must also add execute permission so that the directories can be accessed. It does not want to add execute permission for new files until you debug the code:

```
rwxrwxrwx    # default new directory permission
```

umask acts like chmod in reverse. Each digit in umask tells what default permission to turn off. Assume that umask is 27. New files will then get permission 640. umask of 27 says to turn off write permissions for group and read/write/execute permissions for other:

```
file default: r w - r w - r w -
umask of 27:  - - - - w - r w x
resultant:    r w - r - - - - -
```

If your umask is 27, new directories will get permission 750:

```
dir default: r w x r w x r w x
umask of 27: - - - - w - r w x
resultant:   r w x r - x - - -
```

Thus, to give the owner full access (rwx) for new files, and to give the group and other only read permission, you should use this command:

```
umask 022
```

In general, small values of umask leave most permission bits on, which means that you are very trusting and allow other users great access to the files that you create. Large values of umask turn off more permission bits, which means that you are more security conscious. There are two philosophies for umask:

- Allow great access to your files and turn off permissions for specific files or directories only where security is an issue.

- Allow little access to your files and turn on permissions to specific files or directories on an as-needed basis.

With umask, you can determine which philosophy appeals best to you.

Watching the Dangerous *setuid* and *setgid* Permissions

setuid and setgid files are dangerous because they might give an unauthorized user root access, or at least access to run a program in another user's name.

To make a program setuid root, the user must be root. (Remember, you must be the user to which you want to make a program setuid.) So, if you never mount partitions from other machines, and if you are 100% sure that no one can get to the root, you have no problem. However, it is very difficult to be so sure, as hackers may have cracked root's password.

setuid programs are very convenient for hackers because they might create a back door to the root account, which is still available after root has changed his password to something the hacker does not know.

However, a simple way exists by which to verify that no new setuid program has appeared on your system since last check—use the commands crontab, find, and diff. To use this strategy, you must have a version of the find program, which supports the -perm option. If your version does not support this, you may download one from the gnu archive (URL: http://www.gnu.org/order/ftp.html).

With the command find / -perm ++s, you can recursively traverse the whole filesystem and search for files that have either setuid or setgid permission. The script in Listing 14.1 does this and saves the output in the file called suid.info. This file is compared with the one from the previous run using `diff`, and thus only outputs new setuid/setgid programs (or setuid/setgid programs that have vanished).

Listing 14.1   Program to Search for New *setuid*/*setgid* Programs

```
#!/bin/sh
test -e suid.info && mv suid.info suid.info.old
test ! -e suid.info.old && touch suid.info.old
find / -perm -4000 -print> suid.info
diff suid.info suid.info.old
```

One change you should make to this program is to give it a full path to where you want it to save the `suid.info` file.

If you make this little program a `cron` job, which is executed once each day, you will have set up a system to check for new setuid/setgid files.

You will get an email only as result of the `cron` job when new setuid/setgid program appears because it otherwise will not output anything.

setuid/*setgid* Files When Mounting Filesystems

On some variant of UNIX, the `mount` command supports a `nosuid` option. This means that a filesystem mounted with this option does not give special meanings to a setuid/setgid program (that is, they will not be setuid/setgid files). Without this option, mounted filesystems may be a problem, as the following example shows.

Imagine that you are a system manager on a UNIX system at an institute on a university campus. One day a system manager from another institute asks if you would be so kind as to mount a file system from his UNIX so that your common students can access their files (located on his hard disk) on your system. What should you answer? Will this affect the security at your system?

It will most definitely affect the security at your system if you do not turn off setuid/setgid with the `nosuid` option for `mount`. If the other system manager is hostile, he might create a setuid-root shell on the file system that you mount, and obtain root access to your filesystem. Even if he is not hostile, you should think about what could happen if the root password on his system is not as well planned as on your system. The answer could be that a hacker cracked the root password and thus gained root access at your system.

# chapter 15

System Startup, Shutdown, and Managing Jobs

*By Steve "Mor"
Moritsugu*

Bringing up the system

Shutting down the system

Adding system startup/shutdown jobs

Running jobs periodically
or at a later time

Checking and changing job priorities

Starting and killing background jobs

Suspending and resuming
background jobs

Tip for Beginners

If you run UNIX or Linux on your home computer, bringing up the system and doing a proper `shutdown` are very important sections in this chapter.

You can skip the rest of this chapter until you are more comfortable entering UNIX commands. Then come back to this chapter to read how to automate commands and suspend and resume processing.

Starting Up the System

Systems vary widely in the steps required to fully bring up UNIX and allow users to log in and do their work. This is because UNIX has been ported to many different types of computers and different processors by different computer companies. In the simplest case, you simply turn on the power, and the UNIX system comes up on its own. The system will be ready for use in a few minutes, or it could take much longer depending on firmware diagnostics, restoring network connections, initializing devices and databases, and so on. Other types of UNIX systems will not come up on their own, and you must enter specific commands to bring them up.

Warning: Improper Startup Can Damage the System Severely

On system startup, some UNIX systems require you to enter commands to initialize special hardware or software packages that have been added to the system. Don't bring up a UNIX system unless you have been instructed on the proper steps for that specific computer.

The average user never has to worry about this on most commercial UNIX systems because the system is in a restricted area in the computer room attended by computer operators and administrators. However, on some desktop UNIX systems and home-based UNIX systems the owner/user is the only operator/administrator. I can't tell you the specific steps required to bring up every UNIX system, but I can tell you the general steps or stages that are involved.

Remove Any Bootable Media

Avoiding a Boot Virus

By far, the majority of computer viruses affect Windows and not UNIX systems. However if your UNIX system runs on an Intel processor, a Windows boot virus could prevent UNIX from starting. You could catch this virus if you accidentally leave an infected diskette in the drive and then start the UNIX boot up process. This is another critical reason to make sure there is no diskette in the drive when you start to boot UNIX.

Booting is the process of loading software into memory, which allows a program or an operating system to start running. Most systems can boot from several types of devices. For example, most Intel i86 systems are configured to boot from drive A first (the floppy) and then from drive C (the hard disk) if there is no disk in the floppy drive. Other machines may boot by preference from CD-ROM or tape. Remove such media before bringing up the system because UNIX normally boots from the hard disk.

Power On Auxiliary Subsystems Before the Main Computer

Some systems have external boxes of disk drives, tape drives, or port connections that are connected to the main system by cables. Usually these should be powered up and ready before the main computer is powered up. If you don't do this, the system may not come up at all, or it will be incapable of using those devices until the system is rebooted with those devices online.

Run Power-On Diagnostics

Most computers will run some sort of diagnostics when they are first powered on. This could be just a quick memory test. Some computers will run a suite of tests that could take minutes or hours—or could even go forever—unless you know how to end the diagnostics. You should watch the screen output when you first bring up the UNIX system so that you get a feel for the typical messages. Then if a hardware problem is detected, you will at least recognize that something is different. Often the bootup will scan for all the devices on your system. If a device takes too long to respond or does not respond at all, you might have a hardware problem.

Loading the UNIX Kernel into Memory

The next step in booting is loading the UNIX kernel file into memory. The kernel contains the driver codes needed to access the disk, monitor, keyboard, and other hardware on the system. On some systems, you will receive a boot prompt from which you can specify boot options or special kernels to load. Sometimes booting requires you to enter a complicated command string that includes the device address of the primary disk containing the kernel file.

SEE ALSO

➤ *For more information on the UNIX kernel, see page 24*

Mounting the Root Disk and Checking It

The booting process includes a phase of checking to see whether the operating system was shut down properly the last time. If it was not, there could be damage to the root filesystem, and you may see a message such as this:

```
fsstat: mount failed.  Possibly damaged filesystem.
okay to check the root filesystem (y/n) ?
```

---

fsck and Corrupted Systems

On older UNIX systems, powering off without doing a shutdown command can cause serious data corruption, even if no programs were running at the time. On reboot after a crash, the system will note that it was not shutdown properly and will then run **fsck** to check and clean up the filesystems. It may ask first if it is okay to run **fsck**. This is always a time of great tension, waiting to see if the system is clean or if many corrupted files are found. Newer UNIX systems have more protection against corrupted files but it is still important to always shutdown before poweroff.

This check is performed by a program called fsck. Sometimes fsck is started automatically without waiting for a response from the user. If you are lucky, fsck will report a tight series of phase messages such as the following:

```
Phase 1: Check Blocks and Sizes
Phase 2: Check Path Names
Phase 3: Check Connectivity
```

If you are unlucky, the phase messages will be strewn with ugly-sounding errors like the following:

```
EXCESSIVE BAD BLOCKS I=1432
POSSIBLE FILE SIZE ERROR I=257
35738 DUP I=138273
DUP/BAD I=374 OWNER=17 MODE=700 SIZE=14328 FILE=/data/_maincust
(REMOVE?)
```

Each of these errors indicates possible data corruption or file loss. Sometimes there are thousands of these errors, and the system must be restored from a backup or reloaded from scratch. Some modern UNIX systems offer a journaled filesystem type that makes them much more resistant to such problems as an improper shutdown or system crash. It is also wise to use a UPS (uninterrupted power supply), which contains a battery that will keep the system from crashing in the event of power failure.

Single-User Mode

As UNIX comes up, many systems enable the operator to stop in single-user mode, in which the system is only partially initialized and maintenance functions can be performed. On some systems, a special command sequence must be used to get to single-user mode. Most systems, for security reasons, require that a user enter the root login password to bring the system to single-user mode. In single-user mode, you are running with root (superuser) privilege. If you type `exit` from single-user mode, you will not get another login prompt. Instead, the system will exit single-user mode and usually start up multiuser mode.

Multiuser Mode

If the system does not stop in single-user mode, it goes on to initialize the system and devices for its main run mode, called *multiuser mode*. UNIX is usually quite verbose as it is coming up, giving you startup messages such as the following as each subsystem is activated:

```
Mounting filesystems
cron started, pid=274
Network daemons started: portmap inetd routed
printing subsystem started
```

Again, try to learn your system's bootup messages even if you don't understand what they mean so that you will recognize if something out of the ordinary occurs during bootup. After all initialization is complete, you should be able to log in to the system on any of the system ports.

SEE ALSO

➤ *For some specific examples on bringing up UNIX, see page 338*
Also see page 354

System V Run Levels

System V UNIX uses a number from 0 to 6 to indicate how far the system has been initialized. These numbers are called init levels, or run levels, and they are outlined in Table 15.1.

Table 15.1 Common UNIX System V Run Levels

Run Level	Description
0	Total shutdown state; ready to power off
1	Maintenance mode/single-user mode
2	Multiuser mode
3	Multiuser mode with filesystems exported (Solaris)
3, 4, 5	Customizable run levels (varies by site)
5	Shutdown and cut power (Solaris)
6	Standard shutdown and reboot

AIX and SCO UNIX normally operate in run level 2. Solaris normally operates in run level 3. Sometimes there is an s or S state for single-user mode, which differs from run level 1 only in minor respects. You can display the current run level from the root account by entering the following command:

```
# who -r
   .      run-level 2 Feb 18 08:13      2    0    S
#
```

The preceding example shows that you are currently in run level 2, which you entered on February 18 at 08:13. The previous run level was S (single-user mode), which is a state you pass through each time you bring up the system.

Shutting Down the System

It is vital that UNIX be shut down properly before the power is turned off to prevent file corruption or loss. Use the UNIX shutdown command to do this. There are alternative commands to shut down the system, such as powerdown, reboot, haltsys, or init 0. Beware of such commands. The man pages will tell you that all users must already be logged out, filesystems must be unmounted, and networking must be closed before it is safe to run some of those commands. In general, you should use the shutdown command, which is designed to bring the system down safely.

Warning for DOS/Windows Users

Many users of DOS and old Windows systems have learned that they can usually power off the system without a proper shutdown as long as all programs were closed. Don't try this on UNIX or on newer Windows servers as data and file corruption could result.

How to shut down the system

1. Log in as root.

2. Use the who and ps commands to make sure that users or programs are not in the middle of updating important files on the system.

3. Shut down all databases that require a special shutdown before the system itself can be shut down. Follow the proper steps for that database.

Preventing the UPS from Damaging the Database

Some UPSs will shut down the system in the event of a prolonged power failure. If you have a database that must be shut down before the system is shut down, you must configure your UPS software to properly shut down the database first.

4. Enter cd / to verify that you are in the root directory when you shut down the system. If you are in a mounted directory, you could have problems unmounting that directory later.

5. You will encounter two versions of the shutdown command: a System V version (used on SCO UNIX) and a BSD version (used on AIX). Solaris provides both versions, depending on your PATH variable. Proceed now to either the System V or the BSD shutdown procedure, described next. If you are not sure which version of shutdown to use, try the System V method first and enter all possible options: -g, -i, and -y. If this command receives a syntax error, it will not cause any harm and will confirm that you need to use BSD shutdown options instead.

System V shutdown syntax allows these options:

```
cd /
shutdown -g MIN -i RLEVEL -y
```

MIN specifies the grace period. Replace MIN with the number of minutes to broadcast messages to all users that the system is going down. (If -g is omitted, the default is to wait one minute.) Enter -g 0 to shut the system down immediately, without waiting. Do a shutdown only if you are very sure that no application file updates are in progress (see Appendix A, "UNIX Commands," for a definition of *application file*).

RLEVEL is one of the following run levels:

- 0, to totally shut down the system (ready for power-off)

- 1, to go to maintenance mode/single-user mode. Some systems allow these options to specify single-user mode:
  - `-i s`
  - `-i S`
  - `-i su`
- 5, to shut down and turn off the power (only on some Solaris systems)
- 6, to shut down and automatically reboot

If no `-i` option is specified, most systems will go to run level 0 by default; however, some, such as Solaris, will go to run level 1 (single-user mode) instead.

An optional parameter is `-y`. If you do not include the `-y` option in the `shutdown` command, the system will ask after the grace period has ended if you (still) want to shut down the system. Enter `y` to proceed with the `shutdown` command, or enter `n` to abort the `shutdown` command.

For example, on a System V-type UNIX system, the following command broadcasts a warning periodically for 5 minutes that all users should log off because the system is going down. It will then shut down the system and automatically reboot it:

```
cd /
shutdown -g5 -i6 -y
```

On a BSD type of UNIX system, use these shutdown options:

```
cd /
shutdown STATE WHEN
```

`STATE` can be one of the following:

- `-h` to shut down and halt the processor
- `-r` to shut down and immediately reboot with no operator intervention

`WHEN` can be one of the following:

- `now` if you are sure it is okay to shut down the system immediately
- `+MIN`, where *MIN* is the number of minutes the system is to wait while shutdown messages are broadcast periodically
- `HH:MM`, where *HH* and *MM* are the number of hours and minutes before the system will be shut down

SEE ALSO

➤ *For some specific shutdown examples, see page 337*
Also see page 354

Automating Jobs at System Startup or Shutdown

UNIX provides great flexibility in allowing jobs to run automatically, based either on system events or on time and date. Some of these mechanisms are only for the root user (system administrator), but many of them can be used by all users. The following sections describe the most common functions that can be performed by the root user only.

Automating Jobs at System Startup on System V UNIX

The root user (only) can customize and add to the jobs that are run automatically at system bootup. Some systems use the System V method; others (even some SVR4 systems) use the BSD method.

> **Warning**
>
> The `rc2.d` directory, or other `rc` directories, should not be modified by beginners. Errors could prevent the system from booting.

Look in the directory named /etc. If your system has files called rc, rc0, and rc2, and if it has directories called rc.d, rc0.d, and rc2.d, it is using the System V-type system startup programs, or scripts. These are called *rc scripts* (rc stands for "run control") because these scripts control how you enter or leave certain run levels. (Table 15.1 shows the common System V run levels.) rc2 is a script program that is run when the system changes to run level 2 (multiuser mode). The rc2 script program uses files in directory rc2.d, as in this example from SCO UNIX:

I01MOUNTFSYS*	P21perf	P90RESERVED*	S85nis*	S91manahttp*
P00SYSINIT*	P70uucp*	P93scohttp*	S85tcp*	S95psleeper*
P03RECOVERY*	P75cron*	P95calserver*	S88edge*	S99apcssd*
P04CLEAN*	P86scologin*	S00MDAC*	S89nfs*	messages/
P05RMTMPFILES*	P86sendmail*	S35dlpi	S90atlas*	
P15HWDNLOAD*	P86xdlls*	S60sync*	S90fasttrack*	
P16KERNINIT*	P87USRDAEMON*	S80lp*	S90iproute*	
P20sysetup*	P88USRDEFINE*	S84rpcinit*	S90secure*	

After the first letter, each script has a number that controls the order in which the scripts will run. Table 15.2 shows what the first letter of each script means:

Table 15.2   System V *rc* Script Prefixes

Prefix Letter	Meaning
K	Kills a process by running this script
S	Starts a process by running this script
P	Runs P numbers in parallel if there are no S or K scripts in that range (SCO UNIX only)

For example, in the previous output listing, you can see that the `lp` spooling system is started first, and then `tcp` networking, and then `nfs`.

Modifying the System V startup scripts

1. In this directory, create your own script whose name begins with S99. This will cause your script to execute after the other initialization scripts. Set the owner, group, and permissions to match the other files in this directory. There can be more than one script that starts with S99.

2. In your S99 script, enter the system commands you want to run when the system goes to multiuser mode. Use full pathnames for each command, directory, and file; for example, you would use `/etc/shutdown` instead of `shutdown`.

   If in doubt, use the `type` command to make sure that you have the correct full pathname of commands, as in this example:

   ```
   # type shutdown
   shutdown is /sbin/shutdown
   #
   ```

3. Do not create backup copies of your script in this `rc2.d` directory. If you do, `S99yourscript.bak` (for example) would be executed during every bootup along with `S99yourscript` because both are in `/etc/rc2.d`.

4. Use `&` to run subtasks in the background to prevent the possibility of hanging the system and preventing a reboot; for example, the `stty` command can be used to set the baud rate of a port, but if the device is not ready—if, for example, a modem is waiting for an incoming call—the `stty` can hang until the device is ready. If this `stty` command is in your `rc` script, the system will also hang, and you'll have to reset and go to single-user mode to correct the problem. To prevent such a problem, create a script that accesses the desired port, and call that script from the `rc` script in the background, as shown here:

   ```
   /usr/startup/portsetup &
   ```

5. If your function needs to execute some particular code during system startup and some other code when the system is shut down, you should perform this additional step. Put a copy of your script in /etc/init.d, using a name that does not begin with S99. Solaris uses a hard link to do this; SCO OpenServer 5 uses complex symbolic links. To find out how to do it on your system, look at other scripts in rc2.d and init.d, and follow their examples. The idea is to have one script that handles both the startup and shutdown tasks for this function. The script should save $1 as a mode; then, if that mode is started, the script should execute startup code. When that mode is stopped, the script should execute shutdown code. When you finish, link this script into the multiuser startup directory (/etc/rc2.d) or the shutdown directory (/etc/rc0.d), and add S99 for startup or K## for shutdown.

Automating Jobs at System Shutdown on System V UNIX

To automatically run a job just before the system shuts down, you could write a shell script to run those commands and then invoke shutdown. You must then remind everyone to run your script instead of the standard shutdown command. If your UPS can shut down the system during a prolonged power failure, you must also modify the UPS setup to invoke your script to shut down the system.

On System V type systems, a directory called /etc/rc0.d contains scripts similar to those in /etc/rc2.d. You could add a script (that runs your desired job) to the rc0.d directory so that it automatically runs when the system changes to run level 0 (the totally shutdown state).

Automating Jobs at System Startup on BSD UNIX

If your system uses BSD startup scripts, you will find a number of scripts whose names begin with *rc* followed by a period, such as rc.net. All these rc scripts will be in the /etc directory. However, not all rc scripts are run during system startup.

If you run the following command on an AIX UNIX system:

```
ls -lu /etc/rc*
```

you will see output similar to this:

```
-r-xr-xr--   1 bin      bin         1786 Aug 21 16:03 /etc/rc
-rw-r--r--   1 root     system        48 Feb  4  1996 /etc/rc.bak
-r-xr-xr--   1 bin      bin         2502 Feb  4  1996 /etc/rc.bsdnet
-r-x------   1 root     system     21187 Feb  4  1996 /etc/rc.motpowerfail
```

```
-rw-r--r--   1 root      system        571 Feb  4  1996 /etc/rc.ncs
-r-xr-xr--   1 bin       bin          7352 Aug 21 16:03 /etc/rc.net
-r-xr-xr--   1 bin       bin          4554 Aug 21 16:03 /etc/rc.net.serial
-rw-r--r--   1 root      system        982 Feb  4  1996 /etc/rc.netls
-rwxr-xr-x   1 root      system       4201 Aug 21 16:04 /etc/rc.nfs
-rwx------   1 root      system      29511 Feb  4  1996 /etc/rc.powerfail
-rwxrwxr--   1 root      system       4180 Aug 21 16:04 /etc/rc.tcpip
```

The -lu option to ls shows you when the rc scripts were last accessed. You can see that only five of the scripts were used in the last reboot on August 21 at 16:04. The other rc scripts have not been accessed since 1996.

These are lines from the /etc/inittab file, which executes some of these rc scripts on startup:

```
brc::sysinit:/sbin/rc.boot 3 >/dev/console 2>&1 # Phase 3 of system boot
powerfail::powerfail:/etc/rc.motpowerfail -t 5 2>&1 ¦ alog -tboot >
    /dev/console 2>&1 # Power Failure Detection
rc:2:wait:/etc/rc 2>&1 ¦ alog -tboot > /dev/console # Multi-User checks
...
rctcpip:2:wait:/etc/rc.tcpip > /dev/console 2>&1 # Start TCP/IP daemons
rcnfs:2:wait:/etc/rc.nfs > /dev/console 2>&1 # Start NFS Daemons
...
```

To run a job at system startup, you must insert the job within one of the rc scripts that is run at startup. This is a job for an experienced programmer and should not be attempted by a beginner. Errors could prevent your system from booting correctly later.

Automating Jobs by Any User

Regular users can automate particular jobs to run when they log in, or at certain times, or on certain days. The system administrator can use the same mechanisms to run system processes periodically.

Automating Jobs and Setup Commands When the User Logs In

It is possible to automate commands (and hence jobs) to run automatically whenever you log in to UNIX. These commands may also set up your desired environment by setting shell variables that control the environment. Two files are executed by every Bourne or Korn shell user during login:

- /etc/profile
- .profile (in the user's home directory)

Only the root user can modify /etc/profile because changes in that file affect the logins for all users. For security reasons, you should never give write permission for that file to anyone else.

Run df Every Time Root Logs In

The system administrator (root) must constantly monitor all filesystems to make sure that they are not filling up because that could cause application errors, system errors, and even file corruption. The df command shows the disk-free blocks. Adding df to root's .profile allows the system administrator to see on every login if any filesystems are out of disk blocks.

Users can usually modify their own .profile files to set up their environment preferences on login. (On some systems, the administrator might allow users read access to .profile but not write access to prevent users from making incorrect or undesirable changes to their .profile files.) Execution of the lines in /etc/profile and .profile has the same effect as if the user typed those same lines at the keyboard just after logging in. For example, an exit command from /etc/profile or .profile will put the user back at the login prompt and force a new login.

/etc/profile and .profile are good places to set shell variables such as PATH, CDPATH, TERM, and umask. Preferred stty options for the port can be set automatically also. Changes to /etc/profile affect all users, but those changes can be altered by code in .profile in the user's home directory.

Errors in /etc/profile or .profile Can Prevent Login

It is very embarrassing (and potentially disastrous) to make a change to /etc/profile or .profile and find that you've made an error that prevents you or anyone else from logging back into the system. I always log in on two different stations before I change either of these profiles. I make the change on one station, log off, and log back in. If the login fails, I'm already logged in on the second station and can correct my error or remove my change entirely.

/etc/profile can also be used to add extra security to your system. For example, using standard Bourne shell programming, /etc/profile could check to see if a user is logging in from a modem port and, if so, only allow login at restricted times or ask for an extra password. If the /etc/profile code executes the exit command, the user's login will terminate, and he will go back to the initial login prompt.

Scheduling Jobs to Rerun Periodically

UNIX maintains a set of tables called *crontabs* (chronological tables) that contain jobs scheduled to run periodically. There is one table or file, usually in /usr/spool/cron/crontabs, for each user who has submitted a cron job. The system runs that job using that user's account.

To see if any cron jobs have been submitted and to view them, you use the -1 option (list) with the crontab command. If you are logged in as root, you might see output like this:

```
# crontab -l
17 5 * * 0 /etc/cleanup > /dev/null
0 2 * * 0,4 /usr/lib/cron/logchecker
3 3 * * * /usr/lib/cleantmp > /dev/null
1 3 * * * /etc/setclk -rd1800 > /dev/null 2>&1
5 18 * * 1-5 /usr/lib/sa/sa2 -s 8:00 -e 18:01 -i 1200 -A
30 1 * * 2,3,4,5,6 /etc/edge.nightly -MB -n root -d /dev/null 1>/dev/null 2>&1
5 4 * * 0 /etc/shutdown -g5 -i6 -y
#
```

Each line in the crontabs specifies one UNIX command to run periodically. Each line has six fields, separated by one or more spaces or tabs. Table 15.3 describes the six fields and their contents.

Table 15.3 Fields in Crontabs

Field	Function	Possible Range of Values
1	Minute of the hour	0–59
2	Hour of the day	0–23
3	Day of the month	1–31
4	Month of the year	1–12
5	Day of the week	0–6 (0 refers to Sunday)
6	Command to run	

You can indicate consecutive ranges with a dash, as in 1–5. Multiple values in one field can be specified in any order and should be separated by a comma (and no spaces), as in 1,3,7,2,25.

Tips on Crontab **Field 1: The Minute of the Hour**

If you find an asterisk in field 1 (to run your job 60 times in one hour), it is usually a mistake. Also, don't put a zero in the minute field for every cron job because that could hurt system performance at the start of every hour. Stagger the minute values for those jobs that don't have to start exactly on the hour.

In Table 15.3, the command to run (in field 6) can be a UNIX command or a shell script. Use a full pathname to reference all files and any commands that are not in /bin or /usr/bin. Any standard output or standard error messages that are not redirected to a file will be mailed to the user who submitted the cron job. If the system was down at the time and day it was scheduled to run the job, that job will be skipped. It will run again at the next scheduled time and day if the system is up then.

The easiest way to add, remove, or modify an existing cron line is to run the following:

```
crontab -e
```

This command will invoke the default text editor, usually vi, and enable you to edit your existing cron entries. As described earlier, each line or entry has six fields that describe how often to run the job and which UNIX command to invoke. After you save and exit the editor, your cron editing changes will be activated. If you remove a line while in the crontab editor (and save the file), then that line will no longer execute periodically because it is no longer in your crontab (that is, cron table).

Another way to change your cron tables is like this:

```
crontab FILENAME
```

FILENAME is a text file that contains all the cron job six field entries that you want to have running. Beware: The cron entries in this file replace all your existing cron jobs. To avoid deleting existing cron jobs when you want to submit one additional cron job, use the following procedure if your system does not support the crontab -e option described previously.

crontab -e **Versus the Long Way**

The following procedure shows the long way to add or change a cron job, which is the only procedure that works on older UNIX systems. On newer UNIX systems, use crontab -e instead of this procedure since it is easier and safer to use.

Adding/removing/modifying a `cron` job

1. Log in as the user whose `cron` job you want to modify. (Don't run `cron` jobs as root unless it is absolutely necessary.) If you have never added a `cron` job before, use an account other than root, sys, adm, or uucp so that you can practice adding and removing a test `cron` job first.

2. Enter `cd` to go to your home directory.

3. Unless the command to run via cron is extremely simple, use vi or another editor to create a shell script (called a *cron script* for this procedure). In that cron script, insert the desired command(s) you want to run periodically via cron. You should use a cron script especially if you want to run a sequence of multiple commands from `cron`. Test your cron script by running it directly from your terminal. Use full pathnames within your cron script for any files to be accessed. Use full pathnames for any system commands that are not in `/bin` or `/usr/bin`.

   If you are trying out `cron` for the first time, try using `date` as a test command in field 6. The output of the date command will be mailed to you from `cron`. Another good cron test script is a program to create a small result file in your home directory or `/tmp`, like this:

   ```
   echo cron test `date` > /tmp/fred.cron.tst
   ```

4. At the shell prompt, test your ERASE key as follows. Enter `datex`, but before pressing the Enter key, press the backspace key or Ctrl+H to erase the x. Then press the Enter key. The current date and time should be displayed. If not, your ERASE key is not working; do not proceed further.

5. Next, enter this command slowly and carefully:

   ```
   crontab -l > cronfile
   ```

   Check your command carefully before you press the Enter key. Use your ERASE key slowly and carefully to correct any errors. If you get an error saying either No such file or Can't open file, you have no current cron jobs. Just ignore this error and continue to the next step.

6. In step 5, if you accidentally omit the -l option, you could delete all your current ongoing `cron` jobs. If you lose the root user's `cron` jobs, important system functions will be disabled. The rest of this step discusses how to try to save your cron jobs if you accidentally omit the -l option.

   The missing -l option puts your current crontabs in jeopardy. You will then see the PS2 prompt, usually the greater than sign (>), which means that the shell is waiting for input from the keyboard to replace your current crontabs. Press your INTR key (usually Ctrl+C or DEL) to abort this command. If the INTR key fails, go to another port and run step 5 correctly to save your existing cron jobs in a disk file. Then come back to this port and enter your EOT key (usually Ctrl+D) to wipe out your current crontabs.

7. Enter the following:

```
vi cronfile
```

(You can use any text editor to edit this file.) Now you should see all your current ongoing cron jobs in the six-field format discussed earlier. For example, you might see the following line:

```
17 5 * * 0 /etc/cleanup > /dev/null
```

If your login account has never submitted a cron job before, this cronfile will be empty. If this cronfile is empty but it is not supposed to be empty (for instance, the root's cronfile should not be empty), go back to step 1 and start over. If you have lost your prior cron entries, you will have to key them all in again or restore them from a backup. Cron files are usually saved in /usr/spool/cron/crontabs, where there are several files, each named for a user who has submitted cron jobs to run.

8. Use the text editor (invoked in the previous step) to modify any existing six-field cron lines and to add new ones—in the six-field format—to this file. If you created a cron script in step 3 of this procedure, add a new six-field line to that file, with the full pathname of your cron script in the last field. When you finish editing, save your work and exit from the editor. This cronfile is just a temporary file, so if you don't like your saved results, go back to step 5 and start over.

9. Enter the following:

```
cat cronfile
```

Make sure that this file contains proper six-field entries for all previous cron jobs to be retained, plus any modified or new cron jobs you've added.

10. Enter the following:

```
crontab cronfile
```

This submits your cron changes, replacing all your previous cron jobs. If you get an error saying that you are not allowed to submit cron jobs, see the later section "Enabling and Disabling cron/at/batch by User."

11. Enter the following:

```
crontab -l
```

to display your current crontab entries as submitted. Then review the warnings about this command that appeared earlier in this procedure.

> **Root's** crontab **Should Not Be Empty**
>
> Do not practice with the crontab command while running as root. Get some experience submitting cron jobs and modifying crontab as a non-root user first. root's crontab contains many commands that should be run periodically for proper system maintenance. If you are a beginning system administrator and you accidentally lose all of root's cron jobs, you can usually get them back by restoring /usr/spool/cron/crontabs/root from a backup tape.

SEE ALSO

➤ *For more information on editing with vi, see page 563*

➤ *For more information on using cat to display a file, see page 210*

Using the Asterisk (*) Wildcard in *Crontabs*

crontab allows an asterisk (*) wildcard to be used as shown in Table 15.4. Note that it is a crontab wildcard, not a filename generation wildcard or a regular expression wildcard. In general, the asterisk says to do the job as often as that field allows:

Table 15.4   Using the Asterisk (*) Wildcard in *crontabs*

crontabs Field	What an Asterisk Means in That Field
1. Minute of the hour	Do job every minute, 60 times per hour
2. Hour of the day	Do job every hour, 24 times per day
3. Day of the month	Ignore this field and use field 5 **
4. Month of the year	Do job every month, 12 months per year
5. Day of the week	Ignore this field and use field 3 **

**An asterisk in both fields 3 and 5 means the job is to run every day.

Notice that the asterisk has a special meaning for field 3 (day of the month) and field 5 (day of the week). In the following examples, nightly is a hypothetical application program:

- Case 1: Both field 3 and 5 have asterisks:

```
0 23 * * * /nightly    # run nightly every day at 11 PM
```

- Case 2: Either field 3 or field 5 has an asterisk, but not both:

```
0 23 * * 1,3 /nightly   # run nightly 11 PM on Mondays and Wednesdays
0 23 1,3 * * /nightly   # run nightly 11 PM on the 1st and 3rd of
                        #    each month
```

- Case 3: Neither field 3 nor field 5 has an asterisk:

```
0 23 1,3 * 1,3 /nightly   # run nightly 11 PM on the 1st and 3rd of
                          # each month as well as every Monday and Wednesday
```

Running Early Morning Weekday Jobs

Here is a `crontab` error that novice system administrators often make if the job is to run early every weekday morning:

```
30 1 * * 1-5 /u/backup
```

This company works Monday through Friday and wants to execute a backup at 1:30 AM after every work day. However, with this command, Friday's work will not be backed up until Monday morning at 1:30 AM. Because heavy building maintenance work and power problems are more frequent on weekends, this is not good. Here is the corrected entry, which will also run the backup on Saturday morning:

```
30 1 * * 2-6 /u/backup
```

For the same reason, this would not be a good entry for that company:

```
30 1 * * * /u/backup
```

Because no one is in the office on Saturday and Sunday, the tape will not be changed, and Friday night's backup (which really runs early Saturday) will be rewritten Saturday night and Sunday night. A power problem over the weekend could corrupt files, and then those corrupted files would replace the good Friday night backup.

SEE ALSO

➤ *For more information on backups, see page* *431*

Scheduling One-Time Jobs at a Specific Date/Time

The UNIX at command enables you to schedule a job to run once at a later predetermined time. If you want to run the job more than once (periodically, for example), see the previous section on the `crontab` command.

In this example, you use the at command to defer running the `salestotal` and `invupdate` programs until 11 PM at night:

```
$ at 23
salestotal
invupdate
Ctrl+D
$
```

Following the at command itself, indicate when to run the at jobs using one of these three methods:

- Method 1 is to enter a time only, for example:

```
3       means 3 a.m.
17      means 5 p.m.
0704    means 7:04 a.m.
7:04pm          means 7:04 p.m.
```

The job will run within the next 24 hours at the requested time.

- Method 2 is to enter a time and day, for example:

```
2pm Sat
1923 Aug 24
7:04pm tomorrow
```

The job will run within the next year at the requested time on the requested day.

- Method 3 is to give an offset, for example:

```
now + 5 min
now + 2 days
```

You can use the -l option with the at command to list your current scheduled jobs. You can use the -r option to remove scheduled jobs.

The following example illustrates a quick command you might want to use for testing the at command. It creates a junk file in the current directory in 5 minutes if you don't remove the job:

```
$ at now + 5 min
date > junk
Ctrl+D
warning: commands will be executed using /bin/sh
job 888071220.a-9910:0 at Sat Feb 21 06:27:00 1998
$
```

When you press Ctrl+D to submit your lines to the at command, you may see a warning as in the previous example that /bin/sh, the Bourne shell, will be used to execute your commands instead of your usual shell. You also see a job id number, as in the example.

Use at -l to list all pending at jobs:

```
$ at -l
888071220.a-9910:0      Sat Feb 21 06:27:00 1998
$
```

In the preceding example, notice that at -l shows when the job will run, but it does not show the UNIX command that will be run. Use at -r to remove an at job to prevent it from running:

```
$ at -r 888071220.a
at: 888071220.a does not exist: No such file or directory (error 2)
$ at -r 888071220.a-9910:0
$ at -l
$
```

Notice that the -r option requires that the full job id be entered.

If the system is down at the time and day the at job is supposed to run, the at job will be run as soon as the system is brought up again (unlike cron).

You can even write an at job that will queue itself up to run again periodically. You do so by adding a line like this at the end of the at script:

```
echo "sh jobname" ¦ at 2330 sat next week
```

Scheduling One-Time Jobs to Run When the Load Is Light

The batch command can be used to defer running a job until the system is idle, but this means you can't predict when it will run. If your system is always running user jobs at all hours, batch is not a useful command for you because it may never be capable of starting your job.

In the following example, you can see that the overall batch command is very similar to the at command; however, you do not specify a time or a date to run the jobs.

```
$ batch
salestotal
invupdate
Ctrl+D
$
```

Enabling and Disabling *crontab/at/batch* by User

The root user (system administrator) can modify these two files to allow or deny users to use crontabs:

```
/usr/lib/cron/cron.allow
```

```
/usr/lib/cron/cron.deny
```

The root user also can modify the following two files to allow or deny users to use the at or batch commands:

/usr/lib/cron/at.allow

/usr/lib/cron/at.deny

If the allow files exist, only users listed in that file can use the command. The deny files are used only if the allow files do not exist. In that case, all users can use the command except those listed in the deny file.

SEE ALSO

➤ *For more information on comparing* cron, at, batch, nice, *and* renice, *see page 423*

Assigning Job Priorities

The following sections cover the commands necessary to view and change the priorities of running processes.

Viewing Jobs and Their Priority

You can use the -lf options with ps to show each running process (job) and its current priority. Each line of output has more than 80 characters, so the output can be confusing to read on an 80-character screen. In the following example, there is one heading line followed by process information about three commands: -ksh, ps -lf, and pg. (The dash (-) before ksh indicates that it is a login shell.) The command name is given in the last column of the process information. Check the man page on ps to see what all the columns mean.

```
$ ps -lf | pg
 F S      UID   PID  PPID  C PRI NI   ADDR    SZ   WCHAN    STIME     TTY
    TIME    CMD
20 S    mori  9998  9374  6  73 20 fb11e798  132  fb11e798 06:54:41 ttyR030
    00:00:00 -ksh
20 O    mori 10020  9998  7  48 20 fb11e8f0  160       - 06:55:23 ttyR030
    00:00:00 ps -lf
30 S    mori 10021  9998  2  78 20 fb11ecf8   72  fb11ecf9 06:55:23 ttyR030
    00:00:00 pg
```

The column labeled NI shows the process nice value (in this case, 20). The higher the nice value, the lower its priority to get system resources and time (the nicer it is to everyone else on the system). Table 15.5 gives the minimum and maximum nice values for the two types of UNIX systems you will encounter.

Table 15.5   *nice* (Priority) Values

Type of System	Allowed Range for nice Values	Default Value
System V	0 to 39	20
BSD	−20 to +20	0

See Table 15.6 for another standard property of the ps command.

Table 15.6   Another Property of the *ps* Command:

Property	See page
Allows output to be piped or redirected	116

Starting a Job with Low Priority

The preceding section shows how to view and interpret the nice value for a process. Use the nice command to start another UNIX command at a lower priority so that you are being nicer to other users on the system, as in the following:

```
nice -5 find / -name acme-proposal -print > /tmp/find.out
```

Here, the priority of the find command is lowered so that other users are not slowed down as much while it runs. The following is the general syntax of the nice command:

```
nice -VAL UNIX-CMD
```

-VAL is a measure of how much to lower the job's priority. The larger the value, the nicer you will be to other users on the system and the slower your job will run. The root user (only) can enter --VAL (dash dash) to lower the nice value and hence raise his job priority above other users. The root user must be careful, however, not to raise the priority so high that the job takes over and disables all other system functions.

UNIX-CMD is the desired command to run. If you enter a pipeline, enter a nice command for each stage of the pipeline. (See the next example.)

The following example shows that the nice command must be explicitly invoked for each command in a pipeline. This command pipes the output of ps -lf to pg. The column labeled NI gives the nice value of the running process. Note that ps has a nice increment of 5, and pg has a nice increment of 7. Different values were chosen just to illustrate a point; normally, you would use the same value for both:

```
$ nice -5 ps -lf ¦ nice -7 pg
 F S      UID   PID PPID  C PRI NI     ADDR   SZ    WCHAN    STIME      TTY
   TIME CMD
20 S     mori 10042  9996  5  73 20 fb11e798  132  fb11e798 07:12:35 ttyR029
   00:00:00 -ksh
20 O     mori 10066 10042  9  44 25 fb11e8f0  160         - 07:13:24 ttyR029
   00:00:00 ps -lf
20 S     mori 10067 10042  5  76 27 fb11ecf8   72  f093d7c0 07:13:24 ttyR029
   00:00:00 pg
$
```

Notice that the pg command has a nice value of 27. That's because nice -7 means to raise the nice value 7 points from the default value, which is 20 because this is a System V type of UNIX.

Your nice or renice **May Differ**

Check the man pages on your system for nice and renice to see the maximum and minimum nice value supported. The two possible ranges of nice values you might encounter were listed previously in Table 15.5. Some systems do not support one or both of these commands.

Changing the Priority of an Existing Job

Modern UNIX systems support a renice command to enable you to change the nice value of a process that has already been started. However, you must first look up the PID value for the desired process using the ps command (see the previous ps example). Here is the general syntax of the renice command:

```
renice -n VAL PID
```

VAL is a number between 1 and 19. This represents the amount to raise the nice value and lower the priority of the job.

PID is the process ID number for the process (job) you want to change. For example, if an existing process has PID number 10042, you can lower its priority as follows:

```
renice -n 5 10042
```

Comparing *cron, at, batch, nice,* and *renice*

The following is a comparison of these five commands and how to choose which of them to run:

- cron—Use cron to run a command or job more than once, on some regular basis. If the system is down at the scheduled time for a job, the job will not be run when the system comes back up, until the next scheduled cron date and time. The following four commands only run the command or job one time.

- at—Use at when you want to run a command or job on a specific day at a specific time. If the system is down at the scheduled time for this job, the job will be run as soon as the system comes back up.

- batch—Use batch to postpone a command or job until the system is less busy. There is no way to predict when the job will run.

- nice—Use nice to start a command or job right now but reduce its priority so that it does not slow down other users as much.

- renice—Use renice to change the priority of a command or job that is already running so that it does not slow down other users as much.

Managing Background Jobs

UNIX is a multitasking operating system. This means that, in general, you can start more than one job, and all will run concurrently. Your station is not tied up waiting for them to finish. You can even specify sequences of jobs so that one job will not start until the previous job has completed.

Starting Background Jobs

To start a job in the background, simply end the UNIX command with a space and then an ampersand (&), as shown in this example:

```
$ make acmesys > acme.log 2>&1 &
27903
$
```

Here's a breakdown of the parts of that command:

- make is a command that can take a long time to complete; therefore, you might run it in the background so that it does not tie up your station.

- `>` `acme.log` redirects the output from `make` into a file called `acme.log`. This is often a good idea when you're starting background because the output is saved for later review. If you don't redirect the output in this way, it will still go to your screen, where it could mix with other output.

- `2>&1` redirects any error messages from the `make` command so that they will go to the same file as the standard output (so you're saving output and errors from `make` in the same file).

- `27903` is the job number, which is also called a process id number or PID. If you save this number, you can use it later to check on this job.

Preventing Logoff from Killing Background Jobs

Logoff still Warns about Nohup Jobs

On some UNIX systems, exit will still warn you that you have stopped or background jobs, even if you started those jobs via nohup. If you are sure you started the job with nohup, type `exit` a second time to logoff. Your background job will continue to run, thanks to nohup.

Logging off the system usually terminates all background jobs that you started. Some shells will warn you that you have stopped jobs. If you then type `exit` a second time, you will terminate those jobs and log off. The `nohup` command enables you to start background jobs that will not be killed when you log off. Here is the general syntax to follow:

`nohup UNIX-CMD &`

`UNIX-CMD` is the command to run.

Because this will be running as a background job, you should redirect standard output and standard error. Save them in a file if you want to look at them later. Send them to `/dev/null` to discard them, for example:

`nohup make zImage > /tmp/log 2>&1 &`

If you do not redirect standard output and standard errors, the `nohup` command will automatically create a file called `nohup.out` to save them in.

Killing a Background Job

If you write down the PID that is displayed when you start a background job, it is easy to terminate that job using the following procedure. You can also use the ps command and the who -u command to determine PID numbers for jobs or user sessions to terminate.

How to terminate a job by its PID

1. From the shell prompt, enter kill *PID*, where *PID* is the PID number of the process you want to terminate. Double-check that you have entered the number correctly. Then press the Enter key. This kill command gives the job a chance to terminate gracefully, closing applications and removing lock files and temporary files. No messages will be displayed.

2. Now enter the command kill -9 *PID*, where *PID* is the same number you used in step 1. Double-check that you have entered the number correctly. Then press Enter. This kill ends even uncooperative commands. Although you can execute step 2 immediately after step 1, you might want to wait a few seconds to let step 1 wrap up.

3. If step 2 gives the error No such PID, ignore that error. It just means that step 1 was enough to end the task, and step 2 was unnecessary but not harmful.

If you don't remember your PID number, you can look it up using the ps command:

> **Note**
>
> See Appendix B, "Glossary," for the definition of *PID value*.

Using ps to find a PID number

1. From the shell prompt, enter these two commands:

```
ps -ef
ps aux
```

Some systems support both of these commands, but sometimes only one gives results.

2. Using the command that works on your system, look at the initial heading to find the PID column, the user (UID) column, and the command (CMD) column.

3. If necessary, rerun the command and pipe it to pg, more, or less to see it a page at a time.

Alternatively, you can pipe the output of the ps command to grep to filter out the lines you don't care about. Note that this will also remove the heading.

4. Locate the command that you want to terminate. Check the UID column to make sure that you started this command.

5. Locate the PID for that command. Then you can follow the procedure for terminating a job by its PID.

This is an example of a command used to find a background job. However, the output was cut off in midprocess. Because ps can show so many processes, the command was aborted using ^c (on Solaris):

```
# ps -ef
     UID   PID  PPID  C    STIME TTY      TIME CMD
    root     0     0  0   Feb 20 ?        0:02 sched
    root     1     0  0   Feb 20 ?        0:15 /etc/init -
    root     2     0  0   Feb 20 ?        0:00 pageout
    root     3     0  0   Feb 20 ?        1:02 fsflush
    root   289     1  0   Feb 20 ?        0:00 /usr/lib/saf/sac -t 300
```

Suppose that you were running the previous command to look for a find command that was started earlier. You could use grep to filter out the lines you don't want, as shown here:

```
# ps -ef¦grep find
    root 27961 27955  5 13:53:33 pts/1    0:03 find / -name acme -print
    root 27967 27955  0 13:54:19 pts/1    0:00 grep find
#
```

From the CMD field (the last field), you can see that two processes mentioning find were found. Looking at field 2, you see that PID 27961 is the find process you want to terminate. Notice that PID 27967 is the grep process that was looking for find; in other words, grep saw itself while it was looking for find.

This is a similar example that uses an additional grep -v to remove the extraneous grep process from the output:

```
# ps -ef ¦ grep find ¦ grep -v grep
    root 27961 27955  5 13:53:33 pts/1  0:03 find / -name acme -print
#
```

When you know the PID you want to terminate, you can enter these lines to kill the process:

```
kill 27961
kill -9 27961
```

SEE ALSO

➤ *For more information on* grep, *see page 494*

Applying Extra Job Control Under the Korn Shell

The previous section covered use of background jobs that would apply to all shells, including the Bourne shell. Newer shells have made it much easier to work with background jobs by adding a feature called *job control*. For example, some systems have added job control to the Bourne shell, which can be invoked as jsh. This section describes the other job control commands, which are similar to jsh: They are csh for the C shell and ksh for the Korn shell.

Listing Background Jobs

To list all background jobs in any shell supporting job control, go to the shell prompt and enter jobs.

You will see output like this:

```
$ jobs
[4] +  Running              find / -name acme -print > /tmp/acme.find &
[3] -  Stopped (SIGTSTP)    man find
[2]    Stopped (SIGTSTP)    bc
[1]    Stopped (SIGTSTP)    vi acmereport
$
```

The job number is given in brackets at the start of each line. The job most recently in the foreground (the one that was most recently active on your screen) is indicated by a plus sign (+). The second most recent job is indicated by a minus sign (-). Notice that you no longer have to worry about PID numbers.

Suspending and Resuming Jobs

One of the most powerful applications of job control is to take a foreground job (one that is tying up your keyboard and screen), suspend it in the background so you can enter other commands, and then retrieve the suspended job later. You can even cause that job to continue running in the background while you do other commands in the foreground at the standard shell prompt.

In some older UNIX operating systems, very few utilities honor the Ctrl+Z to suspend the current job; in those systems vi is the only command that works. Under Solaris, UnixWare 7, and AIX, however, Ctrl+Z seems to work for every utility. You can use it to move jobs very easily between the foreground and the background. This was true in the Korn shell, but not under jsh.

Moving a job to the background and back to the foreground

1. Make sure that you are in a shell that supports job control, such as the Korn shell (not the Bourne shell). If you are not sure, invoke the Korn shell with the command exec ksh.

   Enter any UNIX command that will take some time to complete. Do not enter a final ampersand (&) to the command; the job will run in the foreground and tie up your keyboard and screen.

2. To move that job to the background, press Ctrl+Z. You should see an acknowledgment like this, specifying the command you were running:

   ```
   ^Z[1] + Stopped (SIGTSTP)   find / -name acme_-print
   ```

   If you do not see such a message, either your shell does not support job control or your version of UNIX does not support the use of Ctrl+Z to suspend all jobs.

   You will now have a system prompt, at which you can enter other commands. Your previous job is suspended (it's no longer running).

3. Enter jobs, and you will see output like this:

   ```
   [2] + Stopped (SIGTSTP) find / -name acme -print > /tmp/acme.find &
   [1] - Stopped (SIGTSTP) man find
   ```

4. To allow the job to continue running in the background, at the shell prompt, enter bg %JOBID, where *JOBID* is the job number shown by the jobs command. If the job is the most recent job—as denoted by the plus sign (+)—you can omit %JOBID altogether.

5. Enter jobs again. Now you should see output like this, indicating that your job is running:

   ```
   [2] +  Running        find / -name acme -print > /tmp/acme.find &
   [1] - Stopped (SIGTSTP) man find
   ```

6. To bring your job back to the foreground, at the shell prompt, enter fg %JOBID, where *JOBID* is the number of the job you want to bring to the foreground. The command being run will appear on the screen, and the specified job will again have control of your keyboard and screen.

Killing a Background Job Under the Korn Shell

With job control, it is easy to terminate a background job:

Terminating a background job using job control

1. At the shell prompt, enter `jobs` to determine the job number of the job you want to terminate. This should be a small number, no greater than the total number of jobs displayed. This is *not* a PID number.

2. Enter the command `kill %JOBID`, where *JOBID* is the number of the job to be terminated.

   Or, to terminate the most recent job, you can enter `kill %%`.

   Or, to terminate the second most recent job, you can enter `kill %-`.

Pausing Background Jobs Just Before They Output

Some background jobs will compute for a long time and then display a result. You may want the compute phase to continue in the background but then have the job suspend itself until you are ready for the output.

Suspending jobs just before they output

1. At the shell prompt, enter `stty tostop`. This will cause any new background jobs to suspend just before they start any output. This mode lasts until you log off.

2. Enter your desired UNIX command, ending in an ampersand (`&`) so that it runs in the background. Press `Enter`.

3. At the shell prompt, enter `jobs`. From the output of the `jobs` command, determine whether the background job is running. If the state of the background job is running, it is not yet ready to display any output.

4. When the `jobs` command shows that your desired background job is stopped, it is ready to provide some output. Enter `fg %JOBID`, where *JOBID* is the number of the stopped job. This will bring the job to the foreground and start the output so that you can see the output on your screen at a time of your choosing.

SEE ALSO
➤ *To avoid having to manually issue this command each time you login, see page 410*

chapter

16

System and File Backups

Accessing UNIX devices such as
tape and disk

Backing up and restoring using `tar`

Backing up and restoring using `cpio`

Steve "Mor" Moritsugu

Tip for Beginners

It is important to back up your files periodically to disk or tape. `tar` and `cpio` are the most common UNIX commands used for this purpose. You will need to ask someone knowledgeable about your system for help the first time you do this because the device name and access method can differ among UNIX systems. If you run your own UNIX system at home, read the section "Backing Up and Restoring the Operating System."

Backing Up User Files

Backing up files means to make copies of those files so that the files can be recovered later if needed. The files may be copied to the hard disk, but more often backups are made to tape or disk so that your data is protected if the hard disk is physically damaged. Backups can be done over a network to a tape drive on a different system. *Archiving* is another word for backing up. Files backed up onto tape or disk are called *archive copies* of your data. These tape or disk archives can also be used to transfer copies of your data to another system.

This section discusses how a user can back up files, either to protect the data or to transfer it to another system. The root user can back up the entire system. This chapter also discusses system backups, which are similar to user backups but with some extra considerations.

If your UNIX system is in a restricted area in the computer operations area, you may not be allowed to go near the actual computer. In that case, you cannot insert a tape or disk for backup purposes. You may have to put in a request for this backup and schedule it with your system administrator or computer operations department. The administrator may tell you that all files on the system are backed up periodically, so there is no need for you to get your own special backups. If so, find out the procedure if you need to restore some files.

Network users can become confused about tape and floppy devices. I have seen Windows users `telnet` into UNIX, which allows the user to log on and run UNIX commands. Then, the confused user puts a disk into the Windows floppy drive and tries to access it from UNIX by typing in UNIX commands. This doesn't work because the UNIX commands access the floppy drive on the UNIX system. The magic of networking and `telnet` allow you to run commands on that distant UNIX system, but any UNIX floppy commands access the floppy on that distant UNIX system, not on your own Windows PC. In this situation, you could use a utility such as Windows `ftp` to bring the UNIX file to your local system and then back it up to your local floppy drive.

This chapter is not for network users who access UNIX from a remote system. This chapter is for those users who have physical access to the UNIX computer itself. To back up files, put your own floppy disk or tape into the UNIX machine. You then run UNIX commands that are discussed in this chapter to back up the files to that floppy or tape. Finally, remove the floppy or tape and store it in a safe place until you need to restore these backup copies of your files, if ever.

Be careful when you insert a floppy or tape with important files that you want to restore. Another user on the system, even a remote user in a different city, could start a floppy or tape operation that will overwrite your tape. Floppies and tapes usually have a little slider that can be moved to write-protect your media and prevent writing.

SEE ALSO

➤ *For more information on* ftp *file transfer, see page 693*

UNIX Device Files

In UNIX, special files enable you to access physical devices. These files are called *device files* or *device nodes*. If you redirect output to a special device file, the output goes to that physical device. If you redirect input from a special device file, the input (if any) comes from that physical device. Some devices are more complicated, and their device nodes can be accessed only in certain ways or by special programs.

By convention, all the special device files are stored in the /dev directory. This causes the full pathname of the device file to start with /dev/, which indicates that this is not a regular UNIX file. Each device file is a pointer to a driver for that device. A *driver* is a software program that contains subroutines that can be called depending on what device function is desired (for example, read, write, rewind, seek, and so on).

Let's examine some device files on Solaris 2.6. The files that access the floppy happen to contain the word *diskette* (which is not usually true for other UNIX systems). These files are actually symbolic links to much longer device names, so I have added the -L option to ls to follow the symbolic links and look at the actual device files.

```
$ ls -lL /dev/*disket*
brw-rw-rw-  1 root     sys       36,  2 Apr 10 16:57 /dev/diskette
brw-rw-rw-  1 root     sys       36,  2 Apr 10 16:57 /dev/diskette0
crw-rw-rw-  1 root     sys       36,  2 Apr 27 11:24 /dev/rdiskette
crw-rw-rw-  1 root     sys       36,  2 Apr 27 11:24 /dev/rdiskette0
$
```

In the preceding example, note that the first character in the line (which stands for the file type) is either the letter b or c. b stands for *block* device file; c stands for *character* device file. A character device is also called a *raw* device. This is a driver that simply passes characters one after the other. This is called *sequential access*. A block driver is used for more complicated situations—in this case, allowing random access to specific blocks of the disk. Some devices have only a character device and no block device (for example, tape drives allow only sequential access).

In the same example, note that the size of the file is missing. File size is normally listed after the group and before the date of last access. In place of the size, device files have two numbers separated by a comma: a major number and a minor number. In this example, all the files listed have major number 36 and minor number 2. These device files contain no code or data about the device. In fact, device files are totally empty, which is why no size is listed. The driver code to access all devices on the system is linked together to form one large UNIX kernel. A device file major number indicates which driver in the kernel should be used to access this device. The minor number gives the driver additional information about this device.

Some people mistakenly copy /dev files from one UNIX system to another, thinking they are transferring the driver code to the new system. Because the /dev files are only pointers into the kernel, you can understand why their attempts fail.

Determining What UNIX Device Name to Use

This chapter explains how to use tar and cpio to back up and restore files. You can use these commands on all UNIX systems. However, you must determine what device name to use. This can differ from system to system.

The best course of action is to contact the system administrator and ask what device names are available for backups and whether any special rules must be followed.

Unfortunately, system documentation often does not cover device names. However, some man pages are useful for looking up device names:

- Solaris:
  ```
  for floppy devices: man -s 7D fd
  for SCSI tape devices: man st
  ```

- SCO UNIX OpenServer:
  ```
  for floppy devices: man fd
  for SCSI tape devices: man Stp
  ```

- SCO UNIX UnixWare 7:

```
for floppy devices: man 7 fd
for SCSI tape devices: man 7 tape
```

- AIX 4.x:

```
for floppy devices: man fd
for SCSI tape devices: man rmt
```

- Linux:

```
for floppy devices: man fd
for SCSI tape devices: man st
```

Other UNIX systems support man -k to look up man topics by keywords. If this is the case, try these commands to find likely man pages covering devices:

```
man -k flop
man -k disket
man -k tape
man -k scsi
```

On Solaris, use the following command:

```
man -k tape
```

This command produces output that includes these lines:

```
rmt       rmt (1m)     - remote magtape protocol module
st        st (7d)      - driver for SCSI tape devices
stli      stli (8)     - Silo Tape Library Interface
```

On AIX 4.x, this is a useful command:

```
lsdev -C | pg
```

This command shows information about each of the device names on the system. Here is some example output from that command:

```
hdisk0    Available 04-B0-00-0,0 4.0 GB SCSI Disk Drive
hdisk1    Available 04-B0-00-1,0 4.0 GB SCSI Disk Drive
rmt0      Available 04-B0-00-4,0 Travan TR-4 4GB Tape Drive
cd0       Available 04-B0-00-5,0 CD-ROM Drive
```

There is no easy way to determine on your own the exact device names to use on an unfamiliar UNIX system. This section has looked at several commands you can use to get some clues as to these device names. Again, the best advice is to ask your system administrator or anyone on the system who uses a device you want to use.

Tape Drives

The most common type of tape drive found on UNIX systems is a SCSI tape drive. These require a SCSI controller card in your computer. SCSI disk drives, SCSI tape drives, and SCSI CD-ROM drives can then be cabled to the SCSI controller. The system administrator must set up each new SCSI device, although some UNIX systems autosense new SCSI devices upon bootup. Any administrative setup process will vary from system to system.

These are some of the most common types of SCSI tape drives:

- **Quarter-inch cartridge (QIC)streamer tape drives**—The term *quarter-inch* refers to the width of the tape. Different models of these tape drives exist. Some hold as little as 250MB of data; others hold up to 26GB of data. Many of the larger tape drives can read tapes written on the smaller QIC tape drives.

- **4-mm DAT drives**—A common model of this drive holds 4GB of raw data and up to 8GB due to compression. Tapes come in lengths of 90 meters or 120 meters. Longer tapes can hold more data. Several styles of tapes exist, such as DDS or DDS-II, so it is important to get the correct type of tape for your drive.

- **8-mm Exabyte helical scan drives**—Two commonly used types of this drive have capacities of 2.3GB or 5GB.

- **9-track half-inch magnetic tape drives**—These drives often have settings for Low (800 bpi), Medium (1600 bpi), or High (3200 bpi) density. They are also called *reel to reel* drives. Due to their cost, they are rarely used except to exchange or submit data, especially in government agencies.

New tape drives and changes to this list occur frequently. For example, there are now also Trevan, AIT, and DLT tape drives. If you are planning to purchase a tape cartridge to back up your files, be careful to get the correct type and length of tape for your tape drive. The best way to do this is to write down the brand and model of tapes that are currently being used.

UNIX Tape Device Names

The UNIX driver name for a SCSI tape simply numbers each SCSI tape drive in the order in which it was added to the system. This tape drive number is a logical number that has no relation to any physical values such as the SCSI target id number. These are the SCSI tape device names for some specific types of UNIX systems:

- **Solaris**—`/dev/rmt/0`, `/dev/rmt/1`, `/dev/rmt/2`, and so on
- **SCO UNIX OpenServer**—`/dev/rStp0`, `/dev/rStp1`, `/dev/rStp2`, and so on

- **SCO UNIX UnixWare 7**—/dev/rmt/ctape1, /dev/rmt/ctape2, and so on
- **AIX 4.x**—/dev/rmt0, /dev/rmt1, /dev/rmt2, and so on
- **Linux**—/dev/st0, /dev/st1, and so on

This list shows that to use the first tape drive on a Solaris system, you would use /dev/rmt/0. To use the second tape drive added to a SCO UNIX OpenServer system, you would use /dev/rStp1.

Most systems allow several device names for a given tape drive. Each name has the same major number (because it uses the same kernel driver) but has a different minor number to modify how the tape drive functions. The most common alternative device name is the nonrewinding tape device name. When using the standard tape device name, the UNIX command accessing the tape does not complete until the tape operation has completed and the tape is completely rewound. If you use the nonrewinding tape device instead, then this final rewind operation is not done. This leaves the tape positioned just after the last file accessed so that new files can be read or written at that point and the tape drive hardware will support this.

Following are some alternative names for a SCSI tape device 0:

- Solaris:

/dev/rmt/0	Standard device name
/dev/rmt/0n	Nonrewinding device
/dev/rmt/0l	Select low density
/dev/rmt/0m	Select medium density
/dev/rmt/0h	Select high density
/dev/rmt/0u	Select ultra
/dev/rmt/0c	Select compressed
/dev/rmt/0b	Select BSD behavior

These options can be combined.

These are the available device files in the directory /dev/rmt:

0	0bn	0cb	0cn	0hb	0hn	0lb	0ln
0b	0c	0cbn	0h	0hbn	0l	0lbn	0m
0mn	0u	0ubn	0n	0ub	0un	0mb	0mbn

- SCO UNIX OpenServer:

`/dev/rStp0`	Standard device name
`/dev/nrStp0`	Nonrewinding device
`/dev/xStp0`	To issue special commands

- SCO UNIX UnixWare 7:

`/dev/rmt/ctape1`	Standard device name
`/dev/rmt/ntape1`	Nonrewinding device
`/dev/rmt/nrtape1`	Retension instead of rewinding device
`/dev/rmt/utape1`	Unload on close

- AIX 4.x:

	Low Capacity	Retension on Open	Rewind on Close
`/dev/rmt0`	N	N	Y
`/dev/rmt0.1`	N	N	N
`/dev/rmt0.2`	N	Y	Y
`/dev/rmt0.3`	N	Y	N
`/dev/rmt0.4`	Y	N	Y
`/dev/rmt0.5`	Y	N	N
`/dev/rmt0.6`	Y	Y	Y
`/dev/rmt0.7`	Y	Y	N

- Linux:

`/dev/st0`	Standard device name
`/dev/nst0`	Nonrewinding device

Tapes do not have to be formatted before use. Some applications, however, must initialize a tape the first time it is used for that application, but the application should prompt you as needed. Periodically, quarter-inch cartridges (QIC) should be retensioned to ensure smooth tape flow while reading or writing for maximum data reliability. After using the nonrewinding device node, you should issue the `rewind` command before you remove the tape. The following list gives the complete shell commands to retension or rewind the first tape drive on several types of UNIX systems:

- Solaris 2.x:

```
mt -f /dev/rmt/0 retension
mt -f /dev/rmt/0 rewind
```

- SCO UNIX OpenServer:
  ```
  tape reten /dev/rStp0
  tape rewind /dev/rStp0
  ```

- SCO UNIX UnixWare 7:
  ```
  tape reten /dev/rmt/ctape1
  tape rewind /dev/rmt/ctape1
  ```

- AIX 4.x:
  ```
  (no retension command)
  mt -f /dev/rmt0 rewind
  ```

- Linux:
  ```
  mt -f /dev/st0 retension
  mt -f /dev/st0 rewind
  ```

Disk Drives

Floppy disks provide a convenient way to back up or transport files or programs, but they hold far less data than a tape backup. The most common floppy disk drive is the 3.5-inch floppy drive. Each double-sided high-density floppy has a capacity of 1.44MB. In the past, you could also find boxes of lower-capacity single-sided or low-density floppy disks, but these are rare now. Some systems use the older 5.25-inch floppy drives. Double-sided high-density 5.25-inch disks could hold only 1.2MB. The 5.25-inch disks also used to come in the lower-capacity single-sided or low-density varieties. You might encounter the newer 2.88MB floppy disks, which require special drives to hold that 2.88MB capacity. Some UNIX systems have no floppy drive at all.

UNIX Disk Device Names

Usually a number of floppy device files exist in the /dev directory to handle these single-sided and low-density disks. On SCO UNIX OpenServer, for example, the floppy device names contain phrases such as 48, 96, or 135 to indicate the number of tracks per inch in the floppy disk; ss or ds to indicate single-sided or double-sided; and 9, 15, 18, 21, or 36 to indicate the number of sectors per track. The following shows the various devices files for the A: floppy (floppy drive 0 [fd0] on SCO UNIX OpenServer):

```
$ cd /dev
$ ls -CF *fd0*
fd0          fd048        fd096ds15    rfd0135ds21    rfd048ss8
```

```
fd0135ds15    fd048ds8     fd096ds18    rfd0135ds36   rfd048ss9
fd0135ds18    fd048ds9     fd096ds9     rfd0135ds9    rfd096
fd0135ds21    fd048ss8     rfd0         rfd048        rfd096ds15
fd0135ds36    fd048ss9     rfd0135ds15  rfd048ds8     rfd096ds18
fd0135ds9     fd096        rfd0135ds18  rfd048ds9     rfd096ds9
$
```

You can ignore most of these device names because floppies with less than 1.44MB are rarely used anymore. The following list gives the device files for the 1.44MB 3.5-inch floppy, which is the most common. It also gives the 2.88 MB 3.5-inch floppy device names, in case you encounter this extended capacity drive. Most UNIX systems now also provide an autosensing floppy device file that automatically adjusts to the formatted capacity of the disk. You can use these autosensing device files for most floppy operations, but some UNIX systems do not allow the autosensing device to be used when formatting. Also included are the complete shell commands to format a floppy in this list of floppy device files:

- Solaris:

`/dev/diskette`	Autosensing block device file
`/dev/rdiskette`	Autosensing character or raw device file
`fdformat/dev/rdiskette`	To format a 1.44MB disk

  Note that under Solaris there is a Volume Management Daemon (vold) that wants full control of all disk and CD-ROM drives. You cannot access these devices from the command line while vold is running.

- SCO UNIX OpenServer:

`/dev/fd0`	Autosensing block device file
`/dev/rfd0`	Autosensing character or raw device file
`/dev/fd0135ds36`	2.88MB block device file
`/dev/rfd0135ds36`	2.88MB character or raw device file
`/dev/fd0135ds18`	1.44MB block device file
`/dev/rfd0135ds18`	1.44MB character or raw device file
`format /dev/rfd0135ds18`	To format a 1.44MB disk

- SCO UNIX UnixWare 7:

`/dev/dsk/f0t`	Autosensing block device file
`/dev/rdsk/f0t`	Autosensing character or raw device file

`/dev/dsk/f03et`	2.88MB block device file
`/dev/rdsk/f03et`	2.88MB character or raw device file
`/dev/dsk/f03ht`	1.44MB block device file
`/dev/rdsk/f03ht`	1.44MB character or raw device file
`format /dev/rdsk/f03ht`	To format a 1.44MB disk

- AIX 4.x:

`/dev/fd0`	Autosensing block device file
`/dev/rfd0`	Autosensing character or raw device file
`/dev/fd0.36`	2.88MB block device file
`/dev/rfd0.36`	2.88MB character or raw device file
`/dev/fd0.18`	1.44MB block device file
`/dev/rfd0.18`	1.44MB character or raw device file
`format -d /dev/rfd0`	To format a 1.44MB disk

- Linux:

`/dev/fd0`	Autosensing block device file
(none)	Autosensing character or raw device file
`/dev/fd0E2880`	2.88MB block device file
(none)	2.88MB character or raw device file
`/dev/fd0H1440`	1.44MB block device file
(none)	1.44MB character or raw device file
`fdformat /dev/fd0H1440`	To format a 1.44MB disk

Choosing `tar`, `cpio`, **or Other Backup Programs**

Warning: Restoring a Complete Backup Is Not Trivial

You may think that your system is safe because you have a complete backup. However, on many types of UNIX, before you can restore your backup you must completely reinstall and reconfigure the operating system (which can be as difficult as it sounds, if not more so). When evaluating backup programs, give high marks to utilities that can automatically restore your whole system in an emergency.

The tar and cpio utilities are found on all types of UNIX systems and enable you to save and restore files. Many other backup utilities on UNIX systems do a better job and are easier to use than tar or cpio. They have names like dump, ufsdump, LoneTar, BackupEdge, bru, mksysb, Solaris Data Backup, ARCserve, Legato Networker, and so on. Some of these are standard utilities on one particular type of UNIX; some are extra-cost software available from third-party vendors. For your own UNIX system, you should survey the backup programs available for your type of UNIX and choose the one that gives you the best features.

Why consider tar or cpio at all if better programs are available? The answer is that tar and cpio are valuable because you will find them on virtually all UNIX systems. Assume that you are going on the road and will visit 10 different UNIX systems and want to load a demo program at each site. What type of backup of the demo program will you take with you? If these are unknown systems, your safest bet is to take a tar or cpio backup of the demo. For the same reason, if you need to ship software to many diverse UNIX systems, tar or cpio is a sensible choice. If you receive software from a vendor who supports several different types of UNIX systems, the software you receive is likely to be in tar or cpio format.

It is valuable for you to learn both tar and cpio because you could receive data in either form. tar is the easier utility to use, however, and many vendors choose this format for sending out their software products. tar is very convenient for backing up specific files or directories. It backs up any directory recursively, which means that it backs up all files and subdirectories of that directory, and all files and subdirectories of those subdirectories, and so on.

On the Internet, you will sometimes see download files with the extension .tar, which indicates a tar archive. This means that tar has been used to save a group of files as a single disk file, so there is only one file to download instead of many. You may also see the extension .tgz, which is a tar archive that has been compressed by gzip so it will be faster to download.

Historically, tar has had some significant limitations that argue against its use in backing up a complete UNIX system (see the later section "tar Limitations"). cpio offers better flexibility and control in choosing what is backed up, for example. However, this makes cpio more complicated to use. With cpio, you can choose to back up just portions of a directory, or you can choose to exclude portions of a directory, which tar cannot do. cpio also gives you much greater flexibility when selectively restoring files from a backup that tar gives you. cpio enables you to do incremental backups, which means that you back up only files that have changed since the last backup; tar does not. Despite its added complexity, cpio is a better choice for doing a complete backup than tar, especially on older UNIX systems.

The following sections discuss the use of `tar` and `cpio` in your system backups and restores.

Using `tar` to Back Up and Restore Files

You will find that this section on `tar` uses much of the same wording as in the following section on `cpio`. The two commands have similar functionality, and only some specific details and examples change the two sections. The `tar` and `cpio` sections are complete in themselves without complicated references to one another, but if you read them both, you'll get a strong sense of déjà vu.

Backing Up a Directory Subtree

`tar` stands for *tape archive* utility because typical UNIX backups are done on a tape drive. `tar` can also back up to a disk or a disk file. This is an example of a basic `tar` command to back up one complete directory:

```
$ cd /usr/fred/projects
$ tar cvf /dev/XXX? .
```

First use `cd` to change to the directory to back up. `tar` backs up that directory recursively, automatically including all files and subdirectories and their contents. Following are descriptions of the other elements of this `tar` command:

$	A representation of the shell prompt. Your shell prompt may be different.
tar	A UNIX command to back up files to a tape archive. This `tar` archive is usually saved on a tape or disk but can also be saved in a disk file.
cvf	Three separate options for the `tar` command. `tar` historically did not allow a dash (-) before the first option, but newer versions allow it for compatibility with other UNIX commands. Take a look at each letter separately:
c	Creates a backup. The first letter in this `tar` option list must be c, x, or t.
v	Is verbose (shows filenames being backed up).
f	Allows the specification of the device or file to back up to.

Give `tar` a Valid /dev Device Name

Don't assume that a valid device name for one system will work on another system. When you enter your `tar` command, double-check your spelling of the /dev device to back up to. If you use a wrong device name or a misspelled name, `tar` will create and output everything to a disk file with that name, which could use up all available disk blocks and crash your system.

/dev/XXX? It is very important to replace this with the tape or disk device name that you want to back up to. (These device names were covered at the start of this chapter.) You could also specify a disk filename to hold the tar archive.

. A period is a relative pathname indicating that the current directory is the one to back up. Some users mistakenly put an asterisk (*) here rather than the period, but an asterisk does not back up hidden files (files that start with a period) in this directory.

When you run this tar command, you might see output similar to the following:

```
$ cd /usr/fred/projects
$ tar cvf /dev/XXX? .
a ./ 0K
a ./acme/ 0K
a ./acme/report6 1K
a ./pegasus/ 0K
a ./pegasus/1997/ 0K
a ./pegasus/1997/expenses 1K
a ./pegasus/1997/sales 4K
a ./pegasus/1998/ 0K
a ./pegasus/1998/expenses 8K
a ./pegasus/1998/sales 10K
$
```

Because you used the tar v option, you see each directory and filename as it is being backed up, along with the size of the file. The letter a at the start of each line tells you that the file is being archived (saved on the backup disk or tape). If there is a large amount of data, backups can take hours to complete. When the tar backup has completed, you can refer to the media that contains the backup as a tar archive. Depending on the type of media, you can also refer to the backup as a tar disk or a tar tape.

If you omit the v option, then no filenames are displayed during the tar backup:

```
$ cd /usr/fred/projects
$ tar cf /dev/XXX? .
$
```

Backing Up Selected Directories or Files

You can specify a list of specific files or directories for tar to back up by using the following command:

```
$ cd /usr/fred/projects
$ tar cvf /dev/XXX? ./acme* ./reports/1997 ./reports/1998
```

./acme* illustrates that shell filename wildcards can be used to generate a list of files—in this case, all files and directories that start with acme. ./reports/1997 illustrates that directories can be specified. These are backed up recursively.

The preceding example specifies relative pathnames to back up, which is the recommended procedure.

SEE ALSO

➤ *For more information on the asterisk (*) wildcard, see page 292*

Listing the Table of Contents of an Archive

Enter the following command to display (to standard output) the contents of a tar archive (the filenames that have been saved on this tar disk or tape):

```
$ tar tvf /dev/XXX?
```

Here, t shows the table of contents of the backup. The first letter in this tar option list must be c, x, or t. No files are saved or restored by this operation. /dev/XXX? should be replaced with the tar device or backup filename.

When you run this tar command, you might see output such as the following:

```
$ tar tvf /dev/XXX?
drwxr-xr-x 1001/10          0 Apr 28 21:23 1998 ./
dr-xr-x--- 1002/10          0 Apr 28 21:24 1998 ./acme/
-r--r--r-- 1002/10         29 Apr 28 21:24 1998 ./acme/report6
drwxr-xr-x 1001/10          0 Apr 28 21:25 1998 ./pegasus/
drwxr-xr-x 1001/10          0 Apr 28 21:26 1998 ./pegasus/1997/
-rw-r--r-- 1001/10        135 Apr 28 21:26 1998 ./pegasus/1997/expenses
-rw-r--r-- 1001/10       3281 Apr 28 21:27 1998 ./pegasus/1997/sales
drwxr-xr-x 1001/10          0 Apr 28 21:27 1998 ./pegasus/1998/
-rw-r--r-- 1001/10       7995 Apr 28 21:26 1998 ./pegasus/1998/expenses
-rw-r--r-- 1001/10       9463 Apr 28 21:27 1998 ./pegasus/1998/sales
$
```

Let me pick the third line of this output and explain each field. This line ends in `report6`.

`-r--r--r--`	This is the file type and permissions just as `ls -l` would show them.
`1002/10`	`1002` signifies the owner of this file (the UID number). `10` signifies the group of the file (the GID number).
`29`	This is the size of the file in bytes.
`Apr 28 21:24 1998`	This is the date and time of the last modification of the file.
`./acme/report6`	This is the filename from the backup.

If you omit the v option, only the filenames are displayed:

```
$ tar tf /dev/XXX?
./
./acme/
./acme/report6
./pegasus/
./pegasus/1997/
./pegasus/1997/expenses
./pegasus/1997/sales
./pegasus/1998/
./pegasus/1998/expenses
./pegasus/1998/sales
$
```

Note that it takes as long to list the table of contents as it does to write the `tar` archive in the first place.

Restoring Archives

To use any file from a `tar` backup, you must first restore the desired file or files from the `tar` tape or disk to the hard disk. Before using `tar` to restore a large `tar` archive, however, you must check several important details. The following sections address such concerns as checking for disk free (available) blocks and absolute and relative pathnames, planning where the files are to be restored, working around absolute filename limitations, and changing to the proper directory.

Checking for Disk Free Blocks

It is important to check for disk free (available) blocks in the various filesystems because if any of the UNIX filesystems run out of available disk blocks, application programs may give errors and abort, which could leave databases in a corrupted state. If the root filesystem runs out of blocks, the whole UNIX system could crash.

In the same way, only a limited number of files can be created in any filesystem. df also shows how many more files can be created in each filesystem. Before you restore an archive, check first that the filesystem is not running out of available files.

This is an example of the df command:

```
$ df
/                   (/dev/dsk/c0t0d0s0 ):  154776 blocks    46382 files
/usr                (/dev/dsk/c0t0d0s6 ):  240348 blocks   254137 files
/proc               (/proc            ):       0 blocks      940 files
/dev/fd             (fd               ):       0 blocks        0 files
/export/home        (/dev/dsk/c0t0d0s3 ): 3456112 blocks   427351 files
/opt                (/dev/dsk/c0t0d0s5 ):  382996 blocks   268002 files
/tmp                (swap             ):  198216 blocks     9636 files
/export/home/data   (/dev/dsk/c0t0d1s0 ): 8231524 blocks   933162 files
$
```

You will see one line in df for each filesystem that exists in your UNIX system. In this example, there are eight filesystems. Each filesystem is known by the directory at the start of the line. The /export/home/data filesystem in this example has the most available blocks (8231524) and the most available files (933162), so that is where you would want to restore any large backups. root (/) has the fewest available blocks (154776), and /tmp has the fewest available files (9636), so you should not restore any large archives to those filesystems. Disregard /proc because it is not a disk filesystem.

You can determine which filesystem a directory is in by finding the longest starting directory in df. For example, /export/home/data/acme is in the /export/home/data filesystem, not the /export/home filesystem, because you use the longest df directory that applies.

SEE ALSO

➤ *For more information on* df *and filesystems, see page* 477

Checking for Absolute versus Relative Pathnames

Before you restore any files from a tar backup, list the tar table of contents and check whether the filenames begin with a slash (/). Absolute or full pathnames begin with a slash; relative pathnames do not.

Take a look at the following example:

```
$ tar tvf /dev/XXX?
drwxr-xr-x 1001/10     0 Apr 28 21:23 1998 /mori/
```

```
dr-xr-x---  1002/10        0 Apr 28 21:24 1998 /mori/acme/
-r--r--r--  1002/10       29 Apr 28 21:24 1998 /mori/acme/report6
drwxr-xr-x   001/10        0 Apr 28 21:25 1998 /mori/pegasus/
drwxr-xr-x  1001/10        0 Apr 28 21:26 1998 /mori/pegasus/1997/
-rw-r--r--  1001/10      135 Apr 28 21:26 1998 /mori/pegasus/1997/expenses
-rw-r--r--  1001/10     3281 Apr 28 21:27 1998 /mori/pegasus/1997/sales
drwxr-xr-x  1001/10        0 Apr 28 21:27 1998 /mori/pegasus/1998/
-rw-r--r--  1001/10     7995 Apr 28 21:26 1998 /mori/pegasus/1998/expenses
-rw-r--r--  1001/10     9463 Apr 28 21:27 1998 /mori/pegasus/1998/sales
$
```

In this example, all the filenames begin with a slash (for example,
/mori/acme/report6). Therefore, this tar backup contains absolute pathnames rather
than relative pathnames.

Now consider this example:

```
$ tar tvf /dev/XXX?
dr-xr-x---  1002/10        0 Apr 28 21:24 1998 ./acme/
-r--r--r--  1002/10       29 Apr 28 21:24 1998 ./acme/report6
drwxr-xr-x  1001/10        0 Apr 28 21:25 1998 ./pegasus/
drwxr-xr-x  1001/10        0 Apr 28 21:26 1998 ./pegasus/1997/
-rw-r--r--  1001/10      135 Apr 28 21:26 1998 ./pegasus/1997/expenses
-rw-r--r--  1001/10     3281 Apr 28 21:27 1998 ./pegasus/1997/sales
drwxr-xr-x  1001/10        0 Apr 28 21:27 1998 ./pegasus/1998/
-rw-r--r--  1001/10     7995 Apr 28 21:26 1998 ./pegasus/1998/expenses
-rw-r--r--  1001/10     9463 Apr 28 21:27 1998 ./pegasus/1998/sales
$
```

In the preceding example, all the filenames begin "dot slash" (./). Because they do
not start with a slash, these are relative rather than absolute pathnames.

Finally, take a look at this example:

```
$ tar tvf /dev/XXX?
dr-xr-x---  1002/10        0 Apr 28 21:24 1998 acme/
-r--r--r--  1002/10       29 Apr 28 21:24 1998 acme/report6
drwxr-xr-x  1001/10        0 Apr 28 21:25 1998 pegasus/
drwxr-xr-x  1001/10        0 Apr 28 21:26 1998 pegasus/1997/
-rw-r--r--  1001/10      135 Apr 28 21:26 1998 pegasus/1997/expenses
-rw-r--r--  1001/10     3281 Apr 28 21:27 1998 pegasus/1997/sales
drwxr-xr-x  1001/10        0 Apr 28 21:27 1998 pegasus/1998/
-rw-r--r--  1001/10     7995 Apr 28 21:26 1998 pegasus/1998/expenses
-rw-r--r--  1001/10     9463 Apr 28 21:27 1998 pegasus/1998/sales
$
```

In this example, all the filenames again are relative because none begins with a slash.

SEE ALSO

➤ *For more information on relative and absolute pathnames, see page 70*

Planning Where `tar` **Files Will Be Restored**

In the preceding section, you saw that the `tar` backup will either contain absolute or relative pathnames. If the pathnames begin with a leading slash, then the pathnames are absolute. This means that you can restore the files from the backup only to the original directory where they came from. This can be dangerous because you would be restoring old versions of each file, wiping out any new versions and losing any updates done since the `tar` backup was made.

For example, assume that you display the `tar` table of contents and see this line among the output lines:

```
-rw-r--r-- 1001/10   135 Apr 28 21:26 1998 /mori/pegasus/1997/expenses
```

`/mori/pegasus/1997/expenses` is an absolute pathname. `tar` can usually restore this file only to that absolute pathname on disk. Before restoring this file, it would be a good idea to copy the current version of that file to ensure that all the new updates are retained.

If the files in the `tar` archive use relative pathnames, however, you can restore the files to many different directories. This is useful, for example, when you want to look up information in the old file from the `tar` backup without overwriting the current version of that file. In this case, you would restore the backup file to a temporary working directory, look up the desired information, and then delete the old file when you are done.

Assume that you display the `tar` table of contents and see either filenames that begin with dot slash (`./`) or filenames that begin with neither dot nor slash, such as the following:

```
-rw-r--r-- 1001/10   135 Apr 28 21:26 1998 ./mori/pegasus/1997/expenses
-rw-r--r-- 1001/10   135 Apr 28 21:26 1998 mori/pegasus/1997/expenses
```

In either case, the backup files use relative pathnames. You can predict where `tar` will restore these files by inserting the current directory at the start of the relative pathname to be restored.

For example, if my current directory is `/tmp`, then `tar` would restore the expenses file from the previous paragraph to this absolute pathname:

```
/tmp/mori/pegasus/1997/expenses
```

In another example, if my current directory is /mori/pegasus, then tar would restore the expenses file from the previous paragraph to this absolute pathname:

/mori/pegasus/mori/pegasus/1997/expenses

Finally, if my current directory is / (the root directory), then tar would restore the expenses file from the previous paragraph to this absolute pathname:

/mori/pegasus/1997/expenses

In summary, if the tar archive contains absolute pathnames, tar restores those files (from tape or disk) back to their original location. If the archive contains relative pathnames, tar restores the files to pathnames determined by adding the current directory to the tar pathname.

Considering Absolute Filename Workarounds

If you create your tar archive using absolute filenames, you can restore those files only back to their original location (usually). This is a very great and frustrating limitation of tar. For this reason, the documentation on tar usually advises you to use relative pathnames when doing a tar backup. The earlier section of this chapter on using tar for "Backing up a Directory Subtree" documents only how to back up using relative pathnames.

Under Linux/GNU systems, tar automatically strips the leading slash when the tar backup is created so that the tar archive always uses relative pathnames. However, you can still encounter the frustration of absolute pathnames under Linux/GNU tar in two ways: You can use a special Linux/GNU tar -P option to preserve the leading slash, or you might receive a tape from another system written using absolute pathnames.

Under SCO UNIX, tar has a very useful -A option that suppresses the leading slash on restore. You can then restore absolute pathnames as though they were relative pathnames in the tar archive. You can add the -A option anywhere in the list of tar options as long as it is after the initial x option. This -A option does not exist on AIX, Solaris, or Linux/GNU.

If absolute pathnames in tar are a big problem for you, see whether your system supports the pax command, which should be capable of reading tar archives and which supports an -s option to modify the filenames found.

Changing to the Proper Directory

If the files in the tar archive use absolute pathnames, it makes no difference what directory you change to before doing the tar restore command.

If the files in the `tar` archive are relative, one of the most crucial and dangerous decisions when restoring relative files using `tar` is to choose what directory to change to before you start the `tar` restore. Because you are restoring one or more old archive files, there is a danger of unintentionally overwriting the current version of those files. To determine what directory to change to, compare the pathname on tape with the absolute pathname of the location in which you want to restore the files:

```
Example 1
    pathname on tar archive:
        ./mori/pegasus/1997/expenses
    desired absolute pathname after restore:
        /tmp/restoredata/mori/pegasus/1997/expenses
    directory to change to before doing the tar restore:
        /tmp/restoredata
Example 2
    pathname on tar archive:
        ./mori/pegasus/1997/expenses
    desired absolute pathname after restore:
        /mori/pegasus/1997/expenses
        i.e. we do want to restore the file to its original location
    directory to change to before doing the tar restore:
        /
Example 3
    pathname on tar archive:
        ./mori/pegasus/1997/expenses
    desired absolute pathname after restore:
        /pegasus/1997/expenses
    directory to change to before doing the tar restore:
        We cannot complete this example by just setting our current
        directory. It could be done by more complex procedures_such as
        creating a subdirectory mori as a symbolic link to root (/), or
        by restoring the files to some temporary directory and then
        moving them to the desired location.
```

Restoring All Files to the Original Directory

Restoring files can be tricky and dangerous: There is a possibility that you will overwrite the wrong files. This section shows you several ways of restoring and discusses their good and bad points.

You probably won't want to use the easiest restore, which is to put all the files back where they came from. If you do this, you destroy your files that have up-to-date information and replace them with files from the backup that have old information.

This operation is done only rarely. For example, if something goes wrong with a major update operation and all the current files are corrupted, you may want to restore all the files from older but uncorrupted versions from the backup.

To restore all files in the `tar` backup to their original directory, change to the directory where you originally made your backup. Then issue the `tar` restore command shown here:

```
$ cd /usr/fred/projects
$ tar xvf /dev/XXX?
```

Here, `/usr/fred/projects` is just an example directory name. Enter in its place the directory where you made the backup. If the `tar` archive contains absolute pathnames, it does not matter what directory you change to.

x means to extract files from the backup. The first letter in this `tar` option list must be c, x, or t. Extracting (restoring) files is always a dangerous option because you must make sure that you do not overwrite the wrong files.

`/dev/XXX?` should be replaced with the file or device name for your `tar` archive.

This example shows what the screen looks like when you run this command:

```
$ cd /usr/fred/projects
$ tar xvf /dev/XXX?
x ., 0 bytes, 0 tape blocks
x ./acme, 0 bytes, 0 tape blocks
x ./acme/report6, 29 bytes, 1 tape blocks
x ./pegasus, 0 bytes, 0 tape blocks
x ./pegasus/1997, 0 bytes, 0 tape blocks
x ./pegasus/1997/expenses, 135 bytes, 1 tape blocks
x ./pegasus/1997/sales, 3281 bytes, 7 tape blocks
x ./pegasus/1998, 0 bytes, 0 tape blocks
x ./pegasus/1998/expenses, 7995 bytes, 16 tape blocks
x ./pegasus/1998/sales, 9463 bytes, 19 tape blocks
$
```

Notice that each line begins with an x, indicating that the file shown on that line is being extracted from the `tar` archive to the disk.

Restoring All Files to a Different Directory

Be forewarned that the procedure of restoring all files from a tar archive to a different directory can be used only if there are relative pathnames in the `tar` archive. Review the earlier sections to check absolute versus relative pathnames, check the disk free blocks, and choose a filesystem that has plenty of available blocks. Then change to the proper directory. Here is an example:

```
$ cd /tmp
$ tar xvf /dev/XXX?
x ., 0 bytes, 0 tape blocks
x ./acme, 0 bytes, 0 tape blocks
x ./acme/report6, 29 bytes, 1 tape blocks
x ./pegasus, 0 bytes, 0 tape blocks
x ./pegasus/1997, 0 bytes, 0 tape blocks
x ./pegasus/1997/expenses, 135 bytes, 1 tape blocks
x ./pegasus/1997/sales, 3281 bytes, 7 tape blocks
x ./pegasus/1998, 0 bytes, 0 tape blocks
x ./pegasus/1998/expenses, 7995 bytes, 16 tape blocks
x ./pegasus/1998/sales, 9463 bytes, 19 tape blocks
$
```

In this example, the acme and pegasus directories from the tar backup are restored in the /tmp directory. You can choose some directory other than /tmp if another file-system has enough available disk blocks.

Again, be warned: If the tar archive contains absolute pathnames, your current directory is ignored and the files are restored to their original location, which could be disastrous.

Restoring Only Selected Directories or Files

It is possible to restore only selected directories or files, as this example shows. It is very important to specify the directories or files exactly as they appear in the tar table of contents, including any leading slash (/) or dot slash (./). Any directories are restored recursively.

Consider the following command:

```
$ cd desired-dir
$ tar xvf /dev/XXX? ./acme/report6 ./pegasus/1997
```

Here, desired-dir should be replaced with the desired directory in which you want to issue the tar command.

/dev/XXX? should be replaced with the tar file or device name.

./acme/report6 illustrates how to restore a file.

./pegasus/1997 illustrates how to restore a directory and all its files and subdirectories.

Note that it takes as long to restore selected files as it takes to write the tar archive in the first place.

453

Setting and Using the `tar` Table of Backup Devices

Many UNIX systems such as Solaris and SCO UNIX allow the common `tar` devices to be placed in a file called `/etc/default/tar`.

This is an example of that file from Solaris 2.6:

```
#          device          block    size
archive0=/dev/rmt/0         20       0
archive1=/dev/rmt/0n        20       0
archive2=/dev/rmt/1         20       0
archive3=/dev/rmt/1n        20       0
archive4=/dev/rmt/0        126       0
archive5=/dev/rmt/0n       126       0
archive6=/dev/rmt/1        126       0
archive7=/dev/rmt/1n       126       0
```

The system administrator can enter the commonly used `tar` device names in place of the device names shown in this file. This allows entering a single digit to specify the target device in the `tar` command:

```
$ tar cv2 .
```

In the preceding example, 2 refers to the `archive2` entry in `/etc/default/tar`. Given the `/etc/default/tar` file shown, the `tar` command would be equivalent to the following:

```
$ tar cvf /dev/rmt/1 .
```

If no digit is specified, Solaris defaults to the `archive0` device. SCO UNIX looks for a line that starts `archive=`. Use this default case for the most commonly used `tar` device:

```
$ tar cv .
```

Setting the `tar` Blocking Size

`tar` allows a `b` option to set the block size, ranging from 1 to 20 blocks of 512 bytes per tape record. The default value is 20 if no `b` option is specified. `tar` is unique among UNIX commands in that all the option letters are specified first, and then any arguments to those options are listed in the order of the option letters:

```
$ tar cvfb /dev/XXX? 10 .
```

Notice in the preceding command that the `f` option is specified before the `b` option, so `/dev/XXX?` (the argument to the `f` option) must be specified before the `10` (the argument to the `b` option).

The only time that the `b` option should be specified is when trying to read a tape that was written with a block size that was not set to the standard default of 20.

`tar` **Limitations**

Historically, `tar` has had a number of limitations, which are listed in the following paragraphs. Newer versions of `tar` have removed many of these, but you should be aware of these possible limitations and test for them.

Beware of multivolume backups (`tar` backups that take more than one tape). Older versions of `tar` did not allow continuation to a second tape or did not handle this reliably. Test this procedure thoroughly before you use it, or just back up each group of files onto a single tape.

In addition, `tar` does not back up directories. It creates them as needed on restore, but the owner, group, and permissions will not be restored as they were originally.

`tar` did not back up empty directories. It created directories only when there were files to restore to that directory.

`tar` did not back up `/dev device` files. This made `tar` a poor choice for a complete system backup.

`tar` could not salvage files after a bad spot on the tape.

Using `cpio` to Back Up and Restore Files

You will find that this section on `cpio` uses much of the same wording as in the previous section on `tar`. The two commands have similar functionality, and only some specific details and examples change the two sections. The `tar` and `cpio` sections are complete in themselves, without complicated references to one another, but if you read them both, you'll get a strong sense of déjà vu.

Backing Up a Directory Subtree

`cpio` stands for *copy in/out* and it enables you to back up files to tape, disk, or a disk file. Here is an example of a basic `cpio` command to back up one complete directory:

```
$ cd /usr/fred/projects
$ find . -print | cpio -ocvaB > /dev/XXX?
```

First use `cd` to change the directory to back up. Then use the `find` command to feed all the pathnames to `cpio` to back them up. Following are descriptions of the other elements of the `cpio` command:

`$`	This represents the shell prompt. Your shell prompt may be different.
`find . -print`	This `find` command lists the relative pathname of all files and subdirectories in the current directory.
`cpio`	This is a UNIX command to back up files by doing copy in or out. This `cpio` archive is usually saved on a tape or disk but can also be saved in a disk file.
`-ocvaB`	These are options for the `cpio` command. Take a look at each letter individually:

o	Outputs files to the archive. The first option letter to `cpio` should be either i (input) or o (output).
c	Writes an ASCII header for portability to better read this tape on another system.
v	Is verbose (shows filenames being backed up).
a	Resets the last access date of each file that is backed up to what it was before the `cpio` was run.
B	Sets a tape block size of 5120 bytes. Some tape drives, such as DAT tapes or Exabyte tapes, require a block size larger than 1.

Give cpio a Valid /dev Device Name

Don't assume that a valid device name for one system will work on another system. When you enter your `cpio` command, double-check your spelling of the `/dev` device to back up to. If you use a wrong device name or a misspelled name, `cpio` will create and output everything to a disk file with that name, which could use up all available disk blocks and crash your system.

`/dev/XXX?`	It is very important to replace this with the tape or disk device name that you want to back up to. (These device names were covered at the start of this chapter.) You could also specify a disk filename to hold the `cpio` archive.

When you run this cpio command, you might see output like this:

```
$ cd /usr/fred/projects
$ find . -print | cpio -ocvaB > /dev/XXX?
.
acme
acme/report6
pegasus
pegasus/1997
pegasus/1997/expenses
pegasus/1997/sales
pegasus/1998
pegasus/1998/expenses
pegasus/1998/sales
50 blocks
$
```

Because you used the cpio v option, you see each directory and filename as it is being backed up. If there is a large amount of data, backups can take hours to complete. After the cpio backup has completed, you can refer to the media that contains the backup as a cpio archive. Depending on the type of media, you can also refer to the backup as a cpio disk or cpio tape.

Notice that at the end of the backup, cpio tells you how many blocks the backup took up (50 blocks, in this example). It is a good idea to write this on the tape label. If you ever want to restore this entire tape, you will then know how many free blocks you need on the hard disk.

If you omit the v option, then no filenames are displayed during the cpio backup—only the size of the backup is displayed at the end:

```
$ cd /usr/fred/projects
$ find . -print | cpio -ocaB > /dev/XXX?
50 blocks
$
```

cpio also allows a V option, which simply prints a dot (.) each time a file is backed up. This enables you to watch the progress of the backup and make sure it is proceeding without displaying so much output that you slow down the backup:

```
$ cd /usr/fred/projects
$ find . -print | cpio -ocaB > /dev/XXX?
..........
50 blocks
$
```

Backing Up Selected Directories or Files

cpio backs up only the filenames that you pipe to it. If you give it a directory name, it backs up only the directory, not its contents. To back up a complete directory, you must use a utility such as find to provide all the file pathnames within that directory. You can back up individual selected files like this:

```
$ cd /usr/fred/projects
$ ls ./acme* ./pegasus/report7 | cpio -ocaB > /dev/XXX?
```

Here, ls lists the files to back up by cpio. This does not work on Linux/GNU systems, in which ls can add special indicators to the end of the filenames.

./acme* illustrates that shell filename wildcards can be used to generate a list of files—in this case, all files that start with acme.

./pegasus/report7 illustrates another file to be backed up.

The preceding example specifies relative pathnames to back up, which is the recommended procedure.

You can back up multiple directories to cpio as follows:

```
$ cd /usr/fred/projects
$ (
> find ./expenses -print
> find ./pegasus -print
> ) | cpio -ocaB > /dev/XXX?
```

Parenthesis (()) are used to group multiple find commands and send the combined output to cpio.

The greater than sign (>) at the start of a line is the PS2 prompt. The shell prints this (not the user) to indicate that it is expecting the continuation of a command started on the previous line.

You can back up individual files and complete directories as follows:

```
$ cd /usr/fred/projects
$ (
> echo ./acme* ./pegasus/report7
> find ./expenses -print
> find ./pegasus -print
> ) | cpio -ocaB > /dev/XXX?
```

You can then exclude selected files using grep -v, as follows:

```
$ cd /usr/fred/projects
$ (
> echo ./acme* ./pegasus/report7
> find ./expenses -print
> find ./pegasus -print
> ) | grep -v /tmp/ |
> grep -v junk |
> cpio -ocaB > /dev/XXX?
```

The preceding example backs up the following files:

- All files that start with acme in the current directory
- report7 in the pegasus subdirectory
- All files and directories in the expenses directory
- All files and directories in the pegasus directory
- However, from the preceding files, exclude the following from the backup:
  - Any files or directories that contain /tmp/ in their pathname
  - Any files or directories that contain junk in their pathname

Listing the Table of Contents of a cpio Archive

Enter the following command to display (to standard output) the contents of a cpio archive (the filenames that have been saved on this cpio disk or tape).

```
$ cpio -itcvB < /dev/XXX?
```

In this command, i is input from an already made cpio archive. The first letter in this cpio option list must be i or o. t shows the table of contents of the backup. No files are saved or restored by this operation.

On some UNIX systems, cpio autosenses if the tape was written using the c option, so the c option is not needed when reading from the tape. On other UNIX systems, you get an error if you don't use the c option on cpio.

When you run this cpio command, you might see output like this:

```
$ cpio -itcvB < /dev/XXX?
drwxr-xr-x   4 mori    staff       0 Apr 28 21:23 1998, .
dr-xr-x---   2 jane    staff       0 Apr 28 21:24 1998, acme
-r--r--r--   1 jane    staff      29 Apr 28 21:24 1998, acme/report6
```

```
drwxr-xr-x   4 mori    staff       0 Apr 28 21:25 1998, pegasus
drwxr-xr-x   2 mori    staff       0 Apr 28 21:26 1998, pegasus/1997
-rw-r--r--   1 mori    staff     135 Apr 28 21:26 1998, pegasus/1997/expenses
-rw-r--r--   1 mori    staff    3281 Apr 28 21:27 1998, pegasus/1997/sales
drwxr-xr-x   2 mori    staff       0 Apr 28 21:27 1998, pegasus/1998
-rw-r--r--   1 mori    staff    7995 Apr 28 21:26 1998, pegasus/1998/expenses
-rw-r--r--   1 mori    staff    9463 Apr 28 21:27 1998, pegasus/1998/sales
50 blocks
$
```

This output contains the same fields as `ls -l` would display.

If you omit the v option, only the filenames are displayed:

```
$ cpio -itcB < /dev/XXX?
.
acme
acme/report6
pegasus
pegasus/1997
pegasus/1997/expenses
pegasus/1997/sales
pegasus/1998
pegasus/1998/expenses
pegasus/1998/sales
50 blocks
$
```

Note that it takes as long to list the table of contents as it takes to write the `cpio` archive in the first place.

Restoring Archives

To use any file from a `cpio` backup, you must first restore the desired file or files from the `cpio` tape or disk to the hard disk. Before using `cpio` to restore a large `cpio` archive, however, you must check several important details. The following sections address such concerns as checking for disk free blocks and absolute and relative pathnames, planning where the files are to be restored, working around absolute filename limitations, and changing to the proper directory.

Checking for Disk Free Blocks

It is important to check for disk free blocks in the various filesystems because if any of the UNIX filesystems run out of available disk blocks, application programs may give errors and abort, which could leave databases in a corrupted state. If the root filesystem runs out of blocks, the whole UNIX system could crash.

Review the previous `tar` section "Checking for Disk Free Blocks." The comments on the `df` command are applicable to `cpio`.

One advantage of `cpio` over `tar` in this area is that `cpio` tells you the number of blocks in the full backup, so you know approximately how many available blocks are needed to restore the full backup.

Checking for Absolute versus Relative Pathnames

Before you restore any files from a `cpio` backup, list the `cpio` table of contents and check whether the filenames begin with a slash (/). Absolute or full pathnames begin with a slash; relative pathnames do not.

Consider the following example:

```
/mori/acme/report6
```

This filename is absolute. The following filename is relative:

```
acme/report6
```

`cpio` removes any leading dot slash (`./`) from the filename, so `./acme/report6` is saved as `acme/report6`, which is an equivalent form.

Planning Where the Files Will Be Restored

In the preceding sections, you saw that the `cpio` backup will contain either absolute or relative pathnames. If the pathnames begin with a leading slash, then the pathnames are absolute. This means that `cpio` can restore the files only from the backup to the original directory where they came from, regardless of the current directory. This can be dangerous because you would be restoring old versions of each file, wiping out the new versions and losing any updates done since the `cpio` backup was made.

For example, assume that you display the `cpio` table of contents and see this line among the output lines:

```
-rw-r--r--  1 mori  staff 135 Apr 28 21:26 1998, /mori/_pegasus/1997/expenses
```

Here, `/mori/pegasus/1997/expenses` is an absolute pathname. `cpio` can usually restore this file only to that absolute pathname on disk. Before restoring this file, it would be a good idea to copy the current version of that file so that all the new updates are retained.

If the files in the cpio archive use relative pathnames, you can restore the files to many different directories. This is useful, for example, when you want to look up information in the old file from the cpio backup without overwriting the current version of that file. In this case, you would restore the backup file to a temporary working directory, look up the desired information, and then delete the old file when you are done.

Assume that you display the cpio table of contents and see filenames that begin with no dot or slash:

```
-rw-r--r--  1 mori  staff 135 Apr 28 21:26 1998, mori/pegasus/1997/expenses
```

In this case, your backup files are using relative pathnames. You can predict where cpio will restore these files by inserting the current directory at the start of the relative pathname to be restored.

For example, if my current directory is /tmp, then cpio would restore the expenses file from the previous paragraph to this absolute pathname:

```
/tmp/mori/pegasus/1997/expenses
```

For another example, if my current directory is /mori/pegasus, then cpio would restore the expenses file from the previous paragraph to this absolute pathname:

```
/mori/pegasus/mori/pegasus/1997/expenses
```

For another example, if my current directory is / (the root directory) then cpio would restore the expenses file from the previous paragraph to this absolute pathname:

```
/mori/pegasus/1997/expenses
```

In summary, if the cpio archive contains absolute pathnames, cpio restores those files (from tape or disk) back to their original location. If the archive contains relative pathnames, cpio restores the files to pathnames determined by adding the current directory and the cpio pathname.

Considering Absolute Filename Workarounds

If you create your cpio archive using absolute filenames, you can restore those files only back to their original location (usually). This is a very great and frustrating limitation of cpio. For this reason, the documentation on cpio usually advises you to use relative pathnames when doing a cpio backup. The earlier section of this chapter on using cpio for "Backing up a Directory Subtree" documents only how to back up using relative pathnames.

Under SCO UNIX, cpio has a very nice -A option that suppresses the leading slash on restore. You can then restore absolute pathnames as though they were relative pathnames in the cpio archive. You can add the -A option anywhere in the list of cpio options as long as it is after the initial i option. This -A option is not found on AIX, Solaris, or Linux/GNU.

If absolute pathnames in cpio are a big problem for you, see whether your system supports the pax command, which should be capable of reading cpio archives and which supports an -s option to modify any filenames found.

Changing to the Proper Directory

If the files in the cpio archive use absolute pathnames, it makes no difference what directory you change to before doing the cpio restore command.

If the files in the cpio archive are relative, one of the most crucial and dangerous decisions when restoring relative files using cpio is to choose what directory to change to before you start the cpio restore. Because you are restoring one or more old archive files, there is a danger of unintentionally overwriting the current version of those files. To determine what directory to change to, compare the pathname on tape with the absolute pathname where you want to restore the files, as in the following three examples:

- **Example 1**

  Pathname on cpio archive:
  ```
  mori/pegasus/1997/expenses
  ```

  Desired absolute pathname after restore:
  ```
  /tmp/restoredata/mori/pegasus/1997/expenses
  Directory to change to before doing the cpio restore:
  ```

  ```
  /tmp/restoredata
  ```

- **Example 2**

  Pathname on cpio archive:
  ```
  mori/pegasus/1997/expenses
  ```

  Desired absolute pathname after restore (restore the file to its original location):
  ```
  /mori/pegasus/1997/expenses
  ```

  Directory to change to before doing the cpio restore:
  ```
  /
  ```

- **Example 3**

  Pathname on `cpio` archive:

  `mori/pegasus/1997/expenses`

  Desired absolute pathname after restore:

  `/pegasus/1997/expenses`

You cannot complete this example by just setting your current directory. It could be done by more complex procedures, such as creating a subdirectory `mori` as a symbolic link to root (`/`), or by restoring the files to some temporary directory and then moving them to the desired location.

Restoring All Files to the Original Directory

Restoring files can be tricky and dangerous: There is a possibility that you will overwrite the wrong files. This section shows you several ways to restore and discuss their good points and bad points.

You probably won't want to use the easiest restore, which is to put all the files back where they came from. If you do this, you destroy your files that have up-to-date information and replace them with files from the backup that have old information. This operation is done only rarely. For example, if something goes wrong with a major update operation and all the current files are corrupted, you may want to restore all the files from older but uncorrupted versions from the backup.

To restore all files in the `cpio` backup to their original directory, change to the directory where you originally made your backup. Then issue the `cpio` restore command shown here:

```
$ cd /usr/fred/projects
$ cpio -icvdum < /dev/XXX?
```

Here, `/usr/fred/projects` is just an example directory name. Enter in its place the directory in which you made the backup. If the `cpio` archive contains absolute pathnames, it does not matter what directory you change to.

`i` inputs files from the backup. The first letter in this `cpio` option list must be `i` or `o`. Inputting (restoring) files is always a dangerous option because you must make sure that you do not overwrite the wrong files.

You have already looked at `c` (ASCII header) and `v` (verbose).

`d` creates directories as needed. `u` unconditionally restores—otherwise, an older file from the backup is not allowed to overwrite a newer file on disk.

m preserves the file date and time of the last modification as it was when the file was backed up. Otherwise, this restore operation is a file modification.

/dev/XXX? should be replaced with the file or device name for your cpio archive.

Here is an example showing what the screen looks like when you run this command:

```
$ cd /usr/fred/projects
$ cpio -icvdum < /dev/XXX?
.
acme
acme/report6
pegasus
pegasus/1997
pegasus/1997/expenses
pegasus/1997/sales
pegasus/1998
pegasus/1998/expenses
pegasus/1998/sales
50 blocks
$
```

Restoring All Files to a Different Directory

Be forewarned that the procedure of restoring all files from a cpio archive to a different directory can be used only if there are relative pathnames in the cpio archive. Review the earlier sections to check absolute versus relative pathnames, check the disk free blocks, and choose a filesystem that has plenty of available blocks. Then change to the proper directory:

```
$ cd /tmp
$ cpio -icvdum < /dev/XXX?
.
acme
acme/report6
pegasus
pegasus/1997
pegasus/1997/expenses
pegasus/1997/sales
pegasus/1998
pegasus/1998/expenses
pegasus/1998/sales
50 blocks
$
```

In this example, the `acme` and `pegasus` directories from the `cpio` backup are restored in the `/tmp` directory. You can choose a directory other than `/tmp` if that filesystem has enough available disk blocks.

Again, be warned: If the `cpio` archive contains absolute pathnames, your current directory is ignored and the files are restored to their original location, which could be disastrous.

Restoring Only Selected Directories or Files

It is possible to restore only selected directories or files, as the following example shows. It is very important to specify the directories or files exactly as they appear in the `cpio` table of contents, including any leading slash (/). Directories are not restored recursively (`cpio` does not restore the contents of a directory). You must use wildcards if you want to restore a whole directory.

```
$ cd desired-dir
$ cpio -icvdum < /dev/XXX? acme/report6 'pegasus/1997/*'
```

Replace `desired-dir` with the desired directory where you want to issue the `cpio` command. Replace `/dev/XXX?` with the `cpio` file or device name.

`acme/report6` illustrates how to restore a file. `'pegasus/1997/*'` illustrates how to restore a directory and all its files and subdirectories. (Notice the single quotes: You must prevent the shell from manipulating the asterisk [*] as if this were a filename generation wildcard.)

Note that it takes as long to restore selected files as it takes to write the `cpio` archive in the first place.

Setting the `cpio` Blocking Size

`cpio` allows a `B` option to set the block size to 5120 bytes. Larger block sizes can be set by using the `-C` option instead of `-B`. Larger block sizes may help performance in backing up to high-performance tape drives:

```
$ cd desired-dir
$ find . -print | cpio -ocvaC40960 > /dev/XXX?
```

Notice in the preceding command that `-C` is used to set a tape block size of 40960 bytes. The same `-C` value must be used to read this tape:

```
$ cpio -icvdumC40960 < /dev/XXX?
```

Saving Files on a DOS-Formatted Disk and Restoring Them

Many UNIX systems can save and restore files using a DOS-formatted floppy disk. However, remember that UNIX runs on many types of non-Intel computers, some that have no floppy disk drive.

Usually, special utilities are required for UNIX to access a DOS disk. Sometimes these are not part of the standard UNIX distribution and must be found and downloaded for your version of UNIX. Because of this, the commands and arguments may differ on various machines. Following are some example commands. Look for similar commands in the man pages on your machine.

To list the DOS directory on diskette, your UNIX system may support commands like these:

```
mdir a: or mdir /dev/fd0
dosdir a: or dosdir /dev/fd0
```

To copy a UNIX file to diskette, your UNIX system may support commands like these:

```
mcopy unix-file a:dos-file
mwrite unix-file a:dos-file
doscp unix-file a:dos-file
```

To copy a DOS file from diskette to UNIX, your UNIX system may support commands like these:

```
mcopy a:dos-file unix-file
mread a:dos-file unix-file
doscp a:dos-file unix-file
```

UNIX text and DOS text files use different character sequences to mark the end of the lines. Often the DOS disk copy utilities will have an option to convert DOS end of line to UNIX, and vice versa. It is important to use that feature only for text files and not for binary files.

You may also find similar commands to create a DOS directory on disk, remove files, remove a directory, and so on.

Backing Up and Restoring the Operating System

Backing up and restoring the primary system disk drive is much more difficult than other disk drives on your system. The primary disk drive contains the root filesystem, where the UNIX operating system files reside. This drive has special codes stored near the beginning of the disk drive to allow UNIX to start running when you bring up the system after a shutdown. It contains the UNIX kernel, which resides on a special place on the primary disk drive so that it can be read into memory early in the bootup process to allow access to all the system devices.

Traditional UNIX Complete Restore

If you have a tape backup of all the files on the system, you may think you are secure in case of problems. However, if your primary disk drive becomes unbootable, the traditional UNIX complete restore involves these steps:

- Find your original UNIX media and licenses.
- Find all driver disks and updates.
- Reinstall UNIX, making sure that you partition the disk drives about the same as before.
- Configure your system tape drive.
- Install and configure your backup software.
- Restore your backup.

This is not a simple process, especially if you have never done it before or can't locate all the pieces.

Some UNIX systems allow you to make boot/root floppies:

- The boot disk contains the UNIX kernel. It can boot even if the hard disk is corrupted and cannot boot. The boot disk loads the kernel into memory and then requests you to insert the next diskette.
- The root filesystem disk contains a mini-UNIX system that runs totally in memory and does not use the hard disk. This mini-UNIX often contains useful utilities to repartition your disk drive, to reinitialize the disk filesystems, and to restore them from tape.

Experts can put a system back together if there is a boot/root floppy set, but this is usually beyond the average user.

mksysb **on AIX**

IBM's version of UNIX, called AIX, comes standard with a very useful utility called mksysb (make system backup). You run it like this:

```
mksysb -i /dev/rmt0
```

It will back up your root volume group to tape. Individual files can be restored from this tape if needed. If your system becomes unbootable, insert the AIX operating system CD-ROM (used to load the system) and boot it. This works like the boot/root disks mentioned earlier in that the AIX CD-ROM can boot up even if the hard disk cannot boot and contains a mini-UNIX system with utilities designed to restore the whole primary disk drive from the last `mksysb` backup.

Emergency Recovery on UnixWare 7

UnixWare 7 from SCO provides a similar catastrophic restore capability. Use a utility like this to make a special backup:

```
/sbin/emergency_rec ctape1
```

Also create emergency recovery disks using a command like this:

```
/sbin/emergency_disk diskette1
```

If your system becomes unbootable, use the emergency recovery disks to restore your last emergency backup.

BackupEDGE **and** LoneTar

A number of companies sell useful utilities to the UNIX marketplace. BackupEDGE from Microlite and LoneTar from Cactus International are good examples of products that can be purchased to provide catastrophic recovery for UNIX. This section describes these two examples to give you some understanding of these types of products.

BackupEDGE has a component called RecoverEDGE. LoneTar has a component called AirBag. Both require that you make special emergency disks before your UNIX system is in trouble. You use these products to make full backups of the system every night. They provide menuing programs to help you restore desired files and directories from any backup.

If your UNIX system becomes unbootable, you can use the emergency disks you created earlier and restore your last night's backup directly to disk automatically. The advantage these products offer is that you can do catastrophic recovery from last night's backup, instead of requiring a special backup that might be months old.

# chapter 17

Managing System Resources

Sanjiv Guha and
Steve "Mor" Moritsug

Disk space management

Mounting and unmounting the
file system

System performance management

> **Tip for Beginners**
>
> Read the initial part of this chapter so that you understand what filesystems are and how to determine how much disk space is available in each one. Skip the rest of the chapter. You will probably not have to mount or unmount any filesystems as this is usually done automatically. `lost+found`, quotas, and the remaining topics are for more advanced users.

Managing Disk Space

A UNIX system has a number of resources attached to it. These resources are the I/O subsystem (which manages the disk), terminals, CPU, memory, and so on. This chapter concentrates on how to manage the disk space on a UNIX system. The various system resources are managed by the system administrator, who can log on as the root superuser and add, modify, or delete resources. To try to manage resources is inherently dangerous because a mistake can crash your system and corrupt your data. Sometimes it is necessary to take the system out of multiuser mode and run in single-user mode (maintenance mode) to change some critical system resources. Consult your system documentation.

> **UNIX Honor System**
>
> All users have the potential to create too many files, or use up too many disk blocks, or create too many processes. UNIX expects that users will use these common resources responsibly. Even if you are not logged in as root, you can still use up too many resources and, in extreme cases, crash the system. Quotas, described later in this chapter, are one way to prevent users from using too many disk blocks.

It is very important to avoid running out of disk blocks on a UNIX system. Processes and applications can die in the middle of transactions if the disk suddenly becomes 100% full. If transactions or updates fail in the middle, it can be impossible to recover without restoring from a backup tape. For this reason, all UNIX users—and, of course, the system administrator—should keep an eye on the system disk space, as described in this section

What Is a Filesystem?

All system disk space is grouped into one or more filesystems. On some systems, each separate disk drive is a separate filesystem. A file or a directory cannot span across filesystems. When a filesystem is full, you cannot create files in it or expand existing files, even if there are available disk blocks on other filesystems.

Perhaps you are familiar with DOS, in which each disk drive gets a drive letter such as C: or D:. You can also create multiple logical drives on one physical drive. These logical drives divide up the available disk space. Files usually cannot span logical drives. The UNIX filesystem is very much like a DOS logical drive.

A UNIX filesystem is one physical disk drive or a contiguous section of a disk drive (that is, a logical drive). Unlike DOS, UNIX filesystems are not denoted by drive letters. Instead, two important values reference a filesystem:

- A device node to access the filesystem, such as /dev/sda3
- A mount point, or mount directory, such as /data

The *device node* is a special file in the /dev directory that accesses the proper kernel driver to read and write disk blocks in the physical disk section reserved for that filesystem. Each disk section has a unique device node and driver to access that section.

The *mount point* is a normal UNIX directory that becomes a special access point to the filesystem. For example, if /data is the mount point directory to a different filesystem, you can access the report7 file in that filesystem as follows:

/data/report7

This example looks like a normal UNIX pathname. However, any pathnames that begin with /data, in this example, will really be in a different disk section—that is, a different filesystem.

A mount command transforms the mount point directory from being a normal directory. After it is mounted, the mount point is like a space warp: Passing through it takes you to the other disk section or filesystem. Each filesystem has only one mount point or point of access. If the filesystem is not mounted, you cannot access the files in that section of the disk.

RAID Controllers

A RAID controller allows multiple disk drives to be combined into one logical system pack or disk. The idea of RAID is to provide the disk capacity of one large disk drive by combining several smaller, less expensive disk drives. Since multiple drives have a higher probability of failure compared to a single drive, redundancy is provided. This is either through mirroring or by maintaining data parity information that allows the system to regenerate the data if any single drive fails.

Usually, a filesystem cannot span physical disk drives; however, many UNIX systems offer special utilities or hardware options that can do this, such as Redundant Array of Independent/Inexpensive Drives (RAID).

In addition, a filesystem generally also cannot be expanded in size. To remove blocks from one filesystem and put them into another, you must save all the data in both filesystems, re-create fresh filesystems with the new sizes, and then restore the data in both filesystems. The Veritas filesystem, IBM's AIX UNIX, and some others enable you to leave parts of the disk unallocated to any current filesystem. If a filesystem fills up, you can simply enlarge it by adding some of the unused disk space to it.

SEE ALSO

➤ *For more information on device nodes, see page 433*

The Filesystem Table

Look but Don't Make Any Changes

UNIX has a number of configuration files, like the filesystem table. It is useful to look at these files to get a better insight into UNIX; however, don't modify such files unless you know what you are doing. Incorrect files could be disastrous to your data and the whole system.

The filesystem table is a file that contains one entry for each filesystem to be mounted. This file gives the device node and mount point for each filesystem, plus any special mount options needed.

The name of this table varies on different types of UNIX systems. Here are some examples:

```
/etc/fstab      (filesystem table)
/etc/vfstab
/etc/default/filesys   (SCO OpenServer)
/etc/filesystem
```

Use the man command for each of these possible names to see which one is used on your system.

The Root Filesystem

The main filesystem for every UNIX system is called the root filesystem, which contains the root directory. On some small, simple UNIX systems, this is the only filesystem.

The root filesystem may be documented in the filesystem table, but it is mounted very early in the system bootup procedure, using a process much different than the other filesystems.

Mounting the Filesystem

Before you can access the directories set up in your UNIX system, the system administrator must mount the filesystem. The filesystem table designates which filesystems are to be mounted automatically when the system goes to multiuser mode. At other times, the system administrator can mount or unmount a filesystem manually.

You can get a list of the currently mounted filesystems by using the following command:

```
mount
```

The system will respond with something like this:

```
node        mounted   vfs   date            options  over
----        -------   ---   ------------    -------  ----------
/dev/hd0    /         jfs   Dec 17 08:04    rw, log  =/dev/hd8
/dev/hd3    /tmp      jfs   Dec 17 08:04    rw, log  =/dev/hd8
/dev/hd1    /home     jfs   Dec 17 08:06    rw, log  =/dev/hd8
/dev/hd2    /usr      jfs   Dec 17 08:06    rw, log  =/dev/hd8
```

For each filesystem, the mount command lists the node name, the device name, the name under which it is mounted, the virtual filesystem type, the date and time it was mounted, and its options. You can use the following options:

rw   Grants read and write capabilities.

ro   Grants read only capabilities.

bg   Enables you to process the mount in background. If the mount fails, the system will keep trying to mount the specified filesystem.

If you want to mount a filesystem called xyz, with the read and write option, you can use the following command:

```
mount -o rw /dev/hd4 /xyz
```

In this example, /dev/hd4 is the device node to access the section of the disk where the filesystem resides. /xyz is the mount point.

Note that before mounting, /xyz is a normal UNIX directory that may contain files and subdirectories, all in the root filesystem. After it's mounted, those files and subdirectories vanish and are replaced by files and directories in the /dev/hd4 filesystem. If you unmount the filesystem, then the original files and subdirectories reappear.

If you want to mount all the filesystems defined in the filesystem table, you can use either of the following commands:

```
mount -a
```

```
mountall
```

Unmounting the Filesystem

If you want to do any maintenance on a filesystem, your system documentation may tell you to take the filesystem offline first. You can use the umount command to unmount a filesystem. (Notice that the first letter *n* is missing in the command: umount) If you want to unmount the filesystem mounted as /xyz, for example, you can use the following command:

```
umount /xyz
```

The umount command will find the corresponding device node from the filesystem table. Similarly, you could give umount just the device node name.

You cannot unmount a filesystem, however, if even a single file under that filesystem is in use. The umount command will not provide you with any details of which files are in use or who is using them.

If you use the cd command to change to any directory in a filesystem, you will keep that directory open and prevent unmounting that filesystem. The following is a command sequence:

```
cd /
umount /xyz
```

In this example, a change is made to the root directory, thus making sure that no directory in the /xyz filesystem is held open, which would prevent unmounting it.

In very extreme emergencies, you can use the -f option to force the unmount with this command:

```
umount -f xyz
```

If you do this, however, the program using the files will not terminate properly and you may lose some of the information. In fact, this is so dangerous that it is advised that you never do this.

Disk Space Information

Running out of Disk Space is Serious

Many UNIX commands and programs need to create new files or enlarge existing ones. If a filesystem runs out of disk space, these programs can terminate, leaving updates partially completed. Sometimes the only way to bring the files to a consistent state is to restore all files from the last backup.

To assess the amount of space available on a filesystem, you can use the df command. If you want to find out about the details of all filesystems, you can use the command with no options:

```
df
```

The system will respond with this:

Filesystem	512-blocks	Free	%Used	Iused	%Iused	Mounted on
/dev/hd0	19368	9976	48%	4714	5%	/
/dev/hd1	24212	4808	80%	5031	19%	/usr2
/dev/hd2	9744	9352	4%	1900	4%	/u
/dev/hd3	3868	3856	0%	986	0%	/u/archive

In this example, the root filesystem (mounted on /) has 9976 free or available disk blocks for creating new files. Because it has a total of 19368 blocks, it is 48% filled up. Iused refers to how many inodes are in use. You need an inode to create a new file, so the %Iused tells you how many more file names (roughly) can be created in this filesystem.

On some systems, the space displays as 512-byte blocks. If desired, you can use a -k flag with the df command to display space in 1024-byte blocks. On other systems, the space displays in 1024-bytes blocks by default.

If you want to display the space usage of the current filesystem, you can use the following command:

```
df .
```

The system will respond with this:

Device	512-blocks	free	%used	iused	%iused	Mounted on
/dev/hd4	19368	9976	48%	4714	5%	/

If you determine that a filesystem is running out of space (using the df command), you can use the du command to find out which files are taking up most of the space. The du command has a number of flags you can use to get different information.

You can use the following command to get the disk usage of the current directory:

```
du -k
```

You will get the following response from the system:

```
240    ./test
8 ./info
16 ./info/lost
 264 .
```

Each line displays the number of 1024-byte blocks being used by the subdirectory, with a total at the end.

If you want to find the size of each and every file in the directory and the subdirectories, you can use the following command:

```
du -k -a
100 ./test/file1
120 ./test/file2
20 ./test/file3
8 ./info/file1
16 ./info/lost/file1
264    .
```

You can also use the `find` command, covered in Chapter 7, "Listing and Finding Directories and Files," to find all the large files in the filesystem and also to look for large files that have not been accessed or modified in a long time.

How to Determine Which Filesystem a File Is In

In several situations you will need to know which filesystem a particular file is in. For example, in the section "Linking Files" in Chapter 9,Copying, "Moving, Renaming, Removing, or Linking Files," it mentions that you cannot create a hard link from one filesystem to another. Another example that requires understanding of filesystems would be if you are about to create a large file and want to check how many available blocks are left in that filesystem. Run the `df` command, as shown here:

```
$ df
Filesystem  512-blocks Free  %Used  Iused  %Iused  Mounted on
/dev/hd0    19368      9976  48%    4714   5%      /
/dev/hd1    24212      4808  80%    5031   19%     /usr2
/dev/hd2    9744       9352  4%     1900   4%      /u
/dev/hd3    3868       3856  0%     986    0%      /u/archive
```

In this example, there are four filesystems. The four mount points are shown here:

- `/`

- `/usr2`

- `/u`

- `/u/archive`

To determine the filesystem for a file, find the longest mount point that matches the beginning of the file's absolute pathname, such as the following:

```
/u/archive/reports/acme
```

The example filename matches both `/u` and `/u/archive` at the start of the pathname. The rule says that the longest match prevails, so this file is in the `/u/archive` filesystem. Here are some more examples:

```
/u/reports/acme is in the /u filesystem
```

```
/usr2/u/archive is in the /usr2 filesystem
```

```
/usr/reports/acme is in the root filesystem (/)
```

```
/reports/acme is in the root filesystem (/)
```

Limiting Disk Space for Users

Many UNIX Systems Don't Use Quotas

It is common to find UNIX systems where disk quotas are not set up. Sometimes this feature is not even available. However, if disk space is tight and users are not good about voluntarily limiting their disk usage, quotas can be a useful administrative tool.

As a part of management of disks, you can limit the amount of disk space a user can use or the size of a file a user can create.

To do this, use the `quota` command. You can find out about the current quota of a user with this command:

```
quota -u user1
```

The system will respond with this:

```
User quotas for user user1 (uid 502):
Filesystem  blocks  quota  limit  grace  Files  quota  limit  grace
     /u       20      55     60            20     60     65
```

You can also look up quotas for the filesystem user and quotas for user keith (uid 502) similarly.

You can get a list of quotas for all users for the filesystem /u by using the repquota command, as shown here:

```
repquota -u /u
```

The system will respond with this:

	Block limits				File limits			
User		used	soft	hard	grace	used	soft	hard	grace
root	--	3920	0	0		734	0	0	
davec	+-	28	8	30	3 days	3	0	0	
keith	--	48	0	0		7	0	0	

The + printed in the first column next to davec indicates that the user has exceeded established block limits.

You can modify disk quotas for a user by using the edquota command. If you want to make the disk quota of user2 the same as that of user1, you can use the following command:

```
edquota -p user1 user2
```

You can set the maximum file size a process can create, and this helps manage the disk space. You can use the following command to display the file size limit of a process:

```
ulimit -f
```

The system will respond with the following:

```
4194303
```

This means that the maximum file size is 4194303 blocks of 512 bytes.

The system administrator can modify the file size limit by using the following command:

```
ulimit -f 5000000
```

Checking and Clearing the lost+found Directory

After a system crash, the next reboot automatically runs the fsck utility (filesystem check) to diagnose and repair file, directory, and inode problems in all filesystems. The fsck utility creates an entry in the lost+found directory for any file or directory inode that is not referenced by an entry in any directory in that filesystem. Each filesystem has its own lost+found directory, including the root filesystem. This directory should be checked and cleared periodically.

These "unreferenced inodes" are often complete files or directories that have lost their name. This can occur if the system crashes while a file is being created or deleted. fsck saves these unreferenced inodes in the lost+found directory of the corresponding filesystem. Because they are files that have lost their names, entries in lost+found are given a numerical name that corresponds to the inode number.

```
# cd /lost+found
# ls
007367
010340
012487
016524
016714
$
```

The system administrator (root) should look at the files and directories created in the lost+found directories and either delete them or move them to a different directory and give them a real name. Because you don't know the original filename, you must gather clues about the file to decide if it is worth saving.

A long listing shows that these files are several years old. If these haven't been needed in all this time, they probably can be deleted. You can also see the file owner, group, and size. Any large files might be application data that could be valuable to preserve:

```
# ls -l
total 42
-rw-------   1 mori     group        4210 Feb 27  1997 007367
-rw-rw----   1 mori     group         705 May 21  1997 010340
-rw-------   1 fred     group        4380 Mar 10  1997 012487
-rw-------   1 mori     group        4866 Dec  5  1996 016524
-rw-------   1 mori     group        4106 Dec 12  1996 016714
#
```

The ls -c option is described in Chapter 7. It shows the last time the inode was modified. In the following example, all these files show the same date of last inode change on February 21, 1998. This probably is the date when the system was rebooted after a crash, and these unreferenced files were all saved in lost+found by fsck:

```
# ls -lc
total 42
-rw-------   1 mori     group        4210 Feb 21  1998 007367
-rw-rw----   1 mori     group         705 Feb 21  1998 010340
-rw-------   1 fred     group        4380 Feb 21  1998 012487
-rw-------   1 mori     group        4866 Feb 21  1998 016524
-rw-------   1 mori     group        4106 Feb 21  1998 016714
$
```

Use the `file` command to look for any text files in the `lost+found` directory.

```
# cd /lost+found
# file *
007367:         ksh history file
010340:         data
012487:         ksh history file
016524:         ksh history file
016714:         ksh history file
$
```

In this example, most of these files are the Korn shell history files that enable you to repeat previous commands. These are not important and can be deleted.

For text files, use any text editor or pager utility to view the file contents. If it is a text file that belongs to a user on the system, I usually just email that file to that user and let the user decide if it is worth keeping.

If it is not a text file, use `cat -v`, `od`, or the `strings` command to view its contents. Use any recognizable text within the file to make your decision on whether to save the file elsewhere or delete it.

```
# strings 010340|pg
Gn#ac/
Acme Sales Volume
Eastern Region
50#7/6
Western Region
```

It is important to check and purge all `lost+found` directories periodically because `fsck` can utilize only unused entries that already exist in `lost+found`. If `lost+found` is full, `fsck` cannot save unreferenced files in that filesystem and must discard them. Another reason to purge these files periodically is that some of them may be huge. Delete the ones you don't need to recover that disk space.

SEE ALSO

➤ *To learn more about the* `file` *command, see page 179*

➤ *For more information on the* `fsck` *command, see page 402*

➤ *For more information on inodes, see page 248*

ALSO LOOK UP THE TERM INODE IN THE GLOSSARY.

➤ *For more information on using the vi text editor, see page 563, 587*

➤ *For more information on using the emacs text editor, see page 625*

➤ *For more information on using a pager utility, see page 211*

➤ *For more information on displaying files containing control characters, see page 218*

Some Other Commands for Disk Management

You can use compress, gzip, or bzip2 to compress files that you do not use very often, such as archival files. These files can then be uncompressed if you need to access them.

compress, gzip, and bzip2 are covered in more detail in Chapter 10, "Comparing, Sorting, Modifying, Combining, and Splitting Files."

Another way to free up disk space is to save files that you don't need very often to tape and then delete those files from disk. You can use tar, cpio, or other utilities covered in Chapter 16, "System and File Backups," to do this. If the data is critical, make two backup copies in case the first is not fully readable.

Also be aware that technology changes constantly. Many systems today have evolved and have been upgraded to the point where they can no longer read the backup tapes made several years ago on older technology tape drives. Some installations keep a running version of an old computer system just in case they need to access old backups that can be read only on that system.

Writable CD-ROM drives are becoming more common today. They can currently hold more than 600MB of data and are very durable. You will have a much better chance of reliably recovering data from a five-year old CD-ROM compared to a five-year old magnetic tape.

Managing System Performance

The system administrator should monitor system performance to see if any bottlenecks or other system problems are developing. Several system utilities are useful in this regard.

System Activity Reports

The sar command is a very powerful way to look at various aspects of system performance. Run this from the root account. The following is the general syntax of sar:

```
sar -REPORT LEN CNT
```

The following are your available options:

- REPORT is a single-letter option to tell what report to run. Here are three of the most useful reports:

    - -u reports CPU usage.

    - -b reports disk buffer and cache access.

    - -d reports disk drive usage.

There are many more reports as well. Check the man page on sar.

- LEN tells how long to monitor the system in seconds.

- CNT tells how many times to repeat the monitoring and reporting process.

In the following example, CPU usage is monitored starting at 9:26:32. Five seconds later, the monitoring is stopped and the results are displayed. The output shows that nothing was going on during those 5 seconds because the system was idle 99% of that time:

```
# sar -u 5

SCO_SV unix01 3.2v5.0.4 Pentium     10/15/97

09:26:32    %usr    %sys    %wio    %idle (-u)
09:26:37      0       1       0      99
#
```

In the following example, some user has started an intensive compute-bound program. The system idle time goes to 0%:

```
# sar -u 5

SCO_SV unix01 3.2v5.0.4 Pentium     10/15/97

09:26:06    %usr    %sys    %wio    %idle (-u)
09:26:11     100      0       0       0
#
```

In the next example, the compute-bound job is gone and a heavy disk access job is running. Most of the time is in wio, which means *waiting on input/output*. In most business computer systems, wio is usually the time spent waiting for disk accesses to complete:

```
# sar -u 5
```

```
SCO_SV unix01 3.2v5.0.4 Pentium    10/15/97


09:27:10   %usr   %sys   %wio   %idle (-u)
09:27:15      0      3     97       0
#
```

> **System Tuning Is Complex**
>
> Analyzing system performance, identifying bottlenecks, and tuning the system or upgrading the hardware is a complex process. Whole books are available on the subject. Some companies provide software to monitor the system and locate bottlenecks. If some of your processes involve communication with other systems and shared resources, this adds another significant layer of complexity to the problem.

Because the disk is the bottleneck in this case, sar -b (see the example that follows) will show disk buffer access and caching statistics. In the 5-second monitoring period, the program made 429 read requests and only 46 write requests every second. It is typical for a program to read a number of blocks before it is ready to write a block. These read and write requests are called logical requests because they don't always result in a physical disk access. If the requested block is still in the disk cache from some previous operation, you don't have to do a disk read, which saves time and improves performance.

In the following example, 429 read requests were made every second, but only 224 disk blocks every second were necessary. $rcache shows that the cache was 48% efficient because 429–224, or 205, read requests were satisfied from cache. The cache prevented 205/429 accesses, which equals 47.8%. The cache is usually much more efficient in a normal business environment because critical blocks are often reread a high percentage of the time:

```
# sar -b 5


SCO_SV unix01 3.2v5.0.4 Pentium    10/15/97


09:27:26 bread/s lread/s %rcache bwrit/s lwrit/s %wcache pread/s pwrit/s (-b)
09:27:31    224     429      48       0      46     100       0       0
#
```

The sar -d shows access statistics for each disk drive on the system:

```
# sar -d 5
```

```
SCO_SV unix01 3.2v5.0.4 Pentium    10/15/97

09:27:41  device   %busy    avque    r+w/s   blks/s   avwait   avserv (-d)
09:27:46  wd-0     69.86    1.53     75.25   590.42   4.88     9.28
#
```

In this example, there is only one disk drive:

- %busy 69.86 means that the drive was busy 69.86% of the monitoring period.

- avque 1.53 means that there were, on average, 1.53 disk requests pending all the time.

- r+w/s 75.25 is the average number of data transfers to and from the disk per second. Each transfer could involve multiple 512-byte blocks.

- blks/s 590.42 is the number of 512-byte blocks transferred per second.

- avwait 4.88 means that each request spent an average of 4.88 milliseconds on the queue before being serviced.

- avserv 9.28 means that each request took about 9.28 milliseconds to seek the correct address, wait for the correct sector, and then transfer the data. This value will be larger on slower disk drives.

The sar -d and sar -b data don't correlate exactly because they were measured at different times. You can monitor several options at one time.

In the following example, you monitor CPU (-u), buffers (-b), and disk (-d) in the same 10-second interval:

```
# sar -ubd 10

SCO_SV unix01 3.2v5.0.4 Pentium    07/28/99

19:15:11    %usr    %sys    %wio    %idle (-u)
        bread/s lread/s %rcache bwrit/s lwrit/s %wcache pread/s pwrit/s (-b)
         device   %busy    avque    r+w/s   blks/s   avwait   avserv (-d

19:15:21      10       8       0      82
               0     146     100       0      15      99       0       0
#
```

Notice at 19:15:11, the monitoring starts and prints out all three headers. At 19:15:21, 10 seconds later, the monitoring ends and displays the results. The -d showed no results because no accesses occurred. This example shows that the system was 82% idle and that there were 0 physical reads or writes during that period.

In the following example, the system spent 100% of its time running user programs. Again no disk accesses were done:

```
# sar -ubd 10

SCO_SV unix01 3.2v5.0.4 Pentium    07/28/99

19:15:42   %usr    %sys    %wio   %idle (-u)
        bread/s lread/s %rcache bwrit/s lwrit/s %wcache pread/s pwrit/s (-b)
         device  %busy    avque    r+w/s    blks/s   avwait    avserv (-d)

19:15:52    100      0       0       0
              0      2     100       0      2     100       0       0
#
```

In the following example, the system spent 94% of the time waiting on I/O. The average number of requests was higher than you saw previously, and so was the average wait on the queue. With more requests pending, the system could service them in a more efficient order, so the average time to service a request actually went down from before:

```
# sar -ubd 10

SCO_SV unix01 3.2v5.0.4 Pentium    07/28/99

19:16:29   %usr    %sys    %wio   %idle (-u)
        bread/s lread/s %rcache bwrit/s lwrit/s %wcache pread/s pwrit/s (-b)
         device  %busy    avque    r+w/s    blks/s   avwait    avserv (-d)

19:16:39      3      3      94       0
             64    542      88       8     39      81       0       0
           wd-0  49.40    4.94    70.06   143.51   27.81    7.05
#
```

The next example shows what sar would report when you access the same small file repeatedly. All the blocks of the file are in the cache, so the cache becomes 100% efficient for reads; thus, no physical reads are needed. Notice that the system spends 62% of its time in system routines, not user code. In this case, the system routines are doing the cache lookup and memory to memory buffer transfers:

```
# sar -ubd 10

SCO_SV unix01 3.2v5.0.4 Pentium    07/28/99

19:18:02   %usr    %sys    %wio   %idle (-u)
```

```
          bread/s lread/s %rcache bwrit/s lwrit/s %wcache pread/s pwrit/s (-b)
           device  %busy    avque    r+w/s   blks/s   avwait   avserv (-d)

19:18:12      34      62        4        0
               0    3357      100        5       24       81        0        0
             wd-0    4.39    19.45     3.69     9.38   219.46    11.89
#
```

sar History

The system usually keeps about 10 days' worth of sar statistics in the directory
/usr/adm/sa:

```
# cd /usr/adm/sa
# ls -CF
sa06    sa08    sa10    sa12    sa14    sar07   sar09   sar13
sa07    sa09    sa11    sa13    sa15    sar08   sar10   sar14
#
```

Here, the sa## files are the history files. ## is the day of the month on which that
history was taken. The example shows sar history from the 6th of the month to the
15th. The last day is the current day and will be incomplete until the day is over.

To display sar reports for a previous day, use this general syntax:

```
sar -REPORT -f /usr/adm/sa/DAY
```

The following are your available options:

- REPORT is a single-letter option to tell what report to run.
- DAY is a file sa## found in that directory.

For example:

```
# sar -uf sa11
```

The vmstat Command

Some BSD-type UNIX systems provide vmstat instead of sar. However, because sar
is so powerful, many of these systems offer both vmstat and sar today. vmstat reports
statistics since the last system reboot, such as in the following code:

```
# vmstat
kthr      memory              page                  faults         cpu
-----  -----------  ------------------------  -------------  -----------
 r  b   avm   fre   re  pi  po  fr   sr  cy    in   sy   cs  us sy id wa
 0  0  7415  5774    0   0   0   4   13   0   138 3819  30   9 13 70  9
#
```

man `vmstat` provides the following legend:

- **r**—Number of kernel threads placed in run queue
- **b**—Number of kernel threads placed in wait queue
- **avm**—Active virtual pages
- **fre**—Size of the free list
- **re**—Pager input/output list
- **pi**—Pages paged in from paging space
- **po**—Pages paged out to paging space
- **fr**—Pages freed (page replacement)
- **sr**—Pages scanned by page-replacement algorithm
- **cy**—Clock cycles by page-replacement algorithm
- **in**—Device interrupts
- **sy**—System calls
- **cs**—Kernel thread context switches
- **us**—User time
- **sy**—System time
- **id**—CPU idle time
- **wa**—CPU cycles if waiting on pending disk input/output

The `iostat` Command

Along with `vmstat`, another utility that you may find available is `iostat`:

```
# iostat
tty:    tin    tout avg-cpu:  % user   % sys   % idle  % iowait
        3.3    56.0               8.7    12.7    69.8     8.8
Disks:         % tm_act     Kbps     tps   Kb_read   Kb_wrtn
hdisk1            7.2       52.8     4.6   9868291   1932212
hdisk0            5.3       23.2     4.7   1210536   3973271
cd0               0.0        0.0     0.0         0         0
#
```

man `iostat` explains the columns as follows:

- **tin**—Shows the total number of characters read by the system for all ttys
- **tout**—Shows the total number of characters written by the system to all ttys

- **% user**—Shows the percentage of CPU utilization that occurred while executing at the user level
- **% sys**—Shows the percentage of CPU utilization that occurred while executing at the system level
- **% idle**—Shows the percentage of time that the CPU or CPUs were idle and the system did not have an outstanding disk I/O request
- **% iowait**—Shows the percentage of time that the CPU or CPUs were idle, during which the system had an outstanding disk I/O request
- **% tm_act**—Indicates the percentage of time the physical disk was active
- **Kbps**—Indicates the amount of data transferred (read or written) to the drive in Kbytes per second
- **tps**—Indicates the number of transfers per second that were issued to the physical disk
- **Kb_read**—The total number of Kbytes read
- **Kb_wrtn**—The total number of Kbytes written

part

IV

UNIX TEXT PROCESSING

chapter

18

Searching for Lines in a File or Pipeline

Steve "Mor" Moritsugu

Finding lines that contain a pattern, that are missing a pattern, or that contain two patterns

Regular expression wildcards that can be used to find patterns

Extra pattern search capabilities in egrep, perl, fgrep, and awk

Tip for Beginners

This chapter covers searching for lines that contain patterns within files or output. The chapter first covers `grep` and its options in order of usefulness. Then, it covers special pattern-matching wildcards called regular expressions. These are a perfect example of why some people love the elegance and power of UNIX commands so much, and why others hate them for being cryptic and complex.

You should learn to use `grep` and some of its most useful options now. Postpone regular expressions and the remainder of the chapter until you are comfortable with the filename generation wildcards that are covered in Chapter 11, "Generating and Using File Lists."

Finding/Displaying Lines That Contain a Pattern

To find and display lines in a file that contain a name or pattern, you can use the `grep` command (you learn where it gets its name later). For example, assume that you have an employee file in which each line contains the name and information about one employee. To display just the lines from that file that contain the name *Smith*, you would enter this:

```
$ grep Smith employee-file
Smith, Carl - 555-6379, hired 3-7-92, dept 6
Smith, Dennis - 555-3291, hired 8-27-96, dept 2
Smithers, Jane - 619/555-1720, hired 4-4-89, dept 2
$
```

In this output, notice that only lines containing the word *Smith* are displayed. The other lines are not displayed. Also notice in the last line that *Smith* was found as part of the string `"Smithers"`.

The general syntax for the `grep` command is as follows:

```
grep pattern file1 file2 ...
```

`grep` displays (to standard output) any lines from the given files that contain the pattern, even if the pattern is part of a larger word or string.

This pattern can be a name, number, or any sequence of characters. The pattern is called a *regular expression* and can include special wildcards (covered later in this chapter). If the pattern contains any punctuation or spaces, you will need to enclose the pattern in single or double quotation marks. (That's also discussed later in this chapter.) In general, a good rule of thumb is to always enclose the pattern in single quotation marks.

If you specified more than one file in your grep command, the grep output will include the filename as well as the text of the lines that contain the pattern, as shown here:

```
$ grep Acme report*
report3:    Acme Enterprises    1,373,383,234  world-wide
report3:Martin, President of Acme Toys, confirmed the project
report.acme:of the four Acme divisions, it is the least
$
```

If you do not provide a list of files, grep reads its input from standard input, so grep can be used in a pipeline, as in this example:

```
$ who | grep smith
leesmith    tty3     Mar  6 19:48
smith       ttya03   Mar  6 17:23
$
```

In this command line, who shows which users are currently logged in. The output from the who command is piped to grep, which looks for lines that contain the name *Smith* as either a complete word or as part of a larger word. Notice that to use grep in a pipeline, you cannot specify any filenames after the pattern to search for.

grep is the quintessential UNIX filter. Think of a paper filter in a coffeemaker. The filter holds the coffee grounds and the hot water. The filter allows the liquid coffee to pass through, but it retains the grounds. The job of a filter is to selectively allow things you want to pass through and to block the things you don't want so that they can't get through. This is what grep does, especially when you use it in a pipeline. In the previous example, you start with the who command. But because you want to see only the lines that reference Smith, grep passes those lines through. grep blocks all the lines that don't contain Smith—you could say it filters them out because you don't want to see them. Because some output can contain tens of thousands of lines or more, grep is an extremely important and often used utility under UNIX so that you can concentrate on just the lines you are interested in.

See Table 18.1 for other standard properties of the grep command.

Table 18.1 Other Properties of the `grep` Command

Property	See page
Allows relative and absolute pathname arguments	70
Processes either filename arguments OR standard input	115
Changes only the output, not the file	111
Allows a list of filenames and filename wildcards	292
Allows output to be piped or redirected	116

Ignoring Uppercase and Lowercase When Selecting Lines

To ignore case when searching for patterns with `grep`, you add the `-i` option to `grep`, as in the following example:

```
$ grep -i acme report7
The Acme account is currently handled by Linda. It is
once they merged with ACME INDUSTRIES, their stock value
Pauley, Mr. Robert Kacmeth, Ms. Jean Bensen, and other notable
$
```

When you use the `-i` option with `grep`, it does not matter whether you specify the pattern in uppercase, lowercase, or mixed-case characters. In the previous example, the `-i` option instructs `grep` to find all lines containing the pattern, regardless if the pattern appears in uppercase, or lowercase, or mixed case. Without the `-i` option, `grep` shows a line only if the case of the pattern in the line exactly matches the upper- and lowercase letters of the pattern.

In older versions of UNIX, use `-y` instead of `-i` to ignore case. Some newer versions of UNIX allow `-y` to ignore case (for backward compatibility), but `-i` is preferred.

Saving the Selected Lines in a File

You can use redirection (`>` or `>>`) to save the output of `grep` in a file, like this:

```
grep 'Acme Shoes' /usr/fred/report* > acme/shoefile
```

In this example, you are looking for the pattern Acme Shoes. Because it contains a space, you must enclose the pattern in single or double quotation marks. The list of files to look in is indicated by a filename generation wildcard pattern that specifies all files in the directory /usr/fred that start with the name *report*. The command then tells grep to save all the matching lines to a file called shoefile in the acme subdirectory of your current directory. grep does not display the lines onscreen because the output is being redirected.

This is another similar example:

```
who | grep fredp >> fredplog
```

Here, you are checking to see whether the user fredp is currently logged in. If so, you want grep to append his login information—as reported by who—to the fredplog file.

Piping the Selected Lines to Other Commands

grep is often used in a pipeline to filter out unwanted lines so that other commands can process the desired lines. To see how this works, consider the following example:

```
$ who | grep fredp | wc -l
    3
$
```

In this example, who generates a list of every user who is currently logged in. grep cuts down that list to only the lines that mention fredp. wc -l counts the lines that it receives. From the output, you can see that the user fredp is currently logged in simultaneously on three different ports.

> **Building Complex Command Lines**
>
> Piping to the wc command can give wrong results if the lines to count are not the correct lines. Build up complex command lines one step at a time, so you can see the output. Once you are sure the output is correct, then repeat the previous command and pipe it to the next command in the pipeline. Chapter 22 shows how you can repeat the previous command without retyping it and gives an example of building a complex command sequence step-by-step.

This result may be misleading, though, because grep considers a line to be matching even if the pattern found is part of a larger word. In the example, suppose that there is a user named alfredpenn. Notice that the string fredp is found within alfredpenn. What if alfredpenn were logged in on three ports, and fredp was not logged in at all? You would get the same result:

```
$ who | grep fredp | wc -l
    3
$
```

Choosing Your Pattern

Much of the skill of using grep comes from wisely choosing what pattern to search for, especially the start of the pattern and the end of the pattern. For example, using the following grep command might not be a very good idea:

```
$ grep 'acme' report*
```

This command requires a space before acme in the pattern, in an effort to avoid words such as "Dacmer." However, requiring a starting space is not a good idea because grep will not find acme if it is at the start of a line or if it is in quotation marks (because "acme" does not start with a space).

Assume that you have a very large phone list file containing lines such as this:

Bower, Linda 714/555-8182

Decker, Tom 818/714-6192

Mellinger, Fred 714/639-1215

Smith, Will 714/909-3818

Smithson, Charlie 818/603-2194

To quickly look up people with the last name of Smith, you would enter:

```
$ grep Smith, phone-list
Smith, Will 714/909-3818
$
```

Notice that you can add a comma at the end of the grep pattern only because the file contains a comma after the last name. The comma allows you to display Smith while avoiding Smithson. This comma is not a feature of grep; it simply results from how the file is set up.

To count the number of people whose phone number is in area 714, you would enter this command:

```
$ grep 714/ phone-list | wc -l
```

You can specify a slash (/) after 714 only because your file has a slash (/) between the area code and the phone number. Using the slash (/) in the pattern allows you to ignore 714 if it is part of the phone number but not if it's the area code. Again, the slash (/) is not a feature of the grep command; it is an example of how you can look at the data and wisely choose a pattern that will return the lines you want to see.

Displaying Lines That Don't Contain the Pattern

grep is also useful as a reverse filter: You can use it to remove unwanted lines that contain a specified pattern so that you can see what is left over. To display lines that don't contain the pattern, use the -v option with grep to make it work as a reverse filter, as in this example:

```
$ who | grep -v guest | wc -l
```

Here, who displays one line for each person logged in to the system. The grep command then uses a reverse filter to exclude lines that contain the word *guest* so that all other logins will pass through but guest logins will be ignored. The output of grep is then piped to wc -l, which counts the number of logins excluding the guest login.

Adding the Line Number to the Found Lines

To make grep show the line number as well as the line that contains the pattern, add the -n option to grep:

```
$ grep -n Acme report8
13: Acme Industries
246:Pacific Acme Ltd
1202:Paul Acmeersch
$
```

As you can see, grep –n displays the line number first, followed by the line that matches the pattern.

If the -n option to display the line number is used with multiple files, the output of grep begins with the filename and then the line number, as shown in the following example:

```
$ grep -n Acme report*
report2:25:Acme Enterprises
report8:13: Acme Industries
report8:246:Pacific Acme Ltd
report8:1202:Paul Acmeersch
report.acme:45:whose former name was Acme Inc. until they merged
$
```

Displaying Just Filenames That Contain the Pattern

Sometimes, you just want to know which files reference a particular name or pattern. If the pattern is mentioned on thousands of lines in each file, the normal grep output would be too long to easily analyze. To display just the filenames that contain the pattern, use the -l option with grep to list the filenames, not the lines that contain the pattern:

```
$ grep -l Acme report*
report2
report8
report.acme
$
```

---

grep -c Counts Lines, Not Occurrences

When looking at grep -c output, people often make the common mistake of thinking that the number next to the filename is the number of times the pattern occurs in the file. Note, however, that grep -c counts the number of lines, not occurrences. If the pattern occurs 10 times but all on one line, grep -c will show a countcountc of 1, not 10 for that file.

To display each filename and a count of the number of lines in that file that contain the pattern, you can use the -c option with grep, like this:

```
$ grep -c Acme report*
report2:1
report4:0
report8:3
report12:0
report.acme:1
report.pegasus:0
$
```

Finding Lines That Contain Two Patterns

You can use grep twice to make a double filter. Lines must then contain two patterns to pass through, as shown here:

```
$ grep -in acme report* | grep merge
report7:246:once they merged with ACME INDUSTRIES, their stock value
report.acme:45:whose former name was Acme Inc. until they merged
$
```

In this example, you pipe grep to grep to make a double filter. To pass through the first filter, lines must contain the word *acme* in either uppercase or lowercase. To pass through the second filter, lines must also contain the word *merge*. The output displays lines that contain both patterns within the line. It does not matter whether the second pattern comes before or after the first pattern in the line. Piping grep to grep sets up a logical AND condition, which means that a line must satisfy both conditions to pass through.

Which Filter Should Come First?

If you pipe the output of one grep to another grep, you will get the same result, no matter which pattern you search for first. For better efficiency, however, the first filter should be the one that eliminates the most lines. Then, the second filter will have less work to do.

Notice that the second grep command must not specify any files so that it will read from standard input and process the output from the first grep command. The following example shows a mistake people sometimes make:

```
$ grep -i acme report* | grep merge report*
```

Don't make this mistake. This example will not generate an error, but it will not do what you intended. Because the second grep command has been given a list of files, it ignores the output from the first grep. What you have here is a failure to communicate. The second grep command is its own single filter, which looks only for lines that contain *merge* and displays them—even if they don't contain *acme*. The first grep command does all that work for nothing because its output is ignored.

You can also combine a regular filter with a reverse filter, as in this example:

```
$ grep -i Acme report* | grep -vi Dacmer
```

Here, you first use a regular filter to find lines that contain acme in either upper- or lowercase. Note, however, that the first filter also finds lines that contain *Dacmer* because *Dacmer* contains *acme*. The second grep is a reverse filter that removes lines from the first filter. The end result is lines that contain *acme* but not *Dacmer*. However, there is still one potential problem here: Any lines that contain both *acme* and *Dacmer* will be removed by the reverse filter. Later you will see how perl can filter out whole words by ignoring patterns within other words.

Wildcard Pattern Matching in Lines (Regular Expressions)

One of the things that makes UNIX very powerful is the way that patterns can be used to specify what you are looking for in a general way. You saw this with filename generation wildcards, which enable you to form a list of files based on a pattern. In this section, you will meet a totally different form of UNIX wildcard that I call a regular expression wildcard. UNIX neophytes often confuse filename generation wildcards with regular expression wildcards and then wonder why things do not work as they expect.

> **Where Does grep Get Its Name?**
>
> The text editor ed was commonly used before vi was available. In the ed editor, g/re/p is a command used to globally search for the regular expression enclosed in slashes (/), and then p says to print each line found. When a separate utility was developed to do the same thing, it was given the ed command name g/re/p without the slashes.

A regular expression is a string of characters that you want to search for. Short regular expressions can be combined to make one larger regular expression. A regular expression then can be either a complete pattern or a single element of a pattern. Regular expressions can contain special characters or metacharacters that have special pattern-matching capabilities. These special characters will be referred to as regular expression wildcards to differentiate them from filename generation wildcards.

In this chapter, you will see how to use regular expressions to find desired lines in a file or a pipeline. In the following chapter, you will learn how to use regular expressions to modify a file or pipeline. Although regular expressions are complex, it's important that you know about them because they are a basic tool of UNIX that gives it much of its power and elegance.

Selecting Lines That Contain a Pattern

This is a typical grep command:

```
grep acme report7
```

If you enter this command, grep will search the contents of the file report7 and will display all lines that contain the string *acme* even if *acme* is part of a larger word. Note that the pattern *acme* can be positioned anywhere in the line, and grep will display that line.

Selecting Lines That Start with a Pattern

What if you want to see only lines if they start with *acme*? You can specify this by adding a regular expression wildcard. You add the circumflex (^), also called the caret, to the start of your pattern, as shown here:

```
grep '^acme' report7
```

Notice the single quotation marks around the search pattern. It is generally a good idea to put single quotation marks around the pattern (but there is one case in which you should use double quotation marks; you'll learn about that later). As you might recall, you usually put single quotation marks around the pattern if the pattern contains any punctuation or spaces. But it doesn't hurt to use single quotation marks even if there's no punctuation or spaces.

In the previous example, the circumflex (^) is a regular expression wildcard that stands for the start of the line. Thus, only lines that begin with acme will match the pattern. In its output, grep will display those lines, including any text that follows acme on the lines.

The circumflex is not a wildcard character unless it occurs at the start of the pattern. For example, consider this command:

```
grep '2^4' mathproblems
```

Here, grep will display all lines that contain 2^4 anywhere within the line. The circumflex is just another character to search for because it does not occur at the start of the pattern.

To search for lines that begin with a circumflex, you would have to enter a command like this:

```
grep '^^' filename
```

In this example, the first circumflex is a regular expression wildcard indicating the start of the line. The second circumflex is not at the start of the pattern so it is not a wildcard; it indicates a literal circumflex character.

To specify that a leading circumflex is a literal circumflex and does not indicate the start of the line, you can precede it with a backslash (\):

```
grep '\^acme' report7
```

In this example, `grep` searches for and displays all lines that contain ^acme anywhere within the line.

Note that every line has a beginning. Therefore, the following command would match every line in the file:

```
grep '^' report7
```

> **UNIX Documentation Avoids the Term _Wildcard_**
>
> In cards, a wildcard is usually a special card that counts as whatever card you need most. You can see that it is a stretch to call the circumflex (^) and dollar sign ($) wildcards by that definition. Therefore, UNIX documentation usually avoids the term _wildcard_ and calls them special characters or _metacharacters_. In practice, UNIX users seem to have no trouble referring to any character with a special meaning as a wildcard, as I do in this book.

Selecting Lines That End with a Pattern

What if you want to see only lines that end with acme? You can do this by adding another regular expression wildcard, the dollar sign ($), to the end of your pattern:

```
grep 'acme$' report7
```

Here, the dollar sign is a regular expression wildcard that stands for the end of the line. Thus, only lines that end with _acme_ will match the pattern. `grep` then displays those lines, including any text that precedes acme on the lines.

The dollar sign is a wildcard only if it occurs at the end of the pattern; otherwise, it indicates a literal dollar sign character. To indicate that you want to search for a literal dollar sign as the last character of a pattern, precede the dollar sign with a backslash so that it will not indicate the end of a line.

Specifying the Contents of the Entire Line

To specify that you want to search for an entire line, you can use the leading circumflex (^) and the trailing dollar sign ($) wildcards in the same pattern, as in this example:

```
grep '^acme$' report7
```

To understand this example, you must know that regular expressions are compared character by character from left to right with each line of the file or pipeline. For a line to match the pattern in the given example, it must have these elements in this order:

- The start of the line
- The word *acme*
- The end of the line

For example, this line does not match the pattern previously specified:

```
acme acme
```

Even though the line starts with `acme` and ends with `acme`, it does not match. If you compare the regular expression `^acme$` with the line `acme  acme` left to right, it's easy to see that the regular expression allows for only one *acme* in the line.

Here is another example of using the circumflex and dollar sign characters together:

```
grep '^$' report7
```

Given this command, `grep` searches for and displays all empty lines—lines in which the end of the line immediately follows the start of line.

Now consider this other example:

```
grep '$^' report7
```

Here, the circumflex (^) is not a wildcard because it does not occur at the start of the pattern. Similarly, the dollar sign ($) is not a wildcard. Thus, this `grep` command searches for and displays all lines in the file `report7` that contain a dollar sign ($) followed by a circumflex (^) anywhere within the line.

Test Your UNIX Skills

Give a UNIX command sequence that counts the number of lines in file prog1 that start with the word REM and also end with the word Acme.

The answer is on the next page.

Answer to test on previous page

```
grep '^REM' prog1 | grep 'Acme$' | wc -l
```

Including Shell Variables in Regular Expressions

You can use shell variables within your regular expressions, as shown here:

```
who | grep $LOGNAME
```

In this example, $LOGNAME usually contains a user ID name. who displays all logins, and grep filters out unwanted lines to show only those lines where the user is logged in.

If shell variables are adjacent to other pattern elements, enclose them in curly braces ({}) like this:

```
grep "${prefix}acme${SUFFIX} Inc" report7
```

For this example, suppose that $prefix contains g4 and $SUFFIX contains UK. The example would then execute the following command:

```
grep "g4acme-UK Inc" report7
```

Because the pattern contains a space, you must enclose it in double quotation marks. See the later section on quoting regular expressions for more information.

SEE ALSO

➤ *For more information on shell variables, see page 27*

➤ *For more information on quoting rules, see page 119*

Including Command Substitution in Regular Expressions

Regular expressions can also contain elements that you specify using shell command substitution indicated by backquotes (`) or $(). For example, take a look at the following command:

```
grep "report`date '+%Y'`" report7
```

In this example, the regular expression is made up of two elements:

- The word report
- This command in backquotes: `date '+%Y'`

Within the second element, `'+%Y'` is an option to the date command, telling it to display the current year in four-digit format. The backquotes (`` ` ``)substitute the output of the enclosed command into the current command line and remove the backquoted command.

Therefore, if the current year is 1998, the previous grep command is equivalent to this:

```
grep "report1998" report7
```

When you use command substitution, a regular expression can contain elements generated by any other UNIX command or pipeline.

SEE ALSO

➤ *For more information on backquotes and command substitution, see page 308*

Quoting Regular Expressions to Prevent Problems

If your regular expression pattern does not contain any punctuation characters or spaces, it does not matter whether you enclose the pattern in single quotes, double quotes, or no quotes at all. None are needed.

If there are punctuation or spaces within the pattern, review the basic quoting rules in Chapter 4, "Rules for Entering UNIX Commands." The rest of this section contains more complex quoting situations for advanced users.

If your regular expression pattern needs to include one or more single quotation marks, do not enclose the pattern in either single or double quotes. Instead, just put a backslash in front of each punctuation character and a space in your regular expression. For example, suppose that you want to search for the following string:

```
'73 Canyon[46]'
```

To do so, you could use this grep command:

```
grep \'73\ Canyon\[46\]\' filename
```

Alternatively, you can escape just the pattern single quotes and enclose the other characters in single quotes:

```
grep \''73 Canyon[46]'\' filename
```

To search for one backslash (\), you must put two backslashes in your pattern (\\) if the whole pattern is enclosed in single quotes. The pattern backslash must be preceded by a backslash for grep to treat it as a literal search character instead of a special character. If the pattern is not enclosed in single quotes, you must use four backslashes (\\\\) in your pattern to search for one backslash (\). This is because the shell will preprocess the line and remove two of them. For example:

```
$ grep "a\\\\b" filename
Ana\Belle
$ grep 'a\\b' filename
Ana\Belle
$
```

SEE ALSO

➤ *For more information on quoting rules, see page 119*

UNIX Commands That Allow Regular Expressions

Only the following UNIX commands allow the use of regular expressions:

- grep, egrep, fgrep
- sed
- awk
- perl
- vi (when searching and substituting)
- ed (when searching and substituting)

Comparing Filename Wildcards with Regular Expression Wildcards

Sometimes, people are confused about when to use regular expressions and when to use Filename Generation Wildcard patterns. The following guidelines should alleviate some of the confusion:

- Use regular expressions when you want to search the contents of files or pipelines for patterns. Only a handful of commands support the use of regular expressions; see the previous section.
- Use Filename Generation Wildcard patterns when you want to create a list of filenames based on a pattern. Many UNIX commands will accept a list of files on the command line.

Allowing Any Characters in Certain Pattern Positions

The period (.) is a regular expression wildcard. It represents any single character, which enables you to specify exactly how many character positions to allow before, after, or between other pattern elements. The following command shows an example of the period character in use:

```
grep 'dog.bone' report7
```

Given this command, grep would display all lines that contain *dog*, followed by any single character, followed by *bone*. For example, it might return lines that contain the following strings:

- dog-bone
- dog bone
- dog/bone
- dogEbone

It would not, however, display a line containing *dogbone* because there is no character separating *dog* and *bone* in that case.

To specify that you want to match an actual period (.) in a regular expression, you precede the period with a backslash, like this:

```
grep '5\.25' report7
```

This command would display any lines containing 5.25. The backslash is needed before the period to prevent grep from thinking that the period is a regular expression wildcard that matches any character.

Specifying Allowed Characters in Pattern Positions

Test Your UNIX Skills

Give one UNIX command sequence that will display all lines from file acme that mention any report from report23 to report27.

The answer is on the next page.

Answer to test on previous page

```
grep 'report2[3-7]' acme
```

The following answer is wrong because the square brackets match only a single character, not a sequence:

```
grep 'report[23-27]' acme    # wrong
```

Square brackets allow you to specify a set of alternatives for the character in that position within a regular expression, as shown in the following example:

```
grep 'dog[- EZ1-3]bone' report7
```

Given this command, grep would display lines that contain any of the following strings:

- dog-bone
- dog bone
- dogEbone
- dogZbone
- dog1bone
- dog2bone
- dog3bone

Note, however, that unless other allowed *dog bone* references were included in the lines, grep would not display lines that contain the following strings:

- dog4bone (because 4 is not an allowed alternative)
- dogEZbone (because the square brackets represent only a single character within the pattern)
- dogbone (because there is no single character between *dog* and *bone*)

Inside the brackets ([ ]), a dash (-) between two letters or digits indicates an inclusive range. To indicate a literal dash as a character in the list, you must place it first or last in the list. To indicate a right bracket (]) as a character in the list, place it as the first list element, as in []abc]. A period (.), asterisk (*), left bracket ([), or backslash inside the brackets is treated as a literal character without special meaning. Consider, then, the following command:

```
grep '[0-9][0-9][0-9]' report7
```

Here, grep displays any lines containing three (or more) consecutive digits. Even if you are searching for only three digits, grep might find more than three digits because the pattern does not prohibit more digits before or after the three digits.

Here is another example:

```
grep '^[A-Z]' report7
```

Given this command, grep will display all lines that begin with a capital letter.

Specifying Characters Not Allowed in Pattern Positions

If the list in square brackets begins with a circumflex (^), it will match any single character except for the ones in the list. For example, given the following command

```
grep 'acme[^0-9]' report7
```

grep will display all lines containing *acme* followed by one character, as long as that character is not a digit. It will not display lines that end with *acme* because there must be one character following *acme* in this pattern.

Have You Seen This Before?

The square brackets this chapter covers in regular expressions are very similar to square brackets in filename generation wildcards, which are discussed in Chapter 11.

Regular Expressions	Filename Generation Wildcards	Description
[...]	[...]	Matches any character in list
[^...]	[!...]	Matches any character not in list

Here is another example:

```
grep '^[^a-zA-Z]' report7
```

This command will display all lines that start with some character other than a letter. It will not display empty lines, however, because some non-letter character must be present.

Specifying Number of Occurrences of a Regular Expression Element

When using repeated regular expressions, you can use a shorthand method of specifying the number of occurrences of the previous regular expression element. This shorthand method uses escaped braces: \{ and \}, which means that you must put a backslash (\) before each brace character. Here's an example of a command with escaped braces:

```
grep '2[0-9]\{10\}000' report7
```

In this command, the regular expression tells grep to look for a 2, followed by exactly 10 digits (not 11 digits), followed by 000.

The following syntax is allowed within the escaped braces:

- \{x\} means to match a total of x occurrences of the previous pattern element (not 1 + x occurrences).
- \(x,\} means to match x or more occurrences.
- \(x,y\} means to match at least x occurrences, but not more than y occurrences.

Consider the following example:

```
grep '$[0-9]\{3,5\}\.' report7
```

Given this command, grep would display all lines that contain a dollar sign ($), followed by at least three digits but not more than five digits, followed by a period (.). Note that because the period is escaped, it is not a wildcard.

Here's another example:

```
grep '[a-zA-Z]\{20,\}' report7
```

This command would display all lines that contain words of 20 or more uppercase or lowercase letters. Note that the comma is superfluous here; you'll learn why in the section on unbounded "or more" wildcards.

Specifying Zero or More Occurrences of a Regular Expression Element

The asterisk is a regular expression wildcard that you can use as a shorthand method for this expression:

```
\{0,\}
```

The asterisk (*) tells grep to allow zero or more occurrences of the previous regular expression element. Don't confuse this with the asterisk (*) filename generation wildcard, which means something different and is used in a totally different context.

The following command shows you how to use the asterisk regular expression wildcard:

```
grep 'ab*c' report7
```

In this command, b* indicates that grep should allow zero or more b's. Given this command, grep would display lines that contain any of the following strings:

- ac (0 occurrences of b)

- abc (1 occurrence of b)

- abbc (2 occurrences of b)

- abbbc (3 occurrences of b)

- abbbbc (4 occurrences of b)

- And so on, including abbbbbbbbbbbbbbbbbbbbbbbbbbbbbbbbbbbbbbbbbbbbbbbbbbbbbc

---

What Do These Brackets ([   ]) Contain?

Because spaces within text can contain combinations of spaces and tabs, some grep commands can contain a pattern such as '^[   ]*acme'. You might think there are four spaces within the brackets, but this makes no sense. The only contents that would constitute a valid and reasonable regular expression inside the brackets are one space and one tab. This pattern looks for *acme* at the left margin or as the first printable text after some initial spaces or tabs.

To indicate zero or more occurrences of any character, you can use the period and the asterisk together (.*), as in this example:

```
grep 'dog.*bone' report7
```

This command would display lines that contain the following strings:

- dogbone

- dog-bone

- doggy bone

- My dog has a bone

- My dog is named Rover. Please add a soup bone to the grocery list.

This command would not display cases in which *dog* is on one line and *bone* is on the next. The whole regular expression must be on one line.

As another example, this command would display all lines that contain zero or more digits:

```
grep '[0-9]*' report7
```

This command will display all lines of report7, even if they do not contain any digits. Each line either contains some digits or no digits (that is, zero digits). In general, every possible line file contains zero or more occurences of any character.

The following command displays any line containing one digit followed by zero or more digits:

```
grep '[0-9][0-9]*' report7
```

Essentially, this finds and displays all lines with one or more digits.

Given the following command, grep displays any lines that contain a dollar sign, followed by one or more digits, followed by a period (.):

```
grep '$[0-9][0-9]*\.' report7
```

This command is also equivalent to the following one:

```
grep '$[0-9]\{1,\}\.' report7
```

Anytime you see two consecutive occurrences of a regular expression element followed by an asterisk (*), that wildcard pattern will match one or more of those elements, as in this example:

```
grep 'abb*c' report7
```

This command tells grep to display any lines that contain a, followed by one or more b's, followed by a c.

Dropping Unbounded "Or More" Regular Expression Wildcards

UNIX offers several ways for you to indicate that an element is to be used a certain number of times—or more. For example, you could use any of the following expressions:

a\{6,\}	(6 or more of the letter a)
b*	(0 or more of the letter b)
cc*	(1 or more of the letter c)
ddd*	(2 or more of the letter d)

Compare these two commands:

```
grep '[0-9]\{3,\}' report7
```

```
grep '[0-9]\{3\}' report7
```

The first of these commands will display lines that contain three or more digits. The second command will display lines that contain three digits. However, the second command does not specify limitations on what characters may come after those three digits. Thus, the second command will allow more digits after the three digits. It will also display lines containing three or more digits. In other words, the two commands will both display the exact same output, even though you specified "or more" in the first command but not in the second.

The same is true for these two commands:

```
grep 'abb*' report7
grep 'ab' report7
```

The first command will display lines containing a, followed by one or more b's. The second command will display lines containing ab. The two commands are equivalent, however, because any line that contains a, followed by one or more b's also contains a, followed by one b (and vice versa). The command without the "or more" is better, though, because it is more efficient and easier to understand, and you can predict the results.

I call these unbounded "or more" situations because you are not specifying pattern elements before and after the "or more" element. If the "or more" element is unbounded, either before or after the element, omit the "or more" part from your grep command. This makes the grep command more efficient, and you will better understand what lines your grep command will output.

Here are some bounded "or more" situations:

```
grep "abb*c" report7
grep '^[0-9]*$' report7
grep '$[0-9]\{5,\}\.' report7
```

In each of these commands, pattern elements have been specified both before and after the "or more" wildcards. Here, the "or more" is significant, however; if you leave it out, you will change the output from the command.

Extra Regular Expression Wildcards Available in egrep

The egrep command is an extended version of grep that allows some regular expression wildcards that grep doesn't allow. However, egrep does not support the braces {} wildcard to specify the number of occurrences. Sometimes the set of egrep regular expression wildcards are called *extended regular expressions* or *full regular expressions*. The syntax for egrep is the same as that for grep.

See Table 18.2 for other standard properties of the egrep and fgrep commands. fgrep is discussed in a later section of this chapter.

Table 18.2 Other Properties of the `egrep` and `fgrep` Commands

Property	See page
Allows relative and absolute pathname arguments	70
Processes either filename arguments OR standard input	115
Changes only the output, not the file	111
Allows a list of filenames and filename wildcards	292
Allows output to be piped or redirected	116

Specifying One or More Occurrences of an Element with egrep

To specify that the previous pattern element is to be used one or more times, you use the plus sign (+) wildcard with `egrep`, as shown here:

```
egrep 'ab+c' report7
```

This command would display lines that contain a, followed by one or more b's, followed by c. The plus sign (+) wildcard is not supported by `grep`.

Using a Regular Expression Element Zero or More Times with egrep

To specify zero or one occurrence of an element, you can use the question mark (?) with `egrep`:

```
egrep 'Mrs?. Smith' report7
```

This command would display lines that contain strings such as these:

- `Mr. Smith`
- `Mrs. Smith`

However, it would not display lines with Mrs. Smith. The question mark (?) must be preceded by a backslash (\) or must be enclosed in double or single quotation marks (as shown). The question mark (?) wildcard is not supported by `grep`.

Searching for One of Several Patterns

Test your UNIX skills

Give one UNIX command sequence that will display all lines from file acme that mention any report from report27 to report73.

The answer is on the next page.

Answer to test on previous page

```
egrep 'report(2[7-9]|[3-6][0-9]|7[0-3])' acme
```

In the above answer, 2[7-9] matches 27 through 29, [3-6][0-9] matches 30 through 69, and 7[0-3] matches 70 through 73.

Using egrep, you can search for and display lines that contain one of several patterns. You separate those patterns with the vertical bar, which is also used as the pipe sign. Here's an example:

```
egrep 'acme|pegasus|apollo' report7
```

This command will display lines that contain *acme*, *pegasus*, or *apollo*. The vertical bar (|) must be preceded by a backslash or enclosed in double or single quotation marks (as shown).

Parentheses [()] can be used to group the vertical bar choices, as shown here:

```
egrep 'project (acme|pegasus|apollo)' report7
```

This command will display lines that contain *project acme*, *project pegasus*, or *project apollo*.

Extra Regular Expression Wildcards Available Only in Perl

Perl is a complete programming language that runs under UNIX and Windows. While it usually does not come with any commercial UNIX distribution, it is readily available via the Internet for most UNIX systems. If Perl is available on your system, you can use it as a grep-like command-line utility that provides search and display capabilities not available in grep or egrep.

Perl is most commonly used as a programming language, but it does have command-line options that allow it to be used as a command-line filter (such as grep, sed, and awk) with this general syntax:

```
perl -ne 'print if /re/opt' file1 file2
```

The following are the options:

- -ne are command options. The -e option to perl enables you to enter a line of Perl code on the command line. The -n option allows perl to process each line of standard input or any files specified on the command line.

- *re* stands for any regular expression pattern to search for. You can include any of the regular expressions for grep and also extended expressions for egrep. Braces to indicate a repeat count should not be escaped by a backslash as they are with grep.

- *opt* stands for search options that may be specified, such as the following:

  - i says to ignore case.

  - x says to ignore non-escaped spaces allowing the pattern to expand for readability.

Here is an example:

```
perl -ne 'print if /acme/i' report7 report8
```

This example will ignore case while looking for the string *acme* in report7 and report8.

Here is another example:

```
perl -ne 'print if /^acme [0-9] {3,} \ /ix' report7 report8
```

This command illustrates that complex regular expressions are easier to read using perl. The regular expression is found between the slashes (/) in the command. If you use the Perl x option after the closing slash, spaces are ignored in the regular expression unless they are escaped—that is, preceded by a backslash. Think of the x as allowing you to expand the pattern, using spaces freely to make it more readable. The other Perl feature that improves readability is that backslashes are not used before braces indicating repeat counts.

See Table 18.3 for other standard properties of the perl command

Table 18.3 Other Properties of the perl Command

Property	See page
Allows relative and absolute pathname arguments	70
Processes either filename arguments OR standard input	115
Changes only the output, not the file	111
Allows a list of filenames and filename wildcards	292
Allows output to be piped or redirected	116

Finding Words That Are Not Parts of Larger Words

Using `perl`, you can search for words that are not part of larger words. This is difficult or impossible using `grep` or `egrep`.

To specify a word boundary, enter `\b` in the regular expression for `perl`:

```
perl -ne 'print if /\b in \b/ix' report7
```

With Perl, a word can contain upper- or lowercase letters, digits, or the underscore character (_). In this example, the regular expression is placed within slashes. Again, the x option following the final slash is being used so that spaces can be inserted in the regular expression to improve readability. This command will display any lines in `report7` that contain the word *in*. By placing `\b` before and after the word *in*, you can specify that the word *in* cannot be part of a larger word. Therefore, the output will not display lines that contain the words *tin*, *bin*, *dinner*, or *into*, for example. However, it will display the word *in* if it is at the start of a line, if it is at the end of a line, or if it has punctuation around it.

In the following command, the `\b` occurs only before the word *in*:

```
perl -ne 'print if /\b in /ix' report7
```

The command will display all lines that contain words that start with *in*, including larger words such as *into* or *intend*.

To specify that a position not be on a word boundary, you use `\B` (with a capital B), as in this example:

```
perl -ne 'print if / in \B /ix' report7
```

This command will display all lines that contain the string *in* as part of a longer word such as *inn* or *into* or *dinner*. However, the words *tin* and *bin* would not match the pattern because they have a word *boundary* after the word *in*.

SEE ALSO

➤ *For more information on* `perl`, *see Chapter 29.*

Turning Off Regular Expression Wildcards

To turn off the special nature of a regular expression wildcard, precede it with a backslash, as in this example:

```
grep '2\*3' mathreport
```

Here, you are looking for the string 2*3, so you have to turn off the special meaning of the asterisk.

Two Reasons to Avoid *fgrep*

fgrep is supposed to be the fast grep because it does not have to handle regular expressions. However, it is often the slowest of the grep commands. The X/Open (Ver 2) spec calls fgrep obsolete and prefers the equivalent command grep -F.

If you have a large number of wildcards to turn off, you can use the fgrep command, which does not allow any regular expression wildcards. All characters are regular characters to fgrep. Therefore, with this command, you can look for all lines with five or more asterisks:

```
fgrep '*****' report7
```

You don't have to precede each one with a backslash, though, because you used the fgrep command instead of grep.

fgrep is also useful for ignoring wildcards in the contents of shell variables, as in the following example:

```
fgrep "$USERINPUT" report7
```

Checking Only Specific Fields to Select a Line

awk is an extensive programming language that is available on all commercial UNIX systems. You can use a subset of it as a grep-like command-line utility that provides search and display capabilities not available in grep or egrep.

See Table 18.4 for other standard properties of the awk command.

TABLE 18.4 Other Properties of the awk Command

Property	See page
Allows relative and absolute pathname arguments	70
Processes either filename arguments OR standard input	115
Changes only the output, not the file	111
Allows a list of filenames and filename wildcards	292
Allows output to be piped or redirected	116

Displaying a Line if Exact Match in One Field

grep checks the whole line for a match. If you want to check only a specific field of the line, you can do that using awk, as in the following:

```
awk '$3 == "acme"' file1 file2
```

This example will display any lines from *file1* or *file2* where field 3 is exactly the word *acme*. The following are the options:

- $3 indicates field 3 in the line. Fields are separated by one or more spaces or tabs. The first field is $1. The last field may be indicated as $NF.
- == indicates that you are looking for an exact match.
- "acme" indicates the string to search for, as contained within the quotation marks. It may not contain wildcards because you are using the == test for an exact match.
- *file1 file2* are files that awk will search in.

Displaying a Line Based on Numeric Value in One Field

You can use the following format to display a line if a particular field contains a numeric value. This example displays lines from *file1* and *file2* only if the third field of each line contains the value 5:

```
awk '$3 == 5' file1 file2
```

No quotation marks are required around the numeric value. You can replace == with the following tests:

```
==   equal to
!=   not equal to
>    greater than
>=   greater than or equal to
<    less than
<=   less than or equal to
```

The following command will display all lines in yearend.rpt in which the first field of the line contains a number larger than a negative 3.6:

```
awk '$1 > -3.6' yearend.rpt
```

If the field starts with a letter (that is, it is not numeric), awk treats it as an impossibly large numeric value. In the previous example, the value -3.6 illustrates that the numeric values can have decimal fractions and can be negative.

Displaying a Line if There Is a Regular Expression Match in One Field

To use regular expressions when checking for a matching string, change the test from == to tilde (~), and put slashes around the regular expressions, as shown here:

```
awk '$3 ~ /^acme[0-9]/' report7
```

This command will display all lines from report7 in which field 3 starts with acme, followed by a digit.

awk allows the same regular expression wildcards as egrep, which include the following:

+	For one or more occurrences of previous element
?	For zero or one occurrence of previous element
|	For allowed alternative patterns
()	For grouping patterns

Like egrep, awk does not allow the use of \{ \} to specify the number of occurrences.

Displaying a Line Based on Multiple Conditions

To check for two conditions before displaying a line, use && to indicate a logical AND. For example, in this command, awk is checking field 3 from ls -l, which is the owner of each file:

```
ls -l | awk '$3 == "fred" && $5 > 2300'
```

awk is also checking field 5, which is the size of the file in bytes. This command will display only files owned by fred that are larger than 2300 bytes.

To check for one condition or another being true, use || to indicate a logical OR, as in this example:

```
ls -l | awk '$3 == "fred" || $5 > 2300'
```

This command will display all files that are either owned by fred or are greater than 2300 bytes.

To group conditions, use parentheses, like this:

```
ls -l | awk '( $3 == "fred" || $3 == "jane") && $5 > 2300'
```

This command will display files owned by either fred or jane, provided that the size is greater than 2300 bytes.

chapter

19

Replacing or Removing Text from a File or Pipeline

Steve "Mor" Moritsugu

Extracting/removing characters by column position

Replacing one string with another

Special replacement capabilities in *perl* and *awk*

Conditional replacement based on field values

Formatting output into columns

Translating characters: uppercase to lowercase

Deleting punctuation or control characters

Removing duplicate lines

> **Tip for Beginners**
>
> Read about the `cut` command and the `sed` command to make simple replacements at the start of this chapter.
> Before you tackle regular expressions in the `sed` command, make sure that you are comfortable with all the
> regular expression rules covered in the previous chapter using the `grep` command.

Extracting/Removing Characters by Column Positions

You can use the UNIX `cut` command to remove selected column positions from a
list of files or a pipeline and then display the results. The –c option to `cut` enables
you to specify a range of column positions to extract. The way to think about this
command is that you are going to `cut` this range out of the output and keep it in the
output; the rest gets thrown away, as follows:

```
$ date
Sun Mar 22 17:58:40 PST 1998
$ date | cut -c5-10
Mar 22
$
```

In the preceding example, –c5–10 specifies that you want to cut out and keep
columns 5 through 10 and throw the rest away. You can specify more than one
range, separated by a comma, as follows:

```
$ date | cut -c5-10,24-28
Mar 22 1998
$
```

Omit the ending number in the range to allow that range to go to the end of the
line, as follows:

```
$ date | cut -c5-10,24-
Mar 22 1998
$
```

The –f option to `cut` can be used to specify a field number if a tab character separates each field, as follows:

```
$ cat data2
acme    1978    24.6
saturn  1953    8.3
wondra  1981    16.7
$ cut -f1,3 data2
acme    24.6
```

```
saturn  8.3
wondra  16.7
$
```

In this example, –f1,3 tells cut to cut out and keep fields 1 and 3.

If some character other than a tab is used as the field separator, you can use the –d option to specify that field separator character. The following example uses the same data fields, but the field separator is a colon (:), not a tab:

```
$ cat data3
acme:1978:24.6
saturn:1953:8.3
wondra:1981:16.7
$ cut -d: -f1,3 data3
acme:24.6
saturn:8.3
wondra:16.7
$
```

Although it is possible to set the –d field separator to a space, this is not useful in most situations because cut does not allow multiple spaces to be regarded as a single field separator. For example:

```
$ cat data4
xxx yyy   zzz
$ cut -d' ' -f1,3 data4
xxx
$
```

In the preceding example, there are three spaces between yyy and zzz. Therefore, cut considers the file data4 to have these fields:

```
field 1: xxx
field 2: yyy
field 3: empty
field 4: empty
field 5: zzz
```

Wherever two separators are together, there is an empty field between them, like this:

```
xxx yyy <empty> <empty> zzz
 1   2     3       4      5
```

You might normally expect a group of spaces or tabs to be one field separator. For cases in which fields may be separated by more than one space or tab character, you will need a more powerful command than cut. Later in this chapter, you will see how to use the awk command to extract fields from output. Notice that it has no trouble extracting field 1 ($1) and field 3 ($3) even though there are multiple spaces.

```
$ cat data4
xxx yyy   zzz
$ awk '{print $1, $3}' data4
xxx zzz
$
```

See the following Table 19.1 for other standard properties of the cut command:

Table 19.1 Other Properties of the *cut* Command:

Property	See page
Allows relative and absolute pathname arguments	70
Processes either filename arguments OR standard input	115
Changes only the output, not the file	111
Allows a list of filenames and filename wildcards	292
Allows output to be piped or redirected	116

SEE ALSO

➤ *For more information on determining when to use* awk *or* cut *to extract fields, see page 554*

Replacing or Removing Strings (Using Regular Expression)

The preceding chapter showed how to use regular expression wildcards to find lines containing a pattern within a file or pipeline. That chapter also showed that regular expression wildcards can look similar to filename generation wildcards, but these are two different sets of wildcards used for totally different purposes even though they use some of the same wildcard characters. This section teaches you how to replace a substring within a line and how to use regular expression patterns to define the string to be replaced.

SEE ALSO

➤ *For more information on regular expression wildcards, see page 502*

> **Global Search and Replace**
>
> Search and replace is another way to refer to the **sed** command being presented in this section. It is global because the command operates on the whole file. Keep in mind that the replacements only occur in the output and not in the original file.

Replacing One String with Another

To replace one string with another when displaying the output of a file, use the `sed` command, like this:

```
sed 's/Mr. Smith/Ms. Wilson/g' report7
```

`sed`	This is the stream editor. It makes any editing changes you specify as it processes the data stream one line at a time.
`'s/Mr. Smith/Ms. Wilson/g'`	This is the editing command you give to `sed`. This command is usually enclosed in single quotation marks to protect the punctuation inside from shell interpretation. Use double quotation marks rather than single quotation marks if you want to include any shell variables as part of the editing command.
`'s/Pattern/Repl/g'`	This is the general format of the `sed` substitute command. `Pattern` is the string for which to search, and `Repl` is the string with which to replace it. `Pattern` may contain regular expression wildcards, but `Repl` may not. The example searches for the string `Mr. Smith` and replaces all occurrences of it with the string `Ms. Wilson`. This is true even if the `Pattern` is part of a larger word—for example, `Mr. Smithson` would become `Ms. Wilson`. You will see later in this chapter how Perl can prevent this problem.
`report7`	This is the file for `sed` to process. You can also specify a list of files, and `sed` will display the contents of each of them, making the substitution indicated. Filename generation wildcards can be used to generate the list of files.

Note that `sed` displays the changed output to standard output; it does not modify the file itself. The output from this command can then be piped to another command, or it can be redirected to a file.

Here is the same sed command used in a pipeline situation:

```
cat report* | sed 's/Mr. Smith/Ms. Wilson/g' | pg
```

report* is not a regular expression wildcard; it is a filename generation wildcard that generates a list of all files that start with the word *report*. The cat command will output these files on the standard output that is piped to the same sed command just analyzed. The output from sed will then be displayed one page at a time onscreen.

sed displays the replaced lines to standard output. The changes are not made in the source file. If you want to replace the contents of a file, you must use two UNIX commands and a temporary file. For example:

```
sed 's/pattern/repl/g' report7 > /tmp/sed$$
mv /tmp/sed$$ report7
```

This technique is explained under the property "Changes only the output, not the file" in the following Table 19.2. This table lists a number of standard properties that apply to the sed command.

Table 19.2 Other Properties of the *sed* Command:

Property	See page
Allows relative and absolute pathname arguments	70
Processes either filename arguments OR standard input	115
Changes only the output, not the file	111
Allows a list of filenames and filename wildcards	292
Allows output to be piped or redirected	116

Making the Replacement Only Once per Line

Remove the g flag from the substitute command to make the replacement a maximum of once per line. Without the g flag, the same replacement would be made once on every line where the pattern occurs, but never more than once on any given line. For example:

```
sed 's/IBW/MCC/' partslist
```

Assume that the file partslist, mentioned in the preceding command, contains lines like this:

```
402     IBW-10    IBW(4),IBW(5)
403-6   IBW-11-6  IBW(3),MNT(16)
527     GRV-6     GRV(13,MNT(14)
```

The preceding `sed` command would replace those lines as follows:

```
402      MCC-10     IBW(4),IBW(5)
403-6    MCC-11-6   IBW(3),MNT(16)
527      GRV-6      GRV(13,MNT(14)
```

Notice that only the first occurrence of IBW on each line has been replaced.

You should omit the g flag whenever you use the circumflex (^) R.E. wildcard or the dollar sign ($) R.E. wildcard. For example:

```
sed 's/^[    ]*Chapter/Section/' book3
```

In this example,

```
[    ]
```

this is an R.E. wildcard that indicates either a space or a tab. There is a space and a tab character within the square brackets.

```
^[    ]*
```

This line indicates zero or more spaces or tabs at the start of a line.

```
^[    ]*Chapter
```

This line indicates the word *Chapter* on the left margin—that is, it can be indented and still match the pattern.

The preceding `sed` command will replace the word *Chapter* with *Section*, but only if *Chapter* is the first word on the line, ignoring any leading spaces. The replacement word, *Section*, will not be indented even if *Chapter* was indented. You will see in the next section how to preserve what wildcards matched, which would allow the replacement to have the same indentation.

Your command will still work if you include the g flag with the circumflex (^) or dollar sign ($) R.E. wildcards. The g flag is just unnecessary and slightly inefficient because there cannot be more than one match per line when you use either of these two R.E. wildcards.

Changing the Delimiter

The character immediately following

```
sed 's
```

is the delimiter that marks the start and end of the search pattern and replacement string. Slash (/), colon (:), and percent sign (%) are the most commonly used delimiters. These three commands all do the same thing:

```
sed 's/xxx/yyy/g' report7    # delimiter is slash (/)
sed 's:xxx:yyy:g' report7    # delimiter is colon (:)
sed 's%xxx%yyy%g' report7    # delimiter is percent sign (%)
```

Choose a delimiter that is not a character in the search pattern or the replacement string. To change all occurrences of /usr/fred to /usr/jane, for example, you would choose a delimiter other than slash (/). For example:

```
sed 's:/usr/fred:/usr/jane:g' report7
```

Instead of changing the delimiter character, you can put a backslash (\) before the delimiter character to use it within the source or the destination. The following line is equivalent to the preceding example, but it is more difficult to read:

```
sed 's/\/usr\/fred/\/usr\/jane/g' report7
```

You can choose any character to be the delimiter by escaping it. In the following example, the first \a sets the delimiter. Any nonescaped letter *a* characters will delimit the search and replacement strings. Escape the letter *a* to include it as a part of the search or replacement string:

```
sed 's\a/:$\aa\aag' report7
```

In this example, \a sets the delimiter. You are searching for these four characters in sequence: slash (/), colon (:), dollar sign ($), and the letter a. Any time this four-character sequence is found, it will be changed to just the letter a. Here is a breakdown of the fields in the previous example:

```
sed 's\a/:$\aa\aag' report7
    s\a          (sets the delimiter as being the letter a)
       /:$\a      (search string where \a indicates the letter a)
            a     (delimiter)
             \a   (replacement string is just the letter a)
              a   (delimiter)
              g    (flag)
```

Removing (Deleting) a String from a Line

To remove or delete a string, use the sed replacement command and specify an empty replacement string. For example:

```
sed 's/ (LPX)//g' report
```

This example searches for a space followed by LPX in parentheses and deletes those six characters wherever found.

Using Selective Replacement or Deletion

You can limit which lines sed acts on to do replacement or deletion. One way to do that is to specify a starting and ending line number. For example:

```
sed '14,253 s/Mr. Smith/Ms. Wilson/g' report7
```

Here, 14 specifies the starting line number for sed to start making replacements. Line 1 is the first line of the file or pipeline.

The number 253 specifies the last line number for sed replacements.

Use a dollar sign ($) to specify the last line of the file, as follows:

```
sed '14,$ s/Mr. Smith/Ms. Wilson/g' report7
```

This command is useful when you want to process most of a file, but it has a header section that you don't want to process.

Another way to selectively replace or delete a pattern is to specify a qualifying pattern that must appear on the lines to be processed. For example:

```
sed '/Acme/ s/Mr. Smith/Ms. Wilson/g' report7
```

Here, the replacement will occur only on lines that contain the qualifying string Acme. Instead of *Acme*, you could also have specified a qualifying pattern containing R.E. wildcards. If the qualifying pattern contains a slash (/), precede it with a backslash (\), as follows:

```
sed '/\/usr\/fred/ s/Mr. Smith/Ms. Wilson/g' report7
```

In this example, the replacement will occur only on lines that contain the qualifying string /usr/fred. You can also use an initial \x to select any character *x* as the delimiter for the qualifying pattern. For example:

```
sed '\:/usr/fred: s/Mr. Smith/Ms. Wilson/g' report7
```

In the preceding example, the replacement will occur only on lines that contain the qualifying string /usr/fred.

If you want to process a section of consecutive lines but don't know the starting and ending line number, you can use patterns to specify start and end, as follows:

```
sed '/^ *Chapter 2/,/^ *Chapter 3/ s/Mr. Smith/Ms. Wilson/g' report7
```

In this example, the replacement will occur on all output lines in the section of report7 whose first line has the words *Chapter 2*, which may come after some leading spaces. The section for replacement ends on the line that contains *Chapter 3* (again, leading spaces are allowed). Notice that both patterns are in slashes (/) and are separated by a comma (,).

Using Regular Expression Wildcards in the *sed* Search String

The preceding chapter discussed regular expression (R.E.) wildcards. (For a quick reference of all the special symbols, see Appendix B.) All the rules for regular expressions given in the previous chapter also may be used in the sed search pattern (but not in the replacement pattern). The next sections go over each of the regular expression rules quickly and see how these apply to sed. Go back to the previous chapter and review the corresponding rule for a more complete description of that wildcard rule.

Replacing Patterns Only at the Start of a Line

Use the caret (^) at the start of a pattern if you want the pattern to be replaced only if it occurs at the start of a line:

```
sed 's/^Line/Line #/' report7
```

In this example, the word *Line* will be changed to *Line #*, but only if the word *Line* is at the start of a line. *Line* will not be changed if it is indented. That can be fixed as follows:

```
sed 's/^\([    ]*\)Line/\1Line #/' report7
```

This example will replace *Line* even if it is preceded by zero or more spaces or tabs. This is a complex example because it uses a technique you will see later in this chapter to remember what spaces or tabs were found and to insert them into the replacement string. In the following command, the first caret (^) at the start of the pattern is a wildcard that indicates the start of line:

```
sed 's/^^/x/' report7
```

A caret anywhere else in the pattern is not a wildcard. This command will replace a caret (^) with the letter x, but only if the caret is at the start of a line.

Replacing Patterns Only at the End of a Line

The following example will replace the word VOID with the word Cancel, but only if VOID is found at the end of a line.

```
sed 's/VOID$/Cancel/' report7
```

In the following command, the second dollar sign ($) at the end of the pattern is a wildcard that indicates the end of line:

```
sed 's/$$/x/' report7
```

A dollar sign ($) anywhere else in the pattern is not a wildcard. This command will replace a dollar sign with the letter x, but only if the dollar sign is at the end of a line.

Replacing an Entire Line

This command will look for any lines whose total text is just the word VOID and will replace that word with the word Cancel:

```
sed 's/^VOID$/Cancel/' report7
```

Pattern matching is checked character by character, going left to right, so the following line would not be changed by the previous command:

```
VOID VOID
```

In the following example, the caret (^) and the dollar sign are not wildcards because of their placement within the pattern:

```
sed 's/$VOID^/Cancel/' report7
```

This command will look for the six characters: dollar sign, VOID, and caret. If it finds those six characters anywhere within a line, it will change those six characters to the word Cancel.

Including Shell Variables in the Pattern or Replacement

In the following example, you want sed to search for the username found in the $LOGNAME variable:

```
sed "s/$LOGNAME/Cancel/g" report7
```

Here, double quotes had to be used around the sed command instead of single quotes, which would not have allowed the contents of $LOGNAME to be substituted.

In the following example, you want the first dollar sign to be replaced by the shell. You want the shell to pass the final dollar sign without interpretation to the sed command, where it indicates that you are looking for the username only at the end of a line. Notice that you escape the second dollar sign by putting a backslash (\) before it so that the shell will pass it as is:

```
sed "s/$LOGNAME\$/Cancel/g" report7
```

SEE ALSO

➤ *For more information on shell variables, see page 27*

➤ *For more information on quoting rules, see page 119*

Including Command Substitution in the Pattern or Replacement

All the comments in the previous section also apply to command substitution using backquotes (`). In the following example, the head command is used to access the first name in a namelist file. You then use sed to search for that name at the end of a line and change it to the word Cancel:

```
sed "s/`head -1 /usr/fred/namelist`\$/Cancel/g" report7
```

SEE ALSO

➤ *For more information on backquotes, see page 124*

Also see page 308

Allowing Any Characters in Certain Pattern Positions

The period (.) regular expression wildcard matches any single character, as in the following:

```
sed 's/dog.bone/dog-bone/g' report7
```

This previous command will replace any of these words if found in report7:

- dog-bone
- dogEbone
- dogsbone
- dog*bone

Many other words would be replaced by that pattern. It would not replace the word *dogbone* because the pattern requires one character between *dog* and *bone*.

Specifying Allowed Characters in Pattern Positions

Use the square bracket wildcard to list the allowed characters to match for one pattern position:

```
sed 's/dog[eE-]bone/dogbone/g' report7
```

The previous example will replace only the following three words with the word *dogbone*:

- dogebone
- dogEbone
- dog-bone

Specifying Disallowed Characters in Pattern Positions

Put a caret at the start of the square bracket wildcard list to show disallowed characters to match for one pattern position:

```
sed 's/dog[^eE-]bone/dogbone/g' report7
```

The previous example will replace any word that starts with *dog* and ends with *bone* and that has exactly one character in between except for the following three words:

- dogebone
- dogEbone
- dog-bone

Specifying the Number of Occurrences of a Regular Expression Element

Use \{n\} to specify *n* repetitions of the previous regular expression element:

```
sed 's/[0-9]\{5\}/*****/g' report7
```

This command will change any five-digit sequence into asterisks (*). A 10-digit or 15-digit sequence would also be changed to an equal-length string of asterisks. A six-digit sequence would appear as five asterisks (*) but the sixth digit would remain unchanged. Similarly, a seventh, eighth, or ninth digit would remain unchanged because the command changes only blocks of five digits, going left to right, in the output.

Use \{n,\} to specify *n* or more repetitions of the previous regular expression element:

```
sed 's/[0-9]\{5,\}/*****/g' report7
```

This command will replace any strings of five or more digits with exactly five asterisks (*).

Use \{n,m\} to specify *n* or more repetitions (but not more than *m* repetitions) of the previous regular expression element:

```
sed 's/[0-9]\{5,10\}/*****/g' report7
```

This command will replace any sequence of 5 to 10 digits with exactly five asterisks (*). Then, any remaining sequence of 5 to 10 digits will be replaced by exactly five more asterisks (*), and so on.

Specifying Zero or More Occurrences of a Regular Expression Element

---

Test Your UNIX Skills

Question 1: Give a UNIX command to display file acme but remove any indentation, which means remove any leading spaces.

Question 2: Display lines from file acme with a consistent 4 space indentation. You must first remove any existing indentation.

Answers on next page.

The asterisk (*) regular expression wildcard is frequently confused with the filename generation asterisk (*) wildcard, covered in Chapter 11, "Generating and Using File Lists." Assume that you want to replace the phrase *dog bone* no matter how many of any characters are between *dog* and *bone*. The following is not the correct way to do this:

```
sed 's/dog*bone/dogbone/g' report7   # wrong
```

Answers to test on previous page

Answer 1: sed 's/^ *//' acme

Answer 2: sed 's/^ */ /' acme

The asterisk (*) regular expression wildcard matches zero repetitions of the previous regular expression element, so the previous command will replace only the following words:

- dobone
- dogbone
- doggbone
- dogggbone
- dogggggggggggggbone

Use the regular expression .* to match zero or more of any characters:

```
sed 's/dog.*bone/dogbone/g' report7    # correct
```

Ignoring the Unbounded "Or More" Wildcard Rule from Previous Chapter

The previous chapter discussed a rule to drop unbounded "or more" wildcards in line-oriented situations because they are superfluous. That chapter discussed grep, and grep is line-oriented. If you search for lines with five digits, you will get the same result as searching for lines with five or more digits.

However, sed is pattern-oriented, not line-oriented, so unbounded "or more" wildcards do make a difference. Both of the following examples were analyzed earlier in this chapter. The second example is an unbounded "or more" wildcard at the end of the pattern. Its presence does make a difference and so cannot be dropped as unnecessary, as in the following:

```
sed 's/[0-9]\{5\}/*****/g' report7
sed 's/[0-9]\{5,\}/*****/g' report7
```

Using & to Embed the Found String in the Replacement

If the replacement string contains an unescaped ampersand (&), whatever string matched the pattern will substitute for the ampersand (&) in the replacement. In the following example, you are searching for any strings of one or more digits. When these are found, sed will replace them in the output with exactly the same string of digits that were found but will enclose them in parentheses:

```
sed 's/[0-9][0-9]*/(&)/g' report7
```

To insert a literal ampersand in the replacement, precede it with a backslash (\).

Understanding a More Complex *sed* Example Using Regular Expressions

This example shows a more complex regular expression pattern and how it is useful:

```
sed 's/JPC[^A-Za-z]*SPR/JPC-SPR/g' report7
```

In this example, `[^A-Za-z]` is a regular expression wildcard that indicates any one character that is not an uppercase or lowercase letter.

`[^A-Za-z]*` is a regular expression wildcard that indicates zero or more occurrences of any nonletter character.

`JPC[^A-Za-z]*SPR` is the pattern to search for in the preceding `sed` command. It looks for JPC, followed by SPR, with zero or more of any nonletter characters in between. That pattern can be found in each of the following lines except for the last line:

```
The JPCSPR company
long history of JPC-SPR relations
many JPC/SPR employees
JPC*SPR company president
four JPC(-)SPR votes
negotiate JPC SPR contracts
two companies, JPC and SPR, merged
```

In these lines, the writer has not been consistent in referring to the company name, but you can use an R.E. wildcard pattern to match all the different references and replace them with one consistent reference. The following shows how the preceding lines would be displayed after running the example `sed` command, which is repeated here:

```
sed 's/JPC[^A-Za-z]*SPR/JPC-SPR/g' report7
```

```
The JPC-SPR company
long history of JPC-SPR relations
many JPC-SPR employees
JPC-SPR company president
four JPC-SPR votes
negotiate JPC-SPR contracts
two companies, JPC and SPR, merged
```

Notice that the last line did not match the R.E. pattern, so no replacement was made in that line.

Using Special Characters

To search for a literal asterisk (*) or period (.) in the search pattern, precede that character with a backslash (\) so that `sed` will not take it as a wildcard. For example:

```
sed 's/321\.43/421.43/g' report7
```

Here, the backslash (\) indicates that the following period is not a wildcard, so `sed` will search for `321.43` and replace all occurrences of that exact string with `421.43`.

There is no way to search for a pattern that begins on one line and ends on the next line. You cannot use \n in either the search pattern or the replacement string. You can use an escaped newline to start a new line in the replacement string, as follows:

```
$ date | sed 's/ /\
>/g'
Sun
Mar
22
11:38:09
PST
1998
$
```

In this example, you are changing each space in the output to a new line. Notice that a backslash was entered before pressing the Enter key for the new line in the `sed` replacement string. You then get the PS2 prompt (>), which indicates that you are still entering part of a previous command. You then enter the rest of the `sed` command.

To include a literal single quotation mark (') in either the search or the replacement strings, you cannot use single quotation marks to enclose the strings as in previous examples. Also, using a preceding backslash to quote the internal single quotation mark (') does not help. You must change to double quotation marks around the `sed` command, as follows:

```
sed "s/it's/it is/g" report7
```

See the following section for other issues when using `sed` with double quotation marks rather than single quotation marks.

Using Shell Variables in the Search or Replacement String

If you often use a specific phrase in the search or replacement string, you can save it in a shell variable for easy reuse, as follows:

```
CO="Acme"
```

To use shell variables in your `sed` command, use double quotation marks rather than single quotation marks, as follows:

```
sed "s/president of $CO/chairman of $CO/g" report7
```

This command searches for president of Acme and changes those words to chairman of Acme.

If a shell variable is adjacent to other letters or digits or underscore, enclose the variable in curly braces {}, as follows:

```
sed "s/president of ${CO}Ltd/chairman of ${CO}Ltd/g" report7
```

The preceding command searches for president of AcmeLtd and change those words to chairman of AcmeLtd.

When using double quotation marks rather than single quotation marks, you must also put a backslash (\) before the following:

A dollar sign ($), if not beginning a shell variable

A backquote (`), if not enclosing command substitution

A double quotation mark inside your string

You must also change any literal backslashes (\) in your search or replacement string into four backslashes (\). (This is because the shell will remove two of them, and the backslash must be preceded by a backslash to indicate a literal backslash.)

SEE ALSO

➤ *For more information on shell variables, see page 27*

Avoiding Replacing 0 or More Occurrences

Assume that report7 contains these lines:

```
five trucks XXX
three XX cars
```

Assume that you want to replace any group of X's with a question mark (?). This is the wrong way to do that:

```
sed 's/X*/?/g' report7          # wrong way
```

This is the output from the preceding command:

```
?f?i?v?e? ?t?r?u?c?k?s? ??
?t?h?r?e?e? ?? ?c?a?r?s?
```

The reason you see the replacement string so many times is because there are always zero occurrences of any character between any two other characters. If you have the letters *ab*, for example, there are zero occurrences of the letter *X* between those two characters. To correct the preceding sed command, you should specify one or more *X*'s, not zero or more *X*'s.

This is the correct sed command to use:

```
sed 's/XX*/?/g' report7          # correct way
```

XX* specifies one *X* followed by zero or more *X*'s, which is equivalent to one or more *X*'s. This is the output from that command:

```
five trucks ?
three ? cars
```

Using What a Wildcard Matched in the Replacement String

Test Your UNIX Skills

Output file report7 but enclose in square brackets any string of digits found at the end of any line.

Answer on next page.

If you enclose part or all of the R.E. pattern in escaped parentheses, sed remembers the exact characters that matched that part of the pattern. You can then use the remembered string in the replacement pattern as \1. Use \2 for a second remembered pattern, and so on. This is an example analyzed previously in this chapter:

```
sed 's/^[    ]*Chapter/Section/' book3
```

Here, *Chapter* is changed to *Section*, but, as you saw, the replacement string loses the left margin it had previously. You can correct that as follows:

```
sed 's/^\([    ]*\)Chapter/\1Section/' book3
```

\(\)   These are the escaped parentheses.

\([   ]*\)   This uses escaped parentheses to remember how many spaces or tabs were found at the left margin before the word *Chapter*.

\1   In the destination string, this restores the remembered string.

Now consider a different example. Assume that report7 contains lines that contain numbers up to six digits. For example:

```
12345 cartons and 534723 sets
73293 boxes of 24 items
1837 containers of 144 packages
```

You can use sed to put a comma in the numbers to make them more readable, as follows:

```
sed 's/\([0-9]\{1,3\}\)\([0-9]\{3\}\)/\1,\2/g' report7
```

Answer to Test on Previous Page

```
sed 's/\([0-9][0-9]*\)$/[\1]/' report7
```

[0-9][0-9]* illustrates that regular expressions are greedy. It will match the longest possible string of digits.

---

sed Can Use Lots of Punctuation

When I first started using UNIX, I automatically ignored any **sed** commands with lots of punctuation. This is a prime example of where UNIX can seem to be cryptic. I wish someone had shown me then how to break such patterns down into simple elements. Pattern matching on the command line is one of the things that gives UNIX its elegance and power.

`\( [0-9] \{ 1,3 \} \)`	This is the first part of the pattern to search for. It matches one, two, or three consecutive digits. These are wildcards discussed in the preceding chapter. Spaces have been added so that you can see the elements within the pattern, but spaces are not allowed in the actual command. The actual digits matched are remembered as the first remembered string (\1).
`\( [0-9] \{ 3 \} \)`	This is the second part of the pattern to search for. It matches three consecutive digits. These must immediately follow the first part of the pattern. Putting the two patterns together causes the command to look for (and replace) any occurrences of four to six consecutive digits. The actual digits matched by this R.E. pattern are remembered as the second remembered string.
`\1,\2`	This is the replacement string. It consists of the first remembered string, then a comma (,), and then the second remembered string. Thus, you are putting back the original numbers with a comma in between.

This is the output of that command:

```
12,345 cartons and 534,723 sets
73,293 boxes of 24 items
1,837 containers of 144 packages
```

Eliminating All but the Search Pattern

Assume that `report7` contains lines like this:

```
Income in Jan 52384 as reported in accounting report.
Income in Feb 63283 as reported in accounting report.
Income in Mar 61966 as reported in accounting report.
```

Also assume that you want to display only the month and the amount, and you want to delete the rest of the text on the line. Rather than try to form a pattern for the rest of the text to delete, you also have the option to form a pattern for the text to keep, if that is easier. You can then eliminate all but the search pattern by remembering the text found as the search pattern, as follows:

```
sed 's/.*\([A-Z][a-z][a-z] [0-9]\{5\}\).*/\1/' report7
```

`.*`	This begins and ends the search pattern. This specifies zero or more characters before and after the pattern, so the whole line will be replaced.
`\( ... \)`	This remembers the characters that match the pattern so that you can use them in the replacement.
`[A-Z][a-z][a-z]`	This matches the three-letter month that begins with a capital letter.
`[0-9]\{5\}`	This matches five consecutive digits.
`\1`	In the replacement string, this puts back only the matched month and amount in place of the entire line.

This is the output from that `sed` command:

```
Jan 52384
Feb 63283
Mar 61966
```

This technique is also useful when setting shell variables with values from some UNIX commands. You can use `sed` to extract just the pattern you want and save it in the variable, as discussed in the next section.

Remembering the Rule: Regular Expressions Wildcards Match the Longest Possible Span

R.E. Wildcards Are Greedy

The technical term "greedy" can be used to describe the fact that wildcards match the longest possible string of characters in the line.

This is the output from the UNIX `id` command:

```
$ id
uid=501(mori) gid=100(users) groups=100(users),11(floppy)
$
```

You can use `sed` to extract the current logon name from the `id` output, which is given in the first set of parentheses. Here is the wrong way to do that:

```
$ id | sed 's/.*(\(.*\)).*/\1/'        # wrong way
floppy
$
```

`.*`	This begins and ends the pattern so that you can replace the whole line, as discussed in the preceding section.
`( ... )`	This tells `sed` that you are looking for text within parentheses.
`\(.*\)`	This tells `sed` to remember all the actual characters found within the parentheses.
`\1`	In the replacement string, this tells `sed` the replacement is to consist of only what was found inside the parentheses.

The preceding command found the word inside the last parenthesis because of the rule that R.E. wildcards always match the longest possible span. At the start of the pattern to search for is `.*` (which indicates zero or more characters before a parenthesis). This could match everything in the line up to the first parenthesis, or the second parenthesis, or the last parenthesis. You can come closer to the correct result by replacing the first `.*` with `[^(]*`, which indicates zero or more of any character except for a left parenthesis. For example:

```
$ id | sed 's/[^(]*(\(.*\)).*/\1/'        # still wrong
mori) gid=100(users) groups=100(users),11(floppy
$
```

Now, the problem is that the middle `.*` matches all characters from the first left parenthesis to the last right parenthesis because of the longest span rule. You can correct that problem by replacing the middle `.*` with `[^)]*`, which indicates zero or more of any character except for a right parenthesis, as follows:

```
$ id | sed 's/[^(]*(\(([^)]*\)).*/\1/'        # correct
mori
$
```

Now, you have extracted the contents of the first parenthesis. You can use the same construction to place the result in a shell variable, as follows:

```
MYLOGIN=`id | sed 's/[^(]*(\(([^)]*\)).*/\1/'` # extract 1st parenthesis
```

This command is useful for those UNIX systems that do not automatically set a $LOGNAME variable to your login name.

Using Perl to Replace or Delete Strings

Perl is a complete programming language that runs under both UNIX and Windows. Although it usually does not come packaged with any commercial UNIX distribution, it is readily available via the Internet for most UNIX systems. If Perl is available on your system, you can also use it as a simple command-line utility that provides replacement capabilities not available in sed.

For simple replacement, perl is just like sed if you use the –pe option to perl. The following two commands are equivalent:

```
    sed 's/Mr. Smith/Ms. Wilson/g' report7
perl -pe 's/Mr. Smith/Ms. Wilson/g' report7
```

Earlier, this chapter discussed the g flag for sed. It means the same thing to perl: process all patterns on the line, not just the first occurrence on a line. As in sed, you can omit the g flag to perl, as follows:

```
perl -pe 's/Mr. Smith/Ms. Wilson/' report7
```

The preceding command will replace Mr. Smith only the first time it is found on a line. Any other occurrences of Mr. Smith on the same line will not be replaced. Let me say this in another way: Without the g flag, multiple replacements can be done in the file, but only one replacement can be done on any line.

perl does not use backslashes (\) before braces {} for repeat counts or before parentheses () for remembered strings as sed, grep, and awk do. You must then use preceding backslashes in perl if you want to indicate parentheses as literal characters in the pattern. Preceding backslashes are needed only before literal braces if they take the form {n}, {n,}, or {n,m}, which could be confused with R.E. wildcards.

Although perl can accomplish a large number of things, this section looks only at command-line replacement capabilities in perl that can't be done in sed.

SEE ALSO

➤ *For other standard properties of the perl command, see page 518*

➤ *For more information on Perl programming, see 801*

Matching the Shortest Possible Span

One of the wildcards supported in perl but not in sed is the question mark (?). Use this after another wildcard (for example, * or +) to limit the scope of that wildcard to the shortest possible span. Now you can solve the `id` extraction problem from the preceding section much more easily. For example:

```
$ id | perl -pe 's/.*?\((.*?)\).*/\1/'
mori
$
```

`.*?\(`	This indicates zero or more characters before a left parenthesis. The `?` says to match the shortest possible span, so the pattern matches everything up to and including the first parenthesis on the line.
`( ... )`	This remembers the actual characters matched. `perl` does not use backslashes (`\`) here.
`\(.*?\)`	This indicates the shortest span between a left and right parenthesis. This limits you to the contents of one set of parentheses.

Expanding Patterns for Readability

The `x` flag (available only in `perl`) allows spaces to be put into the search pattern so that the elements can be separated for readability. All spaces in the pattern are ignored unless preceded by a backslash (`\`). You can apply this to the `id` extraction command in the preceding section:

```
$ id | perl -pe 's/.*?\((.*?)\).*/\1/'
```

Here is the same command with the x flag and spaces for readability:

```
$ id | perl -pe 's/.*?  \( ( .*? ) \)  .*/\1/x'
```

Replacing Words That Are Not in Larger Words

Earlier, this chapter looked at this command:

```
sed 's/Mr. Smith/Ms. Wilson/g' report7
```

You saw that it would also change `Mr. Smithson` to `Ms. Wilson`. You can avoid that if `perl` is on your UNIX system by using the `\b` wildcard that matches a word boundary in `perl`, as follows:

```
perl -pe 's/Mr. Smith\b/Ms. Wilson/g' report7
```

`Mr. Smith` matches the pattern and will be replaced. `Mr. Smithson` does not match the pattern and so will not be replaced. If `Mr. Smith` is followed by punctuation or the end of the line, it still satisfies the `\b` (word boundary) condition and so would be replaced. Multiple `\b` wildcards can be used at the start, end, and inside one search pattern.

SEE ALSO

➤ *For more information on the* \b perl *wildcard, see page 519*

Replacing One String or Another

Use the vertical bar (|) to separate one alternative from another in the search pattern, as follows:

```
perl -pe 's/cars|trains|planes/vehicles/g' report7
```

The preceding command will search for the words *cars*, *trains*, or *planes* and replace each of them with the word *vehicles*.

You can use parentheses for grouping alternatives, as follows:

```
perl -pe 's/in (two|four) (cars|trains)/by freight/g' report7
```

The preceding command would look for the following phrases:

- in two cars
- in four cars
- in two trains
- in four trains

It would replace all occurrences of those four phrases with the words *by freight*.

These parentheses also remember the actual text that matches the pattern that can be referenced as \1 or \2. Use (?:...|...) if you don't want to remember the pattern, as follows:

```
perl -pe 's/in (?:two|four) (cars|trains)/in three \1/g' report7
```

(?:two|four)	This allows either the word *two* or *four* here. It does not remember what was matched.
(cars|trains)	This allows either the word *cars* or *trains* here and does remember what was matched.
\1	This enables you to put the remembered string (*cars* or *trains*) in the replacement.

Ignoring Case When Matching the Regular Expression Pattern

It is cumbersome to ignore uppercase and lowercase when using sed to make replacements. For example:

```
sed 's/[aA][cC][mM][eE] [cC][oO][rR][pP]\./Acme Inc./g' report7
```

Using the /i flag (in the same position in the command as the g flag) causes perl to ignore case and enables you to write the equivalent command, like this:

```
perl -pe 's/acme corp\./Acme Inc./gi' report7
```

Selective Replacement or Deletion

In Perl, you can first check if the line contains some qualifying regular expression. Only in those lines will a second regular expression be substituted with a replacement string. Q.R.E. is my abbreviation for a qualifying regular expression. Here is the general syntax:

```
perl -pe 's/R.E./replacement/g if /Q.R.E/' file1 file2
```

In the next example, if /acme/ sets acme as the Q.R.E. so that the replacement of Ms. Wilson for Mr. Smith will occur only on lines that contain acme somewhere in that line.

```
perl -pe 's/Mr. Smith/Ms. Wilson/g if /acme/' report7
```

Using *awk* to Replace or Delete Strings

awk is an extensive programming language available on all commercial UNIX systems. As discussed in the preceding chapter, awk can be used in a simple command-line form when you want to selectively process lines based on the contents of specific fields.

SEE ALSO

➤ *For more information using* awk *to display selected lines, see page 520*

➤ *For other standard properties of the* awk *command, see page 520*

➤ *For more information on* awk *programming, see page 801*

Replacement or Deletion Based on Fields

In a previous chapter, you saw how to display lines from a file if a specific field was equal to a specified value. For example:

```
awk '$3 == "acme"' report7
```

In this example, lines from report7 will be displayed only if the complete field 3 of that line exactly matches the word acme. You can modify that command to search for and replace a regular expression (R.E.) pattern on lines where field 3 exactly matches the word acme, as follows:

```
awk '$3 == "acme" { gsub ("R.E.","repl") } {print}' report7
```

$3	This is the field number to check. $1 is the first field. $NF would indicate the last field in any line. Each field is separated by one or more spaces or tabs.
acme	This is an example string to check for. It may not contain any R.E. wildcards because of the ==.
R.E.	This is the pattern to search for that may contain R.E. wildcards.
repl	This is the string that is to replace the search pattern everywhere it is found on the line. An & in this repl string will be replaced with the characters that matched the whole R.E. pattern.
report7	This is an example file to process. A list of files could also be specified here, including filename generation wildcards. If no files are given, awk will read from standard input, so you can pipe to it from other commands.

No spaces are required inside the single quotation marks. They have been added because they are permitted for readability.

If you want to delete the R.E. pattern on just the selected lines, change the repl string to the empty string, as follows:

```
awk '$3 == "acme" { gsub ("R.E.","") } {print}' report7
```

To make the replacement only on the first occurrence in a line but not on other occurrences on that same line, use sub rather than gsub, as follows:

```
awk '$3 == "acme" { sub ("R.E.","") } {print}' report7
```

As you saw with grep in the previous chapter, you can test numeric values in fields using ==, !=, >, >=, <, or <=, and so on.

```
awk '$3 > 6.7 { gsub ("R.E.","repl") } {print}' report7
```

In the preceding command, the replacement will occur only if field 3 contains a numeric value larger than 6.7. You can also limit the replacement to lines that contain a regular expression pattern in a particular field, as follows:

```
awk '$3 ~ /Q.R.E./ { gsub ("R.E.","repl") } {print}' report7
```

Q.R.E. is my abbreviation for a qualifying R.E.—that is, an R.E. that must be present somewhere in the line for the replacement to occur. You can combine several conditions using || for "OR" and && for "AND", as follows:

```
awk '$2<=3.14 && $3~/acme/ {gsub ("R.E.","repl")} {print}' report7
```

In the preceding example, the replacement will not occur unless both conditions are true: field 2 is less than or equal to 3.14 and field 3 equals or contains acme, which is the pattern specified as the Q.R.E.

Displaying Only Selected Fields

I frequently use awk when I want to display only selected fields from a line. Use { print $n } to display just field *n* from the output, as follows:

```
$ ls -l report7
-rw-r--r--   1 mori     users          2966 Mar 22 15:08 report7
$ ls -l report7 | awk '{print $5}'
2966
$
```

In the preceding example, you used awk to print just field 5 from ls —l, which gives the size in bytes of the report7 file. You can use the same command to save the size in a variable, as follows:

```
$ SIZE=`ls -l report7 | awk '{print $5}'`
```

In the preceding command, you use backquotes to save the size of report7 in variable SIZE. You can display both the name from field 9 and the size from field 5 as in this example:

```
$ ls -l | awk '{print $9, $5}'
acme 17263
report7 2966
report8 34238
$
```

You can specify literal strings in the output in double quotation marks. You can also use tabs to make the columns line up better. In the following example, a tab is specified as the sole character in the double quotation marks between $9 and $5:

```
$ ls -l | awk '{print "file: " $9 "    " $5}'
file:
file: acme      17263
file: report7   2966
file: report8   34238
$
```

Consider another example. In the output of ls —l, field 3 is the file owner. You have already seen how to cause awk to process fields based only on the contents of a particular field. For example:

```
$ ls -l | awk '$3 == "root" {print "file: " $9 "    " $5}'
```

In this example, you will display the filename and size only if the owner of the file is root. In the next example, you check field 2 to see whether the link count for the file is greater than 4, as follows:

```
$ ls -l | awk '$2 > 4 {print "file: " $9 "    " $5}'
```

In the next example, you display information about the file only if field 4, the group name, contains an R.E. pattern. For example:

```
$ ls -l | awk '$4 ~ /^work/ {print "file: " $9 "      " $5}'
```

In the preceding example, you will display the filename and size only if field 4, the group of the file, starts with the word work. Also, as you have seen before with awk, you can use || as an OR condition and && and as an AND condition, as follows:

```
$ ls -l | awk '$2 > 4 && $4 ~ /^work/ {print "file: " $9 "      " $5}'
```

Conditionally Replacing a Particular Field Value

You can conditionally replace the value of a field of output by adding an awk action with this general format:

```
{if (condition) $n = value} {print fields}
```

Often, this is used to modify a field if it is either below or above a certain threshold. In the following example, note the use of \t within double quotes to tab to the next field to line up the output.

```
$ ls -l |
awk '{if ($5 > 20000) $5=20000} {print "file: " $9 "\t" $5}'
file:
file: acme      17263
file: report7   2966
file: report8   20000
$
```

In the preceding example, report8 had a value larger than 20000, but you used the awk command to set the largest reported value at 20000. You could also set the value to some word in double quotation marks, as follows:

```
$ ls -l |
awk '{if ($5 > 20000) $5="overflow"} {print "file: " $9 "\t" $5}'
file:
file: acme      17263
file: report7   2966
file: report8   overflow
$
```

Formatting Fields into Straight Columns

awk has many features of the C language, including the printf function. For example:

```
$ ls -l |
> tail +2 |
> awk '{printf("Name: %16s, Size: %5d, Blocks: %6.2f\n", $9, $5, $5/512)}'
```

```
Name:           acme, Size: 17263, Blocks:  33.72
Name:        report7, Size:  2966, Blocks:   5.79
Name:        report8, Size: 34238, Blocks:  66.87
$
```

---

printf Available Outside of awk

printf is available even when you are not using the awk command. printf is usually available as a separate UNIX command that can be used at the shell prompt and in shell scripts to control the format of your output and line them up in columns (as you see for the awk command here).

`ls -l |`	This is the first line of the example. Notice that shell pipelines may be split after the pipe sign (|), to be continued on the next line.
`tail +2 |`	This enables you to ignore the first line of the ls –l output, which is a heading that contains the total number of blocks before the file information begins.
`printf("format string", v1, v2, ...)`	This is the general form of the printf function. The format string can contain literal words such as Name: in the example. It should end in \n, which indicates a new line.
`%16s`	In the example, this indicates that the first variable listed following the format string should be displayed using at least 16 character positions. The s after the 16 says to display the value as a string. This specification is used to display the filename in the example.
`%5d`	This indicates that the next variable or value following the format string should be displayed using at least five character positions. The d after the 5 says to display the value as a decimal integer—that is, a whole number without a fractional part. This specification is used to display the size in bytes in the example.

...continued

`%6.2f`	This indicates that the next value following the format string should be displayed using at least six character positions. The f after the `6.2` says to display the values as a floating-point number—that is, a number with a decimal fraction. The `.2` says to display two decimal places to the right of the decimal point. This specification is used to display the calculated size in blocks in the example.
`$5/512`	This is a calculation for the size in blocks. `$5` is the size in bytes, so `$5/512` is the size in blocks.

You can enter a minus sign (`-`) after the percent sign (`%`) to cause `printf` to left-justify the output in the field, as follows:

```
$ ls -l |
> tail +2 |
> awk '{ printf("Name: %-16s, Size: %-5d, Blocks: %-6.2f\n", $9, $5, $5/512)}'
Name: acme          , Size: 17263, Blocks: 33.72
Name: report7       , Size: 2966 , Blocks: 5.79
Name: report8       , Size: 34238, Blocks: 66.87
$
```

When left-justifying the output in the fields, it no longer looks nice to follow the field with a comma, so you can remove the commas from the format string, as follows:

```
$ ls -l |
> tail +2 |
> awk '{ printf("Name: %-16s  Size: %-5d  Blocks: %-6.2f\n", $9, $5, $5/512)}'
Name: acme          Size: 17263  Blocks: 33.72
Name: report7       Size: 2966   Blocks: 5.79
Name: report8       Size: 34238  Blocks: 66.87
$
```

Numbers are easier to compare when they are right-justified, which causes the decimal points to line up again down the column. Let's go back to right-justifying the two numeric fields and put back the comma after the second field, as follows:

```
$ ls -l |
> tail +2 |
> awk '{ printf("Name: %-16s  Size: %5d, Blocks: %6.2f\n", $9, $5, $5/512)}'
```

```
Name: acme               Size: 17263, Blocks:  33.72
Name: report7            Size:  2966, Blocks:   5.79
Name: report8            Size: 34238, Blocks:  66.87
$
```

Now, note that the columns of numbers are easier to compare. If any of the values are longer than the size you specified, the full value will be displayed and the other columns will be offset, as follows:

```
$ ls -l |
> tail +2 |
> awk '{ printf("Name: %-16s  Size: %5d, Blocks: %6.2f\n", $9, $5, $5/512)}'
Name: acme                     Size: 17263, Blocks:  33.72
Name: long-long-long-filename  Size: 1993126, Blocks: 3892.82
Name: report7                  Size:  2966, Blocks:   5.79
Name: report8                  Size: 34238, Blocks:  66.87
$
```

Determining When to Use *awk* or *cut* to Extract Fields

If you want to extract a field from the output of a UNIX command, should you use awk to extract by field number, or cut to extract by column positions? Many commands allow fields to be extracted by either method. Take, for example, ls –l:

```
$ ls -l
-rw-r--r--  1 mori     users        2966 Mar 22 15:08 report7
$
```

The filename is the field in this output where you find the most variation in size of the field, so it is fortunate that it is the last field. If it were the first field, very long filenames would move all the other fields out and change their column positions.

In the /dev directory, the number of fields in ls –l changes, as follows:

```
$ ls -l /dev | head -5
total 13
crw-------  1 root     root     10, 134 Jan 20  1997 apm_bios
crw-------  1 root     sys      16,   1 Feb 18  1994 arp
crw-rw-rw-  1 root     sys      10,   3 Jul 17  1994 atibm
crw-rw-rw-  1 root     sys      14,   4 Jul 18  1994 audio
$
```

In this directory, files don't have a size in field 5. Rather, they have two values, separated by a comma and a space(s). This puts the filename in field 10 rather than 9, as in other directories. Therefore, to write a program to extract the filename from `ls` `-l` output, which includes the `/dev` directory, it would be better to use `cut` than `awk`. Then again, on some systems, you may encounter very long group names or very large file sizes, which causes you to have to adjust the column positions that you use.

```
-rwxr-xr-x   1 root     bin        2688 Oct 15  1995 arch
-rwxr-xr-x   1 root     bin       61201 Aug  6  1995 ash
-rw-rw----   1 mori     group      1828 Mar 19 14:56 Main.dt
-rw-rw----   1 mori     group       231 Feb 19 19:04 Personal.dt
```

In the preceding example, you see `ls` `-l` output from two different systems. The first two lines are from a Linux system. The second two are from SCO UNIX. Notice that the column positions for `ls` `-l` are different between these two versions of UNIX. If you wanted to write one program to extract the filename from `ls` `-l` and you wanted it to work on both Linux and SCO UNIX, you would use `awk` to extract field 9 (as long as the program does not have to work with `ls` `-l` from the `/dev` directory).

It is common to find programs that extract information from fields in UNIX command output. Some will use `awk`, and some will use `cut`. Problems can develop when values in the fields get very large or when you want to run the same program on a different system. As long as you are aware of these trouble spots, you can often quickly find the problem and solve it by modifying the extraction code. You might have to change the column positions being used in a `cut` command, for example, or change the field number used in an `awk` command.

Replacing/Removing Characters in a File or Pipeline

The `tr` command enables you to translate every occurrence of one specific character into a different character. It also enables you to delete every occurrence of a specific character. `tr` does not allow any files on the command line, so you must pipe any data for `tr` to translate.

Determining Which Type of *tr* Is on Your UNIX System

Unfortunately, there are two different versions of `tr`. They differ in whether they require brackets [ ] around ranges of characters. Some versions of UNIX have one type of `tr`; other versions have a different type of `tr`.

This is how the nonbracket version of tr works:

```
$ echo abcdefaabbcc | tr 'a-c' '1-3'
123def112233
$
```

In this command, echo sends the letters abcdefaabbcc to the tr command. tr looks up each letter in its first list. If it finds a letter, it translates it to the corresponding character in its second list. If the character is not found in the first list, it is passed as is to the output.

The bracket version of tr works the same way, except that it requires square brackets around any ranges, as follows:

```
$ echo abcdefaabbcc | tr '[a-c]' '[1-3]'
123def112233
$
```

The following versions of UNIX require brackets for tr ranges:

- HP-UX
- SCO UNIX 3.2v4
- Solaris 2.x (SunOS 5.x)

The following versions of UNIX do not require brackets:

- SCO UNIX 3.v5 (OpenServer 5)
- Linux (Slackware 3.0.0)
- IBM AIX 4.x

This is a simple test that you can run on your system to see which type of tr command you have:

```
echo abc[] | tr '[a-c]' '12345'
```

If tr requires brackets, you will see this output:

```
123[]
```

The square brackets in "[a-c]" just enclose a range and are not part of the list. Therefore, tr maps abc to 123 and passes the input square brackets as is. If your version of tr does not require brackets, the same command line will give this output:

```
23415
```

Because brackets are not required around ranges, their presence in the list is treated just as any other character; therefore [will map to 1, a will map to 2, b to 3, c to 4, and] to 5.

See the following Table 19.3 for other standard properties of the tr command:

Table 19.3 Other Properties of the *tr* Command:

Property	See page
Does not allow filename command-line arguments	765
Allows output to be piped or redirected	116

Don't Use `tr` to Replace Strings

```
tr 'wilson' 'smith'
```

This command will translate all w's to s's, all i's to m's, all l's to i's, and so on. Use **sed** when you want to replace strings, as follows:

```
sed 's/wilson/smith/g'
```

Changing Uppercase to Lowercase, or Vice Versa

One of the most common uses of `tr` is to map (that is, translate) all uppercase characters to lowercase, as follows:

```
$ echo ABCdef[] | tr "[A-Z]" "[a-z]"
abcdef[]
$
```

Use the square brackets in the preceding example even if your version of `tr` does not require brackets. If your version does require brackets, 26 characters in the first list map to the 26 corresponding elements in the second list. If your version does not require brackets, 28 characters in the first list map to the 28 characters of the second list. In both cases, the left bracket ([) will be passed as a left bracket ([), and the same is true for the right bracket (]).

You can convert lowercase to uppercase as follows:

```
$ echo ABCdef[] | tr "[a-z]" "[A-Z]"
ABCDEF[]
$
```

Setting/Zeroing the Eighth Bit of Each Character

Text files normally have the eighth bit of each character set to zero. This is also called the most significant bit. If set to 1, it changes the meaning of the character to some extended character set, which can cause strange symbols to appear or even lock up your terminal. When downloading a file, you may end up with a file that you can't display because it has some characters with the eighth bit on—that is, set to 1. You can use tr to turn off the eighth bit, as follows:

```
$ tr "[\201-\376]\377" "[\001-\176]\177" < file1 > file2
```

file1   This is the file where some characters have the eighth bit on.

file2   This will be created by the tr command, which is a copy of file1, but the eighth bit will be off on all characters.

Use the brackets even if your version of tr does not require them because then the same command will work on all UNIX systems. Most UNIX systems will let you include \377 in the range, but SCO UNIX 3.2v5 will not. Therefore, I have specified \377 separately from the range in brackets in the preceding command so that the command will work on all types of UNIX systems, including SCO UNIX 3.2v5.

You can use a similar command if you need to turn the eighth bit on all characters:

```
$ tr "[\001-\176]\177" "[\201-\376]\377" < file1 > file2
```

Removing Selected Characters

You can use the –d option with a single list to remove selected characters from the pipeline, as follows:

```
tr -d '!@#$%^&*()' < file1 > file2
```

This command removes the selected punctuation characters from file1 and saves the result in file2.

Control characters can cause problems if they occur within data or text files. End users can accidentally input control characters into the data by using the arrow keys in applications that do not support the arrow keys. The next tr example shows how to remove all control characters except for tab and newline:

```
$ tr -d '[\001-\010][\013-\037]\177' < file1 > file2
```

The preceding command should be used on systems where tr requires brackets. If used on the other type of system, this command will also remove brackets from the output that is not what is desired. For systems that do not require brackets, this is the same command to remove all control characters except for tab and newline:

```
tr -d '\001-\010\013-\037\177' < file1 > file2
```

Translating Most Control Characters into One Error Character

Rather than deleting all control characters, you may want to translate them into some character as an error indication that something has been modified. Use '[X*]' as the second string to translate all characters in the first list to character x, as follows:

```
tr '[\001-\010][\013-\037]\177' '[^*]' < file1 > file2
```

The preceding command translates all control characters except for tab and newline to a circumflex (^). If your system does not require brackets, use this form of the tr command:

```
tr '\001-\010\013-\037\177' '[^*]' < file1 > file2
```

Notice that brackets are required around [^*], even in the second case where brackets are not used around ranges.

Replacing/Removing Whole Lines

You can replace or remove whole lines in several ways. The next sections examine these in more detail.

Replacing Whole Lines

To completely replace any line that contains a pattern, you can use the sed command, like this:

```
sed 's/.*acme.*/  ***canceled***  /'
```

acme   This represents the pattern to look for. You can replace this with any desired R.E. pattern.

.*acme.* This matches the whole line that contains acme, so the whole line will be replaced.

Removing Lines Containing a Regular Expression Pattern

To totally remove any lines containing a pattern, use the –v option to grep, as follows:

```
grep -v 'R.E.'
```

The –v option to grep reverses the sense of grep. Instead of showing lines that contain the pattern, grep will then show only lines that do not contain the pattern, effectively removing any lines from the output that do contain the pattern.

SEE ALSO

➤ For more information on the grep command, see page 494

Removing Repeated Lines

Use the uniq command to remove from the output any lines that exactly match the preceding line. Assume that you have a file called cars, which contains different brands of automobiles, as follows:

```
$ cat cars
ford
ford
pontiac
BMW
ford
pontiac
$
```

Here is the output from the uniq command on that file:

```
$ uniq cars
ford
pontiac
BMW
ford
pontiac
$
```

In the preceding file, only line 2 exactly matches the preceding line, so it was removed. You can see that there are other matching lines in this file, but uniq does not remove them because they are not adjacent. Notice that the sort command does put identical lines adjacent to each other, as follows:

```
$ sort cars
BMW
ford
ford
ford
pontiac
pontiac
$ sort cars | uniq
BMW
ford
pontiac
$
```

In the previous example, you have made uniq work more effectively by first sorting the lines. You can count the number of different cars in the file by piping the output from the preceding example to wc –1 to count the lines, as follows:

```
$ sort cars | uniq | wc -l
      3
$
```

The –u option to uniq displays just the lines that are unique—that is, that have no adjacent matching lines. For example:

```
$ sort cars | uniq -u
BMW
$
```

The –d option shows one copy of just the duplicated lines, as follows:

```
$ sort cars | uniq -d
ford
pontiac
$
```

The –c option counts the number of duplicates for each line, as follows:

```
$ sort cars | uniq -c
      1  BMW
      3  ford
      2  pontiac
$
```

Here is a more advanced example of using uniq -c to count adjacent matching lines. It begins with the who command to see who is logged in. This is piped to awk to extract just the user name (field 1) in each line of who output. The result is sorted so that matching lines are adjacent. This is piped to uniq -c to count the duplicate, adjacent matching lines. The result is then sorted one more time so that the last users displayed are the ones who are logged in the most times.

```
$ who | awk '{print $1}' | sort | uniq -c | sort
    1 jane
    1 peter
    1 root
    3 mary
    7 fred
$
```

The preceding output shows that fred is logged in 7 times and mary 3 times. The rest of the users are only logged in once.

See the following Table 19.4 for other standard properties of the uniq command:

Table 19.4 Other Properties of the *uniq* Command:

Property	See page
Allows relative and absolute pathname arguments	70
Processes either filename arguments OR standard input	115
Changes only the output, not the file	111
Allows a list of filenames and filename wildcards	292
Allows output to be piped or redirected	116

SEE ALSO

➤ *For more information on the* sort *command, see page 266*

chapter

20

Steve "Mor" Moritsugu

Using vi to Edit a Text File

Tip for Beginners

Every UNIX user should know the basics of how to edit text files using vi, because vi is the only editor that is standard on all UNIX systems. While vi has more than 75 separate commands, you can edit anything if you learn just the first 10 commands this chapter give you. This chapter covers all the basics of vi. The next chapter shows how to use these basics to automate repetitive editing tasks that can make you far more productive than using a mouse.

Introducing the vi Text Editor

A text editor enables you to create and modify text documents that contain just the letters and characters that you can type on your keyboard. A word processor, on the other hand, not only allows text editing but also accommodates changing the presentation of that text by selecting the font size and style. Simple text files are extremely important under UNIX. With few exceptions, all UNIX system administration is ultimately done by editing text files that customize the system and control how it operates. Shell scripts and C programs are keyed in as text files by a programmer. Even Internet Web pages are simple text files with fonts, colors, and graphics indicated as textual directives to the Web browser.

vi is the one text editor that is available on all UNIX systems. Don't look for font choices in vi because it is not a word processor. Some UNIX users also do not like vi because you have to memorize all the commands. There are no drop-down menus to help you cut and paste or replace text. There also is no help facility inside vi (but you'll soon learn how to fix that).

Some types of UNIX systems do provide alternatives to vi, such as emacs, pico, or WordPerfect for UNIX. Some users edit text under Windows and then download it to UNIX. If you work on only one UNIX system and can guarantee that you will never have to work on a different one, choose any text editor that is available on your system. If you work with more than one type of commercial UNIX system, however, you may find that porting your favorite editor to each one is a losing battle. In that case, read this chapter on vi to learn the basics. vi is like UNIX: It is difficult to get started, but after you do start, you can do powerful things that make it worth the effort.

Starting vi

The usual way to start vi is to specify the filename to edit:

`vi filename`

If the file does not already exist, vi will create it for you. If the file to edit is in another directory, enter its pathname. After you enter this command, your screen will clear and then show you the contents of the file. You might see lines at the bottom of the screen that begin like this:

```
~
~
~
~
```

If a line starts with a tilde (~), this means that the screen is showing lines that are beyond the end of the file. For example, if your file contains only 10 lines, then your vi screen will contain these sections (assuming a typical 24-line screen):

- 10 lines of file contents
- 13 lines with just a tilde (~)
- 1 line at the bottom to enter special vi commands

If you are creating a new file, all the lines will start with a tilde (~) until you enter some text.

When you start vi, the contents of the file are read into vi's workspace. All your changes modify only the local workspace, not the file itself. When you are done editing, there are two ways to end vi:

- `:wq`—To save your work and exit vi
- `:q!`—To abort (that is, throw away) your changes and exit vi The vi command ZZ may be used instead of `:wq` to write and quit vi. Advanced users sometimes enter vi without specifying a filename. In that case, they must use commands such as `:r` or `:e` to read or edit desired files, and `:w filename` to save this work.

Creating a File for vi Practice

If you are new to UNIX, you probably don't have any files that are safe for you to edit yet; therefore, follow this procedure to create a scratch file that you can use to practice vi.

> **Never Practice on** /etc/passwd
>
> Other books and articles sometimes use /etc/passwd as an available text file to practice on. However, this is a critical system file that you should not play with, especially if you are logged on as root. In fact, don't practice on any files in /etc, and don't practice as root.

How to practice with vi

1. Log on to UNIX.

2. At the shell prompt, enter cal 1998 > cal-junk.

   Press Enter to execute this line. The word *junk* is used in any filenames that are just for practice and that can be killed later. This step will create a text file that contains a calendar that you can practice editing.

3. When you want to practice with vi, at the shell prompt enter vi cal-junk.

   Press Enter to execute this line.

4. When done practicing with vi, press Esc and then enter the following:

   :wq (to save your work and exit vi)

   :q! (to abort—that is, throw away—your changes and exit vi)

   Press the Enter key to complete this step.

   To remove this practice file, enter the following:

   ```
   rm cal-junk
   ```

   Press Enter to execute this line. It is good manners to clean up after yourself, but you may delay deleting this file for several days or weeks while you practice with vi.

Edit Anything with Just 10 vi Commands

There are more than 75 separate letter and punctuation commands to learn in vi. Where should you start? This section covers the first 10 vi commands to learn, and they will enable you to edit anything. If you are new to vi, follow the preceding procedure to create a cal-junk practice file so that you don't accidentally change an important file.

Moving Around Using the h, j, k, and 1 Commands

In vi, you can move the cursor by entering the commands listed in Table 20.1. Some people think that the letter l should move left, so this command also has been added.

Table 20.1	Moving Around Using the h, j, k, and 1 Commands		
vi Command	Description	Mnemonic	Alternative
h	Move left	Leftmost char	Left arrow key
j	Move down	j goes below line	Down arrow key
k	Move up	k loops up	Up arrow key
1	Move right	Rightmost char	Right arrow key

These four keys—h, j, k, and l—occur next to each other on your keyboard. The mnemonic in the table will help you remember which key does what. For example, a lowercase j goes below the line to remind you of down.

Don't depend too much on the arrow key alternatives. Sometimes, you will find that everything will work in vi except for the arrow keys because they require that the terminal settings, the keyboard, and certain system files (such as `termcap` or `terminfo`) all be properly coordinated. Even if the arrow keys work most of the time, they can become unreliable over a slow connection or on a heavily loaded system or network. Learning to use h, j, k, and l rather than the arrow keys will also help you later with mapping sequences to keys and command-line editing in the Korn shell, a very useful feature.

When you enter h, j, k, or 1 in vi, it should not echo to the screen. Instead, the cursor should just move in the desired direction. You do not have to press Enter to execute the command. If the h, j, k, or l appear onscreen, somehow you have gotten into Insert mode and have inserted those characters into your workspace. Press Esc to end Insert mode; now h, j, k, and l should work correctly.

vi will not let you move to a position on the screen unless there is text in the workspace at that position. You cannot move past the end of a line, and you cannot move down from the last line. If you edit an empty file, you will not be able to move at all until you enter some text.

Assume that your vi screen looks like this:

```
Hello
~
~
~
```

Here, there is only one line in the file. You cannot move up (k) or down (j) because you can move only to lines that exist. You can move to the right only four times (l), and then you reach the end of the line and can move no further. You will not be able to move off this line until you use the i command to insert additional lines or the A command to append additional lines, as you shall see later in this chapter.

SEE ALSO

➤ *For more information on command-line editing in the korn or bash shell," see page 613*

Getting vi Beeps on Errors

If you try to do an illegal command in vi (such as moving down from the last line), vi will beep to signal an error. It is possible to turn this off (:set noerrorbells), but vi beginners should listen for the error beeps and learn from these mistakes.

Using a Repeat Count

You can put a repeat count directly before most vi commands. For example, 50h will move left 50 characters, and 999j will move down 999 lines. With a repeat count, it is easy to move up or down large distances, which is a necessity in huge files.

If the repeat count given for the cursor movement is too large, you will get differing results depending on which type of UNIX you are on. If vi beeps, the cursor will not move at all because you cannot move beyond the end of the line or past the last line. If there is no beep, vi on that system has moved you as far as possible and has stopped at the last character or last line in the workspace.

If the h, j, k, and l commands move the cursor, how do you enter those characters into the document? Read on.

Using the i Command to Insert

Tip: Beware of Arrow Keys in Insert Mode

If you try to use the arrow keys while in Insert mode, this may not produce the changes you expect on some systems. Before moving the cursor, press Esc to end Insert mode. Then, move the cursor to the next section and enter i to re-enter Insert mode.

Now you'll learn the fifth vi command. First, enter i to turn on Insert mode. In Insert mode, all the text that you type is entered just before the current cursor position into the workspace. Press Esc to turn off Insert mode; this puts you back into vi Command mode. You can input multiple lines in one insert by pressing Enter after each line. Here is a summary of some key points:

In Command mode:

- Every letter or character you type is a vi command that causes some action to occur.

- What you type does not echo (that is, the letters you type do not appear on the screen).

In Insert mode:

- Every letter or character you type is inserted into the workspace as part of your text file.

- What you type does echo.

- Press Esc to end Insert mode and return to Command mode.

Using x **and** dd **to Delete**

Where Does dd **Gets Its Name?**

A convention in vi specifies that a double-letter command operates on the whole line. For example, cc changes the whole line; yy yanks the whole line; and **dd** deletes the whole line.

Here is the sixth vi command to learn: Enter x to delete one character where the cursor is. For example, 25x will delete 25 characters. vi reduces any repeat count larger than the rest of the line so that the rest of the current line is deleted but the following lines are not affected.

Now, here's the seventh vi command to learn: Enter dd to delete the current line. You can be anywhere in the line when you enter dd. As an example, 25dd will delete 25 lines, including all of the current line.

How to insert text after the last line of the file

1. Move your cursor to the last character of the last line of the file. For this example, assume that your screen looks like this:

```
Hello
~
~
~
```

2. Enter the letter i to start Insert mode.

3. Re-type the last character of the last line, and then press Enter. Now your screen looks like this:

```
Hello
o
~
~
~
```

4. Enter the new line contents.

```
Hello
Everyoneo
~
~
```

5. Press Esc to end Insert mode.

6. Press x to delete the extra character in the last line.

```
Hello
Everyone
~
~
```

Later, you will learn easier ways to do this using the append command (A) and the open new line command (o). The previous procedure is needed only if you never learn more than the first 10 vi commands.

Using the J Command to Join Lines

Beware of Caps Lock When Using the J Key

If you accidentally leave your Caps Lock key on and use h, k, or 1 to move around, it is harmless. A j to go down, however, would become J to join lines. Multiple J's will join many lines—and before you know it, you have a mess. The next chapter, which covers mapping a key, shows you a way to prevent this.

Here's the eighth vi command to learn: Unlike some editors, vi has no end-of-line character that you can delete to join two lines. The only way to join two lines is to use the J command. As an example, 5J will join five lines. J, 1J, and 2J all do the same thing—they join two lines. Any leading spaces in the second line will be reduced to a single space.

Using :wq to Save and Exit

This is the ninth vi command to learn. So far, all your changes have modified the vi workspace, which is a temporary file. To save your work and exit, enter the following:

```
:wq
```

The leading colon causes the cursor to go down to the last line where the w and q will echo onscreen. Press Enter to complete this command and any other vi command that starts with a colon (:).

Using :q! to Abort Changes

> **Tip: Use Backspaces to Abort a Colon (:) Command**
>
> If you type a colon (:) command such as :q! and then change your mind, do *not* press Esc because this will execute the :q! command and throw away all your changes. To abort a colon command, press the Backspace key or Ctrl+H repeatedly until the cursor has left the last line. The left-arrow key will not work for this.

Now here's the 10th vi command to learn. If you don't like your changes, you can exit vi without saving them back to the original file by entering the following:

```
:q!
```

This returns you to the shell prompt and throws away all the editing you have done. Be aware that after you throw away your editing changes by :q!, you cannot change your mind later and get them back again.

This completes the 10 commands you need to use vi. You can now edit anything. Practice with these 10 for a while. Then read the following section in this chapter to see the next group of vi commands you should master.

Adding a Help Facility to vi

There is no help facility within vi, which makes vi difficult to use—especially if you use it only occasionally. Here is a way to add a help facility to use while you are in vi.

How to add a help facility to vi

1. Use vi to create a text file, /tmp/vihelp, with these contents:

```
echo "
(You may put repeat count BEFORE most commands.)
:q!     -- abort vi without saving
```

```
cW         -- change word(s) until ESC
x    dd    -- delete char(s) or line(s)
G          -- go to end of file
1G         -- go to line one of file
i          -- insert text until ESC
A          -- insert at end of line until ESC
J          -- join lines
h,j,k,l -- move left,down,up,right
Ctrl+L Ctrl+R  -- repaint the screen
r          -- replace one char
:wq        -- save and exit vi
:f         -- show filename, current line, size
u          -- undo"
```

2. Make sure that you have included the quotation marks (") in the first and last lines.

3. Log on as root, or ask your system administrator to do the next steps.

4. Enter this line:

   ```
   ls -l /usr/bin/vihelp.
   ```

   Make sure that this file does not already exist. If it does, choose a different name that does not exist, such as `helpvi`.

5. Enter these commands:

   ```
   cd /usr/bin
   mv /tmp/vihelp vihelp
   chmod 755 vihelp
   ```

6. Now exit and log back on as a nonroot user.

7. Enter `vi` to edit any test file, and check out the new help facility by entering the following:

   ```
   :!vihelp
   ```

8. Press Enter when you are done reading the help file and are ready to resume vi editing.

9. You can use vi to expand the help message in file `/usr/bin/vihelp` as desired. Make sure that the final quotation marks occur at the end of the last line.

Learn These Eight vi Commands Next

While the first 10 commands given previously enable you to complete any editing task, the job is much easier if you learn these next eight vi commands.

Press Ctrl+L Ctrl+R to Repaint the Screen

The Real Repaint Command

Some terminals require only `Ctrl+R`, and some require only `Ctrl+L` to repaint the screen. If you use them both (in any order), however, it works for all cases and you don't have to remember which command to use on which terminal types.

Sometimes over a modem line or slow network, garbage may appear on your screen or the cursor will end up on a different line than vi thinks it is. If the cursor is on the wrong line, you will see characters from a different line appear at the cursor when you space to the right. To clear up this problem, press these two control characters, Ctrl+L and Ctrl+R, to repaint your screen to match the workspace.

Undo Changes Using the u Command

vi remembers the last insert, delete, or modification done. If you want to undo it, enter the u command in vi Command mode. You do not have to be near the line where the change was made when issuing the u command. Commands to move the cursor are ignored by the u command and cannot be undone. (Actually, many cursor motion commands can be undone by entering backquote backquote [``].) A second u command will undo the undo command, reinstating the last change again. A third u command will toggle the undo and remove the last change. A fourth u command will reinstate the last change, and so on.

If you join five lines with the 5J command, a u command will separate them into their original lines. A second u will join them again. You can watch the lines magically join and then separate each time you enter the u command. This is a great way to learn about more complex vi commands.

Using the u command if something goes wrong

1. Sometimes an accidental control character or line noise will cause garbage on the vi screen. Press Ctrl+L and Ctrl+R to repaint the current screen and remove the garbage.

2. Enter the u command to undo the last change. The cursor will move to the location of that change.

3. Enter u several times to watch the change toggle. If the change is an undesirable side effect of the accident, enter u one or two more times to undo the bad change.

Using A to Append Text at the End of Line

The capital A command first moves the cursor to the end of the current line. It then enables you to start inserting text after the last character on the line. Press Esc to end Insert mode.

Using :w to Save Your Work Periodically

If you are making a lot of changes in your vi session, it is prudent to save your work periodically. Enter :w to write the current workspace to the disk file. Then, if you accidentally hit the wrong keystroke or your system connection dies, you can log back on and your disk file will have the last-saved contents.

Using :w File to Save in a Different File

You can save your work to a different file than you are editing by entering the following:

```
:w newfile
```

If you are editing a critical document, for example, you might enter the following:

```
:w doc1
```

After more editing, you might enter this:

```
:w doc2
```

In this way, you can save many versions of this one file. This gives you more chances to recover information in case you accidentally delete some text and then save the file without that text.

Handling Write Permission Failure

When trying to save your work, vi may return an error such as Permission Denied or Read Only.

Two Directories You Can Write To

Non-root users cannot create or delete files in most directories on a UNIX system. You can start vi even if you cannot write into the current directory. vi will not give an error until you try to save your work in this directory. To save your work in a different directory as shown in this procedure, use a full pathname to save into a directory where you have write permission. There are usually only two directories a new user can write to. The user's home directory is one and /tmp is the other.

Handling errors when saving a file in vi

1. Try saving the file using this command:

```
:w!
```

2. If that fails, save your work temporarily like this:

```
:w /tmp/cantwrite
:q
```

3. Now you can move your changes in /tmp/cantwrite to your desired filename or directory.

Using r to Replace One Character

Enter r to replace one character. The next character typed will appear onscreen, replacing the character that was at that cursor position. Then you will be back in Command mode, ready to enter new vi commands.

Using cW to Change Words

Use the cW command in vi when you want to replace the current word. Your replacement string can be one or more words. The replacement can be longer or shorter than the original word.

How to use cW to change words

1. Move the cursor to the start of the desired word or words to change.

2. If you want to change more than one word, enter the number of words to change. Do not press Enter.

3. Enter cW.

A dollar sign ($) will appear at the end of the last word to change. Do not press Enter.

4. Start typing your replacement text. It can be shorter or longer than the words being changed, and it can also have fewer or more words. You may use the Enter key to input multiple lines. If the new text is longer, the remainder of the line will move to the right to accommodate it as you type.

5. Press Esc after you have entered all the replacement text. If the new text is shorter than the words being replaced, the remainder of the line will move to the left to fill up the gap automatically.

6. Here is an example command:

```
3cWacmeESC
```

The preceding command changes (replaces) three words (including the word where your cursor is). It replaces those three words with the single word *acme*.

Using 1G/G to Go to the Start/End of a File

Enter a number and then capital G to go to that line number. For example, 1475G will move the cursor to line 1,475 of the workspace. If the file does not have that many lines, it will give an error beep. Moving quickly to a specific line number in a file can be useful for a C programmer because the compiler often reports the line number in the source where an error occurs.

The two most common uses of the G command are 1G to go to the start of the file and G to go to the end of the file.

Using :f to See the Filename, Size, and Where You Are

Enter :f to see the name of the file you are currently editing, what line you are on, and how many lines are in the file. For example, consider this code:

```
"report7" [Modified] line 43 of 335 --12%--
```

Ctrl+G is an alternative that will show the same information as :f.

Tips to Help You Use vi

This section covers the third group of vi commands to learn. It includes the standard UNIX command to spell check a text file, which is very crude as you will see. It includes a procedure on how to format a paragraph if some lines are too short or too long. It covers how to recover your changes if vi terminates before you save your work. The last tip shows how to invoke vi in read-only mode.

Restoring the Whole Line Using the U Command

In vi Command mode, capital U will undo all changes on the current line since you moved to it. After you leave a line, you lose the ability to restore it to its original state.

Using `spell` to Find Misspelled Word

Standard UNIX has only minimal spell-checking capability. The following steps demonstrate how to use it.

`ispell` **is Better**

There is a free, open source utility called `ispell` that does a better job than `spell`. It shows you each misspelled word and the sentence that contains it. It gives you various options on how to correct or ignore the flagged word. `ispell` is not found on most commercial UNIX systems but can often be downloaded for your type of UNIX system.

Finding misspelled words

1. From the shell prompt, enter `spell < filename | pg`.

   (`Filename` is the file to spell-check.)

   Replace `pg` with your preferred utility to view results one page at a time.

2. All unknown words will be displayed onscreen, one per line. The context (that is, the complete line) in which the misspelled words appear is not shown.

3. Mentally flag any misspelled words, and then manually use vi to find and correct them in the file, one by one.

See Table 20.2 for other standard properties of the `spell` command.

Table 20.2   Other Properties of the `spell` Command

Property	See page
Allows relative and absolute pathname arguments	70
Processes either filename arguments OR standard input	115
Changes only the output, not the file	111
Allows a list of filenames and filename wildcards	292
Allows output to be piped or redirected	116

Formatting Paragraphs

If you are using standard English paragraphs, one of the frustrating limitations of vi occurs when you have to lengthen or shorten an internal line in the paragraph. An odd-sized line looks out of place in the middle of the paragraph. You can fix the odd line by moving text to or pulling text from the next line, but now the next line has an odd size. You then have to hand-adjust each line to the end of the paragraph.

Here are two easier ways to handle that situation.

How to format paragraphs using `fmt`

1. At the shell prompt, enter the following:

   ```
   type fmt
   ```

   If you get the error `Not found`, `fmt` is not supported on your version of UNIX. Skip this procedure and use the following procedure to format if `fmt` is not found. `fmt` was not available on SCO UNIX OpenServer 5, but it is on Solaris 2.x, AIX 4.x, and Linux.

2. To format a paragraph in vi, move your cursor to the start of the paragraph. Enter the following:

   ```
   !}fmt
   ```

   This should adjust the rest of the lines of your paragraph so that no lines are too long or too short. If this does not work, enter u to undo that change, and follow the next procedure instead.

3. The `fmt` command assumes that the left margin is correct for the paragraph. If the left margin also needs to be adjusted, enter this:

   ```
   !}fmt -c
   ```

This next procedure helps you to format paragraphs that works well even if `fmt` is not on your system and if there are no tabs in the line.

How to format paragraphs

1. Enter cd to go to your home directory.

2. Enter cp .exrc .exrcbak to back up your current .exrc file. Ignore any cp errors that .exrc does not exist. (In that case, there is no need to back it up.)

3. Enter vi .exrc.

4. Look at the full contents of this file and make sure that there is no line that starts with map g.

   If there is such a line, do *not* continue with this procedure.

5. Make sure that there is a line that starts with set wrapmargin=, or that starts with set wm=.

   If you do not find such a line, enter this line at the end of the file:

   ```
   set wm=10
   ```

6. Press Esc and then Q.

The cursor will go to the last line, and a colon will appear.

7. Enter map g 0721Bi.

Do not press Enter.

8. Press Ctrl+M.

Press Esc.

Press Ctrl+V.

Press Esc.

Now press Enter.

9. Enter vi.

The word *vi* should echo on the bottom line of the screen. Press Enter.

10. Enter :wq to save your changes to .exrc and exit vi.

11. Check that all went well by entering cat -v .exrc.

At the end of the file, you should see this line:

```
map g 0721Bi^M^[
```

If something went wrong, use vi to correct that line. If necessary, restore .exrc from the backup and start over.

12. The preceding steps prepare the .exrc file and need to be done only once for each logon user. Now use vi to edit a test file with a paragraph that needs to be formatted. Make sure that the file is backed up in case something goes wrong. Move the cursor to the start of the paragraph that needs to be formatted.

13. Count the number of lines in the paragraph. Enter that number followed by J to join all the lines of the paragraph into one long line.

14. Enter g repeatedly until all the lines of the paragraph have been formatted correctly.

Recovering a Lost Edit

If vi ever terminates abnormally, there is a chance that you can recover some or all of the text you were editing, even if you didn't save it to disk.

Recovering your changes if vi terminates abnormally

1. From the shell prompt, enter this line:

```
vi -r
```

You will see a list of files that vi has preserved because it aborted abnormally while editing them. These are actually the vi workspace files that may contain some edits that had not been saved to the disk file.

2. If you see a file you want to look at, enter the following:

```
vi -r filename
```

Filename must appear exactly as shown in the list—that is, type in any preceding directory names exactly as shown.

3. After looking at the text with vi, enter the following line if you decide that you want to keep this information:

```
:w absfile
```

`absfile` represents the full pathname of the file you want to save it as.

4. Exit from vi, as follows:

```
:q
```

5. After you recover a file in this way and exit vi, that file is removed from the preserved list, and you cannot try to recover it again. It is a good idea to check your preserved files periodically and either recover and save or discard them to prevent vi from preserving files that accumulate in the preserve areas.

Starting vi in Read-Only Mode

To edit a file in Read-only mode, substitute the `view` command for vi in your command line. `view` starts vi in Read-only mode. If you try to write the file, `view` will give an error saying that the file is read-only. This is a good precaution for those cases in which you are just looking at the contents and don't intend to make any changes. Root (that is, system administrator) users are especially advised to use `view` when just looking at system configuration files.

You can override `view`'s Read-only mode and save changes, as follows:

```
:w!
```

Table 20.3 Text Insertion Commands in vi

vi Command	Description
i	Insert text just before cursor until `Esc`
I	Insert text at start of line until `Esc`
a	Insert text just after cursor until `Esc`

vi Command	Description
A	Insert text at end of line until Esc
o (lowercase o)	Open a new line below the current line, insert until Esc
O (capital O)	Open a new line above the current line, insert until Esc

Moving Around in vi

Many cursor commands in vi enable you to move to different parts of the screen or the file you are editing. First, it's necessary to go over how to count words, which is useful for moving, deleting, and replacing text.

Using Separated Words Versus Contained Words Versus Non-Words

Separated words (or space-delimited/delineated words) are any groups of characters separated by one or more spaces, tabs, or ends of lines. Contained words are any groups of letters or digits separated by punctuation, spaces, tabs, or ends of lines. The W command moves to the next space-separated word. The w command moves forward by contained words and non-words.

In the following example, if the cursor is at the start of the line, you can get to the word *is* using one W command. It takes nine w commands to do the same thing. The letter w has been added under the start of each contained word and non-word that you would encounter.

```
Hudson(2)--on--the--Bay is our destination.
       www  w w w  w w    w
```

```
Hudson     <contained word>
(          <non-word>
2          <contained word>
)--        <non-word>
on         <contained word>
--         <non-word>
the        <contained word>
--         <non-word>
Bay        <contained word>
```

The next chapter shows more about how differentiating separated words versus contained words can be useful.

Table 20.4 Motion Commands in vi

vi Command	Description
h/j/k/1	Move left/down/up/right.
0	Move to the start of the current line.
^	Move to the start of the first word on the current line.
$	Move to the last character of the current line.
w/b	Move forward/backward one contained word or non-word.
W/B	Move forward/backward one separated word.
e E	Move to the end of the current contained/separated word.
L/M/H	Move to the lowest/middle/highest line on the screen.
{/}	Move to the start of the preceding/next paragraph.
Ctrl+F/Ctrl+B	Move forward/backward one full screen.
Ctrl+D/Ctrl+U	Move down/up one half-screen.
*n*G	Go to line *n*.
1G/G	Go to first/last line.

Moving by Searching for a String

In this section, you will find several commands that allow vi to move the cursor to the next occurrence of a word or string of characters. Slash (/) searches forward while question mark (?) searches backward in the file. To move on the line more easily, use the f command to go forward to a particular character in the current line. Use the percent sign (%) to move to the matching enclosure character. The last method is to set a mark at a useful spot in your file so vi can return there whenever you wish.

Moving the cursor to a pattern

1. In vi Command mode, enter / to search forward in the workspace. Enter ? to search backward in the workspace. The cursor will move to the last line of the screen and echoes the / or ?. Do not press Enter until instructed.

2. Enter the pattern to search for. Press Enter to execute. The cursor will move to the next occurrence of the pattern. Your pattern may contain regular expression wildcard patterns, as described in Chapter 18, "Searching for Lines in a File or Pipeline."

3. If the pattern is not found in the rest of the file, vi will wrap around and start searching at the other end of the file. If vi has to wrap around, this message usually appears: Wrapped. If the pattern does not exist anywhere within the whole file, the cursor will remain where it was and this message will appear: Not found.

4. To repeat the last search, enter n.

This will find the next occurrence of the same pattern.

To repeat the last search but in the opposite direction, enter N.

If you were previously searching forward in the file, N will find the next occurrence backward in the file.

Moving in the Line to a Specific Character

If you are logged on to a UNIX system over the Internet, you may find that responses to your vi keystrokes have almost incapacitating delays. Rather than counting how many characters or words to move, you can use the vi f command when you have to move right to a desired character in one command.

Moving the cursor forward or backward to a particular character

1. Determine the letter or digit you want to move to. You usually should avoid vowels because they are too common in the line.

2. To move to the right, enter f, followed by the desired character. To move to the left, enter F, followed by the desired character.

3. The cursor will move to the next occurrence of that character.

4. Enter semicolon (;) to move to the next occurrence of that same character on that line.

Finding a Matching Enclosure Symbol

If you are a programmer, you may need to enter complicated formulas using nested enclosure symbols, such as: ({ [ ] }). For example:

```
{ printf("%d",tbsz(r7y[4])) }
```

vi understands such nesting and can automatically find the matching closing or opening parenthesis, bracket, or brace even if it is on a different line. Place the cursor on the desired enclosure symbol, and press % to move the cursor to the matching enclosure symbol at that nesting level.

Setting a Mark So That You Can Return There

vi offers the capability for dealing with huge text files. vi can mark and return to up to 26 different places within the file.

Setting a mark and returning to the marked spot

1. Move the cursor to a desired spot in the file, and enter ma. m is the vi command to mark this spot, and a is the name or label you can use to refer to this spot later. You can use any letter of the alphabet; therefore, you can set up to 26 marks.

2. To return to mark a later, enter <single quote><a> ('a) to go to the start of line containing mark a. You may also enter <backquote><a> (`a) to go to the line and character position for mark a.

3. Note that editing a line containing a mark often erases the mark.

Table of vi Commands for Deleting Text

In Table 20.5, notice how vi delete commands are based on the cursor motion commands.

You may precede most of these commands with a repeat count.

Table 20.5 Text Deletion Commands in vi

vi Command	Description
x/dd	Delete character(s)/whole line(s).
D	Delete from the cursor to the end of the line.
dw dW	Delete forward to the next contained/separated word.
db dB	Delete backward to the next contained/separated word.
de dE	Delete to the end of the current contained/separated word.
d0/d$	Delete to the start/end of the current line.
dh/dl	Delete character(s) to the left/right.
d{/d}	Delete to the start of the previous/next paragraph.
d'a	Delete to (and including) the start of the line containing mark a. This mark must have been set previously. All 26 lowercase letters may save different marked positions.
d`a	Delete to the line and character position of mark a.

Recovering Deleted Text

vi automatically saves the previous nine deletions in numbered buffers. If you delete the wrong thing, you may be able to get it back if you realize it soon enough. Note that many UNIX systems save only text deleted by the d command, not the x command.

Recovering deleted text from numbered buffers

1. Move the cursor to some empty lines where you can easily see any text that might be recovered.

2. Enter "1p.

   The most recently deleted text will be inserted at the cursor.

3. If this is not what you are looking for, enter u to undo the insert and remove the unwanted text.

4. Enter a period (.). This inserts text from the next most recent deletion.

5. If this is not what you are looking for, enter u to undo the insert and remove the unwanted text.

6. Continue entering these two characters, period (.) and u.

   This enables you to view all nine of the numbered delete buffers to see whether your desired text can be recovered.

Table of vi Commands for Changing Text

The following table shows how much text will be changed by the c command. A dollar sign ($) sign will appear at the end of the region to be changed. Enter the new replacement text, and press Esc when done. The remaining text on the line will move left or right as needed.

If the dollar sign showing the end of the region to change is not where you expect, press Esc, and the whole region will disappear. Then immediately press the u key, and the line will be restored to its original text.

In Table 20.6, notice how vi change commands are based on the cursor motion commands.

You can precede most of these commands with a repeat count.

Table 20.6   Table of vi Commands for Changing Text

vi Command		Description
cc		Change whole line(s).
C		Change from cursor to the end of the line.
cw	cW	Change forward to the next contained/separated word.
cb	cB	Change backward to the next contained/separated word.
ce	cE	Change to the end of the current contained/separated word.
c0/c$		Change to the start/end of the current line.
ch/cl		Change character(s) to the left/right.
c{	c}	Change to the start of the preceding/next paragraph.
c'a		Change all text to (and including) the start of the line containing mark a. This mark must have been set previously. All 26 lowercase letters may save different marked positions.
c`a		Change to the exact character containing mark a.

Replacing Text

Enter r to replace one character. Enter the new desired character. vi will then be ready for a new command. Do not press Esc.

Enter R to go into Replacement mode. Now anything you type will replace the current text. Press Esc to end this mode.

Letting the vi Editor Work for You

Steve "Mor" Moritsugu

How to zip through repetitive editing

How to map a sequence of vi
commands to one key

Mapping J to prevent accidents

Conditional text substitution, global
and partial

Cut, copy, and paste between files

vi special editing modes

Harnessing other UNIX commands
in your vi editing

> **Tip for Beginners**
>
> Many UNIX experts do not like the vi editor, so UNIX provides a number of standard and downloadable alternatives. If you do use vi, hopefully you will learn the basic vi commands in Chapter 20, "Using vi to Edit a Text File," well enough to tackle this chapter, which covers what makes vi worth all the hassle. In this chapter, you will see how all the various vi commands can be used to speed through any repetitive editing chore. You'll see how the power of all the other UNIX commands can be harnessed as if they were local vi editing commands.

Zipping Through Repetitive Editing

The preceding chapter covered the mechanics of using vi. This chapter shows how vi uses the tools from that chapter to automate almost any situation in which, in other editors, you would have to manually enter the same set of keystrokes (or worse, mouse drags) over and over again.

Using . to Repeat an Edit

The period (.) command repeats the last insert, delete, or modification but applies it to the current cursor position. The catch is, it repeats only the very last change. Assume, for example, that you are composing a letter and want to change a three-word company name (such as Acme Computer Products) to some other name repeatedly. If you first delete the old three-word name, then insert the new name, and then replace one character that you mistyped, the last change that you made is to replace one character. The period command can now repeat this last change repeatedly, but replacing that one character would not be a useful thing to repeat.

> **Name That Tune**
>
> A popular show gives the prize to the person who can Name That Tune after hearing the fewest musical notes. Similarly, vi gives a prize if you can complete an edit using one vi command instead of several commands. The prize is that you can then repeat this edit as often you desire by going to the next location and pressing the period key. As you learn more vi commands, you will find more opportunities to use the period key shortcut.

This next example shows the wrong way to prepare to use the period command in vi. A total of four vi commands are used to change the company name so the period command cannot be used to change the next occurrence of the old name. It would repeat only the last insert and would not delete the old name.

```
/Acme Computer Products
dw
dw
dw
iWondra Data CorpESC
```

The period command is one of the vi power tools. To use it, you must be able to first accomplish your change by using a single vi command. You can precede that command with a repeat count. Then the period command can repeat that useful command as needed. The preceding example involved replacing three words, so the following command should be used:

```
3cw
```

The 3 is a repeat count because you want to change three words. The c command enables you to type in new input of any length to replace the indicated text until you press Esc. The w indicates contained words, which means that any punctuation following the third word would not be changed. Separated words versus contained words were covered in the preceding chapter. 3cW would change three separated or space-delineated words, which would also change any following punctuation.

```
/Acme Computer Products
3cwWondra Data CorpESC
```

In this example, the 3cw command replaces the old name and inserts the new name in one operation. This operation can now be repeated as often as desired by the period (.) command.

Having successfully executed 3cw once, you can now find the next occurrence of any three words that you want to change and move the cursor there. Press the period (.), key and the current three contained words will be replaced by the same text you typed previously. Move the cursor to the next occurrence, and press the period to replace all the three-word sequences throughout the document as needed. This is selective replacement because you can look at each occurrence and either press the period there or not, as desired. Avoid the temptation to do other editing as you move along, because that will cause the period command to forget your three-word change and remember a new change. The next section shows you how to automate this selective find and replace even more. But first, a couple more points.

Notice that 3cw is a syntactic command that does not specify the original contents—that is, the period (.) command can then be used on any desired three words. If there are several three-word company names, the period command can change any of them to the new text. Just move the cursor to any three-word pattern and press the period key.

Sometimes the text to be changed may contain a variable number of words, but it always fits into the same number of characters, such as an entry in a table. Assume that your table entry is 15 characters long and you want to type in the same new entry to replace several different entries. The key to successfully using the period command is to construct a single vi command to repeat. In this case, the first command could be either of the following:

```
15cl
```

```
R
```

15cl uses the l command to move right, so 15cl changes 15 characters to the right of the cursor, including the current character. Because this is a table, you would need to type in exactly 15 characters so that the new text exactly fits the table size. You can also use the R command to replace exactly 15 characters in one command.

Using *n* and . to Search and Selectively Repeat an Edit

You can combine the n command to repeat the last search with the period command to really zip through repetitious editing chores.

Note that this procedure is useful when you want to view each line to decide whether you should change it. If you don't need to view each occurrence, use the procedure for global or partial text substitution, as discussed later in this chapter.

Using two-finger editing

1. Invoke vi to edit the document where you want to selectively replace some text.

2. Enter 1G to make sure that you are at the start of the document.

3. Enter /pattern, where pattern is the word(s) that you want to selectively replace. This moves the cursor to the first occurrence of that word.

4. Decide whether you want to retain any punctuation immediately following the pattern, such as a period or quotation marks. If so, you use contained words. If not, you use separated words. (This is discussed more in the preceding section on the period command.)

5. Count the number of words to replace. For separated words, each word is separated by spaces or tabs. For contained words, count the number of words and non-words to be replaced. Enter that count now. Do not press Enter.

6. Enter c.

   Do not press Enter.

7. For contained words, enter w.

For separated words, enter W.

A dollar sign ($) should appear, showing you the end of the text to change.

8. If the dollar sign does not appear in the correct place, press Esc, and then enter u.

This restores the original text. Go back to step 4 and try again.

9. Type in the new replacement text; it can be longer or shorter than the original text. Press Esc when done.

10. Press n to go to the next occurrence of the pattern to replace. Look it over, and decide whether you want to make the replacement there.

11. If you want to make the replacement, enter a period.

Your new text replaces the pattern.

Don't Forget That You Can Undo a Mistake

As you are doing your two-finger editing, you may press the period when you meant to press the n key. The period will cause your last change to be applied again. To correct this mistake, just enter u to undo the last change.

---

12. For real editing speed, place one index finger on the period key and the other index finger on the n key. Press n to go to the next occurrence of the pattern and look it over. Press period only if you want to replace it. With this two-finger editing, you can literally selectively replace hundreds of occurrences in a few minutes.

Mapping a Key to a Commonly Used Command Sequence

The period command is limited in that it can repeat only the very last insert, delete, or modify editing command that you performed. There will be times when repetitive editing cannot be accomplished by the n command and the period command because several editing commands or motion commands must be done for each repetition.

You can handle this situation by mapping an unused command key to a sequence of vi editing commands or motion commands in sequence. In the preceding chapter on vi, you saw how to map the letter g to a sequence of commands that can format a paragraph. After a letter has been mapped, position the cursor and press that letter. Then the commands mapped to that letter will be executed.

Before you can map a key, however, you must find out whether your terminal supports Ctrl+V in Visual mode. The Ctrl+V is important for mapping because it enables you to enter control characters as part of the sequence to be mapped. Some terminals require a special sequence to use Ctrl+V, so you need to check that first.

Checking whether Ctrl+V is supported in Visual mode

Why is Ctrl+V a Problem on Some Terminals?

If your TERM is set to tvi925, a down arrow sends a Ctrl+V. If you press Ctrl+V while in vi on that terminal, vi will think that a down arrow key has been pressed, so vi gets confused. You can eliminate the problem by using **Q** to exit from Visual mode temporarily. Alternatively, you will not have problems with Ctrl+V if you set your TERM to vt100>$I~commands;vi text editor;motion> or ANSI.

---

1. At the shell prompt, type `vi`.

Press Enter to execute this command. Note that no filename is to be specified.

2. When in vi, enter a colon (:). The cursor should go to the bottom line, and a colon should appear there.

3. Press Ctrl+V as you would any control character.

4. Look at your screen. If the bottom line looks like this:

```
:^
```

and the cursor is directly under the circumflex (^), your terminal supports Ctrl+V in Visual mode. If your screen has any other result, such as a blank line at the bottom, your terminal does not support Ctrl+V in Visual mode.

5. Press Esc twice.

6. Enter a colon.

7. Enter q!, and then press Enter. You should now be back at the shell prompt.

Now you are ready to map a character. Here is an example mapping to give you a feel for what mapping can do. Imagine that you want to map the available v key so that every time you enter a v in Command mode, it does the following:

```
Go down to next line: j
Go to the start of the line: 0
Move right 15 characters: 15l
```

```
Replace the next 10 characters with acme: 10clacmeESC
    10cl says change the next 10 characters to the right
        with whatever I type in until I press ESC
Go to the end of the line and insert a dash (-): A-
    Notice we use the capital A command to insert at the end of line.
Then insert Dept 2 and terminate the insert: Dept 2ESC
```

This is the map command that will accomplish all this:

```
:map v j015l10clacme^[A-Dept 2^[
```

In the preceding command, notice the following:

- Multiple vi commands can be strung together to form the mapping. Do not put any spaces between the commands.

- The Esc character appears as ^[. Control characters often appear preceded by a circumflex. If you insert the Enter key within a mapping, it will appear as ^M. You must press Ctrl+V before each control character or Enter key that is part of your mapping command. Pressing Ctrl+V causes vi to display a circumflex to alert you that the very next character input, if it is a control character, will be treated as just another data character in the line.

Now you are ready to actually set up a mapping.

How to map a key to a sequence of commands

1. From vi's Command mode (that is, not Insert mode), enter a colon. The cursor should go down to the last line on the screen, and a colon prompt will appear there. Do not press Enter until instructed.

2. In the preceding procedure, you determined whether your terminal supports Ctrl+V in Visual mode. If your terminal does not support Ctrl+V in Visual mode (or if you are not sure), from vi Command mode enter Q. (Notice that this is a capital Q.)

    Do not press Enter. The cursor will go to the bottom of the screen and a colon (:) prompt will appear. You have now left Visual mode. This step is not needed, but it is harmless if your terminal does support Ctrl+V in Visual mode.

3. Type map.

    Do not press Enter until instructed.

Don't Map the K Key

The most common commands used to move the cursor are the arrows keys and the equivalent h, j, k, and l keys. Even experienced vi users sometimes forget to turn off the Caps Lock key before pressing h, j, k, and l repeatedly to move around. If you map the capital K key to a sequence of vi commands, you may accidentally invoke this mapping repeatedly by pressing the k key with Caps Lock on.

---

4. Enter a space, and then enter the desired command letter to map. You should avoid any letter that is a vi command because you will not be able to do that command anymore after that letter is mapped. Actually, only five upper- or lowercase letters are not vi commands: g, K, q, v, and V. (I usually map g to format paragraphs, as shown in the preceding chapter. I recommend against mapping capital K because h, j, k, and l are used to move the cursor, and you don't want usage of those cursor motion letters to disturb text if the Caps Lock has been accidentally left on. Therefore, I recommend that you use lowercase v or uppercase V as the desired command letter to map.)

5. Enter a space, and then enter the vi command sequence to enter every time the mapped letter is pressed. As you saw earlier, enter a Ctrl+V before any control characters or Esc or the Enter key in your command sequence. The Ctrl+V will cause a circumflex to appear before your control character.

6. Now press Enter to complete your map command. Because you did not precede it with a Ctrl+V, this Enter key terminates the map command.

7. If your terminal does not support Ctrl+V, you will still be on the last line with a colon prompt. In that case, type vi and then press Enter. This returns you to Visual mode.

8. Your cursor should now have left the bottom line, and you should be in vi Command mode ready to enter vi commands, including the new command letter that you just mapped.

When you have hundreds of repetitive editing changes to make, the best way to speed this up is to set up two-finger editing (as discussed earlier) using the n command to search for the next pattern to change and the period (.) command to repeat the last change. If the last change is too complicated to be done by a single command, set up a mapping so that the whole command sequence can be done by a single letter, such as the v key. Use the slash (/) command to find the first occurrence to change. Now put one index finger on the n key and the other index finger on the v key. Press n to find the next occurrence to change. Press v only if you want to change it.

You will lose your mapping when you exit from vi. In the preceding chapter on vi, in the section on formatting paragraphs, you saw how to put the letter g mapping into a file called .exrc in your home directory. Notice that in this file, you put the complete map command, but you do not put a colon (:) before the word map. Any mapping set up in .exrc in your home directory is available to you every time you use vi.

Preventing *J* from Turning Your Text to Mush

If you use h, j, k, and l to move the cursor instead of the arrow keys, you will discover that, if the Caps Lock is accidentally on, it is harmless to type H, K, and L:

H moves the cursor to the highest line on the screen.

K is not a command (as long you don't map this character).

L moves the cursor to the lowest line on the screen.

If you wanted to go down 10 lines and so pressed the j key 10 times but did not notice that your Caps Lock was on, you would now find that you joined 10 lines. You would have created one long line that probably takes up more than one line and looks like mush. To fix it, you must painstakingly insert the missing Enter key at the end of each of the original lines. The J command also trims any leading spaces in the line, so you would have to re-enter any leading spaces. After you have made this mistake a couple of times, you may wish there was a way to prevent this problem. There is.

Preventing problems with accidental J's

1. Put this mapping in your .exrc file in your home directory:
   ```
   map J J:
   ```

2. Having done that, if you enter several capital J's by mistake, the first J will join two lines and then go into Colon mode on the bottom line. The rest of the J's will harmlessly appear on the bottom line. After you realize your mistake, just press Backspace or Ctrl+H until you have moved all the way to the left and are off the last line.

3. Enter u if you want to undo the effect of the single J command that was executed. You have now fully recovered from your mistake.

If you do want to join several lines, you can still do so by preceding the J with a repeat count. This will join the requested number of lines and then go into Colon mode on the bottom line. Just press Backspace or Esc to leave the bottom line and continue your other editing.

On some versions of UNIX, mapping J to a pattern that contains J will cause an infinite loop. In that case, typing J will cause vi to hang and not accept any more commands. Press your interrupt key (either Delete or Ctrl+C) and exit vi. The hang tells us that you cannot use this mapping on your system.

Global and Partial Text Substitution

vi has a built-in colon command g to globally search for and replace all occurrences of one pattern with another. You learned how to use sed and awk in the previous chapters; however, this next section shows you how to use other UNIX commands to modify your whole file or any part of your file. After you learn this technique, you can do much more than the global g command can do.

Substituting Regular Expressions Patterns Throughout the File

How to globally replace a pattern in your document

Why Not Use the Built-in vi Replacement Commands?

vi supports two built-in colon commands: g (global) and s (substitution, which aren't covered in this book because calling the external sed command fills the same function as both these built-in commands). This gives you more practice with sed, which is an important UNIX command, and shows you how to call other external UNIX commands to manipulate your text (as you shall see).

1. In vi Command mode, enter a colon. This should move the cursor to the last line, where a colon prompt is waiting.

2. Enter the following:

   `%! sed 's/R.E./newstring/g'`

   %! tells vi to apply the following UNIX command to all lines of your file.

   sed is the stream editor that you studied in detail in Chapter 19, "Replacing or Removing Text from a File or Pipeline."

   s is the sed command to substitute one string for another.

   R.E. stands for regular expression. Enter the string to search for; you may include R.E. wildcards.

   newstring stands for the replacement string to be put in place of the R.E. string, wherever it is found.

g tells sed to do this substitution multiple times on one line, as needed. Without the g flag, sed will do multiple substitutions, but only one on any given line.

3. Press Enter to execute your command.

4. The changes will be made to all lines, and you should now be back in vi Command mode. On some types of UNIX systems, you may be prompted to press Enter or Return to continue.

5. Check the lines of your file to see whether you are happy with the changes made. If not, you can remove all the changes by entering the u command to undo them. Remember, the u command can undo only the preceding change, so check the file immediately after doing these replacements.

SEE ALSO

➤ *For more information on R.E. patterns, see page 502*

Substituting Regular Expression Patterns in a Portion of the File

Using the technique in the preceding section, you can also do the replacement only in a section of the file (which is not possible with the global g command that this book does not cover). The following procedure uses the fact that you can set marks in the file to reference that line, as you saw in the previous chapter on vi.

How to substitute strings in just a section of the file

1. In vi, move the cursor to the start of the section where the text substitution is desired.

2. Type ma.

   This sets mark a at that line. If mark a is already in use to mark another line of the file, you can choose any other lowercase letter for your mark. You can have up to 26 marks set at one time.

3. Move the cursor to the last line of the section to be modified.

4. Type ! 'a.

   Do not press the Enter key until instructed. Change the letter a in the preceding example if you are using a different mark. Notice that the single quote mark is used, not a backquote. This should take the cursor to the bottom screen line, and a bang sign (!) prompt should appear there.

5. Enter the following:

```
sed 's/R.E./newstring/g'
```

   This is the same sed command that was analyzed in the preceding step-by-step procedure.

6. Press Enter to execute your command.

7. The changes will be made to the section of your file, and you should now be back in vi Command mode. On some types of UNIX systems, you may be prompted to press Enter or Return to continue.

8. Check the lines of your file to see whether you are happy with the changes made. If not, you can remove all the changes by entering the u command to undo them. Remember, the u command can undo only the preceding change, so check the file immediately after doing these replacements.

To summarize:

```
:%! sed ...    replaces throughout the file
!'a sed ...    replaces back to or forward to mark a
```

SEE ALSO

➤ *For more information on setting a mark so that you can return there, see page 584*

Conditionally Substituting Text in vi

You can replace the sed command in the preceding section with other sed commands or other different commands entirely to give you great control over how text is substituted in vi. All the following examples use :%! to replace text in the whole file, but the !'a could also be used in the following examples to make the replacement in just a portion of the file.

```
:%! sed '/R.E.1/ s/R.E.2/newstring/g'          # general form
:%! sed '/acme$/ s/^president/chairperson/g'    # example
```

In the previous examples, the first line shows the general form of a modified sed command that you can also use in vi to conditionally substitute text. In this form of the sed command, sed searches for *R.E.2* and replaces it with *newstring*, but only in lines that contain *R.E.1* somewhere within the line. In the second line, you can see an example using this form of sed. In that example, if *president* occurs at the start of a line, it will be replaced with chairperson, but only if the line ends in the word acme.

The following line shows the general form of an awk command that you can also use in vi to conditionally substitute text. Using awk, you can check a particular field to decide whether you should do the text substitution in that line. In this form of the awk command, awk searches for all occurrences of *R.E.2* and replaces them with *newstring*, but only in lines where field n exactly matches sstring:

```
:%! awk '$n == "sstring" {gsub("R.E.2","newstring")} {print}'
```

In the following line, you can see an example using this form of awk. In that example, any time that D is followed by three characters, the D and those three characters will be replaced with M46253, but only if field 3 of the line contains K6697:

```
:%! awk '$3 == "K6697" {gsub("D...","M46253")} {print}'
```

In the following lines, you see the general form and an example that is similar to the preceding awk command. Use this awk form when you want to do a substitution, but only if a particular field contains a value greater than or equal to numval:

```
:%! awk '$n >= numval {gsub("R.E.2","newstring")} {print}'
:%! awk '$3 >= 16.2 {gsub("D...","M46253")} {print}'
```

You can replace >= with the following operators:

>= (greater than or equal to)

<= (less than or equal to)

== (equal to)

!= (not equal to)

>   (greater than)

<   (less than)

The following example again shows the general form and an example that is similar to the two previous awk commands. Use this awk form when you want to do a substitution, but only if a particular field contains an R.E. pattern. In the specific example here, any time that D is followed by three characters, the D and those three characters will be replaced with M46253, but only if field 3 of the line ends with a P followed by a digit:

```
:%! awk '$n ~ /R.E.1/ {gsub("R.E.2","newstring")} {print}'
:%! awk '$3 ~ /P[0-9]$/ {gsub("D...","M46253")} {print}'
```

Changing the Indentation of Your Lines

Test Your UNIX Skills

Assume that the number of spaces at the start of each line has not been consistent in your file. Enter a vi command to change all lines from the current line (forward or backward) to mark c so that any group of one or more spaces at the start of a line are changed to exactly five spaces. Don't change lines that do not start with a space.

Answer on next page.

Answer to Test on Previous Page

```
!'c sed 's/^  */         /'
```

The above answer has two spaces before the asterisk (*) and five spaces after the * /.

You can change the indentation by using the sed command to either add spaces to the left margin or remove them.

```
:%! sed 's/^ *//'
```

The preceding sed command removes all leading spaces (but not tabs) for all lines of the file.

```
!'a sed 's/^ *//'
```

The previous sed command removes all leading spaces (but not tabs) from the current line to mark a.

```
:%! sed 's/^/   /'
```

The preceding sed command adds three leading spaces to each line of the file.

```
!'a sed 's/^/   /'
```

This sed command adds three leading spaces to the section, starting from the current line to mark a.

Moving/Copying Sections of Text in vi

Moving and copying sections of text can by done in several ways. The next section shows you how to use marks to do this because it gives you the best control and the most successful results.

Moving/Copying Text in the Same File

To move or copy text within the same file with vi

1. In vi, move the cursor to the start of the text to move or copy.

2. Type ma.

   This command executes without pressing Enter. It sets mark a at that line. If mark a is already in use to mark another line of the file, you can choose any other letter for your mark. You can set up to 26 marks.

3. Move the cursor to the last line of the section to be moved or copied.

4. To move the text, type d'a.

This command executes without pressing Enter. It deletes all text from the current line to and including mark a and saves it in what is called an unnamed buffer.

5. To copy the text, type y'a.

This command executes without pressing Enter. It yanks—that is, copies—all text from the current line to and including mark a and saves it in what is called an unnamed buffer.

6. Move the cursor to the line just above the desired place to put the moved or copied text. If you want to move or copy text to the beginning of the file, you must insert a blank line at the start of the file so that you can be in the line just above where you want to do the insert.

7. Enter p.

This command executes without pressing Enter. It will paste—that is, insert—all text saved in the unnamed buffer by the previous steps 4 or 5.

Moving/Copying Text Between Different Files

To move or copy text between different files using vi

1. Use vi to edit the source file—that is, the file that contains the text to be moved or copied.

2. Move the cursor to the start of the text to move or copy.

3. Type ma.

This command executes without pressing Enter. It sets mark a at that line. If mark a is already in use to mark another line of the file, you can choose any other letter for your mark. You can set up to 26 marks.

4. Move the cursor to the last line of the section to be moved or copied.

5. To move the text, type "bd'a.

This command executes without pressing Enter. It deletes all text from the current line to and including mark a and saves it in buffer b. If buffer b is already in use saving other text, you can choose any other letter for your buffer. You can save text in up to 26 buffers, named for each letter of the alphabet (hence, they are also called named buffers). Named buffers are always preceded by double quotation marks ("). The letter of the mark used and the letter of the named buffer do not have to be the same.

6. To copy the text, type `"by'a`.

This command executes without pressing Enter. It yanks—that is, copies—all text from the current line to and including mark a and saves it in buffer b. If buffer b is already in use saving other text, you can choose any other letter for your buffer. You can save text in up to 26 buffers, named for each letter of the alphabet (hence, these are called named buffers). Named buffers are always preceded by double quotation marks (`""`). The letter of the mark used and the letter of the named buffer do not have to be the same.

7. If you have done any text modifications in this file that you want to preserve, save your changes now.

Then type `:w`.

The preceding vi command writes the vi workspace to the file. Do not exit from vi at this point because that would clear all of vi's unnamed and named buffers.

8. Type `:e file2`.

Colon (:) e changes the file you are editing while preserving the text in named buffers. If you quit vi and restart it, all your buffers will be empty. Replace `file2` in the preceding command with the name of the file to which you want to move or copy the saved text.

9. In this new file, move the cursor to the line just above the desired place in this file to put the moved or copied text. If you want to move or copy text to the beginning of this file, you must insert a blank line at the start of the file so that you can be in the line just above where you want to do the insert.

10. Type `"bp`.

This command executes without pressing Enter. It pastes—that is, inserts—all text saved in the buffer b by the previous steps 5 or 6.

Setting Options for Inserting Text

In vi, the `set` command enables you to turn on or off various modes in vi. This section looks at modes that enhance text input.

Ignoring Case When Searching Using / or ?

To ignore case when searching ahead for strings using the slash or searching backward using the question mark, enter the following:

```
:set ignorecase
```

To turn off this mode, enter this:

```
:set noignorecase
```

You can abbreviate this command as `ic`, as follows:

```
:set ic
:set noic
```

Setting vi to Always Show the Input Mode

---

showmode Is Great for Beginners

It is very common to hear a lot of beeps when beginners first learn to use vi. The beeps indicate errors and many beeps indicate that the beginners are making many errors. One of the most common errors is to enter vi commands while in insert mode and to try to insert text while in command mode. The **showmode** option will show you in the bottom-right corner whenever you are in an insert mode, so you learn more quickly the difference between command mode and text insert modes.

Sometimes people have trouble in vi because they lose track of whether they are in Insert mode or Command mode. For example, some files created by beginners contain lines like this:

```
:wq
:w!q
:wq!
wq
q
:q
```

These lines are inserted into the file because the user was in Insert mode. You must be in command mode for commands like these to function.

vi has a mode that tells you in the bottom-right corner of the screen if you are in Insert mode, Replace mode, Append mode, and so on. To turn on this mode, type the following:

```
:set showmode
```

To turn off this mode, typetypetype this:

```
:set noshowmode
```

Turning On Autowrap at the End of a Line

vi has a mode that will check whether you are near the end of a line when inserting text. If so, it takes the current word and moves it to the start of the next line, as though you had pressed the Enter key just before the start of this word. With this mode on, you never have to press Enter because vi autowraps the line for you. To turn on this mode, type the following:

```
:set wrapmargin=10
```

The preceding command causes any word that gets within 10 characters of the end of the line to autowrap to the start of the next line. You can set a larger or smaller number than 10 to determine where you want to wrap the end of the line.

To turn off this mode, type this:

```
:set wrapmargin=0
```

This command may be abbreviated as wm, as follows:

```
:set wm=10
```

Turning On Autoindent at the Start of a Line

If you are using vi in a document with an indented left margin, it will be useful for you to turn on Autoindent mode. Any time you advance to the next line while in Insert, Append, or Replace mode, vi automatically enters the same number of spaces as on the preceding line.

To turn off this mode, type the following:

```
:set noautoindent
```

You can abbreviate this command as ai, as follows:

```
:set ai
:set noai
```

Turning On the Autowrite Option

If you frequently cut, copy, and paste between different files, you will find the autowrite option useful:

```
:set autowrite
```

When you set this command, any `:e` command to edit a different file will automatically save the current file if there are changes in the workspace that have not been saved.

To turn off this mode, type this line:

```
:set noautowrite
```

Using Abbreviations for Long Strings

If you have a long phrase to enter frequently, you can set up an input abbreviation that vi will expand for you as soon as you insert the abbreviation.

Setting up and using vi abbreviations

1. In vi, enter a colon, and then enter `abbrev`. Do not press Enter until instructed.

2. Enter a space, and then enter the abbreviation you want to use to signal that the long phrase is really to be inserted at the cursor.

3. Enter a space, and then enter the long phrase itself.

4. Press Enter to set up this abbreviation.

5. To make use of the abbreviation that has been set up, from vi, go into Insert mode and start inserting text. As part of the text you enter, insert the abbreviation from step 2. You should see that the abbreviation text is immediately expanded by vi to the longer phrase.

Turning On Line Numbers

In vi, there is a mode to show line numbers before each line of a file. These line numbers are not inserted into the file itself, but they are just displayed to the screen. This can be useful if you compile a C language program and the compiler tells you that you have an error at line 1453.

To turn on vi line numbering, type the following:

```
:set number
```

To turn off this mode, type this:

```
:set nonumber
```

This command can be abbreviated as nu, as follows:

```
:set nu
:set nonu
```

Saving Your Options in *.exrc*

If you have : set options that you want to use every time you enter vi, you can create a file called .exrc in your home directory. It can contain set options, map commands, and abbreviations, as follows:

```
set autoindent
set ignorecase
set showmode
set wm=10
map g 072lBi^M^[
map J J:
abbrev SVR4 UNIX, System V, Release 4
```

Notice that each line in this file does *not* start with a colon.

SEE ALSO

➤ *For more information on home directories, see page 62*

Harnessing Other UNIX Commands to Work in vi

Earlier, you saw how to apply sed to some or all of the lines of the file. You can use that same technique to use other UNIX commands to manipulate lines in vi.

Checking Other UNIX Commands While in vi

While you are editing in vi, you might want to look up some information by running other UNIX commands or pipelines. You can do this from vi Command mode, by entering this:

```
:! cmd
```

Replace cmd in the preceding command with the desired UNIX command or pipeline you want to run. The output from that command will appear on your screen. At the end, it will prompt you to press the Enter key. Then you will be back in vi Command mode, ready to do more editing of your file. You saw this process in the preceding chapter on vi when you wrote a script that displayed a help message for vi. In that exercise, the colon bang (:!) was used to run the vihelp script so that you could see the help message and then resume editing.

```
:! cal 2000 | pg
```

The preceding example displays a calendar of the year 2000, one page at a time. You can now use pg to go back and forth in the calendar for 2000 to look up what day a particular date falls on. After you end this `cal 2000` pipeline, you will automatically resume your editing in vi with the current screen completely refreshed.

Inserting the Output of Other UNIX Commands into Your File

You can insert the output from any UNIX command or pipeline into your file by moving the cursor to a blank line. Then enter this:

```
!! cmd
```

Replace `cmd` in the preceding command with the desired UNIX command or pipeline you want to run. Bang-bang (`!!`) causes the current line you are on to be provided as standard input to the `cmd` you enter. The output from that command will be inserted in your file in place of the current line.

```
!! cal 1999
```

This example inserts a calendar of the year 1999 into your file in place of the current line. Hint: You can enter this type of command on a blank line.

```
!! cat ffile
```

The preceding vi command inserts the contents of `ffile` in place of the current line. `ffile` can be specified as a basename or as an absolute or relative pathname. Alternatively, you can use the built-in vi command `:r ffile` to insert the contents of `ffile` at the current cursor position.

Sorting All or Part of the File

In vi, you can sort all the lines of your file by entering the following:

```
:%! sort
```

You can enter any desired `sort` options (see Appendix A, "UNIX Commands"). All lines of the file will be passed to the `sort` command. The output of the `sort` command will replace the current contents of the file. If you don't like the results, you can enter `u` to undo that last modification.

How to sort a section of your file

1. Move the cursor to the start of the section to sort.

2. Type `ma`.

   This command executes without pressing Enter. It sets mark a at that line. If mark a is already in use to mark another line of the file, you can choose any other letter for your mark. You can set up to 26 marks.

3. Move the cursor to the last line of the section to be sorted.

4. Type `!'a sort`.

Enter any desired options after `sort` (see Appendix A). Press the Enter key to execute this command.

5. Now the lines in the section will be sorted.

SEE ALSO

➤ *For more information on sorting files or pipelines, see page 266*

Deleting Lines That Match a Pattern

Test Your UNIX Skills

Give a vi colon command that will remove all blank lines and lines that contain nothing but spaces and/or tabs.

Answer on next page.

In vi, you can delete all the lines of your file that contain an R.E. pattern by entering the following:

```
:%! grep -v 'R.E.'
```

You can enter any desired `grep` options (see Appendix A). All lines of the file will be passed to the `grep` command. The output of the `grep` command will replace the current contents of the file. If you don't like the results, you can enter u to undo that last modification.

Deleting lines with a pattern from a section

1. Move the cursor to the start of the section where you want to delete lines that contain a pattern.

2. Type `ma`.

This command executes without pressing Enter. It sets mark a at that line. If mark a is already in use to mark another line of the file, you can choose any other letter for your mark. You can set up to 26 marks.

3. Move the cursor to the last line of the section.

4. Type `!'a grep -v R.E..`

Enter any desired options after `grep` (see Appendix A). Follow the standard rules for `grep`, including any needed quotation marks around the R.E. pattern. Press `Enter` to execute this command.

5. Now the lines in the section that contain the R.E. pattern will be removed.

SEE ALSO

➤ *For more information on the* `grep` *command, see page 495*

Answer to Test on Previous Page

`:%! grep -v '^[    ]*$'`

In the above line, the square brackets contain one space and one tab.

Encrypting/Decrypting All or Part of Your File

If your UNIX system supports the `crypt` command, you can apply the technique in the preceding section to `crypt` also.

`:%! crypt`

The preceding vi command will ask you for a key. It will then use that key to encrypt or decrypt the whole file. Safeguard your key carefully because you cannot decrypt the text without it.

`!'a crypt`

The preceding vi command encrypts or decrypts a section of the file from the current line to mark a.

SEE ALSO

➤ *For more information on encrypting a file or pipeline", see page 266*

Inserting a Banner Headline into Your Document

You can use the UNIX `banner` command to change a line so that each character is about 10 characters tall, as follows:

`!! banner`

This vi command pipes the current line of the file to `banner` and replaces that line with the output from `banner`.

You can also create a banner using text that is not found in the file. Create a blank line and enter:

```
!! banner Desired Text
```

Replace Desired Text in this example with your desired text.

SEE ALSO

➤ *For more information on displaying text in large banner letters," see page 220*

Printing a Section of Your File

Printing a section of your file from vi

1. In vi Command mode, type the following:
   ```
   :w
   ```

   This vi command writes the file to disk, which is important to do before the rest of these steps.

2. Set mark a at the start of the section to print.

3. Move to the end of the section to print, and enter the following:
   ```
   !'a lp
   ```

   You can use either lp or lpr, depending on which one your system supports. You can add any desired options, such as selecting the destination printer or the number of copies.

4. The preceding command deletes all the lines to be printed from your file. Enter u to undo the deletion and restore those lines to your file. It is very important that the u command be run immediately after step 3.

SEE ALSO

➤ *For more information on printing files and pipelines, see page 223*

Counting Number of Lines/Words/Characters in Part of Your File

Counting lines, words, or characters in a section of your file from vi

1. In vi Command mode, type the following:
   ```
   :w
   ```

   This vi command writes the file to disk, which is important to do before the rest of these steps.

2. Set mark a at the start of the section to be counted, as follows:
   ```
   ma
   ```

Move to the end of the section to be counted, and enter this:
```
!'a wc
```

3. To do the whole file instead of just a section, replace step 2 with this one command:
```
:%! wc
```

4. The preceding command deletes all the lines to be counted and replaces them with three numbers:

   • Number of lines in that section

   • Number of words in that section

   • Number of characters in that section

   Write down any of these numbers if you need them.

5. Type u to undo the deletion and restore those lines to your file. It is very important that the u command be run immediately after step 3.

SEE ALSO

➤ *For more information on counting lines and other things, see page 158*

Editing Multiple Files

You can give vi a list of files to edit, as follows:
```
vi report*
```

When you finish editing one file, save it (:w) and use :n to start editing the next file in the list. If you have set autowrite, as described earlier, you can omit :w because :n to go to the next file will automatically write the current file.

See Table 21.1 for other standard properties of the vi command:

Table 21.1 Other Properties of the *vi* Command:

Property	See page
Allows relative and absolute pathname arguments	70
Allows a list of filenames and filename wildcards	292

Sanjiv Guha and Steve
"Mor" Moritsugu

Command-Line Editing in the Korn Shell

Editing the command line so that you
don't have to retype it

History of commands

Developing complex pipelines using
command-line editing

The Alias command

> **Tip for Beginners**
>
> The Korn shell and the Bash shell offer many conveniences that the standard Bourne shell lacks. Command-line editing allows you to repeat and modify previous commands or fix wrong characters without retyping the whole command. You will see in this chapter how advanced users use this feature to construct complex command pipelines reliably and quickly one step at a time.

Command-Line Editing in the Korn or Bash Shell

While working with UNIX—or, for that matter, with any other operating system—you must correct any key entry errors by using the available keys on the terminal. However, not all keyboards have the same layout—and they may not even have the same keys. You may find that you cannot erase a wrong character because the Delete or Backspace keys are programmed incorrectly. Because of this, you may not be able to correct keying errors and may find yourself retyping whole command strings.

Korn shell provides two different ways of editing commands in the command line. You either can use keys used by the source editor vi or you can use the source editor emacs. Depending on which editor you are familiar with, you can invoke either of these options for command-line editing. This chapter shows you how to use vi commands to edit your command line.

> **vi Command Set**
>
> The Korn shell allows you to turn on an option to use the same editing commands as you would use in the vi editor. The Korn shell is not the only program that emulates the vi command set so that you can use editing commands that you are already familiar with. For a similar reason, the Lynx browser allows you to select vi commands to navigate. An older utility sledit, to edit disk slices, also used vi commands.

Command-line editing allows you to do the following:

- Re-execute the previous command.
- Retrieve any previous command, modify it, and execute it.
- Find a particular previous command so that you can modify it.
- Correct a mistake at the start of the current command.
- Develop complex pipelines step by step.

Command-Line Editing in Linux

The Linux Bash shell has a very nice way to retrieve and edit commands using the arrow keys and the Insert and Delete keys. This is possible because Linux knows you are on a PC keyboard.

On commercial versions of UNIX, you will encounter many different types of terminals and keyboards. In many situations, the arrows keys are not functional. UNIX command-line editing does not require that you have a PC keyboard and have working arrow keys.

Which is better? Linux command-line editing is very nice, but it works only on Linux. UNIX command-line editing works on all type of terminals, keyboards, and even on Linux. Most UNIX/Linux people today will encounter a variety of systems. I suggest you always use UNIX command-line editing as covered in this chapter, even on Linux systems. Then you can seamlessly move from UNIX to Linux, and vice versa, as needed.

Turning On Command-Line Editing

Before you can do any UNIX command-line editing, you must be in a shell that supports it, and you must tell the shell whether you want to use vi editing commands or emacs editing commands.

If you are familiar with vi, then you can use the following command on the command line or have it in the `.profile` file (which gets executed at logon) to use vi commands for command-line editing:

```
set -o vi          # if already in the Korn or Bash shell
```

On the other hand, if you are familiar with the emacs editor, use the following command:

```
set -o emacs       # if already in the Korn or Bash shell
```

You can have only one of these active at any time. The most recent command is in effect. This chapter describes only vi command-line editing.

If you are on a UNIX system (not Linux) but you are not in the Korn shell, you can start the Korn shell and turn on vi command-line editing in one step, like this:

```
exec ksh -o vi     # start the Korn shell with vi command editing
```

vi Command-Line Editing

Like the vi file editor, the vi command-line editor has two modes:

- Input mode
- Command mode

In *Input mode*, every character you type is inserted into the command line. You see each character as you type it because it is echoed to the screen at the correct location in the command line. You can use the Esc key at any time while in Input mode to switch to end Input mode and change to Command mode. Each time you see the shell prompt, you are automatically put into Input mode so that you can enter UNIX commands.

If you press Esc to end Input mode, you change to Command mode. Then every letter is a command to invoke some sort of vi editing on the command line. What you type does not appear on the screen, but you will see the results of your commands immediately.

While in Command mode, if you press a key that does not translate to a vi command, then you usually hear a beep sound from the terminal. In vi Command mode, lowercase letters have different meanings from uppercase letters. In Command mode, you can navigate to any part of the command you have entered so far and modify it, including inserting new strings in the middle of the command.

How to Re-Execute the Previous Command

If you are in vi command-line Edit mode, you can repeat the previous command by entering these three characters:

Esc k ENTER

Esc ends Input mode, even if you have not entered anything on the command line yet.

k is the vi command to move up one line. This retrieves the previous command and displays it on the command line.

ENTER causes the current command buffer to be executed, even if the cursor is not at the end of the buffer.

How to Edit a Previous Command

After you enter Esc k, as just described, the previous command will appear on the command line, and your cursor will be on the first character of that line, in vi Command mode. You can then use most of the standard vi commands to modify the command line. Table 22.1 shows many of the ways to modify the command line.

Table 22.1   vi Commands to Modify the Command Line

Command	Description
nx	Delete *n* characters; example: 5x
D	Delete from cursor to end of line
dd	Delete all characters in line
p	Insert last deleted text at current cursor
I	Insert at start of line until Esc
i	Insert before cursor until Esc
a	Insert after cursor until Esc
A	Insert at end of line until Esc
rc	Replace current character with character c; example: rg replaces with the letter g
R	Replace all characters until Esc
cW	Change the current word until Esc, pulling in or pushing out all subsequent words as needed
cnW	Change *n* words until Esc
~	Change uppercase to lowercase, and vice versa

You can also use standard vi commands to move around on the command line, as shown in Table 22.2. In Tables 22.1 and 22.2, *n* indicates a repeat count. You can omit this if the value is 1.

Table 22.2   vi Commands to Move Around on the Command Line

Command	Description
0	Move to start of line
$	Move to end of line
nW	Move forward *n* words

continues...

617

Table 22.2 Continued

Command	Description
nE	Move to end of the *n*th word
nB	Move backward *n* words
nh	Move left *n* characters
nl	Move right *n* characters
fc	Move right to character c
Fc	Move left to character c

In Table 22.2, the nW, nE, and nB commands refer to space-separated words. You can also use nw, ne, and nb to move by contained words and non-words, as discussed in the section "Using Separated Words Versus Contained Words Versus Non-words" in Chapter 20, "Using vi to Edit a Text File." Table 22.3 shows other useful vi editing commands.

Table 22.3 Other Useful vi Editing Commands

Command	Description
u	Undo the last modification.
v	Invoke vi to edit the command line as if it were a file. When you write and quit, all lines in your vi file buffer will be executed.
ENTER	Execute the whole current command, even if the cursor is not at end of line and even if you're in Input mode.

How to Correct the Current Line

If you type a long line and see a mistake near the start of the line, it is easy to fix it using vi command-line editing.

Enter Esc to end Input mode, and change to Command mode. Do not press Enter before Esc because this would execute your incorrect line.

Now use any of the vi editing commands to fix your mistake. When the mistake is corrected, press Enter to execute the whole line, even if the cursor is not at the end of the line and even if you are still in Input mode.

History of Commands

The Korn shell keeps a history of the commands across the session. That is, even if you log out, you can still obtain the commands you entered in the previous session by using the Korn shell command `fc`. By default, the history is stored in the `$HOME/.sh_history` file, where `$HOME` is the home directory for the user. If you want to modify the filename for the history file, you can modify the filename specified in the system variable `HISTFILE`. You can include the following command in the `.profile` file to modify the history filename.

```
export HISTFILE=$HOME/myhistoryfile
```

If you want to get a list of the last few commands, enter the following:

```
fc -l
```

`fc` Is Not Part of vi Command Editing

You can do many things with the `fc` command, which is presented here for background information. I never use the `fc` command because I can do the same functions using vi command-line editing, as you will see.

The system responds as follows:

```
116  ls -l
117  ls
118  find . -print
119  vi test.c
120  rm test.c
```

`fc -l` can usually be executed by typing its alias:

```
history
```

The numbers on the left are the line numbers of the commands in the history file. A higher number indicates a more recent command than one with a lower number.

If you want to obtain a list of commands within a specified number of lines, use the following command:

```
fc -l 117 119
```

This command lists the command numbers 117 through 119 in the history file:

```
117  ls
118  find . -print
119  vi test.c
```

You can also use *relative number* to list the commands. The following command lists all commands starting with the second to last command from the most recent command:

```
fc -l -2
```

The system response is as follows:

```
118  find . -print
119  vi test.c
120  rm test.c
```

If you want to obtain the list of commands in reverse order, you can use the following command:

```
fc -l -r -2
```

The system response is as follows:

```
117  rm test.c
118  vi test.c
118  find . -print
```

You can also execute just one of the commands in the history file using the -s flag with the fc command. If you want to execute the most recent command only, use the following command:

```
fc -s
```

If you want to execute the command at line 118, for example, you can use the following command:

```
fc -s 118
```

Moving Around in Command Space

The history of previous commands forms a command space in which you can use more vi commands to retrieve desired commands so that they may be edited and executed. In command space, remember these two directions:

- Up goes back in time toward older commands.
- Down goes forward in time toward the most recent commands.

Command space stops at the last command executed. You cannot go down/forward in time to see future commands you are about to execute (see Table 22.4).

Table 22.4 Retrieving Previous Commands to Edit

Command	Description
nk	Go up/back in time *n* lines and retrieve that command
nj	Go down/forward in time *n* lines and retrieve that command
nG	Retrieve line n from history
/word	Search up/back in time and retrieve last command that contains word
/	Repeat last search, going more up/back in time
n	Same as /, but does not need Enter to run
N	Same as n, but in reverse time direction
?word	Search down/forward in time and retrieve next command that contains word
?	Repeat last search, going more down/forward in time

Developing Complex Pipelines Using Command-Line Editing

Command-line editing enables you to do much more than just correct mistakes on the command line. It allows you to reliably build up complex pipelines on the command line that would not be possible or safe any other way. Let me demonstrate this in an example from real life.

The `lpstat` command shows print requests that I have submitted but that are still in the queue waiting to be printed:

```
$ lpstat
p215-2422            stevemor         1448    Sep 09 19:39
p104-2426            stevemor           29    Sep 11 09:37
p104-2427            stevemor         5347    Sep 11 09:37
p215-2431            stevemor           29    Sep 11 09:37
p215-2432            stevemor           29    Sep 11 09:38
p215-2433            stevemor           29    Sep 11 09:38
p215-2436            stevemor           29    Sep 11 09:46
p215-2437            stevemor           29    Sep 11 09:46
...
```

The `lpstat` command is covered in the section "Checking the Print Queue," in Chapter 8, "Displaying and Printing Files and Pipelines." In this example, notice that each line references one print job, and the first field of each line contains the request ID that starts with the printer name (p215 in this example) and the job request number. p215-2422 is the first request ID shown here.

The UNIX cancel command enables you to cancel a print request. To cancel many requests, you must type each request ID on the command line:

```
$ cancel p215-2422 p215-2431 p215-2432 ...
```

The cancel command is covered in the section "Canceling a Print Job," in Chapter 8. Now assume that there are hundreds of print jobs that I need to cancel, but I don't want to type in each request ID manually to cancel them. Assume that I want to cancel only jobs for p215, not for other printers. Assume that I don't want to cancel the first job p215-2422, so I can't cancel all jobs for p215.

Does it sound difficult to selectively cancel those print requests? Do you think you need a program to do something that complicated? Not at all. Watch how command-line editing allows you to handle this with ease. First, turn on command-line editing in case it was not on already:

```
$ exec ksh -o vi
```

The previous command puts you in the Korn shell with vi-style command-line editing enabled. Now, start the ball rolling by using awk to display just the first field of the lpstat output:

```
$ lpstat|awk '{print $1}'
p215-2422
p104-2426
p104-2427
p215-2431
p215-2432
p215-2433
p215-2436
p215-2437

...
```

Using awk as a filter to remove unwanted text in this way is covered in the section "Displaying Only Selected Fields," in Chapter 19, "Replacing or Removing Text from a File or Pipeline." Next, you want to retrieve the previous command so that you can build on it. Enter Esc and then the letter k. Your previous command will appear with the cursor at the start of the line:

```
$ lpstat|awk '{print $1}'

_
```

Enter A to append at the end of the line. The cursor will move there:

```
$ lpstat|awk '{print $1}'
```

Add a grep command to this pipeline so that you see only requests for p215. Then, press Enter to execute this pipeline:

```
$ lpstat|awk '{print $1}'|grep '^p215-'
p215-2422
p215-2431
p215-2432
p215-2433
p215-2436
p215-2437
...
```

Using grep as a filter to exclude lines in this way is covered in the section "Selecting Lines That Contain a Pattern," in Chapter 18, "Searching for Lines in a File or Pipeline." The caret (^) symbol is described in the section "Selecting Lines That Start with a Pattern," in Chapter 18. Again, do Esc k A and add a tail +2 command to exclude the first request ID, which you don't want to cancel per your original assumptions:

```
$ lpstat|awk '{print $1}'|grep '^p215-'|tail +2
p215-2431
p215-2432
p215-2433
p215-2436
p215-2437
...
```

Using tail to suppress beginning lines is covered in the section "Displaying Just the Ending Lines of a File or Pipeline," in Chapter 8. Now, do Esc k A to recall the previous command so that you can add on to the end of it. Add xargs cancel to the pipeline to cancel all the request IDs you have selected through this pipeline. Notice in the example that follows that the requests are canceled as you wanted. When you run lpstat again, you see that the requests you did not want to cancel are still there:

```
$ lpstat|awk '{print $1}'|grep '^p215-'|tail +2|xargs cancel
request "p215-2431" canceled
request "p215-2432" canceled
request "p215-2433" canceled
request "p215-2436" canceled
request "p215-2437" canceled
```

```
...
$ lpstat
p215-2422           stevemor          1448     Sep 09 19:39
p104-2426           stevemor            29     Sep 11 09:37
p104-2427           stevemor          5347     Sep 11 09:37
p104-2430           stevemor            29     Sep 11 09:37
$
```

Using xargs to process a list of items in this way is covered in the section "Using xargs to Process a List of Files," in Chapter 11, "Generating and Using File Lists." xargs was needed here because cancel normally wants the request IDs on the command line and will not look for them from standard input. On commercial UNIX systems, xargs will automatically run several cancel commands if there are too many request IDs that might overflow the command line if done in one command.

All the request IDS to be canceled are now gone, so your job is done. In the previous sequence, notice how command-line editing allowed you to develop complex pipelines one step at a time, testing each step to make sure that it was doing what you wanted.

Aliases

You can use the alias command to define a shortcut for a command string. There are two types of aliases: regular alias and tracked alias. A *tracked* alias shows you the complete path of the command.

You can use the alias command by itself to generate a list of all aliases set up in the current environment. If you use the -t command, as follows, then you will get a list of all tracked aliases:

```
alias -t
```

You can use the alias command to define an alias for a command or for a number of commands. In the following example, an alias is set up for the ls command as the ls command but with the -l option:

```
alias ls="ls -l"
```

chapter

23

Introducing the Emacs Editor

By Jesper Pedersen and
Steve "Mor" Moritsug

Starting Emacs

Binding keys

Defining macros

Searching and replacing text

Spell-checking documents

Major and minor modes

Getting help about Emacs

> **Tip for Beginners**
>
> This chapter describes a text editor called Emacs. It is usually not provided on most commercial versions of UNIX, but it often can be downloaded via the Internet. Learn the basics of vi first in Chapter 20 because vi is the one editor available on all flavors of UNIX. While not as wide spread as vi, Emacs offers many powerful features and is the editor of choice for many UNIX experts.

A text editor enables you to create and modify text documents that contain the letters and characters that you can type on your keyboard. With a word processor, on the other hand, you can not only edit text, but you can also change the presentation of that text by selecting the font size and style.

This chapter introduces you to the most advanced text editor available: Emacs. A common saying about Emacs illustrates its versatility: *If it can't be done in Emacs, it ain't worth doing at all.* The following list of some of Emacs' basic features gives you an idea about what this utility offers:

- An extremely useful undo facility.
- Autosaving files periodically. This guarantees that you lose only a minimal amount of your work in case of program/power/human failure.
- A lot of online help through the Info System (a hypertext format similar to the one used on the World Wide Web).
- Modes for different assignments, including functions and keyboard bindings to speed your work (for example, modes for writing HTML documents, C programs, and LaTeX documents).
- Spelling facilities (the `ispell` program, for example).
- Powerful macros that may speed up your work considerably.
- Incremental searches.
- Search and replace, using regular expression.
- Binding keys on your keyboard to your specific needs.

Emacs enables you to do almost anything—and everything—on your computer. The following list presents just some of the tasks worth doing in Emacs:

- Finding differences in text files.
- Reading/composing mail.
- Editing files on other filesystems.

Most important of all, Emacs is extremely configurable, which means that you can customize it to whatever your needs might be. This chapter presents a number of customization examples for your review.

Technical Terms

To really explain Emacs, it is necessary to introduce a few technical terms. The subject will become easier and more accessible when you understand these terms. A good understanding of these terms will also serve as a solid foundation on which to further build your knowledge about Emacs. Armed with an understanding of the following rudimentary terms, you can start searching constructively for information in the Emacs info pages:

- **Buffer**—A buffer is the basic editing unit in Emacs. One buffer corresponds to one text file being edited. Although you can have several buffers, you edit only one at a time. However, you can have several buffers visible simultaneously. Most often a buffer contains the text of a file you are editing.

- **Point**—The point refers to the place where text would appear if you inserted it into a given buffer. Each buffer has exactly one point.

- **Region**—The region is the text selected. Numerous functions may work either on the whole buffer or only on the region (for example, spell-checking).

- **Ctrl+X**—This is what Ctrl+X means: You press the Ctrl key and keep it down while you press X; then you release both.

- **M+X**—This is what Meta+X means: You press the key labeled Meta (or Alt, if no keys are labeled Meta) and keep it down while you press X; then you release both. If your keyboard does not have a Meta key, or if you are logged on using Telnet (where the Meta key might not work), you can use an alternative key sequence: Esc+X. You press the Escape key (often labeled Esc), release it, and then press X.

Starting Emacs

Emacs can run both with and without the presence of X windows. This chapter assumes that you have X windows, but don't worry if you don't; the following information doesn't require that you have it.

The Emacs Menu Bar

One difference between running Emacs with and without X is the presence of a menu bar at the top of the window. In newer versions of Emacs, however, you may find a menu bar when running in non-X mode (also called Text mode).

If your version of Emacs is earlier than 19.22, you should consider updating your Emacs installation. The newer versions have many features that make the upgrade worthwhile.

To start Emacs, just type `emacs`. This brings up a window that looks like the one in Figure 23.1.

```
 Buffers Files Tools Edit Search Help
 GNU Emacs 19.34.1 (i386-debian-linux-gnu, X toolkit) of Sun Mar 16 1997 on depre\
 ciation
 Copyright (C) 1996 Free Software Foundation, Inc.

 Type C-x C-c to exit Emacs.
 Type C-h for help; C-x u to undo changes.
 Type C-h t for a tutorial on using Emacs.
 Type C-h i to enter Info, which you can use to read GNU documentation.
 (`C-' means use the CTRL key.  `M-' means use the Meta (or Alt) key.
 If you have no Meta key, you may instead type ESC followed by the character.)

 C-mouse-3 (third mouse button, with Control) gets a mode-specific menu.

 If an Emacs session crashed recently,
 type M-x recover-session RET to recover the files you were editing.

 GNU Emacs comes with ABSOLUTELY NO WARRANTY; type C-h C-w for full details.
 You may give out copies of Emacs; type C-h C-c to see the conditions.
 Type C-h C-d for information on getting the latest version.

-----Emacs: *scratch*       (Lisp Interaction)--L18--All----------------------
 For information about the GNU Project and its goals, type C-h C-p.
```

FIGURE 23.1
The Emacs startup window.

The toolbar is at the top of the window. You can use this toolbar just like a toolbar in Microsoft Windows. Its content changes depending on what you are doing.

Below the toolbar is the buffer. At first, it contains some startup information. As you start to type, however, the buffer's content is replaced with your text.

At the bottom of the window is the status line, in reversed video. At the beginning of an Emacs session, this status bar contains the following information:

- To the left of the text `Emacs:` are five dashes. This indicates that the buffer is synchronized with the file on disk (that is, the content of the buffer is the same as the content of the file on disk). If the content of the buffer is changed, the five dashes will be replaced with the text `--**-`.

- Next to the text Emacs: is the name of the buffer. Because you haven't loaded any file yet, the buffer is just a dummy buffer named *scratch*. When you open a file, the filename will be located here.

- Next is information about which mode you have started (the text Fundamental). This could have been HTML, for example, if you had loaded the HTML mode.

- Next is the number of the line at which the point is located (the text L1).

- Finally, you see information about which part of the buffer you are looking at. All indicates that all the buffer is visible. Alternatives are: Bot at the bottom of the text; Top at the top of the text; and 8%, which means the current screen shows lines found 8% into the file.

Below the status line is an empty line. This line is used to interact with you when Emacs wants information from you.

Opening/Saving Files and Exiting Emacs

Emacs can open files using a mouse, if one is active on your UNIX station, or via keystrokes.

How to open a file using the mouse

1. From the Files menu, choose Open File.

2. Type the name of the file you wish to edit. (If you type a name of a file that does not exist, a new one will be created; then this new file will be opened.)

Now the file is loaded into a buffer, and you can edit it to your heart's content. To move around within the buffer, you use the cursor keys.

Entering Commands and Inserting Text

In contrast to vi, Emacs does not have an Editing mode and a Command mode. In Emacs, you enter commands by using the Ctrl key and the Meta key; you insert text by just typing it.

When you choose an item in the menu bar, you should be very attentive to the shortcut listed next to the item. If you learn these shortcuts, your interaction with Emacs will be substantially faster, and thus you will get more work done.

How to open a file without using the mouse

1. Press Ctrl+x, Ctrl+f.

2. Type the name of the file you wish to edit.

After you are finished editing your file, you can save it by pressing Ctrl+x, Ctrl+s, or by choosing Files, Save Buffer from the menu bar.

To exit Emacs, choose Exit Emacs from the Files menu, or use the shortcut Ctrl+x, Ctrl+c.

Using the Undo Facility

Emacs has a very powerful undo mechanism that can help you when you regret a modification. To undo a modification, go to the Edit menu and choose Undo. (Bound to Ctrl+_; this is the Ctrl key and then underscore.) If you perform several undo actions in succession, you will undo just as many corrections. Note that Emacs may collect several text insertion commands into one entity. This means that one undo command may remove several words.

A very important point to note about the Undo facility is that the undo actions may be undone as well. (That is, undo and redo are the same function.) An example may clarify the matter.

An example of an undo command

1. Start Emacs.
2. Type 1 2 3 4 on four separate lines.
3. Now undo until you have removed 3 and 4.
4. Type 5.
5. Now start undoing, and observe.

You will see that 5 is removed, and then 3 and 4 are inserted again. If you continue undoing, you will see that 4, 3, 2, and finally 1 will be removed.

Cut and Paste

A capability that makes the computer so much better than an ordinary typewriter is cut and paste: the possibility of moving text around in your documents, copying text into several places, and so forth. To mark a section of the text, you can use either the mouse or the keyboard.

Copying/cutting text using the mouse

1. Place the mouse over the beginning of the text you want to mark.
2. Press the left mouse button. While you keep the mouse button pressed, drag to the location where the selection should end.

Using the Mouse

You can use the mouse in Emacs or XEmacs only in one of its newer versions under X Windows.

3. Release the mouse button.

4. If you want to copy the text to the Clipboard (and don't want to delete it from the buffer), select the Edit menu and choose Copy. If you want to cut the text to the Clipboard (and delete it from the buffer), select the Edit menu and choose Cut.

Copying/cutting text using the keyboard

1. Place the point (the insertion cursor) at the start of the text you want to select.

2. Press Ctrl+spacebar (that is, the Ctrl key and the spacebar). At the bottom of the buffer, the text Mark set should appear.

3. Go to the location where you want the selection to end.

4. If you want to copy the text to the clipboard, press M+w. (M is the Meta key.) If you want to cut the text to the clipboard, press Ctrl+w.

Although remembering the key bindings may seem difficult, you should try very hard to do so; it will make your interaction with Emacs much faster. You won't need to grab the mouse, for example, when you want to cut and paste.

Pasting the most recent selection into the buffer using the mouse

1. Place the mouse over the point where you want to paste the text.

2. Press the middle mouse button.

Pasting the most recent selection into the buffer using the keyboard

1. Place the point at the location to which you want to paste.

2. Press Ctrl+y.

Remember that Emacs saves more than one step of undo information. The same is true regarding selections: You can paste a selection that is not the most recent one.

Pasting what is not the most recent selection into the buffer using the mouse

1. Place the point where you want to paste the text (either by moving with the cursor keys or by pressing the left mouse button at the location).

2. From the Edit menu, choose Select and Paste, and then choose the selection that you want to paste.

Pasting what is not the most recent selection into the buffer using the keyboard

1. Place the point at the location to which you want to paste.

2. Press Ctrl+y to paste the most recent selection.

3. Now you may go through the list of older selections by pressing M+y until you reach the selection you want.

Automatic Backups

Autosave Based on Key Strokes

Emacs determines when to autosave your program based on how many key strokes you have input since the last autosave. This can be changed in a parameter called auto-save-interval which is set by default to 300.

Emacs saves your buffers periodically to disk, to ensure that if by accident you should not save a buffer before exiting, it is not lost forever. When Emacs opens a file for which the backup file is newer, it suggests that you recover data from the autosaved file.

If you get the backup notification message, it might be a good idea to see what the difference is between the original file and the autosaved file, using the `diff` command. (The autosaved file has the same name as the original, except that the autosaved file has a pound sign (#) character at the beginning and at the end of its name.)

Recovering an autosaved file

1. Press M+x.

2. Type `recover-file` and press Enter.

3. Type the filename and press Enter.

4. Emacs asks whether you really mean it. If you still do, type `yes` and press Enter.

Binding Keys

You probably have three important questions on your mind right now:

- Why are the bindings so difficult and so nonintuitive?
- Is there any chance that I will ever learn all these strange bindings?
- Can I change the binding so that undo is bound to Ctrl+backspace, for example?

The short answers are "Don't you have more important things to worry about?," "Yes," and "Yes."

The more detailed answers follow.

To the question of whether you will ever learn all these different bindings, yes, you will. It will come with time, if you just force yourself not to use the mouse when alternatives are available.

The reason for the bindings is not very clear, but a good guess might be that it is because Emacs was not designed from scratch, but rather is a result of years of development. Because of backward-compatibility issues, the bindings are the way they are. There seems to be a general plan, however:

- All letters, numbers, and symbols on the keyboard insert the label given on the key, if pressed without either the Control or Meta key.

- A function that is used very often is available with either the Control or the Meta key pressed. (For example, *go to end of line* is bound to Ctrl+e, *undo* is bound to Ctrl+_ (that is, Control and underscore), and *paste* is bound to Ctrl+y.)

- If the Control prefix is bound to a function that works on characters for a given key, the Meta prefix works on words (if this gives any meaning for the given function). Likewise, if the Control prefix works on lines, the Meta prefix will work on sentences. Examples of this include the following: Ctrl+t transposes two characters; M+t transposes two words. Ctrl+e moves the point to the end of the line; M+e moves the point to the end of the sentence.

- Functions that are used more seldom are bound with a prefix Ctrl+x. Examples of this include the following: Ctrl+x, Ctrl+c exits Emacs; Ctrl+x 2 splits the window in two, with a buffer in each one.

- Function, which is specific to a given mode, is prefixed with Ctrl+c.

- Function, which is very seldom used, or which it would not be a good idea to have bound on the keyboard, is not bound at all but is accessible by pressing M+x and typing the name of the function.

How to see a list of all keyboard bindings

1. Press Ctrl+h, Ctrl+b. This should split the window. In one of the windows, a description of all bindings should appear.

2. Press Ctrl+x, o. This moves the selection to the window that contains the description.

3. Browse through the text with the arrow keys.

4. When you are finished, press Ctrl+x, 0 (zero) to bury the help buffer.

When you have found a function that sounds interesting, you can get more information about it.

How to see the description of a given function

1. Press Ctrl+h, f.

2. Type the function name that you want more information about (for example, `open-line`).

3. Press Ctrl+x, 1 to bury the window after you finish. (It is Ctrl+x, 1 this time because the selection is in the window that you want to keep.)

Now you're almost ready to rebind the keyboard to your personal preference. Before you do that, however, it is very useful to know which binding already exists for a given key. This information is retrieved by pressing Ctrl+h, c, and then pressing the key in mind. This action displays the function name for the function bound to this key. To get more information about the function, follow the previous instructions.

How to rebind a key

1. Press M+x.

2. Type `global-set-key` to bind the key in all buffers, or type `local-set-key` to bind only the key in the given buffer.

3. Press Enter.

4. Press the key that you want to rebind.

Key Binding with Ctrl+Shift

Different modes may rebind keys in defiance of that to which you have already bound them. This might be avoided by using Ctrl+Shift as a prefix for your own key bindings.

---

5. Type the function name you want to bind to the given key.

Now you can bind the keyboard just the way you want it. One thing you still need to learn, however, is how to save the bindings from session to session.

The file called `.emacs` located in your home directory is a setup file for Emacs. Information in this file is read each time Emacs starts. The file is writing in a language called *Emacs LISP*, or *elisp* for short.

The following description applies only to global key bindings. It is much more difficult to bind local keys because some sort of description of which buffers they apply to is needed. This is beyond the scope of this book.

How to save a key binding into the *.emacs* file

1. Create the key binding, as previously described.
2. Press M+x.
3. Type `repeat-complex-command` and press Enter.
4. Browse through the history list either with the up/down arrow keys, or press M+p and M+n until you get to a line that starts with (`global-set-key`).
5. Copy this line into the Clipboard.
6. Press Ctrl+g. (This will give a beep in your speaker, and the buffer should disappear.)
7. Open the file `.emacs` in your home directory.
8. Go to an appropriate location in this file, and paste. This should insert the text (`global-set-key`).
9. Save the file.

Defining Macros

Where Does Emacs Get Its Name?

The ability to define and use macros is a key feature of Emacs, whose name comes from the words *Editor MACroS*. Initially Emacs began as a set of macros, written by Guy Steele, for the TECO editor on a PDP-10. Richard M. Stallman, founder of the GNU Project and President of the Free Software Foundation, developed these initial macros into the Emacs utility.

One of the main things that computers are much better at than humans is trivial, repetitive work. Emacs has macros that help you to do such tasks. A *macro* is a facility that enables you to record a sequence of keystrokes for later playback.

How to record a macro

1. To start recording, enter Ctrl+x.
2. Make the keystrokes that you wish to record.
3. To end recording, enter Ctrl+x.

If you want to keep several macros defined at the same time, you need to name them.

How to name a keyboard macro

1. Press M+x.

2. Type `name-last-kbd-macro` and press Enter.

3. Type a name for the newly defined macro.

You can invoke the last defined keyboard macro (named or not) by pressing Ctrl+x, e. You can invoke a named keyboard macro by pressing M+X and typing it and then pressing Enter.

If you name a macro, you can bind it to a key (as described in the preceding section).

Macros survive only as long as Emacs. When you close Emacs, all the defined macros disappear unless you save them in the `.emacs` file.

How to save a macro into the *.emacs* file

1. Define the macro, as outlined previously.

2. Name the defined macro, as outlined previously.

3. If you want to bind the macro to a key, do so as outlined in the preceding section.

4. Open your `.emacs` file and go to an appropriate location in it.

5. Press Ctrl+1, M+x.

6. Type `insert-kbd-macro` and press Enter.

7. Type the name of the defined macro and press Enter.

Repeating Macros

When you have defined a macro, you want to use it often (maybe even a hundred times). To do this, you can use Emacs' repeating facility. If you press Ctrl and type a number (while keeping Ctrl pressed), the following command executes that many times. (This is not 100% correct, but in most cases it is so.) Thus, if you want to repeat a macro 20 times, press Ctrl+2 Ctrl+0 Ctrl+x, e. (This is Ctrl 20, and the keyboard prefix for executing a macro.)

Often, you will want to execute a macro on several lines. An example of this could be to insert > at the beginning of every line in a region of the text.

Using repeated macros to insert at the start of every line in a region

1. Record a macro that inserts > at the beginning of the line.

2. Go to the starting line of the region.

3. Press Ctrl+ and the key you have bound for this macro (Control+spacebar, for example).

Selecting with the Mouse

You can also complete steps 2 through 4 by using the mouse to select the region.

---

4. Go to the end of the region.

5. Press M+x.

6. Type `apply-macro-to-region-lines` and press Enter.

If you need to create a macro that involves inserting numbers (increasing or decreasing), go to the following FTP site:

`ftp://ftp.cis.ohio-state.edu/pub/emacs-lisp/functions/counter.el.Z`

This utility will not be described further here because it is not part of the standard emacs distribution. It is really easy to install, however, and it proves extremely useful. If the preceding site is busy, try the mirror site at the following:

`ftp://src.doc.ic.ac.uk/gnu/emacs`

If you ever catch yourself in a situation where the sound from the keyboard goes Tik taak tik tik, tik taak tik tik, Tik taak tik tik, it might be worth considering creating a macro!

Searching and Replacing Text

When you are writing programs or documents, you may often want to search for a given text in your document. Emacs has several functions for searching for text. This section describes these functions.

Another task that you often find yourself doing is replacing some text with another. There are three kinds of searches:

- **Ordinary searches**—In this kind of search, you type the text that you want to search for; Emacs will go to the first occurrence of this text. You can then ask it to go to the second occurrence, the third, and so on.

- **Incremental searches**—In this kind of search, Emacs starts the search as soon as you type the first letter. As you type more letters, Emacs searches further on in your document, to reflect the increased level of information about what you are searching for.

- **Regular searches**—In this kind of search, you can add wildcards, just like you do in the shell (although the wildcards are formed in a different way, called *regular expressions*).

You can replace text in two ways:

- **Ordinary search and replace**—In this strategy, you type the text that you want to replace and the text you want it substituted with. Then for each match, Emacs asks whether you want to replace this match.
- **Regular search and replace**—In regular search and replace, you can replace text by using regular expression. This way, you can replace \printf{...} with write ..., for example.

Incremental Searches

The search type most often used is the *incremental search*. Therefore, this section starts with that one.

To search forward using incremental search, press Ctrl+s. To search backward, press Ctrl+r.

After you have pressed either Ctrl+s or Ctrl+r, you can type the letters for which you are searching. Each time you add a new letter, Emacs tests whether the words found match (by searching using the previous letters). If this is not the case, Emacs searches further in your document. When you have added as many letters as you wish, you can press Ctrl+s or Ctrl+r to search further on with the letters typed so far. This way you can switch between typing letters and pressing either Ctrl+s or Ctrl+r.

Incremental search is much faster than ordinary search because you do not need to type the whole word. If you are searching for the word *miscellaneous*, for example, it might be enough just to type misc. If you do that using ordinary search and find that misc also matches the word *miscalculation*, which occurs several times in your document, you may have to start all over again in your ordinary search. In incremental search, however, all you have to do is type the letter e, which will make you search for *misce* (which doesn't match the word *miscalculation*).

Ordinary Searches

In one situation, an ordinary search is preferable to an incremental search—namely, when you have the word to search for on your Clipboard.

How to search using an ordinary search

1. Press Ctrl+s, or Ctrl+r and Return, for an ordinary search forward or ordinary search backward, respectively.

2. Type the letters you wish to search for. Or, in the case that the letters are located on the clipboard, press Ctrl+y.

Ordinary Search and Replace

Emacs has a function for replacing one sequence of letters with another. This function replaces text from the current position in the buffer through to the end of the buffer.

How to search and replace

1. Press M+%. (This is the function `query-replace`.)

2. Type the text that you want to replace, and press Enter.

3. Type the text that you want to insert, and press Enter.

Emacs will now go to the first occurrence of the text and ask what you want to do. You have the following possibilities:

- Press y to replace the occurrence and go to the next one.

- Press n to skip the occurrence and go to the next one.

- Press ! to replace the occurrence and all the following matches.

- Press q to stop the replacing.

- Press the comma key (,) to replace the current occurrence, but not move the cursor point immediately. (To restart replacement, press y.)

Regular Search and Replace

Two functions exist for regular expression incremental searches, bound to Ctrl+M+s and Ctrl+M+s for forward and backward searching. A function called `query-replace-regexp` (not bound to any key) exists for search and replace with regular expressions.

Regular expressions in UNIX have already been covered in previous chapters of this book. The following section shows you how Emacs can use the power of regular expressions.

SEE ALSO

➤ *For more information on regular expressions, see "Wildcard Pattern Matching in Lines," page 502*

➤ *Also see "Using Regular Expression Wildcards in the* sed *Search String," page 531*

Example: Replacing *printf("...")* with *write ...*

Imagine that you are rewriting a program to a different language and want to replace all the occurrences of the pattern `printf("...")` with `write ....`.

The text represented by the three dots should be the same after `write` as it is between the quotation marks. That is, `print("Hello world")` should be replaced with `write Hello world`. Ordinary replacement would not do here because the pattern `")` may occur in statements other than `print(".`

First, we have to create the regular expression, which matches `printf("...")`, where the three dots could be anything. This is done with the regular expression `\bprintf("\([^)]*\)")\b`. To explain this complicated expression, it is shown here broken down into eight numbered parts:

```
    \bprintf("\([^)]*\)")\b
1. \b
2.   printf("
3.           \(
4.            [^)]
5.                *
6.                 \)
7.                  ")
8.                    \b
```

Here is an explanation of each of the numbered parts in this example:

1. `\b` matches a word boundary. This way, the replacement will not replace, for example, `sprintf("...")` because of the s at the beginning.

2. This is just ordinary text to be matched.

3. This starts a regular grouping. This is necessary, if you wish to refer to the text between the brackets in the replacement.

4. The square brackets signal a list of characters to match. The ^ character at the beginning of this list says that the list should be negated. (That is, it is a list of characters that should not be matched.) All in all, this element says that a single character, different from a closing bracket, may be matched.

5. A star says that the preceding element may be matched any number of times. Together with the square bracket, this says that any number of characters may be read, as long as it is not an ending bracket.

6. This ends the group started in line 3.

7. Ordinary text to match.

8. This matches a word boundary (see line 1).

Regular expressions try to match as much as possible. Therefore, if line 4 had not said that an ending bracket was illegal, it would have read from the first `printf` to the very last one (any characters may be matched with a single dot).

Now you are ready to do the replacement that was just discussed.

Replacing *printf...* with *write...*

1. Press M+x.

2. Type `query-replace-regexp` and press Enter.

3. Type `\bprintf("\([^)]*\)")\b` and press Enter.

4. Type `write \1` and press Enter.

Now Emacs will ask you for permission to replace the first occurrences of `printf`....
Note the `\1` in the replacement string. It will be expanded to the text matched
between the `\(` and `\)` in the text that is replaced.

Compiling a List of Matches

Sometimes you want to see the whole list of lines that match a given text search.
This may be done with the function `list-matching-lines`. It is not bound to any key;
to access it, therefore, you need to use M+X. If this function is given a numeric prefix (which is given just like the repeating count, previously described—pressing Ctrl,
and typing the number while holding the Ctrl key), that many lines will be shown as
context.

How to get a list of all matches

1. If you want to see a context (that is, lines around the matching line), press Ctrl,
and while holding it down, press the number of lines to show as context.

2. Press M+x.

3. Type `list-matching-lines` and press Enter.

4. Type the text you are searching for. (Technically speaking, this is in fact a regu-
lar expression. As long as you are not searching for +,*,\(,\),\|, however, you
will never notice.)

Emacs will now split the window in two, where you will see the list in one of the
windows. By pressing the middle mouse button on one of the matches, you will
instruct the other window to update its view to show this match.

When you are finished, you can close the window with the list of matches by pressing either Ctrl+x, 1 (if you are located in the window you want to keep), or Ctrl+x, 0
(if you are located in the window you want to remove.)

Figure 23.2 shows an example of such a list that was created with a context of 1.

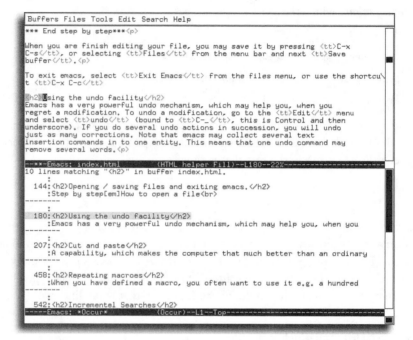

FIGURE 23.2
Showing a list of matches using `list-matching-lines`.

Case in Searches

Emacs is very configurable. You have already seen how the keyboard can be bound to your personal preferences. The built-in functions can be controlled using variables that instruct them how to work.

The `case-fold-search` variable tells Emacs whether searches should be case-sensitive. If its value is set to t (True in elisp), searches will not be case-sensitive. If, however, this is set to nil (False in Elisp), searches will be case-sensitive.

Enabling caseless searches

1. Press M+x.
2. Type `set-variable` and press Enter.
3. Type `case-fold-search`.
4. Type t to enable caseless searches, or nil to get cases in searches.
5. Press Enter.

Spell-Checking Documents

Emacs has a very useful interface called `ispell`: a spell-checker. If you don't have `ispell` installed on your system, you can download it via FTP from this site:

`ftp://ftp.gnu.org/pub/gnu/`

Basically, Emacs offers three functions: `ispell-word` (bound to M+$), `ispell-region`, and `ispell-buffer`.

To start `ispell`, press M+x and type the name of one of the functions (you have seen this process before). Now Emacs will start spell-checking. If you spell-check only a single word and the word is correct, it will display `miscellaneous is correct`. If you spell-check a region or the whole buffer, Emacs will display `Spell-checking done` when it is finished with your buffer.

In case of spelling errors, Emacs highlights the word that it failed to find in its dictionary and gives you a list of possibilities. You can select the correct word from this list by pressing the number listed next to the word, as shown in Figure 23.3.

FIGURE 23.3
Spell-checking with Emacs.

If Emacs doesn't guess the correct word, you can type it yourself by pressing r (for *replace*), typing the word, and finally pressing Enter. If the word is likely to be misspelled many times throughout the document, it might be a better idea to press a capital R, which asks for a replacement and afterward does a query-replace. This way you do not have to type the replacement string for each occurrence of the misspelled word.

On the other hand, if the word is a new technical expression that is spelled correctly, you can either press the spacebar to accept the word this time, press a to accept the word throughout the lifetime of the buffer, or press i (for *insert*) to insert the word into your personal dictionary.

A few extra options are available when using ispell. To see these, press Ctrl+h, f and type ispell-help.

Major and Minor Modes

When you are writing HTML documents, you will find that you want Emacs to be configured in one way. You will want it to be configured in quite a different way when you are writing C++ programs or ordinary letters (that is, such as ones that you send to your mother on her birthday).

Examples of differences between the two configurations include the following:

- The way text is indented. (In C++ mode, the indentation level should increase on opening braces and decrease on closing ones.)
- The set of functions bound to the Ctrl+c key prefix.
- The content of the menus. (C++ mode adds a menu entry called C++.)

All such configurations are saved in packages called *modes*. Modes exist for most programming languages, including C, C++, Java, Python, TCL, Assembler, HTML, LISP, TeX, AmsTeX, LaTeX, and many more.

Modes for a given *language* are called *major modes*. Another sort of modes (called *minor modes*) are those that add minor changes to the behavior of Emacs. You can have only one major mode loaded at a time, whereas you may have many minor modes loaded simultaneously. The set of minor modes that you want to have loaded might be the same in different major modes.

Examples of minor modes include the following:

- **Auto-fill mode**—When this minor mode is turned on, Emacs automatically inserts line breaks. You can configure at which column line breaks should occur by moving the cursor to that column and pressing Ctrl+x, f.
- **Mouse-avoidance mode**—When this minor mode is loaded, the cursor moves away if the point is getting to close.
- **Font-lock mode**—When Font-lock mode is enabled, text is fontified as you type it.

- **Auto-compress mode**—When this minor mode is active, Emacs automatically compresses and decompresses files.

- **Column-number mode**—When this minor mode is enabled, the column number appears in the status line.

To see a list of major modes, refer to the section titled "Getting Help," later in this chapter.

Loading Minor Modes

You can toggle a minor mode on and off by pressing M+X and typing its name.

Two types of minor modes exist: those that are independent of the buffer, and those that are buffer-dependent. In the preceding list, Mouse-avoidance mode, Auto-compress mode, and Column-number mode are buffer-independent; Auto-fill mode and Font-lock mode are buffer-dependent.

Buffer-independent minor modes that you want available by default can be started in the `.emacs` file by typing the mode's name in brackets. Consider the following:

```
; semicolon starts a comment in the .emacs file
(mouse-avoidance-mode) ; start mouse-avoidance-mode
                       ; in its default setup

    ; an alternative way of starting it, this
    ; time with an_argument, which
    ; describes how it should be started.
    ; Only one of these_commands should
    ; be used.
mouse-avoidance-mode 'exile)
```

Some of the minor modes may have an optional argument (such as Mouse-avoidance mode, just described). To see whether a given mode has any options, you should see the description of the function with the name of the mode (using Ctrl+f, f).

The buffer-dependent minor mode is a bit harder to start, by default. There is a general way to start a minor mode when a major mode is started, namely using *hooks*. Hooks are additional functions that can be invoked when a major mode is started. Each major mode has such a hook called *mode-name*-hook. The code needed in the `.emacs` file to start Auto-fill-mode when using the major mode Text mode is as follows:

```
(add-hook 'text-mode-hook
 (function
   (lambda ()
     (auto-fill-mode 1))))
```

Loading Major Modes

You can still select the major mode for a given buffer by pressing M+X and typing its name. However, you cannot turn it off that way (because a buffer always should have exactly one major mode). Therefore, to turn off a major mode, you must turn on another. (One major mode with almost no functionality exists and is called *fundamental mode*. You may switch to this one to turn off a given mode.)

You can tell Emacs to start a given major mode when loading a file by placing a special pattern on the first line of the file, which looks like this:

```
-*-Mode name-*-
```

To start C++ mode for a given file, you can insert this text:

```
// -*- c++-mode -*-
```

Note the two slashes at the beginning of the line, which tells the C++ compiler that this line is just a comment. This way, the C++ compiler will not try to compile the instruction to Emacs.

Another way to get Emacs to start a major mode automatically is to tell it which mode to start, depending on the filename. This way, you can tell Emacs that files ending in .c should be started in Ctrl+*mode*, files ending in .pas should be started in Pascal mode, and files ending in .doc should be started in Text mode. This is done by setting the variable to auto-mode-alist. You might use the following example as a template for this:

```
(setq auto-mode-alist (append (list
    '("\\.html" . html-helper-mode)
    '("Makefile"  . makefile-mode))
  auto-mode-alist))
```

The second line states that files ending in .html should be edited in the major mode called html-helper-mode, and the third line says that files called makefile should be edited in makefile-mode.

Before you start defining a lot of patterns this way, it might be worthwhile to inspect the variable auto-mode-alist first because many mode specifiers are defined by default. Check this out by pressing Ctrl+h, v, typing auto-mode-alist, and then pressing Enter.

Getting Help

Emacs offers a lot of help available online, ranging from descriptions of key bindings to a general introduction to Emacs. Common to it all is that this is available with the key prefix Ctrl+h. In the following list, you can get an overview of the available information:

- **Ctrl+h, Ctrl+h (`describe help`)**—This is the most important key binding for you to remember. This is the entrance to an index of all the key bindings.

- **Ctrl+h, f (`describe function`)**—Given a function name, this gives you documentation about that function. (You have already seen numerous examples of this.)

- **Ctrl+h, v (`describe variable`)**—Given a variable name, this function describes the variable. Variables are used to configure how Emacs works in different situations.

- **Ctrl+h, c (`describe key`)**—With this function, you may find out what a given key does.

- **Ctrl+h, w (`where is command`)**—When you have found a function that you like, you may want to find out whether it is bound to a key, and if so, where. This function helps you with this task.

- **Ctrl+h, a (`apropos`)**—This function proves very useful when you are searching for a function that will do a specific job. It enables you to type part of a command name, and then it gives you a list of all matches.

- **Ctrl+h, p (`find packages`)**—This function enables you to search for packages and modes based on categories. This is a very good way to find enhancements to your Emacs setup.

- **Ctrl+h, i (`load info`)**—This loads the info pages (see the following section).

Info Pages

If you press Ctrl+h, i, you will get into a huge world of information, namely the *info pages*. The info pages are much like HTML pages used on the Web, with hyperreferences between the different documents. If you start this journey by pressing the question mark (?) key, you will get to a page that contains the key bindings in the info system. The following are the four most important ones:

- If you press Enter on top of a reference, you will get to the document it refers to. (References are in bold face.) You can also follow a hyperlink by pressing the middle mouse button on top of the reference, if you have such a mouse.

- When you have followed a hyper-reference, you can go back to the document you came from by pressing the L key.
- The info pages are organized like a book, with sequential pages (in contrast to HTML documents, where several pages are possible as the next page for a given one). This way, you can read the info pages one by one. You can go to the next page by pressing n, and to the previous page by pressing p.
- If you press i, you will be asked for a word to look up in the index of the given info page set. Next, the page that describes this word will be loaded.

Figure 23.4 shows an example of an info page. At the first line, you can see references to the previous page (in page order) and to the page above. Note that there is no Next page; this is the last one in the given section.

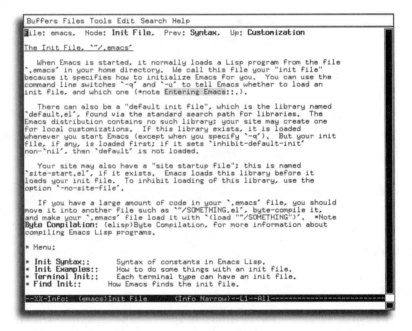

FIGURE 23.4
An info page.

In Figure 23.4, the text "Entering Emacs" is a hypertext reference, which is highlighted because the mouse was placed over the text when the screenshot was done. At the bottom of the window are four references to subsections.

Carrying on with Emacs

On the Web, you can find a reference card for Emacs at this site:

```
http://www.imada.ou.dk/Technical/Refcards/
```

This may help you with all the different key bindings. The author of this chapter, Jesper Pedersen, has written a program called the Dotfile Generator, which is very useful for beginners to Emacs. This is a configuration tool that helps you set up many of Emacs' variables. The Dotfile Generator can be downloaded from its home page at this site:

```
http://www.imada.ou.dk/~blackie/dotfile
```

You can find two manuals about elisp: a reference manual called `elisp-manual` and an introduction called `emacs-lisp-introduction`, at this site:

```
ftp://ftp.gnu.org/pub/gnu/
```

The introduction is for newcomers to programming.

Extra Emacs Packages

You have already seen many of the features of Emacs. However, one of its most powerful features is still to be explored. Namely, Emacs has the capability to be extended with user code. In one of the earlier sections, you saw how you could save your key bindings and macros in the .emacs file from session to session. You can also write entirely new functions, which may be accessible using M+X and another bound key.

Web Addresses Change Constantly

Don't be surprised if some of the Web URL addresses given in this chapter don't work after a while. Web content is constantly evolving and being reorganized. Sometimes the old page will refer you to the new page. Sometimes you just have to hunt around until you find it.

This capability is shared by users, literally. Many people have developed extra functions to be used with Emacs, and many of these functions are already shipped along with Emacs. On the Web, you can find more than a thousand packages for use with Emacs. Check out the following address:

```
ftp://ftp.cis.ohio-state.edu/pub/gnu/emacs
```

These packages include major modes, minor modes, and a lot of user functions.

Useful Emacs Functions

Table 23.1 lists Emacs functions.

Table 23.1	Useful Emacs Commands	
Function	**Bound to Which Key**	**Description**
downcase-word	M+l	Changes all the letters from the starting point to the end of the word to lowercase
capitalize-word	M+c	Makes the first letter uppercase, with the rest of the word in lowercase
upcase-word	M+u	Changes all the letters from the cursor point to the end of the word to uppercase
beginning-of-line	Ctrl+a	Moves the cursor point to the beginning of the line
end-of-line	Ctrl+e	Moves the cursor point to the end of the line
goto-line	Unbound	Queries the user for a line number and goes to that line
kill-line	Ctrl+k	Moves the text to the end of the line if the point isn't at the end of the line; otherwise, removes the line break
kill-buffer	Ctrl+x, k	Removes the current buffer
fill-paragraph	M+q	Rearranges the given paragraph so that all lines will be filled up

Emacs Info on the Web

For more information on Emacs, check out the Emacs home page:

http://www.gnu.org/software/emacs.html

Answers to frequently asked questions about Emacs can be found at the following Web page:

http://www.geek-girl.com/emacs/faq/

part

V

NETWORKING

chapter

24

Accessing Other UNIX Systems by Modem

James Edwards and
Steve "Mor" Moritsugu

Overview of modem communications

Controlling UNIX serial devices

Testing configurations with the
cu program

Configuring dial-in and dial-out
communications

Transferring files with the cu program

Transferring files and executing
programs with uucp

Extending the network through PPP

> **Tip for Beginners**
>
> Modems can be very frustrating and difficult to set up. A correct modem cable is particularly important because the modems use more serial signal lines than other devices. Note the section on Win modems that do not work with UNIX.

Accessing Other UNIX Systems by Modem

This chapter is concerned with the how-to of accessing other UNIX systems over modems. It provides step-by-step instructions to guide you through the more common tasks associated with this form of intersystem communications.

But first, some basics need to be covered. Remember, UNIX is a multiuser operating environment, and as such, it needs to implement some fundamental controls over the available (and shared) system resources. Before you can successfully make use of these resources, you must have a basic understanding of how they have been configured.

This chapter starts with some basic concepts. It begins by looking at some of the generic features and functionality of modem communications and some typical configuration requirements. After that, it focuses directly on how you need to configure your systems. It finishes with some specifics on how you can make use of these resources.

Adding a modem to your UNIX system makes it more available for both friends and foes. If a hacker discovers your modem phone number, there may be an attempt to break in or disrupt your system. Make sure that all user accounts have good passwords that are not easy to guess! Periodically check the Internet and user groups for information on security problems that might affect your system.

Don't Use Win Modems Under UNIX/Linux

Win modems are low-cost internal modems made more cheaply because the Windows driver software handles the function of the missing hardware. UNIX and Linux systems cannot use the Windows driver and thus cannot use these modems at all.

External Modems Are Not Win Modems

External modems plug into the COM1 or COM2 serial port using an external cable. These are not Win modems, so they should work under UNIX or Linux. External modems usually have a nice set of LED signals to help you watch the progress of your call and troubleshoot problems.

This is a list of terms often associated with Win modems and offers a good indication that they will not work under UNIX or Linux:

- Win modems
- Soft modems
- Software modems
- Rockwell HCF modems
- Most PCI modems
- HSP (Host Signal Processor) modems
- MWave modems
- DSP (Digital Signal Processor) modems
- Rockwell RPI modems
- Modems that require a minimum-speed Pentium

An Overview of Modem Communications

Modems are telephones for computers. Like any standard telephone, they can handle both incoming and outgoing data to and from any location. Modems speak their own language, which computers understand but humans don't. As such, when a modem dials a number, the call must be answered by another modem for any meaningful communication to occur. But telephones are like this, too. After all, what would be the point of making a telephone call to somebody who doesn't speak the same language as you?

When two modems are connected, it becomes possible to enable effective communication between the two remote hosts operating the modems. Typically, this communication enables such things as file and printer resource sharing and the execution of remote applications.

Figure 24.1 summarizes the events involved in establishing a connection between two remote hosts. This provides a useful guide for determining what devices are involved at each step of the connection process.

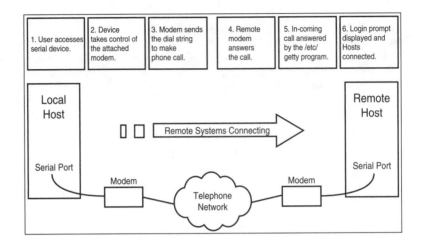

FIGURE 24.1
Connecting remote UNIX hosts.

UNIX Serial Devices

UNIX systems use special files known as *devices* to give users access to system hardware. These devices are commonly stored in the /dev subdirectory, with one or more files providing access to a specific piece of hardware.

The exact number and names of serial ports on any particular system depend on both the hardware configuration and the version of UNIX. Luckily, you can refer to some common standard implementations as a guide.

Typically, most hardware platforms have four serial ports, referred to as COM1, COM2, COM3, and COM4. Under Linux, the corresponding UNIX device files for these ports are commonly called /dev/ttyS0, /dev/ttyS1, /dev/ttyS2, and /dev/ttyS3. The exact names of these devices might vary slightly, depending on the flavor of UNIX you are running.

Thinking back to Figure 24.1, you will need to be able to configure UNIX to handle both dial-in and dial-out modem services. UNIX provides separate device files, depending on which service you want to use, and you should try to remember to use the right device. Devices providing dial-out services are typically called /dev/cua1, /dev/cua2, /dev/cua3, and /dev/cua4. The corresponding /dev/ttyS1 through /dev/ttyS4 devices are normally reserved for dial-in purposes.

Because your modem is physically attached to a serial port, your only access to it is through the corresponding device file. It's important to understand which ports are configured and available on your UNIX system. The tasks outlined in the next section help you check which serial device drivers are present.

Checking Serial Device Files

It's important to know which devices are available on your UNIX system.

Finding the available serial devices

1. Type `ls -l /dev/ttyS?` and press Enter.

2. A list of devices similar to the following appears:

```
crw--w--w-  1 root  root  4, 64 Mar 14 20:56 /dev/ttyS0
crw--w--w-  1 root  root  4, 65 Mar 14 20:56 /dev/ttyS1
crw--w--w-  1 root  root  4, 66 Mar 14 20:56 /dev/ttyS2
crw--w--w-  1 root  root  4, 67 Mar 14 20:56 /dev/ttyS3
```

3. Type `ls -l /dev/cua?` and press Enter.

4. A list of devices similar to the following appears:

```
crw--w--w-  1 root  uucp  5, 64 Mar 14 20:56 /dev/cua0
crw--w--w-  1 root  uucp  5, 65 Mar 14 20:56 /dev/cua1
crw--w--w-  1 root  uucp  5, 66 Mar 14 20:56 /dev/cua2
crw--w--w-  1 root  uucp  5, 67 Mar 14 20:56 /dev/cua3
```

The exact names of these device files might be different, depending on the UNIX version and flavor. For example, under most SCO UNIX implementations, the serial COM port device files for nonmodem lines are called /dev/ttyn*a*; modem lines are called /dev/ttynA, where *n* represents the serial port number.

Checking Serial Communication Configuration

Now that you have identified the devices that your UNIX hosts can make use of, you have some service configuration tasks to complete. These configuration tasks depend on whether you will be enabling dial-in or dial-out devices or a mixture of the two. One very important consideration is enabling effective access control. You need to ensure that after one user has grabbed a serial device, no other user can access that device until the connection has been dropped and the call has been completed.

Checking Serial Communication Dial-In Configurations

When a user dials in to your host, you want to present him with the standard login prompt, giving him system access following the supply of a valid username and password. UNIX systems achieve this through the interaction of four separate programs: init, getty, login, and shell. Figure 24.2 illustrates the cyclical relationship that exists between these four programs.

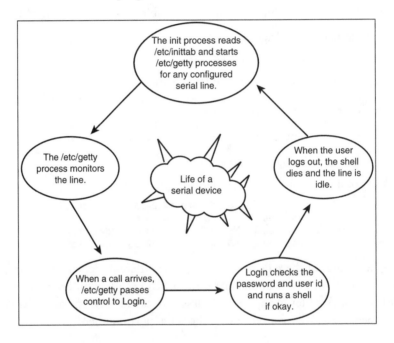

FIGURE 24.2
The SVR3 circle of serial device life: init, getty, login, and shell.

SVR4 and SVR5 Have No getty
UNIX System V Release 4 (SVR4) and Release 5 (SVR5) do not use a getty for each login port anymore. Instead, one tty monitor program controls logins on many ports.

The init process is the first real process to be run whenever you start the UNIX operating system. As such, it is an essential part of the operation of any UNIX system. UNIX relies on the init process to act as a launching pad for all other programs and to control all system devices. In reality, init is pretty dumb. It relies on a special configuration file called /etc/inittab to tell it what to do.

Listing 24.1 is an excerpt from the /etc/inittab file on my UNIX system. It serves as an example of how the init process exercises its power over the available serial devices.

Listing 24.1   A Sample */etc/inittab* File

```
# Serial lines
s1:45:respawn:/sbin/getty 19200 ttyS0
s2:45:respawn:/sbin/getty 19200 ttyS1
s3:45:respawn:/sbin/getty 19200 ttyS2
s4:45:respawn:/sbin/getty 19200 ttyS3
```

The syntax of any entry within the /etc/inittab file is fairly straightforward. Each entry consists of four distinct parts (*fields*) separated by a colon (:). The first field is called a *tag* and is simply an arbitrary value that provides an index within the /etc/inittab file. Listing 24.1 has separate tags labeled s1, s2, s3, and s4, each corresponding to the four available serial devices.

The second field tells the init process at which run level to execute that particular file entry. All the entries in Listing 24.1 are for run levels 4 and 5. The third field tells init what to do when the program indicated in the fourth field has finished. In Listing 24.1, this field contains the word *respawn*, which instructs the system to restart the program after it terminates. The fourth field is the most interesting because it contains the name of the program you want init to run. In this example, this is a program called /etc/getty. This program is run with two options. The first is the maximum bit rate of the attached modem, and the second is a serial device file /dev/ttyS1 through /dev/ttyS4.

Modems on SCO UnixWare 7

UnixWare 7 is UNIX SVR5 that has no gettys. Run scoadmin, hardware, Modem Manager. Modems can be set up as Incoming Only, Outgoing Only, or Incoming and Outgoing.

/etc/getty is a monitoring program. It reads the file called /etc/gettydefs, which is used to store configuration settings for any attached modems, including such things as the modem's supported data rate, flow control, and parity settings. The /etc/getty process reads /etc/gettydefs and waits for the modem to receive a call. When an incoming call arrives, /etc/getty fires up a login process, displays a login prompt to the user who is dialing in, and then terminates.

Having init assign /etc/getty to any of your serial device files provides an effective method of servicing dial-in user requests. When a call has been completed, the shell program terminates, and the init process respawns another /etc/getty process to watch for the next incoming call. In this manner, the circle of life for your serial devices continues.

Checking Serial Configuration for Dial-Out

To be able to dial out of your UNIX system, you need to be able to get control of a serial device from the /etc/getty process. This can be best achieved by editing the /etc/inittab entry for a particular serial device, changing the respawn setting in the third field to off:

```
S3:45:off:/etc/getty 19200 ttyS3
```

What if you want to make both outgoing and incoming calls? With the configuration just shown, you have no option but to install two modems and two telephone lines: one inbound and the other outbound. There is an alternative, however. It makes use of lock files that record when a serial device is in use, for either an inbound or an outbound call, preventing any other access to that device until the call has been completed. This alternative approach uses a program called /etc/uugetty and its associated configuration file, /etc/conf.uugetty.

Newer gettys are uugettys

On many newer UNIX systems, all the gettys are the equivalent of uugetty. If the port is configured as a modem in the Devices file, it uses the lock files to allow both dial-in and dial-out use.

Configuring a single serial device for both inbound and outbound access

1. Edit the /etc/inittab file using the vi command by typing vi /etc/inittab and pressing Enter.

2. Scroll through /etc/inittab to locate the existing entry for the serial device controlling the attached modem.

3. Place a # character at the start of the line to comment out the entry. The resulting line should look like this:
   ```
   #s2:45:respawn:/etc/getty 19200 ttyS2
   ```

4. Enter o to start a new line using the vi editor, and then enter the following text:

`S2:456:respawn:/etc/uugetty ttyS2 19200`

5. Save the /etc/inittab file and exit the vi program by pressing the Esc key and then Shift+ZZ.

6. After you have finished editing the /etc/inittab file, you must instruct the init process to read your new configurations. To do this, enter the following command at the shell prompt:

`kill -HUP 1`

The preceding procedure demonstrated how you can configure your UNIX system through the use of the /etc/uugetty program to accept and answer dial-in requests. It's important to note that, by running the /etc/uugetty program against any of your serial devices, that device will no longer be available for dialing out of your system. In the example, by running /etc/uugetty against the /dev/ttyS2 device, you effectively reserved that device to handle dial-in requests only. If you have only one modem and one telephone line, handling both dial-in and dial-out requests could prove tricky.

All is not lost, however. UNIX provides another set of serial device files that you can use for dial-out purposes. Under Linux systems, these files are called /dev/cua#, where # refers to the port number. For example, in the preceding procedure, you configured the /dev/ttyS2 device to accept dial-in calls. To use the same modem and telephone line for dial-out requests, you could use the corresponding dial-out device, /dev/cua2. As long as no one is dialing into the system at the same time, you can make an outbound call using the /dev/cua2 device and still leave /etc/uugetty free to monitor the connection for incoming calls.

Logging in Using the *cu* Program

Now that you have configured /etc/getty to watch for incoming calls, you can try to dial into the system. Most flavors of UNIX provide a standard communication program called cu, which stands for "call UNIX." The cu program is very rudimentary and doesn't have all the bells and whistles associated with many commercially available communication packages. However, cu is fully functional. This section explores how you can make use of this program to complete simple host-to-host communications. Administrators commonly reserve the use of the cu program as a troubleshooting tool because it provides a simple and effective way to test the configuration of serial devices, control files, and modems.

Before investigating the advanced features of cu, you should check your configurations.

Using *cu* to log in to another UNIX system

1. Start the cu program from the shell prompt by typing cu and pressing Enter. The program will return the following syntax statement:

   ```
   Usage: cu [options] [system or phone number]
   ```

2. My modem is attached to my COM3 port, so I would need to instruct cu to use the device /dev/cua2. At the shell prompt, I would type cu -l /dev/cua2 to start cu using this serial device. You should type the same command, substituting the device name you are using.

Only one Login per Port

The file /etc/inittab may have several entries for the same serial device. On SCO UNIX, the modem device file is in uppercase and the non-modem device is lowercase. Make sure that you enable only one login or getty process for any device. If it is mentioned on multiple lines in inittab, make sure only one line is set to respawn.

---

3. If everything has been configured correctly, the cu program will echo the word Connected and will await further instructions. If cu echoes a message similar to this one, you have a problem:

   ```
   cu: open (/dev/ttyS2): Permission denied
   cu: /dev/ttyS2: line in use
   ```

   A message similar to this one means that something else is using that particular serial line. That something else is probably the init process, which will likely be running /etc/getty.

4. Open the /etc/inittab file using the vi program and ensure that the entry for that serial line has been commented out. Remember, if you change the /etc/inittab file, you will need to tell the init process to reread the file. This can be done in one of two ways. Either type init q and press Enter, or type kill -HUP 1 and press Enter.

5. If the cu program responds by initially echoing Connected but then immediately echoes an error message stating cu: Got hangup signal, you are connecting to a serial line without a modem attached. Determine which line your modem is connected to, and rerun cu using the correct device.

6. If you were successful in connecting cu to the modem, type at. You might not see the characters as you type them, but you should see the word OK echoed to your screen. This message comes from your modem, which is telling you that it is alive and working.

7. Type ate1 and press Enter. The modem will echo OK to your screen. Now everything you type will be displayed.

8. Now try to connect to your remote host. Enter atdt, followed by the telephone number of your remote host's modem. The modem will ignore any spaces. If you are dialing through a PBX, you might need to dial a 9 first to access an outside circuit. You can type a comma to indicate a pause, allowing the switch some additional time to allocate the circuit.

9. The modem will dial the number and connect to the remote modem. At the remote host, the /etc/getty or /etc/uugetty program will notice the incoming call and issue a login prompt that will be echoed to your screen. Log in using your username and password.

10. To disconnect, type exit to quit the remote shell program. Then enter ~ (tilde). The system will respond by echoing the system name in parentheses. Ignore this and press .. The cu program will echo Disconnected and will return you to the shell prompt.

Configuring *cu*

It's possible to configure the cu program to place a call to a remote system without having to specify which particular device to use and without having to directly attach to the modem to dial the remote system's telephone number. In such a way, you can configure your system with one or more dial-out lines and ask the cu program to grab the first available line and automatically dial the telephone number you need.

The cu program uses four configuration files associated with the UUCP suite of programs. These configuration files normally reside in the subdirectory /usr/lib/uucp/ and are called Devices, Dialers, Systems, and Permissions.

Change to the /usr/lib/uucp/ subdirectory and type ls -l to display the files within the subdirectory. Look for the presence of your UUCP configuration files. If no files exist, you can create them from scratch. It is important to remember that these four configuration files are interrelated and must cross-reference each other in order to work successfully. The following procedure walks you through a sample configuration of these files.

Configuring *cu* files

1. Enter vi Devices (note the capital D in the filename). In this file, you need to define which serial ports you want to make available and set up references to these ports that can be used by the /usr/lib/uucp/Systems and /usr/lib/uucp/Dialers configuration files. The following code illustrates the syntax of entries within the Devices file:

```
# /usr/lib/uucp/Devices
#add a definition for each serial device that will be
used for dial out
modem   cua1    -    19200   hayes
modem   cua2    -    19200   hayes
modem   cua3    -    19200   hayes
modem   cua1    -    19200   hayes
```

Each line in the Devices file refers to a defined dial-out device within /dev. You identify the modem and the highest available modem speed, as well as a key word to identify the type of device attached to this port. Notice that all the entries use the same keyword, modem. In this way, a dial-out request will be capable of simply grabbing the first available port rather than waiting for a specific device to become free.

2. Enter a new line within the /usr/lib/uucp/Devices file by typing o and then modem *device* - 19200 hayes (replacing the word *device* with the name of your dial-out device file). Press Esc and then press Shift+ZZ to exit and save the /usr/lib/uucp/Devices file.

3. Now edit the /usr/lib/uucp/Dialers file by entering vi Dialers (again, note the uppercase D in the filename). In this file, you need to define the initialization settings that you want the cu or uucp program to send the modem. Here's an example:

```
# /usr/lib/uucp/Dialers
#add a definition for each modem defined in the
Drivers file
hayes  =W-,   ""ATZ OK ATDT\T CONNECT
```

4. You need to make a reference to the hayes keyword you placed in the /usr/lib/uucp/Devices file. Enter a new line by pressing o, and then enter the following line:

```
hayes   =W-,    "" ATZ OK ATDT\T CONNECT
```

The ATZ command resets the modem, with the expected return of OK from the modem. The ATDT command should be familiar from the previous section "Logging in Using the cu Program." The \T refers to the telephone number that is defined for the specified system and passed from the `/usr/lib/uucp/Systems` file.

5. Save and exit the `/usr/lib/uucp/Dialers` file by pressing Esc and then entering ZZ.

6. The `/usr/lib/uucp/Systems` file defines the name of the system to dial, the type of port that should be used, a schedule for allowing unattended connection (specifically, for uucp program use), the telephone number to dial, and some script commands to allow for automatic login once connected. Here's an example:

```
# /usr/lib/uucp/Systems
#add a definition for each remote system that users
will wish to access.
Horse MoTuWe0800-1700 modem 19200 123456 "" \n login:
-login: name word:pass
Jupiter Any modem 19200 123456 "" \n ogin:-ogin:
username word:password
Remote Any  modem 19200 12345678
```

7. Enter vi `/usr/lib/uucp/Systems` to edit this file. Press o to enter a new line, and type this line:

```
remote  Any  modem  19200 12345678
```

This defines an entry for the cu program to use to connect to your remote UNIX system at any time of day, using any device of type modem, as indicated in the `/usr/lib/uucp/Devices` file. In addition, you specify the bit rate at which to connect and the telephone number to dial. Save and exit the file by pressing Esc and ZZ.

8. On the remote UNIX system, you need to configure the `/usr/lib/uucp/Permissions` file to enable yourself to remotely log in and to define given read and write privileges that you want to make available. Open or create the `/usr/lib/uucp/Permissions` file, and add the following lines:

```
LOGNAME=local_machine MACHINE=local_machine
SENDFILES=yes
```

The `/usr/lib/uucp/Permissions` file is critical when you are allowing unattended uucp access to your UNIX host. In those circumstances, an entry for all hosts that you will allow access to should be defined within the file, and entries should be provided against the following keywords:

MACHINE   Gives the system name

LOGNAME   Gives the system name as it will appear in the logfiles

continues...

...continued

CALLBACK	Specifies a number to call back on once a connection has been made at a given number
REQUEST	Specifies whether a remote system can request files
SENDFILES	Specifies whether a remote system can send files
READ	Specifies which directories a remote system can read
WRITE	Specifies the directories a remote system can write to
COMMANDS	Specifies commands that uux can execute

9. Save the Permissions file and exit to the shell prompt by pressing Esc and then ZZ.

Using the *cu* Program

You can now make use of your new configuration files to improve the operation of the cu program. In addition, you can explore some other cu functionalities, such as transferring files.

Using *cu* to transfer a file

Warning

Although the cu program can transfer files between UNIX systems, it does so without employing any error checking or recovery. After the transfer is done, use **sum** -r on each system to checksum the two files. If the checksums do not match, the file was not correctly transferred. You may have to lower the baud rate if your phone lines do not allow a good transfer.

1. Log in to UNIX and type cu -z remote (where *remote* is the system name you specified within the /usr/lib/uucp/Systems file). If your version of UNIX objects to the -z option, leave it out. The cu program automatically connects to the remote system and returns the login prompt for your username and password.

2. Log in to the remote system. Then enter the command ~?. The cu program displays a list of available commands.

3. Enter ~%put to transfer a file to the remote host.

4. The cu program will prompt you for the local file to transfer to the remote system. Enter a local filename.

5. The cu program will prompt you for the name to call the file when it has been transferred to the remote system. You can use the same name by simply pressing Enter.

6. The cu program will indicate when the transfer has been completed.

7. Enter ~. to disconnect and return to the shell prompt.

Listing 24.2 illustrates the execution of the preceding steps, showing the transfer of the file /home/report to a remotely attached system. Note that it is also possible to use other escape sequences to transfer files. Enter the ~? command to list the available commands within your own implementation of the cu program.

LISTING 24.2 Transferring a File Using *cu*

```
~[local_host]?
[Escape sequences]
[~. hangup]    [~!CMD run shell]
[~$CMD stdout to remote]    [~|CMD stdin from remote]
[~+CMD stdin and stdout to remote]
[~# send break]    [~cDIR change directory]
[~> send file]    [~< receive file]
[~pFROM TO send to Unix]    [~tFROM TO receive from Unix]
[~sVAR VAL set variable]    [~sVAR set boolean]
[~s!VAR unset boolean]    [~v list variables]
[~z suspend]
[~%break send break]    [~%cd DIR change directory]
[~%put FROM TO send file]    [~%take FROM TO receive file]
[~%nostop no XON/XOFF]    [~%stop use XON/XOFF]
[connected]
~%put
file to send: /home/report
Remote file name [report]:
...
[file transfer complete]
[connected]
~.
Disconnected.
```

Running commands on the local system

1. Log in to UNIX and connect to a remote host using cu -z *remote* (where *remote* is the hostname of the remote system you configured within the

/usr/lib/uucp/Systems file). If your version of UNIX objects to the -z option, leave it out. After you're connected to the remote host, log in with a valid user name and password.

2. Create a new file called /home/cu_remote_file on the remote host by typing vi /home/cu_remote_file at a shell prompt. Press o and enter This is a test of the cu program. Press the Esc key and then enter ZZ to save the file and return to the shell prompt.

3. Enter the command sum cu_remote_file. The sum program will output two numbers: a 16-bit checksum of the file cu_remote_file, and an approximation of the size of the file. Write down both of these values.

4. Enter ~%take /home/cu_remote_file /home/cu_local_file to transfer the file to the local UNIX host and save it using the same filename.

   When cu indicates that the transfer is complete, you can check that the file has been transferred without errors by running the sum command on the transferred copy of the file.

5. Enter ~! /bin/sh to run a shell on the local system from within the cu program. At the shell prompt, type sum cu_local_file and then press Enter. As before, the sum program will output two numbers. Check these against those generated in step 3. If the transfer occurred with no errors, these numbers will be the same.

6. Type exit to return to the cu program. Log out of your remote connection and press ~. to exit the cu program.

After you have configured your files for cu operation, you can also run uucp commands.

Transferring Files via *uucp*

The initials *UUCP* stand for UNIX-to-UNIX Copy Program. This is not just one program, but it is a suite of utilities that provide a way to transfer files and execute applications across physically distributed UNIX platforms. The UUCP suite is most often employed for unattended file transfers, particularly for the moving of email between systems. However, it is possible for users to use these programs for their own file transfer requirements.

Creating a file transfer program

1. Log in to UNIX and create a test file called uucp_data.

2. At the shell prompt, enter this line:
   ```
   uucp uucp_data remote\!/home/uucp_data
   ```

3. Use vi to edit the /usr/lib/uucp/Systems file and add the following command to the entry you created for the host remote. After the telephone number, add the following test:

   ```
   " "" \r gin:-gin: <userid> word: <password>
   ```

   Replace *<userid>* and *<password>* with a valid username and password on host remote.

4. The uucp command will reference the /usr/lib/uucp/Systems file and locate the entry for host remote. When it finds the reference, a connection will be made to the remote host, and uucp will automatically log in using the username and password pair specified. When login is complete, the file uucp_data will be transferred, and uucp will terminate the connection.

Restricting Where Users Place Files

The /usr/lib/uucp/Permissions file must be edited to enable you to transfer your file to the specified location. In the preceding example, that was the case. However, it's good practice to restrict where on the remote system users are allowed to place files. Normally, this will be /usr/spool/uucp or /usr/spool/uucppublic.

---

5. The uucp program expects a number of parameters that offer useful additional functionality. It is possible to use the -m switch to force the system to return an email informing you when a transfer has been completed. Enter the following command at the shell prompt, and then press Enter:

   ```
   uucp -m uucp_data remote\!/home/uucp_data
   ```

6. Similarly, if you were copying a file to a remote system, you might want to inform a user on that system when the file arrives. You can do this through the -n switch. Use the following command to send an email to user Lauren located on the remote system when the file transfer has been completed:

   ```
   uucp -nlauren uucp_data remote\!/home/uucp_data
   ```

Running Remote Commands

The uux program is part of the uucp suite. It allows users with the proper permission to execute commands on remote UNIX hosts. Again, the execution of this command is controlled via the /usr/lib/uucp/Permissions file.

Running the *date* command remotely

1. Log in to UNIX and issue the command uux `remote\!date`.

2. The program executes the `date` command on the remote host and returns the result to your shell.

Typically, the uux command will not be executed directly by users but will be used as part of applications such as email and network news servers. For this reason, most systems will limit execution of rmail and rnews programs within the `/usr/lib/uucp/Permissions` file.

Checking on the Status of *uucp* Tasks

Users can check the status of any outstanding uucp file transfer request through the use of the uustat program.

Running *uustat*

1. Log in to UNIX; at the shell prompt, type uustat.

2. A list of currently queued jobs will be displayed. Here's an example:
   ```
   jupiter  02/14 - 20:45:00 (POLL)
   mars     02/14 - 20:53 S jupiter filename.txt 48871
   /home/james/docs/sams/uucp/filename.txt
   catfish  02/23 - 10:25:00 (POLL)
   ```

3. By default, uustat displays only those jobs queued by the user issuing the uustat command. To display all the jobs currently scheduled, type uustat -all.

You can run the uustat program with some optional parameters to find out additional information about the performance of the individual uucp programs.

Running *uustat* with parameters

1. Type uustat -e and press Enter. This provides a list of all currently queued program execution requests.

2. Type uustat -m and press Enter. This command generates a summary of the status of making connections to remote hosts. Here's an example:
   ```
   remote      05/23 - 10:15     CALLER SCRIPT FAILED
   dtcg02      05/30 - 11:30     LOGIN FAILED
   jupiter     05/30 - 11:30     CONN FAILED (CALLER
   SCRIPT FAILED)
   ```

The preceding code illustrates failed uucp connections to three hosts; remote, dtcg02, and jupiter.

Canceling a *uucp* Request

You can use the uustat program to cancel an outstanding uucp file transfer or program execution request.

Using *uustat* to cancel a *uucp* request

1. Log in to UNIX. At the shell prompt, edit the /usr/lib/uucp/Systems file by typing this line:

   ```
   vi /usr/lib/uucp/Systems
   ```

2. Press the o key to add a new line, and then type the following text:

   ```
   nohost Never modem 19200 123456
   ```

   This defines a new system called nohost that will never be called by the uucp programs.

3. Put a message into the uucp queue by issuing a transfer request to nohost that you know will never be sent. Enter the following and then press the Enter key:

   ```
   uucp /home/uucp_data nohost\!/home/uucp_data
   ```

4. Type uustat. You will see a code line similar to the following:

   ```
   nohostN001 nohost root 03-15 02:25 Sending
   /home/uucp_data (1864 bytes) to /home/uucp_data
   ```

Watch Caps Lock When Canceling with uustat

The command uustat -K (with an uppercase K) removes all currently queued uucp requests. When canceling jobs with uustat, make sure that the Caps Lock key hasn't been accidentally set.

---

5. To remove the transfer request, enter the following command:

   ```
   uustat -k nohostN001
   ```

Extending the Network by Modem (PPP)

The Point-to-Point Protocol (PPP) provides a way to transmit IP packets over a modem-to-modem connection. A PPP connection between two remote UNIX hosts provides a way for all remote users and applications to access one another over a single modem link rather than restricting communication to individual users at any one time.

In such a way, it is possible to use PPP to extend a network so that remote hosts can interoperate as if they were located on the same local LAN. However, it should be noted that the speed of communication between two systems connected over a dial-up line will be slower than if they were connected by a LAN.

Configuring a Simple PPP Connection

Three distinct parts are involved in configuring the operation of PPP upon any UNIX host: creating a PPP user account on the remote system (on the system accepting the incoming call), developing the chat script, and executing the PPP daemon. This section examines each in turn.

Creating a PPP user account

Editing /etc/passwd

Some UNIX systems, such as SCO UNIX, do not allow you to edit the /etc/passwd file directly. Use the scoadmin program to change the shell for a user.

1. It is advisable to set up and dedicate a special user account to control the execution of the PPP. Log in to UNIX as the root user on the remote system and create a new account. Then edit the /etc/passwd file so that it looks similar to the following:
```
ppp_user:e9prWE5B4fs:501:202:ppp execution account:
/tmp:/usr/lib/ppp/ppp-on
```
It should be noted that the GID and UID values will be system-specific, as will the password you create in the second field. The startup program is indicated as being the file /usr/lib/ppp/ppp-on, which is a configuration script that will turn ppp services on.

2. Before you can turn on PPP services, you must establish connectivity between your modems. This is similar to when you were logging in remotely using the cu program: Before you could enter a username and password on the remote system, you had to connect to get the local modem to dial the telephone number of the remote host. The chat program gives you an effective way to do this for PPP.

   Enter the following to create a new PPP chat script, and then press the Enter key:
```
vi /usr/lib/ppp/ppp-chat
```

3. Enter o to add the following line, substituting the correct username (typically ppp or ppp_user), password, and telephone number for your system:
```
ATZ OK ATDT12345678 CONNECT ogin: ppp word: <password>
```

Notice that the syntax employed by the chat program is very similar to the entries you made within the /usr/lib/uucp/Systems configuration files. The first entry resets the modem, and the modem sends out an OK. Then the chat script dials the telephone number of your remote host. When the CONNECT message and login prompt have been received, the chat script sends the username and again the password at the subsequent password prompt.

Save and exit the new /usr/lib/ppp/ppp-chat file by pressing Esc and then entering ZZ.

4. Create the shell script that will start the PPP connection by entering the following command:

```
vi /usr/lib/ppp/ppp-on
```

Then edit the file to contain the following entries:

```
#!/bin/sh
#script to activate ppp connection
pppd connect "chat -f /usr/lib/ppp/ppp-chat"
/dev/cua2 19200
-detach 130.100.0.5:130.200.0.20 defaultroute
```

Notice that in this example, the dial-out device for PPP has been set to /dev/cua2, and the local and remote IP addresses have been set to 130.100.0.5 and 130.200.0.20. You should amend this to reflect your system's configuration. When you have finished, press the Esc key and then enter ZZ to save the file and return to the shell prompt.

5. You need to set permissions on this file to allow the root user to execute the script and activate the PPP connection. To do this, enter this line:

```
chmod 744 /usr/lib/ppp/ppp-on
```

6. Establish the PPP link by running the shell script.

Stopping the PPP Connection

Removing an existing PPP connection is achieved by sending a hang-up signal to the pppd process ID (PID).

The pppd process will store its PID in the device lock file it creates in the subdirectory /var/lock. This file has a name relating to the serial device name. For my PPP configuration, I used the serial device /dev/cua2, so my lock file is called /var/lock/LCK..cua2.

PPP Connection Scripts

Many flavors of UNIX provide basic shell scripts to manually turn PPP connections on and off. These are used if PPP is not set for bring-up on demand. Although these scripts are commonly called `ppp-on`, `pppattach`, or `ppp-off`, their directory location can vary considerably among UNIX flavors. Type this line to locate these files on your system, and then press Enter:

```
find / -name 'ppp*' -print
```

Removing a PPP connection

1. Log in to UNIX as the root user, and enter `cat /var/lock/_LCK..cua2`. This echoes to the screen a number that is the PID of the `pppd` currently using the `/dev/cua2` serial device.

2. Tell the `pppd` to terminate by sending it the hang-up signal using the `kill` command `kill -HUP PID`, where `PID` is the number returned in step 1.

A Final Note

This chapter explained how you can gain access to the modems connected to your UNIX system. However, it is worth remembering that among the many flavors of UNIX, the filenames of some system devices might have some slight differences.

It should be noted that over the past few years, other more efficient and more effective methods for transferring files between UNIX hosts have steadily replaced the use of UUCP. It would be fair to say that it has become fairly uncommon to find a UNIX host that relies on UUCP as a file-transfer mechanism. Much of the downfall of UUCP can be attributed to the increased adoption of the use of the `sendmail` program to transfer email messages. But the increased ubiquity of the hosts being permanently connected to the Internet hasn't helped its cause. If hosts are to be continuously connected through the Internet, there is value in adopting a batched file transfer method.

In part, UUCP's loss has been PPP's gain, with the adoption of PPP-enabled connections as the favored way of providing connectivity to the Internet. This chapter illustrated how you might configure a UNIX host to establish an ephemeral PPP connection. However, it should be noted that most PPP connections are established as permanent connections and that the `ppp-off` script is never run.

chapter

25

Accessing Other UNIX Systems on the Network or Internet

*James Edwards and
Steve "Mor" Moritsug*

Checking IP addresses and network
connections

Testing a connection with `ping`

Checking whether domain name
services are running

Logging on to UNIX over the network

Transferring files across the network

Executing commands on another
system in the network

Accessing a remote filesystem (NFS)

Using `mailx` to handle email

Tip for Beginners

Many UNIX systems are connected in a local area network using Ethernet cards. This network can be extended using routers to include remote systems. The coverage in this chapter of IP addresses, `ping`, Telnet, and `ftp` will help you in those situations.

The TCP/IP suite of protocols is at the very heart of networking UNIX systems. This chapter addresses the operation of these protocols. Although this one chapter won't turn you into a TCP/IP guru, you will get sufficient information and guidance that will enable you to sufficiently use the protocols and connect into a network.

Some Important Networking Concepts

Before you begin, you need to cover some basics. Networking involves a number of hardware and software components that must be installed and configured. Figure 25.1 provides a useful starting point, illustrating how these components fit together to provide network connectivity.

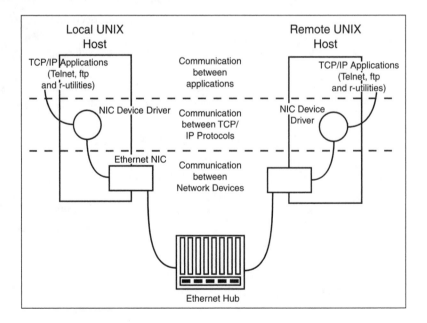

FIGURE 25.1
Components of network connectivity.

Figure 25.1 illustrates a UNIX host connecting to an Ethernet network and using the TCP/IP protocols to communicate with a neighboring host. How does all this fit together? The Ethernet network provides you a foundation for communication, a way for your hosts to be physically connected. After tour hosts are connected, they can communicate through the TCP/IP protocols. These protocols provide the hosts with a way to do things to each other, such as execute remote programs, share resources, and transfer files.

Ethernet is by far the most common form of physical network transport. Other forms do exist, however, including token ring, FDDI, and Asynchronous Transfer Mode (ATM), some of which may sound familiar. Although each of these network types employs distinct features and functionality, and although all require very different configuration, some similarities do exist. In fact, the same general connectivity components outlined in Figure 25.1 hold true across all these physical network types. This chapter examines Ethernet in detail because it is the most likely network form you will need to interface with.

Checking Your Network Connections

You begin by physically attaching your system to the network. This is accomplished through the use of a network interface card, or NIC (pronounced *nick*). The NIC will need to be physically installed within your UNIX system. A number of connection points off the system's motherboard—referred to as *slots*—are specifically reserved for the purpose. In fact, many UNIX systems are commonly shipped from the manufacturer with a NIC already installed.

After the NIC has been physically installed within your system, you must tell UNIX how to identify and communicate with it. In UNIX, all communication to system hardware is handled through special files called devices. These devices must be configured within the UNIX kernel. Therefore, when you add a new NIC, you need to ensure that a corresponding device file has been made available to the kernel.

More often than not, your system will automatically detect the existence and current configuration of an installed NIC upon system boot. With some UNIX flavors, however, it is necessary to run a standard configuration program to tell the system about a freshly added NIC and how to communicate with it.

The configuration program that you will need to run depends on the flavor of UNIX that you are using. These programs are more often than not menu-driven and guide the user through the configuration of a new device.

A relatively simple way to ensure that a new device entry has been recognized by the UNIX kernel is to look at the messages displayed as the system boots. The following tasks illustrate how this might be achieved on a PC-based UNIX system.

As any UNIX system boots, it echoes device configuration and initialization messages to the console. These messages may flash by quickly, making examination very difficult. Thankfully, however, these messages are also written to a special log that can be displayed using the dmesg command.

Displaying internal NIC information

1. Type the command dmesg | more and look for references to the Ethernet devices.

If dmesg Does Not Show Your Devices

On some UNIX systems, dmesg shows very limited output. Look for system bootup messages in /usr/adm/messages, /var/adm/messages, /usr/adm/syslog, or /var/adm/syslog.

---

2. Depending on your system's boot process, it is possible that the dmesg is too big and unwieldy to leaf through looking for a reference to an Ethernet driver. If so, type dmesg | grep eth to pinpoint any defined device. Listing 25.1 illustrates the result of this command on my dmesg file.

Listing 25.1 Searching for an Ethernet Card

```
# dmesg | grep eth
eth0: WD80x3 at 0x300, 00 00 C0 FE 55 28, IRQ 5, 0xca000
#
```

3. The output from dmesg displays the current configuration of the installed NIC. In Listing 25.1, the UNIX device eth0 corresponds to the NIC installed using IRQ 5, at memory address ca000 and using I/O channel 300. These values were the defaults that the manufacturer provided. If you want to change any of these values, you must follow the NIC manufacturer's instructions for doing so.

4. Now that you know how the UNIX system refers to the installed NIC, you can configure it for operation through the use of the interface configuration program called ifconfig (pronounced *i f config*). Many, but not all, flavors of UNIX provide a way to confirm the presence of a defined device through the netstat command. Type netstat −i and press Enter. This command displays the status

of all system interfaces; any unconfigured interfaces will have an asterisk next to their device name.

Checking IP Addresses

Each NIC must be allocated a unique address for the TCP/IP protocols to work. An assigned IP address is taken from an available 32-bit binary address space. For simplicity and ease of use, however, you can reference this address space using a concept referred to as decimal dot notation.

The operation of decimal dot notation calls for a 32-bit IP address to be divided into four equal parts, with each part being 8 bits long. Each of these 8-bit values can then be represented as a decimal number value, with each decimal number separated from the next by a dot (.). Listing 25.2 illustrates this point; notice how it becomes far easier to refer to an address as it is divided and then represented as decimal numbers.

Listing 25.2   Representing Binary IP Addresses Through Decimal Dot Notation

```
00000110000000110000000010000000001      - 32-bit binary value
00000110 00000110 00000010 00000001     - Divided into 4 equal parts
   6  .   6  .   2  .   1               - Represent each as a decimal value
```

Remember that you use TCP/IP protocols to move data between different hosts within networks. To successfully achieve this, each host needs a unique IP address. In fact, a network host can have more than one IP address: one for each NIC installed. You can use a standard program called `ifconfig` to assign an IP address to NIC. The following task list provides a quick example:

1. Log on to UNIX as root (only the root user can execute the `ifconfig` command).

2. At the command line, type `ifconfig eth0 130.100.10.1`, replacing the entry `eth0` with the installed and configured NIC device name, and replacing `130.100.10.1` with the IP address that you want to assign to this interface.

3. You can also run the `ifconfig` command to report the configuration of any installed interface. To do this, type `ifconfig –a`. The use of the –a switch tells `ifconfig` to report the configuration for all installed interfaces. Listing 25.3 provides an example.

Listing 25.3 *ifconfig* Configuration Details

```
#ifconfig -a
le0:flags=63<UP, BROADCAST, NOTRAILERS, RUNNING>
    inet 10.252.10.66 netmask fffffffe0 broadcast 10.252.10.95
eth0: flags=63<UP, BROADCAST, NOTRAILERS, RUNNING>
    inet  130.100.10.1  netmask  ffff0000 broadcast  130.100.255.255
eth1: flags=63<UP, BROADCAST, NOTRAILERS, RUNNING>
    inet  10.252.10.33  netmask  ffffffe0 broadcast  10.252.10.63
```

Notice in Listing 25.3 that `ifconfig` reports back that interface eth0 has an IP address of 130.100.10.1 and a broadcast address of 130.100.255.255. To understand IP addresses, you need to be aware that the address identifies both a host address and a network address. The netmask value is used to tell UNIX which part of the IP address is the host part and which is the network part.

A netmask is constructed to cover the network part of the address with binary 1s, which equals a value of 255 for each of the decimal numbers within Decimal Dot Notation. If you apply the provided netmask value to any IP address, it will reveal both the host and the network portion of an address. The example in Listing 25.4 provides an example of how a mask might be used.

Listing 25.4 Examining the netmask Value

```
00000110 00000110 00000010 00000001  - Divided into 4 equal parts
   6  .  6  .  2  .  1              - Represent each as a decimal value


 255  . 255  .  0  .  0              - the decimal mask value
11111111 11111111 00000000 00000000  - the same mask in binary


              2  .  1              - mask 0's show the host address


   6  .  6                         - mask 1's show the network address
```

Overall, the IP address space is divided into three main groups, referred to as address classes. Each of these classes provides an address space that is suited to a specific type of network. Table 25.1 details the breakdown of these classes, indicating the address range and the typical network use.

Table 25.1 Understanding the Entire IP Address Space

Classes	Address Range	Default Mask	Typical Use and Function
Class A	1.0.0.0 to 127.255.255.255	255.0.0.0	Class A addresses contain a small number of network addresses, but each network can address more than 16 million hosts.
Class B	128.0.0.0 to 191.255.255.255	255.255.0.0	The Class B address space provides for a large number of medium-size networks that each contain more than 64,000 hosts each.
Class C	192.0.0.0 to 223.255.255.255	255.255.255.0	The Class C address space provides for millions of small-scale networks, each holding a maximum of 254 hosts in each network.

The address space above the Class C limit of 223.255.255.255 is reserved and should be ignored.

Table 25.1 indicates that you can tell the class that an IP address belongs to just by looking at the first decimal number of the address; by using the default mask value, you can automatically determine both the network number and the host address.

When you configure IP addresses, you can optionally use the default mask value, or you can alternatively specify your own mask, enabling the capability to refer to more networks, each containing fewer hosts. These additional networks are referred to as subnetworks because they are a subset of the address class; the netmask is now referred to as a subnet mask. You can use the ifconfig program to define subnet mask values.

Setting the IP address and netmask

1. Log on to UNIX as the root administrator. Type ifconfig a to report the current configuration of all the interfaces installed in your system. Select one interface (I use the interface eth0, but you should substitute references to that interface with your own).

2. Type ifconfig eth0 130.100.10.1, and then press Enter.

3. Type ifconfig eth0. Notice that the netmask value is set to the Class B default of 255.255.0.0 or, if your system displays this only in hexadecimal, ffffffff0000.

4. Type ifconfig eth0 130.100.10.1 netmask 255.255.255.0, and then press Enter.

5. Type `ifconfig eth0`. Notice that the netmask value is now set to a value of `255.255.255.0` or, if your system displays this only in hexadecimal, `ffffffffffff00`.

The `ifconfig` program has a number of additional options that enable a user to make changes to the way the TCP/IP protocols operate over a given interface. The details of these settings are beyond the scope of this chapter. For a more detailed break-down of functions, refer to the UNIX man pages. Before leaving the `ifconfig` pro-gram, it is useful to make one last change: to set the broadcast value.

In the development of TCP/IP protocols, two schools of thought developed relating to how an interface should send a packet to all the hosts on any network. Remember from previous discussion that an IP address consists of both a host and a network portion. Both approaches agreed that the network portion of the IP address would need to be identified, but one approach decided that all hosts within this network would be identified using all 1s in the host portion of the address, while the other specified all 0s. Over time, the all-1s broadcast won dominance. By far, it is now the most commonly found setting. Because the option exists, however, it is important that you check your interface configurations to ensure that you are using the correct setting.

Make a task list to illustrate the use of the `ifconfig` program to report interface con-figuration and note broadcast of all 0s and then to change this to all 1s. The list also illustrates the complete use of the `ifconfig` command to include the IP address, the subnet mask, and the broadcast address.

Setting the broadcast address

1. Log on to UNIX as the root administrator, and type the following command (substituting the specified values to match your own configurations and address requirements): `ifconfig eth0 130.100.10.1 netmask 255.255.255.0 broadcast 130.100.10.0`. Then press Enter.

2. Type `ifconfig eth0` and notice that the broadcast address for this interface has been set to `130.100.10.0`.

3. Now configure the interface for an all-1s broadcast (remember that this is the most commonly used setting). To do this, type the following commands: `ifcon-fig eth0 130.100.10.1 netmask 255.255.255.0 broadcast 130.100.10.255`, and then press Enter.

4. Type `ifconfig eth0`, and notice that the broadcast address for this interface now has been set to `130.100.10.255`.

Naming a UNIX Host

Referring to UNIX hosts through IP addresses can and will prove somewhat cumbersome; you can make things easier by giving your host a name. To do this, you provide an entry in the hosts /etc/hosts file:

Viewing and modifying the *hosts* file

1. Log on to UNIX as the root administrator (changing the hostname is one of those things that only root can do).

2. The /etc/hosts file is used to associate a hostname with the IP address of your system. When you refer to this hostname, the system references the /etc/hosts file to determine the corresponding IP address. The /etc/hosts file can be extended to include references to other hosts that you need access to.

3. Now edit the /etc/hosts file. Type in the command vi /etc/hosts, and then press Enter. Listing 25.5 provides an example of an /etc/hosts file. Notice how entries are arranged within this file.

4. Each line in the /etc/hosts file provides a hostname to IP address mapping. Multiple hostnames, known as aliases, can be provided to any individual IP address. Press o to add a new line to the /etc/hosts file. Enter the IP address of one of the interfaces in your host, press the Tab key, and enter a hostname.

5. In the example outlined in Listing 25.5, I added a host entry for IP address 130.100.50.1 of fin.sales.catfish.com. Save and exit the /etc/hosts file by pressing the Esc key and then Shift+ZZ.

Listing 25.5 provides a sample /etc/hosts file. Each entry relates an IP address to a given hostname.

Listing 25.5 Example */etc/hosts* File

```
#
# include and entry for the loopback interface
127.0.0.1               localhost


# include entries for host machines here
# IP address              hostname    alternative    names
#
130.100.10.1            www.catfish.com     web
130.100.10.10           man.catfish.com     manhost     loghost
```

continues...

Listing 25.5   Continued

```
130.100.50.1          fin.sales.catfish.com
10.10.4.2             mars.catfish.com      mars
#
# corporate nameserver
10.193.10.1           dns.catfish.com       dns      namessrv
```

Notice in Listing 25.5 that the entry for IP address 130.100.10.1 contained two hostname entries: `www.catfish.com` and `web`. It is possible to associate multiple names to the same IP address; these alternative names are referred to as aliases. Now edit your `/etc/hosts` file and add an alias to this file. In my example, I add an alias to the host 130.100.50.1 currently called `fin.sales.catfish.com`.

Adding an alias to the *hosts* file

1. Log in to UNIX as root, and type the command `vi /etc/hosts`. Then press Enter.

2. Scroll down to the line you need to add an entry for within the `/etc/hosts` file. You can do this by pressing the `j` key or the down-arrow key. In my example, I move down to the 130.100.50.1 entry and move to the end of the line.

3. Press a to add to this line, and add the new alias. Type the new hostname `accounts`.

Testing a Connection with *ping*

The `ping` program is easily the most commonly used utility within TCP/IP networks. The `ping` program is used to test network connectivity between hosts. This is accomplished through the operation of something called the Internet Control Message Protocol—or more simply, ICMP.

The `ping` program works by sending an ICMP ECHO REQUEST packet to a remote host. When this host receives the packet, it returns an ICMP ECHO_RESPONSE packet. In such a way, you can use the `ping` utility for two purposes: to confirm the end-to-end connectivity between hosts, and to provide a measure of the round-trip delay or how quickly you can reach any remote host.

Testing a connection using *ping*

1. Log on to UNIX. You don't have to use the root account; anyone can run the `ping` command.

2. Now ping the new interface you just added. Type in the following commands (replacing my IP address for the one you used), and then press Enter: ping 130.100.10.1. The ping command should respond with output similar to that in Listing 25.6.

Listing 25.6 An Example of the *ping* Program

```
#  ping 130.100.10.1

ping  130.100.10.1(130.100.10.1):  56 data bytes
64 bytes from 130.100.10.1: icmp_seq=0. ttl=252 time=215. ms
64 bytes from 130.100.10.1: icmp_seq=1. ttl=252 time=216. ms
64 bytes from 130.100.10.1: icmp_seq=2. ttl=252 time=217. ms
64 bytes from 130.100.10.1: icmp_seq=3. ttl=252 time=216. ms
64 bytes from 130.100.10.1: icmp_seq=4. ttl=252 time=216. ms
^c
---PING STATISTICS------------------------------
5 packets transmitted, 5 packets received, 0% packet loss
round-trip min/avg/max = 215/216/217
#
#
```

Depending on the UNIX version, aix, sco, and linux all work as in Listing 25.6. In addition, TCP/IP implementation on other PC OS works in this manner. However, the version of ping found with Solaris works as you outline. (This fact is addressed in the note that follows the task list.)

3. Listing 25.6 illustrates the use of ping to test the connectivity to the IP address 130.100.10.1.

ping Options

The implementation of the ping program can differ somewhat between UNIX implementations, requiring different switch settings to be used to enable certain functionality. If you type ping mars.catfish.com on a Sun workstation, for example, you would expect the response mars.catfish.com is alive. If you wanted to obtain similar statistics as displayed in Listings 25.6 and 25.7, you would need to use the -s switch and specify both the packet data size and the number of ECHO_REQUEST packets that you wanted to send. The command ping -s mars.catfish.com 56 5, for example, would tell ping to send 56 bytes of data in five separate request packets to the remote host mars.catfish.com.

4. It is possible to instruct ping as to how many ICMP packets it should send to the remote destination; in the examples here, you didn't indicate any amounts, so the command needed to be terminated with a control-break. By default, a data packet is 56 bytes in length; to this is added an 8-byte ICMP header. The remote host returns ECHO_RESPONSE packets. For each of these packets, the ping utility displays an increasing sequence number, a time-to-live (ttl) value (which is decremented for every gateway the packet passes through), and a round-trip delay recorded in milliseconds.

5. It is also possible to specify a hostname rather than an IP address. If this is done, ping will need to first look up the hostname before executing the connectivity test. Type in the following command and then press Enter:

```
ping mars.catfish.com.
```

Listing 25.7 Another Example of the *ping* Program

```
#  ping mars.catfish.com

ping  mars.catfish.com(130.100.10.1) :  56 data bytes
64 bytes from 130.100.10.1: icmp_seq=0. ttl=252 time=215. ms
64 bytes from 130.100.10.1: icmp_seq=1. ttl=252 time=216. ms
64 bytes from 130.100.10.1: icmp_seq=2. ttl=252 time=217. ms
64 bytes from 130.100.10.1: icmp_seq=3. ttl=252 time=216. ms
64 bytes from 130.100.10.1: icmp_seq=4. ttl=252 time=216. ms
^c
---PING STATISTICS------------------------------
5 packets transmitted, 5 packets received, 0% packet loss
round-trip min/avg/max = 215/216/217
#
#
```

Checking Whether Domain Name Services Are Running

The preceding section outlined the operation of the /etc/hosts file and indicated how this file provides a convenient way to map between IP addresses and hostnames. One of the limitations of using the /etc/hosts file is that you need to ensure that all hosts within the network have the same address mappings. This obviously raises some potentially huge maintenance issues as the number of hosts of your networks increase. More importantly, imagine how ineffective Internet access would be if you had to create an entry in your /etc/hosts file containing the IP addresses of any host you wanted to access.

Obviously, an alternative approach is necessary. That alternative is the domain name system (DNS). The DNS provides hostname-to-IP-address mapping through a collection of hierarchical databases.

With the aid of DNS, it is possible to query a single host, the domain name server, and locate any networked host. Now a domain name server will track IP addresses and hostnames within its own network, but it will know how and where to forward requests for hostnames outside its own network or domain. In such a way, it becomes possible to locate and maintain the IP-to-hostname mappings of all network hosts—even one as large as the Internet.

So, two questions arise: 1. How do you know whether your host has been configured to use DNS? 2. How do you tell your TCP/IP programs to access this configuration? All TCP/IP programs function if they are supplied with either an IP address or a hostname. If a hostname is supplied, however, the program first must resolve that name into the host's IP address. This resolution process is standard: First check to find a local DNS configuration file is made. If this fails, the program will try to find a matching entry in the /etc/hosts file. If this fails, it will post the error message unknown host.

Using another system as a nameserver

1. Create a resolver file on your UNIX host. Type vi /etc/resolv.conf, and then press Enter. If a resolv.conf file didn't already exist, one will be created when you use vi.

2. Press the o key to start a new line, and type domain catfish.com. Then press Enter.

3. You need to include the IP address of the DNS server within your configuration file. To do this, type in the keyword nameserver, followed by a space and the IP address of your network's DNS server. Save the file and exit the vi program by pressing Esc followed by Shift+ZZ.

4. Listing 25.8 illustrates my /etc/resolv.conf file, which includes references for two DNS servers: a primary and a secondary, or backup, server.

Listing 25.8   An Example */etc/resolv.conf* File

```
#  /etc/resolv.conf
#
#  default domain setting
domain              catfish.com

#available nameservers, primary and secondary
nameserver          130.100.10.10
nameserver          130.100.20.50
#
#  end of file
```

5. Now you have completed your resolver configuration, you can test it. Run the `ping` program. However, instead of specifying an IP address, enter a hostname, for example, `telnet www.catfish.com`.

6. If everything works, the `catfish.com` Web server should respond to the `ping` request.

Checking Whether You Are Connected to the Internet

Many companies connect their networks to the Internet. This means that after you are able to access your local network hosts you may, by default, also be able to access the entire Internet.

Firewalls Block `ping`

Importantly, the `ping` program does not always accurately reflect whether you have Internet connectivity. This is because some companies set up firewalls that restrict the type of application traffic allowed in from the Internet. If your `ping` program fails with an error message of "host unreachable," try connecting to a major Internet site using your Web browser.

You could use the `ping` program to check whether you have Internet access. Type `ping ds.internic.com`. If you get a response, you are connected.

If you still cannot access the Internet, you might need to gain access through a proxy service. A *proxy* provides application services on behalf of a user by a secured third party. This third party is called a *proxy server* and is often, but not always, integrated within the Internet firewall server. The use of a proxy means that individual users are shielded from having to conduct direct communication with external devices, which increases network security.

If your site is using proxies, you need to ensure that your application programs—Telnet, FTP, and Web browser—have been configured to use the proxy service. This configuration involves entering the IP address of the host running the proxy, as well as the port number the application is running on. Figure 25.2 illustrates the configuration of proxy servers and ports for my Web browser program.

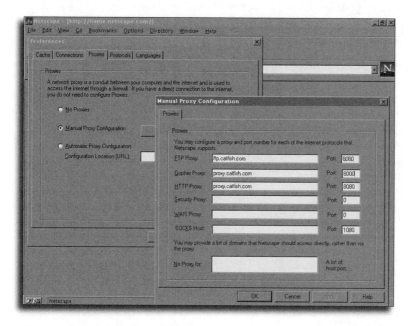

FIGURE 25.2
Configuring a Web browser for using proxy services.

Logging On to UNIX over the Network

After connectivity has been established, you can start to execute some applications over the network. The following section examines the execution of a number of application programs, illustrating what functionality can be achieved.

Using Telnet to Log On

The Telnet program provides the capability to log on and access resources on a remote host. The Telnet program takes the remote hostname or IP address as an argument and attempts to open a connection to the specified host.

Using *telnet* to log in to a remote UNIX system

1. Type in the following commands, replacing the specified hostname with the name of your own host: telnet www.catfish.com. Then press Enter.

2. The Telnet program first tries to resolve the hostname www.catfish.com. Notice in Listing 25.9 how it does this and then uses the IP address to connect to the remote server. Once connected, a logon prompt displays.

Listing 25.9 An Example Telnet Connection

```
#
# telnet www.catfish.com.
Trying 130.100.10.1…
Connected to www.catfish.com.
Escape character is '^]'.

(www.catfish.com.) (ttyp12)


login:
```

3. Log on to the remote host by entering a valid username and password. After logging on, type who to see who else is logged on to this host. To exit, type exit and press Enter.

4. The Telnet program can work in Interactive mode as well. To demonstrate this, type Telnet and then press Enter.

Using *rlogin* Instead of Telnet

The rlogin program is one of a number of r-utilities (the *r* stands for *remote*) developed to run over TCP/IP networks. This program is very similar to the Telnet program in that it enables a user to operate a terminal session on a remote host. Different from Telnet, however, the rlogin program does not require you to provide a user id and a password.

Configuring *hosts.equiv* and *.rhosts*

The r-utility programs make reference to two configuration files: /etc/hosts.equiv and a file optionally stored in a user's home directory called .rhosts. Imagine that you have two hosts in your network—one called jupiter, the other called mars—both of which are in the catfish.com domain.

All network users have an account on each host with a similarly constructed username (both usernames are of the form first initial and surname, such as jedwards). By configuring the /etc/hosts.equiv file, you could allow all users to access either machine by logging on only once to their local machine and then using the rlogin program. The following task list illustrates how to achieve this:

1. Log on to UNIX as the root administrator, type vi /etc/hosts.equiv, and press Enter.

2. Add a new line to the /etc/hosts.equiv file by pressing o and then Enter. On this new line, add an entry for the host you want to provide equivalent user access to. In my example, I would enter the hostname jupiter.catfish.com. Save and exit the /etc/hosts.equiv file.

3. Log off as the root user, and then log back on to the jupiter.catfish.com server using another user account. At the shell prompt, enter the following command: rlogin mars.catfish.com. Then press Enter. The rlogin command forwards a logon request to the remote host. The server checks for equivalency by looking for the user's local hostname within its own /etc/hosts.equiv. If a match is found, the logon is allowed and a shell program is launched on the remote host.

You can enable similar functionality by this time creating a .rhosts file in a specific user's home directory. Consider the same host configuration as before. The following procedure shows how to set up .rhosts to allow a single user to log in to a remote system without a password, assuming there is no /etc/hosts.equiv file.

Setting up *.rhosts*

1. Log on as a user on the host mars.catfish.com. Use the vi program to create a new file called .rhosts in the user's home directory. This will be similar to the following: vi $HOME/.rhosts.

2. Press o to start a new line, and add the following entry, jupiter.catfish.com jedwards, with the first entry being the remote hostname and the second being the logon account name on the host to which you will be giving equivalence. When this is complete, save the file and exit vi.

3. Log off the `mars.catfish.com` host and log on to `jupiter.catfish.com` using the userid `jedwards`. Now, at the UNIX shell prompt, issue the following command: `rlogin mars`. Then press Enter. Again, because you have created equivalence between the hosts, you will be automatically logged on to the mars server without having to supply either a username or a password.

For security reasons, the root account cannot be allowed access through the `hosts.equiv` file. Use the `.rhosts` file in root's home directory (usually `/`) to allow root access without a password.

From these examples, you should be able to see that the configuration of either `/etc/hosts.equiv` or `.rhosts` has the potential to be a very powerful asset, but at the same time it raises some serious security concerns. An unscrupulous user could make a change within either of these files and then gain access to any host account. The following points provide some guidelines for limiting the abuse of providing host equivalence:

- Set effective file permissions on the `/etc/hosts.equiv` file.
- The `/etc/hosts.equiv` file should be set with permissions that enable it to be edited only by `root`. Other users of the system require read access, but it is advisable not to enable the file as readable by the world.
- Never include a plus sign (+) within the `/etc/hosts.equiv` file.
- A plus sign on its own provides equivalency to any and all hosts, meaning that access to any like-named accounts is granted from all networked hosts. Unscrupulous users would simply need to create a similarly named account on their local machine to access a remote host account.
- Include only the names of specific hosts, not individual accounts.
- Refrain from allowing users to create `.rhosts` files. In general, the same security rules examined earlier for the `/etc/_hosts.equiv` file should be applied to `.rhosts` files. Because any user can create an `.rhosts` file within his own home directory, however, it would be an administrative nightmare to ensure the syntax within each of the files. It is recommended that any required equivalence between accounts be set through the `/etc/hosts.equiv` file and that `.rhosts` files not be used. Where equivalence between accounts of dissimilar names is required, an account username and password should always be provided.

Transferring Files Across the Network

The Telnet and rlogin commands provide a way for a remote user to access system resources, but not an effective way to transfer files across the network. These deficiencies are alleviated through the operation of the File Transfer Protocol (FTP).

The following section examines the operation of FTP and illustrates how it can be used to transfer files between UNIX hosts. FTP can operate both from the command line and interactively. Start by looking at using it interactively.

Starting FTP

1. Log on to UNIX as any user, but not to the root account. At a shell prompt, enter the command ftp and press Enter.

2. The ftp program will drop into Command mode and offer the prompt ftp>. Type in the word open, and press Enter.

3. FTP will prompt for the name of the remote host you want to open a connection to. At this prompt, I entered the hostname ftp.catfish.com to access my FTP host machine. Enter the hostname of another UNIX system within your network.

4. If successful, the remote server prompts you to enter a username and then a password. On your system, enter this information. FTP will inform you when you are successful and return you to the ftp> prompt. You are now connected to the remote server and can transfer files. Listing 25.10 provides an illustration of these tasks.

Listing 25.10   Accessing a Remote Host Using *ftp*

```
# ftp
ftp> open
(to) ftp.catfish.com.
Connected to ftp.catfish.com.
220 ftp server (Monday, March 30 12:12:22 EST 1998) ready.
.

Name (ftp.catfish.com. james
331 password required for james.
Password: *******
230 Guest login ok, access restrictions apply.
ftp>
```

5. The ftp program enables you to display remote files and to move around the file systems contained on the remote server. Type in the command ls -l and then press Enter. FTP will transfer a listing of the current directory on the remote machine. The following listing provides a summary of the files on the host ftp.catfish.com.

Listing 25.11 Using *ftp* to List Files

```
ftp> ls -l
200 Okay
150- ftp server ready
150 Opening data connection for /bin/ls
total 6
-rw-rw-r-x  1 root    system    1634   Apr 4  1996  cu_mor
-rw-r--rwx  1 root    system    424    Apr 4  1996  source.c
-rw-rw-r--  1 root    system    3234   Apr 4  1996  fames.c
-rw-rwxr--  1 root    system    634    Apr 4  1996  pigsou.c
-rw-rw-r-x  1 root    system    1634   Apr 4  1996  cracko.4
-rw-r-xrwx  1 root    system    234    Apr 4  1996  seventen
226 Transfer complete.
ftp>
```

6. Now transfer the file source.c from ftp.catfish.com to your local host. Before you do this, change to your home directory on your local host; you can do this through the ftp command lcd. Type the following, replacing the file reference with your own home directory: lcd /home/james.

7. To transfer the file, type get source.c, and then press Enter. The ftp program will then transfer the file, indicating when the transfer has completed.

Transferring Multiple Files with FTP

The ftp program can also transfer multiple files in one go. You can try this by transferring all the files in the remote directory on ftp.catfish.com.

Transferring multiple files via FTP

1. Before you can do this, however, you must make a couple of adjustments to your current FTP session.

2. Notice in Listing 25.11 that some of the files contained in the remote subdirectory are in fact executable files. As such, you need to tell `ftp` to transfer these programs in Binary mode rather than Text mode. This can be done by typing the word `binary` and pressing Enter.

3. Also, instead of transferring files one at a time, you can use the `mget` command to transfer multiple files at once. By default, however, the mget program works in Interactive mode, prompting you for each file. You can overcome this by turning off the FTP Interactive mode. Do this by typing the word `prompt`.

> **Note**
>
> All the available FTP commands can be displayed by pressing the question mark (?) key at the `ftp` prompt. In addition, remember that when setting commands—such as `prompt`, `hash`, and `binary`—these are all toggle commands that can be reset by entering the command again.
>
> The `ftp` utility can be used to transfer files from the local host to a remote host. This is accomplished in a similar way to that outlined earlier. Instead of using the commands `get` and `mget`, however, use the commands `put` and `mput`.

4. Now you are ready to transfer all the files from the remote host. Type the command `mget`, and press Enter. The `ftp` program will prompt for the files to be fetched. Type `*.*` to transfer all files. FTP will transfer the files one by one, indicating when each transfer is completed as well as providing performance statistics such as the transfer time and number of bytes copied between systems.

5. Listing 25.12 provides a summary of these tasks. Notice how I also added the FTP command `hash`. This causes FTP to print a hash mark (#) to the screen for every 1024 bytes it transfers. This can prove very useful, especially if you need to transfer large files. You should note that the number of bytes between hash marks may differ slightly among different UNIX flavors.

Listing 25.12 Transferring Multiple Files Using FTP

```
ftp>
ftp> binary
200 type set to I.
ftp> prompt
Interactive mode off
```

continues...

Listing 25.12 Continued

```
ftp> hash
Hash mark printing on
ftp> mget
(remote-files) *.*
local: cu_mar remote: cu_mar
200 Okay
150 Opening data connection for XXX (XXX bytes).
226 Transfer complete.
local: source.c remote: source.c
200 Okay
150 Opening data connection for XXX (XXX bytes).
####
226 Transfer complete.
4560 bytes received in 0.00467 secs (9.5e+02 Kbytes/sec)
local: frames.c remote: frames.c
200 Okay
150 Opening data connection for XXX (XXX bytes).
################################################################
#############################################
226 Transfer complete.
115695 bytes received in 0.347 secs (3.3e+02 Kbytes/sec)
local: pigsou.c remote: pigsou.c
200 Okay
150 Opening data connection for XXX (XXX bytes).
################################################################
#################################################################
#########################################################
##############################
226 Transfer complete.
1570 bytes sent in 0.01432 secs (1.9e+02 Kbytes/sec)
local: cracko.4 remote: cracko.4
200 Okay
150 Opening data connection for XXX (XXX bytes).
#
226 Transfer complete.
240 bytes sent in 0.00299 secs (1.9e+02 Kbytes/sec)
```

Using *rcp* to Transfer Files

Just as `rlogin` provided an alternative to using Telnet, another of the r-utilities—
rcp—provides an alternative to using FTP for file transfers. The use of `rcp` requires
the configuration of a `.rhosts` file in the user's home directory. The following example leads you through the necessary `.rhosts` configuration before illustrating the
operation of this utility.

Setting up and using *rcp*

1. Log on to the remote host, using an ordinary account, not as the root user.
   Enter the following commands to create a new `.rhosts` file in the account's
   home directory: `vi $HOME/_.rhosts`. Then press Enter.

2. Open a new line in this file by pressing o, and enter the name of your local host
   and the account name on that host to whom you want to grant access. My local
   host is `jupiter.catfish.com`, for example, and my account name on that host is
   `jedwards`. Therefore, I would make the following entry within the `.rhosts` file on
   the remote host: `jupiter.catfish.com    jedwards`.

3. Save the `.rhosts` file, exit from vi, and log off the remote host. Now you are
   ready to execute any of the r-utilities.

4. Log on to your local host (the one you added an entry for in step 2). Type the
   following command to create a new file that you can use for testing the `rcp` utility: `touch testfile`. Then press Enter. Run the `rcp` utility to place a copy of this
   file in the home directory on the remote server `mars.catfish.com` by typing the
   following:
   ```
   rcp testfile mars.catfish.com/home/jedwards/testfile.
   ```

5. After the transfer has completed, log on to the remote host and check that the
   file has been copied. To do this, type `rlogin mars.catfish.com`, and then type `ls
   -l $HOME/testfile`.

6. One advantage of using the `rcp` program to transfer files over and above the `ftp`
   program is a capability to perform recursive copying of entire directory structures. The following command provides an example of this:
   ```
   rsh -r catfish.com:/usr/lib/source   /backup/source
   ```

   This command copies the subdirectory `/usr/lib/source` and all the underlying
   subdirectories and files to the local subdirectory `/backup/source`. The only way
   to achieve a similar functionality using FTP is to tar all the files under
   `/usr/lib/source` and then transfer that one file. Obviously, `rcp` provides a lot
   more flexibility.

Executing Commands on Another System in the Network

The rsh program (sometimes pronounced *rush* or, alternatively, *r-s-h*) provides a method to execute commands on remote hosts without having to log on beforehand. As the program's name suggests, this is another of the r-utilities. As such, the /etc/hosts.equiv and .rhosts configuration covered in previous sections of this chapter must be applied before you can use the command.

Setting up and running *rsh*

1. Create an entry for your local UNIX host in the .rhosts file of the remote host. In my case, I would do this by logging on to the host mars.catfish.com (my remote host) and typing vi $HOME/.rhosts, then adding the entry jupiter.cat-fish.com before saving and exiting the file.

2. Log off the remote host and log on to the local host. Execute the rsh command to execute the /bin/ls program against the remote host by typing the following command line: rsh mars.catfish.com /bin/ls. Then press Enter.

3. The rsh command produces a file listing of the $HOME directory on the remote host. Try executing some other executables on the remote host. The following steps detail some interesting examples.

4. Enter the command line rsh mars.catfish.com/bin/sh to start up a UNIX shell on the remote host.

5. The command rsh mars.catfish.com who displays the users currently logged on to the remote host.

6. Executing the rsh command without specifying a command to execute on the remote host results in the user being logged on the remote host, the same result as if you had used the rlogin command. To try this, enter the command line rsh mars.catfish.com.

Sharing a Directory Between Two UNIX Systems (NFS)

Sun Microsystem's Network File System (NFS) has become a standard feature on all TCP/IP implementations of UNIX and Linux.

An NFS server system can export one or more of its local directories so that they are accessible to other UNIX systems. These directories must be listed in /etc/exports.

Take a look at these example contents of /etc/exports on the system zebra.

```
/projects/acme
/usr/fred/reports      -ro
/usr/fred/documents    -access=lion:rhino
/usr/jane/status       -rw=tiger
```

The /projects/acme directory has no modifiers in the example /etc/exports. This means that any other system in the network can mount that filesystem like this:

```
mount zebra:/projects/acme /acme
```

Assume that system tiger is in the same network as system zebra and runs the previous command. Now any users on tiger can look at local directory /acme and see all the files and directories that are in /projects/acme on system zebra. Users on tiger can make changes to those files. The changes will actually be made on system zebra in the /projects/acme directory.

In this example, /usr/fred/reports is exported read-only (-ro). This means that remote systems can mount and read files in the directory but cannot change them or add new files.

In the previous example, the -access option means that only systems lion and rhino can mount the directory /usr/fred/documents.

In the last line of the previous example, /usr/jane/status can be modified only if mounted from system tiger. Other systems can mount this filesystem, but only as read-only.

To mount the exported filesystem, you may need to add -f NFS to specify that a remote NFS directory is being mounted:

```
mount -f NFS -o soft zebra:/projects/acme /acme
```

In the previous example, -o soft allows the mount command to terminate with an immediate error if the remote system or the remote directory is not currently accessible. Without the soft option, the default is a hard mount. This means that the mount command waits until it is successful. Beware of putting a hard NFS mount into your normal system bootup sequence. If the remote system or remote directory is not available, your system may hang at that point and not come up until the mount is successful.

Using the *mailx* command

You can send mail to other users in the same system and receive mail from them by using the `mailx` commands. If two UNIX systems are connected in a network and can ping, Telnet, and `ftp` to each other, then users on the system can usually send mail to users on the other system using the same `mailx` command. If your system is connected to the Internet, then you can use `mailx` to send mail to anyone in the world and receive replies.

Alternatives to `mailx`

`mailx` is an older, character-based mail program that cannot handle email attachments. UNIX programs such as `pine` or `elm` can be easier to use on character-based terminals. A Windows PC can be used to pop waiting mail from a UNIX system for a particular user, and then the mail and attachments can be viewed using your preferred PC email program. In a similar manner, outgoing email from the Windows PC can be dropped off on the UNIX server.

The `mailx` command provides subcommands to facilitate saving, deleting, and responding to messages. This command also provides facilities to compose and edit messages before finally sending them to one or more users. In the past, a command called `mail` was used. Today, the `mail` command usually invokes `mailx`.

The mail system on UNIX uses *mailboxes* to receive mail for a user. Each user has a system mailbox, in which mail for that user is received. The mail is kept in the mailbox until it is read or deleted by the user. The user can read, save, and delete the mail once the mail is received.

After the user has read the mail, the mail may be moved to a secondary or personal mailbox. The default secondary mailbox is called the *mbox*. The mbox is usually present in the home directory of the user. However, the user may specify the name of a file as a secondary mailbox. All messages saved in the mbox are saved indefinitely until moved to other secondary mailboxes, which are sometimes known as folders. You can use the folders to organize your mail. For example, you might have folders organized by subject matter and can save all mail pertaining to a subject in a particular folder.

You may send messages to one or more users using the `mailx` command. This command enables you to send mail to users on the same host or other hosts in the network to which the local host is connected. If your system is connected to the Internet, you can send mail anywhere in the world. You will not get a positive acknowledgment if the mail delivery is successful. However, if the mail cannot be delivered, you will get notification.

Following is a list of some of the flags that may be used with the mail command:

- `-d` displays debug information.
- `-f` specifies the name of a folder in which you have saved your mail previously. If no folder is given, it defaults to mbox in your home directory.
- `-s "subject"` associates a subject for the mail to be created.
- `-v` displays detailed information by the `mailx` command

Each mail has information associated with it. The following is a list of the information:

- `status` indicates the status of a mail. The following is a list of the various statuses of a mail item:
  - `M` indicates that the message will be stored in your personal mailbox.
  - `>` indicates the current message.
  - `N` indicates that the message is a new message.
  - `P` indicates that the message is to be preserved in the system mailbox.
  - `R` indicates that you have read the message.
  - `U` indicates an unread message. An unread message is the one that was a new message at the last invocation of `mailx` but was not read.
  - `*` indicates that the message has been saved or written to a file or folder.
  - A message without a status indicates that the message has been read but has not been deleted or saved.
- `number` indicates a numerical ID of the message to which it can be referred.
- `sender` indicates the user who sent the message.
- `date` indicates when the mail was received in the mailbox.
- `size` indicates the size of the message by number of lines and number of bytes.
- `subject` indicates the subject matter of the mail if the sender has associated a subject with the mail. If the mail does not have an associated subject, this will not be present.

The following is a list of subcommands you can use while in mail's _> prompt:

- `q` applies mailbox commands entered this session.
- `x` quits without updating the mailbox.

- !command starts a shell, runs a command, and returns to the mailbox.
- cd places you in the home directory. Optionally, you can specify a directory name to place you in the specified directory.
- t displays the current message. Alternatively, you can specify a message list to display that message in the message list.
- n displays the next message.
- f displays headings of the current message. Optionally, you can specify a message list to display its heading.
- e edits the current message. Alternatively, you can specify a message number to modify that message.
- d deletes the current message. Optionally, you can specify a message list to delete the message in the message list.
- u restores deleted messages.
- s file appends the current message, including the heading, to a file. Optionally, you can specify a message list between s and file to append the specified messages to the file.
- w file appends the current message, excluding the heading, to a file. Alternatively, you can specify a message list between s and file to append the specified messages to the file.
- pre preserves (undeletes) messages in the system mailbox. Optionally, you can specify a list of messages to keep in the system mailbox.
- m addresslist creates and/or sends a new message to addresses in the address list.
- r sends a reply to senders and recipients of messages. Optionally, you can specify a list of messages to send replies to senders and recipients of all messages in the list. (Some UNIX systems swap the r and R functions.)
- R sends a reply only to senders of messages for the current message. Alternatively, you can specify a list of messages to send replies to senders of the messages. (Some UNIX systems swap the r and R functions.)
- a displays a list of aliases and their addresses.

While composing mail, you can use a number of escape sequences at the beginning of a line. The following is a list of escape commands prefixed by the default escape character ~ (tilde):

- ~. indicates the end of a mail message.

- ~A inserts the autograph string Sign.

- ~b name adds name to Bcc (blind carbon copy list).

- ~c name adds name to Cc (visible carbon copy list).

- ~e invokes the editor. The default editor is ex. However, you can modify the editor to beviby modifying the EDITOR environment variable.

- ~f message-list forwards either the message being read or the list of messages provided.

- ~m message-list inserts text from the current message or the list of messages provided into the message being composed.

- ~p prints the current message.

- ~q quits the message Input mode.

- ~r filename inserts text from the specified filename into the message being composed.

- ~s sub sets the subject of the mail being composed to sub.

- ~t name-list adds each of the names specified in the list to the list of recipients.

- ~v invokes the visual editor vi.

- ~w filename writes the message being composed to the specified filename.

SEE ALSO

➤ *For information on reading or sending email using the CDE mailer, see page 150*

➤ *For information on the StarOffice application suite, which also allows reading and sending email, see page 162*

➤ *For information on reading and sending UNIX email via Netscape on Windows, see page 725*

Examples

You can invoke the mailx command by itself to put you into the mail > prompt where you can use the subcommands. You will be able to get into the mail > prompt only if you have mail. Otherwise, you will get a message similar to You have no mail. If you have mail, prompts similar to the following will be displayed:

```
mailx
Mail [5.2 UCB] Type ? for help.
"/usr/spool/mail/testuser": 1 message 1 new
>N  1 testuser    Fri Mar 26 22:49  285/9644
&
```

If you now quit `mailx` command using the `quit` subcommand (abbreviated as q), the mail is saved in your personal mailbox (`mbox` file in your home directory).

To delete the current message, you can use the following subcommand while inside the `mail` command:

```
d
```

If you have more than one message and you want to delete a specific message, such as message number 5, you can use the following subcommand while inside the `mail` command:

```
d 5
```

To see the mail you have saved in your personal mailbox, you can use the `mailx -f` command, which results in the following:

```
mailx -f
Mail [5.2 UCB] Type ? for help.
"/home/testuser/mbox": 1 message
>   1 testuser    Fri Mar 26 00:11   162/5175
&
```

To save mail in a folder while in the `mailx` command, you can execute the following subcommand:

```
& save 1 /u/testuser/folder1/file1
```

This creates a `file1` from the first message in the directory `/u/testuser/folder1`. Now, if you invoke the `mailx` command to read the file `/u/testuser/folder1`, it results in the following:

```
mailx -f /u/testuser/folder1
Mail [5.2 UCB] Type ? for help.
"/u/testuser/folder1": 1 message
>   1 testuser    Fri Mar 26 00:11   162/5175
&
```

After you are in `mailx`, you can execute the subcommand m to create and send mail to other users, as in the following:

```
& m friend1
Subject: Testing mailx command
This is test of the mailx command
Here we are trying to send a mail to user friend1 with cc to Âfriend2
Cc: friend2
&
```

The body of the mail is terminated by Ctrl+D (Press Ctrl and D simultaneously). It is possible to send mail to multiple users using the m subcommand.

To send the message stored in a file called letter to the recipient user1@host1 and then send copies of the message to user2@host2 and user3@host3, you can use the following command:

```
mail -c "user2@host2 user3@host3" user1@host1<letter
```

A Final Note

The tasks outlined in this chapter enable you to get your hosts networked. This provides a basis for you to be able to run all the most common network applications and access remote systems.

It is worth remembering that with nearly 30 different flavors of UNIX commercially available, some differences in program operation and syntax will be evident. This chapter has tried to cover the approaches adopted by most of the major UNIX flavors; as always, it is worthwhile referring to your system's man pages for version-specific options of the commands and programs covered throughout this chapter.

chapter

26

Accessing UNIX from Windows

*James Edwards and
Steve "Mor" Moritsugu*

Windows and TCP/IP

Dial-up networking

> **Tip for Beginners**
>
> It is very common to find Windows PCs on people's desks with network access to a UNIX server. Many Windows utilities, such as Netscape, can be used in place of UNIX character-based utilities, providing great synergy. This chapter discusses how to set up that connection.

Most users operate one of the Windows family of operating systems on their PCs—the majority making use of the Windows 95/98 version. It's likely that these same users will need to communicate with UNIX hosts, either located within their own network or in public networks such as the Internet. This chapter addresses the issues of providing Windows 95/98 users with access to UNIX hosts.

The Windows operating system prides itself on its plug-and-play configuration capabilities. What does this mean? Well, when a new device such as a modem is added to a PC, Windows automatically attempts to recognize and configure it. If any additional configuration information is required, Windows automatically starts a simple program to guide and prompt the user for the information needed to complete the configuration.

By and large, the operating system accomplishes these tasks very favorably, especially in comparison to any flavor of UNIX. However, you should be aware of a number of "gotchas"—this chapter helps to identify some of those things.

Windows and TCP/IP

The TCP/IP protocols are very much the de facto standard for networking. Windows offers native support for these protocols, along with a simple program, called a *wizard*, for guiding users through the necessary installation and configuration processes.

To enable effective TCP/IP networking support for LAN connections under Windows, the configuration of three separate components is required: the Microsoft Client for Networking, a Network Interface Card (NIC) adapter, and the TCP/IP protocols. All these configuration steps rely on the Network icon located in the Windows control panel; the following task guides you through the necessary steps required to enable TCP/IP networking within Windows.

Enabling TCP/IP networking

1. Open the Control Panel by clicking the Start button located on the taskbar. Then highlight Settings and click the option Control Panel. When the Control Panel has opened, double-click the Network icon.

2. Within the Network window, click the Configuration tab. Examine the displayed list of components appearing in the window below the words The Following Network Components Are Installed. To connect to a network, you must ensure that three entries are present: Client for Microsoft Networks, NIC Adapter, and TCP/IP Network Adapter.

3. If any of these entries are not present within your configurations, you can add them by first clicking the Add button. You are presented with four options: to add a client, a protocol, an adapter, or service. First, step through adding the networking client.

4. Select Client in the Component Type option box, and then click the Add button. Select Microsoft as the manufacturer; in the Network Clients window, select the option Client for Microsoft Networking. Confirm this selection by clicking OK.

Associating Protocols with Adapters

When more than one network adapter has been installed, Windows 95/98 makes use of an arrow to associate a network protocol with a specific network adapter. If only a single network adapter has been configured, Windows does not provide this association, but instead simply states the protocol name within the Network window.

---

5. Add the NIC Adapter in a similar fashion: Click the Add button, select the option Adapter, and click the Add button. Highlight the manufacturer for the NIC that you have installed in your PC; if your exact NIC is not displayed, click the Have Disk button and follow the instructions for loading the NIC vendors device drivers from disk. Click the Add button and then the OK button to confirm and complete the operation.

6. Next, have Windows load the TCP/IP protocols and configure them for use over the installed NIC. Do this by clicking the Add button, this time selecting the option Protocol. Click the Add button again, and select Microsoft under the list of available manufacturers. Specify TCP/IP as the network protocol to add, and complete the operation by clicking the OK button.

7. At this stage, you have all the networking components loaded, but you haven't configured any of them. First, configure the NIC. In the option window under The Following Network Components Are Installed, click once on the entry for your NIC Adapter.

8. Click the Properties button and then click Driver Type. Choose the Enhanced Mode (32-bit and 16-bit) NDIS Driver option. Click the Bindings tab, and check the box for TCP/IP *NIC* Adapter (where *NIC* reflects your NIC manufacturer). Click the OK button to complete this configuration.

9. Now configure the TCP/IP protocols. Under the title bar The Following Network Components Are Installed window, click once on TCP/IP NIC Adapter and then click the Properties button.

10. Click the IP address tab. If you have been allocated an IP address, click once on the option button Specify an IP Address, and then enter your IP address and the corresponding netmask. If you will be allocated an IP address through a DHCP server, check the option button Obtain an IP Address Automatically.

11. Click the Bindings tab, and check the Microsoft Client option box. Click the OK button to save this change.

Using the Hosts File Instead of DNS

Windows supports the use of a hosts file as an alternative to using DNS. This file is located in the Windows subdirectory, and its syntax is exactly the same as that used on a UNIX host, with individual IP addresses mapping to specified host names. If you don't have access to a DNS server and don't want to refer to your hosts using IP addresses, the \Windows\hosts file provides a useful alternative.

---

12. All the remaining settings are purely optional. However, one other important option is the configuration of DNS. If you plan to use DNS (for example, to connect to the Internet), then click once on the Enable DNS option button. In the configuration boxes provided, add the hostname you want to call your PC, as well as its domain name. I called my host pcclient and my domain catfish.com. Figure 26.1 outlines this configuration.

13. You must also add the IP address of the DNS server in the window DNS Server Search Order. Click the Add button to add the DNS reference, and then click the OK button once to save these settings. Again, Figure 26.1 illustrates this configuration.

FIGURE 26.1
Configuring DNS under Windows 95/98.

14. Click OK at the bottom of each screen until Windows prompts you to reboot. After the reboot, use ping to test the connection, as described next.

Testing the Connection with *ping*

The ping tool ships as part of the standard Windows operating system and provides an excellent tool for both confirming your PC configuration and troubleshooting network connectivity. Unfortunately, the version of ping that ships with Windows is a DOS program and, as such, must run in a Windows DOS box. The following task illustrates how you can make use of this command.

Pinging the IP address

It is important to remember that if you use a hostname, the ping program must resolve this hostname before ping can test host connectivity. If the name you specify cannot be resolved, ping cannot report whether the host is reachable. For this reason, it is preferable to specify a host's IP address rather than its hostname when using ping.

Using the *ping* tool

1. Bring up your Windows taskbar and click once on the Start button. Move the cursor to highlight the Run option, and click once. The Run option box appears. Type the following command line at the Open prompt: ping 130.100.10.2 (replace my IP address with the IP address you used in your own interface configuration).

2. The ping program executes, but because it is a DOS-based program, it first opens a DOS window. ping sends a request packet to the specified interface asking it for an immediate response. If you have correctly configured your PC, you should see a response similar to the one outlined in Figure 26.2.

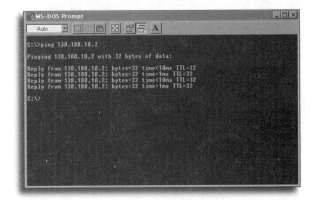

FIGURE 26.2
Pinging a local interface to check network connectivity.

3. If you configured a \Windows\hosts file or have access to a DNS server, you can use a hostname in place of the IP address. To test this, activate a DOS box and type ping *hostname* (replace *hostname* with the name of your remote host).

Viewing Local TCP/IP Settings

Use ipconfig /all **on Windows NT**

winipcfg is found on Windows 95/98 but not on Windows NT. Run ipconfig /all on Windows NT to get the equivalent IP information.

Windows provides a utility that enables you to view detailed information about your current network configurations. This utility, called `winipcfg.exe`, is located in the `\Windows` subdirectory. This task helps you to view some of the functionality provided through this utility.

Using the *winipcfg* utility

1. Bring up your taskbar and click once on the Start button; then click the Run menu option. This brings up a dialog box; type in `\Windows\winipcfg` as the program you want to open, and press Enter.

2. The `winipcfg` program starts and displays a window similar to the one shown in Figure 26.3.

FIGURE 26.3
TCP/IP configuration information with `winipcfg`.

As Figure 26.3 illustrates, the `winipcfg` program displays helpful configuration information that can be used to assist in troubleshooting network connectivity problems.

Troubleshooting with `winipcfg`

The use of `winipcfg` can prove especially useful if your IP address is allocated to you automatically through DHCP. When you know your IP address, you can troubleshoot more effectively. Also notice on the `winipcfg` display two additional buttons: Release All and Renew All. If your interface got its IP address through DHCP, then these buttons provide you with a way to release or renew the IP address you are using.

---

3. The example in Figure 26.3 illustrates the TCP/IP configuration for my Ethernet connection; it is also possible to discover the configuration for other configured interfaces. If you have configured your PC for dial-up networking, click the down arrow to activate the drop-down list and select the option PPP Adapter. `winipcfg` displays the configuration for that interface.

4. Click the More Info button; `winipcfg` expands to include a lot of additional information relating to your current connection. Figure 26.4 provides an illustration for my PPP adapter configuration.

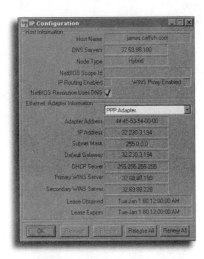

FIGURE 26.4
Use `winipcfg` to display TCP/IP connectivity details.

Transferring Files to and from UNIX with FTP

Windows provides a standard implementation of the FTP program for file transfer. Like the Windows version of the `ping` and `telnet` programs, `ftp` is made available only as a DOS program. However, it is still a useful and effective way to transfer files between Windows and UNIX hosts.

Using *ftp* to transfer files

1. To use `ftp` to transfer a file from a remote host, you must ensure that the host is capable of accepting your `ftp` request. To do this, the host must be running an ftp server process. To confirm this, log on to the remote host and type the following commands: `cat inetd.conf | grep ftp`. If the server can handle inbound `ftp` client requests, a response similar to Listing 26.1 should be displayed:

Listing 26.1 Checking Whether the FTP Server Is Running on the Remote UNIX Host

```
# cat /etc/inetd.conf | grep ftp
ftp       stream  tcp     nowait  root    /usr/sbin/tcpd /usr/sbin/wu.ftpd
#
```

2. To activate the ftp program, move the cursor to the taskbar and click the Start button. Click once on the Run menu option. A dialog box appears, requesting the name of the program you want to execute. Type in ftp and press Enter.

3. A DOS window appears, along with the ftp command prompt ftp>.

Windows Versus UNIX ftp

The standard Windows version of the **ftp** program is identical to the UNIX version of the program, which is illustrated in Chapter 25, "Accessing Other UNIX Systems on the Network or Internet." The additional features and functions outlined in Chapter 25 can also be applied to the Windows version of the **ftp** program.

---

4. Type in ? to display a list of the available commands. You must first open a connection to the remote host. In the following example, I open a connection to my FTP server called ftp.catfish.com. Type the following, replacing the indicated hostname with the name of your remote UNIX server and then press Enter:
   open ftp.catfish.com

5. If successful, the remote server prompts you to enter a username and then a password. Enter this information; FTP informs you when you are successful and returns you to the ftp> prompt. You are now connected to the remote server and are able to transfer files. Figure 26.5 illustrates these tasks.

FIGURE 26.5
Accessing a remote UNIX host using FTP.

6. The ftp program enables you to display remote files and to move around the filesystems contained on the remote server. Type in the command dir and then press Enter. ftp displays a listing of the current directory on the remote host.

7. To transfer a file from the remote host to your Windows PC, type the command get *filename* (where *filename* is the name of the file on the remote host), and then press Enter. The ftp program transfers the file and indicates when the transfer has completed.

8. Similarly, you can transfer a file from your Windows PC to the remote UNIX host. To do this, type put *filename* (where *filename* is the name of the file to transfer). This time, when ftp reports that the transfer is complete, type dir and press Enter. The resulting directory listing should now also include your freshly transferred file.

Logging On to UNIX with *telnet*

If you want to log on to any UNIX host across a TCP/IP connection, you must use the telnet program. This program, which ships as part of the Windows operating system, provides terminal emulation facilities for TCP/IP networks.

Logging on to a UNIX host with *telnet*

1. To start telnet, click the Start button and select the Run menu option. In the Run program dialog box, type telnet and click the OK button to start the program.

2. To connect to a remote host, click the Connect menu option and then the Remote System option.

3. A Connect option box is displayed. Enter the hostname or IP address of your remote UNIX host. Remember, if you enter a hostname, you must either have DNS configured or have an entry for the host in your \Windows\hosts file. Figure 26.6 provides an illustration.

4. Click the Connect button to activate the connection. The remote host's logon screen should be displayed for you to provide your username and password.

5. To disconnect from the host, click the Connect menu item and select the Disconnect option.

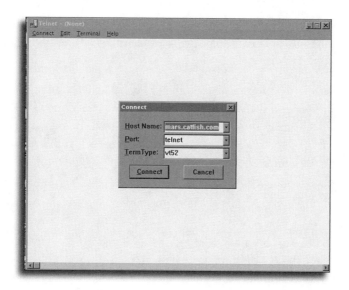

FIGURE 26.6
Using telnet to log on across a TCP/IP connection.

Dial-Up Networking

Windows provides you with two options for accessing UNIX hosts over dial-up connections. One option is to configure your Windows PC to be capable of operating the TCP/IP protocols over a modem connection. This option enables you to run any one of the TCP/IP-based applications outlined so far within this chapter and is typically the route chosen in providing a PC with a connection into the Internet.

An alternative approach is to configure Windows to enable a user with the capability to log on to a remote host. This option enables you to access files and resources on the remote host; however, this option is limited in that it provides access to only a single remote host at any one time. The following sections examine both of these approaches.

Accessing UNIX Hosts via the Internet

To access hosts over the Internet, you must complete four tasks: Install and configure your modem, configure the modem's physical port, configure the networking devices and protocols, and configure a connection script that will dial your Internet service provider's telephone number and initiate communication over your configured devices.

The following task list provides a simple guide through this process, beginning with the installation and configuration of your modem.

Accessing UNIX hosts over the Internet

1. Click the Start button located on the taskbar. Move the cursor to the Settings menu option, and then right-click the Control Panel option. When the Control Panel folder opens, double-click the Modems icon. If you already have a modem installed, the Modems Properties dialog box appears. If this is the case, right-click the Add button before proceeding.

2. The Install a New Modem window opens. Click the Next button to run the Installation Wizard and have Windows guide you through the installation process. Click the Next button to continue with this process.

3. You will be asked if you want Windows to search for the newly installed hardware; select the No option button and click Next. From the displayed Device Type list, select Modem and click Next.

4. Check the option Don't Detect My Modem, I Will Select It from a List, and click the Next button. A new window opens; select both your modem's manufacturer and the model under the provided options.

5. Click the Next button to continue the installation, and select the COM port that the modem will use. Windows attempts to install your modem; the screen may go blank for a few seconds as it completes the process. Upon completion, a window is displayed reporting the success of the installation process; click the Finish button to exit the Installation Wizard.

6. Press the Finish button to bring up the Modem Properties window. To effectively complete the installation process, you must define how Windows is to use the modem; this is done by clicking the Dialing Properties button found within this window.

7. The Dialing Properties screen prompts you to enter your local dialing area code and specify whether you need to dial a special number before being able to dial any location. This might be the case if your modem line connects via a PBX and requires a 9 to be dialed to access an outside telephone line. Make any changes to the Dialing Properties screen required for your own environments.

8. Click the OK button to save and exit the Dialing Properties screen, and again to exit the Modem Properties screen.

The next task list ensures that your COM port settings correspond to those you configured for your modem during its installation. This is achieved through accessing the System icon, again located within the Control Panel. The following tasks summarize the settings you need to make.

Configuring COM port settings

1. To open the Control Panel, click the Start button located on the taskbar. Move the cursor to the Settings menu option, and then right-click the Control Panel option. The Control Panel folder opens; double-click the System icon.

2. The System Properties window opens; click the Device Manager tab and then double-click the COM port to which you connected your modem. Click the Port Settings tab to adjust the displayed values so that they correspond to the ones you configured for your modem.

3. Click OK to save the settings and return to the System Properties window; then click OK to close this window and return to the Control Panel folder.

After you have installed your modem and communication port, you must set up and configure the TCP/IP protocols to be capable of communicating over these devices. This is achieved by the completion of the following steps.

Configuring TCP/IP protocols

1. Open the Windows Control Panel by clicking the Start button and then choosing Settings and then Control Panel. Double-click the Network icon.

2. Click the Configuration tab and examine the list of currently configured components. To configure dial-up networking, the following two entries must be present: Dial-up Adapter and TCP/IP Dial-up Adapter.

   If either of these items is not present, you must add it. If you need to add an item, click the Add button. You are presented with four options of things you can add: a client, a protocol, an adapter, and a service.

   If you need to add a dial-up adapter, click the adapter option and click the Add button. Select Microsoft as the manufacturer, and select Dial-up Adapter under the Network Protocols window. Click the OK button to confirm the operation.

   If you need to add the TCP/IP protocol Dial-up Adapter option, click the Add button, click the protocol option, and then again click the Add button. Select Microsoft as the manufacturer, and select TCP/IP as the network protocol. Complete the operation by clicking the OK button.

3. Now for TCP/IP protocol configuration: In the window The Following Network Components Are Installed, click Dial-up Adapter. Click the Properties button, and then click the Driver Type option and choose Enhanced Mode

(32-bit and 16-bit) NDIS Driver. Click the Bindings tab and then check the box for TCP/IP Dial-up Adapter. Click the OK button to complete this operation.

4. In the window The Following Network Components Are Installed, click TCP/IP Dial-up Adapter and then click the Properties button. This screen then provides a place to configure the TCP/IP protocol parameters. Figure 26.7 provides an example.

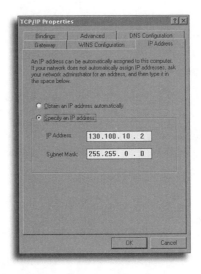

FIGURE 26.7
Configuring TCP/IP parameters.

5. The essential item to configure is the IP address of the Windows PC. To do this, click the IP Address tab. If you have been allocated an IP address to use, click the Specify an IP Address option button and then enter your IP address and associated netmask. If you have not been allocated an IP address, click the Obtain an IP Address Automatically option.

6. If your PC is capable of making use of DNS, click the DNS Configuration tab. Next, check the Enable DNS option button, and then add your PC's hostname and domain name. Then add the IP address of the DNS server in the DNS Server Search Order window and click the Add button.

7. Finally, click the OK button to save the configuration and exit.

Your modem is configured, and your device port and the protocol configuration are set up. Now you must instruct Windows how to establish a connection; this is achieved via the Dial-up Networking option. The following task illustrates the necessary configuration steps.

Configuring dial-up networking

1. Double-click the My Computer icon, the Dial-Up Networking folder, and the Make New Connection icon. This starts a wizard program to guide you through the setup of a new dial-up networking session.

2. Enter a name to describe the session, and select the modem that the wizard should use. Click the Next button to continue.

3. Enter the telephone number of the server you are dialing, including country and area codes as appropriate. Click the Next button, and the wizard informs you that your session configuration is complete. Click the Finish button to save and exit.

4. Your session is saved in the Dial-up Networking folder. Select this icon, and right-click; then select the Properties option and then the Server Type option button. The screen shown in Figure 26.8 is displayed.

FIGURE 26.8
Specifying the server type for dial-up networking.

5. This dialog box enables you to specify which protocols are capable of operating across the established connection. Click the TCP/IP Settings button and enter TCP/IP configuration information for this specific connection, which overrides the values specified in the Control Panel. This enables you to configure TCP/IP differently for any particular connections you might make.

6. To activate this session, double-click the Session icon in the Dial-up Networking folder. A dialog box appears, prompting for your username and password, as well

as the telephone number that is to be dialed. Enter your username and password, and click the Connect button.

7. Windows dials the specified telephone number and attempts to connect using your username and password. After a connection has been established, you can use any of the TCP/IP programs to access remote servers across this connection.

Accessing a UNIX Host over a Terminal Connection

Chapter 24, "Accessing Other UNIX Systems by Modem," illustrated how a UNIX host can provide remote logon support through the use of modems and dial-up lines. Windows provides comparable functionality through its HyperTerminal program. This program allows a PC to be configured to be capable of establishing a terminal connection with a remote host.

Configuring HyperTerminal to access a UNIX host

1. To configure a connection using HyperTerminal, click the Start button and move the cursor to the Programs menu option. Windows displays the available program groups on your PC. Select Accessories and then HyperTerminal.

2. In the HyperTerminal folder, double-click the program called `Hypertrm.exe`. This starts the HyperTerminal configuration program, which guides you through the rest of the necessary configuration steps.

3. Enter a name for the new connection, and select an icon for this connection from the available list. Click OK to continue.

4. HyperTerminal prompts you for the telephone number of the remote host you want to connect to. To complete this information, add the country and area code information by selecting the drop-down box. HyperTerminal helps you to complete these steps.

5. Click the down arrow at the end of the Connect Using window, and select the modem you want HyperTerminal to use. When you have finished entering this information, click the OK button to continue.

6. HyperTerminal displays the number you want to dial, as well as the location you are dialing from within the Connect dialog box (see Figure 26.9).

7. If you must change the configured telephone number of your remote host, you can do so by clicking the Modify button. This action displays the Properties window for your connection (see Figure 26.10).

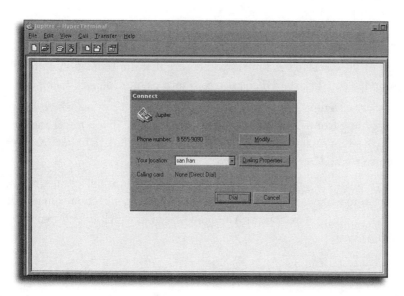

FIGURE 26.9
Accessing the HyperTerminal Connect dialog box.

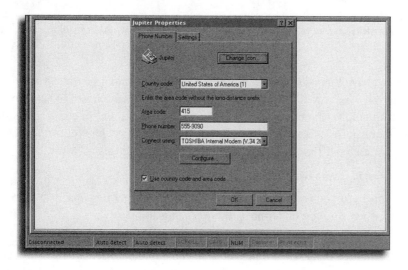

FIGURE 26.10
Changing the dial-in properties of a HyperTerminal connection.

8. Clicking the Phone Number tab enables you to change the telephone number, including the country and area code of the remote host. This tab also provides you with the ability to change connections modem configuration by clicking the Configure button.

9. Click the Settings tab. The options available on this screen enable you to change the look and feel of the terminal session. You shouldn't need to make changes to any of these settings as long as you ensure that the Emulation option is set to Autodetect. Click the OK button to return to the Connect dialog box.

10. Click the Dialing Properties button to tell HyperTerminal which location you are dialing from. This option is particularly useful if you travel and need to access a remote host from many different locations. Click the OK button to return to the Connect dialog box.

11. After you are happy with your connection configuration settings, click the Dial button to make the remote connection. When a connection is made, the remote UNIX host presents you with a logon screen in which to enter your username and password.

Transferring Files to and from the Remote Host

kermit and Xmodem Are Not Standard

kermit and Xmodem are not standardly supported on commercial UNIX. These are widely available as free, nonsupported utilities for most types of commercial UNIX, but they must be downloaded and installed.

After you have logged on to a remote host, HyperTerminal provides you with a simple and effective way to transfer files to and from a remote host. To achieve this, the host must employ a method of downloading files across dial-in connections through the use of communication server software such as kermit. The following steps illustrate how a HyperTerminal user can transfer files using this software.

Transferring files with HyperTerminal

1. Connect to your remote UNIX host by using HyperTerminal as previously described, and log on with a valid username and password.

2. On the remote host, start up the kermit file transfer program by typing kermit. Inform the remote host that you want to upload a binary file from your PC by typing set file type binary and pressing Enter. Then type receive to place the host in the correct mode to receive your file. Press Alt+X to escape back to the HyperTerminal program.

3. Click the Transfer menu option in the HyperTerminal program, and then click the Send Files option. A dialog box appears in which you type the name of the

file to transfer, or you can click the Browse button to locate the file. When you have selected the file, click the Send button to start the transfer.

4. HyperTerminal can also be used to receive files from the remote system. This can be set up by selecting the Receive Files option under the Transfer menu. Use the Browse button to indicate where transferred files are to be placed, and then use the Transfer program on your remote host to send files to your HyperTerminal session.

Reading and Sending UNIX Email via Netscape on Windows

The Netscape Communicator application suite is primarily an Internet browser; however, it also offers Internet email capabilities. The operation of the Netscape application requires a TCP/IP connection from the Windows PC into the Internet. This can be provided though a network connection made via a NIC or a modem.

Configuring Netscape Communicator for email

1. Launch the Netscape Navigator by clicking the Start button, selecting the Programs option, scrolling to the Netscape folder, and clicking the Netscape Navigator icon. Alternatively, if you have created a shortcut to this application, you can launch it by simply double-clicking the shortcut icon.

2. On the Netscape option bar, select Window and then Netscape Mail. Netscape displays the email client and prompts for a user ID and a password to access your remote email account. After Netscape is connected, the email window should look similar to the one in Figure 26.11.

3. New email messages are automatically placed in your Inbox folder. Click the Inbox folder in the top-right window; Netscape indicates the number of unread messages.

4. A summary line for each message within your Inbox appears to the right of this window. You can open any of these messages by clicking them, with the message then appearing in the window at the bottom of the Netscape email client.

5. Move the mouse arrow to any one of the dividers separating these three windows; as you do, notice that the cursor changes shape. Click and hold down the mouse button; as you move the mouse, the individual window sizes change.

6. To send a message, click File and then the New Mail Message menu option. Alternatively, use the shortcut of pressing Ctrl+M.

7. A Message Composition dialog box appears; enter the email address of the recipient, or alternatively click the Mail To button. The Address book appears (see Figure 26.12).

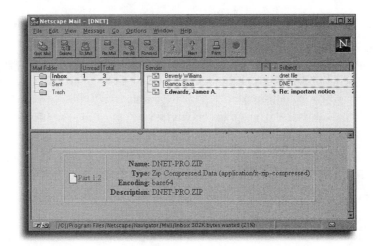

FIGURE 26.11
Netscape email client.

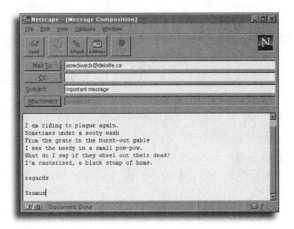

FIGURE 26.12
Creating a new email message using Netscape Navigator.

8. Attach a file to your email message by clicking the Attachment button. Click the Attach File button to locate the file, click the Open button to select a highlighted file, and then click OK to continue.

9. Click the Send button. If you didn't enter anything on the subject line, Netscape again prompts you for a message subject. Enter a subject if you want, and then press OK to continue.

SEE ALSO

➤ *For information on reading/sending email using the CDE mailer, see page 150*

➤ *For information on the StarOffice application suite, which also allows reading and sending email, see page 162*

SMB Shared Directories and Printers

Let UNIX Back Up PC Files

Many Windows PCs do not have a tape drive. Save important Windows files on the UNIX shared directory, and let UNIX back up those files each night automatically.

Many UNIX systems support the SMB protocol that Windows uses to share directories and printers. (The new SMB initiative is now referred to as CIFS—Common Internet Filesystem.) This allows the UNIX system to appear in the Windows Network Neighborhood. The UNIX shared directories can be used to exchange data among Windows PCs. The UNIX printers can be used by the Windows PCs.

chapter

27

UNIX and the Internet

Gordon Marler

> **Tip for Beginners**
>
> There is a great wealth of information about UNIX on the Internet. I'm constantly downloading new drivers, patches, and hardware specifications, and doing research on the Internet. I can often find my own problem solutions even before customer support returns my call. There is a wealth of free, very useful utilities that can be downloaded as you will see.

Surfing the Internet from UNIX

Some of the first machines that could access the World Wide Web were running UNIX. The first Web browser to be widely used was Mosaic, an X-Windows application developed by the National Center for Supercomputing Applications (NCSA) at the University of Illinois. Mosaic runs on several flavors of UNIX and is still available today, even though it does not have some of the nicer features of the latest generation of browsers.

Browsers such as Netscape Navigator/Communicator, Sun's HotJava, and Lynx appeared later. If your flavor of UNIX doesn't have X-Windows, or if you don't have the proper hardware to run it, you can still run Lynx because it requires only a dumb terminal.

The locations mentioned in Table 27.1 probably use a format that you're familiar with because many companies today put uniform resource locators (URLs) in their advertisements; these look something like this: `http://www.somecompany.com/`. The `http` portion of these URLs tells your Web browser which protocol to use when talking with the Web server you specify after `http://`.

Table 27.1 Web Browsers That Run on UNIX and Where to Get Them

Browser	Location
Netscape Navigator/ Communicator	`http://home.netscape.com/`
NCSA Mosaic	`ftp://ftp.ncsa.uiuc.edu/Mosaic/Unix/ binaries/2.6/`
Lynx	ftp://www.slcc.edu/pub/lynx/ release2-8/
Sun HotJava	`http://www.javasoft.com/products/ hotjava/index.html`

To help you become more familiar with these protocols and when you might want to use them, Table 27.2 lists and describes the more common ones.

Table 27.2 URL Protocol Specifiers and Their Purpose

Protocol	Purpose
http://	Used to specify a Web page.
https://	Used to specify a secure Web page, which will be encrypted as it is sent to you.
ftp://	Specifies the use of the file transfer protocol to upload and download files.
news://	Specifies a host that will be used as a Network News (Usenet) server.
file:/<pathname>	Enables you to load a local file into your browser (note only *one* slash after the colon in this protocol).
gopher://	Designates a host offering Gopher services.

It's good to remember that many Web servers on the Internet can provide one, some, or all the services listed in Table 27.2 for different parts of their Web site. Many at least provide the first three.

Finding the Right Site

If you're trying to guess a company's Web site address and you end up on some other company's Web site, you will usually find a link to the place you really want to go. Here's an example.

Imagine that you want to go to the home page of Diamond Multimedia, the manufacturer of PC video cards. You try `http://www.diamond.com`, but you discover that this is the Web site for SI Diamond Technology, Inc. But look! There's a link to the Diamond Multimedia Web site: `http://www.diamondmm.com`.

These links usually come about because the Webmaster of the site you originally ended up on is tired of receiving email asking how to get to the Web sites of companies with names similar to his company.

Usually, if you want to find a company's Web site, you can assume that the URL for it will be very close to `http://www.companyname.com`—unless some other company with a similar name is already using it.

You will find out pretty quickly that the World Wide Web is not very centrally organized, and information is spread out over a vast area. If you're looking for something in particular, you either have to know where it is already, or you need help finding it. Web *search engines* can help you out with that.

These engines are generally extremely large UNIX servers that send out *spiders* or *robots*, which seek out, examine, and catalog every Web page on every Web server they can find. A few of the ones currently available are listed in Table 27.3. You can look them over and pick one that suits you best. Each has its own way of letting you specify what you want to search for in its respective catalogs. Some of these services have better catalogs than others, but that changes over time. Each search engine has a handy help feature that will help you with basic searches. The advanced search features take about a page to explain each server type.

Table 27.3 A Few Web Search Engines

Search Engine	Location
AltaVista	`http://www.altavista.digital.com/`
Yahoo!	`http://www.yahoo.com/`
Lycos	`http://www.lycos.com/`

Depending on where your UNIX machine is, you may have a *firewall* between your machine and the Internet. If you access the Internet from work and your company is of any size at all, this is probably the case. If you access the Internet through an Internet service provider from home, you probably don't have to worry about it.

Automatic Proxies

At some sites, the system administrator will not give you the name of your proxy server, but will instead give you a URL that points to an automatic proxy file, which you will have to enter into your browser's Automatic Proxy Configuration. This file contains a script that loads automatically every time you start your browser and programs your browser to intelligently pick the right proxy server for any request you make.

This facility is used at sites that have more than one proxy server so that you don't have to worry about which proxy to point your browser at all the time. You must use a browser that supports this facility, however. Netscape Communicator definitely supports it now, and others are following suit.

If you do have a firewall, your system or network administrator has probably set up a *proxy server*, and you'll have to take some special steps to get your browser to use the proxy server rather than try to go through the firewall directly and fail. The firewall protects your network from intrusion from the Internet, but it also keeps you from getting out. The workaround is to have a proxy server built, which is the only machine allowed direct access to or from the Internet through the firewall. In effect, your browser will ask the proxy to go get a Web page, and then the proxy will hand that page to your browser when it arrives. Don't worry that this will be slow; the proxy server usually gets information off the Web faster than you could directly anyway, and it's a lot safer.

All you have to know is the name of the proxy server and the port that it's listening to. Then you tell your browser, and away you go! The only tricky part might be that that every single protocol listed in Table 27.1 could have its own separate proxy server. This is common only at sites that have an incredible amount of network traffic coming through. (You'll see an example of this later.)

Downloading Software from the Internet

You may wonder why commercial UNIX systems often lack standard freeware utilities, such as `kermit`, that are usually available on Linux. Commercial UNIX systems sell and support UNIX as a product. If they bundled in many freeware utilities, their customers would expect the same support as for the core UNIX software. To make the distinction clear, most UNIX vendors avoid providing free software as part of the standard distribution. However, most vendors also encourage their customers to download from the Internet and use the free software on their own because it extends the product capabilities. Often, a UNIX vendor's Web site will directly link to free software for that version of UNIX.

You already learned how to download files via FTP from the UNIX command line in Chapter 25, "Accessing Other UNIX Systems on the Network or Internet," but you can also use your Web browser to do the same thing. With the browser, it's much easier because all you need to do is point and click.

Most Internet sites that have software you want will enable you to use *anonymous ftp* to download the files you want. It is the convention in anonymous FTP to use anonymous as your username and then give your email address as your password. Some browsers, such as Netscape Navigator, enable you to select a preference that automatically sends anonymous as your username and your email address as your password if you don't specify a username in your URL.

If you don't have a browser that enables you to set preferences for anonymous FTP—or if you are trying to get FTP access to a site that requires you use a specific username and password—you can explicitly enter your username and password for an FTP session through the browser. The syntax of the URL is this:

```
ftp://username:password@the.ftp.site.com/
```

Downloading Lynx

This example assumes that you don't have a browser yet. Therefore, you will want to use the UNIX command line to do the FTP transfers.

The source code for Lynx is available for FTP at `www.slcc.edu` in the directory `/pub/lynx/release2-8/`.

Reading and Writing Zip Files

This chapter shouldn't have to talk about compression, but the compression tool that the Lynx developers used to compress their source code actually derives from the PC PKZIP utility. Therefore, the tool is not a part of UNIX and wasn't discussed in the chapter that covers compression on UNIX. This also means that the standard UNIX compression tools can't read these PKZIP files.

As is often the case with UNIX, however, someone has taken the time to write a utility to read and write these PKZIP files, and has made it freely available to you. You just have to get it and install it yourself, or ask your system administrator to do it for you.

Because the Lynx source code is distributed as a tarred, zipped file (not compressed or gzipped), you also need to get an unzip utility from the Internet; UNIX doesn't come with one by default. You can find a free one already compiled for almost all flavors of UNIX at `ftp.cdrom.com` in the `/pub/infozip/UNIX/` directory.

In this example, the part of the FTP output that was not especially helpful has been stripped out. Note that these messages on the FTP server can change at any time—and frequently do.

```
% ftp -i ftp.cdrom.com
Connected to wcarchive.cdrom.com.
220 wcarchive.cdrom.com FTP server (Version DG-2.0.12 Tue Mar 24 18:34:00 PST
➥1998) ready.
Name (ftp.cdrom.com:gmarler): anonymous
331 Guest login ok, send your complete e-mail address as password.
Password: username@host.com
230-Welcome to wcarchive - home ftp site for Walnut Creek CDROM.
230-There are currently 3000 users out of 3000 possible.
230-
230-Please send mail to ftp-bugs@ftp.cdrom.com if you_experience any problems.
```

```
230-Please also let us know if there is something we don't have that you think
230-we should!
230-
230 Guest login ok, access restrictions apply.
ftp> binary
200 Type set to I.
ftp> hash
Hash mark printing on (8192 bytes/hash mark).
ftp> cd /pub/infozip/UNIX/
250-This directory contains executables for UNIX systems that generally do not
250-ship with a C compiler.
250-
250-   AIX/                    executables for IBM AIX on RS/6000
250-   CLIX/                   executables for Intergraph CLIX
250-   CONVEX/                 executables for ConvexOS
250-   DEC/                    executables for DEC Digital UNIX (OSF/1) and
➡Ultrix
250-   FREEBSD/                executables for FreeBSD 2.x on Intel
250-   HP/                     executables for HP/UX
250-   LINUX/                  executables for Linux on Intel
250-   QNX/                    executables for QNX on Intel
250-   SCO/                    executables for SCO UNIX on Intel
250-   SGI/                    executables for Silicon Graphics Irix
250-   SUN/                    executables for SunOS and Solaris 2.x on SPARC
250-
250-Send problem reports on Zip and UnZip to: _Zip- Bugs@lists.wku.edu
250-
250-Last updated:  1 December 1997
250-
250 CWD command successful.
ftp> cd SUN
250-This directory contains SunOS and Solaris executables for SPARC and Intel
➡x86
250-hardware.
250-
250-  1856 Dec  4 1997  README           what you're reading right now
250-240193 Jun  3 1996  gzip124x.tar.Z    gzip 1.2.4, SunOS exes/docs, tar
➡archive
250-195440 Feb 10 1994  gzip124x.zip      gzip 1.2.4, SunOS exes/docs, zipfile
250-208685 Nov  8 1997  unz532x-41x.tar.Z UnZip 5.32, SunOS 4.x exes/docs,
➡tarball
```

```
250-162289 Nov  8 1997  unz532x-41x.zip    UnZip 5.32, SunOS 4.x exes/docs,
➥zipfile
250-207751 Nov  8 1997  unz532x-sol.tar.Z  UnZip 5.32, Solaris/SPARC 2.x
➥exes/docs
250-161083 Nov  8 1997  unz532x-sol.zip    UnZip 5.32, Solaris/SPARC 2.x
➥exes/docs
250-204513 Nov  5 1997  unz532x-x86.tar.Z  UnZip 5.32, Solaris/x86 2.x exes/docs
250-152404 Nov  5 1997  unz532x-x86.zip    UnZip 5.32, Solaris/x86 2.x exes/docs
94295 Nov  8 1997  zip22x-41x.zip     Zip 2.2, SunOS 4.x exes (no encryption)
250- 91733 Nov  8 1997  zip22x-sol.zip     Zip 2.2, Solaris/SPARC exes
➥(no encrypt.)
250-
250-Binaries with encryption support are available from
250-ftp://ftp.icce.rug.nl/infozip/UNIX/SUN/ :
250-
250-129862 Nov  9 1997  zcr22x-41x.zip     Zip 2.2, SunOS 4.x exes
➥(with encryption)
250-127574 Nov 15 1997  zcr22x-sol.zip     Zip 2.2, Solaris/SPARC exes
➥(w/encrypt.)
250-103685 Nov  8 1997  zcr22x-x86.zip     Zip 2.2, Solaris/x86 exes
➥(w/encryption)
250-
250-The SunOS 4.x executables have been tested under SunOS 4.1.4 and Solaris
➥2.5.1
250-and are virtually indistinguishable in speed from native Solaris 2.x
➥binaries.
250-There have been reports that they don't work well under Solaris 2.4,
➥however,
250-so both flavors are provided.
250-
250-The x86 binaries were compiled under Solaris 2.4 with SC 2.0.1.
250-
250-All Info-ZIP packages contain documentation.  The sources are in ../../src .
250-
250-Send problem reports on Zip and UnZip to:  Zip-Bugs@lists.wku.edu
250-Send problem reports on gzip to:           gzip@prep.ai.mit.edu
250-
250-Last updated:  4 December 1997
250-
250 CWD command successful.
ftp> get unz532x-sol.tar.Z
```

```
200 PORT command successful.
150 Opening BINARY mode data connection for unz532x-sol.tar.Z (207751 bytes).
#########################
226 Transfer complete.
local: unz532x-sol.tar.Z remote: unz532x-sol.tar.Z
207751 bytes received in 3.4 seconds (60 Kbytes/s)
```

Now that you have the unzip utility, you can pipe it through GNU's gzip utility to decompress it and then extract the information from the enclosed tar file. After you have done this, you will probably want to copy the binaries to /usr/local/bin and the man pages to /usr/local/man/man1, or have your system administrator do it for you:

```
% cat unz532x-sol.tar.Z ¦ gzip -d ¦ tar xvf -
x ., 0 bytes, 0 tape blocks
x COPYING, 11259 bytes, 22 tape blocks
x README, 9901 bytes, 20 tape blocks
x WHERE, 16717 bytes, 33 tape blocks
x unzip, 106844 bytes, 209 tape blocks
x unzip.1, 37276 bytes, 73 tape blocks
x unzip.doc, 44561 bytes, 88 tape blocks
x unzipsfx, 54984 bytes, 108 tape blocks
x unzipsfx.1, 13119 bytes, 24 tape blocks
x unzipsfx.doc, 13657 bytes, 27 tape blocks
x zipinfo symbolic link to unzip
x zipinfo.1, 22013 bytes, 43 tape blocks
x zipinfo.doc, 23897 bytes, 47 tape blocks
x zipgrep, 1157 bytes, 3 tape blocks
x zipgrep.1, 3868 bytes, 8 tape blocks
x zipgrep.doc, 3550 bytes, 7 tape blocks
x funzip, 21196 bytes, 42 tape blocks
x funzip.1, 4649 bytes, 10 tape blocks
x funzip.doc, 3914 bytes, 8 tape blocks
```

After you have all the necessary utilities in place, you can go ahead and download the source code for Lynx:

```
% ftp -i www.slcc.edu
Connected to SOL.SLCC.EDU.
220 sol.slcc.edu FTP server (UNIX(r) System V Release 4.0) ready.
Name (www.slcc.edu:gmarler): anonymous
331 Guest login ok, send ident as password.
Password: username@host.com
```

```
230 Guest login ok, access restrictions apply.
ftp> cd /pub/lynx/release2-8
250 CWD command successful.
ftp> dir
200 PORT command successful.
150 ASCII data connection for /bin/ls (205.172.10.173,48147) (0 bytes).
total 3786
-r--r--r--   1 163       14          204102 Mar 10 10:54 CHANGES
-r--r--r--   1 163       14            2514 Mar 10 04:45 features.html
-r--r--r--   1 163       14            2281 Mar 10 12:14 features.txt
-r--r--r--   1 163       14            3285 Mar 10 04:25 index.html
-r--r--r--   1 163       14            3060 Mar 10 12:14 index.txt
drwxr-xr-x   9 163       14            1024 Mar 10 12:19 lynx2-8
-r--r--r--   1 163       14         1669681 Mar 10 12:07 lynx2-8.zip
-r--r--r--   1 163       14           25671 Mar 10 12:07 lynx2-8.zip-lst
-r--r--r--   1 163       14            2085 Mar 14 19:28 ssl.html
-r--r--r--   1 163       14            1786 Mar 14 19:42 ssl.txt
226 ASCII Transfer complete.
671 bytes received in 0.034 seconds (19 Kbytes/s)
ftp> binary
200 Type set to I.
ftp> hash
Hash mark printing on (8192 bytes/hash mark).
ftp> get lynx2-8.zip
200 PORT command successful.
150 Binary data connection for lynx2-8.zip (205.172.10.173,48148)
↪(1669681 bytes).
##############################################################
#####################################################################
##############################################################
226 Binary Transfer complete.
local: lynx2-8.zip remote: lynx2-8.zip
1669681 bytes received in 67 seconds (24 Kbytes/s)
```

The source code for Lynx is in a zip archive, so just run the unzip utility on it. This creates the Lynx source directory and drops all the source code in it:

```
% unzip lynx2-8.zip
Archive:  lynx2-8.zip
   creating: lynx2-8/
  inflating: lynx2-8/COPYHEADER
  inflating: lynx2-8/COPYING
```

```
inflating: lynx2-8/INSTALLATION
inflating: lynx2-8/LYMessages_en.h
```

.....

Running *make* on Lynx

A couple of assumptions are made for this section:

GNU (and Free!) Software

To find out more about GNU software products such as the GNU C Compiler and GNU make you can go to the Free Software Foundation Web site at `http://www.gnu.org`.

Here you will find documentation and source code for all the GNU products. Not only are they freely available, but they often work better than the tools that came standard with your flavor of UNIX.

- You own the C Compiler suite for your flavor of UNIX, or you have installed the GNU C compiler. For most purposes, the GNU compiler is preferred because it is actually better than most commercial compilers. It's pretty nice, especially because it's free.

- You have the make utility that comes with your C Compiler suite, or you have installed the GNU make utility. Neither one is preferred over the other.

As with many current UNIX source distributions, Lynx is packaged with GNU's autoconfig utility, which analyzes your flavor of UNIX and makes sure that all the proper settings are made to enable you to compile Lynx without trouble. Any package like this will have a configure script in its top-level source tree. All you need to do is run configure, and it creates the proper makefile for your machine:

```
% cd lynx2-8
% ./configure
creating cache ./config.cache
checking host system type... sparc-sun-solaris2.5.1
checking for gcc... gcc
checking whether the C compiler (gcc  ) works... yes
checking whether the C compiler (gcc  ) is a cross-compiler_... no
checking whether we are using GNU C... yes
```

...

```
updating cache ./config.cache
creating ./config.status
creating makefile
creating WWW/Library/unix/makefile
creating src/makefile
creating src/chrtrans/makefile
creating lynx_cfg.h
```

Now that you have configured the Lynx source for your platform, you can have the `make` utility compile it for you:

```
% make
```

If Lynx compiles successfully, you can install it by typing the following:

```
# make install
```

You will need to have root access to `/usr/local/` on your system, or have your system administrator install Lynx for you.

Using a Character-Based Browser (Lynx)

Now that you have gone to all that trouble to build a binary for Lynx that runs on your machine, you actually get to use it!

"Installing" Lynx

1. First, if your site is behind a firewall, you need to make sure that you are set up to use the appropriate proxy server, if available. Check with your system administrator to find out your proxy server's name and the port it talks on. If you are not behind a firewall, go to step 3.

2. After you know your proxy server's name and port number (for this example, call the server `relay.mycompany.com` and the port it talks on `8080`), you need to set a few environment variables before you can run Lynx. Assume for simplicity that your proxy server is a proxy for all the following protocols: HTTP, HTTPS, and FTP. If it is not, your system administrator can tell you.

   If you are using the C shell, put the following in your logon scripts:
   ```
   setenv http_proxy     http://relay.mycompany.com:8080/"
   setenv https_proxy    http://relay.mycompany.com:8080/"
   setenv ftp_proxy     ftp://relay.mycompany.com:8080/"
   ```

   If you are using the Bourne/Korn shell, put the following in your logon scripts:
   ```
   http_proxy=http://relay.mycompany.com:8080/; export http_proxy
   https_proxy=http://relay.mycompany.com:8080/; export https_proxy
   ftp_proxy=http://relay.mycompany.com:8080/; export ftp_proxy
   ```

3. Now, you can run Lynx. At the command line, type `lynx`.

Using Lynx is pretty straightforward. Table 27.4 lists the most frequently used commands.

Table 27.4 Brief Lynx Command Summary

Command	Summary
g	Go to a URL; enables you to type in a URL to go to.
/pattern	Search for a pattern in the current Web page.
Up arrow	Move up through the hyperlinks in the current Web page.
Down arrow	Move down through the hyperlinks in the current Web page.
Return	Go to the currently selected hyperlink.

Finding UNIX Vendor Web Sites

Most UNIX vendors keep a presence on the Web and allow varying degrees of access to the Web site's technical support contents based on how much you have paid them for support. Several vendors keep a separate site for a main entry point into their Web and another for UNIX support.

Finding Support

I have included the main entry points to each vendor's Web site because these never change. If you find that the UNIX support pages in Table 27.5 change, you can always be sure that if you go to the main entry point for that vendor, you can find a link to the new UNIX support page.

Table 27.5 Web Sites of UNIX Vendors

Hewlett-Packard	Main entry point:
(HP-UX)	`http://www.hp.com`
	UNIX support:
	`http://us-support.external.hp.com/`
IBM (AIX)	Main entry point:
	`http://www.ibm.com`

continues...

Table 27.5 Continued	
IBM (AIX)	Main entry point:
	UNIX support: http://www.rs6000.ibm.com/support/
Santa Cruz Operation (OpenServer and UnixWare)	Main entry point: http://www.sco.com
	UNIX support: http://www.sco.com/support/
Silicon Graphics (IRIX)	Main entry point: http://www.sgi.com
	UNIX support: http://www.sgi.com/software/
Sun Microsystems (SunOS, Solaris)	Main entry point: http://www.sun.com
	UNIX support: http://sunsolve1.sun.com

Accessing UNIX Technical Support

Several kinds of technical support are available from each UNIX vendor. Some are provided free of charge, but most require that you have a support contract with the vendor. This section reviews each type of support and how you can obtain it. Although each vendor deals with support in a slightly different way, Sun's support system is used as an example.

Escalating a Service Call

Here's something most vendors don't tell you when you get a service contract, but you should know it anyway. If a problem you have found is severely impacting you, the technical support people aren't calling you back in a timely manner, or they seem to be overly inexperienced, you can *escalate* the call. You do this by calling the tech support center back, giving them your service order number, and asking to speak to the escalation manager. You can explain the poor service to him and ask to have the call escalated in priority. You will want to do this only in cases of extreme emergency, or when a software support engineer just won't call you back. I generally have to do it only once a year or so.

When you purchase your UNIX system(s), you are usually given the option to purchase support for both the hardware and the software, which could include the operating system, bundled software tools, and, additionally, any unbundled tools that you elect to buy, such as special compilers or applications. You generally have the option to purchase one of several levels of service, ranging from assistance five days a week, during business hours, to seven days a week, 24 hours a day. Sun calls these service plans SunSpectrum, and they lay out how their plans work at `http://www.sun.com/service/support/sunspectrum/_index.htm`. Most vendors have something very similar.

Recently, vendors have started to offer software support separately from hardware support. Sun calls this Software Only, or Software Subscription service. The exact components of this offering are discussed at `http://www.sun.com/service/support/sw_only/index.html`. This kind of service will probably become more common as time goes on because many people and businesses just want to purchase support for software and take care of hardware problems as they come up.

Direct support for reporting problems with the operating system or the tools that are bundled with it is reserved for customers with support contracts. To report a problem, you generally make a phone call to the vendor's 800 number and give your contract number; you will be asked to briefly describe your problem. You then will be given a service order number for the problem, and an engineer will get back to you within a time frame specified in your contract. Generally, you will find that the problem you're experiencing has already been dealt with, and the engineer will point you to a patch or other workaround.

Another method of reporting such problems is through electronic mail or the vendor's support Web site, mentioned in the preceding section.

Speaking of Web sites, vendors are making more of their support capabilities available through their support Web sites. If you go to Sun's site, you will see that some support, such as patches, frequently asked questions (FAQs), and documentation, is available free of charge.

Some portions of the Web site are restricted to customers who have support contracts. The services provided here include the capability to use a search engine on the patch database to help you find the problem that happens to bother your exact hardware and software combination, and they point you to the patch that will fix it for you. (More on patches a couple of sections from now.) Other contract services include the capability to download special system diagnostic tools and examine online documentation such as white papers, problem symptom and resolution reports, and information on how to transition from one version of the operating system to another.

A final method of getting technical support is often the most useful—and it's free! Later, this chapter discusses using Usenet, but it's good to mention that there is a set of newsgroups for virtually every computer type and operating system that ever existed. Often, you will find that experts frequent these newsgroups and are usually only too happy to provide you with any help you need. However, it is often the case that any question you may have—especially if you're a beginner— has already been asked hundreds of times. If so, it will generally be included in a FAQ message sent out on each newsgroup once a month or so. This is a single message consisting of every support question that has been asked and answered for a specific newsgroup topic since it was created. You will save yourself a lot of trouble (and hate email) by reading this message before asking everyone in the newsgroup about your particular problem. More about the specific names of such newsgroups at the end of this chapter.

Accessing Free (Nonsupported) Software

All vendors provide some internally developed software for monitoring your system free of charge. These are free because they are not supported officially. If you want to report a problem with these tools, you must take it up with the original author, who may or may not be able to do anything, depending on current workload.

An example of such a tool for Sun is SymBEL, originally known as Virtual Adrian, available from `http://www.sun.com/sun-on-net/_performance/se3/`. This tool enables you to analyze the inner workings of the operating system kernel and reports modifications you could make to get better performance out of it. You will notice that it is explicitly stated that the package is not officially supported but Sun would appreciate feedback via email and will consider any requests for enhancement.

Such tools actually work quite well. The problem is *finding* them, because nonsupported applications are not given prominent exposure. If you know the names of the tools that you want, it's a pretty easy process of feeding these names into a Web search engine and coming up with at least a hint of where to obtain the latest copies of them. It's also worthy of note that not all such programs are created or provided by the vendor. Some are written by experienced programmers who want to share them with everybody.

Usenet is another location to look for or hear about such tools. The groups you should monitor for your particular vendor are discussed later in this chapter.

Checking Patches/Updates

As mentioned earlier, vendors make certain critical patches available free on their Web sites. The freely provided patches are also usually available in *patch clusters*, which are a group of patches targeted at a specific release of the operating system. Periodically checking the vendor's Web site for new releases of individual patches or patch clusters is a good idea because this will keep you up to date on issues that might otherwise bite you unexpectedly.

If you have a support contract with your UNIX vendor, you are in a much better position because you can mark certain patches or patch clusters on the Web site so that you are notified immediately via email when updates to them are released. You also have the option of using sophisticated search engines to locate patches that affect your exact hardware, software, or operating system version configuration.

You also have access to a very nice tool on Sun's Web site to help you determine the right patches to apply to your system (and probably similar tools on other platforms) if you have software support. The tool, called patchdiag, compares the patches currently loaded on your system with the patches that Sun currently recommends that you have loaded. It then produces a report telling you what you have loaded and what you should have loaded. This tool even has a separate section describing patches that affect operating systems and applications, and another section that describes the patches that affect security.

One word about patches on UNIX machines: Many vendors are rightfully paranoid about permanently removing any files replaced by a patch application. So, they take the files that are to be replaced and tuck them away, just in case they ever want to back the patch out. Just be aware that you may lose a bit of disk space because of this.

As different patches for the same problem are updated, applying one patch on top of the other takes up more disk space. If you have the time but not the disk space to spare, you can remove the old patch before applying the new one. Usually, when you upgrade your operating system, such patch remnants are removed completely anyway, so you can reclaim the space.

Checking Security Bulletins

Security bulletins for your particular flavor of UNIX are generally displayed very prominently on your vendor's Web site. An archive of past security alerts is also usually available free of charge. Each bulletin describes a part of the operating system that can be compromised by people with the right information. It also describes the patches or actions necessary to block the threat.

Patches for security holes are almost always freely available. You may choose to manually check occasionally for new security bulletins, or you can get on a mailing list that is prominently mentioned in each individual security bulletin. You will be notified when a bulletin is issued for your particular platform automatically after that.

Checking Year 2000 Issues

Unless you have been asleep for the past couple of years, you have heard of all the problems the year 2000 will bring to the computing world in general. Most of these issues have to do with the fact that many applications and some operating systems were written with the first two digits of the year (that's the 19 in the year 1999) hard-coded everywhere. Only the last two digits of the year actually changed in databases and other files where dates were stored. Therefore, when the year 2000 arrives, these applications will change the last two digits of the year to 00, and the year will appear to be 1900 to them.

As you might imagine, this will cause programs that depend on the date moving *forward* as time progresses to get a little confused and do some nasty things to the data that they have control over. Things such as bank records, billing programs, and others may be affected unless such programs are discovered and repaired prior to December 31, 1999.

This whole thing came about because people working on these applications and operating systems had no idea that anyone would still be using *their* applications or even the same computers when the year 2000 arrived. Some developers are still in the bad habit of coding programs that handle date-sensitive information in the same way.

Most UNIX vendors are very conscious of this issue and have spent a great deal of effort to go through their system administration and general system programs to make sure that all of them are year 2000-compliant. If you are running older versions of an operating system, vendors probably have patches that you can apply to fix these problems today. The newer versions of UNIX claim complete year 2000 compliance. If you have a support contract with your UNIX vendor, these patches are prominently displayed on its support Web sites and can be downloaded directly to your system for application. If you have not purchased a support contract with a UNIX vendor, most will still provide their year 2000 patches via the free services section of their support Web pages because they are critical to keeping you up and running.

Of course, patching your UNIX operating system and the tools that your vendor ships with it may not be enough. You probably have applications that you purchased from other vendors, and you will need to either check with them directly or visit their Web sites. As with the UNIX vendors, most application vendors prominently claim fixes to the year 2000 problem on the first page of their support Web site.

Reading the Network News on UNIX

One of the oldest activities on the Internet is reading the Network News, otherwise known as Usenet. Usenet is essentially a gigantic collection of individual discussion topics that range from job offerings (`misc.jobs.offered`), to how to administer your Sun computer (`comp.sys.sun.admin`), to how to care for your African Grey parrot (`alt.pets.parrots.african-grey`). Often, you can speak with experts in the particular topic, or offer advice if you are an expert in this field. Each newsgroup is very specific in its content, but this is enforced only if the newsgroup is moderated. A moderated newsgroup has an assigned moderator who reads every incoming message to the newsgroup to verify that it belongs there. If it doesn't, the moderator rejects that message. An unmoderated newsgroup is usually a free-for-all, but people generally are polite enough to stick to the topic at hand. If the group gets completely out of control, it can be dropped from all news servers throughout Usenet.

Newsgroups are arranged in a hierarchy, where the first word in the newsgroup name is the least specific. As you proceed into the newsgroup name, it becomes more specific. Table 27.6 lists and explains this convention.

Table 27.6   Top Level of Several Usenet Newsgroup Hierarchies

Hierarchy	Description
`comp.*`	Computer-related newsgroups (for example, `comp.sys.sun`, `comp.sys.hp`)
`rec.*`	Recreational newsgroups (for example, `rec.humor`, `rec.gardens.roses`)
`sci.*`	Science-related newsgroups (for example, `sci.math`, `sci.archaeology`)
`alt.*`	Alternative newsgroups (for example, `alt.binaries.startrek`)
`misc.*`	Miscellaneous topics that don't fit anywhere else

When you select a newsgroup to read or write to, this is called *subscribing* to the newsgroup. When you send a message to be included in a newsgroup, it is called *posting* to the newsgroup. When you do this, it will take a day or so to filter out to all the news servers in the world, and then people will very likely reply to what you have written. Previously, you had to scan the newsgroup each day, manually looking for any reply to your original question or remark. Thankfully, most news readers today provide a facility called *threading*, which finds original postings and places any responses to them in chronological order immediately following them. You will find that trn (threaded readnews) and Netscape provide this feature, although Netscape calls newsgroups *discussion groups,* and calls the portion of their browser which you use to read news *Collabra Discussions*.

Having a news reader client is not enough to enable you to read and post to Usenet. You need to have access to a news server. If you are at a large site, your system administrator has probably set up a news server or has arranged with another site to provide this service. In any case, your system administrator can tell you the name of this server so that you can connect to it. If your UNIX machine is standalone and you are accessing the Internet through an Internet service provider, you can ask what the name of that news server is. After you know the name of the news server, set the environment variable NNTPSERVER so that it points to the news server. Most news reader clients look for this environment variable when they start up and use it to identify the news server they should connect to.

Reading and posting messages with Usenet

1. You want to use trn to read Network News. First, make sure that trn is available. If not, ask your system administrator to install it (or something equivalent) for you; or, if you're on your own, you can download the source code for it and compile it yourself. After trn is installed, you can proceed to the next step.

NNTP

NNTPSERVER stands for Network News Transfer Protocol Server.

---

2. Find out the name of your news server from your system administrator or Internet service provider, and set your NNTPSERVER environment variable accordingly. For this example, assume that the name of the news server is
   news.mycompany.com.

   For Bourne, bash, and Korn shell users:
   NNTPSERVER=news.mycompany.com; export NNTPSERVER

   For C shell users:
   setenv NNTPSERVER news.mycompany.com

3. Now, run trn and subscribe to all the comp.sys.sun.* newsgroups. At the command line, type trn. (The bolded terms at the end of the lines in the following output reflect what you type in as response.)

```
To add new group use a pattern or "g newsgroup.name". To get rid
of newsgroups you aren't interested in, use the 'u' command.
No unread news in subscribed-to newsgroups. To subscribe to a new
newsgroup use the g<newsgroup> command.
***End of newsgroups -- what next? [qnp] a comp.sys.sun

Newsgroup comp.sys.sun.admin not in .newsrc --
subscribe? [ynYN] y
Put newsgroup where? [$^Lq] $
. . .
====== 456 unread articles in comp.sys.sun.admin --
read now? [+ynq] y
```

4. When you type a comp.sys.sun, you instruct trn to search the entire list of newsgroups for any with comp.sys.sun in their title. You are asked whether you want to subscribe to each one in turn. If you said yes, trn asks you where you want to put this new newsgroup in your current list of subscribed newsgroups. Pressing the dollar sign ($) puts this newsgroup at the end of your current list. After you have added all your new newsgroups, you are given the opportunity to read the messages in each one.

5. If you would like to post a message to any newsgroup, you do so from anywhere within trn by typing !Pnews. You will be asked what newsgroup you want to send a message to. You can specify more than one newsgroup at once if you like, by separating the newsgroup names with commas.

6. Press the h key at any time in trn for the Help menu.

As discussed earlier, newsgroups deal with specific flavors of UNIX. Reading the ones specific to your flavor can be very helpful—and even more helpful when you need to ask a question—because you are speaking in a forum that deals only with that topic. However, you need to know what the newsgroups are. The good news is that the name of the newsgroups follow a specific pattern. Table 27.7 shows the major Sun newsgroups and their purposes.

Table 27.7 Sun-Specific Newsgroups

Newsgroup	Description
comp.sys.sun.announce	Major announcements of interest to people who use Sun computers
comp.sys.sun.admin	Information on system administration of Sun computers

continues...

Table 27.7 Continued

Newsgroup	Description
comp.sys.sun.apps	Information on applications that run on Sun computers
comp.sys.sun.hardware	Information on Sun computer hardware
comp.sys.sun.misc	Miscellaneous information on Sun computers that doesn't fit into any other newsgroup
comp.sys.sun.wanted	Usually requests for Sun hardware, but sometimes software, too

If you are using Hewlett-Packard's HP-UX, don't give up hope. Just replace "sun" in the preceding table with "hp," and you have the same newsgroups for your platform. Other flavors of UNIX have newsgroups named similarly.

part

VI

SCRIPT PROGRAMMING

chapter

28

Writing Bourne Shell Scripts

Gordon Marler and
Steve "Mor" Moritsugu

Writing/executing a simple script

Supplying script input on the
command line

Executing code based on test results

Performing arithmetic calculations

Debugging your script

Looping through a list of items

Selecting from a menu of items

Tip for Beginners

Writing your own Bourne shell scripts may sound difficult, but they are easy to create as long as you can use a text editor under UNIX (such as vi). Any time you have to type in the same commands frequently, you can save yourself all that typing by creating a shell script to run those commands for you. If you are familiar with any programming language, you should be able to handle with little difficulty simple shell scripts and some of the more advanced shell programming features in this chapter.

The Bourne shell is the standard shell and can be found on every flavor of UNIX that has ever existed. Although it can be considered a subset of the Korn shell or the Bash shell, many people still write scripts in the Bourne shell because it's guaranteed to be portable among all the different versions of UNIX.

You have already seen that the shell can be used as a command line interface to UNIX, but it also contains programming constructs that enable you to automate repetitive command sequences in a script. An example of this would be finding all the programs you currently have running in the system and reporting them to you. You can also have a script interact with you and make decisions based on your input. An example of this would be a script that asks you for a particular user's name, then finds all the programs in the system that belong to that user, and finally reports them to you.

One simple rule before jumping in: The pound sign (#) character signifies that the rest of the characters following it are part of a comment and will not be interpreted by the shell unless the # is the first character on the first line. You will see why shortly:

```
# this is a comment and not part of a command

rm acme   # This is also a comment after an rm command
```

Writing/Executing a Simple Script

You can begin by creating a very simple Bourne shell script that prints a simple message such as Hello World and then exits.

Executing a "Hello World" script

1. First, you need to start a text editor (such as vi) so you can key in your script in a text file using the vi text editor. Call this file testscript:

   ```
   vi testscript
   ```

If vi is not your preferred text editor, you may use any available text editor to create `testscript` or any shell script.

Using a Word Processor to Create Your Script

It is common to find Windows systems and UNIX in the same network. You can use a Windows Word Processor to edit your script and then upload it to UNIX. Just make sure that you save your script as a simple text file in MS-DOS mode and not as a word processing document.

---

2. On some UNIX systems, your script will not run unless it contains magic text in the first line. Most versions of UNIX understand the `#!` notation. If the first two characters in a file are `#!`, UNIX will assume that everything else on the first line of the file is the command interpreter (usually a shell) that will be used to execute the contents of the file. In this case, you want the Bourne shell to execute the contents of your file, so enter the following as the first line of the `testscript` file:

```
#!/bin/sh
```

If you are using the C shell on older UNIX systems, it is important that the first character of any Bourne shell not be a # sign. On those systems, it is common for the first line of your script to be just a single colon, like this:

```
:
```

3. Printing `Hello World` to the screen is accomplished by entering this as the second line of the file:

```
echo "Hello World."
```

4. Those two lines are all you need, so save and exit from the editor. This can be done from vi as follows:

```
:wq
```

5. Next, you must turn on execute permission for the file by entering the following:

```
chmod +x testscript
```

6. You can test your script by running it:

```
$ ./testscript
Hello World
$
```

If you `cat testscript`, your finished script should look like this:

```
$ cat testscript
#!/bin/sh
```

```
echo "Hello World"
$
```

The next example will show you where a simple shell script would be useful in real life. Assume that you have an important employee file. Before you use vi to edit it, you save the older backup and then make a newer backup, like this:

```
cp employeeOLD employeeOLD2
cp employee employeeOLD
vi employee
```

Any time you have to type in repetitive commands like this, you can make your work easier with a shell script. Put the following four lines into a text file called viemp (or any name you prefer):

```
#!/bin/sh
cp employeeOLD employeeOLD2
cp employee employeeOLD
vi employee
```

Next make your script executable:

```
chmod +x viemp
```

To run your script, go to the directory that holds your script. Many users create a local bin directory to hold their executable programs. In that case, you can run your script like this:

```
cd $HOME/bin
./viemp
```

Your script will make your copies and then invoke vi so that you can edit your file. You can also eliminate the cd command by invoking your script as a full pathname:

```
$HOME/bin/viemp
```

Running Your Scripts Without a Pathname

If you use your script frequently, there are ways to invoke it by just typing the script name, without having to cd to its directory or enter a full pathname. To run a script without having to enter a pathname, the directory that contains the script must be listed in your PATH variable. You can either add the directory of the script to PATH or move the script to a directory that is already in PATH.

Continuing the example from the previous section, assume that your script viemp is in the directory /usr/fred/bin. You can add /usr/fred/bin to PATH like this:

```
PATH=$PATH:/usr/fred/bin
```

Having done this, you can invoke viemp like this:

```
viemp
```

You don't have to be in that directory or enter a pathname to run this command now that PATH has been setup. Your change to PATH will remain until you logoff. If you want this PATH modification to be permanent, add the line that sets PATH to the .profile file in your home directory.

Creating and Using Your Own Variables

You will often find it convenient to store the output of a command you run in your script for use later in the script. Or, you might want to hard-code some information such as a long directory path, but you don't want to type the whole path every time you need to use it in the script. And if this directory path ever needs to be changed, it would be nice to be able to change it in only one place in the script and yet have it take effect throughout the script. To do this, you must create a variable. A shell variable begins with any letter or underscore (_) character, followed by zero or more numbers, letters, or underscores.

UNIX is Case-Sensitive

Remember that UNIX is case-sensitive. You must use the same upper- and lowercase letters each time you reference the same variable. For example, $DIR, $Dir, $dir, $diR, and $DIr are all valid but are different variables.

To assign a value to the variable, you use the equal sign (=) and then the value you want to assign to the variable. Note that you can't use a space before or after the equal sign. Study these examples:

`LocalBinaries=/usr/local/bin`	Valid
`TMP=/tmp`	Valid
`_mybinaries=/home/gmarler/bin`	Valid
`rocket_0=apollo`	Valid
`0_rocket=mercury`	Invalid: First character cannot be a number
`myvar = myvalue`	Invalid: There are spaces around the = sign

To retrieve the value stored in a variable, you place a dollar sign ($) in front of the variable name. To avoid ambiguity, this can also be done by surrounding the variable name with curly braces ({}) and putting a dollar sign ($) in front of the whole thing. You will see when this would be necessary a little later.

Writing a script that sets a variable and then printing its value

1. Use vi to create a new script as you did in the previous section, but call the filename `testscript2`.

2. On the second line of the script, set a variable named `tmp_dir` to `/tmp`, as shown here:
   ```
   tmp_dir=/tmp
   ```
   Note that no spaces are allowed before or after the equal sign.

3. On the next line, print the value of the variable `tmp_dir`:
   ```
   echo " Variable tmp_dir contains: $tmp_dir"
   ```

4. Save your script file. It should now contain the following:
   ```
   #!/bin/sh
   tmp_dir=/tmp
   echo "Variable tmp_dir contains: $tmp_dir"
   ```

5. Make your script executable, and test it:
   ```
   $ chmod +x testscript2
   $ ./testscript2
   Variable tmp_dir contains: /tmp
   $
   ```

Remember that it might be necessary to use the optional `${variablename}` syntax when you want to retrieve the value stored in a variable. The following two lines illustrate both syntax methods, are equally valid, and display the exact same result:

```
echo "Variable tmp_dir contains: $tmp_dir"

echo "Variable tmp_dir contains: ${tmp_dir}"
```

Now revisit your `viemp` script from before. By using a variable, it will be easy to modify the script to do the same function for other filenames. In this new version of `viemp`, only one line has to change if you want to work with a different filename:

```
#!/bin/sh
# New version of viemp
FILE=employee
cp "${FILE}OLD" "${FILE}OLD2"
cp "${FILE}" "${FILE}OLD"
vi "$FILE"
```

In the preceding script program, the `${...}` syntax for variables is required because the variable name is followed immediately by other letters or digits. `$FILE` contains employee so `${FILE}OLD` equates to `employeeOLD`. You could not use `$FILEOLD` (without braces) because this would be a different variable from `$FILE` and its contents would be empty since no value was even assigned to it.

Avoid the temptation to commit the following error:

```
# New version of viemp        # wrong
#!/bin/sh
```

The preceding lines are not in the correct order. The magic `#!/bin/sh` must be in the first line of the script. It is worthless as the second line, and your script may not run because it is not the first line.

Using Backquotes to Set a Variable

Rather than manually setting the values of all your variables, you can run a program and store its output in a variable. You run the command you wish to capture the output of by surrounding it with backquotes (`` ` ``). This is also known as command substitution, because the shell takes the command you type in backquotes, runs it as a separate program as though you had typed it in on the command line, and then substitutes the output for the entire backquoted expression. The backquote is on the same key as the tilde (~) on your keyboard.

Using Quotation Marks Around Backquotes

If the command in backquotes is going to produce multiple lines of output, you need to make sure that you enclose the backquoted command in double quotation marks. Otherwise, the new lines in the output will be stripped out, and you will get one very long, ugly line! Double quotation marks are also necessary if you intend to echo the output from such a command after it has been stored in a variable.

You can test this facility by writing a script that collects your username, the name of the computer you are running the script on, and the current date to print an informational message.

Testing the backquote method for setting a variable

1. Use vi to create a new script, as you did in the previous section "Writing/Executing a Simple Script," but call the filename `system_info`.

2. In this script, you will use backquotes to store the output of the date program in the variable `today`. Remember that no spaces are allowed before or after the equal sign. Enter the following:

   ```
   today=`date`
   ```

3. Find out who you are logged on as by running `whoami`, and store this in the variable identity:

   ```
   identity=`whoami`
   ```

4. Find out the name of your UNIX system, and store it in the variable machine:

   ```
   machine=`hostname`
   ```

5. Print this information in a nice format. Enter these lines:

   ```
   echo "Hello, today is $today. "
   echo "I am logged in as $identity on machine $machine."
   ```

6. Save your script. It should look like this:

   ```
   #!/bin/sh
   today=`date`
   identity=`whoami`
   machine=`hostname`
   echo "Hello, today is $today. "
   echo "I am logged in as $identity on machine $machine."
   ```

7. Make the script executable, and test it:

   ```
   $ chmod +x system_info
   $ ./system_info
   Hello, today is Thu Mar 12 01:03:27 PST 1998.
   I am logged in as gmarler on machine proteon.
   ```

You need to make sure that the commands you want to execute by using the backquotes can actually be found by your shell script. You want to do this because scripts that don't have this variable set will inherit the PATH of the user who runs the script. If that user doesn't have the same PATH as you, the author of the script, the script may mysteriously fail to run for that user. If your script invokes any commands that are not found in the usual PATH variable, use a full pathname for that command in your script so that other users can run your script without problems.

Interacting with the User

The following section further demonstrates some of the script commands discussed earlier in this chapter and adds some new ones to your skill set.

Displaying Headings and Prompts

The echo command just displays the argument words it has been given. As such, it is rarely used at the command line. However, it is very useful in shell scripts. Its simplest use is to provide a heading for your output:

```
#!/bin/sh
echo "Users currently logged in at `date`"
who
```

In this example, the echo command outputs a heading before the output of the who command is shown. The heading uses backquotes so that the current date and time are inserted into the heading.

The echo command allows for the following formatting escape characters that help you customize your headings, titles, and prompts:

\c	Insert this directive at the end of the string to be echoed to suppress adding a new line terminator so that subsequent output will appear on the same line. This is useful for input prompts.
\n	This indicates a new line. It is useful for forcing text after this to be printed on the next line.
\t	This indicates a tab and is useful for formatting headings and prompts.
\\	This is useful for inserting the backslash character in the line.
\0xx	This is useful for inserting unprintable control characters. 0xx is an octal representation of an ASCII character. The zero is required.

The following example illustrates use of \n to start a new line, \t to output a tab to indent the next line, and \c to allow the next output or input to stay on the same line:

```
echo "Acme Systems\n\tFounded in \c"
cat founding-date
```

Notice that a space has been inserted before \c so that the founding date is not run together with the previous message. This example will look like this when it is run:

```
Acme Systems
        Founded in 1982
```

On some UNIX systems, the echo -e option is required to use special escape sequences such as \n and \c. In that case, the previous example will display incorrect output, like this, when run:

```
Acme Systems\n\tFounded in \c
1982
```

If your output looks like the previous example, add the -e option as shown here to correct the problem:

```
echo -e "Acme Systems\n\tFounded in \c"
cat founding-date
```

You might even encounter an old version of UNIX that does not allow \n or any escape sequences. In that case, you can still suppress the new line by using the echo -n option:

```
echo -n "Acme Systems
      Founded in "
cat founding-date
```

The previous example also shows that instead of embedding \n within one line, you have the option to use multiple lines within your echo statement.

Using what you know to write a script to print information about the user

1. First, print a header for your table of information. Use a couple tabs in front of the header to more or less center it, and put an extra blank line after it to distance it from the rest of the table. Because echo already forces you to the next line, you just need to add another new line to the end:

   ```
   echo "\t\tCURRENT USER INFORMATION\n."
   ```

   No whoami?

   If whoami is not available on your UNIX system, it will give a Not Found error. Try echo $LOGNAME instead.

2. You need the username of the person running the script for a command used later, so you will save it in a variable:

   ```
   identity=`whoami`
   ```

3. Now you will print some information about the user. Notice that backquoted commands are used right inside the line to be output. These commands are run, and their output is substituted in the text before it is printed:

```
echo "My Unix username is: `whoami`"
echo "My Unix machine name is: `hostname`"
echo "My current directory is: `pwd`"
```

4. Finally, you print a list of all the programs currently being run in the system by the person running this script. The `grep` command (covered in Chapter 18, "Searching for Lines in a File or Pipeline") removes lines that don't reference this user. The `sed` command (covered in Chapter 19, "Replacing or Removing Text from a File or Pipeline") indents all the process lines by three spaces:

```
echo "Programs I am currently running: "
ps -ef ¦ grep $identity ¦ sed 's/^/   /'"
```

5. The following is the whole script:

```
#!/bin/sh
echo "\t\tCURRENT USER INFORMATION\n"
identity=`whoami`
echo "My Unix username is: `whoami`"
echo "My Unix machine name is: `hostname`"
echo "My current directory is: `pwd`"
echo "Programs I am currently running: "
ps -ef ¦ grep $identity ¦ sed 's/^/   /'
```

Getting User Input into a Shell Variable

Now that you know how to output information from your script to the user, it's time to learn how to accept input from the user and use it in your script.

The `read` command serves this purpose. The thing to remember about this function is that it takes only a single type of input: any amount of text (usually up to 1,024 characters) that must be followed by a return. Until the Return key is pressed, the `read` function won't actually do anything with what the user types in. The script will suspend operation until the user completes all the input and presses the Return key. Then the input will be put into the variable that follows the `read` command.

Use the `echo` command to output a prompt message before the `read` command:

```
echo "Enter your name"      # not a good prompt
read NAME
```

If the user's name is Fred, the previous code will look like this when run:

```
Enter your name
Fred
```

It is customary in prompt messages to suppress the new line using `\c`:

```
echo "Enter your name\c"     # still not quite right
read NAME
```

Now the output and input will look like this:

```
Enter your nameFred
```

You should add a space before the \c so that the output and input are not run together:

```
echo "Enter your name \c"    # a good prompt
read NAME
```

Now the output and input will look like this:

```
Enter your name Fred
```

The following steps show you how to ask the user for any username and then report the programs currently being run in the system by that username.

Reporting on currently running programs

1. First, prompt the user to type in a UNIX username, ending with \c to leave the cursor on the same line. Add a final space so that user input does not run together with this prompt message:

```
echo "Please enter a username: \c"
```

2. Now, read the response into a variable named USERNAME:

```
read USERNAME
```

Notice that it is common to use all capital letters for user variables so that it is easy to differentiate them from UNIX commands, which are usually all lower-case.

3. Now print a nicely formatted header, and use the USERNAME variable to find all the programs being run by that username. That information is stored in the variable programs:

```
echo "\n\t\tCURRENT USER INFORMATION FOR $USERNAME\n"
programs="`ps -ef ¦ grep $USERNAME`"
```

4. Now print a line using the USERNAME variable again, followed by two carriage returns and the contents of the program variable:

```
echo "User $USERNAME is running the following programs: \n\n $programs"
```

5. Here's the whole script:

```
#!/bin/sh
echo "Please enter a username: \c"
read USERNAME
echo "\n\t\tCURRENT USER INFORMATION FOR $USERNAME\n"
programs="`ps -ef ¦ grep $USERNAME`"
echo "User $USERNAME is running the following programs:  \n\n $programs"
```

Another thing to remember about `read` is that it can be used to read values into more than one variable:

```
echo "Please enter your firstname, lastname, age and weight"
read firstname lastname age weight
```

If the user enters more space-separated words than the number of variables in the `read` statement, the last variable in your `read` command will receive all the extra values. In the previous example, if the user were to type this line of input:

```
John Smith 10 and a half 87
```

here is what would go into each variable in the `read` statement in that example:

- `firstname` would get `John`
- `lastname` would get `Smith`
- `age` would get `10`
- `weight` would get `and a half 87`

Supplying Script Input on the Command Line

So far, you have created scripts that either don't need any input from the user at all, or that have to interact directly with the user every time you run them. You will often find it convenient to give a script all the information it needs when you invoke it on the command line so that it won't have to ask you any questions while it runs. This is especially true if you're going to run the script in the background, because you don't have the chance to give any extra input to such a script—running it in the background disconnects it from the terminal. This is also useful when another script is going to be running your script and passing it information.

In general, using `echo` to prompt and `read` to get input are useful for users who don't run your script very often and don't remember what information will be asked. These programs can become tedious to an experienced user. Allowing those users to provide all the information right on the command line enables them to run the command more quickly.

Here is an example of running a script called `myscript` and passing it arguments:

```
myscript 3 acme laser4
```

Inside your script, the special variables $1, $2, $3 through $9, called *positional parameters*, are available to access the words the user typed on the command line, which are called the command-line arguments. In the previous example, the following would go into each variable:

- $1 would get 3
- $2 would get acme
- $3 would get laser4
- $4 through $9 would be empty

If myscript in the previous example contains this line:

```
lp -d "$3" -n "$1" "$2"
```

it would be equivalent to executing this command:

```
lp -d laser4 -n 3 acme
```

The previous command prints three copies of the file acme to printer laser4.

$10 is $1 Plus Zero
The maximum argument you can reference is $9. $10 will not generate an error, but it will give you the contents of $1, followed by a zero.

The maximum directly accessible command-line argument is $9. If you need to handle more than nine arguments, you need to use another method that entails the use of the for directive. That directive is discussed in upcoming sections.

It is also handy to note that $0 gets set to the actual name of your script (myscript, in this case). You may find that handy when you want to print information messages and want to include the name of your script in them.

It is illegal to use the equal sign to try to assign a new value to a positional parameter:

```
$1=Acme     # illegal. Won't work.
```

Positional parameters already contain any command line variables you specified when you ran your script.

Executing Code Based on Test Results

All programming languages have some way of deciding whether to execute code based on whether a condition is true or not. The shell provides this to you as the if statement. A small if statement has the general syntax shown on the right, next to a code example on the left:

```
if [ "$CNT" -eq 25 ]          #     if condition
then                          #     then
    cp acme /tmp/archive      #         command(s)
    rm /tmp/acme              #
fi                            #     fi
```

The full possible general syntax of the if statement is shown on the left, with example code on the right:

```
if [ "$CNT" -eq 25 ]          #     if condition 1
then                          #     then
    cp acme /tmp/archive      #         command(s)
    rm /tmp/acme              #
elif [ "$CNT" -gt 25 ]        #     elif condition 2
then                          #     then
    cp acme2 /tmp/archive     #         command(s)
elif [ "$CNT" -gt 0 ]         #     elif condition 3
then                          #     then
    cp acme0 /tmp/archive     #         command(s)
    cp acme0 /tmp/acme        #
    rm /tmp/acme1             #
else                          #     else
    rm -f /tmp/acme           #         command(s)
    rm -f /tmp/acme1          #
fi                            #     fi
```

Here's how it works: The condition in all cases is any command that you can execute. If the exit status of the command is zero (0) (which means that it was successful), then the commands immediately following the condition are executed, up to the next else, elif, or fi. If the exit status of the command is anything but zero (which means that the command failed in some way), then the commands after the condition are skipped up to the next else, elif, or fi.

The elif statement, if present, stands for else if and enables you to test another condition before falling through to the else statement or out of the whole if statement. This part of the statement is not required and is provided in case you need to use it.

The else statement, if present, is executed only if the previous if condition was not true. This part of the statement is also not required:

```
if cp acme /usr/fred
then
    rm acme
fi
```

In the previous example, the condition is the execution of the cp command. If the copy is successful, the code following the word then will be executed, and the acme file will be removed. This will not occur if the cp is unsuccessful:

```
if cp acme /usr/fred
then
    rm acme
else
    echo "Error: could not copy acme to /usr/fred" >&2
fi
```

The previous example illustrates the either/or nature of then versus else. If the cp is successful, you will remove the file acme. If it is not successful, you will echo an error message.

If you don't like wasting a line of code by putting the keyword then on a line by itself, you have the option to put it on the same line as the if or elif keywords, as long as you use a semicolon to separate it from the condition:

```
if condition; then


elif condition; then
```

You'll notice that the condition can be any command, but it is often the test command. The test command is a real UNIX command with many options that you can read about when you enter this:

```
man test
```

Here is how you can use the test command to see if the variable $CNT contains the value 25:

```
if test "$CNT" -eq 25      # old form of test (rarely used)
then
   ...
fi
```

In most shell scripts today, the word test is replaced by an opening bracket ([), and the closing bracket (]) is appended:

```
if [ "$CNT" -eq 25 ]        # how the test command usually appears
then
   ...
fi
```

The [form of the test command requires spaces. Incorrect spacing will cause the condition to be evaluated incorrectly, but it will not generate an error:

```
if [ "$CNT" -eq 25 ]      # correct spacing
if["$CNT"-eq25]           # wrong spacing
if ["$CNT" -eq 25]        # wrong spacing
if [ "$CNT" -eq 25]       # wrong spacing
if [ "$CNT"-eq25 ]        # wrong spacing
```

Watch Your Spacing

Incorrect spacing in the if condition is an easy mistake to make because it generates no obvious error, except that the program gives the wrong result. Think of this simple rule: The bracket characters ([ ]) should never directly touch any other non-space character.

The following sections give more examples of using the test command in if statements.

Checking File Type, Size, or Permissions

One of the things the test command enables you to do is examine several qualities of any filesystem object (file or directory) and to make decisions in your script based on them. Table 28.1 is not a complete list of the options that test can use for a filesystem object, but it does cover the most commonly used ones.

Table 28.1 Options to *test* Used on Filesystem Objects

-d file	Is the file a directory?
-f file	Is the file a regular (normal) file?
-r file	Is the file readable by the user running this script?
-w file	Is the file writable by the user running this script?
-x file	Is the file executable by the user running this script?
-s file	Does the file have a length greater than zero?

Using the *test* command

1. Here, you will create a file and run several tests on it from a script called testif1. First, make it a zero length file, and set the permissions on it:
```
touch /tmp/testfile
chmod 775 /tmp/testfile
```

2. Now you can write your script. Start by using a couple separate if statements:

```
MYFILE="/tmp/testfile"
if [ -d "$MYFILE" ]
then
  echo "My file $MYFILE is a directory!"
fi

if [ -f "$MYFILE" ]
then
  echo "My file $MYFILE is an regular (ordinary) file!"
fi
```

If you save and run this script as is, you should get the following output:

```
% ./testif
My file /tmp/testfile is an ordinary file!
```

This is what you would expect.

Testing Whether a File Exists at All

The test command under the Bourne shell provides no easy way to test whether a filename exists at all. This is corrected in the Korn and Bash shells, which provide an -e test to check if the file exists, regardless of the type of file.

---

3. Now you create a new script called testif2. Use the elif and else statements here:

```
MYFILE="/tmp/testfile"
if [ -d "$MYFILE" ]
then
  echo "My file is a directory!"
elif [ -f "$MYFILE" ]
then
    echo "My file is an ordinary file!"
    if [ -w "$MYFILE" ]
    then
       echo "This file is writable too!"
    else
       echo "This file is not writable"
    fi
    if [ -r "$MYFILE" ]
    then
       echo "This file is readable!"

    else
       echo "This file is not readable"
    fi
fi
```

Notice that you can put an `if` statement inside another `if` statement. With the current file permissions, this script should output the following:

```
% ./testif2
My file is an ordinary file!
This file is writable too!
This file is readable!
```

4. Now modify the permissions on the file slightly, by turning off the capability to write to it so that you can test the script.

```
chmod -w /tmp/testfile
```

5. Now run the script again:

```
% ./testif2
My file is an ordinary file!
This file is not writable
This file is readable!
```

It's worth noting that you don't have to have a separate `if` statement for every condition that you want to test for. You can combine several `test` commands on one line if you like or if it happens to be convenient for what you're trying to accomplish. In Table 28.2, `exp` stands for any option of the `test` command.

Table 28.2 Operators for Combining Multiple *test* Commands

Operator	Description
[exp$_1$ -a exp$_2$]	The whole condition is true only if both exp$_1$ *and* exp$_2$ are true. If either are false, then the whole condition is false.
[exp$_1$ -o exp$_2$]	If either exp$_1$ or exp$_2$ is true, the whole condition is true.
[! exp$_1$]	If exp$_1$ is true, the whole condition evaluates to false, and vice versa. The ! sign is said to negate or invert true to false, and vice versa.

Here are some examples.

The following condition will evaluate to true only if $CNT is greater than 25 *and* if the file /tmp/acme is readable by the user running this script:

```
if [ "$CNT" -gt 25 -a -r /tmp/acme ]
```

The next condition will be true either if the acme file is writable by the user running the script *or* if file abc is not readable by that user:

```
if [ -w acme -o ! -r abc ]
```

The following example shows how escaped parentheses can be used to group the conditions to prevent ambiguity. The condition evaluates to true only if the acme file is writable *and* $CNT equals 1 or 2:

```
if [ -w acme -a \( "$CNT" -eq 1 -o "$CNT" -eq 2 \) ]
```

The first line of the next example shows an incorrect way to test whether either acme or abc is readable. You must use a complete test on either side of -o or -a:

```
if [ -r acme -o abc ]       # wrong
if [ -r acme -o -r abc ]    # correct
```

Another example of the *test* command

1. You can now write a script called testif3 that's a bit shorter. First, change the permissions of your file back:

   ```
   chmod +w /tmp/testfile
   ```

2. You will test to see whether the file is an ordinary file and is both writable and readable:

   ```
   MYFILE="/tmp/testfile"
   if [ -f "$MYFILE" -a -w "$MYFILE" -a -r "$MYFILE" ]
   then
       echo "My file $MYFILE is an ordinary file,
   and it is writable and readable!"
   fi
   ```

3. Now if the file has nothing in it, it wouldn't make sense to try to run it as a program, even if the execute bit was on. Have the script test for this scenario and tell you about it. Notice that the -s test returns true (0) only if the file has a size greater than zero; it returns false (1) if the file size is exactly zero. Therefore, you can reverse the sense of the test by using the ! operator on it. This makes the logic of the statement read as follows: If the file is executable *and* if the file has zero length, print the message:

   ```
   if [ -x "$MYFILE" -a ! -s "$MYFILE" ]
   then
       echo "This file is executable but empty!
   It will run but it will not do anything."
   fi
   ```

4. The whole testif3 script looks like this:

   ```
   #!/bin/sh
   MYFILE="/tmp/testfile"
   if [ -f "$MYFILE" -a -w "$MYFILE" -a -r "$MYFILE" ]
   then
       echo "My file $MYFILE is an ordinary file,
   and it is writable and readable!"
   fi
   ```

```
if [ -x "$MYFILE" -a ! -s "$MYFILE" ]
then
    echo "This file $MYFILE is executable but empty!
It will run but it will not do anything."
fi
```

5. Take a look at the output of the script:

```
% ./testif3
My file is an ordinary file,
and it is writable and_readable!
This file is executable but empty!
It will run but it will not do anything
```

Checking Variable Contents

In addition to checking file attributes, you can use test to see what's in your variables and to make decisions based on their contents, as shown in Table 28.3. There are separate operators for testing variables you want to interpret as strings and those you want to interpret as integers.

Table 28.3 String Operators for *test*

Operator	Description
-n string	Returns true if string has a value (is not null)
-z string	Returns true if string has no value (is null)
string1 = string2	Returns true if string1 is identical to string2
string1 != string2	Returns true if string1 is not identical to string2

A few examples should clarify how these work. You can use any of these statements as the condition of an if statement in your script. You should remember that any variable you pass to test should be surrounded by double quotation marks.

First, you can check to see whether a variable has any value at all:

```
myvar=
if [ -z "$myvar" ]
then
    echo "This variable has no value"
fi
```

That last example can actually bite you, however, if the variable myvar contains certain non-alphanumeric characters such as the equals sign, because test will think that you're trying to assign a value to a variable. To make sure that this never happens to you, you can use another construct, which you will find is extremely common in shell scripts:

```
myvar=
if [ X = X"$myvar" ]
then
    echo "This variable has no value"
fi
```

Did you see how that works? If myvar has no value, the statement boils down to this: Does string X exactly equal X? This is, of course, true.

Now you can do some comparisons between string variables:

```
animal1="pig"
animal2="cow"
if [ "$animal1" = "$animal2" ]
then
    echo "These animals are the same"
fi
if [ "$animal1" != "$animal2" ]
then
    echo "These animals are different"
fi
```

If the strings stored in your variables are numeric, you must use another set of operators to compare integer values, as shown in Table 28.4.

Table 28.4 Integer Operators for *test*

Operator	Description
int1 -eq int2	int1 is equal to int2
int1 -ne int2	int1 is not equal to int2
int1 -gt int2	int1 is greater than int2
int1 -ge int2	int1 is greater than or equal to int2
int1 -lt int2	int1 is less than int2
int1 -le int2	int1 is less than or equal to int2

test Allows Signed Integers

Integer comparisons using the **test** command work correctly with negative and/or positive numbers.

Remember that operators in Table 28.4 work only on integers. They ignore any characters beginning with the first non-digit, as shown in these examples:

- If int1 contains 36abc, its integer value is 36.

- If int1 contains 36.78, its integer value is 36.

- If int1 contains 36,792.72, its integer value is 36.

- If int1 contains abc, its integer value is 0.

Use -eq to compare numbers and = to compare strings:

```
value1="6 "
value2="00005"
if [ "$value1" -ne "$value2" ]
then
    echo "These values are not equal"
fi
if [ "$value1" -eq 6 ]
then
    echo "value1 is equal to 6"
fi
if [ "$value2" -eq 5 ]
then
    echo "value2 is equal to 5"
fi
```

All the tests in the previous example will evaluate to true, and all the echo statements will be executed. Now, if you had used the string operator = rather than the integer operator -eq in the last two tests, you would not have received output from either one of those tests. That's because there is a space after the 6 in value1, and four zeros before the 5 in value2; the string operators are looking for an exact character match rather than a numerical match.

When Quoting Is Needed in a *test* Condition

The following line looks like a valid if test:

```
if [ -f $FILE ]
```

The previous line will work correctly for most cases, but it contains a quoting error that can cause the whole script to abort with an error message like this:

```
scriptname: test: argument expected
or
scriptname: test: option requires an argument
```

Some scripts from reputable UNIX vendors have failed with this error, all because the programmer failed to use quoting when needed in the test condition. The problem will occur if $FILE in the previous example is empty. The line after shell substitution of an empty $FILE will look like this:

```
if [ -f ]
```

The test command will correctly complain that no argument has been provided for the -f option. The solution is to enclose $FILE within double quotes:

```
if [ -f "$FILE" ]
```

Then if $FILE is empty, the line after shell substitution will look like this:

```
if [ -f "" ]
```

The previous line properly provides the empty string as the argument to the -f option, so the program will run correctly without dying at this point. The test will return a false result because the empty string is not a regular file. Here is a simple rule to help you with quoting in a test condition: Use double quotes around any test arguments that contain $variables or backquotes.

In truth, the quotes are needed only if the argument can evaluate to an empty result, but it does not hurt to double-quote all arguments that contain variables or backquotes. Here are some examples:

```
if [ -f $FILE ]            # wrong
if [ -f "$FILE" ]          # right
```

In the previous example, double quotes are needed around $FILE to prevent a syntax error if $FILE is empty. The double quotes are not required if you have previously tested $FILE and know that it is not empty, but the double quotes do not hurt. Many programs get into trouble when future changes allow any empty variable.

In the following example, the double quotes are not really needed because the argument to the -f option will not be empty even if $PREFIX is empty:

```
if [ -f ${PREFIX}9908 ]             # OK
if [ -f "${PREFIX}9908" ]           # OK
```

This illustrates that it does not hurt to get into the habit of using the double quotes.

In the following example, the argument 32 contains no variables or backquotes:

```
if [ $CNT -gt 32 ]          # wrong
if [ "$CNT" -gt 32 ]        # right
```

It can never be empty, so it does not need any quoting. The $CNT argument, on the other hand, should be double-quoted to prevent a syntax error if it is empty. Note that you cannot use single quotes because this would prevent substitution of the variable's contents.

In the following example, backquotes are used to run the `head` command to get the first filename in the `curfile` file:

```
if [ `head -1 curfile` = acme ]          # wrong
if [ "`head -1 curfile`" = acme ]        # right
```

You then check that filename to see if it is `acme`. The backquotes should be enclosed in double quotes in case `curfile` is empty. The word `acme` does not require any quotes because it can never be empty.

In the previous examples, the wrong way (without quotes) will work most of the time. However, you can prevent any failures through correct quoting.

Double Quote $Variables for Security

There is also a security reason to always double quote any dollar sign ($) variables, including $1, $2, and so on to $9. A hacker may try to compromise your system by leaving files, in common directories such as /tmp, which contain special character(s) and punctuation not normally found in filenames. If this filename with special character(s) is picked up in a $variable in a program run by root, then any non-quoted $variable access could allow the hacker to do some damage. Enclosing these $variables within double quotes prevents almost all the mischief that could occur.

This example uses non-quoted variables and thus opens some security problems:

```
cp $1 $dest
```

Double-quoting all $variables is easy to do and it defeats most hacker booby traps:

```
cp "$1" "$dest"
```

Checking Command Results

Previously, you learned that the `condition` part of an `if` statement is usually a form of the `test` command, but you can use any command or program that returns a zero (0) if it completes successfully—and any other number if it doesn't.

Perl May Not Be on Your UNIX System

Perl is the only UNIX filter that makes it easy to search for a word such as `vi` that is not part of a larger word. Perl is not standard on many versions of UNIX, but it is often available by download from your UNIX vendor's Web site or `www.perl.com`.

An example of this would be if you wanted to find out if anyone was running the vi text editor on the system. Actually, this script will locate any vi program running in the system, as well as anything else generated by ps -ef that has the word vi in it.

```
if ps -ef | perl -ne 'print if /\bvi\b/'
then
    echo "Yep, someone is running vi"
else
    echo "No one is running vi at this time"
fi
```

Notice that these lines ran ps -ef, piped the output into perl, and told it to look for any line that contains the two characters vi that are not part of a larger word. If perl is successful in that search, it will return a status code of zero, and the line acknowledging that vi is running somewhere in the system will be returned. Notice that only the status code of the last command that ran in the condition is examined for success or failure. The status code of ps is ignored.

Take a look at the output of the preceding program:

```
% ./vitest
gmarler 16145 16128  0 17:49:02 pts/10   0:00 vi
Yep, vi is running
```

Where did the first line of output come from? Well, the first line of output was produced by running the test condition:

```
ps -ef | perl -ne 'print if /\bvi\b/'
```

The second line was produced by your script. If you don't want the output of the condition program to be seen by the person running your script, you can redirect the output of such programs to /dev/null. The modified line would look like this:

```
if ps -ef | perl -ne 'print if /\bvi\b/' > /dev/null
```

...

That's fine as long as the programs you run in an if condition send any information to *standard output*. If they also send any informational messages or errors to *standard error*, however, you will have to change the line to send both of them to /dev/null if you don't want to see these messages interspersed with yours. In that case, the line would change to this:

```
if ps -ef | perl -ne 'print if /\bvi\b/' > /dev/null 2>&1
```

...

You don't actually even have to use `if` to get these results. You can use the `&&` and `¦¦` operators to connect a series of commands that you want to execute under certain conditions. First, examine how to look at these operators. You can think of this line:

```
command1 && command2
```

as meaning, "If and only if `command1` executed successfully, execute `command2`." You can think of this line:

```
command1 ¦¦ command2
```

as meaning, "If `command1` did *not* execute successfully, execute `command2`."

You can connect as many commands as you think necessary with these operators. Here's an example of the common task of copying a log file to another location to preserve it for future examination before emptying the current log file. You don't want to allow the current log file to be emptied before you are sure that the copy to another location was successful:

```
cp "${logfile}" "${logfile}.1" && cp /dev/null "${logfile}"
```

You could rewrite this to give a nice little message notifying someone that the script could not make a copy of the log file. The parentheses are used to make sure that the commands connected by `&&` are fully evaluated before the `echo` could possibly have a chance to run. If both of the first two commands are successful, the `echo` will never run:

```
( cp "${logfile}" "${logfile}.1" && cp /dev/null "${logfile}" ) ¦¦  {
    echo "Could not copy ${logfile} to ${logfile}.1" >&2
}
```

The form of these previous commands is difficult to read, so you should use the `if` statement for such complicated cases. Here is the equivalent `if` statement:

```
if cp "${logfile}" "${logfile}.1"
then
    cp /dev/null "${logfile}"
else
    echo "Could not copy ${logfile} to ${logfile}.1" >&2
fi
```

The `&&` and `¦¦` forms are useful for short tests where the `if` statement would take up unnecessary lines:

```
[ ! -w "$FILE" ] && continue
```

```
[ -r "$FILE2" ] && cp "$FILE2" /tmp/archive
```

Performing Arithmetic Calculations

You have probably noticed that all the examples worked with so far have dealt strictly with text, with no mention of how to deal with numeric calculations. That's because the shell thinks that everything *is* text; it sees numbers as only ASCII characters. If you need to perform any kind of numeric calculations, you have to use programs outside the shell to do them for you via the backquote operator. The output of these programs can be assigned to a variable or can be printed directly from the echo command.

If all you need to perform are integer calculations, you can use the expression evaluator program, expr, as shown in Table 28.5.

Escaping the expr **Command**

Multiplication in expr uses the asterisk (*), but you must escape it with a backslash. Why? Because expr is a backquoted command, which is run just as if you had typed it in on the command line. If you did that, the asterisk would have been interpreted as a wildcard and would have been converted into the list of all files in the current directory. That's not what you want.

Table 28.5 Mathematic Operations Used in *expr*

Operator	Description
result=`expr 5 + 4`	Addition: Stores 9 in variable result.
result=`expr 5 - 4`	Subtraction: Stores 1 in variable result.
result=`expr 5 \* 4`	Multiplication: Stores 20 in variable result. Note that the asterisk (*) must be escaped with a backslash.
result=`expr 4 / -2`	Division: Stores -2 in variable result. expr does allow negative values.
result=`expr 5 % 4`	Remainder (Modulus): Stores 1 in variable result. That is, 5 divided by 4 leaves a remainder of 1.
result=`expr 5 / 4`	Division: Stores 1 in variable result. Remember, expr can't do anything except integer calculations.

If you need to use floating point math in your script, you can use bc to do your calculations. You will have to be sure to specify the number of decimal places of accuracy to bc each time you use it because the default is to truncate all fractions.

Using the *bc* command example

1. You want to write a script that will convert the number of kilobytes of disk space a user has into megabytes, with an accuracy of two decimal places.

   Assume that a variable called `diskspace_kb` already contains the user's disk space in kilobytes. This variable could be set in a simple assignment, like this:
   ```
   diskspace_kb=1808071.
   ```

---

bc Is Capable of Infinite Precision

bc can multiply two 100-digit numbers and give you an exact result. You can set the scale for bc to display as large a value as you want, and bc will calculate correctly that many places to the right of the decimal point in its answer.

---

2. To get an accuracy of two decimal places, you must use the `scale` directive to `bc`; to get the number of megabytes, you divide the number of kilobytes by 1,024. Notice how `echo` is used to pass commands to `bc` via piping. The double quotation marks are necessary to protect the `bc` commands from being interpreted by the shell before they get to `bc`:
   ```
   diskspace_mb=`echo "scale=2; $diskspace_kb/1024" | bc`
   echo $diskspace_mb
   ```

3. In this case, you should get the following output:
   ```
   1765.69
   ```

Special Shell Variables

For your convenience, the shell predefines several variables, some of which change as your script runs. Others are permanently set for the life of the script.

Checking the Number of Command-Line Arguments Given

When someone runs your script, it is always good to make sure that the user typed in the correct number of arguments on the command line. When your script is run, the shell sets `$#` to that number. You can check it by using the integer comparison operators already discussed.

If the script requires exactly three arguments, here's how you could check that:

```
if [ "$#" -ne 3 ]
then
    echo "Usage: $0 filename username dirname" >&2
    exit 1
fi
```

You will normally perform this test before checking any of the command-line arguments. If this test is successful, you don't have to check if a required argument is empty.

Checking the Status of the Last Command

After running a command, it is a very good idea to make sure that it executed properly. Whenever a command is executed on UNIX, it returns an exit status code when it stops running. The shell captures the value of this exit status code and stores it in the special $? variable. You must examine this variable immediately, however, because it will be reset as soon as the next command is executed. Also, don't try to run a test on the $? variable; doing so resets its value. Save it in a temporary variable first, unless you just want to echo it to the user.

Usually, the value of the variable will be zero (0) if the command executed successfully, and any number other than zero (usually 1) if it did not.

In the first example, you will try to copy a log file to another location before setting the original log file to zero length and compressing the copy:

```
cd /var/adm
cp messages messages.1
STATUS=$?
if [ "$STATUS" -eq 0 ]
then
    compress messages.1 &     # Run the compress in the background
else
    echo "Could not make a copy of the original log file">&2
fi
```

If the cp command in the preceding example fails, it could be due to directory permissions, a full filesystem, or something that is actually wrong with the disk it is on. Not all commands return values other than zero on this kind of failure. As you have seen, the test comparison commands return 0 or 1 based on whether the comparison is valid:

```
firstname="john"
lastname="smith"
[ "$firstname" = "$lastname" ]
echo $?    # This would print 1, since they are NOT equal
[ "$firstname" = "john" ]
echo $?    # This would print 0, since they ARE equal
```

Using Non-Conflicting Temporary Files

If you write a script that many people find useful, it is possible that many of them will be running it simultaneously. If this script needs to open temporary files while it runs, you need to take steps to prevent one copy of the script from clobbering the temporary files of another copy that is running at the same time. Thankfully, the $$ variable enables you to do this. Whenever you run a script, $$ is set to that script's process ID (PID). Every job running on the system is given a unique PID while that process or program is running. $$ allows you access your own PID number.

Even if two users run the same script at the same time, they will be running under different process ID numbers so any filenames that contain $$ created by one user will not conflict with those created by the other user of the same script. Therefore, you should use this $$ variable as part of any temporary filename that your script needs to create.

Assume that you want to write a script that will take a file and add line numbers to all the lines within the file. The nl command will do part of this job: it will number all the lines, but only those in the output. To change the original file, you have to save the nl output to a temporary file and then replace the original file with the temporary file:

```
if [ "$#" -ne 1 ]
then
    echo "Error: This script needs 1 argument" >&2
    exit 3
fi
nl "$1" > /tmp/nm$$ && mv /tmp/nm$$ "$1"
    # Run the Unix nl command on the file given in $1
    # and save the results in a temporary file that will
    # not conflict with any other users running the same
    # script at the same time. If nl was successful,
    # replace the original file with the nl output.
```

Passing All Arguments to Another Command

Now you know how to count the number of arguments that were passed into your script by using $#, but how do you get the actual list of arguments themselves? The special variable $* contains that list.

If you want a script to perform a long listing of any files that you specify on the command line with ls, you could write it this way:

```
if [ "$#" -eq 0 ]
then
    echo "This script takes at least one argument" >&2
    exit 2
fi
ls -l $*
```

As you can see, ls gets all the command-line arguments that you passed into the script. Therefore, if the script is called lister and you run it like this:

```
./lister core /tmp/test
```

it would be the same as typing the following:

```
ls -l core /tmp/test
```

Ending the Script and Setting Completion Status

When your script has done its job and is about to terminate, it is a good idea to return an exit status explicitly instead of letting the shell return the exit status of the last command executed. This is especially true if you are exiting because of an error condition, because you would like to give notice of it to any script that might be calling *your* script. And it is generally nice to give an exit status of zero (0) if your script exits normally so that any script that might be calling yours can check your exit status and feel confident that everything is okay. Any argument you give exit will be the exit status of your script:

```
cp acme /tmp/archive || {
    STATUS=$?
    echo "Error: copy failed" >&2
    exit "$STATUS"
}
```

No Standard Exit Errors

Each different UNIX command and script returns different exit errors. Often these are not even documented. You are free to choose your own non-zero error statuses. Different versions of UNIX may set different limits on the maximum error code.

In the previous example, note that it is important to save the bad status given by $? before doing the echo statement. If echo is the last statement executed by your script, then your script will return a successful (zero) status, even if previous commands were not successful. You can prevent an erroneous status return from the previous script by saving the bad $? status in a $STATUS variable and then returning that same bad status as the status of the whole script. This way, any program that calls this script will know that it was not successful.

Here's another example that shows how to exit your script happily and unhappily, depending on the result of a couple tests:

```
if cp "${filename}" "${filename}.1"
then    compress "${filename}.1"
   cp /dev/null "${filename}" && {
      echo "Done compressing "${filename}."1" >&2
      exit 0        # Ahh! Exiting happily, mission accomplished
   }
else
   echo "Could not copy ${filename} to ${filename}.1" >&2
   exit 1        # Ack! Exiting unhappily
fi
```

Giving Proper UNIX Usage Errors

Usage messages are displayed as an error message from a command or shell script whenever required options or arguments are missing from the command line or when incorrect ones are given. A message beginning with the word *Usage* always means that you have entered an incorrect command; it then gives the proper usage or syntax for that command or shell script:

```
$ cp abc
Usage: cp [-fip] source_file target_file
$
```

> **"Usage" Means "Error"**
>
> In Chapter 1, "Introduction to UNIX and the Shell," you learned that in UNIX, no news is good news. Many beginners see a Usage message pop up from one of their commands and do not realize that the command has failed. When you see the word *Usage*, think "Error, you have misused this command. Here is the correct usage."

In the previous example, the cp command is invalid because no target_file has been given. A usage error is generated showing the syntax needed to enter the command correctly.

Here's an example of what you should put as the first test in each of your scripts. In this example, you have the first part of a script that will copy files to an archive location, compress the archived files, and then destroy the originals. It requires that you give it at least one filename on which to perform this action:

```
if [ $# -eq 0 ]
then
    echo "Error: no filenames given" >&2
    echo "Usage: $0 filename …" >&2
    exit 1                          fi
```

To construct a proper usage message for your script, note that the message must begin with one of the following:

```
Usage:
```

```
usage:
```

Then put the name of the command in the message. Alternatively, the $0 variable can be used to insert the name of the current script, as in either of the following examples:

```
Usage: myscript
```

```
Usage: $0
```

Then specify any allowed options for the command, followed by all allowed arguments specified as one-word descriptions. Use square brackets to indicate optional elements:

```
Usage: $0 [-fip] filename username dir-to-process
```

The following example is not correct because the last argument is not indicated as a single word and therefore implies that five arguments must follow the options:

```
Usage: $0 [-fip] filename username dir to process
```

Usage messages should be displayed on standard error, not standard output. Append >&2 to the echo statement to redirect the output to standard error. No spaces are allowed within >&2:

```
echo "Usage: $0 [-fip] filename username dir-to-process" >&2
```

Here is an example of an improper Usage message:

```
echo "Usage: filename does not exist" >&2    # wrong
```

The previous example is really an error message, not a Usage message, because it does not give the allowed syntax. Error messages are useful and can be combined with Usage messages. Here is a good use of both messages:

```
echo "Error: filename does not exist" >&2
echo "Usage: $0 [-fip] filename username dir-to-process" >&2
```

Use *exit* to Avoid Heavy Nesting

The following code is poor because it is unnecessarily nested and cumbersome. This is difficult code to follow and is very difficult to modify. Error messages are located far from the test for that error:

```
if [ $# -eq 2 ]
then
    if [ -d $1 ]
    then
        if [ -f $2 ]
        then
            cp $2 $1
        else
            echo Error: $2 not a file >&2
            exit 3
        fi
    else
        echo Error: $1 not a directory >&2
        exit 2
    fi
else
    echo Usage: `basename $0` directory file >&2
    exit 1
fi
```

You can improve the previous example a lot by remembering that `exit` ends the program; therefore, it is not necessary to use the `else` keyword. This realization eliminates the need for nesting (putting one `if` statement within another) and allows you to write modular code that is much more readable and easier to maintain and modify. The following code is functionally equivalent to the previous but is better code:

```
if [ $# -ne 2 ]
    then
        echo Usage: `basename $0` directory file >&2
        exit 1
    fi


if [ ! -d $1 ]
    echo Error: $1 not a directory >&2
    exit 2
fi


if [ ! -f $2 ]
    then
        echo Error: $2 not a file >&2
        exit 3
    fi


cp $2 $1
```

Only Use `exit` for Fatal Errors

You can avoid nesting only for fatal errors that cause the whole script to end. If you want to display a warning but allow the script to continue, you cannot use `exit`, and you may have to use some nesting.

In the previous example, notice how each `if` test is a separate module. Notice how easy it is with this modular programming to delete a test, insert an additional test, or rearrange the order of the tests. Notice how the error message follows immediately after the test for that error.

You can use the same modular coding technique when checking for errors in a `for` loop that cause you to end execution of the current item and go on to the next item:

```
for FILE in `find /usr/fred -type f -print`
do
    if [ -s "$FILE" ]
    then
```

```
        if [ -r "$FILE" ]
        then
            lp $FILE
        fi
    fi
done
```

The previous code is cumbersome and heavily nested. The code that follows is functionally equivalent, but it uses modular coding techniques to eliminate the nesting and make it much easier to add additional tests or rearrange tests:

```
for FILE in `find /usr/fred -type f -print`
do
    [ ! -s "$FILE" ] && continue
    [ ! -r "$FILE" ] && continue
    lp $FILE
done
```

Debugging Your Script

If a script doesn't do what you expect, or if a variable doesn't seem to have the value you think it should, you can do a couple things to debug the problem. The easiest is to use the -x option to the Bourne shell. You can do this by modifying the first line of your script to look like this:

```
#!/bin/sh -x
```

Or, you can run the shell directly on your script with the -x option, like this:

```
sh -x scriptname
```

Debug Info Goes to Standard Error

The shell -x option outputs the commands being executed to standard error. To page this output, do this:

```
sh -x scriptname >&2 ¦ pg
```

To save it in a file, enter this:

```
sh -x scriptname >&2 ¦tee filename
```

Both methods accomplish the same thing; the shell is instructed to print each line in the script one by one, expanding any variables to show the values they contain, and running any backquoted commands to show their results. After each line is printed this way, it is actually executed. Here's an example script called info, which you will run with debugging turned on. Each line of the script has been numbered so that you can refer to specific lines. These line numbers are not in the file:

```
1.   #!/bin/sh -x
2.   machine=`hostname`
3.   identity=`whoami`
4.   date=`date`
5.   echo "Hello, today is $date"
6.   echo "I am logged in as user $identity on machine $machine"
7.   cp $HOME/acme /tmp/archive
```

Here is the output from running the previous info script with debugging turned on. Again, each line of the output has been numbered, but these numbers do not actually appear on the screen. In debugging mode, lines beginning with a plus sign (+) are commands from the script after all shell processing and substitution has been done. For some unknown reason, variable assignment does not begin with a plus sign, nor do lines that are output by the script:

```
1.   $ sh -x ./info
2.   + hostname
3.   machine=proteon
4.   + whoami
5.   identity=gmarler
6.   + date
7.   date=Sat Mar 21 19:22:28 PST 1998
8.   + echo Hello, today is Sat Mar 21 19:22:28 PST 1998
9.   Hello, today is Sat Mar 21 19:22:28 PST 1998
10.  + echo I am logged in as user gmarler on machine proteon
11.  I am logged in as user gmarler on machine proteon
12.  + cp /usr/gmarler/acme /tmp/archive
13.  $
```

The following is a detailed explanation of debugging the previous script:

- The execution of line 2 of the script is represented by lines 2 and 3 of the debugging output. Notice that the backquoted hostname command is marked with a plus sign on line 2 to let you know that it was an externally executed command. Line 3 shows a variable assignment, which for some reason is not denoted with a plus sign. Variable machine now has the value proteon, the name of the machine.

- Line 3 of the script is executed in lines 4 and 5 of the debugging output. Line 4 shows the external command whoami being executed, and line 5 shows the output of that command being assigned to the variable identity.

- Line 4 of the script is shown in lines 6 and 7 of the debugging output. Line 6 shows the external command date being executed, and line 7 shows its output being assigned to variable date.

- Line 5 of the script is shown in lines 8 and 9 of the debugging output. Note that line 8 shows the echo command and its arguments after the date output is substituted in the command. Line 9 is the output generated by the echo command that you would see normally even if you didn't run the script in debugging mode.

- Line 6 of the script is shown in lines 10 and 11 of the debugging output. Line 10 expands the values of the identity and machine variables, and line 11 shows the echo output that you would normally see from this script.

- Line 7 of the script is shown in line 12 of the debugging output. The plus sign in line 12 of the debugging output shows that this is a line from the script, after all shell processing and substitutions have been performed. No other debugging lines are generated because no variable assignment was done by this line 7 of the script and because no output was generated either.

You can also use the -xv option, which produces an even more verbose debugging output from the script.

A more difficult—or at least more tedious—method of debugging is to use echo a great deal, printing out the values of variables that you didn't set in your script, such as command-line arguments that get passed into your script, just to make sure that you're getting the information that you think you ought to.

Looping

You will often have a list of items in your script that will each need to have a particular action performed on them. The for loop construct can help with this. Its general form is as follows:

```
for variable in list-of-items…
do
    command
    …
done
```

Here, variable gets set to each value in the list-of-items, and each command is run for each variable. Here is a simple example:

```
for FILE in acme1 report7 /tmp/junk5
do
```

```
        lp $FILE && rm $FILE
done
```

The previous code will print a hard copy of the three files in the list of items: acme1, report7, and /tmp/junk5. If the lp command does not generate an error, the code will then delete the file.

You can use backquotes to generate a much larger list of items to print and then remove. In the following example, you will print and remove all files in /usr/fred and all its subdirectories:

```
for FILE in `find /usr/fred -type f -print`
do
    lp $FILE && rm $FILE
done
```

Remember that when the variables $1 through $9 were discussed, you learned that you could reference only the first nine arguments to a program with them. Using the for loop without a list of items, you can access all the command-line arguments. Assume that your script is invoked like this:

```
myscript dog cat mouse horse
```

Assume that inside myscript, the code looks like this:

```
for arg
do
    echo $arg
done
```

Therefore, the output from the script will be each command-line argument printed on a separate line:

```
dog
cat
mouse
horse
```

The previous program will print all the command-line arguments even if there are more than nine of them.

You can use the same idea to write a script that compresses all the filenames given on the command line (if they exist):

```
if [ "$#" -eq 0 ]
then
```

```
      echo "This command requires at least one argument" >&2
      echo "Usage: $0 filename-to-compress …" >&2
      exit 1
fi
for FILE
do
   if [ -f "$FILE" ]
   then    # this is a regular file
      echo "Compressing file $FILE now" >&2
      compress $FILE
   else
      echo "Sorry, $FILE is not a regular file" >&2
   fi
done
```

Processing All Files in a Directory

In a previous example, you wrote a script that compressed the files you specified
when you ran the script. You can also write a script that will do "something" to all
the files in a directory, such as compress them. The following script expects the user
to supply one or more directory names on the command line after the script name.
All the files in the given directory (or directories) will be compressed by this script.
First, the script checks $# to make sure that at least one command-line argument has
been typed in by the user. Then the script uses a for statement to process each
directory name given on the command line:

```
if [ "$#" -eq 0 ]; then
   echo "Error: This command requires at least one argument" >&2
   echo "Usage: $0 directory-containing-files-to-compress …" >&2
   exit 1
fi

for DIR
do
   if [ ! -d "$DIR" ]; then
      echo "Error: directory $DIR does not exist" >&2
      continue
   fi
   if [ ! -r "$DIR" -o ! -x "$DIR" ]; then
      echo "Error: permissions of directory $DIR do not allow access" >&2
      continue
   fi
```

```
      for FILE in `ls $DIR`
      do
         if [ -f "$DIR/$FILE" ]; then
            echo "Compressing $DIR/$FILE ..."
            compress "$DIR/$FILE"
         fi
      done
done
```

---

for Loop with ls **Versus** find

Use `ls ...` in your for loop to process only files in the directory but not in subdirectories. Use `find ...` in your for loop to process all files in the directory and in all subdirectories.

Within the for loop in the previous example, the script gives an error message if the argument is not a directory (! -d). The continue statement stops the for loop from processing the bad directory name and allows it to work on the next directory name in the command line, if any. In a similar manner, the script tests if the directory is not readable (! -r) or not executable (! -x) by the user running this script. To access files in a directory, you need both read and execute permission on the directory.

```
for FILE in `ls $DIR`
```

In the previous script, this line allows the script to process all the files in the given directory. Backquotes are used around the ls command so that the output of ls becomes the list of items to process in the for statement. Because there may be subdirectories in the given directory, you should first use -f to make sure that you compress only regular files.

$DIR/$FILE in the previous script shows how you can combine two variables to make one file pathname. If the directory $DIR is /usr/fred/docs and the file $FILE is acme, then the file to process is /usr/fred/docs/acme.

Processing All Files in a Directory Tree

Now that you have processed all the files in a directory, what if the directory itself contains another directory, and so on? You will probably want to process all the files in all the subdirectories, too. Here's an example of how you can handle this situation.

Processing files

1. As always, start your script by making sure that the proper number of arguments has been entered. In this case, just one is sufficient, but it is required:

```
if [ "$#" -eq 0 ]
then
    echo "This command requires at least one argument" >&2
    echo "Usage: $0: directory-containing-files-to-compress …" >&2
    exit 1
fi
```

2. Now make sure that each directory mentioned on the command line actually exists:

```
for DIR
do
    if [ ! -d "$DIR" ]
    then
        echo "Sorry, directory $DIR does not exist" >&2
        continue  # go on to next directory
    fi
```

3. Use the find command to generate the entire list of files under each directory. You can then check each line returned from find to see whether it describes a file (it could be describing a subdirectory, a symbolic link, or a pipe); compress it if it is a file:

```
    for FILE in `find $DIR -type f -print`
    do
        if [ -r "$FILE" ]
        then
            echo "Compressing $FILE now" >&2
            compress $FILE
        else
            echo "Error: file $FILE is not readable" >&2
        fi
    done
done
```

Selecting From a Menu of Items

If you want your script to give someone a set menu of options and then want to act on his responses, the case statement is a convenient way to do it. It takes the following form:

```
case value in
    pattern1 )    command
        …
        ;;
```

```
pattern2 )     command
     ...
     ;;
     ...
patternx )     command
     ...
     ;;
esac
```

Here, `value` is any text string that will be compared with the patterns `pattern₁`, `pat-tern₂`, and so on to `patternₓ`. The `command` list following the first pattern that matches `value` will be executed. Usually, a catch-all pattern (such as `*`) will be used as the last pattern to catch anything that you weren't expecting or that the user mistyped. Note the required double semicolons (`;;`) after the last command in each pattern section. Don't forget these; otherwise, you will end up executing several more commands than you were intending to.

The following example covers a script that enables you to compress, to perform a long listing on, or to delete a file.

Compressing, listing, or deleting a file

1. First, you need to print the menu for the user to pick from. Note the use of the `\c` control character to ensure that the new line is suppressed and that the cursor will remain just after the colon, waiting for input:

```
echo "What would you like to do:

1.    Compress a file
2.    Do a long listing of a file
3.    Delete a file

Please select one of the above (1-3): \c"
```

2. Now you can read the user's selection after he types it, and you can pass it into the `case` statement. You should enclose the variable within double quotes, as shown, to prevent a syntax error if the variable is empty:

```
read SELECTION
case "$SELECTION" in
```

3. Now that you have the user's selection, the `case` statement will cover each contingency. The first one is the selection of a file to compress. You will prompt for the file, check to make sure that it really exists, and then compress it if it does:

```
1)  echo "Enter filename to compress: \c"
    read FILE
    if [ -f "$FILE" ]
    then
```

```
        compress $FILE
    else
        echo "Error: $FILE is not a valid regular file" >&2
    fi
    ;;
```

4. The second possible selection is for a file to perform a long listing on. Again you prompt for the filename, make sure that it exists, and then perform the listing:

```
2)  echo "Enter filename to list: \c"
    read FILE
    if [ -f "$FILE" ]
    then
        ls -l $FILE
    else
        echo "Error: $FILE is not a valid regular file" >&2
    fi
    ;;
```

5. Now for the third scenario: a filename to be deleted. You prompt for the filename, make sure that it exists, and then delete it:

```
3)  echo "Enter filename to delete: \c"\
    read FILE
    if [ -f "$FILE" ]; then
        rm $FILE
    else
        echo "Error: $FILE is not a valid regular file" >&2
    fi;;
```

6. Finally, you want to perform your catch-all and report it as a bad selection from the menu. Then you end the `case` statement:

```
    *)  echo "Incorrect selection" >&2
    ;;
esac
```

7. Here is a listing of the complete script described previously:

```
#!/bin/sh
echo "What would you like to do:

1.  Compress a file
2.  Do a long listing of a file
3.  Delete a file

Please select one of the above (1-3): \c"
read SELECTION
case "$SELECTION" in
    1)  echo "Enter filename to compress: \c"
        read FILE
        if [ -f "$FILE" ]
        then
```

```
            compress "$FILE"
        else
            echo "Error: $FILE is not a valid regular file" >&2
        fi
        ;;
    2)  echo "Enter filename to list: \c"
        read FILE
        if [ -f "$FILE" ]
        then
            ls -l "$FILE"
        else
            echo "Error: $FILE is not a valid regular file" >&2
        fi
        ;;
    3)  echo "Enter filename to delete: \c"
        read FILE
        if [ -f "$FILE" ]
        then
            rm $FILE
        else
            echo "Error: $FILE is not a valid regular file" >&2
        fi
        ;;
    *)  echo "Incorrect selection" >&2
        ;;
esac
```

The cases allow use of the same wildcards that are available for filename generation:

```
echo "Remove file (y/n): \c"
read ANSWER
case "$ANSWER" in
    y*|Y*) rm acme ;;
    *) echo "acme was not removed" ;;
esac
```

Slashes and Leading Periods

Wildcards in the shell case statement differ in two respects from Filename Generation Wildcards. The first is that filename wildcards cannot match a leading period but wildcards in the case statement have no such limitation. The second difference is that filename wildcards cannot match a slash (/) but wildcards in the case statement can.

In the previous example, y* will match any answer that begins with the letter y. Similarly, Y* will match any answer that begins with a capital Y. The vertical bar (¦) functions as a logical OR, allowing you to remove file acme if the user provides any answer that starts with a lower- or uppercase Y.

In this example, *) shows how to provide a default case. The asterisk wildcard will match zero or more of any characters, so it matches anything. Only the first case that matches is used, so this default case must be the last case given. In the previous example, if the user's input does not start with a lower- or uppercase Y, then it displays a message that the file was not removed.

chapter

29

Writing Perl Programs

David Pitts and Steve
"Mor" Moritsugu

> **Tip for Beginners**
>
> Perl is an important language today for both UNIX and Windows, especially for Web site programming (which is beyond the scope of this book). Perl provides nice fixes for many of the limitations of UNIX, but it may be too cryptic and too overloaded with punctuation for the beginner. First learn Bourne shell programming in Chapter 28, "Writing Bourne Shell Scripts." Then come back to this chapter to learn how to write programs in the Perl language.

This chapter gives you an introduction to writing Perl scripts (using Perl version 5). Some of the things mentioned in this chapter will not work with version 4 of Perl; this chapter is meant to give enough information for a Perl novice to begin writing his own programs to enhance his performance in the real world. This chapter basically deals with three areas: user input, processing, and output, with an emphasis on user input and processing. Basic output is covered in the form of writing output to standard output (the monitor) and to files.

First, however, what is Perl? Perl is a programming language that is best for almost everything. The author of Perl, Larry Wall, irreverently says that it stands for "Pathologically Eclectic Rubbish Lister." After you have had the opportunity of using Perl for a while, however, I think that you will agree with the standard definition: "Practical Extraction and Reporting Language." Those of you who are used to C will find the syntax similar but better. You will also find that without the compiling associated with C, designing and changing tools becomes quick and easy. Perl is not compiled; it is an interpreted language of sorts. Perl is compiled at runtime, so it displays a speed much faster than most interpreted programs, but it is as easy to write code in as you would in a shell program. For those who are used to awk or sed, Perl takes advantage of regular expressions for providing pattern matching. Basically, Perl has become a replacement to C, shell scripting, TCL, and other programming languages and techniques normally associated with system administration.

Fortunately, Perl does not end there. It is a complete language ready to handle the complex needs of the programming community. Perl has been used in the genome project for mapping DNA, and Majordomo, the most popular mailing list manager, is written in Perl. Perl is being used for thousands (literally) of other projects. For more information on how Perl is being used, see the Comprehensive Perl Archive Network (www.perl.com). A good reference book on Perl is *Programming Perl*, published by O'Reilly and Associates. (It is often called the "camel" book because each O'Reilly book has an animal on the cover, and the Perl book has a picture of a camel.)

Writing/Executing a Simple Perl Script

Every programming course I have ever taken begins with designing a "Hello World" program. This chapter is no exception. We can begin by running a Perl script explicitly from the command line. Assuming that the location of the Perl executable is in your path, the following program

```
perl -e 'print "Hello world!\n";'
```

prints the following output:

```
Hello world!
```

The -e tells Perl to execute the quoted Perl code that follows on the command line. This method is only for short programs that fit on the command line.

See Table 29.1 for other standard properties of the perl command.

Table 29.1 Other Properties of the *perl* Command

Property	See page
Allows relative and absolute pathname arguments	70
Processes either filename arguments OR standard input	115
Changes only the output, not the file	111
Allows a list of filenames and filename wildcards	292
Allows output to be piped or redirected	116

Larger Perl programs should be saved in a text file. Each Perl text file program should have a magic first line beginning with a pound (#) bang (!) followed by the full pathname of the Perl interpreter. Therefore, your first line of your new program should look something like this:

```
#!/usr/local/bin/perl -w
```

When a modern UNIX shell sees #! as the first two characters of a program, it invokes the UNIX command given after #! and passes to that command all the remaining lines of the file to be executed. The -w Perl option gives warnings about possible errors and incorrect variable usage. Therefore, the "Hello World" program could be saved in a Perl program file that looks like this:

```
#!/usr/local/bin/perl -w
print "Hello World!\n";
```

Admittedly, this is not much of a program. However, it is sufficient for making sure that Perl runs and that you have the correct permissions on the file. For Perl to read and execute the script, the script must have both the read and execute permissions set for the person running the program.

Perl may be found in a different directory on your system, and therefore your Perl scripts will require a different first line. Use the `type` command to find its correct pathname:

```
$ type perl
perl is /usr/bin/perl
$
```

For the system that produced the previous output from the `type` command, I would put `#!/usr/bin/perl` as the first line of any Perl script there.

```
$ type perl
perl not found
$
```

This example shows what happens if Perl is not available on your UNIX system. Perl may be an optional component for your version of UNIX. You must download Perl and compile it from your UNIX vendor's Web site or from the Perl Web site at `www.perl.com`. Perl is available for most types of UNIX systems today because it is such a powerful, efficient language with a wealth of available utility programs and libraries for many specific applications.

A Quick Note on Termination

Each line of code must end with some form of termination. There are two types of termination in Perl. The first is the semicolon (;), which is used to terminate a line of code. The second is the right curly bracket (}), which is used to terminate a block of code. Many beginners (and experts, too) forget their terminators. Did you notice the semicolon (;) at the end of our previous Hello World example? (You probably did if you are a C programmer):

```
print "Hello World!\n";
```

What happens when you forget your terminator? The program tries to compile anyway, but it almost always errors out on the line following the one missing the semicolon, or at the end of the program for a missing right curly bracket.

Why is a terminator so important? A terminator is used to tell Perl when a line or block of code is done so that it knows what to do with that code. To Perl, a hard return means nothing. For example, the following two sets of code are the same from Perl's perspective. The second is just easier for humans to read.

```
$first_name="David"; $last_name="Pitts"; $work="Best Consulting";
```

```
$first_name="David";
$last_name="Pitts";
$work="Best Consulting";
```

Therefore, the motto goes, "Terminate, or be terminated!"

Perl Data Types

Before going on, let me point out the main data types used in Perl: literals, variables (including strings, arrays, and hashes), code references, filehandles, and here-documents. Each of these is given brief descriptions and examples in the following sections.

Literals

Literals are actual values—literally, what they are. There are numeric literals (for example, 1, 2, 3, 4, and so on) and string literals (abc, xyz, Fred, Sylvia, and so on). Some characters are not literals but are metacharacters or regular expression wildcards. These characters match something other than themselves. The metacharacters are \ | ( ) [ ] { } ^ $ * + ?.

An important metacharacter to understand is the backslash (\), which turns a metacharacter into a literal character. It also turns some literal characters into metacharacters; for example, \n is a newline, while \t is a tab character.

Variables

Variables are named storage locations used to hold a value. That value could be a number, a character, a string of numbers and characters, or anything else that the program sees fit. Variables are simple scalars that hold a single value or arrays and hashes that hold multiple values. A scalar variable always starts with a dollar sign ($), whether you are setting its value or using its value.

```
#!/usr/local/bin/perl
$cost = 12.34;
print $cost, "\n";
print "The ";
print "End\n";
```

The previous program would display this:

```
24.68
The End
```

Arrays and Hashes

Perl array names start with the at sign (@) to remind you that they are arrays. Multiple array items can be assigned at one time by giving a list of values within parenthesis:

```
@staffmembers = ("Robert", "Steve", "Jill");
print $staffmembers[0],"\n";
```

The previous code accesses the staffmembers array. It sets element 0 to the string Robert, element 1 to Steve, and element 2 to Jill. In the second code line, notice the dollar sign ($) prefix on the array name to display a single element. This program would display this:

```
Robert
```

Hashes are another type of array that contain multiple values, but each value is associated with a look-up string instead of a number. In the following code, the percent sign (%) prefix indicates that sales is hash. The code sets the first three elements of the hash, using the list notation you saw earlier. "Jan" is the first look-up string, and its associated value in the hash is 25.34. The => sign is a fancy comma separator that clearly shows that the left string is a pointer to the right value.

```
%sales = (
    "Jan" => 25.34,
    "Feb" => 12.12,
    "Mar" => 22.27,
);
print $sales{"Feb"} + $sales{"Mar"}, "\n";
```

The previous program would display this:

```
34.39
```

Global, Local, and *my* Variables

By default, all variables are global variables. This means that if you use a variable in one part of a program or subroutine and then use it in another part, that variable still points to the same location; any changes made to it in one location affect it in the other location as well.

Two ways of declaring a local variable exist: use either the `my` or the `local` declaration. I will not discuss their differences here, with one exception. A locally declared variable will carry its value to another subroutine called from within the current subroutine, whereas a `my` declared variable will not. This means that the subroutine gets its own copies of these variables, and any manipulation of these variables does not affect identically named variables outside that subroutine. The following example shows how to use the `my` and `local` identification.

```
my $name = "David";
local @brothers_family = ("John", "Kathy", "Pat", "Emily");
my ($John, $Kathy, $Pat, $Emily) = @brothers_family;
```

Note that the following is not the correct way of initializing the variables $x and $y to be local variables:

```
my $x, $y = 1;
```

This is the same as writing this:

```
my $x;
$y = 1;
```

This initializes $x as a local variable and sets $y (globally) to be equal to 1.

Here are some examples of all these variables:

- $var—A simple scalar variable.
- @var—The entire array; in a scalar context, the number of elements in the array.
- $var[4]—The fifth element of the array @var (as with most counting with computers, the first element of an array is the number 0 element, not the first).
- $d = \@var—$d is a reference to the array @var.
- $$d[4]—The fifth element of the array referenced by $d.
- $var[-1]—The last element of array @var.

- `$var[$x][$y]`—$yth element of the $xth element of the array @var.

- `$#var`—Last index of array @var.

- `%var`—The entire hash; in a scalar context, true if the hash has elements. (A hash is also called an associative array.)

- `$var{'Name'}`—A value from the hash array %var.

- `$d = \%var`—Now $d is a reference to the hash %var.

- `$$d{'Name'}`—A value from the hash array referenced by $d.

- `@var{'x','y'}`—A slice of %var; same as ($var{'x'},$var{'y'}).

Code References

Code references are subroutines. A subroutine is a snippet of code that can be invoked from a different location in the program to handle some portion of the goal of the program. If the subroutine returns a meaningful value, it is also called a function. There are two parts to a subroutine. First, there is the actual snippet of code; second, there is the thing that invokes the code.

A subroutine is defined using the reserve word sub followed by a space, and then the name of the subroutine. The entire subroutine is enclosed in begin and end brackets ({}), as the following subroutine shows.

A pound sign (#) is used to start a comment.

Comments extend from where the pound sign starts until the end of the line. Therefore, if you want three lines of comments, you must place a pound sign at the beginning of each line. (This is different than comments in C.)

```
sub weekday {
    # determine day of week
    $y=$year;
    $d=$mday;
    $m=$month;
    @d= (0,3,2,5,0,3,5,1,4,6,2,4);
    @day=(Sunday, Monday, Tuesday, Wednesday, Thursday, Friday, Saturday);
    $y-- if $m < 3;
    $weekday = $day[($y+int($y/4)-int($y/100)+int($y/400)+$d[$m-1]+$d) % 7];
} # end of sub weekday
```

To call a subroutine, you place an ampersand (&) sign in front of the name of the subroutine. To call the subroutine weekday, for example, you do this:

```
&weekday;
```

Parameters can also be passed with subroutines by placing them inside parentheses.

```
&subroutine(list);
```

This is the same as passing a list of arguments to the program. Therefore, I will defer a discussion about this to the section titled "Supplying Script Input as a Parameter," later in this chapter.

Filehandles

A *filehandle* is a symbolic name that you give to a file, pipe, socket, or device. These will be covered later in the chapter.

Here-Documents

Here-documents are a line-oriented form of quoting. Typically, this is used for printing multiple lines of text. It is quicker to use one print statement with a here-document reference than to print each line individually. Referencing a here-document is done by using two less-than signs (<<) followed by a terminator string used to close the quoted material (no space between the less-than signs and the string) followed by a semicolon (;):

```
print << terminator;
text line 1
text line 2
...
terminator
```

The following is an example of using a here-document to print multiple lines of code.

```
print <<"EOF";
My name is $f_name $l_name

I live at:   $street
   $city, $state  $zip

EOF
```

If a space is inserted after the two less-than signs, or if no string is used to close the quoted material, the print statement will print until it comes to a blank line. Therefore, had I put a space between the << and the " in the first line, all that would have printed would have been the first line rather than the whole thing.

> **Don't Put Terminator on Last Program Line**
>
> One of the advantages of Perl is that the language is available for both UNIX and Windows systems. On Windows, the terminator of a here-document cannot be put on the last line of a Perl program. This is a good rule to follow even on UNIX so your programs are more portable.

Special Perl Variables

Perl has several special built-in variables. These variables have a certain value, or take on a specific value without having to be told by the program. Table 29.2 lists and describes these special variables.

Table 29.2 Special Perl Variables

Variable	Purpose or Function
$_	The default input and pattern-searching space.
$.	The line number associated with the current line of the last filehandle read.
$/	The input record separator.
$,	The output field separator for the print operation.
$"	The separator that joins elements of arrays interpolated in strings.
$\	The output record separator for the print operator.
$#	The output format for printed numbers.
$*	Set to 1 to do multiline matching within strings.
$?	The status returned by the last ` . . . ` command, close, pipe, or system operator.
$]	The Perl version number.
$[	The index of the first element of an array and of the first character in a substring.
$;	The subscript operator for multidimensional array emulation.
$@	The error message returned from the last eval or do command.
$!	If used in a string context, yields the corresponding error string. In a numeric context, yields the current value of errno.
$:	The set of characters after which a string may be broken to fill continuation fields in a format.
$0	The filename of the Perl script being executed.
$$	The process ID of the Perl interpreter running the current script.

Variable	Purpose or Function
$<	The real user ID of the current Perl process.
$>	The effective user ID of the current Perl process.
$(	The real group ID of the current Perl process.
$)	The effective group ID of the current Perl process.
$^A	The accumulator for formline and write operations.
$^D	The debug flags as passed to Perl using -d.
$^F	The highest system file descriptor.
$^I	Inplace edit extension as passed to Perl using -i.
$^L	Form-feed character used in formats.
$^P	Internal debugging flag.
$^T	The time when the current Perl program started.
$^W	The value of the -w option as passed to Perl.
$^X	The name by which this Perl interpreter was invoked.
$%	The current page number of the currently selected output channel.
$=	The page length of the current output channel.
$-	The number of lines remaining in the current page.
$~	The name of the current report format.
$^	The name of the current top-of-page format.
$l	If set to nonzero (default is 0), it forces a flush after every print or write on the currently selected output channel. Otherwise, output might not start until the program has completed.
$ARGV	The name of the current file when reading from <>.
$&	The string matched by the last successful pattern match.
$'	The string preceding the last successful pattern match.
$`	The string following the last successful pattern match.
$+	The last bracket matched by the last search pattern.
$1..$9..	Contains the subpatterns from the corresponding sets of parentheses in the last pattern successfully matched.
@_	Parameter array for subroutines; also used by split if not an array context. Similar to $_ with strings.

continues...

Table 29.2   Continued

Variable	Purpose or Function
@ARGV	Contains the command-line arguments for the script.
@EXPORT	Names the methods a package exports by default.
@EXPORT_OK	Names the methods a package can export if explicitly requested.
@INC	Contains the list of places to look for Perl scripts to be evaluated by the do and require commands.
@ISA	List of base classes of a package.
%ENV	The current environment variables.
%INC	List of files that have been included with do, require, and use.
%OVERLOAD	Can be used to overload operators in a package.
%SIG	Used to set signal handlers for various signs.

Interacting with the User

Several different ways exist by which a Perl program can interact with the user. Parameters can be passed to the program, or input can come from the command line.

Supplying Script Input as a Parameter

Many programs allow parameters to be passed when the programs are instantiated. The programs must be smart enough to know what to do with these parameters. The same is true for any routine called in Perl. Fortunately, Perl has a built-in array that captures any parameters passed to it from the command line. That array is the @argv array. As in any language, the elements of the array are numbered starting with zero (0). Therefore, if two parameters were passed to the program, the first value would be the 0 element of the array, and the second parameter would be the first element of the array.

The @argv array is the default array. There are several ways of getting the information out of the array. The elements can be referred to, as alluded to earlier; if this method is used, the values stay in the array. Another way of getting the information out of the array is to shift it off the array. Using the shift command, you can remove elements off an array one at a time, moving all other elements in the array down one spot.

The following code checks that the required number of command-line arguments have been given on the command line after the name of the Perl program. If not, it generates a Usage error. Otherwise, it processes each argument by just displaying the argument:

```
#!/usr/local/bin/perl -w
$usage = "Usage: scriptname arg1 arg2\n";
die $usage if ($#ARGV != 1);
    # $ARGV[0] is the first arg    # $ARGV[1] is the 2nd arg
    # $#ARGV is the last arg number = # of args - 1
    # to loop thru all cmd line args:
for (@ARGV) {
        print "Processing command line argument: ", $_, "\n";
}
```

Supplying Script Input on the Command Line

It is not necessary to pass variables to a program when the program is instantiated. It is also possible to read input from the command line. This is done with the use of the angle operator. The angle operator uses a special filehandle called STDIN. By placing the input filehandle between less-than and greater-than signs, you can get input from a command line. The value must be assigned to a variable and does include the hard return used when inputting the data. Use the chop command to remove the last character from the string. If you are not sure whether there is a final return in the string, use the chomp command to remove the last character only if it is a return:

```
#!/usr/local/bin/perl -w
print "Enter first value: ";
$firstval = <STDIN>;
chop $firstval;
print "Enter second value: ";
$secondval = <STDIN>;
chop $secondval;
print "$firstval $secondval\n";
```

When this program is run, it will look like this:

```
Enter first value: 3
Enter second value: 2
3 2
```

The following Perl code shows how to range check the input value. If out of range, it will ask for the value to be re-input until a valid value is given:

```
for (;;) {
   print "Enter first value: ";
   $firstval = <STDIN>;
   chop $firstval;
   if ($firstval < 100) {
      last;
   }
   print "Illegal value. Please try again.\n";
}
```

Control Structures

Control structures provide programs with the capability to make decisions, to perform actions based on criteria. Perl has basically two types of control structures: conditionals and interactives. Conditionals are based on the concept that if something is true, perform some action once. Interactives (also known as loops) are based on the concept that if something is true, perform some action until that something is no longer true. This brings us to the question, what is truth?

What Is Truth?

This is a question that has plagued philosophers for thousands of years. Fortunately, we are programmers, not philosophers, and we know what truth is. Truth can be broken down into two types. The first way of looking at truth is a simple value check. If that value is equal to nil or zero, it is false; otherwise, it is true. Therefore, in the preceding example, if $value was anything other than nil or zero (that is, it has some value), it is printed; otherwise, it is not. Here are some examples, using this basic format, showing the difference between true and false:

```
$value = "";
if ($value) { print $value }
```

Nothing gets printed because $value is nil.

```
$value = "David";
if ($value) { print $value }
```

David is printed, because "David" is not nil or zero.

The other way of looking at truth is with truth tables, looking at how one value compares with another value. To look at these truth tables, you must first have an understanding of how comparisons are done in Perl. They are done differently depending on whether they are comparing strings or numbers. Table 29.3 shows the relational operators for numbers and strings as well as what they mean.

Table 29.3   Relational Operators for Numbers and Strings

Numeric	String	Meaning
>	gt	Greater than (returns " " if false, and 1 if true).
>=	ge	Greater than or equal to (returns " " if false, and 1 if true).
<	lt	Less than (returns " " if false, and 1 if true).
<=	le	Less than or equal to (returns " " if false, and 1 if true).
==	eq	Equal to (returns " " if false, and 1 if true).
!=	ne	Not equal to (returns " " if false, and 1 if true).
<=>	cmp	Comparison (returns -1 if left is less than right, 0 if equal, and 1 if left is greater than right).

Using the preceding table, you can then come up with some more complex if commands.

```
if ($value == 24) { print $value }
if ($value == 24 && $name eq "David") {print $name}
if ($value == 24 || $name eq "David") {print $value}
```

The first line is probably fairly understandable: If the value of $value is 24, then print the value of $value. The next two lines use a logical operator to allow a complex set of checking to determine truthfulness. The double ampersand sign (&&) is a logical AND, and a double pipe (||) is a logical OR. With the logical AND, the values on both sides of the && must be true for the entire statement to be true. With the logical OR, only one side has to be true. They use the following basic truth table.

Comparison	Value
True && True	True
True && False	False
False && False	False
False && True	False
True || True	True
True || False	True
False || False	False
False || True	True

Executing Code Based on Test Results

Now that you have input, either from the command line or from standard input, you can do something with it. The most common thing to do with input is to test the results and do something if the results are a certain thing. This test result is done with the `if` command. The syntax of the `if` command is the verb *if* followed by a truth statement. After the truth statement, a block of code gets executed if the truth statement evaluates to true; otherwise, it skips that section of code. A simple `if` statement, then, would look something like this:

```
if ($value) { print $value }
```

Perl has an `unless` command that is similar to the `if` command, but the code is executed only if the condition is false. Think: If the condition is not true, do the action.

```
unless ($value) { print $value }
```

For short statements, the `if` or `unless` may follow a statement:

```
print $value if ($value);
print $value unless ($value);
```

The general syntax for testing if an R.E. pattern is contained within a string looks like this:

```
if ($string =~ /R.E./flags)
```

A useful flag is the `i` flag that ignores case when checking for a match. The following code gets input from the user. If the input starts with lowercase y or uppercase Y, the program prints "affirmative." Otherwise, the program prints `negative`:

```
$input = <STDIN>;
if ($input =~ /^y/i) {
   print "affirmative\n";
}
else {
   print "negative\n";
}
```

Decision Making

Having the capability to check on the truthfulness of something is okay, but with many processes, the desire is to take it one step further: to say "If something is true, do one thing; if it is not true, do something else." This can easily be done in Perl with the `if-else` statement:

```
if ($value eq "True") { do something }
else { do something else }
```

This is about as basic as it gets: a simple yes or no question, with each receiving a separate set of instructions. Of course, with the `elsif` verb, it is possible to have a hierarchy of work performed based upon certain conditions (that is, if the first condition is false, check the next condition). The following example shows that if the value is true, then Perl does something; if it is false, the program then checks another value and, depending on its value, does one of several things:

```
if ($value eq "True") { do something }
    else { if ($range <= 22) { do something }
    elsif (($range > 22 ) && ($range <= 44)) { do something }
    elsif (($range > 44) && ( $range <= 70)) { do something }
    else {do something }
}  # end else
```

As you can see, with a combination of `if`s, `elsif`s, and `else`s, it is possible to create any conditional type statement that may be necessary.

Looping Through a Series of Code

The `if` statement helps to identify what to do when there is a choice. The `for` command is used when you want to loop through a series of code a certain number of times. Say, for example, that you want to perform a task until a certain variable (such as a counter) reaches a certain value. In English what you would do might look something like this:

> Initialize the counter to 0. If the counter is less than or equal to 10, run the series of commands. After the counter is greater than 10, go on to the rest of the program.

Perl uses the same syntax for the `for` loop as C does. The format is as follows:

```
for (initialize; condition; change loop variable) {
    # loop code line 1
    # loop code line 2
    # ...
}
```

The following is an actual Perl example:

```
for ($counter=0; $counter <= 10; $counter++) { do stuff }
```

The following are your options:

- `$counter=0`: Initializes the loop variable.
- `$counter <= 10`: Evaluates to a true or false condition. If true, you execute the loop code again. If false, you bypass the loop and continue executing the rest of the program.
- `$counter++`: This changes the loop variable so that it is ready to execute the loop code again, with a new variable value each time through the loop.
- `{ do stuff }`: This represents one or more lines of loop code that must be listed inside the curly braces {}.

Notice that the `for` loop has three parts. First, you have the initial state of the `for` loop (`$counter = 0`). Next you have under what conditions you are going to execute the code (while the counter is less than or equal to 10). Finally, you have an expression to modify the state of the loop (increment `$counter`). As long as the truth condition is true (`$counter <= 10`), the loop will continue to execute.

You will probably recognize that the `for` loop is identical in nature to the `while` loop. The syntax is different, but the concept is the same. Just for completeness, however, here is the same loop as a `while` loop so that you can see the difference:

```
while ($counter <=10) {do stuff }
```

The main difference between the two is that there must exist in the "do stuff" code a change to the state variable, or you will wind up with an endless loop.

Looping Through Something in Its Entirety

Similar to the `for` loop is the `foreach` loop. The `foreach` loop is used to perform a set of instructions on an entire scalar quantity, such as an array. The syntax is quite simple; I will again give it in plain English and then in Perl.

In plain English, you would say, "For each entity in my set, perform these instructions." Sound simple? Well, it is. The following is the Perl version of the `foreach` command:

```
foreach $value (@array) { do stuff }
```

In the preceding example, each element of the array `@array` is assigned to the variable `$value`. Then the block of code is executed. It is not necessary to have the variable there (`$value`). If it is missing, the special variable `$_` will contain the value of each element as the loop is executed. Here is a real-world example that may help to shed some light on this.

For example, suppose that you want to open a file, save its contents to an array, and check each line for \n and replace it with <br>. This is a good example of looping. The key that this is a looping function is the "check each line" statement. Such a program could look like this:

```
#!/site/bin/perl
open (FILE,"filename")  || die "File not found:  $!\n";
@file=<FILE>;
close(FILE);
foreach (@file) {
    $_ =~ s/\\n/<br>/g;
    push (@temp, $_);
} # end of foreach  (@file)
open (FILE, ">filename");
print FILE @temp;
close FILE;
```

Commonly Used Functions in Perl

Although it would take 100 pages or more to give a brief description of all the functions of Perl, it is adequate to list some of the common functions dealing with arrays, lists, and scalars, giving the novice the ability to make some very powerful and complex tools. Therefore, this section gives a brief description and provides examples for some of the most commonly used functions. Before this occurs, a few points need to be made about functions in general.

Functions can be used as terms in an expression. Some of these functions take on a *list* as an argument. Such a list can be any combination of scalar and list values, but the entire list will be treated as a single dimensional list value. Elements in a list must be separated by a comma, or by a =>, which is a shorthand version of a comma.

Functions do not need parentheses around their arguments. Many programmers use parentheses around the arguments to help distinguish them from the function name and to help indicate that they are arguments. Caution must be taken, however, because parentheses in the wrong location can give varying—and many times unexpected—results. The following example helps to make this more clear:

```
print 1+1+1;    # prints "3"
print (1+1)  + 1;    # prints "2"
print (1+1)+1;    # prints "2"
```

```
print +(1+1)+1;    # prints "3"
print ((1+1)+1);   # prints "3"
```

As you can see, spacing has little or no effect, but the parentheses have a lot of effect on the output.

The functions examined in this chapter fall into the following categories: array, file, hash, system, and variable manipulation. The functions can be broken down into these categories (realizing that some do fit into multiple categories) like this:

```
Array Manipulation:     pop, push, shift, unshift, splice
File Manipulation:      open, close
Hash Manipulation:      each, keys, values
System Manipulation:    time, localtime, system
Variable Manipulation:    ++, --, ., chomp, split, join
```

An accurate observer would note that some of these are not actually functions (., ++, --) but are important enough to be included anyway.

Array Manipulation

Arrays can be treated as stacks. Therefore, things can be added or removed from either end of the stack. With the capability to add and remove things from the beginning and ending of an array, you can perform first-in-first-out and last-in-first-out functionality. Things can also be removed from the middle of a stack. With this in mind, take a look at the following five functions.

The *push* and *pop* Funtions

My wife told me that if I pushed her too far, she would pop me. This is not a reflection on our relationship, but a reminder of what push and pop do. Obviously she already had a lot to deal with, and I was adding to the end of her list. If I continued to do that, she would remove those things back off her list. Therefore, push and pop add and remove things from the end of an array. The syntax and an example of these follow:

```
push ARRAY, LIST
```

The following example uses a foreach statement to read each line of an array. Each line is then subjected to a search and replace routine, and the result of that line is pushed on to an array called @temp:

```
foreach $line (@ARGV)
        { $line =~ s/$search/$replace/g ;
          push (@temp, $line);
} # end of foreach $line (@stuff)
print @stuff,"\n\n",@temp;
```

The pop function works similarly, as seen here:

```
pop ARRAY
pop
```

If ARRAY is omitted, the function pops @ARGV or @. The following example pops each element off an array and performs the same search and replace routine as the preceding example, and the result is pushed on to a second array:

```
while (@ARGV) {
    $argument = pop;
    $argument =~ s/$search/$replace/g ;
    push (@temp, $argument);
} # end while (@ARGV)
    print @temp, "\n\n\", @ARGV;
```

What is the difference between these two examples? There are two differences. Look at the output of the print statements. In both examples, $search = "David" and $replace = "John", and the arguments passed were "David was here." Output of the push example looks like this:

```
Johnwashere.

Johnwashere.
```

Output of the pop example looks like this:

```
here.wasJohn
```

The differences are that, in the pop example, @ARGV loses all its values because they are popped off the list (removed); in the second example, each is just addressed. The second difference is that, in the pop example, the output is the opposite of the input. Can you figure out why?

The *shift* and *unshift* Functions

shift and unshift are just like push and pop, except they work on the other side of the array. push and pop add and remove items from the end of the array, and unshift and shift add and remove items from the beginning of an array. This section uses examples similar to push and pop so that you can see what the differences are. First, however, here is their syntax:

```
unshift ARRAY, LIST
```

Remember, `unshift` prepends items to an array—that means, it adds them to the beginning of the array:

```
foreach $line (@ARGV)
        { $line =~ s/$search/$replace/g ;
          unshift (@temp, $line);
} # end of foreach $line (@stuff)
print @temp,"\n\n",@ARGV;
```

This is the example's output:

```
here.wasJohn


Johnwashere.
```

Notice, that @temp contains the input parameters, "John was here." in reverse order. The following lines show the general syntax for the shift function. If no array is specified, the default array @_ is used.

```
shift ARRAY
shift
```

Just like its counterpart `pop`, `shift` removes items from @ARGV or @ if no ARRAY is given:

```
while (@ARGV) {
        $argument=shift;
        $argument =~ s/$search/$replace/g;
        unshift (@temp, $argument);
} # end while (@ARGV)


print @temp, "\n\n", @ARGV;
```

This is the example's output:

```
here.wasJohn
```

Notice that even though it took the items from the beginning of the stack first, `shift` also put them back in the beginning first. Therefore, the new array, @temp, now contains all the arguments in reverse order.

The *splice* Function

Sometimes, you want to take a bigger piece of an array, or you want to take something out of the middle. That is what `splice` is for. As a matter of fact, you can use `splice` as a replacement for `shift`, `unshift`, `pop`, and `push`. The syntax of splice looks like this:

```
splice ARRAY, OFFSET, LENGTH, LIST
splice ARRAY, OFFSET, LENGTH
splice ARRAY, OFFSET
```

This function removes elements designated by OFFSET and LENGTH from an array, and replaces them with the elements of LIST, if there are any. splice returns the elements removed from the array. If the LENGTH is omitted, shift removes everything after the OFFSET.

The following table shows how to use splice rather than push, pop, shift, and unshift to remove a piece from the middle of the array.

splice	Equivalent
splice(@array, $#array+1, 0, $x, $y);	push (@array, $x, $y);
splice(@array,(@array, -1);	pop (@array);
splice(@array, 0, 1);	shift (@array)
splice(@array, 0, 0, $x, $y);	unshift (@array, $x, $y);
splice(@array, $x, 1, $y);	$array[$x] = $y;

Did you see that special-looking variable $#array? That value returns the index of the last element in the array. By adding 1 to it, you get the OFFSET value (arrays start counting at 0; OFFSET starts counting at 1).

File Manipulation

The two most common things you will do with a file is open and close it. Closing a file is very simple and is discussed first. Opening a file depends on what you are going to do with the file, so a little extra time is spent explaining it.

The *close* Command

Closing a filehandle is not a necessary step up through version 5 of Perl. A file is automatically closed when the program ends or when a new file is opened with the same FILEHANDLE name. There is no guarantee that this will hold true in future versions of Perl, and it is also good programming etiquette to close any files that you open. If you do not remember what filehandles are, see the previous section that discusses them. The syntax is simple:

```
close FILEHANDLE;
```

I give you an example here, but it should be obvious:

```
open (FILE, $file);
$file=<FILE>;
close FILE;
```

The *open* Command

You open a file by opening it and giving it a filehandle. The filehandle is then referred to in the program. Files can be opened for various reasons: to be read from, to be written to, and to be concatenated to. The following table shows the different ways of opening a file.

Command	What It Does
`open (FILE, "filename");`	Reads from an existing file
`open (DAVID, "<filename");`	Opens a file explicitly (same as previous)
`open (church,">filename");`	Creates a file and opens it to be written to (overwrites an existing file)
`open (log,">>filename");`	Appends to a file (does not overwrite an existing file)
`open(file, "| output-pipe-command");`	Sets up an output filter
`open(file, "input-pipe-command |");`	Sets up an input filter

As you can see, it is important to know what you are going to do with the file; otherwise, you can accidentally delete an existing file or append to a file that you meant to overwrite.

The following Perl program illustrates one of the great strengths of Perl: that multiple files can be accessed for input and output at one time. This is very difficult to do in Bourne shell scripting. This program simply reads a line from each of the source files, concatenates them, and writes the new line to a destination file:

```perl
#!/usr/local/bin/perl -w
open (IN1, "file1") or die "cannot open file1";
open (IN2, "file2") or die "cannot open file2";
open (OUT, ">file3") or die "cannot open file3 for output";
while (<IN1>) {
    $firstfile = $_;
    chomp $firstfile;
    $secondfile = <IN2>;
    chomp $secondfile;
    print OUT "$firstfile $secondfile\n";
}
```

Hash Manipulation

Hash arrays are different from regular arrays. A hash array is an associative array. Where a normal array is an indexed list, with each item referred to by its index number, a hash is a list of value pairs. A value pair is where the first item (key) refers to the second item (value); when the first item is referred to, the second item is the value returned. This can be easily illustrated with the following small hash array for the days of the week:

```
%day_of_the_week =
( 0, Sunday, 1, Monday, 2, Tuesday, 3, Wednesday, 4, Thursday, 5, Friday, 6,
➡Saturday);
```

The hash can also be defined this way:

```
%day_of_the_week=  (
    0 => 'Sunday',
    1 => 'Monday',
    2 => 'Tuesday',
    3 => 'Wednesday',
    4 => 'Thursday',
    5 => 'Friday',
    6 => 'Saturday',
);
```

Note that the comma after the last key/value pair *must be there*.

Now that a hash has been defined, you can look at the three functions—each, keys, and values—and see how they relate to the %day_of_the_week hash.

The *each* Function

The each function returns a two-element list consisting of the key and value for the next value of a hash:

```
each %hash
```

The each function is unique in that you can use successive calls to each to iterate over the entire hash. You should not add elements to a hash while you are iterating it, but you can delete from it.

The *keys* Function

This function returns all the keys of the hash:

```
keys %hash
```

The *values* Function

This function returns all the values of the hash:

```
values %hash
```

The following example shows a listing of each of the values of the %day_of_the_week hash:

```
while (($key, $value) = each %day_of_the_week) {
        print "$key has value $value\n";
}
```

The result of this program is as follows:

```
0 has value Sunday
1 has value Monday
2 has value Tuesday
3 has value Wednesday
4 has value Thursday
5 has value Friday
6 has value Saturday
```

System Manipulation

System manipulation is really not a good term for these functions. Basically, it is reading something from the system or performing a system call. Other functions also could be included here (such as exec, fork, kill, and times), but these are the basic ones.

The *time* Function

time returns the number of seconds since the birth of UNIX, January 1, 1970, Universal Time. It can be used to determine how long it has been since a file was accessed, or how long it takes to complete a task. A common function of time is to use it as a parameter of localtime. An example of how to use this function is shown with the localtime function section.

The *localtime* Function

The localtime function returns a nine-element list with the time corrected for the current time zone. The nine elements are shown in the following table, along with their possible values:

Element	Possible Values
seconds	0..59
minutes	0..59
hour	0..23
month day	1..31
month	0..11
year	current year minus 1900
day of the week	0..6
day of the year	0..364
whether it is daylight savings time	0..1

The following example takes the current date and prints the time, date, day of the week, day of the year, and whether it is daylight savings time. You will notice some modifications to the variables to deal with certain values starting with 0. Also, the daylight savings time is changed to True or False:

```perl
#!/usr/bin/perl
($sec, $min, $hour, $mday, $mon, $year, $wday, $yday, $isdst) = localtime(time);
$year+=1900;
$yday++;
if ($sec < 10) { $sec = "0".$sec }
if ($min < 10) { $min = "0".$min }
if ($hour < 10) { $hour = "0".$hour }
if ($isdst) {$isdst = "True" } else { $isdst = "False" }
%tday = (
        0 => 'Sunday',
        1 => 'Monday',
        2 => 'Tuesday',
        3 => 'Wednesday',
        4 => 'Thursday',
        5 => 'Friday',
        6 => 'Saturday',
) ;

%tmonth = (
        0 => 'January',
        1 => 'February',
        2 => 'March',
        3 => 'April',
```

```
            4 => 'May',
            5 => 'June',
            6 => 'July',
            7 => 'August',
            8 => 'September',
            9 => 'October',
            10 => 'November',
            11 => 'December',
    );


    print "Time:  $hour:$min:$sec\n";
    print "Today:  $tmonth{$mon} $mday, $year\n";
    print "Day of the week:  $tday{$wday}\n";
    print "Day of the year:  $yday\n";
    print "Daylight Savings time?:  $isdst\n";
```

The result of this file is the following output:

```
Time:  20:09:46
Today:  March 24, 1998
Day of the week:  Tuesday
Day of the year:  83
Daylight Savings time?:  False
```

As you can imagine, the `time` and `localtime` functions are great for such things as logs, reports, and other applications where it is handy to know when something happened.

The *system* Command

The `system` command allows a Perl program to have access to the system. There are two ways of calling the system. The first is with the `system` command; the second is by placing the command between back-tics. The problem with making system calls is that it greatly limits the portability of your code. One of the nice things about the `system` command is that it blocks SIGINT and SIGQUIT and keeps it from killing the program. Also, the result of a program called with `system` can be saved with a variable, allowing the program to examine the results and perform any necessary steps from the results. A very simple example is listed here.

This example also illustrates the fact that Perl variables can be used to form the command within backquotes. This is a very powerful feature that makes all the power of UNIX accessible to your Perl programs:

```
$cur_dir = `ls $dir`;
```

Actually calling the `system` command looks like this:

```
$cur_dir = system (ls);   # parentheses not necessary.
```

If you want to write Perl programs that run on both UNIX and Windows, avoid using the backquotes and `system` commands. The Perl libraries allow you to emulate most UNIX commands totally within Perl so that your program is portable.

Perl assumes that you know what you are doing and, therefore, lets you do whatever you want. A command such as `$remove = `rm -r \`;` can just kill a system!

Variable Manipulation

Variable manipulation is grouped into a couple different groups. First there are the increment and decrement symbols (++ and --), the dot (.), substitution, and then `split` and `join`. Finally, there is the `chomp` command. These topics will be discussed in this order.

```
++, --
```

These two symbols increment and decrement the value of a variable by one. The following example shows incrementing the variable `$penny` by one and then decrementing it by one:

```
$penny++;
$penny--;
```

You will find this much quicker and easier than the following:

```
$penny += 1;
```

or

```
$penny = $penny -1;
```

The dot (.) is used to concatenate strings. Given the following two strings:

```
$string1 = "University of Kentucky Wildcats";
$string2 = "are the best basketball players ever!";
```

these strings can be concatenated into one string by using the dot, as in the following example:

```
$string3=$string1.$string2;
```

This produces the following output when printed:

```
University of Kentucky Wildcatsare the best basketball players ever!
```

The concatenation did not put a space between the strings; so you must add it. This can be done like this:

```
$string3=$string1." ".$string2;
```

This produces the following result when printed:

```
University of Kentucky Wildcats are the best basketball players ever!
```

If a string of numbers is concatenated, the numbers are put together just like text is; they are not manipulated. For example, the following lines produce the output 123456:

```
$a=123;
$b=456;
$c=$a.$b;
print $c;
```

Substitution

The following is the general syntax to substitute patterns within a variable:

```
$var =~ s/R.E./repl/flags;
```

The following are your options:

- $var is the variable to be modified.
- s/ indicates substitution where slash (/) is the delimiter.
- R.E. indicates any Regular Expression pattern to look for.
- repl indicates the replacement string to substitute for the found R.E. pattern.
- flags can be any of the following:
    - i to ignore case
    - g global (to substitute all occurrences, not just the first)
    - x to ignore inserted spaces for more readability

The following program gets input from the user. It then searches for any strings of zero or more spaces and removes them throughout the string. Thus, all leading, trailing, and internal spaces are removed.

```
$input = <STDIN>;
$input =~ s/ *//g;
print "$input\n";
```

The *split* Function

The split function is used to turn a delimited string into a list:

```
split /PATTERN/, EXPR, LIMIT;
split /PATTERN/, EXPR;
split /PATTERN/;
split;
```

This function scans a string given by EXPR for delimiters indicated with /PATTERN/. It then splits that string into a set of substrings. If the LIMIT is set to a nonzero, positive number, the string is split into no more than that number of substrings. In the process, the /PATTERN/ being matched goes away.

The following example shows how you could split up the /etc/passwd file into its seven different fields. The account lines are colon delimited, so you search on the pattern of the colon:

```
($user,$password,$uid,$gid,$gcos,$home,$init_prog) = split (/:/, @passwd);
```

split, then, breaks up big strings into smaller strings. The join function takes small strings and joins them together into big strings.

The *join* Function

The join funtion takes strings and joins them into a single string with the EXPR delimiting them:

```
join EXPR, LIST;
```

This is the opposite of the split function. The following example takes the seven elements associated with a password entry and joins them together with a colon as the EXPR:

```
$entry = join (':',$user,$password,$uid,$gid,$gcos,$home,$init_prog);
```

The *chomp* Function

chomp is used to remove trailing newlines only from the selected string(s):

```
chomp VARIABLE;
chomp LIST;
chomp;
```

If VARIABLE or LIST is omitted, this function chomps $. One common use for chomp is to remove the input coming from the keyboard:

```
print "Enter your name:   ";
$answer = <STDIN>;
chomp $answer;
if ($answer eq "Fred" ¦¦ $answer eq "fred") {
    print "Nice to see you, Fred!" }
else { die "Sorry! Invalid entry" }
print "Enter your address:   ";
```

If you comment out the chomp $answer line, then no matter what name you enter, the program will abort (die) with an Invalid entry message. This is because your if statement is looking for either Fred or fred, and there is not a newline in either of these strings.

Debugging Your Script

The Perl debugger is not a separate program. Instead, you invoke Perl with the -d option, and you are in Debug mode. While in Debug mode, you have the capability to examine source code, set breakpoints, dump out your function call stack, change the values of variables, and so forth. This section does not go through all the functionality of the debugger, nor does it give you all the available commands. However, this section does introduce you to the basic debugging commands and shows you how to find out more. Specifically, the things that you are shown here are how to set, list, and remove breakpoints; how to step through a program; how to check and change the value of a variable; and how to get help.

I will be using the following short program as a basis for describing the debugger. This program is called rep.pl and is used to search and replace strings in a file. You will notice that I added the -d option so that Perl would run in Debug mode:

```
#!/usr/bin/perl -d
#
#  Open file, replace every occurrence of a string.
#  Usage:  rep string1 string2 file
$file = @ARGV[2];
$search = @ARGV[0];
$replace = @ARGV[1];

if ($file eq "") {
print "Usage: rep.pl [search] [replace] [file name]\n\n";  }

else    {
```

```
open (FILE, "$file") || die "File not found: $! ";
@stuff = <FILE>;
close FILE;

foreach $line (@stuff)
        { $line =~ s/$search/$replace/g ;
          push (@temp, $line); }

open (FILE, ">$file");
print FILE @temp;
close FILE;


}
```

When I run this program, Perl comes up in Debug mode. This means that the code does get compiled. If there are compilation errors (such as missing semicolons), the debugger will not run. Assuming that there are no compilation errors, the debugger should come up and look something like this:

```
Loading DB routines from perl5db.pl version 1
Emacs support available.

Enter h or 'h h' for help.

main::(./rep.pl:6):     $file = @ARGV[2];
  DB<1>
```

By the way, I ran the program with the following command:

```
rep.pl david
```

This will be important as you look at the values of some of the strings, as well as the final output of the program itself.

Listing Code

The first thing to do is list the code. To list code, you type the letter l. This produces the following results:

```
DB<1> l
6==>    $file = @argv[2];
7:      $search = @ARGV[0];
8:      $replace = @ARGV[1];
9:
10:     if ($file eq "") {
```

```
11:    print "Usage: rep.pl [search] [replace] [file
➥name]\n\n";  }
12:
13:    else    {
14:    open (FILE, "$file") || die "File not found: $! ";
15:    @stuff = <FILE>;
DB<1>
```

The debugger indicates the current line with the ==> pointing to the line (line 6). You will notice that it skipped right over the comments at the beginning of the program and went straight to line 6. By default, the debugger lists 10 lines of code. You can specify any range you wish by placing a starting line number and then a dash followed by the number of lines you want to print. Therefore, if you told it that you wanted it to print the first three lines of the program, it would look like this:

```
DB<2> l 1-3
1        #!/usr/bin/perl -d
2        #
#  Open file, replace every occurrence of a string.
```

Executing a Line of Code

After listing the code, now you will execute the first line. Do so by typing the letter n. This tells the debugger to execute the line and go to the next line. That produced the following results:

```
main::(./rep.pl:7):    $search = @ARGV[0];
  DB<3>
```

Printing Values of Variables

At this point, tell the program to execute the next two lines of code. This gives you something else to work with. Now say that you want to know the value of the variables $, $ARGV[0], $ARGV[1], and $ARGV[2]:

```
DB<3> print $_

  DB<4> print $ARGV[0]
david
  DB<5> print $ARGV[1]

  DB<6> print $ARGV[2]

  DB<7>
```

As suspected, the value of $_ is nothing. The value of $ARGV[0] is "david", and $ARGV[1] and $ARGV[2] is also nothing. Now say that you want to change the value of $ARGV[1] to "David" rather than nothing. You do this by telling the variable what it should be, as follows:

```
DB<7> $ARGV[1]="David"

  DB<8> print $ARGV[1]
David
  DB<9>
```

As a matter of fact, you can execute any Perl command from the debugger command line, and it will affect the program that you are running. The only limitation is that you are limited to one line per prompt, and you do not place a semicolon after the command.

Breakpoints

You can use breakpoints to set up one or more stopping points in your program. Once set, a breakpoint tells the debugger to stop on this line if it reaches it. In the example, say you want to set a breakpoint on the 10th line. You want the program to stop at the if statement so that you can figure out what the values are. To set a breakpoint, you use a letter b followed by a line number. Optionally, you can place a condition there as well. If a condition is placed, the breakpoint will stop the execution of the program only if it reaches the line and the condition is true. Therefore, what you want to do is set a breakpoint that stops the program if $file equals "". That command would look like this:

```
DB<5> b 10 $file eq ""
  DB<6> l 6-15
6==>     $file = @ARGV[2];
7:       $search = @ARGV[0];
8:       $replace = @ARGV[1];
9
10:b     if ($file eq "") {
11:      print "Usage: rep.pl [search] [replace] [file
➥name]\n\n";   }
12
13       else   {
14:      open (FILE, "$file") || die "File not found ";
15:      @stuff = <FILE>;
```

Did you notice that line 10 looks different? It has a b next to the line number. This is how the debugger indicates a breakpoint. Now say that you want the debugger to run until it gets to the breakpoint. You do this by issuing a letter c. Follow the c with a w so that you can see a window of code around the current line:

```
DB<7> c
main::(./rep.pl:10):    if ($file eq "") {
  DB<7> w
7:      $search = @ARGV[0];
8:      $replace = @ARGV[1];
9
10==>b  if ($file eq "") {
11:     print "Usage: rep.pl [search] [replace] [file
name]\n\n";  }
12
13      else    {
14:     open (FILE, "$file") ¦¦ die "File not found ";
15:     @stuff = <FILE>;
16:     close FILE;
  DB<7>
```

Now say that you want to take another look at the variables $ARGV[0] and $ARGV1], so type in the following command:

```
DB<7> print $ARGV[0] $ARGV[1]
```

Remember, I said only one command per line. Here you did two commands: You told it to print out two different values. Here is the result of the command:

```
Scalar found where operator expected at (eval 5) line 2, at end of line
        eval '($@, $!, $,, $/, $\\, $^W) = @saved;package main; $^D = $^D | $DB:
:db_stop;
print $ARGV[0] $ARGV[1];

;' called at /usr/lib/perl5/perl5db.pl line 1153
        DB::eval called at /usr/lib/perl5/perl5db.pl line 1062
        DB::DB called at ./rep.pl line 10
        (Missing operator before ?)
        eval '($@, $!, $,, $/, $\\, $^W) = @saved;package main; $^D = $^D | $DB:
:db_stop;
print $ARGV[0] $ARGV[1];

;' called at /usr/lib/perl5/perl5db.pl line 1153
        DB::eval called at /usr/lib/perl5/perl5db.pl line 1062
```

```
      DB::DB called at ./rep.pl line 10
Segmentation fault
```

Well, this told you two things. First, use one command per line. Second, it tells you that if there is an error, a segmentation fault will occur, and the Perl program will bomb. So, you restart and try again. Add your breakpoint back so that you have the same conditions as before. You should realize that now, however, you don't need that breakpoint; you now need to delete it. To delete a breakpoint, enter a lowercase d. If a line number follows the d, the breakpoint is removed from that line. An uppercase D will delete all installed breakpoints:

```
DB<2> d 10
6:      $file = @ARGV[2];
7:      $search = @ARGV[0];
8:      $replace = @ARGV[1];
9
10==>   if ($file eq "") {
11:     print "Usage: rep.pl [search] [replace] [file name]\n\n";   }
12
13      else    {
14:     open (FILE, "$file") || die "File not found ";
15:     @stuff = <FILE>;
  DB<4>
```

The breakpoint at line 10 is now gone. Say you have added some more breakpoints, and now you want to list them. You do that with a capital L, as follows:

```
DB<7> L
./rep.pl:
 6:      $file = @ARGV[2];
   break if (1)
 11:    print "Usage: rep.pl [search] [replace] [file name]\n\n";   }
   break if (1)
 15:    @stuff = <FILE>;
   break if (1)
  DB<7>
```

It seems that you have three breakpoints set: lines 6, 11, and 15. A capital D will delete them all, and you will be ready to go.

```
DB<7> D
Deleting all breakpoints...
  DB<7>
```

A lot more can be done with the debugger—it would take an entire chapter to go into all the functionality. So, before closing the book on the debugger, let me point you to a source of further understanding: the help facility built into the debugger itself. If you just type an h by itself, you will get a long listing of all the possible command options available. If you are like me, you cannot read fast enough to catch it as it is scrolling off the screen. Therefore, typing h h will give the same list in a different format. This one will be in a two-column list that should fit on a single screen. Following each command is a very short description on what that command does. You can see that the v shows versions of modules, for example:

```
DB<10> v
'Term/ReadLine.pm' => '/usr/lib/perl5/Term/ReadLine.pm'
'dumpvar.pl' => '/usr/lib/perl5/dumpvar.pl'
'perl5db.pl' => '1 from /usr/lib/perl5/perl5db.pl'
  DB<10>
```

Finally, when you are done, a simple q will quit you out of the program.

Some Final Words

Perl is a fully functioning powerful language that is easy to use. It brings together the power of C and the ease of shell programming. Perl does not stop there, however. Perl does object orienting and also can be combined with other languages, including C, TK, and Java. What's more, it is easy to use and has some great support behind it.

For further information on Perl, check out the Perl Web site at www.perl.com. There you will find the latest versions of Perl, along with the Comprehensive Perl Archive Network (CPAN), which has lots of code, most of which falls under the same copyright license as Perl itself. You will also find FAQs there. If you get stuck, you can also go to the comp.lang.perl.misc newsgroup and post questions there as well.

part

VII

APPENDIXES

Appendix
A

UNIX Command Reference

> **Note**
>
> Brackets ([]) indicate optional fields.

=

Sets shell variable

Usage: `variable=new-contents`

Standard Input: Not used

Standard Output: Not used

SEE ALSO

➤ *For more information, see page 757*

apropos

Same as `man -k`

at

Run command a specified date/time

Standard Input: Used to input one or more command lines terminated with EOT key (usually Ctrl+D)

Standard Output: Not used

SEE ALSO

➤ *For more information, see page 417*

> **Note**
>
> To restrict this command, edit `/usr/lib/cron/at.allow` and `at.deny`.

awk

Aho, Weinberger, and Kernighan's C-like programming language

Standard Input: Used only if no list-of-files is given

Standard Output: Used to display results

> **Note**
> On some systems, use nawk (new awk) or gawk (GNU awk).

Using awk from the command line to display selected lines:

```
awk '$n == "string"' [list-of-files]
   (display line if field n equals string)
awk '$n > 3.5' [list-of-files]
   (display line if field n is greater than value.
    can also test ==, !=, >, <, >=, <=)
awk '$n ~ /R.E./' [list-of-files]
```

Using awk to display selected fields:

```
awk '{print $1, $5, $0}' [list-of-files]
awk '{if ($5 > 20000) $5=20000} {print "file: " $9        "      " $5}'
awk '{ printf("Name: %16s, Size: %5d, Blocks:           %6.2f\n", $9, $5,
$5/512)}'
```

Using awk from the command line to replace strings:

```
awk '$3 == "acme" { gsub ("R.E.","repl") } {print}' [list-of-files]
awk '$n > 3.5 { gsub ("R.E.","repl") } {print}' [list-of-files]
awk '$n ~ /R.E./ { gsub ("R.E.","repl") } {print}' [list-of-files]
```

Using awk from the command line to remove strings:

```
awk '$3 == "acme" { gsub ("R.E.","") } {print}' [list-of-files]
```

SEE ALSO

➤ *For more information, see page 520 and page 547*

banner

Display words in banner header size

Usage: `banner [words to display]`

Standard Input: Used only if no words supplied on command line

Standard Output: Used to display results

SEE ALSO

➤ *For more information, see page 220*

> **Note**
> This command puts separate words on separate lines unless spaces are escaped or quoted and truncates each line at 10 characters.

batch

Run command when system is not busy

Usage: `batch`

Standard Input: Used to input one or more commands

Terminated with EOT key (usually Ctrl+D)

Standard Output: Not used

SEE ALSO

➤ *For more information, see page 417*

> **Note**
> To restrict this command, edit `/usr/lib/cron/at.allow` and `at.deny`.

bc

Business calculator

Can do infinite precision arithmetic

For two decimal places, enter `scale=2`.

To quit, enter `quit`.

SEE ALSO

➤ *For more information, see page 160 and page 780*

bg

Start suspended job running in the background

Usage: `bg %JOBID`

SEE ALSO

➤ *For more information, see page 427*

Useful options: Same as `kill` (Korn shell) under `%JOBID`

Bourne shell

See `sh`.

C shell

See `csh`.

cal

Display a calendar

Usage: `cal [year]`

Standard Input: Not used

Standard Output: Used to display results

SEE ALSO

➤ *For more information, see page 157*

> **Note**
>
> 98 is not the same year as 1998.

cancel

Cancel print job

Usage: `cancel JOBID`

Standard Input: Not used

Standard Output: Not used

SEE ALSO

➤ *For more information, see page 228*

cat

Display/concatenate files or pipeline

Usage: `cat [list-of-files]`

Standard Input: Used only if no list-of-files is given

Standard Output: Used to display results

Useful options:

`-n` means include line numbers in the output

`-nb` means number only non-blank lines

`-v` means display control chars as printable characters

SEE ALSO

➤ *For more information, see page 210, page 217, and page 284*

cd

Change directory

Usage: `cd dirname`

Standard Input: Not used

Standard Output: Not used except for `CDPATH` (see following Note)

SEE ALSO

➤ *For more information, see page 62*

> **Note**
>
> If no dirname is given, **cd** takes you to your home directory. If a dirname is a basename, **cd** will check whether dirname is a subdirectory of any parent directory in **CDPATH**. If so, **cd** will change to that directory and output its full pathname to Standard Output.

chgrp

Change the group of a file

Usage: `chgrp newgroup list-of-files`

Standard Input: Not used

Standard Output: Not used

Can be done only by the file owner or root

SEE ALSO

➤ *For more information, see page 393*

chmod

Change the mode (permissions) of a file

Usage: `chmod perms list-of-files`

Standard Input: Not used

Standard Output: Not used

Can be done only by the file owner or root

Perms can be specified in two ways:

Symbolic: [ugoa][+-=][rwxst]

Absolute or numeric:

```
perm = read(4) + write(2) + execute(1)
perms = owner-perm * 100 + group-perm * 10 + other-perm +
setuid(4000)+setgid(2000)+sticky(1000)
```

SEE ALSO

➤ *For more information, see page 389*

chown

Change the owner of a file

Usage: `chgrp newowner list-of-files`

Standard Input: Not used

Standard Output: Not used

Can be done only by the file owner or root

SEE ALSO
➤ *For more information, see page 394*

cmp

Compare two files of any type

Usage: `cmp file1 file2`

Standard Input: Not used

Standard Output: Used to display results

> **Note:**
> cmp stops after finding the first difference. No output means that the files are identical.

SEE ALSO
➤ *For more information, see page 263*

Useful options: `-1` means list all the differences

col

Filter control characters from pipeline

Usage: `col options`

Standard Input: Provides input to col

Standard Output: Used to display results

SEE ALSO
➤ *For more information, see page 221 and page 222*

Useful options:

-b means filter out backspaces (^H).

-x means do not convert consecutive spaces to tabs.

comm

Show common and unique lines between two sorted files

Usage: `comm file1 file2`

Standard Input: Only used if `file1` or `file2` is a dash (–)

Standard Output: Used to display results `col 1` shows lines only in `file1`.

`col 2` shows lines only in `file2`.

`col 3` shows lines in common.

SEE ALSO
➤ *For more information, see page 261*

Useful options:

-1 means suppress `col 1` (lines only in `file1`).

-2 means suppress `col 2` (lines only in `file2`).

-3 means suppress `col 3` (common lines).

compress

Compress a file

Usage: `compress filename`

Standard Input: Not used

Standard Output: Not used

SEE ALSO
➤ *For more information, see page 279*

> **Note**
>
> compress renames the file by adding .Z to the end of the filename.

Useful options:

-H allows better compression on SCO UNIX 3.2v5 (but not SCO UnixWare 7). No special option is needed to uncompress or zcat these files. However, these files cannot be uncompressed on AIX 4.2 or SunOS 5.6. Linux cannot uncompress these files, but it can successfully gunzip them (even with .z extension).

copy

Special file copy command

Not available on all UNIX systems

Usage: Copy options source destination

Useful options:

-m means set destination last modification and last access to match the source.

-o means set owner and group to match the source.

-r means copy directories recursively, so all subdirectories are copied.

cp

Copy files

Usage: cp file1 file2

cp list-of-files dest-dir/.

Standard Input: Not used

Standard Output: Not used

SEE ALSO

➤ *For more information, see page 235*

Useful options:

-i means interact with user and ask permission before overwriting an existing file (not available on older UNIX).

-p means preserve owner, group, and permissions, especially from root account (not available on all UNIX systems).

-r means copy directories recursively, so all subdirectories are also copied (not available on all UNIX systems).

cpio

Copy file in/out, especially to tape

Usage: `generate file names | cpio options`

Standard Input: Used to supply a list of pathnames to `cpio`

Standard Output: Usually redirected to tape device

SEE ALSO

➤ *For more information, see page 243*

Major options (one of these must be the first option):

-o means write (save) files on `cpio` archive.

-it means list files on tape without restoring them.

-i means restore files from `cpio` archive.

-p means pass a subdirectory subtree to another directory.

Options for backup using `cpio`:

-a means reset date and time of last access for each disk file to what it was before `cpio` accessed the file.

-B means block the output 10 blocks (5120 bytes) per record.

-c means write character header for greater portability to other UNIX systems. May not be used with -H odc.

-C XX means set tape blocks size to XX bytes.

-H odc means SVR4 systems will write a `cpio` tape that pre-SVR4 systems can read. May not be used with -c option.

-L means follow symbolic links (not on AIX).

-v means verbose output, which lists each file as it is copied.

-V means just show a period as each file is backed up.

Options for restore using `cpio`:

-A means suppress leading slash so that absolute files can be restored to other directories (SCO).

-c means look for character header for greater portability to other UNIX systems. Some UNIX systems will autosense whether an archive file or tape was written with this option. On other systems, you must include -c on restore if tape was written with -c.

-d means create destination directories as needed.

-k means skip corrupted spot on tape and try to resume reading files.

-m means keep the same date and time of last modification for each file as in the source directory.

-t means don't restore any files; just display the table of contents of the tape.

-u means unconditionally overwrite any existing destination files, or else an older file will not overwrite a newer one.

-v means verbose output, which lists each file as it is copied.

-V means just show a period as each file is backed up.

Options for passing files using `cpio`:

-a means reset date and time of last access for each file to what it was before `cpio` accessed the file. May not be used if -m option is included.

-d means create destination directories as needed.

-L means follow soft links (see next section) so that the file pointed to is copied rather than the pointer file.

-m means keep the same date and time of last modification for each destination file as in the source directory. May not be used if -a option is included.

-u means unconditionally overwrite any existing destination files, or else an older file will not overwrite a newer one.

-v means verbose output, which lists each file as it is copied.

-V means just show a period as each file is backed up.

crontab

Submit a whole new cron table for this user

Usage: `crontab NEWTABLE    # submit new table`

`crontab -l # list current table`

Standard Input: Not used

Standard Output: Used to display output for `-l` option

SEE ALSO

➤ *For more information, see page 412*

Notes

To prevent usage, edit `/usr/lib/cron/cron.allow` and `cron.deny`.

Useful options:

`-e` allows edit and submit of cron jobs.

`-l` means list the current table.

crypt

Encrypt or decrypt a file or pipeline

Usage: `crypt < filename`

Standard Input: Redirect this from file or pipeline

Standard Output: Used to display results

SEE ALSO

➤ *For more information, see page 277*

Note

Decryption requires the same key that was used in encryption.

---

csh

Run the C shell

csplit

Split file into smaller files by context

Usage: `csplit options filename [prefix]`

Smaller files will be `prefix00, prefix01, prefix02`

Default prefix is `xx`

Standard Input: Not used

Standard Output: Not used

SEE ALSO

➤ *For more information, see page 288*

Useful options:

`-k` preserves created files in spite of errors such as using 99 as a repeat count.

Examples:

```
csplit -k filename '/Chapter/' '{99}'
csplit filename '/boundaryword/' '/boundaryword/'
/boundaryword/'
```

cut

Cut and keep columns or fields of output

Usage: `cut options [list-of-files]`

Standard Input: Used only if no list-of-files is given

Standard Output: Used to display results

Useful options:

`-c5-16,42-` means specify columns to keep in output.

`-dX` means set char `X` as the field delimiter.

`-fn` means cut and keep field `n`.

date

Display the system date and time

Usage: Date format

Standard Input: Not used

Standard Output: Used to display results

Format has the form `"+%X"`, where X can be:

S second (0–59)

M minute (0–59)

I hour (1–12)

p A.M. or P.M.

H hour (0–23)

T time (hh:mm:ss)

Z time zone

A complete weekday name

a weekday (three letters)

w day of the week (0–6)

d day of the month (1–31)

j day of the year (1–365 or 1-366 for leap years)

U week of the year (0–53) Note that a year may start with a partial week and end with a partial week.

m month (1–12)

b month (three letters)

h month (three letters)

B complete month

y year (two digits)

Y year (four digits)

D MM/DD/YY

c date/time

df

Shows disk free blocks

diff

Show differences between two text files

Usage: `diff file1 file2`

Standard Input: Used only if `file1` or `file2` is a dash (–)

Standard Output: Used to display results

Note

Output beginning with < sign is from the first file. Lines beginning with > sign are from the second file. No output means that the files are identical.

SEE ALSO

➤ *For more information, see page 256*

Useful options:

`-b` means ignore trailing blanks and treat strings of blanks as a single blank.

diff3

Compare three text files

Usage: `diff3 file1 file2 file3`

Standard Input: Not used

Standard Output: Used to display results

> **Note**
>
> In results, === means all three files differ as shown. ===n means file n (1, 2, or 3) differs from the others as shown.

SEE ALSO

➤ *For more information, see page 259*

du

Show disk Usage

echo

Display text

Standard Input: not used

Standard Output: Used to display results

SEE ALSO

➤ *For more information, see page 761*

Special characters:

\n new line

\c suppress new line

\t tab

\a alarm bell

To suppress the newline at end of line:

```
echo -n some text      # on some UNIX systems
echo "some text\c"     # on other UNIX systems
```

egrep

Like grep, but supports additional regular expression wildcards

See *grep*. See wildcards for regular expressions.

SEE ALSO

➤ *For more information, see page 515*

expr

Evaluate simple calculations

For example: CNT='expr $CNT + 1'

VALUE='expr $VALUE * 2'

SEE ALSO

➤ *For more information, see page 158 and page 780*

fg

Bring background job to foreground

Usage: fg %JOBID

SEE ALSO

➤ *For more information, see page 427*

Useful options:

Same as kill (Korn shell) under %JOBID

fgrep

Like grep, but does not support any regular expression wildcards

See grep.

SEE ALSO

➤ *For more information, see page 519*

file

Show the type of contents of a file

Usage: `file list-of-files`

Standard Input: Not used

Standard Output: Used to display results

> **Note**
> If there is no magic number, the `file` command makes its best guess as to the contents based on the beginning of the file.

SEE ALSO
➤ *For more information, see page 179*

Filename Generation Wildcard

See wildcards for filename generation.

find

Find files based on search options

Usage: `find start-dir(s) options actions`

Standard Input: Not used

Standard Output: Used to display results

> **Note**
> `find` searches all subdirectories of the `start` directory(s).

SEE ALSO
➤ *For more information, see page 187*

Useful options:

-atime [+-]ndays means select only files last accessed ndays ago. option + means more than ndays, - means less than ndays, else means exactly ndays ago.

-ctime [+-]ndays means select only files whose inode was modified ndays ago. option + means more than ndays, - means less than ndays, else means exactly ndays ago.

-depth means list the contents of a directory before the directory itself. Sometimes useful when restoring from a non-root account.

-group GROUP means select only files whose group is GROUP.

-inum NUM means select only files whose inode number is NUM.

-mount means select only files in the same filesystem as the starting directory.

-mtime [+-]ndays means select only files last modified ndays ago. option + means more than ndays, - means less than ndays, else means exactly ndays ago.

-name FNAME means select only files with basename FNAME. FNAME may contain filename generation wildcards but then must be in single quotation marks.

-newer filename means select only files newer than given file (that is, modified more recently).

-perm DDD selects only files whose octal permissions are DDD.

-perm -DDDD selects only files that have the same permissions turned on as in DDDD. It ignores permissions that are off in DDDD.

-size [+-]nblocks means select only files of size nblocks. option + means more than nblocks. - means less than nblocks, and else means exactly nblocks in size.

-type TYPE means select only files of type TYPE where TYPE can be:

    f for regular file

    d for directory

    c for character special device node

    b for block special device node

-user USER means select only files owned by USER.

Option logical grouping:

If you specify two options, both must be true to select file.

-o means logical OR.

\(\) can be used for grouping.

! means reverse test (negation).

Useful actions:

-print means display the names selected. Some UNIX systems do this as the default if no action is specified.

-exec means execute the following UNIX command for each file selected. {} in the command indicates where to place the filename. The command must end in \;.

finger

Display information about one user or all who are logged on

SEE ALSO
➤ *For more information, see page 360*

fsck

Filesystem check

SEE ALSO
➤ *For more information, see page 402*

Useful options:

-b means reboot if checking root filesystem made significant modifications on disk (important).

-s means reconstruct the free list unconditionally.

grep

Globally find R.E. patterns and print (display) that line

Usage: grep R.E.pattern [list-of-files]

Standard Input: Used only if no list-of-files is given

Standard Output: Used to display results

See wildcards for regular expressions.

SEE ALSO
➤ *For more information, see page 494*

Useful options:

-c means to display just filenames and count of lines that contain the pattern.

-i means to ignore upper/lowercase.

-l means just list the filenames that contain the pattern.

-n means to include the line number with each line displayed.

-v means to reverse the test; show lines that do not contain the pattern.

-y same as -i, but only on older UNIX systems.

gzip

Compress a file

Usage: `gzip filename`

Standard Input: Not used

Standard Output: Not used

SEE ALSO

➤ *For more information, see page 279*

Note

`gzip` adds `.gz` to a compressed filename.

---

head

Display initial lines of a file or pipeline

Usage: `head options [list-of-files]`

Standard Input: Used only if no list-of-files is given

Standard Output: Used to display results

SEE ALSO

➤ *For more information, see page 214*

Useful options:

-n means display just n lines.

id

Display your user logon and group

SEE ALSO

➤ *For more information, see page 358*

jobs

Korn shell—display your background jobs

Standard Input: Not used

Standard Output: Used to display the results

SEE ALSO

➤ *For more information, see page 427*

join

Join lines from two files based on a join field

Usage: `join options file1 file2`

Standard Input: Used only if a file is given as a dash (–)

Standard Output: Used to display the results

SEE ALSO

➤ *For more information, see page 285*

Useful options:

`-aN` means include all lines in file N.

`-jN` means use field N rather than 1 as the join field.

`-jN M` means use field M in file N as the join field.

`-o A.B` means display field B from file A.

`-t` means set the field separator to the following character.

kill

Bourne shell—terminate a UNIX process

Usage: `kill -SIG PID`

Standard Input: Not used

Standard Output: Not used

SEE ALSO

➤ *For more information, see page 425*

Useful options:

`-SIG` means send signal `SIG` to the process. If omitted, send `SIGTERM` signal (terminate) or replace `SIG` with 15.

Other useful signals to send via `kill`:

`SIGHUP (SIG = 1)` Line disconnect or parent-terminated

`SIGINT (SIG = 2)` Intr key pressed (Ctrl+C or Del)

`SIGQUIT (SIG = 3)` Quit key pressed

`SIGKILL (SIG = 9)` Force termination

kill

Korn shell—terminate a background process

Usage: `kill -SIG PID` (as in `kill` [Bourne shell] earlier)

or `kill %JOBID`

Standard Input: Not used

Standard Output: Display process information line

SEE ALSO

➤ *For more information, see page 429*

Useful options:

`%JOBID` means job whose number is `JOBID`.

`%+` means job most recently put in background.

`%%` means same as `%+`.

%- means job second most recently put in background.

%CMD means job whose command starts with CMD.

%?CMD means all jobs whose command contains CMD.

ksh

Korn shell

noclobber means prevent redirect over existing files.

>| filename means override noclobber and redirect to existing file shell options.

SEE ALSO

➤ *For more information, see page 614*

ksh shell startup runs /etc/profile, then .profile in user's home directory.

less

Display a file or pipeline one screen at a time

Usage: less [list-of-files]

Standard Input: Used only if no list-of-files is given

Standard Output: Used to display results

SEE ALSO

➤ *For more information, see page 211*

> **Note**
> less is not available on most commercial UNIX systems.

Prompt at end of each screen is line XXX.

Useful commands after you are in less:

h displays a help menu.

space or f or Ctrl+f goes to next page.

b or Ctrl+b goes to preceding page.

G goes to last page.

1G goes to the first page.

nf goes forward n pages.

nb goes backward n pages.

nG goes to line n.

/string goes to next occurrence of that string.

n repeats the preceding search.

d or Ctrl+D goes down a half screen.

r or Ctrl+R or Ctrl+L redisplays the current page.

!CMD executes UNIX CMD as a subshell and resumes less when done.

ln

Create soft/symbolic or hard link

Usage: ln [-s] existing-file link-file

Standard Input: Not used

Standard Output: Not used

SEE ALSO

➤ *For more information, see page 248*

Useful options:

-s means create a soft/symbolic link rather than a hard link.

lp

System V—print a file or pipeline

Usage: lp options [list-of-files]

Standard Input: Used only if no list-of-files is given

Standard Output: Not used

SEE ALSO

➤ *For more information, see page 223*

Useful options:

-n NUM means print NUM copies.

-d PTR means print output on printer PTR. If -d is not given, print on system default printer. If no default, give error.

lpr

BSD—print a file or pipeline

Usage: lpr options [list-of-files]

Standard Input: Used only if no list-of-files is given

Standard Output: Not used

SEE ALSO

➤ *For more information, see page 223*

Useful options:

-# NUM means print NUM copies.

-P PTR means print output on printer PTR. If -P is not given, print on system default printer. If no default, give error.

lpstat

Display print spooling status

Usage: lpstat options

Standard Input: Not used

Standard Output: Used to display results

SEE ALSO

➤ *For more information, see page 227*

> **Note**
> If no options are given, `lpstat` shows pending print requests in the queue.

-p -D means show what printers are available and their description, if any.

ls

List files in a directory

Usage: `ls options [list-of-files-or-directories]`

Standard Input: Not used

Standard Output: Used to display results

> **Note**
>
> If no directory is specified, `ls` lists your current directory.

SEE ALSO

➤ *For more information, see page 180*

Useful options:

`-a` means show all files, hidden, nonhidden, and dot-dot (..).

`-b` means show any control characters in filenames.

`-c` means if long format, show date and time inode was last changed.

`-C` means list output in columns.

`-d` means show any directory names rather than the contents of those directories.

`-F` means show the file type by adding slash (/) to directories, asterisk (*) to executables, and the at sign (@) to symbolic links.

`-i` means include the file's inode number as the first field in each output line.

`-l` means list files in long format; includes date and time of last modification.

`-L` means follow symbolic link and show information for the pointed-to file.

`-r` means list files in reverse of normal order.

`-R` means recursively list subdirectories.

`-t` means list files in order of time and date rather than by name.

`-u` means if long format, show date and time of last usage (last access).

mail/mailx

Read and send email

SEE ALSO

➤ *For more information, see page 700*

man

Display online manual page

Usage: `man unixcmd`

Standard Input: Not used

Standard Output: Used to display results

SEE ALSO

➤ *For more information, see page 88*

Useful options:

`-a` means show all sections containing this command, not just the first.

`-k` `WORD` means show command names whose description contains `WORD`.

mkdir

Make new directory

Usage: `mkdir dirname`

Standard Input: Not used

Standard Output: Not used

SEE ALSO

➤ *For more information, see page 72*

Useful options:

`-p` means create any parent directories needed to create dirname.

more

Display a file or pipeline one screen at a time

Usage: more [list-of-files]

Standard Input: Used only if no list-of-files is given

Standard Output: Used to display results

SEE ALSO

➤ *For more information, see page 211*

> **Note**
> Prompt at end of each screen is --More--.

Useful commands after you are in more:

h displays a help menu.

space or f goes to the next page.

Some of the following commands are not available under the more command in some versions of UNIX, especially if piping to the more command.

Ctrl+B goes to the preceding page.

G goes to the last page.

1G goes to the first page.

nf goes forward n pages.

nb goes backward n pages.

nG goes to line n.

/string goes to next occurrence of that string.

n repeats the preceding search.

d goes down a half screen.

Ctrl+L redisplays the current page.

!CMD executes UNIX CMD as a subshell and resumes more when done.

mt

Issue magnetic tape commands

Usage: `mt -f /dev/XXX? cmd`

Standard Input: Not used

Standard Output: Not used

See the `tape` command.

Useful commands:

```
rewind
retention
```

mv

Move/rename files

Usage: `mv file1 file2`

```
mv list-of-files dest-dir/.
mv dir1 dir2
```

Standard Input: Not used

Standard Output: Not used

SEE ALSO

➤ *For more information, see page 235*

Useful options:

`-f` means force the move without a confirmation request if you don't have write permission to the file but do have write permission to the directory.

`-i` means interact with user and ask permission before overwriting an existing file.

nice

Start a job with a low priority

Usage: `nice -VAL UNIXCMD`

Standard Input: Not used

Standard Output: Used as UNIXCMD uses them

SEE ALSO

➤ *For more information, see page 421*

Useful options:

-VAL means lower priority by VAL points.

—VAL means raise priority by VAL points (root only).

nl

Number lines in file output or pipeline

Usage: `nl [list-of-files]`

Standard Input: Used only if no list-of-files is given

Standard Output: Used to display results

SEE ALSO

➤ *For more information, see page 217*

Useful options:

-ba means number all lines, including blank lines.

nohup

Start background that won't terminate on logoff

Usage: `nohup UNIXCMD &`

Standard Input: Not used

Standard Output: Used as UNIXCMD uses them

SEE ALSO

➤ *For more information, see page 424*

od

Display contents as an octal dump

Usage: `od [list-of-files]`

Standard Input: Used only if no list-of-files is given

Standard Output: Used to display results

SEE ALSO

➤ *For more information, see page 218*

Useful options:

`-b` means show output as bytes, not words.

`-c` means show any printable characters.

`-d` means show output in decimal.

`-x` means show output in hexadecimal.

passwd

Change your password

SEE ALSO

➤ *For more information, see page 362*

paste

Display files side-by-side on each line

Usage: `paste list-of-files`

Standard Input: Used only if dash (–) is given as a filename

Standard Output: Used to display results

SEE ALSO

➤ *For more information, see page 284*

perl

Practical extraction and report language

Standard Input: Used only if no list-of-files is given

Standard Output: Used to display results

SEE ALSO

➤ *For more information, see page 517, page 544 and page 801*

Using `perl` from the command line to display selected lines:

```
perl -ne 'print if /R.E./xi' [list-of-files]
```

/x means ignore spaces in R.E. for better readability.

/i means ignore upper/lowercase.

Using `perl` from the command line for replacement or deletion:

```
perl -pe 's/R.E./repl/gx' [list-of-files]
perl -pe 's/R.E./repl/gx if /acme/' [list-of-files]
```

Preceding example: Do replacement only if the acme R.E. pattern is found in the line.

/x means ignore spaces in R.E. for better readability.

/g means make change globally, not just once per line.

Useful options:

-e means Perl script is on command line.

-n means process each line of Standard Input or files specified, but do not display the lines unless directed.

-p means process each line of Standard Input or files specified and display each line after processing it.

pg

Display a file or pipeline one screen at a time

Usage: `pg [list-of-files]`

Standard Input: Used only if no list-of-files is given

Standard Output: Used to display results

SEE ALSO

➤ *For more information, see page 211*

Note

The prompt at the end of each screen is a colon (:).

Useful commands after you are in pg:

h displays a help menu.

Enter goes to the next page.

- goes to the preceding page.

$ goes to the last page (can crash the system on a huge pipeline).

1 goes to the first page.

+n goes forward n pages.

-n goes backward n pages.

nl goes to line n.

/string goes to the next occurrence of that string.

/ repeats the preceding search.

/string/b put the found string on the bottom so that you catch all occurrences.

d goes down a half screen.

. redisplays the current page.

!CMD executes UNIX CMD as a subshell and resumes pg when done.

pr

Format output for printing

Usage: pr options [list-of-files]

Standard Input: Used only if no list-of-files is given

Standard Output: Used to display results

SEE ALSO

➤ *For more information, see page 229*

Useful options:

-COLS means use number in COLS as number of columns to create on the page for output. Truncate any lines longer than column size.

-eSIZ means expand tabs to spaces. If SIZ is given, use that as number of character positions per tab; otherwise, use 8.

-f means insert form feed at end of each page.

-h "HEAD LINE" means use this heading rather than filename at top of page.

-l LINES means format number of lines per page as LINES.

-nSIZ means number each line in body of output. If SIZ is given, use that many characters in number, right justified; otherwise, use five characters in number.

-p means beep and wait for Enter key after each page.

ps

Show process status

Standard Input: Not used

Standard Output: Used to display status

SEE ALSO

➤ *For more information, see page 420*

pwd

Print working directory

Usage: pwd

Standard Input: Not used

Standard Output: Used to display results

SEE ALSO

➤ *For more information, see page 65*

qcan

Cancel print job on AIX

Usage: `qcan options`

Standard Input: Not used

Standard Output: Not used

SEE ALSO

➤ *For more information, see page 228*

Useful options:

`-P PTR -x JOBID` means cancel job ID for printer PTR.

Regular Expression Wildcards

See wildcards for regular expressions.

renice

Lower the priority of a running job

Usage: `renice -VAL PID`

Standard Input: Not used

Standard Output: Not used

SEE ALSO

➤ *For more information, see page 422*

Useful options:

`-VAL` means lower priority by VAL points.

`—VAL` means raise priority by VAL points (root only).

rm

Remove file(s)

Usage: `rm list-of-files`

Standard Input: Not used

Standard Output: Not used

SEE ALSO

➤ *For more information, see page 244. Also see page 74*

Useful options:

-f means force delete when file is not writable without asking confirmation.

-i means Interactive mode, ask confirmation before each file.

-r means that if list-of-files contains a directory, recursively delete that directory and all its subdirectories and files. (WARNING: This is dangerous! There is no undelete in case of mistakes.)

rmdir

Remove a directory

The directory to remove must be empty except for dot (.) and dot dot (..).

SEE ALSO

➤ *For more information, see page 73*

sed

Stream editor

Usage: `sed cmd [list-of-files]`

Standard Input: Used only if no list-of-files is given

Standard Output: Used to display results

SEE ALSO

➤ *For more information, see page 526*

Useful `sed` commands:

q means quit.

s means substitute.

Using sed from the command line to replace strings in output:

```
sed 's/R.E./repl/g' [list-of-files]
sed 's:R.E.:repl:g' [list-of-files] # can change delimiter
sed '5,23 s/R.E./repl/g'[list-of-files]
    ➥only change lines 5 thru 23, $ means end of line
sed '/acme/ s/R.E./repl/g' [list-of-files]
    ➥only change lines that contain acme
sed '/s1/,/s2/ s/R.E./repl/g' [list-of-files]
    ➥only changes lines from first occurrence of s1
    ➥thru next occurrence of s2
sed 's/.*acme.*/     *** canceled ***     /'
    ➥replace whole line
```

SEE WILDCARDS FOR REGULAR EXPRESSIONS.

Using sed from the command line to delete strings in output:

```
sed s/R.E.//g [list-of-files]
```

sh

Run the Bourne shell

SEE ALSO

➤ *For more information, see page 25*

shutdown **(BSD version)**

Shut down the UNIX system

Standard Input: Not used

Standard Output: Not used

SEE ALSO

➤ *For more information, see page 404*

Note

This **shutdown** command requires root privilege.

Useful options:

-h means halt the system.

-r means shut down and reboot.

now means don't wait to shut down.

+MIN means wait MIN minutes before shutting down.

shutdown **(System V version)**

Shut down the UNIX system

Standard Input: Not used

Standard Output: Not used

SEE ALSO

➤ *For more information, see page 404*

Note

This shutdown command requires root privilege.

Useful options:

-g MIN means broadcast warning and wait MIN minutes grace period before shutdown.

-i STATE means go to run-level STATE.

-y means don't ask user to confirm shutdown after grace period.

sleep

Pause program for n seconds

sort

Sort file or pipeline

Usage: sort options [list-of-files]

Multiple files are merged before sorting.

Standard Input: Used only if dash (–) is in the list-of-files or no list-of-files is given

Standard Output: Used to display results

SEE ALSO

➤ *For more information, see page 266*

Useful options:

Initial options apply to all `sort` keys. Options following a `sort` key apply only to that key.

`-b` means ignore leading blanks in sort field.

`-d` means ignore leading punctuation.

`-f` means fold uppercase and lowercase together.

`-k` means define sort keys using a new method: `-k m opts, n`.

`-n` means sort numbers by magnitude.

`-o` means save output in the following filename.

`-r` means sort in reverse order.

`+m` means skip `m` fields per line and then start sorting.

`+m options -n` defines sort keys within the line.

split

Split file into smaller files of equal lines

Usage: `split options [filename] [prefix]`

Smaller files will be `prefixaa`, `prefixab`, `prefixac`, and so on.

Standard Input: Used only if no filename is given or dash (–) is given as filename

Standard Output: Not used

SEE ALSO

➤ *For more information, see page 287*

Useful options:

`-N` creates smaller files of `N` lines each (except the last one). The default is 1000.

strings

Show printable strings within any type of file

Usage: `strings options [list-of-files]`

Standard Input: Used only if no list-of-files is given

Standard Output: Used to display results

SEE ALSO

➤ *For more information, see page 218*

Useful options:

`-n LEN` means set minimum LEN printable sequence to report.

stty

Set/display terminal characteristics

Useful command options:

`-a` means show all `stty` options, precede with minus sign (–) if turned off.

Useful `stty` options:

`erase` means set/show the erase key.

SEE ALSO

➤ *For more information, see page 107, page 365 and page 429*

`intr` means set/show the interrupt key.

`tostop` means suspend running background jobs when they start any output.

su

Become superuser or another user

SEE ALSO

➤ *For more information, see page 370 and page 382*

sum

Compute checksum on file or pipeline

Usage: `sum options [list-of-files]`

Standard Input: Used only if no list-of-files is given

Standard Output: Used to display results

> **Note**
> A matching checksum indicates a high probability that the data is the same.

SEE ALSO

➤ *For more information, see page 263*

Useful options:

`-l` supports a long 32-bit checksum under SCO UNIX 3.2v5 (but not SCO UnixWare 7).

`-r` means compute rotating checksum that can detect differences in order as well as contents.

tail

Display the last lines of a file or pipeline

Usage: `tail options [filename]`

Standard Input: Used only if no filename is given

Standard Output: Used to display results

SEE ALSO

➤ *For more information, see page 215*

Useful options:

`-f` means follow—that is, continuously display any data appended to file until Enter key is pressed.

`-n` means display just n lines. (Warning: Large values of n can be ignored.)

`+n` means display from line n to end of file.

tape

Issue magnetic tape commands

Usage: `tape cmd /dev/XXX?`

Standard Input: Not used

Standard Output: Not used

See the `mt` command.

Useful commands:

`rewind`

`reten`

tar

Tape archive

SEE ALSO

➤ *For more information, see page 443*

Useful options when backing up:

c means create backup (must be the first option).

b means set tape block size.

f means specify the backup device or file.

h means follow symbolic links (AIX).

L means follow symbolic links (SCO).

v means verbose.

Useful options when restoring:

x means extract files from backup (must be the first option).

A means suppress leading slash in filenames (SCO).

m means set date of last modification to when restore was done; otherwise, set last modification of original tape files.

v means verbose.

tee

Save Standard Input to file and send same information out Standard Output.

Usage: `cmd ¦ tee filename`

Standard Input: Used to read input

Standard Output: Used to display current output

SEE ALSO
➤ *For more information, see page 112*

Useful options:

`-a` means append to file, not overwrite.

test

Evaluate condition as true or false

Usage: `test condition`

or

`[ condition ]`

SEE ALSO
➤ *For more information, see page 766*

File tests:

`-f` name means is name a regular file?

`-d` name means is name a directory?

`-r` name means is name readable?

`-w` name means is name writable?

`-x` name means is name executable?

`-c` name means is name a character device file?

`-b` name means is name a block device file?

`-s` name means is name a file with size is greater than zero?

`-h` or `-L` name means is name a symbolic link?

String tests:

`"string"` means is string not empty?

`-z string` means is string empty (zero size)?

`s1 = s2` means are the two strings the same?

`s1 != s2` means are the two strings not the same?

Numeric tests:

`v1 -eq v2` means is v1 equal to v2?

You can also test `-ne`, `-gt`, `-ge`, `-lt`, `-le`.

Combining tests:

`-a` means logical AND.

`-o` means logical OR.

touch

Update file last access and last modification date and time

This command will create an empty file if it does not exist, but it won't affect the contents of an already existing file.

tr

Translate characters. If character is found in `list1`, replace it with the corresponding character in `list2`.

Usage: `tr "list1" "list2" < file1 > file 2`

Standard Input: Always used; will not accept filenames

Standard Output: Used to display results

SEE ALSO

➤ *For more information, see page 554.*

Useful options:

`-d` means delete the characters found in `list1`.

Examples:

```
tr "[A-Z]" "[a-z]" # convert upper to lower case
tr "[\201-\376]\377" "[\001-\176]\177" < file1 > file2
    # turn off 8th bit
tr '\001-\010\013-\037\177' '[^*]' < file1 > file2
    # translate most control chars to ^
```

type

Show full pathname of command

Usage: `type unixcmd`

Standard Input: Not used

Standard Output: Used to display results

SEE ALSO

➤ *For more information, see page 97*

> **Note**
> **Type** works in both the Bourne shell and the Korn shell.

tty

Display your current system `tty` port name

SEE ALSO

➤ *For more information, see page 364*

umask

Show your current file creation permission mask

SEE ALSO

➤ *For more information, see page 395*

uname

Display the system type and name

uniq

Remove non-unique lines

Usage: `uniq options [list-of-files]`

Standard Input: Used only if no list-of-files is given

Standard Output: Used to display results

SEE ALSO

➤ *For more information, see page 559*

Useful options:

`-d` means show only duplicated lines.

`-u` means show only unique lines.

`-c` means show count for each line of number of duplicates.

uucp

UNIX to UNIX copy over serial lines and modems

SEE ALSO

➤ *For more information, see page 668*

uuencode/uudecode

Transform/restore file to or from printable text

Usage: `uuencode binaryfile destname > textfile`

Standard Input: Used only if binary file is not given

Standard Output: Used to display results

Usage: `uudecode textfile`

Standard Input: Not used

Standard Output: Not used

SEE ALSO

➤ *For more information, see page 282*

`vi`

Visual editor

SEE ALSO

➤ *For more information, see Chapters 20 and 21.*

Starting vi:

`vi -r` means display files that can be restored.

`view file` means run vi in read-only mode.

Colon commands:

`:abbrev word` means new phrase.

`:!cmd` means run UNIX `cmd` in subshell, and then resume vi.

`:f` means show current line number and filename.

`:map c string` means map character `c` to string.

`:q!` means quit without saving.

`:w` means write changes to disk.

`:w file` means save in file.

`:wq` means write (save changes) and quit.

Format for the following:

:set mode	:set abbreviation	:set mode to off
:set autoindent	:set ai	:set noai
:set ignorecase	:set ic	:set noic
:set number	:set nu	:set nonu
:set showmode		:set noshowmode

:set wrapmargin=10, turn off by setting to zero

Replacing in Colon mode:

!! `cmd` means replace current line with output of UNIX `cmd`.

!`a `cmd` means apply UNIX command from cursor to mark a.

!'a `sed` `'s/st1/st2/g'` means replace string st1 with string st2 where found from cursor to mark a.

:%! `sed` `'s/st1/st2/g'` means replace st1 throughout the file. st1 may contain regular expression wildcards.

Copy and paste, and delete and paste:

y'a means yank to start of line that contains mark a.

y`a means yank to mark a.

y... means follow y with a motion command to indicate how much text to yank and save.

"ay... means yank and save in named buffer a.

p means paste unnamed buffer at the current cursor.

"ap means paste named buffer at the current cursor.

"np means paste what you deleted n times ago.

Delete text commands:

dd means delete line.

x means delete character.

D means delete to end of line.

d'a means delete to start of line that contains mark a.

d`a means delete to mark a.

d... means follow d with a motion command to indicate what to delete.

"ad... means delete and save in named buffer a.

Insert text commands:

i means insert at or left of cursor until Esc.

I means insert at start of line until Esc.

a means insert after cursor until Esc.

A means insert at end of line until Esc.

o means open line below and insert until Esc.

O means open line above and insert until Esc.

Miscellaneous commands:

J means join lines; nJ joins n lines.

Most vi commands allow a preceding repeat count.

u means undo last insert, delete, or modification.

U means restore line to when you first got there.

. means repeat last insert, delete, or change.

Modifying text:

c means change to end of line with input until Esc.

cc means change current line until Esc.

r means replace character.

R means replace until Esc.

Moving the cursor:

0,^,$ means start of line, first printable character, end of line.

h,j,k,l means same as left, down, up, right arrow.

H,M,L means move high, medium, low on the current screen.

Gn means go to line n; G means go to end of file.

Ctrl+F/Ctrl+B forward/backward one full screen.

Ctrl+D/Ctrl+U down/up one half screen.

W,B,E means move a word ahead, back, or to end of word.

w,b,e means same as preceding explanation, but go to next contained word or non-word.

mc means set mark c.

'c means go to start of line containing mark c.

`c means go to mark c.

Searching:

/string means move ahead to next occurrence of string. See wildcards for regular expressions.

?string means move back to string. See wildcards for regular expressions.

/ or ? without a string means repeat last search.

n or N means also repeat preceding search.

fc means move to character c.

; means repeat preceding f command.

% means find matching closure symbol—for example [{( )}].

whence

Show full pathname of command

Usage: whence unixcmd

Standard Input: Not used

Standard Output: Used to display results

SEE ALSO

➤ *For more information, see page 97*

> **Note**
> whence works in the Korn shell, but not the Bourne shell.

which

Show full pathname of command

Usage: which unixcmd

Standard Input: Not used

Standard Output: Used to display results

SEE ALSO

➤ *For more information, see page 97*

> **Note**
> which works in the Bourne shell, but not the Korn shell.

who

Display who is on the system and other system information

Usage: who options

Standard Input: Not used

Standard Output: Used to display results

Useful options:

-b means show date and time of last system reboot.

-r means show current run-level and when entered.

SEE ALSO

➤ *For more information, see page 366*

Wildcards for Filename Generation

These wildcards may be used in command lines as a shortcut for a list of all filenames that match the wildcard pattern.

SEE ALSO

➤ *For more information, see page 292*

* means zero or more of any character except slash (/) and leading period.

Contain a Pattern (*)

/? means exactly one of any character except slash (/) and leading period.

Positions (?)

[...] means exactly one of the alternatives listed except (/) and leading period.

[!...] means any one character except for the alternatives listed; cannot match a slash (/) or leading period.

Wildcards for Regular Expressions (R.E.)

These are a second group of wildcards that can be only with commands that allow regular expression wildcard pattern matching.

SEE ALSO

➤ *For more information, see page 502 and page 531*

893

^ indicates start of line but only when found at start of pattern.

$ indicates end of line but only when found at end of pattern.

. means exactly one of any character.

[...] means exactly one of the alternatives listed.

[^...] means any one character except for the alternatives listed.

\{n\} means exactly n occurrences of preceding element (supported in grep and sed; not supported in egrep or awk—use {n} for Perl).

\{n,\} means n or more occurrences of preceding element (supported in grep and sed; not supported in egrep or awk—use {n,} for Perl).

\{n,m\} means between n and m (inclusive) occurrences of preceding element (supported in grep and sed; not supported in egrep or awk—use {n,m} for Perl).

* means 0 or more occurrences of preceding element.

*? matches shortest possible span (perl only).

.* means 0 or more occurrences of any character. This is one specific example of using the * wildcard.

+ means 1 or more occurrences of preceding element (supported in egrep, perl, and awk; not supported in grep and sed).

+? matches shortest possible span (perl only).

? means 0 or 1 occurrences of preceding element (supported in egrep, perl, and awk; not supported in grep and sed).

¦ allows specifying alternative patterns to search for (supported in egrep, perl, and awk; not supported in grep and sed).

( ) allows grouping alternatives (supported in egrep, perl, and awk; not supported in grep and sed).

\(\) remembers what characters matched the enclosed pattern (supported in grep and sed; not supported in egrep or awk—use ( ) for perl).

\1, \2 refers to remembered string 1 or 2. See \(\).

\b indicates word boundary (perl only).

\B indicates non-word boundary (perl only).

\X means put backslash (\) before any wildcard X to use it as a literal character in the string.

xargs

Execute another UNIX command with passed arguments

Usage: `xargs cmd [opts]`

Standard Input: Used to pass a list of arguments for `cmd`

Standard Output: However `cmd` uses it

SEE ALSO

➤ *For more information, see page 311*

Useful options:

`-n` NUMB means limit number of arguments put on each to value specified as NUMB.

GLOSSARY

`[]` Brackets or square brackets, used in various commands and scripts.

`{}` Braces or curly braces, used in various commands and scripts.

`$HOME` Shell environment variable that points to your logon home directory.

`$PATH` The shell environment variable that contains a set of directories to be searched for UNIX commands.

`.bmp` Bitmap graphics file.

`.bz2` File compressed using the bzip2 utility, which usually offers better compression than gzip.

`.c` C source file.

`.gif` GIF graphics file.

`.gz` File compressed using the GNU gzip utility, which usually offers better compression than the `compress` command.

`.h` C header file.

`.htm` HTML document.

`.html` HTML document.

`.o` Compiled object file.

`.ps` PostScript file.

`.tgz` Gzipped tar file.

`.tif` TIFF graphics file.

`.txt` Text document.

`.Z` File compressed using the `compress` command.

`/` Root directory.

`/dev/null` **file** The place to send output that you are not interested in seeing; also the place to get input from when you have none (but the program or command requires something). This is also known as the bit bucket (where old bits go to die).

`/dev` Device directory.

`/etc/group` **file** This file contains information about groups, the users they contain, and passwords required for access by other users. The password might actually be in another file, the shadow group file, to protect it from attacks.

`/etc/inittab` **file** The file that contains a list of active terminal ports for which UNIX will issue the logon prompt. This also contains a list of background processes for UNIX to initialize. Some versions of UNIX use other files, such as /etc/tty.

/etc/motd file   Message of the day file; usually contains information the system administrator feels is important for you to know. This file displays when the user signs on to the system.

/etc/passwd file   Contains user information and password. The password might actually be in another file, the shadow password file, to protect it from attacks.

/etc/profile   The file executed to initialize and set up the shell environment characteristics common to all users of the Bash, Bourne, and Korn shells.

/usr/local   Locally developed or add-on public executables directory.

/var/spool   Various spool directories.

absolute pathname   A method of referring to a file where all directories from the root directory to that file are specified. An absolute pathname always starts with a slash, indicating that it is starting from root (for example, /reports/abc refers to the abc file in the reports subdirectory of root).

administrative control of a directory   Users who have write permission to a directory have effective administrative control over that directory. In addition to creating files,

they can delete and rename files of other users, even if they don't have permission to modify those files. If the directory sticky bit is set, having write permission does not give administrative control of the directory.

ANSI   Acronym for American National Standards Institute.

API   Acronym for Application Program Interface. The specific method prescribed by a computer operating system, application, or third-party tool by which a programmer writing an application program can make requests of the operating system. Also known as Application Programmer's Interface.

application   One or more software programs that provide a capability, such as an accounting application.

application data file   A file, usually one of many, that contains data for that application.

application program   A software program, usually one of a great many, that provides part of the programming for an application.

arguments   See *parameters*.

ARPA   See *DARPA*.

ASCII   Abbreviation for American Standard Code for Information Interchange. Used to represent characters in memory for most computers.

AT&T UNIX   Original version of UNIX developed at AT&T Bell Labs, and then a later entity known as UNIX Systems Laboratories. Many current versions of UNIX are descendants; even BSD UNIX was derived from early AT&T UNIX.

`awk`   Programming language developed by A.V. Aho, P.J. Weinberger, and Brian W. Kernighan. The language is built on C syntax, includes the regular expression search facilities of `grep`, and adds in the advanced string and array handling features missing from the C language. `nawk`, `gawk`, and POSIX `awk` are versions of this language.

background job   A job that you initiated but that is running independently of your keyboard and screen so that you can do other things. Many important UNIX system processes run as background jobs, waiting for user requests or other events. (These are often called system daemons.) See *foreground job*.

backup   The process of storing the UNIX system, applications, and data files on removable media for future retrieval.

basename   The longest rightmost part of a pathname that contains no slashes (/) (for example, in `/usr/fred/reports/acme`, acme is the basename of that pathname). A basename can be any type of file including a directory. Also, as used in this book, basename can refer to a filename that

has no slashes and no directory portion.

bash   Acronym for GNU Bourne Again Shell. Contains most Bourne shell, sh, and Korn shell, ksh, enhancements.

boot or boot up   The process of starting the operating system (UNIX).

Bourne shell   A standard shell on all UNIX systems that supports basic programming but few user keyboard conveniences.

BSD   Acronym for Berkeley Software Distribution.

BSD UNIX   Version of UNIX developed by Berkeley Software Distribution and written at University of California, Berkeley.

C   Programming language developed by Brian W. Kernighan and Dennis M. Ritchie. The C language is highly portable and available on many platforms, including mainframes, PCs, and, of course, UNIX systems.

C shell   A user interface for UNIX written by Bill Joy at Berkeley. It features C programming-like syntax.

CAD   Acronym for computer-aided design.

cast   Programming construct to force type conversion of variables.

CD-ROM   Acronym for compact disc–read only memory. Computer-readable data stored on the same

899

physical form as a musical CD. CD-ROMs have large capacity, are inexpensive, are slower than a hard disk, and are limited to reading. There are versions that are writable (CD-R, CD Recordable) and other formats that can be written to once or many times.

CGI   Acronym for Common Gateway Interface. A means of transmitting data between Web pages and programs or scripts executing on the server. Those programs can then process the data and send the results back to the user's browser through dynamically creating HTML.

character special   A device file used to communicate with character-oriented I/O devices such as terminals, printers, or network communications lines. All I/O access is treated as a series of bytes (characters).

characters, alphabetic   The letters A through Z and a through z.

characters, alphanumeric   The letters A through Z and a through z, and the numbers 0 through 9.

characters, control   Any nonprintable characters. These characters are used to control devices, separate records, and eject pages on printers.

characters, digits   The numbers 0 through 9.

characters, numeric   The numbers 0 through 9.

checksum   A numeric value produced by summing all the characters within a file. This sum enables you to do a quick check that the file matches another file. By comparing the checksums, you can quickly check whether two files (are likely to) contain the same contents or whether a file still has the same contents it had when the checksum was last computed. Often, the sum is shifted or rotated after each character is added (think of multiplying by 2). This is then called a rotating checksum, which can detect file differences where the data is the same but in a different order. The goal of the checksum is that a small difference between two files should generate a large difference between the checksums. If two files have the same checksum, there is a high probability that they contain the same contents. If their checksums differ, the two files are definitely not the same.

child directory   Same as a subdirectory.

child process   A process or job started by another process or job, which is called the parent process. See *subprocess*.

child shell   See *subshell*.

class   A model of objects that have attributes (data) and behavior (code or functions). It is also viewed as a collection of objects in their abstracted form.

command substitution   A shell feature that allows backquotes (`) containing another UNIX command to substitute the output of that command as words in the current command.

command-line editing   UNIX shells support the capability to recall a previously entered command, modify it, and then execute the new version. The command history can remain between sessions. (The commands you did yesterday can be available for you when you log on today.) Some shells support a command-line editing mode that uses a subset of the vi, emacs, or gmacs editor commands for command recall and modification.

command-line history   See *command-line editing*.

command-line parameters   Used to specify parameters to pass to the execute program or procedure. Also known as command-line arguments.

comment   Explanatory words meant for a human reader. Usually, comments have special starting characters so that the computer will ignore them. In UNIX shell programming, use a pound sign (#) to start a comment. Other programming languages can use other starting characters for comments.

configuration files   Collections of information used to initialize and set up the environment for specific commands and programs. Shell configuration files set up the user's environment.

contained words   In vi, contained words are any groups of letters and digits. They are separated from other contained words by punctuation, spaces, tabs, and end of line. For example, abc---def=3 contains three contained words: abc, def, and 3. See *separated words* and *non-words*.

CPU   Acronym for Central Processing Unit. The primary "brain" of the computer; the calculation engine and logic controller.

current directory   The directory that is assumed as the base for any relative pathnames. Many UNIX commands will assume this directory if no directory is specifically given. Use the cd command to change your current directory.

daemon   A system-related background process that often runs with the permissions of root and that services requests from other processes.

DARPA   Acronym for (U.S. Department of) Defense Advanced Research Projects Agency. Funded development of TCP/IP and ARPAnet (predecessor of the Internet).

database server   See *server, database*.

default directory   Same as *current directory*.

device file   File used to implement access to a physical device. This provides a consistent approach to access of storage media under UNIX; data files and devices (such as tapes and communication facilities) are implemented as files. To the programmer, there is no real difference.

901

device node   A type of file used to access hardware devices such as tape drives or floppy disks.

digit   One of the characters 0 through 9. A digit is always a single character. One or more digits make up a number.

directory   A means of organizing and collecting files together. The directory itself is a file that consists of a list of files contained within it. The root (/) directory is the top level, and every other directory is contained in it (directly or indirectly). A directory might contain other directories, known as subdirectories.

directory navigation   The process of moving through directories is known as navigation. Your current directory is known as the current working directory. Your logon directory is known as the default or home directory. Using the `cd` command, you can move up and down through the tree structure of directories.

dirname   The part of a pathname from the start to the last internal slash (/)—for example, in `/usr/fred/reports/acme`, `/usr/fred/reports` is the dirname. If there is no slash (/) in the pathname, its dirname is represented by a period (.), which indicates the current directory. See *basename*.

DNS   Acronym for domain name server. Used to convert between the name of a machine on the Internet (`name.domain.com`) and the numeric IP address (`123.45.111.123`).

DOS   Acronym for Disk Operating System. Operating system based on the use of disks for the storage of commands. It is also a generic name for MS-DOS and PC-DOS on the personal computer. MS-DOS is the version Microsoft sells; PC-DOS the version IBM sells. Both are based on Microsoft code.

double   Double-precision floating point.

dpi   Dots per inch.

EBCDIC   Acronym for Extended Binary Coded Decimal Interchange Code. The code used to represent characters in memory for mainframe computers.

ed   An early simple program used for line-oriented text editing.

elm   Interactive mail program.

Emacs   A freely available editor now part of the GNU software distribution. Originally written by Richard M. Stallman at Massachusetts Institute of Technology in the late 1970s, it is available for many platforms. It is extremely extensible and has its own programming language; the name stands for editing with macros.

email   Messages sent through an electronic medium rather than through the local postal service. Many proprietary email systems are designed to handle mail within a LAN environment; most of these can also send mail over the Internet. Most Internet (open) email systems make use of MIME to handle attached data (which can be binary).

encapsulation   The process of combining data (attributes) and functions (behavior in the form of code) into an object. The data and functions are closely coupled within an object. Instead of all programmers being able to access the data in a structure their own way, they must use the code connected with that data. This promotes code reuse and standardized methods of working with the data.

environment variables   See *variables, environmental*.

escaped characters   Characters preceded by a backslash (\). Usually, you escape a character to take away its special meaning, but sometimes you escape a normal character to give it special meaning. See *quoting*.

Ethernet   A networking method where the systems are connected to a single shared bus and all traffic is available to every machine. The data packets contain an identifier of the recipient, and that is the only machine that should process that packet.

expression   A constant, variable, or operands and operators combined. Used to set a value, perform a calculation, or set the pattern for a comparison (regular expressions).

FIFO   Acronym for First In, First Out. See *pipe, named*.

file   Collection of bytes stored on a device (typically a disk or tape). Can

be source code, executable binaries or scripts, or data.

file compression   The process of applying mathematical formulas to data, typically resulting in a form of the data that occupies less space. A compressed file can be uncompressed, resulting in the original file.

file, indexed   A file based on a file structure where data can be retrieved based on specific keys (name, employee number, and so on) or sequentially. The keys are stored in an index. This is not directly supported by the UNIX operating system; usually, it is implemented by the programmer or by using tools from an ISV. A typical form is known as ISAM.

file, line sequential   See *file, text*.

file, sequential   This phrase can mean either a file that can only be accessed sequentially (not randomly), or a file without record separators (typically of fixed length, but UNIX does not know what that length is and does not care).

file, text   A file containing only behaved control characters such as \n (newline) or \t (tab). Also a file with record separators. Can be of fixed or variable length; UNIX tools can handle these files because the tools can tell when the record ends (by the separator).

filename   The name used to identify a collection of data (a file). If no directory is specified, it is assumed to be in the current directory.

filename, fully qualified   The name used to identify a collection of data (a file) and its location. It includes both the path and the name of the file; typically, the pathname is fully specified (absolute). See *pathname* and *absolute pathname*.

filename generation wildcards Special characters that can be used in pattern words in command lines. The shell will replace pattern words with a list of existing files that match the pattern. Don't confuse these wildcards with regular expression wildcards.

filesystem   A hierarchical directory system built in a section of a disk drive or disk structure such as RAID. Non-root filesystems must be mounted on a directory (sometimes at the root) before they can be accessed. All accesses to the mount point directory access the section of the disk where the filesystem resides. This is in contrast to the DOS convention of specifying disk sections as D: or E:. Filesystems usually cannot grow; hence, some directories on your system can be full while others still have available unused disk blocks. Filesystems are stored in a disk partition and are sometimes referred to as being the disk partition. See *mount* and *mount point*.

finger   User information lookup program.

firewall   A system used to provide a controlled entry point to the internal network from the outside (usually the Internet). This is used to prevent outside or unauthorized systems from accessing systems on your internal network. The capability depends on the individual software package, but the features typically include filter packets and filter datagrams, system (name or IP address) aliasing, and rejecting packets from certain IP addresses. In theory, it provides protection from malicious programs or people on the outside. It can also prevent internal systems from accessing the Internet on the outside. The name comes from the physical barrier between connected buildings or within a single building that is supposed to prevent fire from spreading from one to another.

flags   See *options*.

float   Single-precision floating point.

foreground job   A job that is running on and tying up your keyboard and screen. See *background job*.

FSF   Acronym for Free Software Foundation.

FTP   Acronym for File Transfer Protocol. A system-independent means of transferring files between systems connected via TCP/IP. Ensures that the file is transferred correctly, even if there are errors during transmission. FTP can usually handle character-set conversions

(ASCII/EBCDIC) and record terminator resolution (linefeed for UNIX, carriage return, and linefeed for MS/PC-DOS).

full pathname   Same as *absolute pathname*.

gateway   A combination of hardware, software, and network connections that provides a link between one architecture and another. Typically, a gateway is used to connect a LAN or UNIX server with a mainframe (that uses SNA for networking, resulting in the name SNA gateway). A gateway can also be the connection between the internal and external network (often referred to as a firewall). See *firewall*.

GID   Acronym for group ID number.

globbing   See *filename generation wildcards*.

GNU   Acronym for GNU's Not UNIX. GNU is the name of free useful software packages commonly found in UNIX environments that are being distributed by the GNU project at MIT, largely through the efforts of Richard Stallman. The circular acronym name ("GNU" containing the acronym GNU as one of the words) is a joke on Richard Stallman's part. One of the textbooks on operating system design is titled: "XINU: XINU is not UNIX," and GNU follows in that path.

GPL   Abbreviation for GNU General Public License. A license describes how you may use a computer program or product. It describes your rights and limitations. The GPL applies to many free or open source software programs, allowing unlimited use, modification, and redistribution but limits your ability to make those programs less accessible to others.

grep   A common tool used to search a file for a pattern. egrep allows the use of extended (hence the e prefix) regular expressions; fgrep uses limited expressions for a faster (hence the f prefix) searches.

GUI   Acronym for graphical user interface. A GUI allows user input by selecting pictures (icons) using a pointing device (usually a mouse). A GUI is easier for beginners to use than a command line where all commands, options, and arguments must be typed accurately and must follow syntax rules.

here document   The << redirection operator, known as a here document, allows keyboard input (stdin) for the program to be included in the script.

hidden file   A file or directory whose filename begins with a leading period (.). Some utilities will not process hidden files by default (for example, ls and filename generation wildcards). Hidden files are usually system and configuration files that should not be included when you process data files.

HTML   Abbreviation for Hypertext Markup Language; describes World Wide Web pages. HTML is the

905

document language used to define the pages available on the Internet through the use of tags. A browser interprets the HTML to display the desired information.

I-node   Used to describe a file and its storage (also known as *inode*). The directory contains a cross-reference between the i-node and the pathname/filename combination. A file's entry in disk data structure (`ls -i`).

ICMP   Abbreviation for *Internet Control Message Protocol*. Part of TCP/IP that provides network-layer management and control.

inheritance   A method of object-oriented software reuse in which new classes are developed based on existing ones by using the existing attributes and behavior and adding on to them. If the base object is automobiles (with attributes of engine and four wheels and tires; behavior of acceleration, turning, and deceleration), a sports car would modify the attributes: The engine might be larger or have more horsepower than the default, and the four wheels might include alloy wheels and high-speed-rated tires. The behavior would also be modified for faster acceleration, tighter turning radius, and faster deceleration.

init level   Same as run level or system state.

inode   A table entry where all information about a file is stored except for the filename and the actual file

data itself. The inode contains such fields as the file owner, group, permissions, and date and time of last access or modification. Each UNIX filesystem contains an inode table that keeps track of all the files in that section of the disk. There is also an inode table in memory that keeps track of all files currently being referenced. See *filesystem* and *I-node*.

inode number   The entry number of a given file in the inode table. See *inode*. Each filesystem has its own inode table, so two different files could have the same inode number if they reside in different filesystems on the same system. See *filesystem*.

inode table   See *inode*.

int   Integer.

Internet   A collection of different networks that provide the capability to move data among them. It is built on the TCP/IP communications protocol. Originally developed by DARPA, it was taken over by NSF and has now been released from governmental control.

Internet service provider   A company that specializes in connecting you to the Internet.

IRC   Acronym for Internet Relay Chat. A server-based application that enables groups of people to communicate simultaneously through text-based conversations. IRC is similar to Citizen Band radio or the chat rooms on some bulletin boards. Some chats can be private (between invited people only) or public (where anyone can join in). IRC now also supports sound files as well as text; it can also be useful for file exchange.

ISAM Acronym for Indexed Sequential Access Method. On UNIX and other systems, ISAM refers to a method for accessing data in a keyed or sequential way. The UNIX operating system does not directly support ISAM files but add-on languages and applications may provide these types of files under UNIX.

ISO Acronym for International Standards Organization.

ISP See *Internet service provider.*

ISV Abbreviation for independent software vendor. Generic name for software vendors other than your hardware vendor.

kernel The core of the operating system that handles device- and system architecture-specific tasks such as memory allocation, device input and output, process allocation, security, and user access. UNIX tends to have a small kernel when compared to other operating systems.

keys, control Keys that cause some function to be performed instead of displaying a character. These functions have names: The end-of-file key tells UNIX that there is no more input; it is usually the Ctrl+D (^D) key.

keys, special See *keys, control.*

Korn shell A user interface written by David G. Kron for UNIX with extensive scripting (programming) support. The shell features command-line editing and also accepts scripts written for the Bourne shell.

LAN Acronym for local area network. A collection of networking hardware, software, desktop computers, servers, and hosts all directly connected. A LAN could be an entire college campus.

limits See *quota.*

LISP Acronym for List Processing Language.

logon The process with which a user gains access to a UNIX system. This can also refer to the user ID that is typed at the logon prompt.

lp The line printer command.

lpc The line printer control program.

lpd The Line printer daemon.

lpq The Printer spool queue examination program.

lprm The Printer spool queue job removal program.

ls The list directory(s) command.

magic number A number embedded in some files that allows the system to determine the type of contents of that file by looking up the number in a table of magic numbers.

man page   The output from the man command that displays pages from the UNIX online manual that tells you how to use most UNIX commands and what options are available for that command.

memory, real   The amount of storage that is being used within the system (silicon; it used to be magnetic cores).

metacharacter   A printing character that has special meaning to the shell or another command. It is converted into something else by the shell or command; the asterisk (*) filename generation wildcard is converted by the shell to a list of all files in the current directory, for example.

MIME   Acronym for Multipurpose Internet Mail Extensions. A set of protocols or methods of attaching binary data (executable programs, images, sound files, and so on) or additional text to email messages.

motd   Acronym for message of the day.

mount   The act of making a predefined disk drive or section on a disk subsystem (for example, RAID) available to the system. The system maintains an internal mount table of currently mounted filesystems. Mount commands are normally run automatically when the system is started. See *filesystem*, *mount point*, and *unmount*.

mount directory   Same as a *mount point*.

mount point   A standard UNIX directory (which should not but may contain files and subdirectories) used by a mount command to become the access point for a filesystem in another disk drive or section of a disk subsystem (for example, RAID). The files and directories in the mount point directory disappear after it is mounted. Instead, the files and directories of the mounted filesystem appear to be in the mount point directory. Any accesses or changes within the mount point directory actually occur in the mounted filesystem. See *filesystem* and *mount*.

multitasking operating system   One that supports multiple jobs running concurrently, especially when a single user can initiate multiple jobs running concurrently.

multiuser operating system   One that supports multiple users connected to the system running diverse applications simultaneously.

mwm   Motif window manager.

Netnews   A loosely controlled collection of discussion groups. A message (similar to an email) is posted in a specific area, and then people can comment on it, publicly replying to the same place (posting a response) for others to see. A collection of messages along the same theme is referred to as a thread. Some of the groups are moderated, which means that nothing is posted without the approval of the owner. Most are not, and the title of the group is no guarantee that the discussion will be related. The official term for this is Usenet news.

NFS Acronym for network file system. Means of connecting disks that are mounted to a remote system to the local system as if they were physically connected.

NNTP Acronym for Netnews Transport Protocol. Used to transmit Netnews or Usenet messages over the top of TCP/IP. See *Netnews* for more information on the messages transmitted.

non-words In vi, non-words are any groups of punctuation. For example, `abc---def=3` contains two non-words: `---` and `=`. See *contained words* and *separated words*.

object In the truest sense of the word, something that has physical properties, such as automobiles, rubber balls, and clouds. These things have attributes and behavior. They can be abstracted into data (attribute) and code (behavior). Instead of just writing functions to work on data, they are encapsulated into a package that is known as an object.

operator Metacharacter that performs a function on values or variables. The plus sign (+) is an operator that adds two integers.

options Program- or command-specific indicators that modify the behavior of that program. Sometimes called flags. For example, the `-a` option to the `ls` command modifies

its normal behavior to list hidden files, which are usually ignored. These are used on the command line. See also *parameters*.

OSF Acronym for Open Software Foundation.

parameter substitution Same as *variable substitution*.

parameters Data passed to a command or program through the command line. These can be options (see *options*) that control the command or arguments on which the command works. Some have special meaning based on their position on the command line.

parent directory A directory that contains another directory is said to be the parent directory of that subdirectory.

parent process A process or job that creates or spawns a subtask; also called a child process.

parent shell Shell (typically the logon shell) that controls another, often referred to as the child shell or subshell. See *shell*.

password The secure code that is used in combination with a user ID to gain access to a UNIX system.

pathname A method of referring to a file that contains a slash—that is, the directory containing the file is indicated. See *relative pathname* and *absolute pathname*.

Perl Programming language developed by Larry Wall. (Perl stands for Practical Extraction and Report Language, or Pathologically Eclectic Rubbish Language; both are equally valid). The language provides the capabilities of shell programming, awk and sed, and many enhancements. It is often used to program CGI Web scripts for both UNIX and Windows.

permissions When applied to files, the attributes that control access to a file. There are three levels of access: owner (the file creator), group (people belonging to a related group as determined by the system administrator), and other (everyone else). The permissions are usually r for read, w for write, and x for execute. The execute permissions flag is also used to control who may search a directory.

PGP Acronym for the Pretty Good Privacy encryption system.

PID Acronym for Process ID Number. Every job or process under UNIX is listed in a table called the process table. The job's entry number in that table is its ID number or PID.

Pine Interactive mail program.

pipe A method or the action of redirecting the output of one UNIX command to feed the input to a second UNIX command. This eliminates the need to use a file to store temporary results. The pipe self-regulates its flow so that it uses much less disk space than a temporary file would require.

pipe file See *pipe, named*.

pipe, named An expanded function of a regular pipe (redirecting the output of one program to become the input of another). Instead of connecting stdout to stdin, the output of one program is sent to the named pipe, and another program reads data from the same file. This is implemented through a special file known as a pipe file or FIFO. The operating system ensures the proper sequencing of the data. Little or no data is actually stored in the pipe file; it just acts as a connection between the two.

pipe sign A vertical bar character (|).

pipeline A sequence of UNIX commands each linking through a pipe. See *pipe*.

piping The action of using a pipe. See *pipe*.

POSIX Acronym for Portable Operating System Interface, UNIX. POSIX is the name for a family of open system standards based on UNIX. The name has been credited to Richard Stallman. The POSIX Shell and Utilities standard developed by IEEE Working Group 1003.2 (POSIX.2) concentrates on the command interpreter interface and utility programs.

PostScript Adobe Systems, Inc. printer language.

PPID Acronym for Parent PID. The PID (see *PID*) of the process or job that started the current process or job being considered.

PPP   Acronym for Point-to-Point Protocol. Internet protocol over serial link (modem).

pppd   The Point-to-Point-Protocol daemon.

present directory   Same as *current directory*.

printcap   Printer capability database.

process   A discrete running program under UNIX. The user's interactive session is a process. A process can invoke (run) and control another program that is then referred to as a subprocess. Ultimately, everything a user does is a subprocess of the operating system.

process identifier   The unique number assigned to every process running in the system. See *PID*.

pwd   The print working directory command.

quota   General description of a system-imposed limitation on a user or process. It can apply to disk space, memory usage, CPU usage, maximum number of open files, and many other resources.

quoting   The use of single and double quotation marks to prevent special interpretation of the characters inside the quotes. The backslash may also be used for this purpose; see *escaped characters*.

R.E. pattern   See *regular expression*.

R.E. wildcard   A metacharacter that can match desired patterns. See *regular expression*.

RAID   Acronym for Redundant Array of Inexpensive/Independent Disks. A RAID subsystem enables you to combine several disks into one larger disk structure providing striping (for better performance by equalizing the disk load), mirroring (to protect against media or drive failures), or parity (to provide redundancy protection without having to double the number of data disk drives).

RCS   Acronym for Revision Control System.

recursively processing   Recursively processing a directory means that all its subdirectories are also processed, as are all subdirectories of those subdirectories, and so on. All subdirectories will be processed, no matter how many levels removed from the starting directory.

redirection   The process of directing a data flow from the default. Input can be redirected to get data from a file or the output of another program. Normal output can be sent to another program or a file. Errors can be sent to another program or a file.

regular expression   A pattern that may contain one or more regular expression wildcards. Also a name for a subpattern element of a larger regular expression.

regular expression wildcard Special characters that enable you to specify patterns in a general way within files and pipelines. These wildcard patterns are used by utilities such as `grep`, `sed`, `awk`, and Perl to find desired text to display or modify. Don't confuse these with filename generation wildcards.

regular file A UNIX file that contains user or system data, text, programming, and so on, as distinguished from a directory, device node, named pipe, semaphore, or shared memory file. This is the most common type of file on a UNIX system.

relative pathname A method of referring to a file where the directory portion of the filename is indicated as a relative path from the current directory. A relative pathname never starts with a slash—for example, `reports/abc` refers to the `abc` file in the `reports` subdirectory of your current directory.

remark Same as *comment*.

RFC Acronym for Request For Comment. Document used for creation of Internet- and TCP/IP-related standards.

rlogin (Remote login) Gives the same functionality as Telnet, with the added functionality of not requiring a password from trusted clients, which

can also create security concerns. See *Telnet*.

root directory The main system directory that contains all the other directories and files. It is denoted by a single slash (/).

root user The user who is the UNIX system administrator, also called the superuser. Root is regarded as the co-owner of all files and hence has permission to access all files on the system.

routing The process of moving network traffic between two different physical networks; also decides which path to take when there are multiple connections between the two machines. Routing might also send traffic around transmission interruptions.

RPC Acronym for Remote Procedure Call. Provides the capability to call functions or subroutines that run on a remote system from the local one.

RPM Acronym for Red Hat Package Manager.

run level In System V, a number from 0 to 6 that describes the system state.

script A program written for a UNIX utility, including shells, `awk`, Perl, `sed`, and others. See *shell scripts*.

SCSI Acronym for small computer system interface.

sed A common tool used for stream text editing, having ed-like syntax.

separated words   In vi, separated words are any group of characters separated by spaces, tabs, newlines, or formfeeds. Separated words are also called space-delineated/delimited words. See *contained words* and *non-words*.

server, database   A system designated to run database software (typically a relational database such as Oracle, SQL Server, Sybase, or others). Other systems connect to this one to get the data (client applications).

setgid (Set group ID)   If enabled for a program, the user becomes a member of the program's group while the program is running. Allows the program to access files that are normally restricted.

setuid (Set user ID)   If enabled for a program, the user becomes the user who owns the program while the program is running. Allows the program to access files that are normally restricted.

SGID   See *setgid*.

shell   The part of UNIX that handles user input and invokes other programs to run commands. Includes a programming language (for example, Bourne shell, C shell, Korn shell, tcsh, and bash).

shell environment   The shell program (Bourne, Korn, C, tcsh, or bash) invocation options and preset variables that define the characteristics, features, and functionality of the UNIX command-line and program execution interface.

shell or command prompt   The single character or set of characters that the UNIX shell displays for which a user can enter a command or set of commands.

shell scripts   A program written using a shell programming language, like those supported by Bourne, Korn, or C shells.

signal   A special flag or interrupt used to communicate special events to programs by the operating system and other programs.

sit in a directory   Informal way to refer to your current directory or changing to a directory. (It will be easier to access these files if you sit in /tmp, for example.)

SLIP   Acronym for Serial Line Internet Protocol. Internet over a serial line (modem). The protocol frames and controls the transmission of TCP/IP packets of the line. PPP is usually preferable to SLIP.

SNA   Acronym for System Network Architecture, an IBM networking architecture.

special files   Same as *device nodes*.

spool files   Temporary copies of files queued up for printing that are held until they are done printing. This term can also apply to many temporary files held by other system processes such as uucp.

913

stderr (standard error) Elegant method of outputting error messages that allows the shell to easily redirect the errors from the screen to a file, a device, or another program.

stdin (standard input) Elegant method of inputting characters that allows the shell to easily redirect the input to come from a file, a device, or another program as well as from the keyboard.

stdout (standard output) Elegant method of outputting messages that allows the shell to easily redirect the output from the screen to a file, a device, or another program.

stream A sequential collection of data. All files are streams to the UNIX operating system. To UNIX, there is no structure to a file; that is something imposed by application programs or special tools (ISAM packages or relational databases).

subdirectory A directory contained within another directory. If you refer to all subdirectories of a given directory, you are referring not only to its immediate subdirectories but also to every subdirectory of its subdirectories. See *directory*.

subnet A portion of a network that shares a common IP address component. Used for security and performance reasons.

subprocess Process running under the control of another, often referred to as the parent process. See *process*.

subshell Shell running under the control of another, often referred to as the parent shell (typically the logon shell). See *shell*.

subtree A portion of the UNIX directory tree formed by a directory and each of its files and subdirectories and each of their files and subdirectories, going on like this as far as possible.

SUID See *setuid*.

superuser The root operator who is the all-powerful system administrator.

system administrator The person who takes care of the operating system and user administrative issues on UNIX systems. Also called a *system manager*, although that term is much more common in DEC VAX installations.

system manager See *system administrator*.

tar Acronym for tape archiving utility.

TCP Acronym for Transmission Control Protocol.

TCP/IP Acronym for Transport Control Protocol/Internet Protocol. The pair of protocols and also generic name for the suite of tools and protocols that forms the basis for the Internet. Originally developed to connect systems to the ARPAnet.

tcsh A C shell-like user interface featuring command-line editing.

Telnet   Protocol for interactive (character user interface) terminal access to remote systems. The terminal emulator that uses the Telnet protocol is often known as *telnet* or tnvt100.

telnet   Remote logon program.

termcap   Terminal capability database.

terminal   A hardware device normally containing a cathode ray tube (screen) and keyboard for human interaction with a computer system. Does not support graphics or images.

text processing languages   A way of developing documents in text editors with embedded commands that handle formatting. The file is fed through a processor that executes the embedded commands, producing a formatted document. These include `roff`, `nroff`, `troff`, `RUNOFF`, `TeX`, `LaTeX`, and even the mainframe `SCRIPT`.

TFTP   Acronym for Trivial File Transfer Protocol or Trivial File Transfer Program. A system-independent means of transferring files between systems connected via TCP/IP. It is different from FTP in that it does not ensure that the file is transferred correctly, does not authenticate users, and is missing a lot of functionality (such as the `ls` command).

tin   Interactive news reader.

truncate   To remove or discard the ending portion if it exceeds some limit (for example, truncate names to 14 characters).

UDP   Acronym for User Datagram Protocol. Part of TCP/IP used for control messages and data transmission where the delivery acknowledgment is not needed. The application program must ensure data transmission in this case.

UID   Acronym for User ID. Each logon user has an identifying user number called the UID, as listed in `/etc/passwd`.

UIL   Acronym for Motif User Interface Language.

umount   The command that does an unmount. See *unmount*.

unmount   The act of removing a filesystem from the system mount table, which makes its contents no longer accessible to the system (until it is mounted again). This also transforms the mount point directory back to a normal directory, with its old contents now available. See *filesystem, mount, mount point* and *umount*.

URL   Acronym for Uniform Resource Locator. The method of specifying the protocol, format, logon (usually omitted), and location of materials on the Internet.

Usenet   See *Netnews*.

UUCP   Acronym for UNIX-to-UNIX copy program. Used to build an early, informal network for the transmission of files, email, and Netnews.

variable substitution A shell feature that allows the contents of shell variables to be used in commands and scripts.

variables, attributes The modifiers that set the variable type. A variable can be string or integer, left- or right-justified, read-only or changeable, and other attributes.

variables, environmental A place to store data and values (strings and integers) in the area controlled by the shell so that they are available to the current processes and subprocesses. They can just be local to the current shell or can be available to a subshell (exported).

WAN Acronym for wide area network. A network where some of the network connections involve the phone company (for example, digital lines, ISDN, or T1).

Web See *World Wide Web*.

whitespace One or more spaces and tabs that are normally interpreted to delineate commands and arguments to commands (for example,

filenames unless contained within quotation marks).

World Wide Web A collection of servers and services on the Internet that run software and communicate using a common protocol (HTTP). Instead of the users having to remember the location of these resources, links are provided from one Web page to another through the use of URLs.

working directory Same as *current directory*.

WWW See *World Wide Web*.

WYSIWYG Acronym for What You See Is What You Get.

X See *X Window System*.

X Window System A windowing and graphics system developed by MIT, to be used in client/server environments.

X11 See *X Window System*.

yacc Acronym for yet another compiler.

INDEX

Symbols

X-Z

Macmillan FREE Personal Bookshelf ONLINE

Get FREE books and more...when you register this book online for our Personal Bookshelf Program

http://register.quecorp.com/

 Register online and you can sign up for our *FREE Personal Bookshelf Program*...unlimited access to the electronic version of more than 200 complete computer books—immediately! That means you'll have 100,000 pages of valuable information onscreen, at your fingertips!

 Plus, you can access product support, including complimentary downloads, technical support files, book-focused links, companion Web sites, author sites, and more!

 And you'll be automatically registered to receive a *FREE subscription to a weekly email newsletter* to help you stay current with news, announcements, sample book chapters, and special events, including sweepstakes, contests, and various product giveaways!

 We value your comments! Best of all, the entire registration process takes only a few minutes to complete, so go online and get the greatest value going—absolutely FREE!

Don't Miss Out On This Great Opportunity!

QUE® is a brand of Macmillan Computer Publishing USA.

For more information, please visit *www.mcp.com*

Other Related Titles